Lecture Notes in Computer Science 4346

Commenced Publication in 1973
Founding and Former Series Editors:
Gerhard Goos, Juris Hartmanis, and Jan van Leeuwen

T0223183

Lecture Notes in Computer Science 4916

Luboš Brim   Boudewijn Haverkort
Martin Leucker   Jaco van de Pol (Eds.)

Formal Methods: Applications and Technology

11th International Workshop, FMICS 2006
and 5th International Workshop, PDMC 2006
Bonn, Germany, August 26-27, and August 31, 2006
Revised Selected Papers

 Springer

Volume Editors

Luboš Brim
Masaryk University
Botanicka 68a, 602 00 Brno, Czech Republic
E-mail: brim@fi.muni.cz

Boudewijn Haverkort
University of Twente
P.O. Box 217, 7500AE Enschede, The Netherlands
E-mail: brh@cs.utwente.nl

Martin Leucker
Technische Universität München
Boltzmannstr. 3, 85748 Garching, Germany
E-mail: leucker@in.tum.de

Jaco van de Pol
Centrum voor Wiskunde en Informatica, SEN 2
P.O. Box 94079, 1090 GB Amsterdam, The Netherlands
E-mail: Jaco.van.de.Pol@cwi.nl

Library of Congress Control Number: 2007921124

CR Subject Classification (1998): D.2.4, D.2, D.3, C.3, F.3

LNCS Sublibrary: SL 2 – Programming and Software Engineering

ISSN   0302-9743
ISBN-10   3-540-70951-7 Springer Berlin Heidelberg New York
ISBN-13   978-3-540-70951-0 Springer Berlin Heidelberg New York

Springer is a part of Springer Science+Business Media

springer.com

© Springer-Verlag Berlin Heidelberg 2007
Printed in Germany

Typesetting: Camera-ready by author, data conversion by Scientific Publishing Services, Chennai, India
Printed on acid-free paper   SPIN: 12021901   06/3142   5 4 3 2 1 0

Preface

These are the joint final proceedings of the 11th International Workshop on Formal Methods for Industrial Critical Systems (FMICS 2006) and the fifth International Workshop on Parallel and Distributed Methods in Verification (PDMC 2006). Both workshops were organized as satellite events of CONCUR 2006, the 17th International Conference on Concurrency Theory that was organized in Bonn, August 2006.

The FMICS workshop continued successfully the aim of the FMICS working group – to promote the use of formal methods for industrial applications, by supporting research in this area and its application in industry. The emphasis in these workshops is on the exchange of ideas between researchers and practitioners, in both industry and academia.

This year the Program Committee received a record number of submissions. The 16 accepted regular contributions and 2 accepted tool papers, selected out of a total of 47 submissions, cover formal methodologies for handling large state spaces, model-based testing, formal description and analysis techniques as well as a range of applications and case studies.

The workshop program included two invited talks, by Anna Slobodova from Intel on "Challenges for Formal Verification in an Industrial Setting" and by Edward A. Lee from the University of California at Berkeley on "Making Concurrency Mainstream." The former full paper can be found in this volume.

Following the tradition of previous workshops, the European Association of Software Science and Technology (EASST) supported a best paper award. This award was granted to Michael Weber and Moritz Hammer for their excellent paper "'To Store or Not To Store' Reloaded: Reclaiming Memory on Demand."

The primary goal of the PDMC workshop series is to present and discuss recent developments in the young area of parallel and distributed methods in verification. Several verification techniques, ranging over model checking, equivalence checking, theorem proving, constraint solving and dependability analysis are addressed by the PDMC community. Verification problems are usually very demanding tasks, especially because the systems that we build and want to verify become increasingly complex.

On the other hand, parallel and distributed computing machinery is widely available. Algorithms and tools must be developed to use this hardware optimally for our verification tasks. Traditionally, we studied algorithms for homogeneous situations, such as parallel shared-memory computers and distributed clusters of PCs. Currently, the emphasis is shifting towards heterogeneous GRIDs. But even modern desktop PCs are quite heterogeneous, consisting of multiple core processors, various memory devices and cache levels, all with their own performance characteristics.

This year's PDMC had nine submissions; six papers were selected for presentation, and four papers were accepted for publication in this volume. In addition, Luboš Brim from Masaryk University, Brno, gave an invited lecture on "Distributed Verification: Exploring the Power of Raw Computing Power." The full paper can also be found in this volume.

We would like to thank all authors for their submissions. We would also like to thank the members of both Program Committees, and the additional referees, for their timely reviewing and lively participation in the subsequent discussion— the quality of the contributions in this volume are also due to their efforts and expertise.

The organizers wish to thank CONCUR for hosting the FMICS and PDMC 2006 workshops and taking care of many administrative aspects, and ERCIM for its financial support of FMICS. Additionally, the organizers would like to thank the EASST (European Association of Software Science and Technology), the Faculty of Informatics, Masaryk University Brno and the Technical University Munich, the CWI (Center of Mathematics and Computer Science, Amsterdam) and the University of Twente for supporting these events.

December 2006

Luboš Brim
Boudewijn R. Haverkort
Martin Leucker
Jaco van de Pol

Organization

FMICS

Program Chairs

Luboš Brim   Masaryk University Brno, Czech Republic
Martin Leucker   Technical University of Munich, Germany

Program Committee

Rance Cleaveland   University of Maryland, USA
Wan Fokkink   Vrije Universiteit Amsterdam and CWI, The
                              Netherlands
Stefania Gnesi   ISTI-CNR, Italy
Susanne Graf   VERIMAG, France
David Harel   Weizmann Institute of Science, Israel
Klaus Havelund   Kestrel Technology, USA
Thomas A. Henzinger   EPFL, Switzerland
Leszek Holenderski   Philips Research, The Netherlands
Stefan Kowalewski   RWTH Aachen University, Germany
Marta Kwiatkowska   University of Birmingham, UK
Salvatore La Torre   Universitá degli Studi di Salerno, Italy
Tiziana Margaria   University of Göttingen, Germany
Radu Mateescu   INRIA Rhône-Alpes and ENS Lyon, France
Doron Peled   University of Warwick, UK
Ernesto Pimentel   University of Malaga, Spain
Andreas Podelski   Max-Planck-Institut für Informatik, Germany
Don Sannella   University of Edinburgh, UK
Joseph Sifakis   VERIMAG, France

PDMC

Program Chairs

Boudewijn Haverkort   University of Twente, The Netherlands
Jaco van de Pol   CWI Amsterdam, The Netherlands

Program Committee

Gerd Behrmann   Aalborg University, Denmark
Ivana Černá   Masaryk University Brno, Czech Republic
Gianfranco Ciardo   University of California at Riverside, USA
Joerg Denzinger   University of Calgary, Canada

Table of Contents

Invited Contributions

Challenges for Formal Verification in Industrial Setting 1
   Anna Slobodová

Distributed Verification: Exploring the Power of Raw
Computing Power 23
   Luboš Brim

FMICS

An Easy-to-Use, Efficient Tool-Chain to Analyze the Availability of
Telecommunication Equipment 35
   Kai Lampka, Markus Siegle, and Max Walter

"To Store or Not To Store" Reloaded: Reclaiming Memory
on Demand 51
   Moritz Hammer and Michael Weber

Discovering Symmetries 67
   Hassen Saïdi

On Combining Partial Order Reduction with Fairness Assumptions 84
   Luboš Brim, Ivana Černá, Pavel Moravec, and Jiří Šimša

Test Coverage for Loose Timing Annotations 100
   C. Helmstetter, F. Maraninchi, and L. Maillet-Contoz

Model-Based Testing of a WAP Gateway: An Industrial Case-Study ... 116
   Anders Hessel and Paul Pettersson

Heuristics for **ioco**-Based Test-Based Modelling 132
   Tim A.C. Willemse

Verifying VHDL Designs with Multiple Clocks in SMV 148
   A. Smrčka, V. Řehák, T. Vojnar, D. Šafránek,
   P. Matoušek, and Z. Řehák

Verified Design of an Automated Parking Garage 165
   Aad Mathijssen and A. Johannes Pretorius

Evaluating Quality of Service for Service Level Agreements 181
   Allan Clark and Stephen Gilmore

Simulation-Based Performance Analysis of a Medical Image-Processing
Architecture   195
    P.J.L. Cuijpers and A.V. Fyukov

BLASTing Linux Code   211
    Jan Tobias Mühlberg and Gerald Lüttgen

A Finite State Modeling of AFDX Frame Management Using Spin   227
    Indranil Saha and Suman Roy

UML 2.0 State Machines: Complete Formal Semantics Via Core State
Machines   244
    Harald Fecher and Jens Schönborn

Automated Incremental Synthesis of Timed Automata   261
    Borzoo Bonakdarpour and Sandeep S. Kulkarni

SAT-Based Verification of LTL Formulas   277
    Wenhui Zhang

jmle: A Tool for Executing JML Specifications Via Constraint
Programming   293
    Ben Krause and Tim Wahls

Goanna—A Static Model Checker   297
    Ansgar Fehnker, Ralf Huuck, Patrick Jayet,
    Michel Lussenburg, and Felix Rauch

PDMC

Parallel SAT Solving in Bounded Model Checking   301
    Erika Ábrahám, Tobias Schubert, Bernd Becker,
    Martin Fränzle, and Christian Herde

Parallel Algorithms for Finding SCCs in Implicitly Given Graphs   316
    Jiří Barnat and Pavel Moravec

Can Saturation Be Parallelised? – On the Parallelisation of a Symbolic
State-Space Generator   331
    Jonathan Ezekiel, Gerald Lüttgen, and Radu Siminiceanu

Distributed Colored Petri Net Model-Checking with CYCLADES   347
    Christophe Pajault and Jean-François Pradat-Peyre

Author Index   363

Challenges for Formal Verification in Industrial Setting

Anna Slobodová

Intel
anna.slobodova@intel.com

Abstract. Commercial competition is forcing computer companies to get better products to market more rapidly, and therefore the time for validation is shrinking relative to the complexity of microprocessor designs. Improving time-to-market performance cannot be solved by just growing the size of design and validation teams. Design process automation is increasing, and the adoption of more rigorous methods, including formal verification, is unavoidable because for achieving the quality demanded by the marketplace.

Intel is one of the strongest promoters of the use of formal methods across all phases of the design development. Intel's design teams use high-level modeling of protocols and algorithms, formal verification of floating-point libraries, design exploration systems based on formal methods, full proofs and property verification of RTL specifications, and equivalence checking to verify that transistor-level schematics correspond to their RTL specifications. Even with the best effort to adopt the progress in formal methods quickly, there is a large gap between an idea published at a conference and a development of a tool that can be used on industrial-sized designs. These tools and methods need to scale well, be stable during a multi-year design effort, and be able to support efficient debugging. The use of formal methods on a live design must allow for ongoing changes in the specification and the design. The methodology must be flexible enough to permit new design features, such as scan and power-down logic, soft error detection, etc. In this paper, I will share my experience with the formal verification of the floating-point unit on an Itanium(R) microprocessor design and point out how it may influence future microprocessor-design projects.

1 Introduction

Floating-point (FP) arithmetic is, with respect to functional validation, one of the critical parts of modern microprocessor designs. Even though the algorithms for FP arithmetic are well known, optimization for high performance, reliability, testability and low power, may introduce bugs into a design. The huge input data space that needs to be explored to ensure correctness of floating-point designs is beyond the limits of traditional simulation techniques (hereafter referred to as *simulation*). Fortunately, formal methods are well suited for this area and they can enhance a verification effort substantially. Formal semantics of floating-point

L. Brim et al. (Eds.): FMICS and PDMC 2006, LNCS 4346, pp. 1–22, 2007.

operations can be expressed in a succinct way and the IEEE Floating-Point standard [IEEE] serves as a guide for many instruction-set architectures. In this paper, floating-point algorithms are not our concern. Instead, I focus on the correctness of their register-transfer level (RTL) implementations.

For almost a decade, papers reporting compliance proofs for circuit models with respect to the IEEE standard and particular instruction set architecture have been published. While the early research was focused on answering a principal question of the feasibility of formal proofs for computer arithmetic (e.g., [AS95, CB98, OZ+99]), recent work emanates from commercial industry. Formal tools and methods have reached the maturity necessary for their deployment in real design projects.

There are substantial differences between the methodologies used at different companies, depending on their target and available tools and resources. Intel and AMD were among first companies that applied formal methods, at first to verification of floating-point algorithms and then to RTL design. Methods reported from AMD design team in [Rus98, RF00, FK+02] are solely based on theorem proving using ACL2 system [1]. Although lot of automation has been added to building ACL2 models from RTL descriptions, and an ACL2 library of Floating-Point Arithmetic has been created to avoid repetition of implementation independent proofs, the methodology still requires high-level expertise in theorem proving and a perfect understanding of the design.

A recent paper from IBM by Jacobi *et al.* [JW+05] presents a verification method based on symbolic simulation of a RTL model and its comparison to a high-level model written in VHDL. Although highly automated, the approach is not as rigorous as the one described by AMD, and lacks the scope of the methodology developed at Intel [AJ+00][AJ+00, KA00, KN02, KK03, Sch03]. It skips the verification of the more difficult part of the design - multiplier, by removing it from the cone of influence, hence proving merely correctness of the adder and rounder. In contrast, in our approach, no abstraction or design modification took place. We return to the comparison of their work to our results in Section 7.

At Intel, an important work in the area of the verification of floating-point algorithms, and in particular, floating-point libraries for Itanium[R] has been done by John Harrison (see [Har05] for an overview, and [Har00a, Har00b, Har03] for details). However, in hardware verification, while many papers have been published on verification of Pentium[R] design, the first report on the formal verification of floating-point arithmetic for the Itanium[R] microprocessor family was reported on Designing Correct Circuits (DCC) Workshop [2], in March, 2004, in Barcelona [SN04]. The main result was the first successful formal verification of floating-point fused multiply-add instruction which is in repertoire of the IA-64 Instruction Set Architecture (ISA). Proofs have been constructed for a live project aimed at a next generation of Itanium[R] microprocessor. We continued our work presented at DCC by extending the scope and verifying correctness

---

[1] *http://www.cs.utexas.edu/moore/acl2/*
[2] *http://www.math.chalmers.se/~ms/DCC04/*

of the rest of floating-point instructions (about 40) issued to execution pipe All instructions have been verified with respect to eight precisions and four IEEE rounding modes, including dynamic rounding specified in floating-point status register. The verification was based on symbolic trajectory evaluation and arithmetic libraries previously proven within the same system [KN02]. The proof includes correctness of the result, update of floating-point status register, and correctness of more than a dozen interrupt signals. Behavior of the floating-point circuitry for invalid instructions and/or instructions with false qualifying predicates have been considered as well. All proofs have been regularly rerun as a regression suite to ensure the consistency of any changes in the design. Formal sequential equivalence checking was used to finish the validation of low-level design proving its correctness with respect to the RTL. However this last phase of verification is out of scope of this paper.

In the process of constructing our proofs we found many bugs and issues that required RTL changes. Our work also helped to clarify incomplete and ambiguous parts of our micro-architectural specification, and it contributed to some hardware optimizations. The proofs are automated and portable to other Itanium$^{(R)}$ micro-processor designs.

The goal of this paper is to describe the scope and results of our work, and to provide some insight into challenges of using formal verification in an industrial environment, where a fine balance between rigorous verification methods and traditional simulation-based methods is crucial for success of the validation. Although the approach we choose is a combination of known techniques already documented in context of the verification of floating-point adders and multipliers, we believe that it has many aspects that might be interesting to researchers in academia as well as validation engineers.

The paper is organized in following way: Next section describes tools and methodology developed for formal verification of floating-point arithmetic at Intel Corporation and specifics of our approach. The core of our work is described in Section 3, where we dive into details of the verification of the most interesting operation - fused multiply-add, and report what has been covered by our proofs. Since debugging of failing proofs is one of the concerns in the use of formal methods, we touch this question in Section 4. Section 5 focuses on benefits of our effort for the design project. We describe our experience with proof management in Section 6. Concluding section contains summary of our work and detailed comparison to related published work.

2   Our Approach to Formal Verification of FP Arithmetic

Intel's approach to the validation of floating-point arithmetic includes a huge database of corner test-cases and pseudo-random generators for simulation, as well as Intel's FORTE formal verification tool that combines theorem-proving with model-checking capabilities [3]. The methodology described below does not

---

[3] A publicly available version of the tool that can be used for non-commercial purposes can be downloaded from *http://www.intel.com/software/products/opensource/*

rely on FORTE specifics and can be reproduced using any tool with capability of symbolic trajectory evaluation (STE) and some means of composing results obtained by STE. We believe that formal proofs coupled with traditional pseudo-random and focused simulation is a good way to achieve thorough functional validation. In our project, the formal and simulation based validation teams mutually benefited from their collaboration. However, this is out of the scope of this paper and we will focus on formal verification only.

2.1   FORTE System and STE

The history of formal verification of floating-point arithmetic at Intel has been motivated by two controversial trends: promising results in academia that were followed by proof of concept at Intel Research Lab [OZ+99]; and bugs that escaped to the micro-processor products [Coe96, Fis97]. Today, formal proofs developed for Pentium[R] designs [AJ+00, KA00, KN02, KK03, Sch03] are re-used and even put into hands of validation engineers that are not experts on formal methods. These proofs have been done using FORTE – a system built on top of VOSS. In this section, we give a rather informal description of the technology inside the FORTE system, just enough to understand the paper; details can be found in the referred publications. FORTE includes a light-weight theorem prover and a symbolic trajectory evaluation (STE) engine [STE]. The theorem prover is based on a higher-order logic. The interface language for FORTE is FL - a strongly-typed functional language in the ML family [Pau96]. One good property of FL as a specification language is its executability. While creating specifications, we often ran sanity checks. For instance, the translation from the memory format to register-file format was written as specified by the Software Developers Manual [ISA], and then checked whether consequent inverse translations yield consistent values. FL includes Binary Decision Diagrams (BDDs)[Bry86] as first-class objects and STE as a built-in function. For more information we refer the interested reader to the online documentation for the FORTE system and [KA00]. Here we describe the basic mechanisms of STE and the framework in which we work.

STE is a weak form of model-checking where a formal (gate-level) model is subjected to a symbolic simulation. The idea of a symbolic simulator is similar to that of standard simulator but it differs in that symbolic values (besides explicit binary values) are assigned to each signal and these values propagated through the design model. Results of such simulations are formulas for specified signals at specified times.

STE is an enhancement of symbolic simulation where Boolean logic has been extended to a lattice [STE] with X as a bottom (no information) and T as a top element (overconstrained). X is automatically assigned (by the STE simulator) to signals to which no value has been specified. X can be thought of as an unknown value. Its semantics and use are discussed later. Symbolic values are bound to signals at specified times to form signal trajectories. Trajectories that prune possible computations by restricting the values of some signals at specific times are called *antecedents*; they can be interpreted as assumptions. Trajectories that specify expected responses of the circuit are called *consequents*. A specification is written in a form of Boolean expressions that constrain symbolic values in antecedents and consequents. Trajectory evaluation correctness statement $\models_{ckt} [ant ==\gg cons]$ means: all circuit computations that satisfy antecedent *ant* also satisfy consequent *cons*. If any of consequent is violated, a STE run (proof) fails and a counterexample can be extracted from this failure. In fact, the failed proof provides all possible counterexamples and the user may select one for debugging purposes. If all consequents hold at every point of the simulation, success is reported by the tool.

2.2 Pre- and Post-condition Framework

Because of capacity limitations inherit in the STE engine, we may be forced to break our model into smaller pieces. In this case, we make sure that those pieces perfectly fit together. Informally, this means that the border signals of the decomposition match exactly and that nothing is left out of the design. Also the times at which we extract the values of the signals must be consistent. In terms of STE, consequents that include border signals serve as antecedents in the following step of the proof. In this way, we can use facts proved in one part as assumptions for later proofs.

The idea of proof (de)composition described above comes from the *pre-and-post-condition theory* used for verification of sequential programs. It was first applied to STE by Kaivola and Aagaard [KA00]. It allows one to prove the statements of the form $\{P\}S\{Q\}$, where P and Q are logical properties and S is a program. In our case, the program is replaced by a circuit and trajectories that bind values inputs and outputs of the circuit at specific times. $\{P(x)\}(pretr_x, ckt, posttr_y)\{Q(x,y)\}$ represents the statement: if $pretr_x$ binds the Boolean vector x to signals (usually inputs) of the circuit ckt and $posttr_y$ binds the Boolean vector y to signals of the circuit (usually outputs), then property $P(x)$ guarantees property $Q(x,y)$.

$\{P(x)\}(pretr_x, ckt, posttr_y)\{Q(x,y)\}$ is a shorthand for the following formula:

$$\forall x(P(x) \Rightarrow (\exists y(\models_{ckt} [pretr_x ==\gg posttr_y])) \wedge$$
$$(\forall y((\models_{ckt} [pretr_x ==\gg posttr_y]) \Rightarrow Q(x,y)))) \qquad (1)$$

In our methodology, P is a conjunction of an *initial condition* that describes the restriction of inputs to the circuit, and *an auxiliary pre-condition* that is used to further restrict the simulation. For consistency, we use the same initial conditions throughout all proofs for every instruction analyzed, except when we weaken an initial condition to *true*. An example of an initial input condition is a statement that the specified input signals have value of a specific opcode. Auxiliary pre-conditions are usually used to simplify a particular STE run by restricting symbolic values (meaning that the inputs or internal nodes are restricted). An example of an auxiliary pre-condition is a restriction specifying a case in a case split. Another example of an auxiliary pre-condition is a side-condition (that we prove separately) used by architects to simplify the design. We refer to Q as the *post-condition*. Further, *pretr* is a union of the *initial trajectory* that binds symbolic values to the input signals, and the *pre-trajectory* that binds symbolic values to internal signals. *posttr* is referred to as a *post-trajectory*; it binds symbolic values to signals that we consider as outputs for the purpose of a specific proof.

Intel's proof libraries contain reasoning rules that apply to STE runs [KA00]. Here we mention those rules that were relevant to our proofs:

- Pre-condition strengthening

$$\frac{\{P'(x)\}(pretr_x, ckt, posttr_y)\{Q(x,y)\}, \forall x(P(x) \Rightarrow P'(x))}{\{P(x)\}(pretr_x, ckt, posttr_y)\{Q(x,y)\}}$$

- Post-condition weakening

$$\frac{\{P(x)\}(pretr_x, ckt, posttr_y)\{Q'(x,y)\}, \forall x \forall y(Q'(x,y) \Rightarrow Q(x,y))}{\{P(x)\}(pretr_x, ckt, posttr_y)\{Q(x,y)\}}$$

- Post-condition conjunction

$$\frac{\{P(x)\}(pretr_x, ckt, posttr_y)\{Q_1(x,y)\}, \{P(x)\}(pretr_x, ckt, posttr_y)\{Q_2(x,y)\}}{\{P(x)\}(pretr_x, ckt, posttr_y)\{Q_1(x,y) \wedge Q_2(x,y)\}}$$

- Sequential composition

$$\frac{\{P(x)\}(pretr_x, ckt, midtr_z)\{\lambda x.\lambda z.R(x)\}, \{R(x)\}(midtr_z, ckt, posttr_y)\{Q(x,y)\}}{\{P(x)\}(pretr_x, ckt, posttr_y)\{Q(x,y)\}}$$

2.3   Managing the Size of BDDs

It is important to note that STE uses *Binary Decision Diagrams* (BDDs) [Bry86] to represent formulas produced in the symbolic simulation of a design. BDDs provide a unique representation of Boolean functions, but the space required to represent a Boolean function can critically depend on the order selected for the (decision) variables. Therefore, we need to carefully order the BDD variables. It is well-known that an inappropriate (or random) variable ordering may result in exponential growth of a BDD with respect to the number of input variables. To determine a good variable ordering, we need to know the functionality of particular part of the design. An automatic ordering mechanism called *dynamic re-ordering* is available but it takes additional time and is more suitable for reachability analysis which is not our case. Our rule of thumb in establishing the variable ordering was to put control variables close to the top; and interleave operands' variables.

It can be tricky to find a variable ordering that is suitable for representing the specification and the design model simultaneously as the former is written independently from the latter. This can be solved by writing a provably equivalent specification that does not have this problem.

In the process of symbolic simulation we try to avoid building formulas/BDDs that do not contribute to the result – the formulas of the signals in the post-trajectory. This can be done by *node weakening* – assigning X (don't care values) to some signals. Propagation of X's through the circuit often reduce the complexity of intermediate formulas. Weakening is a safe and conservative way to reduce the complexity of STE simulations. If a node is weakened by mistake, a X will appear as the value for signals in post-trajectory results which causes a proof failure; thus, this is a sound method. Besides user-guided weakening, FORTE has an automatic weakening mechanism that is triggered by the size of the BDD for some nodes.

2.4   Verification Methodology

Our methodology was driven by several factors:

- An unusually early start of the formal verification process: our work started at the same time as our traditional simulation effort, i.e., when first lines of RTL code were written.
- Continuous validation effort: proofs has been kept synchronous with changes in the design;
- Limited resources: engineers with experience in formal verification are scarce in the project development.

We looked for the most effective way to achieve high confidence in the design, balancing between investment (learning new tools, writing new specifications, proof maintenance, etc.) and return (covering functionality that cannot be covered by traditional simulation methods with comparable person/time resources). We wished to make a maximal re-use of the formal proofs, and we wanted modularity for an easy maintainability. Our methodology builds on the experience from other Intel groups [KA00, KN02, KK03]. Arithmetic, floating-point, binary and STE proof libraries created for other Intel projects was an important contributer to our success.

Each proof started with a top-down decomposition of the high-level problem into sub-problems, where sub-problems were mapped to bit-level properties checked by FORTE. Decomposition, if needed, was justified by *STE pre-post condition inference rules* [KA00]. However, some simpler instructions did not require decomposition. The gap between the high-level and bit-level specifications was bridged by proof libraries that include IEEE rounding modes [IEEE] and basic floating-point operations like addition and multiplication [KA00, KN02]. These libraries have a clean separation between floating-point values and their encodings that allows customization to particular architectures and micro-architectures. The use of libraries allowed to redirect our focus on writing bit-level specification, describing a mapping from RTL signals and time to mathematical entities, creating environment for debugging and counter-example generation, and overall proof maintenance.

3   Verification of Fused Multiply-Add

3.1   Floating-Point Multiply-Add

The Itanium$^{(R)}$ ISA defines a floating-point architecture that is fully IEEE compliant for the single, double and double-extended data types, with exponent width 8,11,15 or 17 bits (see [ISA] for details).

Floating-Point Registers (FR) in IA-64 architecture are 82 bits long: The significand field (mantissa) is composed of an explicit integer part (significand{63}) and 63 bits of fraction (significand{62:0}). A 17-bit exponent field defines the magnitude of the number. The exponent is biased. The extreme values of the exponent (all ones and all zeros) are used to encode special values (IEEE Signed Infinity, NaNs, IEEE Signed Zeros [IEEE], the double-extended Real Denormals and double-extended Real Pseudo-Denormals [ISA]). The sign bit indicates whether the number is negative (sign=1) or positive (sign=0).

The value of a finite FP number encoded with non-zero exponent can be calculated from the expression

$$(-1)^{sign} * 2^{(exponent-bias)} * significand\{63\}.significand\{62:0\}_2)$$

where $significand\{62:0\}_2$ denote values represented by a significand$\{62:0\}$ with respect to unsigned binary encodings.

In this paper, we focus on operations applied to normalized operands. Normalized FP numbers have exponents in the range from 1 to 0x1FFFE, and their integer bit is 1. Operations on special values have been covered in our proofs, too. Operations on denormals in considered implementation are deferred to software assist handlers, and our proof obligations consist of raising software assist faults if there is no higher fault.

The floating-point status register (FPSR) is an important element of the architectural state. It contains dynamic control (disabled traps, rounding mode, precision mode, wide-range exponent mode, flush-to-zero mode) and status information indicating traps and faults caused by the the execution of the floating-point operations.

The Floating-Point Multiply-Add (FMA) instruction is one of the most complex IA-64 FP instructions implemented in hardware. One of its important applications is the computation of sums of real and complex matrix products [Nie03]. It is also a basic instruction used for the implementation of division and square root in Intel libraries. The format of fma instruction is:

$$(qp)\quad fma.pc.sf\, f1 = f3, f4, f2$$

The specification dictates that the product of floating-point register (FR) $f3$ and FR $f4$ is computed to infinite precision and then FR $f2$ is added to this product, again in infinite precision. The resulting value is then rounded to the precision indicated by pc (and possibly FPSR controls) using the rounding mode specified by FPSR. The rounded and normalized result is placed in FR $f1$. qp

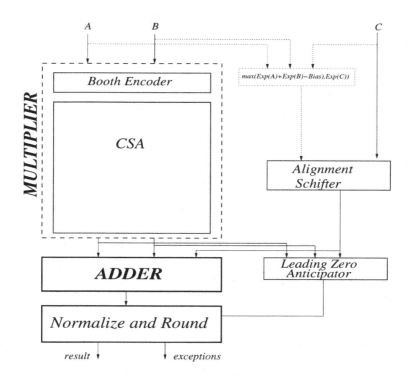

Fig. 1. Floating-Point Fused Multiply-Add Unit

is instruction qualifying predicate. If *qp* is *false*, the instruction has no effect on architectural state.

Considering the range of input values for *fma* instruction (three times 82 bits for operands, 8 precisions, and 4 rounding modes), its validation using exhaustive simulation would require 2^{251} test patterns to, even disregarding additional control flags, e.g., flush-to-zero.

Hardware implementation of the fused-multiply instruction requires a combination of 64-bit multiplier, an alignment shifter, a 128-bit adder, and rounding logic that includes a leading-zero anticipator and a normalization shifter (see Fig. 1). Implementation details are irrelevant for the purpose of the paper and are left out for confidentiality of the design.

After careful proof planning and manual decomposition of the proof goal to low level properties, our main focus became symbolic trajectory evaluation (STE) of those properties and propositional reasoning. All specifications are written in functional language FL.

We will describe the methodology and how we used it to find bugs in the design of an Itanium[R] microprocessor. We will mention the problems associated with using formal verification to verify complex data-intensive instructions.

Several practical issues occur when verifying designs in industrial environment:

- Limited time and human resources;
- Incompleteness of the register-transfer level design;
- Incompleteness of the micro-architectural specification;
- Maintenance of the formal specifications and proofs through the life of the project;
- Need for an efficient regression suite; and
- Complexity of the modern design, which includes features like power management, hardware sharing, scan logic, reset logic, and various levels of abstraction.

In addition to FP exceptions described in IEEE Standard [IEEE], Itanium[R] has a number of faults and traps described in Software Developers Manual [ISA], and many microarchitecture specific interrupts that are described in an Intel internal micro-architectural-level project specification. Besides that, we have to deal with additional complexity due to power management logic, scan logic and reset logic.

Using formal verification in the early phase of the design process means also dealing with the problems related to instability of the model. At the same time, the sooner gets FV involved in the verification process, the more substantial is its impact on finding and fixing bugs right at the beginning. Most problems encountered were found in rounding and the sticky bit computations, and some were a result of incorrect control logic.

Symbolic simulation of all of these constructs in one run is clearly beyond the capacity of todays BDD-based or SAT-based tools. We split the verification task into two subtasks: the correctness of the multiplier and the correctness of adder, rounder and normalizer. Although both tasks have been previously studied, each new design variation provides new verification challenges. In particular, complex power management, scan-out tests, and protection from soft-errors are so much interwind with the main functionality, that the mapping of the mathematical entities to concrete signals at concrete times can be nontrivial. Furthermore, designers use all their experience accumulated during the long years of designing high-performance arithmetic units, e.g. pre-computation of some values, redundancy, taking guess on values and make adjustments later, etc. All these tricks might cause unwelcome surprises to a verification engineer, especially when designer does not provide any mathematical argument for their validity.

Both tasks had to be further decomposed to fit into limitations of the STE engine. Verification of the Multiplier was the harder of the two sub-tasks. The reason for it is that although the algorithm specification gives some indication of further decomposition, it had required a lot of experimentation with symbolic simulation of the model until we found a well-balanced decomposition – a decomposition that was robust to tolerate frequent design changes and fine enough to keep the size of BDDs manageable.

3.2   Verification of Multiplier

We generalize the interpretation of the FP encodings described above. A floating-point number is represented as a 5-tuple $(s, e, m, bias, mfl)$, where s is the sign, e is the exponent bit vector, and m is the significand. mfl stands for mantissa fraction length, and it represents the number of bits after fraction point. Let A, B, and C be FP values of our operands stored in FR $f3$, FR $f4$, and FR $f2$, respectively; we represent them as tuples $(s_a, e_a, m_a, bias, mfl)$, $(s_b, e_b, m_b, bias, mfl)$, and $(s_c, e_c, m_c, bias, mfl)$, respectively, where $mfl = 63$, and $bias=65535$, consistently with the IA-64 floating-point register format.

$$A = (-1)^{\widehat{s_a}} * 2^{\widehat{e_a}-bias} * \widehat{m_a} * 2^{-mfl} \tag{2}$$

$$B = (-1)^{\widehat{s_b}} * 2^{\widehat{e_b}-bias} * \widehat{m_b} * 2^{-mfl} \tag{3}$$

$$C = (-1)^{\widehat{s_c}} * 2^{\widehat{e_c}-bias} * \widehat{m_c} * 2^{-mfl} \tag{4}$$

where $\widehat{x}$ is the integer encoded by the bit-vector x. Consequently,

$$A * B + C = [(-1)^{\widehat{s_a}} * (-1)^{\widehat{s_b}} * (2^{\widehat{e_a}+\widehat{e_b}-2*bias} * \widehat{m_a} * \widehat{m_b} * 2^{-2*mfl}] +$$
$$[(-1)^{\widehat{s_c}} * 2^{\widehat{e_c}-bias} * \widehat{m_c} * 2^{-mfl}] \tag{5}$$

The product $A*B$ can be represented as $P = (s_p, m_p, e_p, bias, pmfl)$, where $s_p = s_a \oplus s_b$ ($\oplus$ is addition mod 2), $\widehat{m_p} = \widehat{m_a} * \widehat{m_b}$ and $|m_p| = 128$, $\widehat{e_p} = \widehat{e_a} + \widehat{e_b} - bias$, and the mantissa fraction length is $pmfl = 126$.

In the first phase, we prove that the Multiplier correctly computes multiplication of significands.

$$\widehat{m_p} = \widehat{m_a} * \widehat{m_b} \tag{6}$$

Correctness of the exponent logic and sign datapath are proved separately. Our implementation uses modified Radix-4 Booth encoder (which interprets significands as unsigned numbers) and a CSA tree [Kor02] that consists of 129-bit $(3, 2)$-counters. Results are provided in redundant form as sum and carry vectors.

The proof follows the idea described by Kaivola and Narasimhan [KN02]. Generic proofs of the high-level multiplication algorithms and their mappings to bit-level specifications are included in their libraries. All we needed to do was to customize the specification of the Booth algorithm for the particular format of our design. However, the verification of bit-level properties involves implementation-specific details. The structure of RTL code is never as regular as the mathematical bit-level specification. Different tricks are used to pre-compute or estimate values and later adjust them to correct values. Since our symbolic simulation engine is based on BDDs, and multiplication is known to be a hard function for BDDs, the proof needed to be further decomposed into subtasks that could pass through the simulator. We split the proof into three steps:

1. Correctness of the Booth encoder (computation of partial products).
2. Correctness of the CSA tree at an intermediate level.
3. Correctness of the result in the redundant form.

It was up to us how we "cut" the tree. We were guided by the capacity of the STE tool and sense of readability and maintainability. Informally, a level is a horizontal (edge) cut through the CSA tree that is defined by a selection of exactly one edge (signal) on each input-to-output path. At first, we symbolically simulated design and observed the growth of BDDs at some sampled levels. The levels were chosen in such a way that they preserved consistency with respect to timing and logical structure. Then we choose a level for which the sum of BDDs had reasonable size.

Step 1: Assuming an initial condition (a valid *fma* instruction with normal operands has been issued to the unit), we proved that the product was correctly encoded into 32 partial products that were multiples of $\widehat{m_a}$:

$$\forall i, 0 \leq i \leq 32 : pp_i = booth(\widehat{m_b}, i) * \widehat{m_a} \tag{7}$$

where

$$booth(s, i) = (-2) * s_{2*i+1} + s_{2*i} + s_{2*i-1}$$

where $[s_{63}, s_{62}, s_{61}, ..., s_1, s_0]$ is the binary representation of s and $s_{-1} = 0$, and $s_{65} = s_{64} = 0$ is a two-bit zero-extension of s. It is well-known [Kor02] that

$$\widehat{m_a} * \widehat{m_b} = \sum_{i=0}^{i=32} pp_i * 2^i \tag{8}$$

In fact, the proof of this equation was carried out by FORTE in a previous project and this fact is a part of the libraries we used.

The correctness of each product has been proved separately because each run required a different BDD variable ordering. Each partial product was expressed using a disjunctive set of variables for consistency reasons. Although it was easy to find a representation of partial products, the first representation we found led to difficulties in consequent proof steps. This was one of several examples where the choice of implementation made a straightforward verification impossible. The cause of the problem was the implementation of partial products as a sum of temporary partial products and a corresponding negate bit:

$$pp_i := tmp\_pp_i + neg_i \tag{9}$$

where the most significant bit of tmp_pp_i and neg_i were inversions of each other. The variable used for the *negate* bit occurs twice in such a representation. While its first occurrence as the sign of the product suggests that is should be put close to the "top" of the variable order, its second occurrence as a a bit that needs to be added to the least significant bit indicates that its best position should be at the tail of the order. The contradictory information content of these variables makes it impossible to find a good BDD variable ordering. Although it wasn't an issue in the proof of the first step, it caused BDDs to grow too large in the subsequent steps. In fact, it was impossible even to build the specification: a sum of partial products.

Our solution to this problem was to use different variables for sign and its inverted representation. Although it was a trivial exercise to prove that the sign and negate bits were complements of each other, it showed to be unnecessary for the proof of our second step; therefore, we left it out of our final proofs. We used a variable ordering, with sign and the encoded bits of $\widehat{m_b}$ at the top, followed by particular partial product interleaved with $\widehat{m_a}$, and the negate bit on the tail.

Step 2: In our second step, we proved that the sum of sum- and carry-vectors at an intermediate level of the CSA tree was equal to the sum of all partial products multiplied by appropriate powers of 2.

$$sum_{int} = \sum_{i=0}^{i=32} pp_i * 2^i \tag{10}$$

This equality was proved under the condition

$$0 \le \sum_{i=0}^{i=32} pp_i * 2^i \le 2^{128} \tag{11}$$

which is weaker than a trivial consequent 15 of the equation 8 and the normality of operands A and B:

$$2^{63} \le \widehat{m_a} \le 2^{64} \tag{12}$$
$$2^{63} \le \widehat{m_b} \le 2^{64} \tag{13}$$

which implies that the product is normal or "slightly above normal", i.e., has two integer bits from which at least one is 1:

$$2^{126} \le \widehat{m_a} * \widehat{m_b} \le 2^{128} \tag{14}$$

$$2^{126} \le \sum_{i=0}^{i=32} pp_i * 2^i \le 2^{128} \tag{15}$$

Step 3: The last level (output) of the CSA tree consists of just two vectors, sum and $carry$ that represent the product:

$$\widehat{m_p} = \widehat{sum} + 2 * \widehat{carry} \tag{16}$$

This redundant form is used as one of the inputs to the Adder. Correctness at this level means that the sum of sum-vectors and carry-vectors is equal to the sum of sum- and carry-vectors at the intermediate level (as specified in step 2).

$$\widehat{sum} + 2 * \widehat{carry} = sum_{int} \tag{17}$$

Similarly to the previous step, this equality was proven under condition that the specified value is in bounds

$$0 \leq sum_{int} \leq 2^{128} \tag{18}$$

which follows from the equality proven in Step 2 and the condition 11.

Putting all steps together and fact 8 we get our target equation 6.

3.3   Verification of Adder and Rounder

Algorithms for floating-point addition can be found in many computer architecture text books (e.g., [Kor02]). In the context of *fma* operations, the addition of the product P and the operand C, the main steps are:

1. Compare exponents of addends ($ediff := \widehat{e}_p - \widehat{e}_c$), to determine left/right shift of m_c, necessary for alignment. Determine exponent of intermediate result as $max(\widehat{e}_p, \widehat{e}_c)$.
2. If $ediff > 0$, shift m_c right; if $ediff < 0$, shift m_c left.
3. Add/subtract $\widehat{m_p}$ and $\widehat{m_c}$, depending on s_p and s_c.
4. Normalize result by shifting it left by number of leading zeros, or right if first non-zero integer bit is more than one place left from the digital point, and adjust exponent.
5. Round to the specified precision using specified rounding mode. Note that post-normalization might be required after rounding-up.

All cases form two groups: true addition and true subtraction. True addition can increase number of integer bits, while true subtraction can lead to a sequence of leading zeros. Considering that our product is normal or slightly above (Equation 15), the latter can happen only if $ediff \in \{-2, -1, 0, 1\}$. All the cases when m_c is shifted too far left (no overlapping occurs) can be reduced to one case where m_p is replaced by the *sticky bit* implemented as an OR of the bits in m_c. Similarly, all cases where m_c is shifted too far right can be reduced to the case where m_c can be replaced by the sticky bit. The notions of sticky bit, *guard* and *round bit* are essential for the computation of a rounded floating point result without computing the precise result first. Further information about these computations can be found in floating-point arithmetic textbooks (e.g. [Kor02]).

Implementation of the rounding can be tricky and it is the most frequent source of bugs. Because rounding is specified independently of the notion of sticky bit, we did not need to know any details of its actual implementation.

Several formalizations of addition and rounding based on IEEE document [IEEE] have been published (see, e.g., [Rus00]). Intel's proof libraries contain all necessary building blocks for the specification.

The problems with verifying floating-point addition were recognized in several works each of which sketched its own solution [CB98, OZ+99, Rus00]. The challenge of the symbolic simulation of the floating-point addition lies in two big shifters – the alignment shifter that in our case aligns the significand of the third operand and the 128-bit significand of the product; and the normalization of the

129-bit significand of the sum. While an equation of a fixed-amount shifter is easily representable using BDDs when an appropriate variable ordering is used, variable-amount shifter causes BDDs to grow exponentially. This observation led to the idea of conditional symbolic simulation: performing the simulation process under restricted conditions expressed as a Boolean function over the input variables [CB98]. Conditional symbolic simulation is implemented in our tool using parametric representations of Boolean constraints [AJ+99].

Parametric representation of a set is an alternative to the characteristic function. It consists of a list of expressions, one for each variable that is in the support of characteristic function. These expressions are defined over a set of new variables. They can be viewed as a mapping of vectors of new variables to the vectors of original variables. The mapping is a surjective mapping onto represented set. In other words, for any assignment of new variables, the mapping provides an assignment of original variables that is in the target set, and for any element in the set, there is an assignment to new variables that is mapped to this element. Therefore, any run of conditional symbolic simulation will exercise only the computational flow defined by the set. At the same time, all inputs that satisfy the conditions will be exercised. In particular, if we run symbolic simulation under restriction that implies a fixed alignment, output of the alignment shifter will be the input shifted by that constant and is easily representable by BDDs. A case split that is appropriate for the verification of floating-point addition has been previously described [AJ+99].

Our proofs for the Adder and Rounder are split into many conditional symbolic simulation runs. Each run uses a variable ordering that is suitable. A good order interleaves bits of the shifted addends and the normalized result. The case split has an additional advantage of the possible parallelization of the task on many computers. Case conditions are functions of the addends - the product and the third operand. The case split follows the scheme below:

- true addition ($s_p = s_c$)
    - extreme cases
        - far-left case: $ediff < \text{EMIN}$
        - far-right case: $ediff > \text{EMAX}$
    - normal cases: $\text{EMIN} \leq ediff \leq \text{EMAX}$
- true subtraction ($s_p \neq s_c$)
    - extreme cases
        - far-left case: $ediff < \text{EMIN}$
        - far-right case: $ediff > \text{EMAX}$
    - close exponent cases: $ediff \in \{-2, -1, 0, 1\}$
        - cases by the number of leading zeros
    - normal cases excluding close cases

The choice of EMIN and EMAX depends on the implementation and the way the specification is written. There was some freedom in the choice up to the point that all extreme cases defined by these values should be treated in the same way. We choose EMIN=-130 and EMAX=130. The completeness of the case split was proven by means of propositional reasoning. The claim has the form: initial condition implies the existence of a case from the considered case list. Cases might even overlap if it simplifies conditional symbolic simulation.

Correctness of a floating-point operation includes faults and flags raised after its execution. There are IEEE mandated exceptions: overflow, underflow, invalid and inexact. We verify these exceptions and the round-up flag that is a part of our micro-architecture as well.

Exceptions cause the respective flag in FPSR to be set. Flags in FPSR are "sticky" - once set, they remain set until the FPSR is reset or changed by instructions used for this purpose. If no traps or faults occurs, the FPSR remains unchanged. In the case that an exception event occurred and that corresponding traps are enabled as stated in FPSR, the appropriate flags are set in Interrupt Status Register. Processing of the exceptions is verified in a separate proof. Besides IEEE FP exceptions, our micro-architecture has additional interrupt signals with a complex prioritization scheme that includes the parity-error fault, reserved register field fault, illegal operation fault, software assist fault, speculative operation fault, serialized re-steer fault, single-step trap, instruction break debug fault, and others. The hardest part of the verification of these signals was to figure out what their specification was as it was unstable during the project and the documentation of the changes was always behind the RTL. Once the specification was established, the STE completed without any intervention, and it did not require any detailed knowledge about the implementation.

Note that the product of normal numbers, can even be a denormal number, when its exponent gets too small. This case was covered by our proofs as well.

Hardware can also take advantage of certain properties of the product of significands that originate from normal numbers. In other words, the Adder does not need to work correctly for arbitrary addends, as long as it works correctly in the context of *fma* instruction. In that case the property used by designers needs to be proven and these facts can be used in the final proof. In particular, we proved and then used in the Adder proofs the fact that there is no carry-out from most significant bit of the sum of sum- and carry-vectors (in the representation of the product) when at least one of the two most significant bits of the product is one.

4   Debugging

The most rewarding part of our formal verification effort was the fact that we were able to help architects find and debug errors in their evolving design. However, a proof failure does not always mean a problem in the design. It might be a consequence of flaws in the specification, proof construction, or the verification tool. In this section we touch on the question of the debugging of failing proofs. We present a partial list of the most common sources of proof failures; hopefully, this list will help future users of this technology to localize their problems.

- **Xs, i.e., don't care values, in post-trajectory.**
  This is the most frequent failure when first running STE. You can observe Xs with the FORTE circuit viewer (*cktviewer*), or list them using some FL functions defined for this purpose. Xs can signal a real bug in the design:
  - Some signals that were not supposed to become a part of a data-flow appear to have an impact on the result.
  - Some signals remain uninitialized. This can happen for many reasons, e.g. missing entry for a truth-table or presence of a multiplexor with incomplete coverage for the combination of enabling signals.

  Occurrence of Xs in post-trajectory can be also caused by a mistake of the verification engineer:
  - Incorrect binding in pre-trajectory: missing signals or incorrect timing.
  - Weakening (dynamic or manual) was too aggressive replacing important signal values with Xs.
  - Some signals that do not contribute to consequents were accidentally included in the post-trajectory.
- **Specification is incorrect.** In most cases this problem becomes clear when you extract a counterexample and compare it with some reliable source (e.g. we had a web-based FP calculator for different architectures). Executability of a specification is crucial for its debugging. A different problem that can occur with the specification is when the constraint under which STE ran was unsatisfied. Our STE is equipped with a checker for such vacuous proof attempts.
- **Tool bug.** Those tool bugs that expose themselves clearly, e.g., a segmentation fault, are not dangerous. We are more afraid of those that hide behind successful proofs. One of the important categories of tool bugs are bugs in RTL-to-STE-model translation tool. An important sanity check for us was to watch for all bugs filed by simulation and analyze any case when formal proofs could not reproduce them.
- **You found a real design bug!** Debugging can be difficult if your translation tool modified RTL. Fortunately, this was not our problem. For each failed proof, STE returns failing condition. First, we extracted a scalar counterexample and ran the STE simulation again to confirm its validity. Afterwards, we reproduced the same error in the traditional simulation environment which is preferable by architects, and finally, we reported the bug to the architect responsible for that particular part of the RTL. When the architect indicated a fix, we reran the proof. Sometimes, when the scalar counter-example did not provide enough information to root the cause of the problem, we helped architects to debug the problem using symbolic values and they found it very useful.

5   Our Impact on the Design Project

Our main goal was to contribute as much as possible to the validation of the floating-point arithmetic in RTL design. While the main focus was on the correctness of the computationally intensive instructions, much more was covered by the proofs, and the design project profited from our effort in variety of ways.

Finding Bugs. Formal verification team found dozens of bugs, some of them months after RTL was considered to be completed and clean. Most of them were related to the rounding logic and to the recognition of floating-point exceptions or their prioritization. Some of them were very hard or practically impossible to find by means of tradition simulation because they occurred only under special conditions.

Clarifying Design Interfaces. One of the contributions of our effort was in helping to clarify interface among FP subunits. Subunits of the FP execution unit were designed by different architects, and we found several mismatches between their understanding of the interface specification. The Micro-Architectural Specification (MAS) was often incomplete regarding this, especially while architects were busy coding RTL code.

Removing Redundant Signals. One of the strengths of STE is that it has the ability to deal with X as a distinguished value (X) for don't care. We used this feature for proving redundancy of some signals in CSA tree. In our project, the multiplier was supposed to handle both signed and unsigned numbers; therefore, our architects were conservative in the choice of the width of the sum and carry vectors in the CSA tree. They wanted to make sure that no information would be lost. We re-ran our proofs with $X's$ assigned to the most significant bits of the vectors and proved that way that they are redundant for the computation of the correct result. After that, the width of the vectors was reduced, and that saved the valuable resources - area and power.

Benefit of the Fast Multiplier Proof. Exhaustive simulation of 64×64 bit multiplier is practically impossible as it involves 2^{128} test cases. In addition, depending on the opcode, multiplication can be performed on signed or unsigned integers, or might be re-directed completely (e.g. in case of multiplication by zero). Therefore, our simulation team was extremely pleased when we reported completion of the formal proof for the multiplier. This gave architects freedom to modify the RTL even in later phases of the project. Such late RTL modifications might have different reasons - timing and power optimization, or refinement of the RTL required by equivalence checker that is used for the verification of the transistor-level schematics against RTL. In order to simplify the verification task for the equivalence checker, architects were modifying RTL to make it structurally closer to the implementation. A quick re-run of formal proofs provided a huge advantage over simulation.

Regressions. The main advantage of the formal proofs is that once created they can be re-run without big manual effort. The continuously changing RTL model was regularly checked by the proofs that we maintained synchronized with RTL until the end of the project. Since many of the proofs could run independently, we could distribute them to idle workstations. We also created a small regression suite that was used on request of architects before they checked their changes in repository. As long as the choice of algorithm implemented in RTL does not change proof maintenance reduces to changes in mapping between signals and time to mathematical entities and occasional node weakening. The amount of work depends greatly on the proof management described in the next section.

6   Proof Management

There are many aspects that need to be taken into account when you create proofs. Some of them are conflicting and you need to find compromise. We had advantage of not to be the first ones who used FORTE for floating-point verification. Since it was expected that the proofs will live throughout the duration of the project they needed to be designed with maintainability in mind. We learned from the teams that worked on the formal verification of Pentium[R] micro-processors [KK03] how to manage evolving proofs so their maintenance would not become a burden. However, we were unable to avoid mistakes. It helped us to understand how important it is to share code among the proofs, and not to over-optimize them. We rearranged our proofs several times in order to simplify the specification or improve readability, and we have never been sorry for doing it. One difference between our project and previous projects was that we started our verification in an earlier phase. As a consequence, we were always facing continuous design changes: repartitioning, change of naming and timing, and structural and interface changes. The other consequence of our early start was incomplete functionality, unstable model, and incomplete specification. The importance of well-structured proofs became clear from the fact that after the *fma* instruction proof had been completed, it took us only about a month to construct the proofs of all other arithmetic instructions.

7   Summary

We described our formal verification effort on next generation Itanium[R] microprocessor. It was the first successful formal verification effort on Itanium[R] in general, and first formal verification of fused multiply-adder. The verification started in an early stage of the project when design was unstable and the specification incomplete. The reward for all difficulties caused by the instability of the model and specification was early discovery of bugs, and, consequently, an acceleration of the design process. Although there is no good way to measure the contribution of early bug detection to the savings of the architect's and the designer's time, it was recognized by the floating-point team. They also felt more comfortable when changing the design in the later stages of the project. Especially appreciated was the proof of the multiplier that gave them a lot of optimization freedom. All proofs were maintained throughout the life of the project. Writing formal specifications also contributed to clarification of the micro-architectural and architectural specification, and this effort inspired several important entries into the Itanium$^{(R)}$ manuals. All of the specifications are re-usable for future Itanium$^{(R)}$ design projects.

The hardest proof was the proof of fused multiply-add instruction. The instruction has been added to several instruction set architectures including Itanium$^{(R)}$. It is a core instruction for different computations including FP division and square-root. The main result reported in this paper was a first proof of this instruction. It combines known techniques applied to the proofs of multiplier [AS95, Rus98, OZ+99, Jac02, KN02] and an adder [CB98, OZ+99, Jac02]. However, the scope of the proof (that included a lot of control) and complexity of the design verified brought unexplored challenges.

The only work published on the formal verification of FMA that we are aware of is [JW+05]. There are several important differences between their and our work:

- In [JW+05], multiplier was excluded from the cone of influence by inserting artificial variables. This way the correctness of multiplication is missing. Roughly speaking the proof is the proof of addition with rounding. Our approach did not change RTL and includes correctness of multiplier.
- The proof in [JW+05] is based on symbolic simulation of two gate-level models; the one derived from RTL and another derived from the reference model that is written in VHDL. The two are compared for equivalence. Although the reference model is quite simple, it has not been formally verified. Our proofs compare formal IEEE models to RTL implementation. Consequently, RTL to transistor-level implementation was compared as a part of our design methodology.
- The scope of our proofs is wider: all arithmetic, logic and miscellaneous instructions, for any legal inputs, with respect to eight precisions (including 3 IEEE precisions), and four rounding modes. Besides the IEEE exceptions, many additional exceptions are considered. At the same time, we must mention that we did not need to deploy specification for denormal operands as those cases are deferred to software assist in our micro-architecture. For our design, the proof obligation was reduced to checking that Software Assist Fault was raised and that the architectural state was preserved. The result of a multiplication can be denormal even for normal input operands and this case is handled in hardware and was covered by our proofs.
- In [JW+05] an assumption of empty pipe is made in order to simulate an instruction in isolation. Our assumption is weaker – we allow other instructions in the pipe unless they cause a flush the pipe (e.g. if there is an older instruction that is raising fault).

All proofs can be customized to another Itanium$^{(R)}$ micro-architecture. Once the case splits and appropriate variable orderings are established and the mapping of the circuit signals and timing to mathematical entities is found, the FORTE system is expected to run fairly automatically. Use of formal methods in the validation of floating-point unit had a considerable impact on the project in terms of acceleration of RTL coding, reduction in validation resources, and at the same time, achievement of higher coverage.

Acknowledgement

I wish to thank Krishna Nagalla, who actively participated on the development of some proofs, Roope Kaivola and Katherine Kohatsu who helped to ramp up on tools and methodology developed for Pentium$^{(R)}$ 4 designs and provided all floating-point proof libraries. Our work would be very hard without collaboration with our architects, in particular Sridhar Samudrala, Kimberly Weier, and Vinodh Gopal; and our validation team, in particular Nick Morgan who was answering our questions on simulation environment in which we created scalar counter-examples.

References

[AJ+99]   M. Aagaard, R. Jones, K.-J. Seger: Formal Verification Using Parametric Representations of Boolean Constraints. *Proc. of the 36th ACM/IEEE conference on Design Automation, 1999, p. 402-407.*

[AJ+00]   M. Aagaard, R. Jones, R. Kaivola: Formal Verification of Iterative Algorithms in Microprocessors. *ACM/IEEE Proc. of Design Automation Conference, 2000, pp.201-206.*

[AS95]   M. Aagaard, K.-J. Seger: The Formal Verification of a Pipelined Double-Precision IEEE Floating-Point Multiplier. *ACM/IEEE Proc. of the International Conference on Computer-Aided Design, 1995, pp.7-10.*

[Bry86]   Bryant, R.E.: Graph-based Algorithms for Boolean Function Manipulation. *IEEE Transactions on Computers*, C-35, pp. 677-691, 1986.

[Coe96]   T. Coe: Inside the Pentium FDIV bug. *Dr. Dobbs Jornal. April 1996, pp. 129-135.*

[CB98]   Y.-A. Chen, R. Bryant: Verification of Floating-Point Adders. *Proc. of conference on Computer-Aided Verification (CAV), LNCS 1427 (Springer), 1998, pp. 488-499.*

[Fis97]   L.M.Fisher: Flaw reported in a new Intel chip. *New York Times, May 6, 1997, D 4:3.*

[FK+02]   A. Flatau, M. Kaufmann, D. Russinoff, E. Smith, R. Sumners: Formal Verification of Microprocessors at AMD. *Designing Correct Circuits 2002.*

[Har00a] J. Harrison: Formal Verification of Floating-point Trigonometric Functions. *Proc. FMCAD, Springer-Verlag 2000, LNCS 1954, pp. 217-233.*

[Har00b] J. Harrison: Formal Verification of IA-64 Division Algorithms. *Proc. TPHOL, Springer-Verlag 2000, LNCS 1869, pp. 234-251.*

[Har03]   J. Harrison: Formal Verification of Square Root Algorithms. *Formal Methods in System Design, Vol. 22, 2003, pp. 143-153*

[Har05]   J. Harrison: Floating-Point Verification. *Proc. of FM 2005, LNCS 3582 (Springer), pp. 529-532, 2005.*

[Jac02]   Formal Verification of a Fully IEEE Compliant Floating Point Unit. *Dissertation, University of Saarbruecken, April 2002.*

[JW+05]   Ch. Jacobi, K. Weber, V. Paruthi, J. Baumgartner: Automatic Formal Verification on Fused-Multiply-Add FPUs. *Proc. of the conference on Design, automation and test in Europe (DATE), 2005.*

[Kor02]   I. Koren: Computer Arithmetic Algorithms. *2nd edition, (A.K.Peters) 2002.*

[KA00]   R. Kaivola, M, Aagard: Divider Circuit Verification with Model Checking and Theorem Proving. *TPHOL 2000, (Springer) LNCS 1869, pp.338-355.*

[KK03]   R. Kaivola, K. Kohatsu: Proof Engineering in the Large: Formal Verification of Pentium[(R)] 4 Floating-Point Divider. *Software Tools for Technology Transfer, (Springer 2003) Vol.4, Issue 3, pp 323-335.*

[KN02]   R. Kaivola, N. Narasimhan: Formal Verification of the Pentium[(R)] 4 Floating-Point Multiplier *Proc. of the conference on Design, automation and test in Europe (DATE), 2002.*

[Nie03]   Y. Nievergelt: Scalar Fused Multiply-Add Instructions Produce Floating-Point Matrix Arithmetic Provably Accurate to the Penultimate Digit. *ACM Transactions on Mathematical Software (TOMS), VOl.29, Issue 1, ACM Press, March 2003, pp. 27-48.*

[OZ+99]   J. O'Leary, X. Zhao, R. Gerth, C.-J. Seger: Formally Verifying IEEE Compliance of Floating-point Hardware. *Intel Technology Journal, Q1 1999.*

[RF00]   D. Russinoff, A. Flatau: Mechanical Verification of Register-Transfer Logic: A Floating-Point Multiplier. In M. Kaufmann, P. Manolios, J. Moore, Editors, *Computer-Aided Reasoning: ACL2 Case Studies, Kluwer Press 2000.*

[Rus98]   D. Russinoff: A Mechanically Checked Proof of IEEE Compliance of a Register-Transfer-Level Specification of the AMD-K7 Floating-Point Multiplication, Division, and Square Root Instructions. *LMS Journal of Computation and Mathematics 1: pp.148-200, 1998.*

[Rus00]   D. Russinoff: A Case Study in Formal Verification of Register-Transfer Logic with ACL2: The Floating Point Adder of the AMD Athlon(TM) Processor. *FMCAD 2000, Springer, LNCS 1954, pp.3-36.*

[Sch03]   T. Schubert: High Level Formal Verification on Next-Generation Microprocessors. ACM/IEEE Proc. of Design Automation Conference, 2003, pp.1-6.

[STE]   C.-J.H. Seger, R.E. Bryant: Formal Verification by Symbolic Evaluation of Partially-Ordered Trajectories. *Formal Methods in System Design, 6(2):147-189,1995.*

[SN04]   A. Slobodová, K. Nagalla: Formal Verification of Floating-Point Multiply-Add on Itanium[(R)] Processor. *Designing Correct Circuits (Unpublished Proc.), March 2004, Barcelona.*

[Pau96]   L. Paulson: ML for the Working Programmer. *Cambridge University Press, 1996.*

[IEEE]   IEEE Standard for Binary Floating-Point Arithmetic. *ANSI/IEEE Std 754-1985.*

[ISA]   Intel[(R)] Itanium[(R)] Architecture Software Developer's Manual. Revision 2.1, Document numbers: (245317-245319)-004, Intel Corporation. 2002.

Distributed Verification: Exploring the Power of Raw Computing Power*

Luboš Brim

Faculty of Informatics, Masaryk University, Brno, Czech Republic

1   Brute-Force in Distribute Verification

With the increase in complexity of computer systems, it becomes more important to develop formal methods for ensuring their quality and reliability. Various techniques for automated and semi-automated analysis and verification have been successfully applied to real-life computer systems. However, these techniques are computationally hard and memory intensive in general and their applicability to extremely large systems is limited. The major hampering factor is the state space explosion problem due to which large industrial models cannot be efficiently handled by a single state-of-the-art computer.

Much attention has been focused on the development of approaches to battle the state space explosion problem. Many techniques, such as abstraction, state compression, state space reduction, symbolic state representation, etc., are used to reduce the size of the problem to be handled allowing thus a single computer to process larger systems. There are also techniques that purely focus on increasing the amount of available computational power. These are, for example, techniques to fight memory limits with efficient utilisation of an external I/O device [2,19,24,28,32], or techniques that introduce cluster-based algorithms to employ aggregate power of network-interconnected computers.

Cluster-based algorithms perform their computation simultaneously on a number of workstations that are allowed to communicate and synchronise themselves by means of message passing. Cluster-based algorithms can thus be characterised as parallel algorithms performing in a distributed memory environment. The algorithms prove their usefulness in verification of large-scale systems. They have been successfully applied to symbolic model checking [22,23], analysis of stochastic [25] and timed [6] systems, equivalence checking [8] and other related problems [7,9,21].

The idea of parallel verification appeared already in the very early years of the formal verification era. However, inaccessibility of cheap parallel computers together with negative theoretical complexity results excluded this approach from the main stream in formal verification. The situation changed dramatically during the past several years. Computer progress over the past two decades has measured several orders of magnitude with respect to various physical parameters such as computing power, memory size at all hierarchy levels from caches to disk, power consumption, physical size and cost. In particular, the focus of

---

* Supported by the Grant Agency of Czech Republic grant No. 201/06/1338.

L. Brim et al. (Eds.): FMICS and PDMC 2006, LNCS 4346, pp. 23–34, 2007.

novel computer architectures in parallel and distributed computing has shifted away from unique massively parallel systems competing for world records towards smaller and more cost effective systems built from personal computer parts. In addition, recent shift in the emphasis of research on parallel algorithms to pragmatic issues provided practically efficient algorithms for solving computationally hard problems. As a matter of fact, interest in parallel verification has been revived.

Asymptotic complexity analysis has turned out to be a surprisingly effective technique to predict the performance of algorithms, to classify some of the problems as computationally hard. In complexity theory, the class NC (for "Nick's Class") is the set of problems decidable in polylogarithmic time on a parallel computer with a polynomial number of processors. Just as the class P can be thought of as the tractable problems, so NC can be thought of as the problems that can be efficiently solved on a parallel computer. NC is a subset of P because parallel computers can be simulated by sequential ones. It is unknown whether NC = P, but most researchers suspect this to be false, meaning that there are some tractable problems which are probably "inherently sequential" and cannot be sped up significantly by using parallelism. Just as the class NP-complete can be thought of as "probably intractable", so the class P-complete can be thought of as "probably not amenable to efficient parallelisation".

Many efficient parallel algorithm can be found for selected subclasses of P-complete problems. Most problems of practical importance call for compute-intensive methods. Accordingly, the attitude towards "inherently sequential" began to change. Not all "inherently sequential" problems are equally difficult to parallelise. There are many problems where the average, or typical, instance is relatively easy to solve, and only the worst-case instances are computationally very demanding. For example, several efficient and highly parallel algorithms are known for solving the maximum flow problem, which is P-complete. The standard complexity theory for P-complete problems asserts the non-existence of algorithms that are efficiently parallelised across an entire problem class, but ignores the possibility that many instances, perhaps including those of interest, can be solved efficiently.

Efficient parallel solution of many problems often requires invention of original, novel approaches radically different from those used to solve the same problems sequentially. Classical examples are list rankings, connected components, depth-first search in planar graphs etc. The rules of algorithm design and analysis have to be changed drastically: we still have to devise and implement clever algorithms, but complexity is not measured asymptotically in terms of the size of the problem: it is measured by actually counting operations, disk accesses, communications, and seconds. In addition, development of methods, tools, and practises for assessing and refining algorithms through experimentation is unavoidable, extensive use of various techniques for efficient implementation as known from algorithm engineering for parallel computation (see e.g.[1]) underpins the new approach.

One of the simplest approach to parallel problem solving is brute-force parallel exploration of the state space. All possible states are generated in some systematic way and checked for the desired property. If the state space is finite, a success is guaranteed provided we can wait long enough. Although exhaustive search is conceptually simple and often effective, such an approach to problem solving is sometimes considered inelegant. The continuing increase in computing power and memory sizes has revived interest in brute-force techniques. Many "real" problems exhibit no regular structures to be exploited, and that leaves exhaustive enumeration as the only approach in sight.

Model checking finite state systems in practise is bug hunting by exhaustively searching a seemingly "chaotic" state space for failed assertions. Hence, brute-force approach to verification is in some sense quite natural and, more importantly, in fighting the practical limitations caused by the state explosion problem the exhaustive search appears to be the only viable approach. *Reachability* is a simple verification problem that is tractable in parallel as the exhaustive enumeration of the state space can be divided into independent subtasks. Reachability is thus one of the basic techniques for the distributed verification.

As a demonstration of the effectiveness of parallel reachability for solving theoretically intractable problems we consider parallel LTL model-checking. The state space to be explored is a directed graph with an initial state and a set of accepting states. In this state space we want to search for accepting cycles. The simplest brute-force approach is first to search for accepting states reachable from the initial one and then for each accepting vertex to test the reachability of the vertex from itself. However, we can do significantly better by using extra information.

The amount of additional information stored is a major issue for the space complexity. We need to be careful in achieving a good balance between space and speed, ideally we use storage space proportional to the logarithm of the number of states.

We present several algorithms for parallel enumerative LTL model-checking that are based on performing repeated reachability. The demonstration includes algorithms presented in [5,10,11,14,3,4,12,13]. The state space is searched for states carrying a particular information, states might be re-visited as the information changes. To guide the search various data structures are used. Besides the traditional stacks and queues, more complicated data structures might be employed as well.

2   Algorithms for Accepting Cycle Detection

Although the algorithms are meant for cluster-based computing we describe the main ideas primarily as sequential, leaving thus many technical details related to distributed computation out.

The problem we consider comes out from the automata-based procedure to decide LTL model checking problem as introduced in [34]. The approach exploits the fact that every set of executions expressible by an LTL formula is an ω-regular set and can be described by a *Büchi automaton*. In particular, the approach suggests to express all system executions by a *system automaton* and all executions not satisfying the formula by a *property* or *negative claim automaton*. These automata are combined into their synchronous product in order to check for the presence of system executions that violate the property expressed by the formula. The language recognised by the *product automaton* is empty if and only if no system execution is invalid.

The language emptiness problem for Büchi automata can be expressed as an *accepting cycle detection problem* in a graph. Each Büchi automaton can be naturally identified with an *automaton graph* which is a directed graph $G = (V, E, s, A)$ where V is the set of vertexes ($n = |V|$), E is a set of edges ($m = |E|$), s is an initial vertex, and $A \subseteq V$ is a set of accepting vertexes ($a = |A|$). We say that a reachable cycle in G is accepting if it contains an accepting vertex. Let $\mathcal{A}$ be a Büchi automaton and $G_{\mathcal{A}}$ the corresponding automaton graph. Then $\mathcal{A}$ recognises a nonempty language iff $G_{\mathcal{A}}$ contains an accepting cycle. The LTL model-checking problem is thus reduced to the accepting cycle detection problem in automaton graphs.

The best known enumerative sequential algorithms for detection of accepting cycles are the *Nested DFS* algorithm [17,27] (implemented, e.g., in the model checker SPIN [26]) and *SCC-based algorithms* originating in Tarjan's algorithm for the decomposition of the graph into strongly connected components (SCCs) [33]. While Nested DFS is more space efficient, SCC-based algorithms produce shorter counterexamples in general. Here, for simplicity reasons, we will not be dealing with the counterexample generation subtask.

It is a well known fact that computing depth-first search postorder is P-complete [31], hence probably inherently sequential. This means that none of the two algorithms can be easily adapted to work on a parallel machine. A few fundamentally different cluster-based techniques for accepting cycle detection appeared though. They typically perform repeated reachability over the graph. Unlike the postorder problem, reachability is a graph problem which can be well parallelised, hence the algorithms might be transformed to cluster-based algorithm that work with reasonable increase in time and space.

2.1   Maximal Accepting Predecessor (MAP)

A vertex u is a predecessor of a vertex v if there is a non-trivial path from u to v. The main idea behind the algorithm is based on the fact that each accepting vertex lying on an accepting cycle is its own predecessor.

Instead of expensive computing and storing of all accepting predecessors for each (accepting) vertex, the algorithm computes a single representative accepting predecessor for each vertex. We presuppose a linear ordering $\prec$ of vertexes (given e.g. by their memory representation) and choose the *maximal accepting predecessor*. For a vertex u we denote its maximal accepting predecessor in the graph G by $map_G(u)$. Clearly, if an accepting vertex is its own maximal accepting predecessor ($map_G(u) = u$), it is its own predecessor and it lies on an accepting cycle. Unfortunately, the opposite does not hold in general. It can happen that the maximal accepting predecessor for an accepting vertex on a cycle does not lie on the cycle. Such vertexes can be safely deleted from the set of accepting vertexes (by applying the *deleting transformation*) and the accepting cycle still remains in the resulting graph. Whenever the deleting transformation is applied to automaton graph G with $map_G(v) \neq v$ for all $v \in V$, it shrinks the set of accepting vertexes by those vertexes that do not lie on any cycle.

As the set of accepting vertexes can change after the deleting transformation has been applied, maximal accepting predecessors must be recomputed. It can happen that even in the graph $del(G)$ the maximal accepting predecessor function is still not sufficient for cycle detection. However, after a finite number of applications of the deleting transformation an accepting cycle is certified. For an automaton graph without accepting cycles the repetitive application of the deleting transformation results in an automaton graph with an empty set of accepting vertexes.

Time complexity of the algorithm is $\mathcal{O}(a^2 \cdot m)$, where a is the number of accepting vertexes. Here the factor $a \cdot m$ comes from the computation of the *map* function and the factor a relates to the number of iterations.

One of the key aspects influencing the overall performance of the algorithm is the underlying ordering of vertexes used by the algorithm. In order to optimise the complexity one aims to decrease the number of iterations by choosing an appropriate vertex ordering. Ordering $\prec$ is *optimal* if the presence of an accepting cycle can be decided in one iteration. It can be easily shown that for every automaton graph there is an optimal ordering. Moreover, an optimal ordering can be computed in linear time.

An example of an optimal ordering is depth-first search postorder. Unfortunately, the *optimal ordering problem*, which is to decide for a given automaton graph and two accepting vertexes u, v whether u precedes v in *every* optimal ordering of graph vertexes, is P-complete [12] hence unlikely to be computed effectively in a distributed environment. Therefore, several heuristics for computing a suitable vertex ordering are used. The trivial one orders vertexes lexicographically according to their bit-vector representations. The more sophisticated heuristics relate vertexes with respect to the order in which they were traversed. However, experimental evaluation has shown that none of the heuristics significantly outperforms the others. On average, the most reliable heuristic is the one based on breadth-first search followed by the one based on (random) hashing.

2.2   Eliminating Bad States (OWCTY)

The accepting cycle detection problem can be directly reformulated as a question whether the automaton graph contains a nontrivial accepting strongly connected component.

A *strongly connected component* (SCC) of $G = (V, E, s, A)$ is a maximal (with respect to set inclusion) set of vertexes $C \subseteq V$ such that for each $u, v \in C$, the vertex v is reachable from u and vice versa. The *quotient graph* of G, $Q(G)$, is a graph (W, H) where W is the set of the SCCs of G and $(C_1, C_2) \in H$ if and only if $C_1 \neq C_2$ and there exist $r \in C_1, s \in C_2$ such that $(r, s) \in E$. The *height* of the graph G, $h(G)$, is the length of the longest path in the quotient graph of G (note that the quotient graph is acyclic). A strongly connected component is *trivial* if it has no edges, *initial* if it has no predecessor in the quotient graph, and *accepting* if it contains an accepting vertex.

The inspiration for the distributed SCC-based algorithm for detection of accepting cycles is taken from symbolic algorithms for cycle detection, namely from SCC hull algorithms. SCC hull algorithms compute the set of vertexes containing all accepting components. Algorithms maintain the approximation of the set and successively remove non-accepting components until they reach a fixpoint. Different strategies to remove non-accepting components lead to different algorithms. An overview, taxonomy, and comparison of symbolic algorithms can be found in independent reports [20] and [30].

As the base for the enumerative algorithm presented here the *One Way Catch Them Young* strategy [20] has been chosen. The enumerative algorithm works on individual vertexes rather than on sets of vertexes as is the case in symbolic approach. A component is removed by removing its vertexes. The algorithm employs two rules to remove vertexes of non-accepting components:

- if a vertex is not reachable from any accepting vertex then the vertex does not belong to any accepting component and
- if a vertex has in-degree zero then the vertex does not belong to any accepting component.

Note that an alternative set of rules can be formulated as

- if no accepting vertex is reachable from a vertex then the vertex does not belong to any accepting component and
- if a vertex has out-degree zero then the vertex does not belong to any accepting component.

This second set of rules results in an algorithm which works in a *backward* manner and we will not describe it explicitly here.

The presented SCC-based algorithm in its forward version requires the entire automaton graph to be generated first. The same is true for the backward version. Moreover, the backward version actually needs to store the edges to be able to perform backward reachability. This is however payed out by relaxing the necessity to compute successors, which is in fact a very expensive operation in practise.

Time complexity of the algorithm is $\mathcal{O}(h \cdot m)$ where $h = h(G)$. Here the factor m comes from the computation of *Reachability* and *Elimination* functions and the factor h relates to the number of external iterations. In practise, the number of external iterations is very small even for large graphs. This observation is supported by experiments in [20] with the symbolic implementation and hardware circuits problems. Similar results are communicated in [29] where heights of quotient graphs were measured for several models. As reported, 70% of the models has height smaller than 50.

A positive aspect of SCC-based algorithms is their effectiveness for *weak automaton graphs*. A graph is weak if each SCC component of G is either fully contained in A or is disjoint with A. For weak graphs one iteration of the SCC-based algorithm is sufficient to decide accepting cycles. The studies of temporal properties [18,15] reveal that verification of up to 90% of LTL properties leads to weak automaton graphs.

Last but not least, SCC-based algorithms can be effortlessly extended to automaton graphs for other types of nondeterministic word automata like generalised Büchi automata and Streett automata.

2.3 Maximal Number of Accepting Predecessors (NEGC)

Consider *maximal number* of accepting vertexes on a path from the source to a vertex, the maximum being taken over all paths. For vertexes on an accepting cycle the maximum does not exist because extending a path along the cycle adds at least one accepting vertex.

For computing the maximal number of accepting predecessors the algorithm maintains for every vertex v its "distance" label $d(v)$ giving the maximal number of accepting predecessors, parent vertex $p(v)$, and status $S(v) \in \{unreached, labelled, scanned\}$. Initially, $d(v) = \infty, p(v) = nil$, and $S(v) = unreached$ for every vertex v. The method starts by setting $d(s) = 0$, $p(s) = nil$ and $S(s) = labelled$, where s is the initial vertex. At every step a *labelled* vertex is selected and scanned. When scanning a vertex u, all its outgoing edges are *relaxed* (immediate successors are checked). Relaxation of an edge (u, v) means that if $d(v)$ is an accepting vertex then $d(v)$ is set to $d(u) + 1$ and $p(v)$ is set to u. The status of u is changed to *scanned* while the status of v is changed to *labelled*. If all vertexes are either *scanned* or *unreached* then d gives the maximal number of accepting predecessors. Moreover, the *parent graph* G_p is the graph of these "maximal" paths. More precisely, the parent graph is a subgraph G_p of G induced by edges $(p(v), v)$ for all v such that $p(v) \neq nil$.

Different strategies for selecting a labelled vertex to be scanned lead to different algorithms. When using FIFO strategy to select vertexes, the algorithm runs in $\mathcal{O}(m \cdot n)$ time in the worst case. For graphs with reachable accepting cycles there is no "maximal" path to the vertexes on an accepting cycle and the scanning method must be modified to recognise such cycles. The algorithm employs the *walk to root* strategy which traverses a *parent graph*. The walk to root strategy is based on the fact (see e.g. [16]) that any cycle in parent graph G_p corresponds to an accepting cycle in the automaton graph.

The walk to root method tests whether G_p is acyclic. Suppose the parent graph G_p is acyclic and an edge (u, v) is relaxed, i.e. $d(v)$ is decreased. This operation creates a cycle in G_p if and only if v is an ancestor of u in the current G_p. Before applying the operation, we follow the parent pointers from u until we reach either v or s. If we stop at v a cycle is detected. Otherwise, the relaxation does not create a cycle. However, since the path to the initial vertex can be long, the cost of edge relaxation becomes $\mathcal{O}(n)$ instead of $\mathcal{O}(1)$. In order to optimise the overall computational complexity, amortisation is used to pay the cost of checking G_p for cycles. More precisely, the parent graph G_p is tested only after the underlying scanning algorithm performs $\Omega(n)$ relaxations. The running time is thus increased only by a constant factor. The worst case time complexity of the algorithm is thus $\mathcal{O}(n \cdot m)$.

2.4 Back-Level Edges (BLEDGE)

The algorithm builds on breadth-first search (BFS) exploration of the graph. BFS is typically used in graph algorithms that work with distances and distances can also be used to characterise cycles in a graph.

Distance of a vertex $u \in V$, $d(u)$, is the length of a shortest path from the initial vertex to the vertex u. The set of vertexes with the same distance is called *level*. An edge $(u, v) \in E$ is called a *back-level edge* if $d(u) \geq d(v)$.

The key observation connecting the cycle detection problem with the back-level edge concept is that every cycle contains at least one back-level edge. Back-level edges are therefore used as triggers which start a cycle detection. However, it is too expensive to test every back-level edge for being a part of a cycle. The algorithm therefore integrates several optimisations and heuristics to decrease the number of tested edges and speed-up the cycle test.

The BFS procedure which detects back-level edges runs in time $\mathcal{O}(m + n)$. Each back-level edge has to be checked to be on a cycle, which requires linear time $\mathcal{O}(m + n)$ as well. In the worst case there can be $\mathcal{O}(m)$ back-level edges, hence the overall time complexity of the algorithm is $\mathcal{O}(m \cdot (m + n))$. Its space complexity is $\mathcal{O}(m + n)$.

3 Comparing the Algorithms

To compare the algorithms we can use the standard asymptotic complexity measures. In Table 1 we summarise time and space complexity of the algorithms, where n is the number of vertexes, m is the number of edges, h is the height of the SCC tree, and a is the number of accepting vertexes in the graph. It seems that Nested DFS and Tarjan's algorithm are asymptotically the best algorithms, both sharing the first place. However, Nested DFS needs only two additional bits, while Tarjan's algorithm needs to store more data to handle DFS and completion numbers. Despite being asymptotically the same, and in fact optimal, in reality Nested DFS is more space efficient than Tarjan's algorithm. All the other algorithms are generally worse. This is true for the worst case analysis when considering these algorithms as sequential ones.

Table 1. Asymptotic time and space complexity

	Time complexity	Space complexity
Nested DFS	$\mathcal{O}(m + n)$	$\mathcal{O}(n)$
Tarjan's algorithm	$\mathcal{O}(m + n)$	$\mathcal{O}(n)$
MAP	$\mathcal{O}(a^2 \cdot m)$	$\mathcal{O}(n)$
BLEV	$\mathcal{O}(m \cdot (m + n))$	$\mathcal{O}(m + n)$
NEGC	$\mathcal{O}(m \cdot n)$	$\mathcal{O}(m + n)$
OWCTY	$\mathcal{O}(h \cdot (m + n))$	$\mathcal{O}(n)$

The situation looks quite different if we want to adapt the algorithms for the distributed environment. Both, the Nested DFS and the Tarjan's algorithm perform badly, because they rely on depth first search postorder of vertexes and in a distributed environment we need to use very expensive techniques to assure the postorder. On the other hand, all the other algorithms can be parallelised easily. The reason is that they do not use any particular order of vertexes and the graph can be explored using local information only.

Still, despite the purely theoretical asymptotic worst case differences, there are many other, often more practical, aspects that may make a difference. Typical example is, when we consider some particular instances of the problem, like graphs with or without accepting cycles. Consider the algorithm MAP. If there is no accepting cycle in the graph, the number of iterations is typically very small in comparison to the size of the graph (up to 40–50). Thus, the algorithm exhibits nearly linear performance. Some other points have been also made when describing the algorithms.

Often we do not know the problem belongs to the specific instance class. However, sometimes we might be able to classify the problem instance in advance and use the most appropriate algorithm to solve the problem.

In the case of automata-based approach to LTL model checking the product automaton that originates from synchronous product of the property and system automata. Hence, vertexes of product automaton graph are ordered pairs. An interesting observation is that every cycle in a product automaton graph emerges from cycles in system and property automaton graphs.

As the property automaton origins from the LTL formula to be verified, it is typically quite small and can be pre-analysed. In particular, it is possible to identify all strongly connected components of the property automaton graph. Cluster-based algorithms use a *partition function* which distributes vertexes of the graph among the participating workstations so that every workstation maintains only a part of the graph. Respecting strongly connected components of the property automaton, a partition function preserving cycle locality can be defined. The partitioning strategy is to assign all vertexes that project to the same strongly connected component of the property automaton graph to the same workstation. Since no cycle is split it is possible to employ localised Nested DFS algorithm to perform local accepting cycle detection simultaneously on all participating workstations.

Yet another interesting information can be drawn from the property automaton graph decomposition. Maximal strongly connected components can be classified into three categories:

Type F: (*Fully Accepting*) Any cycle within the component contains at least one accepting vertex. (There is no non-accepting cycle within the component.)

Type P: (*Partially Accepting*) There is at least one accepting cycle and one non-accepting cycle within the component.

Type N: (*Non-Accepting*) There is no accepting cycle within the component.

Realising that a vertex of a product automaton graph is accepting only if the corresponding vertex in the property automaton graph is accepting it is possible to characterise types of strongly connected components of product automaton graph according to types of components in the property automaton graph. Classification of components into types N, F, and P is useful in other cluster-based algorithms presented in this paper.

It is evident, and we have already explicitly highlighted this with the algorithm presentation on several places, that performing *empirical studies* for comparing actual relative performance of algorithms so as to study their amenability for use in LTL model checking is of crucial importance and in some sense even more important than the traditional asymptotic view. This may lead to the discovery of problem instances for which the performances of solving algorithms are clearly different. Other important results of empirical investigations include assessing heuristics for hard problems, characterising the asymptotic behaviour of complex algorithms, discovering the speed-up achieved by parallel algorithms and studying the effects of the memory hierarchy and of communication on real machines, thus helping in predicting performance and finding bottlenecks in real systems. Experiments can thus help measure many practical indicators that may be extremely difficult to predict theoretically.

A careful tuning of the code, as well as the addition of ad-hoc heuristics and local hacks, may dramatically improve the performances of some algorithms, although the theoretical asymptotic behaviour may be not affected. Unfortunately, it may be sometimes difficult to draw general conclusions about algorithms from experiments. One of the common pitfall is the irreproducibility of experimental results for distributed algorithms.

4   Conclusions

Distributed verification is a new emerging field. Extending the techniques as known from the sequential world adds significant complications and often requires entirely new approaches. In designing practical parallel solutions for distributed verification we need to change our attitude. The key steps for their effective deployment in industry and real applications is to forget about asymptotics, use algorithm engineering techniques and experimental algorithmics, consider often overlooked, yet practically important issues such as hidden constant factors, effects of the memory hierarchy, implications of communication complexity, numerical precision, and use of heuristics. The new demand for distributed verification algorithms that are of practical utility has raised the need to refine and reinforce the traditional theoretical approach.

References

1. D. Bader, B. Moret, and P. Sanders. Algorithm Engineering for Parallel Computation. In *Experimental Algorithmics*, volume 2547 of *LNCS*, pages 1–23. Springer-Verlag, 2002.

2. T. Bao and M. Jones. Time-Efficient Model Checking with Magnetic Disks. In *Proc. Tools and Algorithms for the Construction and Analysis of Systems*, volume 3440 of *LNCS*, pages 526–540. Springer-Verlag, 2005.

3. J. Barnat, L. Brim, and J. Chaloupka. Parallel Breadth-First Search LTL Model-Checking. In *Proc. 18th IEEE International Conference on Automated Software Engineering*, pages 106–115. IEEE Computer Society, 2003.

4. J. Barnat and I. Černá. Distributed Breadth-First Search LTL Model Checking. *Formal Methods in System Design*, 2006. to appear.

5. Jiří Barnat. *Distributed Memory LTL Model Checking*. PhD thesis, Faculty of Informatics, Masaryk University Brno, 2004.

6. G. Behrmann, T. S. Hune, and F. W. Vaandrager. Distributed Timed Model Checking – How the Search Order Matters. In *Proc. Computer Aided Verification*, volume 1855 of *LNCS*, pages 216–231. Springer, 2000.

7. A. Bell and B. R. Haverkort. Sequential and distributed model checking of petri net specifications. *Int J Softw Tools Technol Transfer*, 7(1):43–60, 2005.

8. S. Blom and S. Orzan. A Distributed Algorithm for Strong Bisimulation Reduction Of State Spaces. *Int J Softw Tools Technol Transfer*, 7(1):74–86, 2005.

9. B. Bollig, M. Leucker, and M. Weber. Parallel Model Checking for the Alternation Free μ-Calculus. In *Proc. Tools and Algorithms for the Construction and Analysis of Systems*, volume 2031 of *LNCS*, pages 543 – 558. Springer-Verlag, 2001.

10. L. Brim, I. Černá, P. Krčál, and R. Pelánek. Distributed LTL Model Checking Based on Negative Cycle Detection. In *Proc. Foundations of Software Technology and Theoretical Computer Science*, volume 2245 of *LNCS*, pages 96–107. Springer-Verlag, 2001.

11. L. Brim, I. Černá, P. Krčál, and R. Pelánek. How to Employ Reverse Search in Distributed Single-Source Shortest Paths. In *Proc. Theory and Practice of Informatics (SOFSEM)*, volume 2234 of *LNCS*, pages 191–200. Springer-Verlag, 2001.

12. L. Brim, I. Černá, P. Moravec, and J. Šimša. Accepting Predecessors are Better than Back Edges in Distributed LTL Model-Checking. In *Formal Methods in Computer-Aided Design (FMCAD 2004)*, volume 3312 of *LNCS*, pages 352–366. Springer-Verlag, 2004.

13. L. Brim, I. Černá, P. Moravec, and J. Šimša. How to Order Vertices for Distributed LTL Model-Checking Based on Accepting Predecessors. In *4th International Workshop on Parallel and Distributed Methods in verifiCation (PDMC'05)*, July 2005.

14. I. Černá and R. Pelánek. Distributed Explicit Fair cycle Detection (Set Based Approach). In *Model Checking Software. 10th International SPIN Workshop*, volume 2648 of *LNCS*, pages 49–73. Springer-Verlag, 2003.

15. I. Černá and R. Pelánek. Relating Hierarchy of Temporal Properties to Model Checking. In *Proc. Mathematical Foundations of Computer Science*, volume 2747 of *LNCS*, pages 318–327. Springer-Verlag, 2003.

16. B. V. Cherkassky and A. V. Goldberg. Negative-Cycle Detection Algorithms. *Mathematical Programming*, 85:277–311, 1999.

17. C. Courcoubetis, M.Y. Vardi, P. Wolper, and M. Yannakakis. Memory-Efficient Algorithms for the Verification of Temporal Properties. *Formal Methods in System Design*, 1:275–288, 1992.

18. M. B. Dwyer, G. S. Avrunin, and J. C. Corbett. Property Specification Patterns for Finite-State Verification. In *Proc. Workshop on Formal Methods in Software Practice*, pages 7–15. ACM Press, 1998.

19. S. Edelkamp and S. Jabbar. Large-Scale Directed Model Checking LTL. In *Model Checking Software: 13th International SPIN Workshop*, volume 3925 of *LNCS*, pages 1–18. Springer-Verlag, 2006.
20. K. Fisler, R. Fraer, G. Kamhi, M. Y. Vardi, and Z. Yang. Is there a best symbolic cycle-detection algorithm? In *Proc. Tools and Algorithms for the Construction and Analysis of Systems*, volume 2031 of *LNCS*, pages 420–434. Springer-Verlag, 2001.
21. H. Garavel, R. Mateescu, and I. Smarandache. Parallel State Space Construction for Model-Checking. In *Proc. SPIN Workshop on Model Checking of Software*, volume 2057 of *LNCS*, pages 216–234. Springer-Verlag, 2001.
22. O. Grumberg, T. Heyman, N. Ifergan, and A. Schuster. "achieving speedups in distributed symbolic reachability analysis through asynchronous computation". In *Correct Hardware Design and Verification Methods, 13th IFIP WG 10.5 Advanced Research Working Conference, CHARME 2005*, Lecture Notes in Computer Science, pages 129–145. Springer, 2005.
23. O. Grumberg, T. Heyman, and A. Schuster. Distributed Model Checking for μ-calculus. In *Proc. Computer Aided Verification*, volume 2102 of *LNCS*, pages 350–362. Springer-Verlag, 2001.
24. M. Hammer and M. Weber. "To Store or Not To Store" reloaded: Reclaiming memory on demand. In Luboš Brim, Boudewijn Haverkort, Martin Leucker, and Jaco van de Pol, editors, *Formal Methods: Applications and Technology (FMICS + PDMC)*, volume 4346 of *Lecture Notes in Computer Science*, pages 52–67. Springer, August 2006.
25. B. R. Haverkort, A. Bell, and H. C. Bohnenkamp. On the Efficient Sequential and Distributed Generation of Very Large Markov Chains From Stochastic Petri Nets. In *Proc. 8th Int. Workshop on Petri Net and Performance Models*, pages 12–21. IEEE Computer Society Press, 1999.
26. G. J. Holzmann. *The Spin Model Checker: Primer and Reference Manual*. Addison-Wesley, 2003.
27. G. J. Holzmann, D. Peled, and M. Yannakakis. On Nested Depth First Search. In *Proc. SPIN Workshop on Model Checking of Software*, pages 23–32. American Mathematical Society, 1996.
28. S. Jabbar and S. Edelkamp. Parallel External Directed Model Checking with Linear I/O. In *Verification, Model Checking, and Abstract Interpretation: 7th International Conference, VMCAI 2006*, volume 3855 of *LNCS*, pages 237–251. Springer-Verlag, 2006.
29. R. Pelánek. Typical Structural Properties of State Spaces. In *Proc. of SPIN Workshop*, volume 2989 of *LNCS*, pages 5–22. Springer-Verlag, 2004.
30. K. Ravi, R. Bloem, and F. Somenzi. A Comparative Study of Symbolic Algorithms for the Computation of Fair Cycles. In *Proc. Formal Methods in Computer-Aided Design*, volume 1954 of *LNCS*, pages 143–160. Springer-Verlag, 2000.
31. J. Reif. Depth-first Search is Inherently Sequential. *Information Proccesing Letters*, 20(5):229–234, 1985.
32. U. Stern and D.L. Dill. Using magnetic disc instead of main memory in the murφ verifier. In *Proc. of Computer Aided Verification*, volume 1427 of *LNCS*, pages 172 – 183. Springer-Verlag, 1998.
33. R. Tarjan. Depth First Search and Linear Graph Algorithms. *SIAM Journal on Computing*, pages 146–160, Januar 1972.
34. M.Y. Vardi and P. Wolper. An automata-theoretic approach to automatic program verification. In *Proc. IEEE Symposium on Logic in Computer Science*, pages 322–331. Computer Society Press, 1986.

An Easy-to-Use, Efficient Tool-Chain to Analyze the Availability of Telecommunication Equipment

Kai Lampka[1], Markus Siegle[1], and Max Walter[2]

[1] Universität der Bundeswehr München, Institut für Technische Informatik
{kai.lampka,markus.siegle}@unibw.de
[2] Technische Universität München, Lehrstuhl für Rechnertechnik und
Rechnerorganisation
max.walter@in.tum.de

Abstract. The tool OpenSESAME offers an easy-to-use modeling framework which enables realistic availability and reliability analysis of fault-tolerant systems. Our symbolic engine, which is based on an extension of binary decision diagrams (BDDs), is capable of analyzing Markov reward models consisting of more than 10^8 system states. In this paper, we introduce a tool chain where OpenSESAME is employed for specifying models of fault-tolerant systems, and at the back end our symbolic engine is employed for carrying out numerical Markov reward analysis. For illustrating the applicability of this approach, we analyze a model of a fault-tolerant telecommunication service system with N redundant modules, where the system is available as long as at least K modules are available. Based on this model, it is shown, that the suggested tool chain has more modeling power than traditional combinatorial methods, e.g. simple reliability block diagrams or fault trees, is still easy-to-use if compared to other high-level model description techniques, and allows the analysis of complex system models where other tools fail.

Keywords: Reliability and Availability Analysis, Markov Reward Model, State Space Explosion Binary Decision Diagram, Reliability Block Diagrams.

1 Introduction

Motivation: Obtaining measurement data in order to quantify the reliability and availability (RA) of a system is often very difficult in practice, or even impossible. Thus one is restricted to analyzing a system (or high-level) model, rather than analyzing the system directly. Reliability block diagrams (RBD) are an adequate technique for describing systems, when RA-issues are emphasized. Furthermore, RBDs are a well accepted method in industrial practice. However, using RBDs assumes that, firstly, all failure and repair events in the system are stochastically independent, and secondly, that each component can be in two

L. Brim et al. (Eds.): FMICS and PDMC 2006, LNCS 4346, pp. 35–50, 2007.

states only (active or failed). In contrast, Markov Reward models (MRMs) provide a powerful mathematical framework for computing system state probabilities and thus quantifying a system under study. The modeling power of MRMs is much higher than that of RBDs: Each component can be described by an arbitrary number of states (e.g. active, passive, and several failed states), and arbitrary inter-component dependencies (such as failure propagation, failures with a common cause, or limited repair capacities) can be specified. In contrast to empirical evaluation as provided by simulation studies, which is the most accepted technique in industry, MRM-based studies are restricted to models where events occur with an exponential or zero delay. However, this restriction comes at the benefit that MRMs allow an extensive (!) analysis, such that rare events of fatal impact can also be assessed, where simulation studies may fail to do so. Consequently, MRMs are an adequate formal model for analyzing in particular industrial critical systems.

In this work we consider a tool chain, in which the tool OpenSESAME (simple but extensive structured availability modeling environment) is used as the user interface. In this tool, systems are modeled using RBDs, which can be enriched with intercomponent dependencies. Thus, the traditional limitations of these easy-to-use models were overcome. OpenSESAME automatically converts these diagrams into a high-level model specification (e.g. a stochastic Petri net (SPN)). The interleaving semantics of standard high-level model description methods, such as SPN among others, applied for transforming the obtained high-level model into its low-level representation (commonly denoted as state graph (SG)), may lead to an exponential blow-up in the number of system states. This phenomenon, commonly addressed as *state space explosion* problem, often hampers the analysis of complex and large systems, if not making it impossible at all. Here symbolic methods have shown to ease the problem, such that system models consisting of more than, say, 10^8 system states are still treatable and their RA-measure are still obtainable on commodity computers. Therefore, in the approach presented here, OpenSESAME diagrams are first converted into stochastic activity networks (SAN) as accepted by the tool Möbius [DCC$^+$02]. Internally, the generated SANs are analysed by the *zero-suppressed multi-terminal decision diagram* (ZDD)-based symbolic framework as presented in [LS06a, LS06b]. In this paper we show, that

1. using OpenSESAME, it is much easier to create sophisticated availability models than by e.g. directly creating the corresponding SAN manually, and
2. the proposed tool chain, which is based on ZDDs, is much more efficient in terms of time and space compared to traditional solution methods. The advantages stem from the fact that the traditional methods require the explicit generation of the system's complete state space and the storage of its transition matrix in a sparse matrix format.

Organization: The paper is organized as follows: Sec. 2 introduces the employed tool infrastructure. The model world is introduced in Sec. 3 by giving basic definitions. The general idea of symbolically representing and numerically solving MRMs is introduced in Sec. 4. An industrial case study for evaluating our framework is presented in Sec. 5. Sec. 6 concludes the paper by indicating some related work, by summarizing the achieved innovations and mentioning future steps.

2 Tool Chain

For analyzing systems we employ the tool chain as illustrated in Fig. 1. Via the process of abstraction and simplification one builds a system model, specified as an extended RBD within the tool OpenSESAME. The obtained RA-model is then mapped onto a Stochastic Activity Network (SAN). A SAN is a form of extended Generalized Stochastic Petri Net (GSPN), which also contains reward functions, employed here for describing the RA-measures of interest. The modeling tool Möbius supports the specification of high-level models of that kind. Our new symbolic engine, which possesses an interface to Möbius, can then be employed for generating a symbolic representation of the specified MRM (SAN + reward functions). The numerical solution of the symbolically represented low-level MRM allows finally the computation of the RA-measures of interest. In the following we briefly introduce the different components as employed in the suggested tool chain.

OpenSESAME [WT04, WT05]: The graphical user interface of OpenSESAME allows for the creation of traditional combinatorial availability models, which can be enriched with inter-component dependencies. In these models, a system is defined by its *components*, each specified by a *Mean Time To Failure (MTTF)* and *Mean Time To Repair (MTTR)*. In addition, *reliability block diagrams* specify the redundancy structure of the system, i.e. they determine which components have to be available at the same time to make the overall system available. Several kinds of inter-component dependencies can be specified in an OpenSESAME input model which greatly increases the modeling power without compromising its usability as shown in Sec. 3.1 of this paper.

Möbius Modeling Tool: Möbius is a software tool for performance and reliability evaluation of discrete event systems. Currently, Möbius supports several model specification formalisms [DCC+02], including *Stochastic Activity Networks* (SAN),

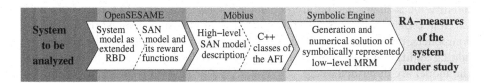

Fig. 1. Tool chain

an extension of GSPNs. Since OpenSESAME can generate GSPNs out of its input diagrams, Möbius can be used in our tool chain.

Within Möbius, the SANs are mapped onto the *Abstract Functional Interface* (AFI), which is implemented in C++ and constitutes the interface between the state graph generator and the (high-level) SAN model specification. Each place of the SAN is hereby mapped onto a *state variable* (SV). Consequently, during state graph exploration, a state of the system model is represented by the values of the SVs, where the ordered tuple of n SVs is commonly denoted as the *state vector*. However, rather than specifying now the RA-measures directly on the level of the state graph, one may define reward functions on the level of the SAN model specification. In the tool chain presented here, these rate rewards are created automatically by OpenSESAME.

Symbolic Engine: The new symbolic engine for analyzing Möbius models with very large state graphs is based on ZDDs, where the implementation consists of the following four modules:

1. A module for the explicit generation of states, which make uses of Möbius' AFI and thus constitutes the interface between the symbolic engine and Möbius.
2. The symbolic state graph generation engine, which generates a symbolic representation of the CTMC of the low-level MRM.
3. A ZDD-library, which is based on the CUDD-package [Som]. This library mainly contains the C++ class definition of ZDDs, the new recursive algorithms for manipulating them and their operator-caches.
4. A library for computing the desired RA-measures on the basis of the symbolically represented MRM. This module contains:
   (a) steady state and transient numerical solvers for computing the state probabilities.
   (b) algorithms for efficiently generating symbolic representations of rate reward functions and for computing the first and second moment of their probability distributions.

3   Model World

3.1   OpenSESAME Input Model

An OpenSESAME model as seen by the user comprises component tables, reliability block diagrams, failure dependency diagrams, repair group tables, and variable tables. Not all model parts are necessary, usually one starts with one component table and a block diagram only. Then the model can be refined by adding additional tables and diagrams. In the following, the individual parts of the model are described.

The *component tables* list all components of which the system consists. Each component type has a unique name, a mean time to failure (MTTF), and a mean time to repair (MTTR). If the system contains several components of the

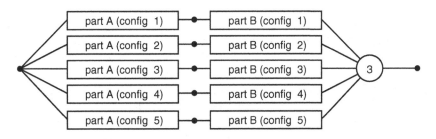

Fig. 2. *"3-out-of-5:G"* system. The system is available, if at least 3 out of 5 configurations are available. In this case, each configuration comprises two components: part A and part B.

same type, the table also lists the number of components of this type. Furthermore, each component may have either a dedicated repair person or is allotted to a repair group (see below). For small and medium sized models, a single component table will be sufficient. For large models, several tables can be used to group related components. An extended version of *reliability block diagrams* (RBD) is used to model the redundancy structure of the system. RBDs are undirected graphs where each edge is labeled with a component. A component may appear several times in the same RBD. Two special nodes s and t define a Boolean system which is available, if there is a connection between these nodes and unavailable otherwise. As components can be unavailable so can the edges: calculating the probability whether s and t are connected yields the availability of the modeled system. In OpenSESAME, several modern extensions to traditional RBDs were implemented. First, the user may specify more than two border nodes. This allows for calculating the availabilities of subsystems in addition to the overall availability. Second, edges may be labeled with a sub-RBD instead of a component. This allows for building a hierarchy of RBDs. Thus, even large systems can be modeled in a concise way. Third, so-called *"k-out-of-N:G"* edges are supported.

As an example, Figure 2 shows a *"3-out-of-5:G"* system which is available if at least 3 of its 5 so-called configurations are available. A configuration may be a simple component, or an arbitrarily large sub-diagram. Alternatively, the system could be modeled using regular RBDs without *"k-out-of-N:G"* edges, however, such an RBD would comprise 30 edges.

Finally, as a unique feature of OpenSESAME, the model can be enriched with inter-component dependencies. Because some dependencies are related to the redundancy structure of the system, it makes sense to add these dependencies to the RBD. For example, in many systems fault tolerance is achieved using fault recovery techniques. In these systems, the redundant components are in passive or standby mode as long as the system is fault free. In contrast to so-called active-active systems which are based on fault masking, the redundant components can be used for non-critical tasks. Furthermore, in systems with fault recovery, a redundant component can possibly replace several components, which allows the construction of N+1 redundant systems. However, such systems also have a drawback compared to systems based on fault masking: the failure of an active component must be detected, localized and isolated, and the redundant component must be activated after the failure of the primary component. During this so-called fail-over time, the system is unavailable. To avoid over-optimistic results and unfair comparisons, availability models should therefore take into account possible fail-over times of fault recovery mechanisms. In OpenSESAME, k-of-N:G edges can therefore be attributed with a fail-over time.

A detailed description of all features of OpenSESAME is outside the scope of this paper. Instead, the interested reader is referred to previous publications [WS05, WT05]. For an overview on the transformation process of OpenSESAME input models into GSPNs and SANs one may refer to [WT04].

3.2 Properties of High-Level MRMs

Via state graph generation a high-level model description and its set of user-defined rate rewards can be mapped to a continuous time Markov chain (CTMC), where each system state is equipped with a rate reward[1]. This yields what is commonly denoted as (low-level) Markov reward model (MRM). In the following we define some properties of high-level model descriptions, as required for our symbolic framework for efficiently generating symbolic representations of MRMs.

Static Properties: A high-level model M consists of a finite ordered set of discrete state variables (SVs) $s_i \in \mathcal{S}$, where each can take values from a finite subset of the naturals. Each state of the model is thus given as a vector $\vec{s} \in \mathbb{S} \subset \mathbb{N}^{|S|}$. A model has a finite set of activities ($\mathcal{A}ct$), where the enabling and execution of an activity l depends on a set of SVs ($\mathcal{S}_l^{\mathcal{D}}$). Two activities are defined to be dependent if their sets of dependent SVs are not disjoint. We also define a projection function $\chi \colon (\mathcal{S}_l^{\mathcal{D}}, \mathbb{N}^{|S|}) \longrightarrow \mathbb{N}^{|\mathcal{S}_l^{\mathcal{D}}|}$ which yields the sub-vector consisting of the dependent SVs only. We use the shorthand notation $\vec{s}_{d_l} := \chi(\mathcal{S}_l^{\mathcal{D}}, \vec{s})$, where $\vec{s}_{d_l}$ is called the activity-local marking of state $\vec{s}$ with respect to activity l.

Dynamic Properties: When an activity is executed, the model evolves from one state to another. For each activity $l \in \mathcal{A}ct$ we have a transition function $\delta_l \colon \mathbb{S} \longrightarrow \mathbb{S}$, whose specific implementation depends on the model description method. Concerning the target state of a transition, we use the superscript of a state descriptor to indicate the sequence of activities leading to that state. It is assumed that the computation of δ_l depends solely on those positions of $\vec{s}$ referring to the SVs contained in $\mathcal{S}_l^{\mathcal{D}}$. By state graph exploration one can construct the successor-state relation as a set of quadruples $T \subseteq (\mathbb{S} \times \mathcal{A}ct \times \mathbb{R}^{>0} \times \mathbb{S})$, which is the set of transitions of a stochastic labeled transition system (SLTS), i.e. the

---

[1] The presented methodology can also take care of impulse rewards, but these are not used for the considered application case study.

underlying activity-labeled CTMC. If activity labels are removed, transitions between the same pair of states are aggregated via summation of the individual rates.

Rate Rewards: Rate rewards enable the modeler to define complex performance measures on the basis of the high-level model, rather than on the level of the underlying CTMC [SM91]. A rate reward defines the reward gained by the model in a specific state. This gives us the following setting: A rate reward r defined on a high-level model is specified by the rate reward returning function $\mathcal{R}_r : \mathbb{S} \to \mathbb{R}_+$, and where $\mathcal{S}_r^{\mathcal{D}} \subseteq \mathcal{S}$ is the set of SVs on which the computation of r actually depends. Analogously to activity-local markings we will also employ the shorthand notation $\vec{s}_{d_r} := \mathcal{X}(\mathcal{S}_r^{\mathcal{D}}, \vec{s})$. The set of all rate rewards defined for a given high-level model, will be denoted as $\mathcal{R}$.

4 Symbolic Representation and Solution of MRMs

4.1 Symbolic Representation of Low-Level Markov Reward Models

In this section, zero-suppressed multi-terminal binary DDs (ZDDs) are introduced, and it will be shown how this symbolic data structure can be employed for representing CTMCs and their reward functions.

The ZDD Data Structure: Different types of symbolic data structures have been employed successfully for compactly representing very large labeled Markov chains. In a Zero-suppressed BDD (ZBDD) [Min93], the skipping of a variable means that this variable takes the value 0. Thus, ZBDDs are more compact than the original BDDs [Bry86] when representing Boolean functions whose satisfaction set is small and contains many 0-assignments. A previous paper [LS06a] introduced the multi-terminal version of ZBDDs, which we call zero-suppressed multi-terminal binary decision diagrams (ZDD). Analogously to algebraic decision diagrams (ADDs) [ADD97], ZDDs permit the representation of pseudo-Boolean functions. It has been found that, for our area of application, the ZDD-based representation is more compact than the ADD-based representation by a factor of approximately two to three, which has the positive effect that the construction and manipulation times of the symbolic representations, as well as the times for the numerical solution of the represented MRM are reduced by about the same factor [LS06a, LS06b].

ZDD-Based Representation of SLTS: By state graph exploration one can construct the set of transitions of the stochastic labeled transition system (SLTS). Each transition within an activity-labeled SLTS T can then be encoded by applying a binary encoding scheme which represents the transition $(\vec{s} \xrightarrow{l,\lambda} \vec{s}^l)$ as the bit-vector $(\mathcal{E}_{Act}(l), \mathcal{E}_S(\vec{s}), \mathcal{E}_S(\vec{s}^l))$. The rate λ is hereby unaccounted, since it will be stored in a terminal node of the ZDD. The individual bit positions of the obtained vectors correspond to the Boolean variables of the ZDD. Given a ZDD-based representation of a SLTS, one simply has to abstract over the binary encoded activity labels, in order to obtain a symbolic representation of the corresponding transition rate matrix. Hereby the boolean variables holding the binary encoded row and column indices are ordered in an interleaved way. Such an ordering is a commonly accepted heuristics for obtaining small BDD sizes, and it also works well for ZDDs.

Symbolic Representation of Rate Reward Functions: Having pairs of binary encoded system states and rate rewards, one obtains a pseudo-boolean function for each reward specification. This function can once again be represented by means of a ZDD.

4.2   Generating and Solving the Low-Level Markov Reward Model

The top-level algorithm for generating and solving low-level Markov reward models can be divided into three main phases: At first one derives a symbolic representation of the CTMC from the high-level model. Secondly one computes steady-state or transient state probabilities. In the third phase, the symbolically represented CTMC enables one to generate symbolic representations of the rate reward functions. Their different stochastic moments can be efficiently computed via BDD-traversal. The main idea of our approach is to limit the explicit exploration and explicit execution of reward functions only to fractions of the low-level MRM, where the missing parts are generated via ZDD manipulations. In contrast to standard methods, this strategy leads to significant runtime-benefits, where the employment of ZDDs yields significant reductions in memory space.

Phase 1: Constructing a Symbolic Representation of a CTMC [LS06a]: The main idea of the activity-local state graph generation scheme is the partitioning of the CTMC or the SLTS T to be generated into sets of transitions with label $l \in \mathcal{Act}$, where each state is reduced to the activity-dependent markings:

$$T^l := \{(\vec{s}_{d_l}, l, \lambda, \vec{s}_{d_l}^{\,l}) \mid \vec{s}_{d_l} = \chi(\mathcal{S}_l^{\mathcal{D}}, \vec{s}) \wedge \vec{s}_{d_l}^{\,l} = \chi(\mathcal{S}_l^{\mathcal{D}}, \vec{s}^{\,l}) \wedge (\vec{s}, l, \lambda, \vec{s}^{\,l}) \in T\} \quad (1)$$

During state graph generation the activity-local transitions T^l are successively generated, where each is encoded by its own (activity-local) ZDD Z_l, which solely depends on the Boolean variables encoding the dependent SVs of activity l. The overall transition relation is then obtained by executing a symbolic composition scheme:

$$\mathsf{Z}_T := \sum_{l \in \mathcal{Act}} \mathsf{Z}_l \cdot \mathbb{1}_l,$$

where in the above equation $\mathbb{1}_l$ represents the pairwise identity over the Boolean variables encoding activity l's set of independent SVs ($\mathcal{S}_l^{\mathcal{I}} = S \setminus \mathcal{S}_l^{\mathcal{D}}$). One may note, that due to the `Apply`-algorithm of [Bry86] and derivatives thereof, that $\mathsf{Z}_l \cdot \mathbb{1}_l$ may in general not yield the Kronecker-product of the encoded matrices. The ZDD Z_T thus constructed encodes a set of potential transitions, therefore at this point it is necessary to perform symbolic reachability analysis. On the other hand symbolic composition might also result in states triggering new model behavior. In case where such states exist, a new round of explicit state graph exploration, encoding, composition and symbolic reachability analysis follows. Several rounds may be required until a global fix point is reached and a complete representation of the user-defined CTMC is constructed.

The advantages of the activity-local scheme can be summarized as follows:

1. In general, only a small fraction of the transitions of the Markov chain needs to be generated explicitly, whereas the bulk of the transitions is generated during symbolic composition.
2. The scheme does not require any particular model structure. In particular, the method is not restricted to structures that can be represented by a Kronecker descriptor.
3. The model is partitioned automatically at the level of the individual activities, i.e. a user-defined partitioning is not necessary.
4. The composition of the individual "activity-local" portions of the Markov chain is carried out efficiently at the level of the symbolic data structure.

Phase 2: ZDD-Based Solution [LS06b]: Once the symbolic representation of the CTMC, i.e. its transition rate matrix, is generated, probabilities for each system state are computed. The solvers considered in this paper employ an approach in which the generator matrix is represented by a symbolic data structure and the probability vectors are stored as arrays [Par02]. If n Boolean variables are used for state encoding, there are 2^n potential states, of which only a small fraction may be reachable. Allocating entries for unreachable states in the vectors would be a waste of memory space and would severely restrict the applicability of the algorithms (as an example, storing probabilities as doubles, a vector with about 134 million entries already requires 1 GByte of RAM). Therefore a dense enumeration scheme for the reachable states has to be implemented. This is achieved via the concept of offset-labeling. In an offset-labeled ZDD, each node is equipped with an offset value. While traversing the ZDD encoding the matrix, in order to extract a matrix entry, the row and column index in the dense enumeration scheme can be determined from the offsets, basically by adding the offsets of those nodes where the **then**-Edge is taken.

The space efficiency of symbolic matrix representation comes at the cost of computational overhead, caused by the recursive traversal of the ZDD during access to the matrix entries. For that reason, Parker [Par02] introduced the idea of replacing the lower levels of the ADD by explicit sparse matrix representations, which works particularly well for block-structured matrices. In the context of our work, we call the resulting data structure *hybrid offset-labeled* ZDD. The level at which one switches from symbolic representation to sparse matrix representation, called *sparse level s*, depends on the available memory space, i.e. there is a typical time/space tradeoff.

For numerical analysis, it is well-known that the Gauss-Seidel (GS) scheme and its over-relaxed variants typically exhibit much better convergence than the Jacobi, Jacobi-Over-relaxation or Power method. However, Gauss-Seidel requires row-wise access to the matrix entries, which, unfortunately, cannot be realized efficiently with ZDD-based representations. As a compromise, Parker [Par02] developed the so-called pseudo-Gauss-Seidel (PGS) iteration scheme, where the matrix is partitioned into blocks (not necessarily of equal size). Within each block, access to matrix entries is in arbitrary order, but the blocks are accessed in ascending order. PGS requires one complete iteration vector and an additional vector whose size is determined by the maximal block size. Given a ZDD which represents the matrix, each inner node at a specific level corresponds to a block. Pointers to these nodes can be stored in a sparse matrix, which means that effectively the top levels of the ZDD have been replaced by a sparse matrix of block pointers. The ZDD level at which the root nodes of the matrix blocks reside is called *block level b*. Overall, this yields a memory structure in which some levels from the top and some levels from the bottom of the ZDD have been replaced by sparse matrix structures. We call such a memory structure a block-structured hybrid offset-labeled ZDD. The choice of an adequate s and an adequate b is an optimization problem. In general, increasing b improves convergence of the PGS scheme (but also increases the time per iteration), and replacing more ZDD levels by sparse structures improves speed of access.

Phase 3: Generating Symbolic Representations of Rate Reward Functions: After the system state probabilities are computed, one needs to generate the symbolic representations of the rate reward functions. Hereby the main idea is once again to exploit locality, so that the explicit evaluation of each reward function is limited to a fraction of states of the CTMC, rather than evaluating the reward functions for each state. I.e. similar to activity-local transition systems one restricts oneself to processing rate-reward-local states. The symbolic representation R_r of the characteristic (pseudo-boolean) function of the set:

$$\mathbb{S}_r := \{ \vec{s}_{d_r} \in \mathbb{S} \mid \mathcal{R}_r(\vec{s}_{d_r}) \neq 0 \}$$

gives hereby a rate-reward-local reward function, such that $R_r \cdot \mathbb{S}$ yields the rate reward for each system state concerning rate reward definition r. Once state probabilities and also symbolic representations of all rate reward functions have been constructed, their moments can be computed via BDD-traversal. Due to the nature of the traversal, one only visits hereby those states individually whose reward value is not zero. The obtained stochastic moments are the desired RA measure, e.g. unavailability.

5   Case Study: Fault-Tolerant Adjunct Processor

In the digital telephone network, so-called adjunct processors translate easy-to-remember, location-independent virtual phone numbers (used e.g. by emergency departments) into their location-dependent physical equivalent.[2] Because adjunct processors play a crucial role in the network, they must be highly available.

---

[2] For example, if one calls 112 in Germany, one will be connected to the closest fire department.

Table 1. Default parameters of the I/O-unit submodel investigated in this paper

parameter	default value	description
N	6	number of configurations
K	4	number of initially active configurations
MTTF-SBC$_i$	$5 \cdot 10^4$ hours	mean time to failure of SBC i
MTTF-RTB$_i$	$1 \cdot 10^5$ hours	mean time to failure of RTB i
MTTR-SBC$_i$	1 hour	mean time to repair of SBC i
MTTR-RTB$_i$	1 hour	mean time to repair of RTB i
FOT$_{ij}$	0.1 hours	fail-over-time from configuration i to configuration j

Typically, an availability of 99.999% is demanded for such a system which corresponds to a mean downtime of less than 5 minutes per year. In a previous work, we investigated the availability of an adjunct processor implementation [GLW00] by a SPN-based model. We will now apply the proposed method to this model to point out its benefits.

5.1   System Description

From a top-level view, the adjunct processor is a series system comprising host units, I/O-units, hot-swap controllers, power supplies, a RAID system and so on. Due to place restrictions, we will evaluate the I/O-subsystem only, as it is the most complex part of the system. The other parts can be evaluated in a similar way which is not shown here.

The I/O-unit consists of N configurations, each comprising a single board computer (SBC) and a so-called rear transition board (RTB). All cabling is connected to the RTB which allows for a quick replacement of the SBC in case of a failure. We assume, that $K <= N$ configurations have to be available at the same time to make the I/O-unit available. Furthermore, we assume that each configuration can be in three states: active, failed, or passive. A passive (or stand-by) configuration does not perform any work but waits until an active configuration fails. After failure detection and localization, the I/O-unit is reconfigured which means that one of the passive configurations becomes activated. The overall time interval which lies between a failure and the completion of the reconfiguration is called the fail-over-time.

A configuration fails, if either its SBC or RTB fails. This can happen to both the active and the passive configurations. Modern architectures in the telecommunication systems are open systems and may contain boards from different vendors. Thus, in general, all components of the system will have different failure and repair rates and also the fail-over times may vary. The parameters of our model are given in Table 1. For the sake of simplicity, we assume exponentially distributed time intervals in the following evaluations. This is acceptable for the mean time to failures, because the effects of aging can be neglected in electronic devices. Analytic evaluation of models with non-exponentially distributed time-intervals is an active area of research.

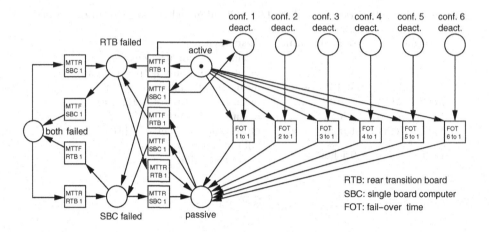

Fig. 3. Single component specified as SPN

Using OpenSESAME, the I/O-unit can be modeled using the RBD shown in Fig. 2 for the case $N = 5$. This model is enriched with information on the respective fail-over-times which are necessary to switch from one configuration to another. We think that the OpenSESAME model is quite intuitive and easy to modify. In contrast, a SPN-based model as sketched in Fig. 3 is much more complex. The figure shows only one sixth of the overall SPN structure for the case $N = 6$. It represents configuration 1 which is one of the configurations which are active after system startup. The remaining five configurations are modeled with equivalent subnets, however, all subnets share the six places `conf. 1-6 deact.`. As it can be seen, even a small fraction of the overall net is much less readable than the RBD from Fig. 2. Moreover, changing the parameters N or K requires a work-intensive and error-prone modification of the SPN structure. This exemplifies the benefit of the proposed method, where OpenSESAME is used to generate the SPN from an OpenSESAME input model which comprises the RBD from Fig. 2, attributed with the respective fail-over-times.

5.2 Model Evaluation

Table 2.A shows the evaluation results in terms of the I/O unit's unavailability for the default values given in Tab. 1 and different fail-over-times. As can be seen, the fail-over time has a significant impact on the result. Please note that if traditional combinatorial methods like a simple RBD or fault tree analysis were used, this would imply the assumption that the fail-over-time is zero. Thus, the result would be highly over-optimistic as it is several orders of magnitude lower than the correct results even for small fail-over-times.

For evaluating the efficiency of our symbolic framework, we analyzed the adjunct processor for two different parameter sets. In the first set, we investigated a *"4-out-of-6"* system (i.e. $N = 6$ and $K = 4$) whereas in the second set a

Table 2. Data as obtained for analyzing the case study

(A) Model specific RA-measures (system unavailability)

	mean fail-over time				
	0 sec	10 sec	1 min	5 min	6 min
"4-out-of-6"	$< 5.99 \cdot 10^{-13}$	$1.67 \cdot 10^{-7}$	$9.97 \cdot 10^{-7}$	$4.93 \cdot 10^{-6}$	$5.91 \cdot 10^{-6}$
"6-out-of-8"	$< 1.60 \cdot 10^{-12}$	$2.49 \cdot 10^{-7}$	$1.49 \cdot 10^{-6}$	$7.40 \cdot 10^{-6}$	$8.86 \cdot 10^{-6}$

(B) Model specific data

	states	trans	$trans_e$
"4-out-of-6"	$9.48720 \cdot 10^5$	$1.45607 \cdot 10^7$	240
"6-out-of-8"	$2.61671 \cdot 10^8$	$5.86973 \cdot 10^9$	544

(C) Solution times

	DSPNexpress				Symbolic Approach			
	peak mem.	SG time	iter. time	# iter.	peak mem.	SG time	iter. time	# iter.
"4-out-of-6"	7.4 GByte	123.014	0.7315	12	36 MByte	2.50562	0.093181	46
"6-out-of-8"	xxx	xxx	xxx	xxx	4105 MByte	15.8026	40.533267	49

"6-out-of-8" system was analyzed ($N = 8$ and $K = 6$). The numerical values were equal to the ones presented in Tab. 1. We stress that the sub-units were not assumed to be symmetric, which resulted in Markov reward models of substantial size to be analyzed. If sub-units were symmetric, lumping techniques for state space reduction could be exploited.

Table 2.B shows the size of the analyzed low-level MRM models as derived from the OpenSESAME input model, via the translation to a SAN and finally applying the symbolic state graph generation scheme. Consequently, Table 2.B contains the number of system states (*states*), the number of transitions among these system states (*trans*) and the number of transitions explicitly established by our activity-local ZDD-based state graph generation scheme ($trans_e$). The latter is extremely small, which is the main source of efficiency of the approach.

Table 2.C shows the memory and CPU-times as required for generating and solving the MRM. Hereby the two different configurations were analyzed on a 64-bit Opteron system with 8 GByte of RAM and a Linux OS. For demonstrating the effectiveness of our ZDD-based framework, we also exported and analyzed the system models with the GSPN-based tool *DSPNexpress* [Lin98]. Table 2.C gives the *peak memory* consumption, the CPU time in secs. required for generating the CTMC (*SG time*), the CPU times in secs. required for each numerical iteration for computing the state probabilities (*iter. time*) and their number (# iter.) as executed under the respective numerical solution method. As numerical solution method, we decided to employ the pseudo-Gauss-Seidel method of [Par02] in case of ZDDs, whereas *DSPNexpress* employs the generalized minimal residual method (GMRES). As convergence criteria a relative convergence of 10^{-6} was taken. The data of Table 2.C indicates that the ZDD-based framework is much more efficient than the standard sparse matrix approach employed within the *DSPNexpress*-tool.

In case of the *"6 out 8"*-configuration, *DSPNexpress* was unable to analyze the system model, due to a lack of RAM. Even for the smaller configuration (*"4-out-of-6"*), our ZDD-based framework is more efficient. Hereby, and in contrast to sparse matrix techniques, the bottleneck is the state-probability vector, since even for very large systems the block-structured hybrid ZDD-based representation of the transition rate matrix of the Markov reward model is still very compact. E.g. for the *"4-out-of-6"*-configuration the ZDD-based representation of the transition rate matrix requires 0.226 MByte only, whereas the probability vector, the iteration vector and the vector holding the diagonal entries of the generator matrix require 14.5 MByte of RAM. Consequently the ZDD-based methodology clearly eases the restriction on Markov reward analysis. Thus it is not surprising that the suggested ZDD-based tool chain is still capable of computing the desired RA-measures in approx. 34 minutes, where standard methods as employed within the *DSPNexpress*-tool fail to do so.

6   Conclusion

Related Work: Several techniques have been proposed to simplify the creation of state-based dependability models. One possibility is to combine several modeling methods in one user-interface (see, e.g. [STP96, THMH98]). Another possibility is to extend Boolean methods (e.g. [DSC00]). The approach favored in our work, i.e. automatically creating the models from a high-level input can also be found (see [MPB03, BB03]). Please refer to our previous work [WT04] for a detailed comparison with OpenSESAME. However, none of these methods uses symbolic data structures for the representation of the state space.

Based on the original Binary Decision Diagram (BDD) data structure [Bry86], several extensions have been developed for representing not only Boolean but also pseudo-Boolean functions, i.e. functions of the type $f : \mathbb{B}^n \mapsto \mathbb{R}$, where Algebraic Decision Diagrams (ADDs) [ADD97] are one of the best known types. In recent years, powerful state space generation algorithms based on symbolic data structures have been developed and implemented in software tools such as PRISM [KNP05] and SMART [CJMS03]. While PRISM is based on ADDs, SMART employs multi-valued decision diagrams and matrix diagrams. Using these techniques, generating the state space and transition structure of the underlying Markov model from the high-level specification is extremely fast, and the resulting symbolic representation can be very memory efficient. Numerical analysis based on the symbolic representation is still an active area of research. Using the approach of offset-labeling, combined with hybrid matrix representation, as first proposed for ADDs in [Par02], it has been demonstrated that iterative solution techniques based on symbolic data structures can be almost as fast as sparse matrix approaches, while being much more memory efficient and therefore able to solve much larger systems.

Summary: In this paper we presented a tool chain which takes a set of high-level diagrams as its input. These diagrams, which comprise component tables, reliability block diagrams, failure dependency diagrams, repair group tables, and variable tables, yield an input model for the tool OpenSESAME. The tool automatically converts this high-level model specification into a SAN as accepted by the tool Möbius. In a second step, the obtained SAN is converted by our ZDD-based symbolic engine into a symbolic representation of a MRM. On the basis of this symbolic representation numerical analysis is carried out, finally yielding the desired reliability- and availability measures of the system under study.

For illustrating the advantages of such an approach, we presented a model of a fault-tolerant telecommunication service system with N redundant modules, where the system is available as long as at least K modules are available. Each module comprises two components and can be either in failed, stand-by or active mode. Reconfiguring the system after a failure takes some time during which the system is not available. All failure-, repair- and reconfiguration-rates can be different. Considering a *"4 out of 6"* and *"6 out of 8"* configuration, where in case of the latter the obtained MRM already consist of more than 2.61×10^8 system states, we illustrate, that our tool chain is capable of computing the relevant measures of interest without problems, where standard techniques, such as included in the tool *DSPNexpress*, are less efficient or even fail.

Future Work: Since we develop our implementations in the context of Möbius, we are currently implementing an efficient symbolic realization of the "Replicate" feature [SM91], so that modeled symmetries lead to much smaller Markov reward models to be solved. Furthermore, an adaptation of aggregation methods for the approximate solution of CTMCs to the case of ZDD-represented MRMs seems to be a promising starting point for future research.

References

[ADD97]   *Formal Methods in System Design: Special Issue on Multi-terminal Binary Decision Diagrams*, Volume 10, No. 2-3, April - May 1997.

[BB03]   M. Bouissou and J. L. Bon. A new formalism that combines advantages of fault-trees and Markov models: Boolean logic driven Markov processes. *Reliability Engineering and System Safety*, pages 149–163, November 2003.

[Bry86]   R.E. Bryant. Graph-based Algorithms for Boolean Function Manipulation. *IEEE ToC*, C-35(8):677–691, August 1986.

[CJMS03] G. Ciardo, R.L. Jones, A.S. Miner, and R. Siminiceanu. Logical and stochastic modeling with SMART. In *Proceedings of Tools 2003*, pages 78 – 97. Springer, LNCS 2794, 2003.

[DCC+02] D. Deavours, G. Clark, T. Courtney, D. Daly, S. Derisavi, J. Doyle, W.H. Sanders, and P. Webster. The Moebius Framework and Its Implementation. *IEEE Transactions on Software Engineering*, 28(10):956–969, 2002.

[DSC00]   J.B. Dugan, K.J. Sullivan, and D. Coppit. Developing a low-cost high-quality software tool for dynamic fault-tree analysis. *IEEE Transaction on Reliability*, 49(1):49–59, March 2000.

[GLW00]   G. Graf, M. Leberecht, and M. Walter. High Availability Commodity Computing - A CompactPCI-System Evaluation. In *Proceedings of the International Conference on Parallel and Distributed Processing Techniques and Applications*, volume 4. CSREA Press, 2000.

[KNP05]   M. Kwiatkowska, G. Norman, and D. Parker. Quantitative analysis with the probabilistic model checker PRISM. *Electronic Notes in Theoretical Computer Science*, 153(2):5–31, 2005.

[Lin98]   C. Lindemann. *Performance Modelling with Deterministic and Stochastic Petri Nets*. Wiley and Sons, 1998.

[LS06a]   K. Lampka and M. Siegle. Activity-Local Symbolic State Graph Generation for High-Level Stochastic Models. In *Proc. of MMB Conference 2006*, pages 245–264, 2006.

[LS06b]   K. Lampka and M. Siegle. Analysis of Markov Reward Models using Zero-suppressed Multi-terminal Binary Decision Diagrams, 2006. To appear in *Int. Conf. Valuetools 2006*.

[Min93]   S. Minato. Zero-Suppressed BDDs for Set Manipulation in Combinatorial Problems. In *Proc. of DAC*, pages 272–277, Dallas (Texas), USA, June 1993. ACM Press.

[MPB03]   I. Majzik, A. Pataricza, and A. Bondavalli. Stochastic Dependability Analysis of System Architecture Based on UML Models. *Lecture Notes in Computer Science*, 2677:219–244, 2003.

[Par02]   D. Parker. *Implementation of Symbolic Model Checking for Probabilistic Systems*. PhD thesis, University of Birmingham, 2002.

[SM91]   W. H. Sanders and J. F. Meyer. A unified Approach for specifying Measures of Performance, Dependability, and Performability. In *Dependable Computing for Critical Applications*, Vol. 4, pages 215–237. Springer-Verlag, 1991.

[Som]   F. Somenzi. CUDD Package, Release 2.4.x. http://vlsi.colorado.edu/~fabio.

[STP96]   R.A. Sahner, K.S. Trivedi, and A. Puliafito. *Performance and Reliability Analysis of Computer Systems*. Kluwer Academic Publishers, 1996.

[THMH98]   D. Tang, M. Hecht, J. Miller, and J. Handal. MEADEP: A dependability evaluation tool for engineers. *IEEE Transaction on Reliability*, 47(4):443–450, 12 1998.

[WS05]   M. Walter and W. Schneeweiss. *The modeling world of Reliability/Safety Engineering*. LiLoLe Verlag, 2005.

[WT04]   M. Walter and C. Trinitis. How to Integrate Inter-Component Dependencies into Combinatorial Availability Models. In *Proc. Ann. Reliability and Maintainability Symp. (RAMS 2004), Los Angeles, USA*, pages 226–231. IEEE, 2004.

[WT05]   M. Walter and C. Trinitis. OpenSESAME: Simple but Extensive Structured Availability Modeling Environment. In *Proc. 2nd International Conference on the Quantitative Evaluation of Systems (QEST) 2005*. IEEE Computer Society Press, 2005.

"To Store or Not To Store" Reloaded: Reclaiming Memory on Demand

Moritz Hammer[1] and Michael Weber[2,*]

[1] Ludwig-Maximilians-Universität München, Institut für Informatik
hammer@pst.ifi.lmu.de
[2] CWI, Dept. of Software Engineering, Amsterdam, The Netherlands
Michael.Weber@cwi.nl

Abstract. Behrmann et al. posed the question whether "To Store or Not To Store" [1] states during reachability analysis, in order to counter the effects of the well-known state space explosion problem in explicit-state model checking. Their answer was to store not all but only some strategical states. They pay in run-time if the answer too often is "Not To Store". We propose a different strategy to *adaptively* trade time for space: "To Store" as many states as memory limits permit. If free memory becomes scarce, we gradually swap states out to secondary storage. We are careful to minimize revisits, and I/O overhead, and also stay sound, i.e. on termination it is guaranteed that the full state space has been explored. It is also available for counterexample reconstruction. In our experiments we tackled state spaces of industrial-scale models with more than 10^9 explicit states with still modest storage requirements.

1 Introduction

Model checking of industrial-scale models is usually restricted by memory size. The research addressing this issue can be divided into two groups: Automatically making models smaller by abstraction, and getting more out of the memory available. While the former direction has seen significant improvements with the advent of CEGAR model checking [2], large-scale model checking still remains an important area of research.

In explicit-state model checking, memory size is mostly restricted by the hash table used to detect state revisits. Among the many solutions to this problem, disk-based model checking and lossy hash tables have been proposed. Disk-based model checking basically tries to maintain a bigger hash table by swapping states to disk. As disk space is much cheaper than RAM, larger state spaces can be checked on normal systems. Disk storage is of course much slower, especially in random-access mode, which establishes the need for adapted algorithms.

* This research has been partially funded by the Netherlands Organisation for Scientific Research (NWO) under FOCUS/BRICKS grant number 642.000.05N09.

L. Brim et al. (Eds.): FMICS and PDMC 2006, LNCS 4346, pp. 51–66, 2007.

Lossy hashing makes use of the observation that the hash table is used for avoiding revisits of parts of the state space that have been visited before. While revisiting is costly with respect to runtime, it does not void the correctness of the search result, as long as the hash table is sufficient to ensure termination. Therefore, it can be attempted to remove states from the lossy hash table in order to reclaim their memory and make room for further, hopefully newly discovered states. Behrmann et al. [1] claim that only 10% of the state space might need to be stored, allowing for much larger search spaces; however this will lead to extensive revisits in our experience.

Both directions have been given much research, but they have not yet been combined. Disk-based model checking usually does not make attempts to check a model in RAM only, should it turn out to be small enough. Lossy hashing, on the other hand, does not attempt to avoid revisits. By combining both strategies, we obtain an algorithm that avoids extensive revisits by performing disk lookups, but runs in RAM only as long as this is sufficient. This leads to a smoothly degrading algorithm, which adaptively changes its use of memory: For smaller models, it is little different from a RAM-only model checker, and it gradually becomes a disk-based model checker if memory becomes scarce.

Contributions. We present an external-memory algorithm for explicit-state space generation. We make novel use of a combination of well-known data structures like lossy hash tables and Bloom filters [3] to reduce expensive disk input and output (I/O). For each generated state, we obtain a three-valued answer: whether a state has surely been seen before, whether it has not been seen so far, or whether the answers requires a costly lookup on disk. Naturally, we aim to keep the number of states in the last class as low as possible to make our method feasible in the presence of high disk latency for random access.

Previous uses of the aforementioned data structures lead to reachable states not being visited, thus rendering the results unreliable. In contrast, a design goal of our algorithm was to ensure that the whole reachable state space is visited, thus enabling its post-processing.

Our experiments show that we can easily handle state spaces of more than 10^9 states. A distinguishing feature of our algorithm is that it performs well if entire state vectors of all states are stored on disk, i.e. we do not apply lossy compression. The stored states can be used in off-line analysis, and graph minimization with existing tools [4,5].

Overview. In Section 2 and 3, we discuss the ingredients of our algorithm: Lossy hashing and Bloom filter. In Section 4 we describe how they are combined, and how disk storage is used to resolve the states that cannot be resolved with this two in-memory data structures. Section 5 describes some optimizations that can be done in order to speed up the disk lookups. Section 6 shows results we obtained from a prototype implementation of our algorithm. We finish with a discussion of related work in Section 7, and conclude with a view on further steps in Section 8.

2   Safe Lossy Hashing

In an explicit-state model checker, the hash table containing the *closed set*, i. e. the set of states already visited, is the most memory-demanding component. In fact, in the SPIN model checker [6], it is the only component to allocate memory once the search has been started. As such, it becomes the limiting factor for model size, and various ways of extending it have been proposed: using under- and over-approximations of the visited set, or making it larger by swapping states to disk.

In our approach, we maintain a chained hash table in memory. But once the table fills up, we choose states that are less likely to be visited again according to some strategy, and swap them to disk, thus freeing the memory they (and the hash table buckets that contain them) claim. The hash table then still serves as an under-approximation of the closed set, i.e. any state that is found to be stored in the hash table is known to have been visited previously, but a miss will have to be checked against disk.

For storing states on a disk a data structure supporting random access may seem the best choice. However, due to the large number of requests and the unpredictable distribution of states, this structures (like a hash table on disk) tend to become prohibitively slow due to disk latency times: As a lookup of any given state is likely to require the reloading of a new block on disk, each state lookup is paid for by the disk's latency time. We thus take the approach taken by most disk-based model checking tools in some way or other: We group our read and write accesses, so that entire *pages of states* can be read and written at once. For writing states, this is easily achieved by collecting states in an in-memory staging area prior to writing them to disk. For reading states, we need to collect states that have been found to be possibly unvisited in a *candidate set*, which will eventually be checked against disk at once. This technique is known as *delayed duplicate detection* (DDD), as for a conflicting state, resolution is postponed until it may be conducted efficiently.

2.1   Selecting Victim States to Swap Out

Once the lossy hash table takes up all memory, each addition of a freshly discovered state needs to be accounted for by the removal of a state in the hash table. For reasons of efficiency, we cannot evaluate all states each time this occurs, but rather select a set of states (with arbitrary size, we used 10% of the total states in the hash table) at once and use states from this set for reclamation of memory. This can be done by assigning to each state a value that indicates how likely we estimate a revisit to be, and calculate the k-median; all elements lesser than the k-median can be scheduled for reclamation. This can be done in $O(n \log n)$ by sorting and selecting, or by an $O(n)$ expected time adaption of quicksort.

There are several candidates for evaluating functions. Behrmann et al. [1] provide some which include a static analysis of the model. We try to avoid a static analysis to remain independent of the state space generator. Also, the

Table 1. Comparison of *cache failures* with different reclaiming strategies. Column "LHT size" indicates the size of the lossy hash table with respect to the total state space size.

LHT size	Cache Failures for Reclaiming Strategy				
	Random	Incoming	Outgoing	Age	Combination
Dining Philosophers (n = 9): 4,685,071 states, 12,234,622 transitions					
2%	7, 569, 757	7, 799, 983	7, 965, 160	7, 657, 372	7, 702, 798
25%	3, 282, 324	4, 913, 862	4, 366, 858	3, 251, 002	5, 143, 714
80%	178, 254	429, 148	403, 077	9, 481	9, 481
LUNAR *scenario 4(b):* 3,335,917 states, 3,923,209 transitions					
2%	225, 960	233, 010	259, 499	228, 485	194, 332
25%	70, 126	62, 733	97, 652	59, 272	43, 221
80%	8, 124	4, 861	13, 249	64	4

purpose of our heuristic differs: While they try to detect states that cut off large subgraphs and avoid revisits to them, we try to measure the likelihood of a direct revisit of a state to avoid the cost of the disk lookup.

Among the candidates for heuristic functions are:

- No evaluation at all – purely **random** replacement. This can be done by just reclaiming the state that happens to collide with the new state in the hash table.
- **Incoming** edges – we maintain a counter for each state in the hash table that counts how often it was revisited. It is hoped that a state that has already been visited several times will be visited further times again.
- **Outgoing** edges – contrary to the incoming edges, the number of outgoing edges is readily available for fresh states. Both the incoming and outgoing edge criteria hope that a *hub state* effect is experienced: that there are states that lie on many paths, while most other states lie on few paths only.
- **Age** – due to *transition locality* often exhibited by models of communication protocols, a new state is more likely to be revisited than is an old state. This assumption is already used in the general layout of our algorithm: Freshly discovered states are added to the lossy hash table, without considering any heuristics on their revisit likelihood.
- A **combination** of said functions, e. g., keeping new states and states that have many outgoing edges.

Table 1 shows the efficiency of different reclaiming strategies for a *Dining Philosophers* model with 9 philosophers, and a model of LUNAR routing protocol scenario 4(b) [7]. The "LHT size" column indicates the size of the lossy hash table with respect to the total state space size. Both, age and the combined measure (evaluating incoming, outgoing and age values evenly) perform well, but neither can produce a significant improvement over the other. With sufficiently small lossy hash tables, any strategy effectively degrades into random replacement.

2.2   Single-Successor States

Apart from reclaiming memory, we can take another measure towards keeping memory requirements of the hash table tractable: We may choose only to store states that have more than one successor. While states with one outgoing transition may be target of multiple incoming transitions, the cost of revisiting them is limited: the previously visited chain of single-successor states is followed again, until a state with multiple successors is found and the revisit is detected. This optimization is used for example in the SPIN model checker [6]. It is very easy to implement and independent of the state space generator as it does not need to take the actual semantics of the state vector into consideration.

Behrmann et al. [1] also mention it as one of their strategies to decide which states not to store. They solve the problem of cycles consisting solely of chained states leading to non-termination by ensuring that every k^{th} state is stored unconditionally. They recommend setting k to a high value.

Contrary to them, we did encounter such cycles in our experiments (e. g., GIOP1 protocol [8], or the Leader Election protocol from SPIN). With a different strategy, we avoid spinning in loops with small diameter (due to k). On encountering a single successor state, we perform a local (degenerated) depth-bounded reachability search from that state. It continues until either a cycle is found (which then can serve as input for further analyses), or by finding a state with more than one outgoing transition. In the latter case the search stops as well, and all states found during its run are thrown away, except for the last one. The same is done if the search hits a memory limit, in order to avoid problems with extremely large chains. However, in practice we observed only short chains of less than 100 states.

We found that the single-successor optimization in some cases vastly reduces the number of states that need to be stored, yet it comes not always for free: in our experiments we sometimes witnessed a high number of revisits, resulting from chains of states with in-degree greater than one. Combining this technique with a static *loop coverage* analysis as proposed by Behrmann et al. [1] would be beneficial, however this is out of scope for this work, as we focus on methods *independent* of the modeling formalism. Note that even if states are revisited, they are not stored to disk a second time, nor do they produce additional disk lookups. If the state space generator is fast enough, the cost of calculating revisited states is easily outmatched by the decreased cost in storing these states.

The single-successor optimization is very effective on models exhibiting a high degree of determinism, that is, in many states exactly one transition can be executed. Models created by experts are often in this class [9], however this is also dependent on the modeling problem at hand. Means to manually make models more deterministic are language constructs like atomic regions and mutexes.

It is worth noting that such mostly deterministic models often do not benefit much from *partial order reduction* techniques, an otherwise very effective technique for state space reduction.

3   Bloom-Filter Cache

Lossy hashing enables us to reclaim memory, in case the state space becomes too large to be kept in memory. Using disk lookups will prevent us from repeatedly searching parts of the state space. However, once states have been removed from the in-memory hash table, we can no longer predict whether a state that was not found in the hash table has indeed not been visited yet, or has been swapped to disk. A query to the lossy hashing will be answered with either "visited" or "don't know", and the "don't know" answers need to be checked againstdisk.

Since this procedure entails a disk lookup for each unvisited state, it is quite costly. An inexpensive way of reducing the number of lookups for new states is offered by Bloom filters [3]. Basically, a Bloom filter is a set representation consisting of an array of m bits and k hash functions $f_1, \ldots, f_k$. To add an element e, the bits $(f_1(e) \mod m), \ldots, (f_k(e) \mod m)$ are set. For $k = 1$ or $k = 2$, this is the same as the bit-state hashing method employed in SPIN [10], but if the state space can be guessed to be roughly of size n, a Bloom filter's k parameter can be optimized for the ratio m/n, producing superior results [11].

While coverage of Bloom filters is notably good, the filter maintains an over-approximation of the set of visited states. If we were to rely purely on the Bloom filter, hash collisions might prevent some parts of the state space to be visited. Dual to the lossy hashing, a *miss* in the Bloom filter will be sufficient to know that a state is unvisited yet, whereas a *hit* will not always be reliable, as it can be a *false positive*. Thus, our Bloom filter will answer with either "unvisited" or "don't know".

It should be noted that, when choosing the right number of hash functions, collisions are exceedingly rare with Bloom filters. For example, only 9 collisions are encountered when checking a model with $\approx$ 800,000 states, using a Bloom filter with 50 Mbits and four hash functions).

Using a Bloom filter is quite cheap: a small portion of memory will provide good coverage, and at least one of the hash functions utilized is required for the lossy hash table lookup anyway (Dillinger and Manolios discuss how to maximize hash function reuse [11]). Together with a lossy hash table, we obtain a cache that gives a three-valued answer on whether a state was visited: either "visited" due to a hit in the lossy hashing, "unvisited" due to a miss in the Bloom filter, or "don't know" if both filters fail to give a definitive answer. The cost of this combined filter is little more than the lossy hashing alone. We need, however, memory to organize the states which are subject to DDD.

Fig. 1 shows the complete algorithm in pseudo-code. While the order in which the Bloom filter and the lossy hashing are queried is arbitrary with respect to the correctness of the algorithm, it is more efficient to precede the lossy hashing check by the Bloom filter check, which is cheaper and may make a check of the lossy hashing (which sometimes involves the processing of a chain of hash buckets and comparing the state vectors) obsolete. The algorithm may further be refined by storing whether a state was reclaimed from the lossy hashing yet,

```
open ← {initialState}                      bloom.add(s)
candidate ← ∅                              if lossy.isFull()
disk ← ∅                                       then State s' ← lossy.reclaim()
while (true) do                                    disk ← disk ∪ {s'}
        if open = ∅ then diskLookup() fi   fi
        State s ← open.removeState();       lossy.add(s)
        for s' ∈ succ(s) do                 .
                if (bloom.isUnvisited(s'))  proc diskLookup() ≡
                        then addToOpen(s')  for s ∈ disk do
                        else if ¬lossy.isVisited(s')    if s ∈ candidate
                                then candidate ←              then candidate ← candidate \ {s}
                                        candidate ∪ {s'}       fi
                        fi                  od
                fi                          if candidate = ∅ then terminateSearch() fi
        od                                  for s ∈ candidate do
od                                                  addToOpen(s)
                                            od
proc addToOpen(State s) ≡                   .
        open ← open ∪ {s}
```

Fig. 1. Pseudo-code for the RECLAIM algorithm

for as long as this has not been done, the visited status of any state may be decided solely by the lossy hashing.

4   Implementation

We have implemented the proposed algorithm as a part of a model checker named CMC[1]. CMC, for "Component-based Model Checker", has been developed as a show-case for component technology. Using different components (like lossy hashing, Bloom filter etc.) proved effective for testing new ways of handling states.

4.1   The Life-Cycle of States

In CMC, states are passed between components as indicated in Fig. 2. We maintain different sets of states:

- the *open set* consists of all states that have been constructed, found to be unvisited but not yet processed,
- the *candidate set* is a set of states that need to be checked against the disk to verify that they have not yet been visited,
- the *reclaim set* is a set of states that are stored in the lossy hashing, but have been scheduled for writeout to disk in order to free memory.

New states are constructed as either the initial state or successor states to a state taken from the open set. These states are passed to the main search

---

[1] http://www.pst.informatik.uni-muenchen.de/~hammer/cmc/

algorithm (①). The main search then queries the caches (②) and obtains a three-valued answer: either the state is not visited, in which case it is added to the open set, or it has been visited already, in which case it is discarded, or we cannot obtain a definitive answer from the caches, in which case we add the state to the candidate set (③). Any state that enters the open set is immediately added to the caches (④). This ensures that no duplicates ever enter the open set.

By adding new states to the caches, the lossy hashing finally runs full, and a reclaim set is chosen. This set is written to disk (⑤) and states from the set are removed if room is needed for new states sent from the open set. Writing states to disk is done in pages, which can be compressed by ZLIB (Section 5.3).

Once the open set becomes empty, or the candidate set becomes too large, a disk lookup is triggered. We use the seemingly inferior technique of checking the complete set of states written to disk in a linear fashion, comparing each state against an index built from the candidate set. Unvisited states are added to the open set, while visited states are discarded (⑥). It is imperative to maintain the invariant of having no duplicates within the open set. This is easily achieved by removing duplicates when building the index.

In order to maintain a definitive upper bound on memory consumption, we still need to avoid uncontrolled memory usage by the open set. Since each state enters the open set only once, this is easy to do by dumping parts of it to disk, should it become too large, and reloading them if the in-memory open set becomes empty (⑦).

Finally, states are taken from the open set by the search algorithm to have their successors computed (⑧).

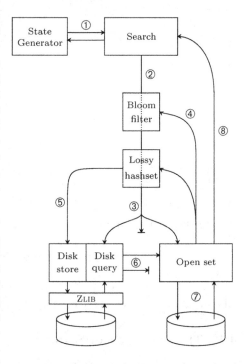

Fig. 2. Life-cycle of states; arrows depict the data-flow of states

5   Speedups Through I/O Reduction

5.1   Partitioning the Closed Set

As described above, disk lookups are done by comparing the candidate set with every state on the disk. While this seems extremely expensive, it proved to be superior to building hash-tables that operate on disk, as usual disk-page caching fails due to the unpredictable position of states within the hash table (and thus on disk).

Table 2. A comparison of I/O effort for different forms of state storage for the `pftp` protocol. "Preparation" describes the part of the algorithm that processes data that is written to or read from disk; for hash compaction, this consists of calculating hash values for the state, whereas for the ZLIB-using algorithm, this contains de- and inflating disk pages.

Method	Pages		Runtime	Relative time for	
	written	read	[min.]	I/O	Preparation
`pftp`: queue size = 11, 12.9M states stored					
Hash compaction, 5 byte	896	6872	9:21	7.89%	2.13%
Hash compaction, 8 byte	1472	11285	9:48	12.36%	2.02%
ZLIB	2880	23205	14:03	4.13%	22.27%
Plain disk	56816	438896	47:12	74.84%	−

By using disk partitions, the cost of looking up a single state may be cut, but this only takes effect at the very end of the run, when a few remaining states need to be checked against the disk. We use n disk partitions (with n being rather small, i.e., $32 \leq n \leq 128$) and a hash function to assign each state to one of them. In our experience, this leads to a very even distribution of states, so that each partition accounts for an n-th of the total set of stored states. The cost of a single-state lookup is then divided by n. However, this does not help for bulk lookups. Due to the even distribution of states by hashing, a lookup with more than n states is likely to require all partitions, and in our setting, a normal lookup contains a few million states.

A lookup is conducted by first building a hash set of candidate states, eliminating duplicates within the candidate set in the process. Then, we load each page into memory at full linear-read disk speed, and compare each state against that hash set. If the state from disk is found in the hash set, it is removed from the hash set. After all pages have been processed, the states remaining in the hash set are added to the open set: they have been found to be unvisited. This is in essence done like in Stern and Dill's CHECKTABLE function [12].

5.2 Hash Compaction

Of course, the above scheme involves reading rather many pages from disk, and reducing I/O traffic becomes of importance. The disk-based MURφ implementations achieve this by employing hash compaction, i.e. not store the state itself, but a hash code (sized 40 bit in case of HOPPER [13]). As state vectors encountered with large models easily exceed 500 bytes, only a hundredth of I/O traffic is produced, at the cost of possibly under-approximating the search space due to collisions and losing state information for those states that are written to disk. We take a different, albeit less efficient approach in terms of I/O traffic: lossless compression of disk pages. The I/O overhead produced by the three approaches is given in Tab. 2. For hash compaction, we employ the SHA1 cryptographic hash function [14].

Table 3. Model statistics for smaller models

Model	States	Non-1-Succ.	Edges	1-succ. revisits	ZLIB compr.	Avg. state size [byte]	State zeroes
HUGO: Hot Fail[†]	4.5M	3.8M	8.5M	5.1M	3.20%	756.6	68%
Peterson, $n = 5$	68.9M	68.9M	378.9M	0.0M	9.06%	148.5	72%
pftp, qsize=11	14.3M	12.9M	38.7M	5.8M	4.15%	298.0	56%
LUNAR, 4(b)	3.3M	0.7M	3.9M	0.9M	5.04%	595.5	42%
Dining Phil., $n = 9$	4.6M	4.5M	12.2M	3.2M	9.95%	95.0	51%
Leader, $n = 11$	8.2M	8.2M	58.4M	0.0M	2.42%	788.0	70%

[†] This is a scaled-down model. For the full model, see Table 4

5.3   Compression

Disk lookups are largely dominated by disk I/O time. Thus it seems sensible to trade CPU time to reduce the disk I/O time, and we can do so by compressing the states.

Compressing states by either using *entropy encoding* or *state collapsing* methods has been investigated in model checking for quite some time. State collapsing maintains a table of process states, from which a state is assembled, and this table cannot be set a definitive memory bound (without further effort). Huffman coding offers a two to three-fold compression.

We can, however, take advantage of the bulk character of our disk I/O operations: We use paging to write sets of states to disk, and also read sets of states during disk lookups. The size of such sets can be chosen arbitrarily, and they are a good target for dictionary-based compression, as used by the Lempel-Ziv LZ77 algorithm [15], which in turn is used in the DEFLATE algorithm as implemented by ZLIB [16].

Using ZLIB brings vast improvements: A compression to 5% of the original state size can be achieved on most of our models (Tab. 3, where a compression level of 8 was used), which not only *decreases* disk lookup times, but also allows to check for state spaces twenty times as large with the same disk space. In our experiments, the overhead of running the ZLIB on the state sets was easily outmatched by the lower time spent on I/O operations.

The benefit of using the ZLIB can be explained from two facts: Our encoding of states produces many zeroes, e.g., rarely changed most significant bits of variables (Tab. 3, last column). Secondly, successive states tend to differ only in a small number of places. Therefore, they are ideal input for any compressor, and since we consider sets of states at once, are even more suitable for dictionary-based compression.

Hash compaction can achieve even higher compression rates; compression is approximately five times higher than with the ZLIB. This is paid for by losing state information and risking collisions. Using 40 bits we found collisions in state spaces with as little as 15M states.[2]

---

[2] We use 'M' and 'G' as abbreviations for multipliers *Mega* (10^6) and *Giga* (10^9), respectively.

Our algorithm offers the guarantee to be exact (optionally allowing for revisits of states due to the single-successor pruning) and also maintains each visited state in a form that can be used to extract the original space, should anyone have need to investigate it.

6   Results

We tested our approach with different kinds of models: standard (parametric) models distributed with SPIN, as well as hand-written and generated PROMELA models. In the latter two categories are some of the largest case studies (state space-wise) we could find.

For state space generation the NIPS Virtual Machine (VM) [17] is used, and an accompanying PROMELA compiler to translate our models into byte-code suitable for execution. Our measurements are done without partial-order reduction, but a version of *statement merging*.

All experiments were carried out on a 64 bit AMD Opteron^{TM} 248 Dual Processor machine with 16 GB RAM and a single 200 GB Serial-ATA hard-disk, running Linux 2.6.4. Only one of the processors is used by CMC.

Effectiveness of Caches. The effectiveness of the caches directly influences the number of states that need to be checked against disk. We measured the number of cache failures, i.e. the number of states that need to be checked against disk, for two different models: the LUNAR scenario 4(b) [7], which is rather deterministic, i.e. it contains 3.3M states and 3.9M transitions, and the Dining Philosophers model for $n = 9$ processes, which has 4.6M states but 12.2M transitions and thus is much more nondeterministic.

The resulting number of cache misses is shown in Fig. 3. For the Dining Philosophers, the lossy hashing cache is more important than for the much more deterministic LUNAR protocol. Caches misses dominate the runtime for large models, since they need to be processed on disk.

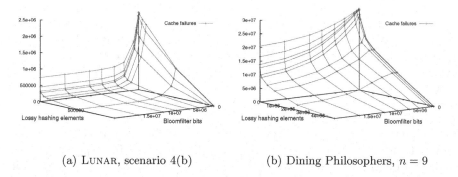

(a) LUNAR, scenario 4(b)   (b) Dining Philosophers, $n = 9$

Fig. 3. Effectiveness of caches with different parameters. Line intersections represent actual measurements. Lower is better, as cache failures result in disk lookups.

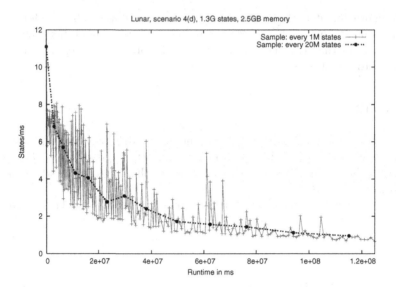

Fig. 4. Smooth degradation illustrated by the states/millisecond development

Smooth Degradation. An advantage of our algorithm is its ability to degrade smoothly, i.e. run without much overhead as long as memory is sufficient and start trading time for memory afterwards. Fig. 4 shows the development of a model checking run for the LUNAR 4(d) example, which consists of 1.3G states (including some revisits), of which 248M are non-single-successors. RAM consumption was restricted to 2.5 GB, with 256 MB given to the Bloom filter, 1 GB given to lossy hashing, and the remainder used up for open and candidate sets, as well as I/O buffers, ZLIB buffer and some smaller data structures. 8.0 GB got written to disk (compressed by ZLIB; the raw data amounts to 153.0 GB). Total runtime is approx. 35.5 hours. For the first 90 seconds, memory was sufficient and allowed for 11 states per millisecond (taken from the open set and processed). Afterwards, the disk had to be used. The bulk operations of reading and writing states do not distribute evenly into short measurement intervals, which explains the peaks, but with a sample interval chosen large enough a clear trend can be identified. The converging behavior can be explained from three effects: First, caches are degrading and resolve less requests, second, as the model is explored exhaustively, revisits become more likely, and third, disk lookups become more expensive.

Large Runs. Tab. 4 shows the results of some large models. For the first and third model, a limit of 2.5 GB RAM was set, whereas the other models were given 16 GB RAM. We always use the Linux O_DIRECT flag for files opened on disk to disable operation system caches. Otherwise, spare memory would be used for caching disk I/O, thus leading to artificially better results, which break down if memory is indeed maxed out. The two LUNAR scenarios exceeded the capabilities of SPIN with 4 GB RAM and both partial-order reduction and COLLAPSE

Table 4. Runs for large models. States visited are all states, including single-successor states, whereas states stored are only states with more than one successor.

Model	States visited	States stored	Edges	Time [h]	ZLIB compr.	Uncompr. stored	Bloom Cache failures
GIOP1	192.9M	162.5M	664.6M	13:34:21	4.81%	79.2GB	363.3K 91.2M
HUGO: Hot fail	555.6M	205.3M	864.9M	15:18:16	3.79%	166.9GB	127.9K 32.1M
LUNAR 4(d)	1.3G	248.3M	1.9G	35:37:29	5.27%	153.0GB	1.7M 150.8M
LUNAR 4(f)	1.6G	334.6M	2.6G	38:36:02	5.73%	230.0GB	12.7M 387.0M

enabled [7]. The GIOP1 protocol [18] has been reported as only checkable with bit-state hashing (although this has been checked on a machine with much less memory than we use). The hot fail-over protocol has been implemented as an example in HUGO [19] and also fails to check in SPIN (for a queue size of 6, which is required; the smaller model in Tab. 3 does not satisfy certain liveness properties).

For all four models, the single-successor criterion works quite well, as can be seen by comparing the number of states actually stored to the number of states visited, which is the sum of the former number and those states discarded due to the single-successor criterion. The visited states number is an over-approximation of the actual number of states in the state space, as is the number of edges, but we still need to store only a fraction of states. Also, ZLIB compression performs very well. We consider both properties to be specific for industrial protocols, which are not too nondeterministic (comparing the number of edges to the number of states covered) and rely on rather large state vectors (more than 500 bytes for all models, with 895 bytes for the hot fail-over protocol).

It should be noted that due to the modularization of our model checker, runtimes are not very optimized and provide a rough outline only. We are confident that they can be significantly improved. The runs support our claim that we can trade runtime for memory, e. g. for the LUNAR scenario 4(d), we require approximately 15 hours with 16 GB of RAM provided, but are also able to finish a run with 2.5 GB in less than 36 hours.

Furthermore, none of our runs came even close to completely using the 200 GB disk we had at our disposal (LUNAR scenario 4(f) required just slightly more than 13 GB). Since RAM consumption stays completely stagnant after the first disk lookup have been triggered, up to ten times larger models can be checked, given enough patience on behalf of the researcher. However, for very large models, our algorithm can be expected to degrade until a dedicated disk-based model checker will be the better choice.

7 Related Work

In this section we review some of the related work on disk-based (explicit) state exploration.

Bao and Jones [13] analyze existing disk-based algorithms. They consider MONO proposed by Stern and Dill [12] and LOCAL by Della Penna et al. [20], and propose their own disk-based algorithm, PART, for state space exploration.

All three algorithms have in common that they can explore larger state spaces than can be handled with purely memory-based algorithms. Parts of the state space is stored on harddisk. In these algorithms several strategies are used to reduce I/O, or to group it so that data can be read linearly from disk, as this can be done much more efficient.

The MONO algorithms uses disk regardless whether enough memory for the full state space is available. At least once per breadth-first level, all states stored in memory are compared for duplicates on disk, and removed if they are. Remaining states have not been visited before, and thus are moved to the breadth-first *open set*. They are also written to disk unconditionally. An overflow situation due to excessively growing *open set*, which we have witnessed in dense models (our run of LUNAR scenario 4(f) had a temporary open set size exceeding 5.8 GB), is not taken care of.

The LOCAL algorithm is a modification of MONO. It does not always compare against all states on disk, but only the most recently stored. Only occasionally, older states are compared against. The scheme works because state spaces of protocol models exhibit *transition locality* [20]. It allows large savings in I/O operations, however states may be revisited and also stored multiple times on disk.

The PART algorithm tries to reduce delayed duplicate detection time even at the expense of increased disk I/O time. Overall run-time is significantly reduced. It simulates *parallel state exploration* [21] on a single processor by partitioning the open list and hashtable and into several pieces, with only one active at a time (*multitasking* without *multiprocessing*). Thus, not all states on disk need to be checked during DDD, but only a fraction. Due to the partitioning of hashtables, either the number of partitions must be guessed upfront to accomodate all reachable states, or a potentially costly scheme for growing the hashtable must be devised. In this algorithm the open lists are not sets, states can enter them several times, leading to significant overhead, both in time and memory, in particular for models with high *locality*.

All three algorithms use *hash compaction* for their largest tests, to reduce I/O bandwidth requirements manifold: instead of full state vectors only a short hashcode (40–48 bit) is stored. However, without having states vectors available to resolve hash collisions, this leads to reachable states accidentally being left unexplored.

Edelkamp et al. [22] accelerate their External A* algorithm with *bitstate hashing*, yielding a partial search algorithm. The A* algorithm is targeted towards finding a *goal state* with heuristics. We see its main use in the early development process when checked properties are frequently not satisfied. If a goal state cannot be found the algorithm would degrade into an exhaustive search. The modification making it a partial search is not helpful in that case.

Behrmann et al. [1] chose a different way to tackle state spaces which do not completely fit into memory. Instead of storing states on disk, they investigated different criteria which allow not to store states *at all*. The savings in space are paid with increased run-time due to revisits, even if enough memory would be available.

8 Conclusions

In this paper, we presented a novel algorithm for state space exploration using external memory. It makes novel use of a combination of Bloom filters, lossy hash tables and compression to reduce disk I/O, while still ensuring that all reachable states are indeed explored. Additionally, states are stored to disk for off-line post-processing. Our experiments confirm that our method is practical. We can easily handle large case studies in the order of 10^9 states.

Future Work. Our implementation still uses some suboptimal algorithms which penalizes checking on disk more than necessary. We would like to address these in the near future, including an analysis of the I/O complexity of the updated algorithms.

We have only addressed reachability problems which do not depend on *depth-first post-order*. Two possible future lines of research suggest themselves at this point. We would like to address how to combine these algorithms with checking of arbitrary temporal formulas. We are confident that we can build on work done for parallel and distributed model checking algorithms [23]. This also leads to the next logical step, namely combining disk-based and distributed model checking, allowing faster results, and possibly pushing towards the Tera-state (10^{12}) scale.

References

1. Behrmann, G., Larsen, K.G., Pelánek, R.: To store or not to store. In Jr., W.A.H., Somenzi, F., eds.: CAV. Volume 2725 of Lecture Notes in Computer Science., Springer (2003) 433–445
2. Clarke, E.M., Grumberg, O., Jha, S., Lu, Y., Veith, H.: Counterexample-guided abstraction refinement. In Emerson, E.A., Sistla, A.P., eds.: CAV. Volume 1855 of Lecture Notes in Computer Science., Springer (2000) 154–169
3. Bloom, B.H.: Space/time trade-offs in hash coding with allowable errors. Commun. ACM **13**(7) (1970) 422–426
4. Garavel, H., Lang, F., Mateescu, R.: An overview of CADP 2001. EASST Newsletter **4** (2002) 13–24
5. Holmén, F., Leucker, M., Lindström, M.: UppDMC – a distributed model checker for fragments of the μ-calculus. In Brim, L., Leucker, M., eds.: Proc. 3rd PDMC. Volume 128(3) of ENTCS., Elsevier Science Publishers (2004)
6. Holzmann, G.J.: The SPIN model checker: primer and reference manual. Addison-Wesley, Boston, MA 02116 (2003)
7. Wibling, O., Parrow, J., Pears, A.: Automatized verification of ad hoc routing protocols. In: FORTE. Volume 3235 of Lecture Notes in Computer Science., Springer (2004) 343 – 358

8. Kamel, M., Leue, S.: Formalization and validation of the General Inter-ORB Protocol (GIOP) using PROMELA and SPIN. STTT **2**(4) (2000) 394–409

9. Pelánek, R.: Evaluation of on-the-fly state space reductions. In: Proc. of Mathematical and Engineering Methods in Computer Science (MEMICS'05). (2005) 121–127

10. Holzmann, G.J.: An analysis of bitstate hashing. Form. Methods Syst. Des. **13**(3) (1998) 289–307

11. Dillinger, P.C., Manolios, P.: Fast and accurate bitstate verification for SPIN. In: SPIN. Volume 2989 of LNCS., Springer (2004)

12. Stern, U., Dill, D.L.: Using magnatic disk instead of main memory in the murphi verifier. In: Computer Aided Verification. (1998) 172–183

13. Bao, T., Jones, M.: Time-efficient model checking with magnetic disk. In Halbwachs, N., Zuck, L.D., eds.: TACAS. Volume 3440 of Lecture Notes in Computer Science., Springer (2005) 526–540

14. Eastlake, D.E., Jones, P.E.: US secure hash algorithm 1 (SHA1). Internet informational RFC 3174 (2001)

15. Ziv, J., Lempel, A.: A universal algorithm for sequential data compression. IEEE Transactions on Information Theory **23**(3) (1977) 337–343

16. Gailly, J., Adler, M.: zlib data compression library. http://www.zlib.net/ (1995)

17. Weber, M., Schürmans, S.: NIPS virtual machine and compiler implementation. http://www.cwi.nl/~weber/nips/ (2005)

18. Kamel, M., Leue, S.: Formalization and validation of the general inter-orb protocol (giop) using promela and spin. STTT **2**(4) (2000) 394–409

19. Knapp, A., Merz, S.: Model Checking and Code Generation for UML State Machines and Collaborations. In: Proc. 5th Wsh. Tools for System Design and Verification, Technical Report 2002-11, Institut für Informatik, Universität Augsburg (2002) 59–64

20. Penna, G.D., Intrigila, B., Tronci, E., Zilli, M.V.: Exploiting transition locality in the disk based murphi verifier. In Springer-Verlag, ed.: Proc. of FMCAD. Volume 2517 of LNCS. (2002) 202–219

21. Stern, U., Dill, D.L.: Parallelizing the Murφ verifier. In Grumberg, O., ed.: Computer-Aided Verification, 9th International Conference. Volume 1254 of LNCS., Springer (1997) 256–267 Haifa, Israel, June 22-25.

22. Edelkamp, S., Jabbar, S.: Accelerating external search with bitstate hashing. In: 19. Workshop on New Results in Planning, Scheduling and Design. (2005)

23. Barnat, J., Brim, L., Černá, I., Šimeček, P.: DiVinE the distributed verification environment. In Leucker, M., van de Pol, J., eds.: 4th International Workshop on Parallel and Distributed Methods in verifiCation (PDMC'05), Lisbon, Portuga (2005)

Discovering Symmetries[*]

Hassen Saïdi

Computer Science Laboratory
SRI International
Menlo Park, CA 94025, USA
Tel.: (+1) (650) 859-3810
Fax: (+1) (650) 859-2844
hassen.saidi@sri.com

Abstract. When analyzing concurrent software applications, symmetry reduction techniques dramatically narrow the size of the state space search by identifying computations that, because of symmetries in the system, are redundant. While analysis algorithms exploiting symmetry reduction are well developed, little has been done in *discovering* the nature of the symmetries of a system. What is even less researched is discovering symmetries that are particular to a temporal property. This paper proposes a general framework for discovering symmetries in systems that exhibit *absolute* or *relative* symmetries depending on the property of interest. Our work extends previous symmetry reduction techniques by making advances in automating generalized model automorphism discovery. Generalized model automorphisms capture exact abstractions and therefore preserve both the validity and the violation of any property of the analyzed system while achieving dramatic state space reduction.

1   Introduction

For over half a century, formal verification has been used to help show that computer systems will behave as they are intended to. The most popular verification technique being used today is model checking, where, given a mathematical model M of the computing system and a logical formula φ that expresses a desired property of the system, the truth value of φ in M is determined by exhaustive exploration of the state space of M. The state spaces of complex systems are many orders of magnitude larger than automated model checking tools can handle. Therefore, the mathematical models of computing systems used in model checking must be much simpler than the systems that are modeled. Yet, the models must contain all the detail that is essential to the analysis being performed, because omission of relevant detail can invalidate the results of the analysis. The only obvious way of ensuring that analysis of these simple models will produce accurate results is to generate them by *abstraction*, the process

---

[*] This research was sponsored by NSF under contract number SA4102-10097PG/CCR-0325274.

L. Brim et al. (Eds.): FMICS and PDMC 2006, LNCS 4346, pp. 67–83, 2007.

of eliminating detail that has been shown to be irrelevant from more detailed models that are more obviously accurate and faithful.

Symmetry reduction is an abstraction technique that reduces the size of the state space search by identifying computations that, because of the symmetry in the model, are redundant. Models of distributed systems comprising many identical components exhibit considerable symmetry. Since multiple components play the same functional role, and therefore interact with their environment in the same way, the identity of a component during analysis is often irrelevant. Multi-threaded programs can also be amendable to symmetry reductions to overcome the potential unbounded number of threads.

At least two natural notions of symmetry — what might be called *absolute* and *relative* symmetry — can be explicated in terms of frame automorphisms, which are, roughly speaking, one-to-one homomorphisms that map the frame $\langle S, R \rangle$ of a model M that represents a set S of states and a transition relation R, onto itself. This allows the construction of a quotient M_G formed by the construction of equivalence classes among states that are not distinguished by elements of the group G of permutations. The size of the model M_G can potentially be exponentially smaller than the size of M. The more symmetries are captured in G, the smaller M_G is. Since M_G is bisimilar to M, then for a property φ, checking whether M_G satisfies φ is equivalent to checking whether M satisfies φ.

The symmetries that can be exploited during model checking are essentially the intersection of the symmetries exhibited by the system and the symmetries exhibited by the property. These sources of symmetries characterize much of the large body of literature that studies symmetry reduction in model checking [4, 9, 16, 6, 5, 11, 10, 17]. The original work of Emerson and Sistla [10] focuses on systems with global symmetries where all components are *permutable* and where the permutations of process identity preserve the valuation of atomic predicates in the property of interest. In [6], a syntactic restriction is imposed on the description language of the system, so that the permutations of components in the system are trivially determined, but also requires a restriction on the syntax of the properties as well. Recent work [11, 17, 9] tackles systems with little or no symmetry at all. In this case, the construction of M_G is done by first computing an approximation of M_G that assumes global symmetry, and then refining it until only the relevant symmetries that guarantee bisimulation for a given property are considered. In [17], model automorphisms are extended to more than just permutations of process identity, but also to local variable-value pairs. This more general notion is better captured by the notion of generalized frame automorphism.

While state-exploration algorithms exploiting symmetry reduction by exploring M_G instead of M are well developed, little has been done in *discovering* the symmetries of a system, and automating the construction of M_G using those symmetries. What is even less researched is discovering symmetries that are particular to a temporal property. If we can automate and speed up the process of discovering the symmetries that are possible for every single property, we would achieve better state-space reduction and provide a much more flexible framework for the analysis of a large class of distributed systems. What is of interest to us is not to exploit only symmetries that induce a bisimulation of the state graph so that all properties are preserved, but to provide an automated way of discovering some or all of the symmetries that can be exploited for every single property of interest, achieving therefore better reduction than classical symmetry reduction methods.

This paper proposes a general framework for discovering symmetries in systems that exhibit global or local symmetries depending on the property of interest. Our work extends previous symmetry reduction techniques by making significant advances in automating generalized model automorphism discovery. Generalized model automorphism allows us to discover symmetries between states satisfying arbitrary predicates while preserving the property of interest. Therefore, we do not only discover symmetries in systems composed of several identical processes, but we can discover symmetries in the state space of a single process. Even when processes are not symmetric and their identities cannot be permuted, part of their local state space can be permuted. The contribution of this paper can be summarized as follows:

- An anytime symbolic algorithm for discovering symmetries in systems that exhibit global, local symmetries, or no apparent symmetries at all.
- Generalization of symmetry reduction to model automorphisms that preserve a particular temporal property.
- Our schema for discovering symmetries is both incremental and conservative. At any time, the set of already computed symmetries is guaranteed to define a generalized model automorphism that guarantees the preservation of the property. This guarantees that no spurious counterexample will be generated.
- The techniques developed have been applied to a real-life system that represents the largest implementation of a distributed multiagent system up to this date, and help improve its architecture. As a result of our analysis, flaws in the architecture of the system could be identified, and a set of test cases has been generated from the model checking of an abstraction of the systems that exploits symmetries. Furthermore, changes in the architecture have been suggested so that relative symmetries can be extended into absolute symmetries, making the analysis simpler and the construction of an argument of the correctness of the architecture easier.

In the larger context of automated abstraction, our approach represents a fundamentally different alternative to current automated abstraction approaches based on abstract interpretation techniques [8], where an initial coarse abstract domain is successively refined until the property is proved correct or a counterexample is exhibited. This is the case of predicate abstraction [13] where an initial partition of the state space using an initial set of predicates is refined by adding more predicates when necessary [15] and therefore obtaining a more precise description of the state space. Our approach can be viewed as a bottom-up abstraction methodology that consists of first considering the system itself and collapsing equivalent states without loss of information. The advantage is that there is no need for refinement since there is no overapproximation of the transition relation that might lead to spurious counterexamples. Our philosophy consists of achieving enough state space reduction in order to be able to model check the system rather than drastically reducing the state space by means of overabstraction and then refinement.

In the rest of the paper, we first introduce our motivating application in Section 2, followed by an illustrative example in Section 3. In section 4, we define the notion of symmetry and model automorphism. In section 5, we describe a generalization of model automorphism. In section 6 we describe our technique for discovering generalized model automorphisms for a given property and describe our algorithm for discovering symmetries, and in Section 7, we discuss the details and results of the analysis.

2   Motivating Application

Our motivating example is UltraLog, a complex distributed multiagent system, built using the Cougaar technology [3], and that represents the largest implementation of an agent system known today. Agents in UltraLog are organized in enclaves that are under different administrative supervision. Enclaves are related by wide area network connections, and every enclave includes a set of administrative agents that are used to enforce security and robustness policies. The mission of the UltraLog system requires that most agents are available when they are solicited. To ensure such a fundamental property, UltraLog relies on the following robustness mechanisms:

- *Intelligent mobility:* Agents are moved to machines where the necessary resources required to perform their tasks are guaranteed to be available.
- *Failure recovery:* Failure of individual agents or machines is dealt with by restarting agents on different machines using the following mechanisms: automatic restart when agents fail, migration of an agent when the machine on which it runs fails, and restoration of the state of the agents after failure using local and replicated storage

Every set of agents in an enclave is monitored by a set of management agents, also called *managers*. The role of a manager is to monitor a set of agents by checking that every single one of them emits regular heartbeats. When an agent's heartbeat is not received, the agent is restarted on a different node along with all the agents that were on the same node. Each agent, manager, and node requires an authentication certificate that enables it to interact with its environment. Authentication certificates are delivered by a set of certificate authorities (CAs) organized in a hierarchical manner. CAs are themselves implemented as agents with the appropriate plug-ins to play their role as CAs, and they therefore require other CAs. There is one root certificate authority. When a node, a manager, an agent, or a CA is restarted, it combines a built-in certificate with the certificate of the manager that initiated the restart into a single request for a new certificate from its CA. Our model of UltraLog is an abstraction of the current implementation in which timing and network information is abstracted away.

The model is parametrized by the number of agents, robustness managers, security managers, certificate authorities, nodes, replicated storage locations, and enclaves. For simplicity, an agent, a manager, or a certificate authority can be in either its *init*, *alive*, or *dead* state, and a node can be either *up* or *down*. The global state is the composition of the states of all agents, managers, certificate authorities, their respective locations, and the state of every node.

Many aspects of the UltraLog architecture break the symmetry that one might exploit among agents, managers, CAs, or nodes. Agents, for instance, need to be distinguished depending on their managers, their CAs, and their locations, and similarly for managers, and CAs. Furthermore, depending on the property, more symmetries can be exploited. Consider, for instance, the property stating that every agent playing the role of a certificate authority that dies is eventually restarted and becomes available:

$$\varphi = \forall (i : CA) : \Box(\Diamond(alive(i)))$$

Each CA i is initially an agent in its *init* state. If i's CA defined by the predicate $certificate(i)$ is running, that is, it is in its *alive* state, then it requests a certificate from it. Once the certificate is delivered, the agent i moves to its *alive* state and starts playing its role as a CA. i can move to state *dead* in two cases: if the node on which it runs goes from its state *up* to *down*, or if i's manager is no longer receiving i's heartbeat. In either case, i is declared dead and its certificate revoked. i is then moved to another node if its original node is compromised, or restarted on the same node otherwise. Nodes on which agents run can go down in a nondeterministic way, and are restarted in a nondeterministic way as well.

Let us assume for a moment that there are three CAs such that CA 1 is the root certificate, and plays the role of certificate authority for CA 2 and CA 3. It is clear from the description of the transition relation of each CA, that the three CAs are not symmetric, and that the permutation of CA 1, CA 2, and CA 3 does not induce an automorphism of the model. So, instead of assuming that all CAs are symmetric or *permutable* until proven otherwise following the approach of [17], we start by considering all CAs as being nonpermutable, and discovering incrementally what possible permutations they might allow. Furthermore, it is possible that even if no permutation among the CAs is possible, there exists some predicate $p(i)$ such that any state where $p(i)$ holds is symmetric to a state where $p(j)$ holds where i and j are different CAs. In fact, we can find arbitrary pairs of predicates p and q that may or may not refer to component identity, or to local variables of components so that the permutation of a state satisfying p by a state satisfying q defines a model automorphism. Using our approach, we are able to discover that CA 2 and CA 3 are permutable. Our approach determines that since CA 2 and CA 3 have the same dependencies up to permutation, they are themselves permutable. The justification is in the fact that both CA 2 and CA 3 depend on CA 1, and on their local nodes on which they run. Since the states of individual nodes depend only on the environment, node identities are permutable as well. Another important condition that allows the permutation of CA 2 and CA 3 is that permuting 2 and 3 in φ leaves the property unchanged.

The symmetry reduction techniques in the literature cannot handle the dynamic aspect of the Ultralog architecture where agents, managers, and CAs are mobile and are moved from node to node. This makes the permutation of agents, managers, CAs, and nodes respectively very tricky. Multiagent systems as well as new emerging architectures such as sensor networks are a challenge to the state-of-the-art abstraction techniques such as symmetry reduction techniques, and tool support for automatically computing useful abstractions is necessary. Traditional symmetry reduction techniques view systems composed of identical components in isolation. In a multiagent system or mobile sensor network, these components operate in a dynamic environment that is constantly changing for each component. Therefore, a much finer analysis is required to discover what aspect of the behavior of these components, and their environment can be safely considered symmetric for a particular property of interest.

3   An Illustrative Example

Following (Figure 1) is a toy example that illustrates the techniques for computing generalized model automorphisms. The example is a program with three boolean variables p, q, and r, and two transitions τ_1 and τ_2. All the variables are true in the initial state.

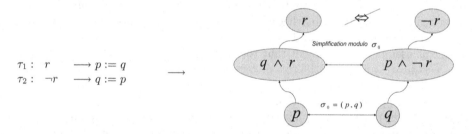

$$\tau_1 : \quad r \quad \longrightarrow p := q$$
$$\tau_2 : \quad \neg r \quad \longrightarrow q := p$$

Fig. 1. A simple example of failed symmetry computation

We can exploit symmetries in this program by finding pairs of arbitrary predicates (p_1, p_2) such that we can permute states that satisfy p_1 and states that satisfy p_2. We denote by $\sigma_0 = (p_1, p_2)$ such a permutation. Let us consider the pair (p, q). We first compute the dependencies for each predicate. The validity of p depends on the predicate $q \wedge r$ and the validity of the predicate q depends on the predicate $p \wedge \neg r$. If p and q have the same dependencies, then we can consider that p and q are permutable. If not, we check whether the dependencies are themselves permutable predicates. Notice that it is not necessary to check whether $q \wedge r$ and $p \wedge \neg r$ are permutable, but only to check whether r and $\neg r$ are, because the predicates $q \wedge r$ and $p \wedge \neg r$ can be simplified modulo the initial permutation (p, q) since the dependencies of p and q have already been computed. The predicates r and $\neg r$ are not permutable since they do not depend

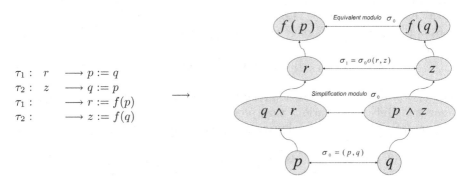

$$
\begin{aligned}
\tau_1 : \quad & r \quad \longrightarrow p := q \\
\tau_2 : \quad & z \quad \longrightarrow q := p \\
\tau_1 : \quad & \quad \longrightarrow r := f(p) \\
\tau_2 : \quad & \quad \longrightarrow z := f(q)
\end{aligned}
\qquad \longrightarrow
$$

Fig. 2. A simple example of successful symmetry computation

on any other predicate except the initial state. At the initial state r is true and therefore $\neg r$ is false. We then conclude that (p, q) is not a valid permutation.

Consider now the second example in Figure 2 where now the program has four variables p, q, r, and z. The dependencies of p and q are respectively $q \wedge r$ and $p \wedge z$. These dependencies are simplified modulo the permutation $\sigma_0 = (p, q)$ and yield the pair (r, z). The dependencies of r and z are respectively the expressions $f(p)$ and $f(q)$. These dependencies are equivalent modulo the permutation $\sigma_0 = (p, q)$. Therefore, p and q are permutable because all their dependencies are either equivalent or permutable modulo the permutation $\sigma_0 = (p, q)$. However, this is not enough since we have to make sure that in the initial state both p and q hold the same value. If the initial values of p and q are unknown, which is the case where p and q contain input variables, then p and q are permutable for input values that make both p and q true.

The permutation $\sigma = (p, q) \circ (z, r)$ induces a generalized model automorphism. Therefore, for any temporal logic property where the permutation of p and q results in an equivalent property, it is only necessary to explore the successor of a single representative state instead of the successors of all the states that are equivalent modulo the permutation σ.

4   Defining Symmetry

Before describing our procedure for discovering symmetries, we recall some preliminary definitions and define symmetry reduction. The state space of a concurrent system is represented by a transition system. Let us say that a transition system M is a quadruple $\langle S, R, L, P \rangle$ where S is a nonempty set, called the set of *states* of M, R is the transition relation of M, P is a set of atomic predicates, and $L : S \rightarrow 2^P$ is a labeling function. We denote by $L(s)$ the values of the predicates of P in s. We also denote by $L(s)_{|Q}$ the values in the state s of the predicates of a subset Q of P with the convention that $L(s)_{|\emptyset} = \emptyset$. A *permutation* on a state S is a bijection of S into itself. We designate by $\mathcal{P}$ the group of permutations of S.

Definition 1 (symmetry Group). *Given a transition system* $M = \langle S, R, L, P \rangle$, *a subgroup* G *of* $\mathcal{P}$ *is called a symmetry group of* M *if for all permutations* σ *of* G:

$$(s_1, s_2) \in R \text{ iff } (\sigma(s_1), \sigma(s_2)) \in R$$

That is, G preserves the transition relation R. Not all permutations are property preserving. Only permutations that preserve certain atomic predicates — that is, permutations that form an invariance group — are useful.

Definition 2 (Invariance Group). *Given a transition system* $M = \langle S, R, L, P \rangle$, *and let* Q *be a subset of the set of predicates* P. *A symmetry group* G *of* M *is called an invariance group of* M *for* Q *if for all permutations* σ *of* G *and for every atomic proposition* β *in* Q, $L(s)_{|\{\beta\}} = L(\sigma(s))_{|\{\beta\}}$. *In other words:*

$$L(s)_{|Q} = L(\sigma(s))_{|Q}$$

That is, G preserves the transition relation R and the atomic predicates of Q. The symmetry group G defines an equivalence relation on S where the equivalence class of a state s is designated by its representative $[s]$ defined by $[s] = \{s' \in S | \exists \sigma \in G, \sigma(s) = s'\}$. This equivalence defines a quotient of the transition system M.

Definition 3 (Quotient Transition System). *Given a transition system* $M = \langle S, R, L, P \rangle$, *and an invariance group* G *of* M *for* P, *a quotient transition system for* M *modulo* G *is the transition system* $M_G = \langle S_G, R_G, L_G, P \rangle$ *where*

1. $S_G = \{[s] | s \in S\}$
2. $R_G = \{([s_1], [s_2]) | (s_1, s_2) \in R\}$
3. $L_G : S_G \to 2^P$ *is such that* $\forall s \in S : L_G([s]) = L(s)$

The transition systems M and M_G are bisimilar. Therefore, G strongly preserves every CTL* property φ with atomic predicates in P.

Theorem 1. *Given a transition system* $M = \langle S, R, L, P \rangle$ *and* G *an invariance group of* M *for* P, *then for any CTL* property φ *where only atomic predicates of* P *appear in* φ:

$$M \models \varphi \Leftrightarrow M_G \models \varphi$$

5 Generalized Invariance Groups

Invariance groups capture the symmetries in a transition system and allow the preservation of all properties that use only atomic predicates in P. This restriction can be removed by allowing that symmetric states s and $\sigma(s)$ do not necessarily agree on the predicates of P.

Definition 4 (Generalized Invariance Group). *Given a transition system* $M = \langle S, R, L, P \rangle$, G *an invariance group of* M *for* P, *and a mapping* $\gamma : P \to P$, *the pair* $\langle G, \gamma \rangle$, *denoted by* G_γ, *is called a generalized invariance group of* M *if for all permutations* σ *of* G:

$$\forall s \in S, L(s) = \gamma(L(\sigma(s)))$$

In the definition above, $L(\sigma(s))$ is the set of all atomic predicates that are true in the state s, and $\gamma(L(\sigma(s)))$ replaces each of those predicates by its corresponding permutation. The generalized invariance group defines a generalized automorphism of M where equivalent states are not required to agree on the set of atomic predicates. This generalization that admits swapping of arbitrary predicates will achieve more symmetry reduction for some properties. The most trivial ones are the properties φ such that φ and $\gamma(\varphi)$ are equivalent, where $\gamma(\varphi)$ is defined as the property φ where every atomic predicate β appearing in φ is substituted by $\gamma(\beta)$. Considering generalized invariance groups is a powerful approach to state space reduction. Permutations between states are not restricted to permutation of process indices anymore. Even if two processes i and j are not symmetric, some of their respective behaviors might be. Therefore it is possible that two predicates $p(i)$ and $p(j)$ can be symmetric but not i and j. Another consequence of considering generalized invariance groups is that symmetry reduction cannot be restricted to concurrent systems defined by the composition of identical processes, but can be defined in general for arbitrary systems.

Theorem 2. *Given a transition system* $M = \langle S, R, L, P \rangle$, *a generalized invariance group* G_γ *of* M *for* P, *and any temporal property* φ *where only atomic predicates of* P *appear in* φ. *If* φ *is invariant under* γ, *that is,* $\varphi = \gamma(\varphi)$ *then:*

$$M \models \varphi \Leftrightarrow M_{G_\gamma} \models \gamma(\varphi)$$

From now on, we consider φ to be a Linear Temporal Logic (LTL) formula. The main importance of G_γ and similar sorts of structure-preserving mappings is that a computation

$$\tau = \langle s_0, s_1, s_2, \ldots \rangle$$

and its image under σ

$$\sigma(\tau) = \langle \sigma(s_0), \sigma(s_1), \sigma(s_2), \ldots \rangle$$

cannot be distinguished by a certain class of logical formulas. Hence, there is no need for considering both τ and $\sigma(\tau)$ when searching for a refutation of φ. In other words, after a (generalized) model automorphism has been discovered, each state s can be identified with its image $\sigma(s)$ under σ to reduce the size of the state space prior to model checking.

6 Computing Symmetries

We propose an algorithm that takes as input a system description and a temporal property φ and produces a generalized invariance group G_γ. Since G_γ is computed so that it preserves only the property φ, dramatic state space reduction can be achieved. For a given property φ, our approach consists of finding a pair (p_i, q_i) of predicates such that the corresponding permutation $\sigma_i = (p_i, q_i)$ defines a generalized automorphism. That is, it preserves the property φ. Once such pair is found, it is possible to find a new pair (p_j, q_j) of predicates such that its corresponding permutation $\sigma_j = (p_j, q_j)$ defines also a generalized automorphism. The composition of σ_i and σ_j is therefore also a generalized automorphism.

Definition 5 (Program). *A program Prog is a tuple $< \mathcal{V}, \mathcal{T} = \{\tau_1, \cdots, \tau_n\}, I >$, where $\mathcal{V}$ is a set of program variables, $\mathcal{T}$ is a set of transitions or guarded commands, and I is a predicate characterizing the set of initial states.*

Each transition τ is a guarded command

$$guard \longrightarrow v_1 ::= e_1, \cdots, v_n ::= e_n$$

where $\{v_1, \cdots, v_k\} \subseteq \mathcal{V}$. The boolean expression *guard* is the guard of the transition τ. Each variable v_i is assigned with an expression e_i of a compatible type. A state of a program *Prog* is a valuation of the system variables of $\mathcal{V}$. We also recall the definitions of predicate transformers over transition systems. The predicate transformer *pre* expressing the precondition by a transition τ of a predicate p over the state variables of $\mathcal{V}$ is defined as follows:

$$pre[\tau](p) \;=\; \exists \mathcal{V}'.action_\tau(\mathcal{V}, \mathcal{V}') \wedge p(\mathcal{V}')$$

where $action_\tau(\mathcal{V}, \mathcal{V}')$ is defined as the relation between the current state and next state, that is, the expression

$$guard \wedge \bigwedge_{i=1}^{k} v_i' = e_i$$

The semantics of a program P is given by its computational model M represented by a transition system defined in Section 4. We denote by $DNF(e)$ the disjunctive normal form of the expression e. We also denote by $[e]^{\sigma=(p,q)}$ the expression e where the predicate p and the predicate q are simultaneously substituted by the predicate q and the predicate p respectively. For instance, $[p \wedge q]^{\sigma=(p,q)}$ is the expression $q \wedge p$. We also have $[q]^{\sigma=(p,q)} = p$. That is, the expression p and the expression q are equivalent modulo the permutation σ. We also define the simplification of an expression modulo a permutation. In Figure 1, the expressions $q \wedge r$ and $p \wedge \neg r$ are simplified to r and $\neg r$ respectively modulo the permutation $\sigma = (p, q)$. The simplification is done by translating both expressions to a disjunctive normal form, and then eliminating disjuncts that are equivalent modulo σ. The remaining disjuncts are conjunctions of atomic expressions and are further simplified by eliminating conjuncts that are equivalent modulo σ. We denote by $Simp(e, \sigma)$, the simplification of e modulo σ. For instance, we have

$$Simp(p \vee (q \wedge r), \sigma = (p, q)) \;=\; r \;=\; Simp(q \vee (p \wedge r), \sigma = (p, q))$$

6.1   Property-Based Permutations

Definition 4 is our starting point in finding symmetries. Let us first define permutations of states that preserve a given property φ.

Definition 6 (φ-Permutation). *Let φ be an LTL formula. A mapping $\sigma : S \to S$ is a φ-permutation if for every infinite sequence τ*

$$\tau \models \varphi \quad iff \quad \sigma(\tau) \models \varphi$$

By definition, φ-permutations preserve the property φ. Given a model M and a temporal logic property φ, the problem of discovering symmetries is the problem of finding a set of φ-permutations. We propose an algorithm for finding permutations by computing and then successively refining an initial permutation. Our incremental approach allows us to provide users with a tradeoff between the amount of reduction they want to achieve and the amount of symbolic computation that is required to generate the permutations. Our algorithm will find a set of permutations that define a generalized invariance group. By showing that these permutations preserve by construction the property φ, we ensure that these permutations are φ-permutation.

6.2   Exploiting Dependencies

One obvious way of discovering φ-permutations is to exploit dependencies. Intuitively, for every sequence of states, any state that does not influence the property φ can be substituted by another state that also does not influence the validity of φ.

Definition 7 (dependency of a predicate). *Let p be a predicate. The dependency of a predicate p with respect to a transition τ, noted $dep(p)[\tau]$, is*

$$dep(p)[\tau] = \begin{cases} pre[\tau](p) & \text{if the assignments of } \tau \text{ affect } p \\ p & \text{otherwise} \end{cases}$$

The dependency of p with respect to a program, noted $dep(p)$, is defined as

$$\bigvee_{i=1}^{n} dep(p)[\tau_i]$$

We extend the definition of dependency to temporal formulas as follows:

$$dep(\varphi) = \bigvee_{p_i \in pred(\varphi)} dep^*(p_i)$$

That is, the union of the transitive closure of the dependency computation for every atomic predicate p_i appearing in φ.

Proposition 1. *Let s and t be two states such that $L(s)_{|dep(\varphi)} = L(t)_{|dep(\varphi)}$. The permutation σ that maps s to t and vice versa, and maps every other state to itself, is a φ-permutation.*

Computing a first set of dependencies can be used to slice a model, and therefore reduce the state space. This can be expressed as a permutation σ_0 defined as follows:

$$\forall s \in S \quad \sigma_0(s) = \begin{cases} t \text{ if } L(s)_{|dep(\varphi)} = L(t)_{|dep(\varphi)} \\ s \text{ otherwise} \end{cases}$$

that is, σ_0 does not distinguish states that agree on the valuation of predicates in $dep(\varphi)$. We consider σ_0 to be the first φ-permutation to be extracted from the property φ.

6.3   Refining Symmetries

Exploiting dependencies allows the permutation between sequences of states that do not affect the property φ. While this can sometime lead to a significant reduction in the state space to explore, it basically exploits a very simple case of symmetry. We propose to further exploit dependencies by refining the already computed symmetries and discovering more symmetric states. Given a φ-permutation σ_0 such as the one computed previously, we know that σ_0 does not distinguish states that agree on the valuation of predicates in $dep(\varphi)$. Our approach for refining σ consists in finding a pair of predicates p and q in $dep(\varphi)$, such that the permutation between states that agree on all the valuations of predicates in $dep(\varphi)$ but p and q is a φ-permutation. That is, the permutation of states s_1 and s_2 satisfying respectively p and q is a φ-permutation.

Definition 8 (permutability). *Let p and q be two arbitrary predicates. p and q are permutable if and only if one of the following is true:*

- *$dep(p)$ and $dep(q)$ are equivalent.*
- *$dep(p)$ and $dep(q)$ are permutable.*

In other words, states satisfying p and q can be permuted if and only if their dependencies are the same up to symmetry. That is, they depend on the same states, or they depend on states that are themselves permutable.

Definition 9 (permutation induced by permutable predicates). *Let p and q be two permutable predicates. The permutation induced by p and q noted $\sigma_{(p,q)}$ is the permutation defined recursively as follows:*

$$\sigma_{(p,q)} = \begin{cases} (p,q) & \text{if } dep(p) \equiv dep(q) \\ (p,q) \circ \sigma_{(dep(p),dep(q))} & \text{if } dep(p) \text{ and } dep(q) \text{ are permutable} \end{cases}$$

That is, the permutation of p and q and their dependencies.

While Definition 8 allows us to define what states are permutable, the following proposition provides a way of finding p and q that are relevant to a particular property φ and such that $\sigma_{(p,q)}$ is a φ-permutation.

Proposition 2. *Let s and t be two states such that s and t satisfy respectively the predicates p and q. Let σ be the permutation such that $\sigma(s) = t$, and $\sigma(s') = s'$ for every state s' satisfying neither p nor q. The permutation σ is a φ-permutation if and only if both of the following are true:*

Begin
$\mathcal{X} = \mathcal{X}_0 \cup pred(\varphi)$;
$\sigma = \sigma_0$;
while $\mathcal{X} \neq \emptyset$ **Do**
chose $q \in \mathcal{X}$ and $p \in \mathcal{X}$
if $permutable?(p, q, \sigma) \wedge [\varphi]^{\sigma(p,q)} = \varphi$
    then
        $\sigma = \sigma \circ \sigma_{(p,q)}$;
        $\mathcal{X} = \mathcal{X} \setminus \{p\} \cup \{q\} \cup dep^*(p) \cup dep^*(q)$;
endif
Od
End

Fig. 3. Algorithm for computing symmetries

- p and q are permutable
- $[\varphi]^{\sigma=(p,q)} = \varphi$

That is, p and q are permutable and permuting p and q leaves the property unchanged.

Proof. The proof is by induction on the structure of the dependencies of p and q.

The initial permutation and its successive refinements can be combined to form a single permutation that can be applied to the entire state space. The following proposition shows that the composition of all permutations computed by our algorithm is a permutation that allows symmetry reduction.

Proposition 3. *Let σ_i be a φ-permutation and let σ_j be a φ-permutation. The composition $\sigma_i \circ \sigma_j$ is also a φ-permutation.*

6.4 An Algorithm for Computing Symmetries

Our algorithm for computing permutations is described in Figure 3. We consider an initial arbitrary set $\mathcal{X}$ of candidate predicates that includes the predicates in the property φ. We pick two predicates p and q and check if they are permutable by computing their dependencies. If p and q are permutable, then p and q are removed from $\mathcal{X}$. We also remove the predicates appearing in $dep^*(p)$ and $dep*(q)$ from $\mathcal{X}$ since if two permutable predicates p' and q' appear in $\mathcal{X}$ and also appear in the dependencies of p and q, then the permutation $\sigma_{(p,q)}$ subsumes the permutation $\sigma_{(p',q')}$.

Figure 4 describes the procedure *permutable?* that checks if two predicates are permutable. First we compute the dependencies of p and q and put those expressions in disjunctive normal form. We check if the dependencies are equivalent modulo the permutation of p and q. If so, we establish that p and q are permutable if and only if p and q are equivalent in the initial state. If not, we

$permutable?(p, q, \sigma)$
Begin
$e_1 := DNF(dep(p))$
$e_2 := DNF(dep(q))$
if $e_1 \equiv [e_2]^\sigma$
  then $I \Rightarrow p \equiv q$
  else $permutable?(Simp(e_1, \sigma), Simp(e_2, \sigma), \sigma)$
End

Fig. 4. Procedure for checking if two predicates are permutable

simplify the dependencies modulo the permutation of p and q and check if the simplified dependencies are themselves permutable.

From the description of the algorithm, it seems that the complexity of computing permutations is reduced to the complexity of a symbolic *pre* computation. However it is much simpler since we propagate the permutations backward and use them in simplifying the dependency predicates. In practice this amounts to a much faster computation of dependencies. Another practical approach is to weaken the notion of *pre* computation and only consider a guard as being the precondition of any predicate by any transition for which the guard is not equal to *true*.

Theorem 3. *Let σ a permutation computed by the algorithm of Figure 3 for a property φ. The permutation σ is a φ-permutation, and for every infinite sequence τ of the corresponding transition system M, $\sigma(\tau)$ is also a sequence of M.*

Proof. First, we can establish that for a given p and q, $\sigma_{(p,q)}$ is a φ-permutation. We can also establish that the composition of two φ-permutations is a φ-permutation. Finally, the definition of $dep(p)$ and $dep(q)$ allows us to show that $\sigma_{(p,q)}$ preserves the transition relation R.

7   Experimentation

UltraLog is modeled using the SAL specification and verification environment [1]. SAL stands for Symbolic Analysis Laboratory. It is a framework for combining different tools for abstraction, program analysis, theorem proving, and model checking toward the calculation of properties (symbolic analysis) of transition systems. A key part of the SAL framework is an intermediate language for describing transition systems. This language serves as the target for translators that extract the transition system description for popular programming languages such as Java, and Statecharts. The intermediate language also serves as a common source for driving different analysis tools through translators from the intermediate language to the input format for the tools, and from the output of these tools back to the SAL intermediate language. Our dependency analysis uses the SAL slicer developed in [12]. The input of the slicing algorithm consists of the slicing criterion and a SAL description of the system in the form of the parallel composition of modules. The slicing criterion is in our case a set of local and global variables appearing in the set of atomic predicates in the formula. The output of the slicing algorithm is another SAL description of the same system wherein irrelevant code from each module has been sliced out. When considering two predicates p and q, the slices with respect to the variables appearing in p and the variables appearing in q are compared for equivalence or for permutability. As a result of using the slicing program as a dependency analysis tool, we can guarantee that the permutations generated by our algorithm correspond to runs in the system. The following is the description of the results of the algorithm for two different properties. The first property expresses that every agent playing the role of a certificate authority that dies is eventually restarted and becomes available:

$$\varphi_1 = \forall(i : CA\_id) : \Box(\Diamond alive(i))$$

The dependency computation allows us to generate the following predicates that appear in the SAL description of UltraLog:

- $location(i) = n$
- $location(ca^*(i)) = n$
- $ca^*(i) = c$

These predicates refer to the free variables n and c representing respectively nodes and certificate authorities. These predicates indicate that in order to verify theproperty above, it is not necessary to consider the behavior of any agent nor any manager, but only the certificate authorities and their associated certificate authorities, and the nodes on which they run. This allows us on the one hand to consider all possible permutations among agents as well as among all managers, and on the other hand to exploit a symmetry among certificate authorities. Since $ca(i)$ designate the certificate authority of agent i, we realize that if i and j are two CAs agents, then i and j are permutable if they have the same CA. A similar property can be verified for application agents.

$$\varphi_2 = \forall(i : Agent\_id) : \Box(\Diamond alive(i))$$

The analysis of the dependencies of the predicate $alive(i)$ leads to the following predicates, and their corresponding permutations.

- $location(i) = n$
- $\exists j : Agent.\ location(i) = location(j) \wedge manager(j) = manager(i)$
- $location(ca^*(i)) = n$
- $location(manager(i)) = n$
- $location(ca^*(manager(i))) = n$
- $enclave(n) = enclave(location(i))$
- $ca^*(i) = c$
- $ca^*(manager(i)) = c$

That is, agents i and j are permutable if and only if, their corresponding CAs and managers are permutable, and if their locations are permutable. We experimented with an agent society of about 15 agents and 3 managers and 3 CAs. The total number of states is about 66×10^6. The reduced model for φ_1 contains only about 10^3 states. The reduced model for φ_2 has about 25×10^3 states. The reduced models for various properties have been used for the purpose of test case generation based on the techniques described in [14]. The test cases have been useful in identifying flaws in the UltraLog implementation and architecture. More details about the example can be found in [2].

8   Discussion

We have presented an automated approach for computing symmetries that are induce by generalized model automorphisms. Our work generalizes previous work on symmetry reduction and allows the discovery of symmetries in systems that exhibit relative or global symmetry in the forms of permutations of states satisfying predicates. Our approach is incremental and is implemented as an anytime algorithm. Our approach is applicable to models of a wide variety of complex systems and architectures such as multiagent systems, mobile sensor networks, and multithreaded software, and has been demonstrated on a large industrial-size system. Since our approach produces exact abstractions, it can be combined with any other abstraction technique.

References

1. http://sal.csl.sri.com.
2. http://www.csl.sri.com/users/saidi/symmetry.
3. Cognitive agent architecture (Cougaar) open source project. www.cougaar.org.
4. K. Ajami, S. Haddad, and J.-M. Ilié. Exploiting symmetry in linear time temporal logic model checking: One step beyond. *Lecture Notes in Computer Science*, 1384:52–62, 1998.
5. E. M. Clarke, T. Filkorn, and S. Jha. Exploiting symmetry in temporal logic model checking. In Courcoubetis [7], pages 450–462.
6. C.N. Ip and D.L. Dill. Verifying systems with replicated components in Murphi. In Rajeev Alur and Thomas A. Henzinger, editors, *Proceedings of the Eighth International Conference on Computer Aided Verification CAV*, volume 1102 of *Lecture Notes in Computer Science*, pages 147–158, New Brunswick, NJ, USA, July/Aug. 1996. Springer Verlag.
7. C. Courcoubetis, editor. *Fifth International Conference on Computer-Aided Verification*, volume 697 of *LNCS*, 1993.
8. P. Cousot and R. Cousot. Abstract interpretation: A unified lattice model for static analysis of programs by construction or approximation of fixpoints. In *popl77*, pages 238–252. ACM Press, Jan. 1977.
9. E. Emerson, J. Havlicek, and R. Trefler. Virtual symmetry reduction. In *15th Symposium on Logic in Computer Science (LICS' 00)*, pages 121–131, Washington - Brussels - Tokyo, June 2000. IEEE.

10. E. A. Emerson and A. P. Sistla. Symmetry and model checking. In Courcoubetis [7], pages 463–478.
11. E. A. Emerson and R. J. Trefler. From asymmetry to full symmetry: New techniques for symmetry reduction in model checking. In *Proceedings of the Conference on Correct Hardware Design and Verification Methods*, volume 1703 of *lncs*, pages 142–156, 1999.
12. V. Ganesh, N. Shankar, and H. Saïdi. Slicing SAL. Technical report, Computer Science Laboratory, SRI International, Menlo Park, CA 94025, 1999.
13. S. Graf and H. Saïdi. Construction of abstract state graphs with PVS. volume 1254, pages 72–83, Haifa, Israel, June 1997.
14. G. Hamon, L. deMoura, and J. Rushby. Generating efficient test sets with a model checker. In *2nd International Conference on Software Engineering and Formal Methods*, pages 261–270, Beijing, China, Sept. 2004. IEEE Computer Society.
15. H. Saïdi. Model-checking guided abstraction and analysis. In *7th International Static Analysis Symposium, SAS 2000*, volume 1824, pages 377–396, June 2000.
16. Sistla, Gyuris, and Emerson. SMC: A symmetry-based model checker for verification of safety and liveness properties. *ACMTSEM: ACM Transactions on Software Engineering and Methodology*, 9, 2000.
17. A. P. Sistla and P. Gedefroid. Symmetry and reduced symmetry in model checking. In *Proceedings of the Thirteenth International Conference on Computer Aided Verification CAV*, volume 2102 of *LNCS*, pages 91–103, 2001.

On Combining Partial Order Reduction with Fairness Assumptions*

Luboš Brim, Ivana Černá, Pavel Moravec, and Jiří Šimša

Department of Computer Science, Faculty of Informatics
Masaryk University, Czech Republic
{brim,cerna,xmoravec,xsimsa}@fi.muni.cz

Abstract. We present a new approach to combine partial order reduction with fairness in the context of LTL model checking. For this purpose, we define several behaviour classes representing typical fairness assumptions and examine how various reduction techniques affect these classes. In particular, we consider both reductions preserving all behaviours and reductions preserving only some behaviours.

1 Introduction

Fairness and partial order reduction are often indispensable for the verification of liveness properties of concurrent systems. The former is mostly needed in order to eliminate some "unrealistic" executions, while the latter is one of the most successful techniques for alleviating the state space explosion problem.

In model-based verification the adequacy of the model is important. As the model is a simplification of the system under consideration, some behaviours exhibited by the model may not be real ones. To tackle this problem the model can be refined or, alternatively, some assumptions that disqualify fictional behaviours in the model are used. For example, when modelling a multi-process concurrent system with a shared exclusive resource we may want to assume, for the sake of simplicity, that no process can starve though some behaviours of the model may not satisfy this assumption. This concept is commonly known as fairness assumptions or simply fairness.

The most common form of fairness [4,7] is *unconditional fairness* that considers only behaviours with some action occurring *infinitely* many times. Further it is reasonable to take into account *enabledness* of actions. This gives rise to even finer concepts. First, *strong fairness* that considers only behaviours where every action *enabled infinitely* many times is *taken infinitely* many times. Second, *weak fairness* that disqualifies behaviours with some action continuously enabled from a certain moment and subsequently never taken.

It might appear that the reason for using fairness is that it allows for simpler models. However, this simplicity is often outbalanced by the complexity of algorithms operating on a model with fairness. In fact, the main reason for using

---

* This work has been partially supported by the Grant Agency of Czech Republic grant No. GACR 201/06/1338. and by the Academy of Sciences of the Czech Republic grant. No. 1ET408050503.

L. Brim et al. (Eds.): FMICS and PDMC 2006, LNCS 4346, pp. 84–99, 2007.

fairness is that it simplifies the modelling process—work that has to be done by a human and not by a computer.

By contrast, partial order reduction allows for reduction of a state space of a modelled system [5,8,9,11]. A particular instance of the concept consists of a set of conditions that the reduction must satisfy. The idea behind partial order reduction is that it might not be necessary to consider *all* enabled transitions at a given state, but only a certain *ample* subset.

The justification for such reduction varies and depends on the nature of properties being examined. For example, we may select only one of mutually *independent* actions if we are interested in deadlocks. In general, a behavioural equivalence over a set of behaviours is defined and the reduction is required to contain a representative of each equivalence class.

In our previous work [2] we have proposed a combination of *distribution* and *partial order reduction*; concepts that push back the frontiers of practical verification, both fighting the state space explosion in its own way. In this paper we examine a combination of *partial order reduction* (and distribution) with *fairness*—a concept used for simplifying the process of modelling. We define four behaviour classes reflecting typical fairness assumptions and two partial order reduction techniques. For each behaviour class and reduction technique we prove or disprove that the reduction preserves behaviours of the class.

Closest to our work on combination of partial order reduction and fairness is that of Peled [8]. Peled uses equivalence robustness of properties to ensure that all fair runs in the original state space have at least one stuttering equivalent *fair* run in the reduced state space. Since fairness assumptions are not generally equivalently robust, one has to add more dependencies among transitions in order to achieve equivalence robustness. In author's later work [9] the discussion continues and on-the-fly state space generation is taken into account.

To contrast with our results, Peled considers only strong and weak fairness and aims at preservation of all behaviours. Whereas we examine more fairness assumptions and also study possibilities for better reduction.

This paper is organized as follows. Section 2 lays theoretical foundations for modelling of a system, reviews partial order reduction, and formulates two of its instances. The main theoretical contribution of the paper follows in Section 3 where we identify four behaviour classes and resolve whether they are preserved under the proposed reductions. After these results are established, we discuss their practical use in Section 4.

2   Partial Order Reduction

As a model we use labelled transition system. Let S be a set of *states* and *transition* be a partial function $\alpha : S \to S$, that is, a transition "can be taken" between different pairs of states. A *labelled transition system (LTS)* is then defined as a tuple $M = (S, s_0, \Delta, L)$, where $s_0 \in S$ is an *initial state*, Δ is a set of transitions over S, and $L : S \to 2^{AP}$ is a labelling function that assigns to each state a subset of some set AP of *atomic propositions*.

Furthermore, a set of transitions *enabled* at a state s, denoted $enabled(s)$, is a set of all $\alpha \in \Delta$ such that $\alpha(s)$ is defined. A *reduction* of M is then defined as a pair $(M, ample)$ where $ample$ is a function assigning to each state s a subset of $enabled(s)$.

A *path* in M from a state s_1 is a finite or infinite sequence $\pi = s_1 \xrightarrow{\alpha_1} s_2 \xrightarrow{\alpha_2} \ldots \xrightarrow{\alpha_{n-1}} s_n \xrightarrow{\alpha_n} \ldots$ of states interleaved with transitions—ending with a state in the finite case—such that $s_i \in S$, $\alpha_i \in \Delta$ and $\alpha_i(s_i, s_{i+1})$ for each index i.

Let $\eta = r_1 \xrightarrow{\alpha_1} r_2 \xrightarrow{\alpha_2} \ldots \xrightarrow{\alpha_{m-1}} r_m$ be a finite path and $\sigma = s_1 \xrightarrow{\beta_1} s_2 \xrightarrow{\beta_2} \ldots \xrightarrow{\beta_{n-1}} s_n \xrightarrow{\beta_n} \ldots$ a finite or infinite path. Then $first(\sigma) = s_1$ denotes the *first* state of σ and $last(\eta) = r_m$ denotes *the last state of* η. If $last(\eta) = first(\sigma)$ then the path $\eta \circ \sigma = r_1 \xrightarrow{\alpha_1} r_2 \xrightarrow{\alpha_2} \ldots \xrightarrow{\alpha_{m-1}} s_1 \xrightarrow{\beta_1} s_2 \xrightarrow{\beta_2} \ldots \xrightarrow{\beta_{n-1}} s_n \xrightarrow{\beta_n} \ldots$ is the *concatenation* of the paths η and σ.

Finally, let $\gamma = (\gamma_1, \gamma_2, \ldots, \gamma_n)$ be a sequence of transitions from Δ. We say that γ is a *cycle* if for every state s, $\gamma_1 \in enabled(s), \gamma_2 \in enabled(\gamma_1(s)), \ldots, \gamma_n \in enabled(\gamma_{n-1}(\ldots(\gamma_1(s))\ldots))$ implies $\gamma_n(\ldots(\gamma_1(s))\ldots) = s$.

In order to simplify the presentation of the particular instance of the partial order reduction technique we are going to suggest, we define two relations which will help to formulate conditions constituting the instance.

Definition 1. *An* independence *relation* $\neg D \subseteq \Delta \times \Delta$ *is a symmetric, anti-reflexive relation, satisfying the following three conditions for each state* $s \in S$ *and for each* $(\alpha, \beta) \in \neg D$:

1. *Enabledness – If* $\alpha, \beta \in enabled(s)$, *then* $\alpha \in enabled(\beta(s))$.
2. *Commutativity – If* $\alpha, \beta \in enabled(s)$, *then* $\alpha(\beta(s)) = \beta(\alpha(s))$.
3. *Neutrality – If* $\alpha \in enabled(s)$ *and* $\beta \in enabled(\alpha(s))$, *then* $\beta \in enabled(s)$.

The dependency *relation* D *is the complement of* $\neg D$.

Note that our definition of $\neg D$ differs from the standard definition of $\neg D$ given in the literature. In particular, we add the *neutrality* condition and therefore our definition of $\neg D$ is more strict. We argue that, in practice, the relation $\neg D$ is approximated using rules conforming to our definition, which allows for more concise proofs.

Definition 2. *An* invisibility *relation* $\neg V \subseteq \Delta$ *is a unary relation with respect to a set of atomic propositions* AP, *where for each* $\alpha \in \neg V$ *and for each pair of states* $s, s' \in S$ *such that* $\alpha(s, s')$, $L(s) \cap AP = L(s') \cap AP$ *holds. The* visibility *relation* V *is the complement of* $\neg V$.

The *reduction* of a given state space is defined by providing a set of conditions the *ample* function has to fulfil to guarantee that behaviours with certain properties are preserved. In the case of properties expressed as formulas from a fragment of *Linear Temporal Logic without any next modalities* (LTL$_{-X}$) the following conditions are used [3].

C0. $ample(s) = \emptyset$ iff $enabled(s) = \emptyset$.

C1. Along every path in the model starting from s, the following condition holds: a transition that is dependent on a transition in $ample(s)$ cannot occur without a transition in $ample(s)$ occurring first.

C2. If $enabled(s) \neq ample(s)$, then every $\alpha \in ample(s)$ is invisible.

C3. A cycle is not allowed if it contains a state in which some transition α is enabled, but is never included in $ample(s)$ for any state s on the cycle.

Theorem 1 ([3]). *Let φ be a LTL_{-X} formula, $M = (S, s_0, \Delta, L)$ be a LTS and $M' = (M, ample)$ a reduction of M satisfying conditions **C0** through **C3**. Then $M \models \varphi \Leftrightarrow M' \models \varphi$.*

We now formulate a new condition that is supposed to replace the condition **C3** and consequently allow for better reduction. Downside of the new condition is that reduction based on it may not preserve all behaviours.

C4. From every state s there is reachable a fully expanded state i.e. state such that $ample(s) = enabled(s)$.

In practice conditions **C3** and **C4** are ensured using provisos based on particular state space exploration algorithm. For example, when using depth first search the following provisos are used.

P3. If $ample(s) \neq enabled(s)$, then none of $ample(s)$ transitions points back to stack.

P4. If $ample(s) \neq enabled(s)$, then at least one of $ample(s)$ transitions does not point back to stack.

It can be shown by a simple argument that provisos **P3** and **P4** indeed imply conditions **C3** and **C4** respectively. Clearly, proviso **P4** is weaker than proviso **P3** and thus generally yields better reductions. Further advantage of condition **C4** over condition **C3** comes to light when combining partial order reduction with distribution; to ensure condition **C4** cycle detection is not necessary.

Based on the above conditions we can consider two reduction techniques. The first one uses the original set of conditions and the second one makes use of the new condition **C4**. In particular, when a reduction satisfies conditions **C0** through **C3** we say it is *safe* and when it satisfies conditions **C0** through **C2** and **C4** we say it is *aggressive*.

3   Behaviour Classes

In this section we identify several behaviour classes and investigate whether they are preserved by safe and/or aggressive reduction techniques. As we are interested in preservation of properties expressed in LTL_{-X}, we use stuttering equivalence as the behavioural equivalence.

Definition 3. *Two infinite paths $\eta = r_1 \xrightarrow{\alpha_1} r_2 \xrightarrow{\alpha_2} \ldots \xrightarrow{\alpha_{n-1}} r_n \xrightarrow{\alpha_n} \ldots$ and $\sigma = s_1 \xrightarrow{\beta_1} s_2 \xrightarrow{\beta_2} \ldots \xrightarrow{\beta_{n-1}} s_n \xrightarrow{\beta_n} \ldots$ are stuttering equivalent, denoted $\sigma \sim_{st} \eta$,* *if there are two strictly increasing infinite sequences of integers $(i_0, i_1, i_2, \ldots)$ and $(j_0, j_1, j_2, \ldots)$ such that $i_0 = j_0 = 0$ and for every $k \geq 0$:*

$$L(s_{i_k}) = L(s_{i_k+1}) = \ldots L(s_{i_{k+1}-1}) = L(r_{j_k}) = L(r_{j_k+1}) = \ldots L(r_{j_{k+1}-1})$$

Definition 4. *Let M is an LTS. An LTL_{-X} formula φ is invariant under stuttering iff for each pair of paths π and π' such that $\pi \sim_{st} \pi'$, $M, \pi \models \varphi$ iff $M, \pi' \models \varphi$.*

Theorem 2 ([10]). *Any LTL_{-X} formula is invariant under stuttering.*

3.1 Paths with Infinitely Many Visible Transitions

Let $trans(\pi)$ denotes the *sequence of transitions* on a path π and $vis(\pi)$ denotes the *sequence of visible transitions* on a path π.

Theorem 3. *Let M be an LTS and $M' = (M, ample)$ be a safe reduction. Then for each path σ in M such that $|vis(\sigma)| = \infty$ there is a path η in M' such that $\sigma \sim_{st} \eta$ with $|vis(\eta)| = \infty$.*

For the proof we refer to the construction of infinite sequence of infinite paths $\pi_0, \pi_1, \pi_2, \ldots$ from the proof of Theorem 1 (see [3], Section 10.6). For the hint on the construction see appendix A.

Theorem 4. *Let M be an LTS and $M' = (M, ample)$ an aggressive reduction. Then for each path σ in M such that $|vis(\sigma)| = \infty$ there is a path η in M' such that $\sigma \sim_{st} \eta$.*

There are two key steps to prove Theorem 4. The first step is an observation that it is sufficient to consider only paths without *scattered cycles*. The next step is a construction of stuttering equivalent path for a path without scattered cycles.

Definition 5. *A path σ contains a* scattered cycle *$\gamma = (\gamma_1, \gamma_2, \ldots, \gamma_n)$ iff:*

- *γ is a cycle*
- *every transition from γ is invisible*
- *there are paths $\theta_1, \ldots, \theta_{n+1}$ such that all transitions in $\theta_1, \theta_2, \ldots \theta_i$ are independent on the transition γ_i and $\sigma = \theta_1 \circ (last(\theta_1) \xrightarrow{\gamma_1} first(\theta_2)) \circ \theta_2 \circ \ldots \circ \theta_n \circ (last(\theta_n) \xrightarrow{\gamma_n} first(\theta_{n+1})) \circ \theta_{n+1}$.*

Lemma 1. *For each path σ in M with $|vis(\sigma)| = \infty$ there is an infinite path σ' in M such that $\sigma \sim_{st} \sigma'$, $first(\sigma) = first(\sigma')$ and σ' does not contain any scattered cycle.*

Proof: Let us suppose that σ contains a scattered cycle $\gamma = (\gamma_1, \gamma_2, \ldots, \gamma_n)$ and $\sigma = \theta_1 \circ (last(\theta_1) \xrightarrow{\gamma_1} first(\theta_2)) \circ \theta_2 \circ \ldots \circ \theta_n \circ (last(\theta_n) \xrightarrow{\gamma_n} first(\theta_{n+1})) \circ \theta_{n+1}$.

According to the definition of the scattered cycle, the transition γ_2 is enabled in the state $first(\theta_2)$ and is independent on all transitions in θ_2. Therefore there is a path in M containing the scattered cycle γ and such that the transition γ_2 precedes all transitions from θ_2. Using the same argument repeatedly we show that there is a path $\theta_1 \circ (last(\theta_1) \xrightarrow{\gamma_1} \ldots \xrightarrow{\gamma_n} last(\theta_1)) \circ \theta_2' \circ \ldots \theta_n' \circ \theta_{n+1}$ in M where $trans(\theta_i) = trans(\theta_i')$ for all $i = 2, \ldots, n$.

As γ is a cycle, $\theta_1 \circ \theta_2' \circ \ldots \theta_n' \circ \theta_{n+1}$ is a path in M stuttering equivalent to σ. It seems that in this manner we could iteratively remove all scattered cycles appearing in σ. However, by removing a scattered cycle from a path we could create a new one. Therefore to prove existence of stuttering equivalent path without scattered cycles we consider all existing as well as potential scattered cycles on the path σ simultaneously.

Let $\delta = (\delta_1, \delta_2, \ldots)$ be a subsequence of $trans(\sigma)$ such that either δ_i is a transition of a scattered cycle in σ or there is a finite number of scattered cycles that can be removed from σ—through the construction above—with δ_i becoming a transition of a scattered cycle afterwards.

Let $(\alpha_1, \alpha_2, \ldots)$ be a sequence of transitions which remain in $trans(\sigma)$ after removing the subsequence δ. We prove that there is an infinite path σ' in M such that $first(\sigma) = first(\sigma')$ and $trans(\sigma') = (\alpha_1, \alpha_2, \ldots)$ as these together guarantee $\sigma \sim_{st} \sigma'$.

We show that for all i, $\alpha_i \in enabled(\alpha_{i-1}(\ldots(\alpha_1(first(\sigma)))\ldots))$. Let δ_j occurs in σ before α_i. Then δ_j can be removed from the path together—with the cycle it belongs to—and α_i still remains enabled thanks to the arguments mentioned above. Consequently, σ' is a path in M and as $vis(\sigma) = vis(\sigma')$ and $|vis(\sigma)| = \infty$, it is infinite. □

It can be shown that any aggressive reduction contains a path stuttering equivalent to a given path in M without any scattered cycle. The construction of the stuttering equivalent path is suspended until Appendix.

3.2 Process Fair Paths

In this subsection we assume, that LTS M is modelling a multi-process system and $\mathcal{P}$ denotes the set of its processes. Further, let $\pi_{\geq i}$ denotes the *suffix* of a path π that is a subsequence of π starting at i-th state.

Definition 6. *Let σ be an infinite path and M an LTS. Then for $\mathcal{X} \subseteq \mathcal{P}$, $trans(\mathcal{X}, \sigma)$ denotes the set of all transitions on σ of a process from $\mathcal{X}$.*

For every $\mathcal{X} \subseteq \mathcal{P}$ such that all $\alpha \in trans(\mathcal{X}, \sigma)$ are independent on all $\beta \in trans(\mathcal{P} \setminus \mathcal{X}, \sigma)$ that is $(\alpha, \beta) \in \neg D$, we define a path $proj(\mathcal{X}, \sigma)$ as a path resulting from σ after removing all transitions of processes from $\mathcal{P} \setminus \mathcal{X}$.

Definition 7. *An infinite path σ is process fair if for every $P \in \mathcal{P}$ the number of P's transition on σ is infinite.*

Theorem 5. *Let M be an LTS and $M' = (M, ample)$ a safe reduction. Then for each process fair path σ in M there is a process fair path η in M' such that $\pi \sim_{st} \eta$.*

Again, for the proof we refer to the construction of infinite sequence of infinite paths $\pi_0, \pi_1, \pi_2, \ldots$, from the proof of Theorem 1 and we omit the rest.

Theorem 6. *Let M be an LTS and $M' = (M, ample)$ an aggressive reduction. Then for each process fair path σ in M there is a path η in M' such that $\pi \sim_{st} \eta$.*

Similarly to the proof of Theorem 4, there are two key steps to prove Theorem 6. The first step is an observation that it is sufficient to consider only *non-reducible paths*. The next step is the construction of stuttering equivalent path path for a non-reducible path.

Definition 8. *Let $\sigma = s_1 \xrightarrow{\alpha_1} s_2 \xrightarrow{\alpha_2} \ldots \xrightarrow{\alpha_{n-1}} s_n \xrightarrow{\alpha_n} \ldots$ be a path in M. If exists $k \in \mathbb{N}$ and a non-empty set of processes $\mathcal{X} \neq \mathcal{P}$ such that*

- *all $\alpha \in trans(\mathcal{X}, \sigma_{\geq k})$ are independent on all $\beta \in trans(\mathcal{P} \setminus \mathcal{X}, \sigma_{\geq k})$,*
- *all transitions from $trans(\mathcal{P} \setminus \mathcal{X}, \sigma_{\geq k})$ are invisible,*
- *both $proj(\mathcal{X}, \sigma_{\geq k})$ and $proj(\mathcal{P} \setminus \mathcal{X}, \sigma_{\geq k})$ are infinite,*

then σ is k-reducible and the path $\sigma' = s_0 \xrightarrow{\alpha_1} \ldots \xrightarrow{\alpha_{k-1}} s_k \circ proj(\mathcal{X}, \sigma_{\geq k})$ is a k-reduction of σ. If no such k and $\mathcal{X}$ exists then σ is called non-reducible.

Lemma 2. *Let σ be a path in M and σ' be a k-reduction of σ. Then σ' is a path in M and $vis(\sigma) = vis(\sigma')$.*

Proof: By a simple argument from definition of $\neg D$ and k-reducibility. □

Lemma 3. *Let σ be a process fair path in M. Then there is an infinite path σ' in M such that $\sigma \sim_{st} \sigma'$ and σ' is non-reducible.*

Proof: We inductively construct a finite sequence of paths $\sigma_0, \sigma_1, \ldots, \sigma_n$ such that $\sigma_0 = \sigma$ and $\sigma_n = \sigma'$ and show that σ_i is a k-reduction of σ_{i-1} for every $i = 1, \ldots, n$.

We start with $\sigma_0 = \sigma$. If σ_i is k-reducible for some k and $\mathcal{X}$ we take the smallest k and subsequently smallest possible $\mathcal{X}$ and we let σ_{i+1} to be the respective k-reduction of σ_i. Otherwise, the construction is finished.

Note that the construction is deterministic – as we choose the smallest possible k and $\mathcal{X}$ – and finite since the sequence is strictly decreasing in the number of processes which take a transition infinitely many times. □

Let σ be a non-reducible path in M resulting from the process fair path transformation outlined above. The construction of a path stutter equivalent to σ in an aggressive reduction $(M, ample)$ can be found in Appendix.

3.3 Weakly Fair Paths

Definition 9. *Let $\sigma = s_1 \xrightarrow{\alpha_1} s_2 \xrightarrow{\alpha_2} \ldots \xrightarrow{\alpha_{n-1}} s_n \xrightarrow{\alpha_n} \ldots$ be a path. If there do not exist i and β such that for all $j \geq i$, $\beta \in enabled(s_j)$ and $\beta \neq \alpha_j$, then σ is weakly fair.*

It can be shown by a simple argument using induction, that every weakly fair path in a model has stuttering equivalent weakly fair path in any safe reduction

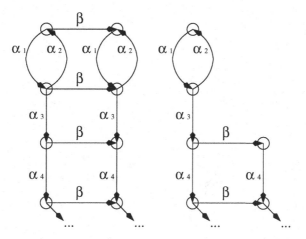

Fig. 1. Model and its reduction

of the model. For the idea of the proof we refer once again to the construction of infinite sequence of infinite paths $\pi_0, \pi_1, \pi_2, \ldots$, from the proof of Theorem 1.

As Figure 1 demonstrates, weakly fair behaviour does not have to be preserved in aggressive reductions. On the left there is a part of the model state space and on the right there is a part of its reduction state space. Let α transitions be mutually dependent and transitions β and α_4 be visible. Then weakly fair path $\beta \cdot (\alpha_1 \cdot \alpha_2)^\omega$ in the model has no stuttering equivalent path in the reduction.

3.4 Strongly Fair Paths

Definition 10. *Let* $\sigma = s_1 \xrightarrow{\alpha_1} s_2 \xrightarrow{\alpha_2} \ldots \xrightarrow{\alpha_{n-1}} s_n \xrightarrow{\alpha_n} \ldots$ *be a path. If for every* β *enabled in infinitely many states on* σ *there exists infinitely many* j's *such that* $\beta = \alpha_j$ *then* σ *is* strongly fair.

It can be shown by a simple argument using induction, that every strongly fair path in a model has a stuttering equivalent path in a safe reduction. However, this path may not be strongly fair as Figure 2 demonstrates.

On the left is a part of model state space and on the right is a part of its reduction state space. Let α transitions be mutually dependent as well as β transitions and γ be dependent on all α and β transitions. Further let α_1, α_2 and γ be visible transitions. For the strongly fair path $(\alpha_1 \cdot \alpha_2 \cdot \beta_1 \cdot \beta_2)^\omega$ in the model state space, there is no stuttering equivalent strongly fair path in the reduction state space.

Furthermore, Figure 3 demonstrates that a strongly fair behaviour does not have to be preserved in aggressive reductions. On the left is a part of the model state space and on the right is a part of its reduction state space. Let α transitions be mutually dependent and transition β and α_3 be visible. Then a strongly fair path $\beta \cdot (\alpha_1 \cdot \alpha_2)^\omega$ in the model has no stuttering equivalent path in the reduction.

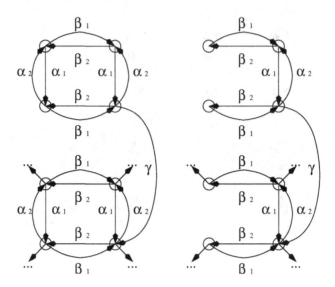

Fig. 2. Model and its reduction

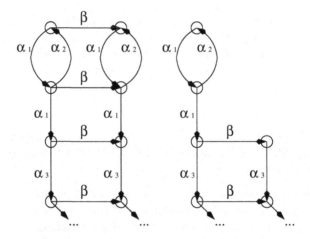

Fig. 3. Model and its reduction

4   Applications

In this section, we identify typical fairness assumptions and relate them, one by one, to results established in the previous section. We try to point out situations where either aggressive or safe reduction may be of use.

Another issue to be discussed is related to usage of fairness model checking algorithms. Although a reduction may preserve all fair behaviours, it may not preserve them "fairly". Therefore, a fairness model checking algorithm may return different results when applied on the model and on the reduction.

Situation 1. Certain subset of actions of modelled system is considered and each of them is taken infinitely many times.

If at least one of the relevant actions is visible, we can apply an aggressive reduction as every behaviour of our interest is preserved in such a reduction. Moreover, the same fairness model checking algorithm can be applied on the reduction.

Otherwise, aggressive reduction does not guarantee that the desired behaviours are preserved in the reduction. On the contrary, safe reductions preserve all behaviours. Furthermore, as the respective construction of a stuttering equivalent path for this set of conditions does not remove any transition from the original path, the same fairness model checking algorithm can be applied.

Situation 2. Certain subset of processes of multi-process system is considered and each of them performs some action infinitely many times.

First, if the subset is equal to the set of all processes, the result for *process fair* paths can be applied. Unfortunately, a *non-reducible* representative of a process fair path might not be fair. Consider the example on Figure 4. On the left there is a part of model state space and on the right there is a part of its reduction state space. Let α transitions be mutually dependent as well as β transitions. Further let β_1, β_2 and α_4 be visible transitions. Finally, let $\{\alpha_1, \beta_1\}$ be the fairness assumption.

The path $(\beta_1 \cdot \beta_2 \cdot \alpha_1 \cdot \alpha_2)^\omega$ in the model state space satisfies the assumption. However, there is no stuttering equivalent path in the reduction state space, which would satisfy the assumption. Thus, one cannot use the same fairness

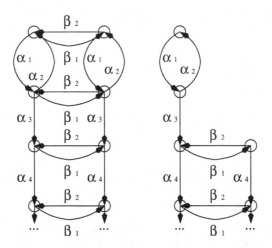

Fig. 4. Model and its reduction

model checking algorithm both for a model M and its aggressive reduction M_R and the equivalence $M \models_F \varphi \Leftrightarrow M_R \models_F \varphi$ does not hold in general.

Nevertheless, this approach can be used for checking validity of φ as $M_R \models \varphi \Rightarrow M \models_F \varphi$. Actually, we find this result to be quite interesting, as checking validity is generally more "space and time demanding" task than checking invalidity—which can be partially dealt with using approximation and stochastic techniques. Again, a safe reduction preserves all behaviours. Moreover, the respective construction of a stutter equivalent path in a safe reduction does not remove any transition from the original path and thus the original fairness model checking algorithm can be used as well.

Alternatively, if we somehow guarantee that every time a process performs infinitely many actions, it performs infinitely many visible actions as well, then all desired behaviours are preserved even by an aggressive reduction and the same fairness model checking algorithm can be applied. However, the more visible actions there are, the smaller the reduction generally is.

Situation 3. Only weakly fair behaviours are considered.

As a weakly fair path might not have a stuttering equivalent path in an aggressive reduction, we discuss this assumption in the context of safe reductions.

These reductions preserve all behaviours and as the respective construction of a stuttering equivalent paths does not remove any transition from the original path, the original fairness model checking algorithm can be applied.

Situation 4. Only strongly fair behaviours are considered.

In general aggressive reductions do not preserve strongly fair behaviours. On the contrary, safe reductions preserve all strongly fair behaviours, but the resulting stuttering equivalent paths do not have to be strongly fair. Therefore the same fairness model checking algorithm cannot be applied.

In order to use the same fairness model checking algorithm the dependency relation can be modified as described in [8]. Alternatively, any model checking algorithm can be used for checking the validity of φ as $M_R \models \varphi \Rightarrow M \models_F \varphi$.

Finally, if the model represents a multi-process system where every process has always enabled at least one action, strong fairness implies process fairness and aggressive reductions can be used for checking validity.

5   Conclusions

The paper explores a combination of two concepts: partial order reduction and fairness, both used in the context of LTL model checking. While the first one is essential in alleviating the state space explosion, the second one simplifies the modelling process.

For the partial order reduction we consider a well-known safe variant together with a new variant represented by condition **C4** which is supposed to replace condition **C3**. It allows for better reduction in general and yet ensures that certain subset of behaviours is preserved. We have defined safe reduction as any reduction satisfying conditions **C0** through **C3** and we have used the new condition to define aggressive reduction. Then we have defined four behavioural classes motivated by typical fairness assumptions. The paper gives a detailed analysis of fairness concepts and demonstrates how they are affected by safe and aggressive reductions.

For several reductions we have encountered the following problem. Even though fair behaviour is preserved by the reduction it does not have an equivalent *fair* behaviour representative in the reduced model. This disables the possibility to use the same fairness model checking algorithm. On the contrary, as all fair behaviours in a model M have a stuttering equivalent behaviour in a reduction M_R and $M_R \models \varphi \implies M \models_F \varphi$, we can actually check formula validity under fairness assumptions. Whether our results can be extended to checking invalidity is left as an open problem.

References

1. D. Bosnacki. Partial order reduction in presence of rendez-vous communications with unless constructs and weak fairness. In *Theoretical and Practical Aspects of SPIN Model Checking (SPIN 1999)*, volume 1680 of *Lecture Notes in Computer Science*, pages 40–56. Springer, 1999.
2. L. Brim, I. Černá, P. Moravec, and J. Šimša. Distributed Partial Order Reduction. *Electronic Notes in Theoretical Computer Science*, 128:63–74, April 2005.
3. E. M. Clarke, O. Grumberg, and D. A. Peled. *Model Checking*. The MIT Press, Cambridge, Massachusetts, 1999.
4. N. Francez. *Fairness*. Texts and Monographs in Computer Science. Springer, 1986.
5. P. Godefroid and D. Pirottin. Refining dependencies improves partial-order verification methods. In *Proc. of the 5th Conference on Computer-Aided Verification*, volume 697 of *LNCS*, pages 438–449. Springer, 1992.
6. G.J. Holzmann, P. Godefroid, and D. Pirottin. Coverage preserving reduction strategies for reachability analysis. In *Proc. 12th Int. Conf on Protocol Specification, Testing, and Verification, INWG/IFIP*, Orlando, Fl., June 1992.
7. T. Latvala and K. Heljanko. Coping with strong fairness. *Fundamenta Informaticae*, pages 175–193, 2000.
8. D. Peled. All from one, one from all: on model checking using representatives. In *Proceedings of the 5th International Conference on Computer Aided Verification, Greece*, number 697 in Lecture Notes in Computer Science, pages 409–423, Berlin-Heidelberg-New York, 1993. Springer.
9. D. Peled. Combining partial order reductions with on-the-fly model-checking. In *Proceedings of CAV'94*, pages 377–390. Springer Verlag, LNCS 818, 1994.
10. D. Peled and T. Wilke. Stutter-invariant temporal properties are expressible without the nexttime operator. *Information Processing Letters*, 1997.
11. A. Valmari. A stubborn attack on state explosion. In *Proc. of the 2nd Workshop on Computer-Aided Verification*, volume 531 of *LNCS*, pages 156–165. Springer, 1991.

A   Appendix

Proof of Theorems 4 and 6 follow the same direction. Thus, we present it just once and we distinguish between different context only when necessary.

Our goal is the following. Given a path σ in M and a reduction $M' = (M, ample)$ satisfying conditions **C0** through **C2** and **C4**, show that there is a path in M' stuttering equivalent to σ.

First, we inductively describe an infinite sequence of paths π_0, π_1, π_2, ..., where $\sigma = \pi_0$ and for every i, $\pi_i = \eta_i \circ \theta_i$ is a path in M, η_i is a path in M', and $| \eta_i | = i$.

Basic step. Let $\eta_0 = \varepsilon$, $\theta_0 = \sigma$.

Inductive step. Let $s_0 = last(\eta_i) = first(\theta_i)$, $\theta_i = s_0 \xrightarrow{\alpha_1} s_1 \xrightarrow{\alpha_2} s_2 \ldots$

There are two possibilities:

A If $\alpha_1 \in ample(s_0)$ then $\eta_{i+1} = \eta_i \circ (s_0 \xrightarrow{\alpha_1} s_1)$, $\theta_{i+1} = s_1 \xrightarrow{\alpha_2} s_2 \ldots$

B The case $\alpha_1 \notin ample(s_0)$ divides into two subcases:

    B1 There is k such that $\alpha_k \in ample(s_0)$ and (α_j, α_k) are independent for all $1 \leq j < k$. We choose the *smallest* possible k. Then $\eta_{i+1} = \eta_i \circ (s_0 \xrightarrow{\alpha_k} \alpha_k(s_0))$. As transitions α_j are independent, $\alpha_k(s_0) \xrightarrow{\alpha_1} \alpha_k(s_1) \xrightarrow{\alpha_2} \alpha_k(s_2) \ldots$ is a path in M. Let $\theta_{i+1} = s_0 \xrightarrow{\alpha_k} \alpha_k(s_0) \xrightarrow{\alpha_1} \alpha_k(s_1) \xrightarrow{\alpha_2} \ldots \xrightarrow{\alpha_{k-1}} \alpha_k(s_k) \xrightarrow{\alpha_{k+1}} s_{k+2} \xrightarrow{\alpha_{k+2}} \ldots$

    B2 $\alpha_k \notin ample(s_0)$ for any k. Then from the condition **C1** all transitions in $ample(s_0)$ are independent on all transitions in θ_i. Let ξ be the shortest path in M' from s_0 to a fully expanded state (the existence of such a path is guaranteed by **C4**) and let β be the first transition of ξ.

    Then $\eta_{i+1} = \eta_i \circ (s_0 \xrightarrow{\beta} \beta(s_0))$, $\theta_{i+1} = \beta(s_0) \xrightarrow{\alpha_1} \beta(s_1) \xrightarrow{\alpha_2} \beta(s_2) \ldots$

Cases **B1** and **B2** cover all possibilities conforming to **C1**.

Notice that a simple argument based on the definition of $\neg D$ yields that the rule **B1** cannot be applied after the rule **B2** without the rule **A** being applied in the meantime. This fact is implicitly employed in proof of Lemma 7.

Next, we characterise properties of the path η and then we prove the stuttering equivalence between η and σ.

Properties of η

Lemma 4. *For every i, $\pi_i = \eta_i \circ \theta_i$ is a path in M, η_i is a path in M', and $| \eta_i | = i$.*

Proof: By induction. Induction basis for $i = 0$ holds trivially. In induction step, we first prove that π_i is a path in M. It obviously holds for the case **A**. In the case **B1**, (α_j, α_k) are independent, for all $j < k$. Hence there is a path $\xi = s_0 \xrightarrow{\alpha_k} \alpha_k(s_0) \xrightarrow{\alpha_1} \alpha_k(s_1) \xrightarrow{\alpha_2} \ldots \xrightarrow{\alpha_{k-1}} \alpha_k(s_k) \xrightarrow{\alpha_{k+1}} s_{k+2} \xrightarrow{\alpha_{k+2}} \ldots$ in M, where α_k is moved before $\alpha_1 \alpha_2 \alpha_3 \ldots \alpha_{k-1}$. Note that $\alpha_k(s_k) = s_{k+1}$. Therefore, $\alpha_k(s_k) \xrightarrow{\alpha_{k+1}} s_{k+2}$ is the same as $s_{k+1} \xrightarrow{\alpha_{k+1}} s_{k+2}$. In the case **B2** we execute a transition which is independent on all transitions in θ_{i-1}, hence θ_i is obviously a path in M. Certainly η_i is a path in M' and $| \eta_i | = i$ in all cases, as we append to η_{i-1} exactly one transition from $ample(last(\eta_{i-1}))$. $\qquad\square$

Lemma 5. *Let $\eta = \lim_{i \to \infty} \eta_i$. Then η is a path in M'.*

Proof: By induction to i. $\qquad\square$

Stuttering equivalence

Lemma 6. *The following holds for all i, j such that $j \geq i \geq 0$.*

1. $\pi_i \sim_{st} \pi_j$.
2. $vis(\pi_i) = vis(\pi_j)$.
3. *Let ξ_i be a prefix of π_i and ξ_j be a prefix of π_j such that $vis(\xi_i) = vis(\xi_j)$. Then $L(last(\xi_i)) = L(last(\xi_j))$.*

Proof: It is sufficient to consider the case where $j = i + 1$. Consider three ways of constructing π_{i+1} from π_i. In case **A**, $\pi_{i+1} = \pi_i$ and the statement holds trivially.

In case **B1**, π_{i+1} is obtained from π_i by executing a invisible transition α_k in π_{i+1} earlier than it is executed in π_i. In this case, we replace the sequence $s_0 \overset{\alpha_1}{\to} s_1 \overset{\alpha_2}{\to} \ldots \overset{\alpha_{k-1}}{\to} s_{k-1} \overset{\alpha_k}{\to} s_k$ by $s_0 \overset{\alpha_k}{\to} \alpha_k(s_0) \overset{\alpha_1}{\to} \alpha_k(s_1) \overset{\alpha_2}{\to} \ldots \overset{\alpha_{k-1}}{\to} \alpha_k(s_{k-1})$. Because α_k is invisible, corresponding states have the same label, that is, for each $0 < l \leq k$, $L(s_l) = L(\alpha_k(s_l))$. Also, the order of the visible transitions remains unchanged. Parts 1, 2, and 3 follow immediately.

Finally, consider case **B2**, where the difference between π_i and π_{i+1} is that π_{i+1} includes an additional invisible transition β. Thus, we replace some suffix $s_0 \overset{\alpha_1}{\to} s_1 \overset{\alpha_2}{\to} \ldots$ by $s_0 \overset{\beta}{\to} \beta(s_0)) \overset{\alpha_1}{\to} \beta(s_1) \overset{\alpha_2}{\to} \ldots$. So, $L(s_l) = L(\beta(s_l))$ for $l \geq 0$. Again, the order of visible transitions remains unchanged and parts 1, 2, and 3 follow immediately. $\qquad\square$

In the following lemma we have to differentiate between individual cases.

Lemma 7. *During the construction of η, the case **A** is chosen infinitely often.*

Proof: for paths with infinitely many visible transitions

First, we prove that for every i, θ_i does not contain any scattered cycle.

By induction to i. For $\theta_0 = \sigma$ the statement holds trivially. If θ_i is constructed applying **A** or **B2** it does not contain any cycle as θ_{i-1} does not contain any. In case of **B1**, a presence of a scattered cycle in θ_i would imply a presence of a scattered cycle in θ_{i-1}

Now, let us assume that there is an index j such that during the construction of $\pi_j, \pi_{j+1}, \ldots$ only the rule **B** is applied. Then either **B1** or **B2** is applied infinitely many times.

In case rule **B1** is applied infinitely many times there is an infinite sequence of transitions which are added to the prefix η_{j-1}. These transitions are invisible and independent on all other transitions in θ_j. From finiteness of the set of states we have that some of the considered transitions form a cycle, which is moreover a scattered cycle in θ_j. Hence a contradiction.

This gives us an existence of an index $k \geq j$ such that for the construction of $\pi_k, \pi_{k+1}, \ldots$ only the rule **B2** is applied. But this is a contradiction to the fact that in **B2** we always choose a transition from the shortest path to a fully expanded state. □

Proof: for process fair paths

First, we prove that for every i, θ_i is non-reducible.

By induction to i. For $\theta_0 = \sigma$ the statement holds trivially. If θ_i is constructed applying **A**, **B1** or **B2** it is non-reducible as θ_{i-1} is.

Now, let us assume that there is an index j such that during the construction of $\pi_j, \pi_{j+1}, \ldots$ only the rule **B** is applied. Then either **B1** or **B2** is applied infinitely many times.

In case rule **B1** is applied infinitely many times there is an infinite sequence of transitions which are added to the prefix η_{j-1}. These transitions are invisible and independent on all other transitions in θ_j. Let P be the process taking α transition on θ_j. If $| proj(\{P\}, \theta_j) | = \infty$, then θ_j is 0-reducible and we get a contradiction. Therefore $| proj(\{P\}, \theta_j) |$ must be finite and θ_j is not reducible for any k. Moreover, σ is a result of process fair path transformation described in Lemma 3. The original process fair path contained infinitely many P's transitions. Thus, during the construction of σ, P's transitions were removed because of some k-reduction. But in that particular moment of the construction a j-reduction removing transitions selected by **B1** rule would be possible too. Finally, as j is strictly smaller than k, this is a contradiction as well.

This gives us an existence of an index $k \geq j$ such that for the construction of $\pi_k, \pi_{k+1}, \ldots$ only the rule **B2** is applied. But this is a contradiction to the fact that in **B2** we always choose a transition from the shortest path to a fully expanded state. □

Lemma 8. *Let α be the first transition of θ_i. Then there exists $j > i$: α is the last transition of η_j and $\forall k : i \leq k < j$: α is the first transition of θ_k.*

Proof: The rules **B1** and **B2** leave the first transition α of θ_i unchanged, the rule **A** shifts the transition α to η_i. Thus it is sufficient to prove that during the construction of η, the rule **A** is applied infinitely often. This follows from Lemma 7. □

Lemma 9. *Let δ be the first visible transition on θ_i, $prefix_\delta(\theta_i)$ be the maximal prefix of $trans(\theta_i)$ that does not contain δ. Then **either** δ is the first transition of θ_i and the last transition of η_{i+1} **or** δ is the first visible transition of θ_{i+1}, the last transition of η_{i+1} is invisible and $prefix_\delta(\theta_{i+1})$ is a subsequence of $prefix_\delta(\theta_i)$.*

Proof:

- If θ_{i+1} is constructed according to **A**, then δ is the last transition of η_{i+1}.
- If **B1** is applied then an invisible transition α_k from θ_i is appended to η_i to form η_{i+1} and δ is still the first visible transition of θ_{i+1}. The prefix $prefix_\delta(\theta_i)$ is either unchanged or shortened by the transition α_k.
- Otherwise an invisible transition β is appended to η_i to form η_{i+1} and $prefix_\delta(\theta_{i+1}) = prefix_\delta(\theta_i)$. □

Lemma 10. *Let v be a prefix of $vis(\sigma)$. Then there exists a path η_i such that $v = vis(\eta_i)$.*

Proof: By induction to the length of v. For the basic step $\mid v \mid = 0$ the statement holds trivially. For the induction step we must prove that if $v \cdot \delta$ is a prefix of $vis(\sigma)$ and there is a path η_i such that $vis(\eta_i) = v$, then there is a path η_j with $j > i$ such that $vis(\eta_{i+1}) = v \cdot \delta$. Thus, we need to show that δ will be eventually added to η_j for some $j > i$, and that no other visible transition will be added to η_k for $i < k < j$. According to the case **A** in the construction, we may add a visible transition to the end of η_k to form η_{k+1} only if it appears as the first transition of θ_k. Lemma 9 shows that δ remains the first visible transition in successive paths θ_k after θ_i unless it is being added to some η_j. Moreover, the sequence of transitions before δ can only shrink. Lemma 8 shows that the first transition in each θ_k is eventually removed and added to the end of some η_l for $l > k$. Thus, δ as well is eventually added to some sequence η_j.   □

Proof: of Theorems 4 and 6

We will show that the described path $\eta = \lim_{i \to \infty} \eta_i$ is stutter equivalent to the original path σ.

First note that $vis(\sigma) = vis(\eta)$. It follows from Lemma 10 that for every prefix of σ there is a prefix of η with the same sequence of visible transitions. The opposite follows from Lemma 6.

Next we construct two infinite sequences of indexes $0 = i_0 < i_1 < \ldots$ and $0 = j_0 < j_1 < \ldots$ that define corresponding stuttering blocks of σ and η, as required in Definition 3. For every natural n, let i_n be the length of the smallest prefix ξ_{i_n} of σ that contains exactly n visible transitions. Let j_n be the length of the smallest prefix η_{j_n} of η that contains the same sequence of visible transitions as ξ_{i_n}. Recall that η_{j_n} is a prefix of π_{j_n}. Then by Lemma 6, $L(s_{i_n}) = L(r_{j_n})$. By the definition of visible transitions we also know that if $n > 0$, for $i_{n-1} \le k < i_n - 1$, $L(s_k) = L(s_{i_{n-1}})$. This is because i_{n-1} is the length of the smallest prefix $\xi_{i_{n-1}}$ of σ that contains exactly $n - 1$ visible transitions. Thus, there is no visible transition between i_{n-1} and $i_n - 1$. Similarly, for $j_{n-1} \le l < j_n - 1$, $L(r_l) = L(r_{j_{n-1}})$.   □

Test Coverage for Loose Timing Annotations

C. Helmstetter[1,2], F. Maraninchi[1], and L. Maillet-Contoz[2]

[1] Verimag, Centre équation - 2, avenue de Vignate, 38610 GIÈRES, France
[2] STMicroelectronics, HPC, System Platform Group,
850 rue Jean Monnet, 38920 CROLLES, France

Abstract. The design flow of systems-on-a-chip (SoCs) identifies several abstraction levels higher than the Register-Transfer-Level that constitutes the input of the synthesis tools. These levels are called *transactional*, because systems are described as asynchronous parallel activities communicating by transactions. The most abstract transactional model is purely functional. The following model in the design flow is annotated with some timing information on the duration of the main components, that serves for performance evaluation. The timing annotations are included as special `wait` instructions, but since the timing information is imprecise, it should not result in additional synchronizations. We would like the functional properties of the system to be independent of the precise timing. In previous work [1], we showed how to adapt dynamic partial order reduction techniques to functional models of SoCs written in SystemC, in order to guarantee that functional properties are scheduler-independent. In this paper, we extend this work to *timed* systems with bounded delays, in order to guarantee timing-independence. The idea is to generate a set of executions that covers small variations of the timing annotations.

1 Introduction

The Register Transfer Level (RTL) used to be the entry point of the design flow of hardware systems, but the simulation environments for such models do not scale up well. Developing and debugging embedded software for these low level models before getting the physical chip from the factory is no longer possible at a reasonable cost. New abstraction levels, such as the *Transaction Level Model (TLM)* [2], have emerged. The TLM approach uses a component-based approach, in which hardware blocks are modules communicating with so-called *transactions*. The TLM models are used for early development of the embedded software, because the high level of abstraction allows a fast simulation. SystemC is a C++ library used for the description of SoCs at different levels of abstraction, from cycle accurate to purely functional models. It comes with a simulation environment, and is becoming a *de facto* standard.

As TLM models appear first in the design flow, they become reference models for SoCs. In particular, the software that is validated with the TLM model should remain unchanged in the final SoC. The TLM abstraction level comes with new synchronization mechanisms that often make existing methods for RTL validation inapplicable. In particular, recent TLM models do not have clocks

L. Brim et al. (Eds.): FMICS and PDMC 2006, LNCS 4346, pp. 100–115, 2007.

at all. In this paper, we concentrate on testing methods for SoCs written in SystemC.

The current industrial methodology for testing SoCs in SystemC is the following. First, we identify what we want to test (the *System Under Test*, or SUT), which is usually an open system. We make it closed by plugging *input generators* and a *result checker*, called *oracle*. SCV [3] is a testing tool for SystemC. It helps in writing input generators by providing C++ macros for expressing constraints: `SCV_CONSTRAINT((addr()>10 && addr()< 50)||` `(addr()>=2 && addr()<= 5));` is an SCV constraint for which the SCV solver will generate random values of `addr` satisfying it. In most existing approaches, the SUT writes in memory, and the oracle consists in comparing the final state of the SUT memory to a reference memory. As usual, the main difficulty is to get a good quality test suite, i.e., a test suite that does not omit *useful* tests (that may reveal a bug) and at the same time avoids *redundant* tests (that can expose the same bugs) as much as possible. Specman [4] is a commercial alternative of SCV which uses the *e* language for describing the constraints.

1.1   Partial Order Reduction Techniques for Scheduler-Independence

In [1], we have presented an automatic technique for the exploration of schedulings in the case of SystemC. It is an adaptation and application of the method for *dynamic* partial order reduction presented in [5]. We assume that the choice of relevant data for the testing phase has already been done: we consider a SoC written in SystemC, including the data generator and the oracle. For each of the test data, the system has to be *run*, with a particular *implementation* of the scheduler. Since the *specification* of the scheduler is non-deterministic, this means that the execution of tests may hide bugs that would have appeared with another valid implementation of the scheduler. Moreover, the scheduling is due to the simulation engine only, and is unlikely to represent anything concrete on the final SoC where we have true parallelism. We would like the SoC description, and in particular the embedded software, to be scheduler-independent. Exploring alternative schedulings is a way of validating this property.

Our tool is based on forking executions: we start executing the system for a given data-input, and as soon as we suspect that several scheduler choices could cause distinct behaviors, we fork the execution. We use an *approximate* criterion to decide whether to fork executions. The idea is to look at the actions performed by the processes, in order to guess whether a change in their order (as what would be produced by distinct scheduler choices) could affect the final state. This criterion is approximate in the following sense: we may distinguish between executions that in fact lead to the same final state; but we cannot consider as equivalent two executions that lead to distinct final states. The result is a complete, but not always minimal, exploration of the scheduling choices for the whole data-input.

1.2   The Hierarchy of TLM Models

There are several levels of transactional models. The more abstract transactional model is purely *functional*. The following model in the design flow is enriched with some timing information on the duration of the main components, that may serve for performance evaluation during simulation. This timing information is quite imprecise: it may be given by previous measures on existing IPs (IP stands for "*Intellectual Property*"; an IP block is a reusable hardware component). For instance, we may have approximate values for the time it takes to write an image in memory. Note that this kind of loose timing is still very far from the precision of cycle-accurate models, and this is why timed transactional models are interesting: they simulate much faster than cycle-accurate models, but they can already give some hints on the performance of the SoC.

Practically, a SystemC description annotated by timings uses a special instruction `wait (duration)`. The interpretation of this instruction by the simulation engine simulates the amount of time taken by the components. When executing such a SoC description enriched with timings, the SystemC execution engine has to take precise values of the timings. There is a risk of producing spurious synchronizations by interpreting the timings too strictly. In other words, the embedded software will be more robust if it works correctly for slightly distinct timings. It is therefore useful to explore alternative timings during testing. It can be done by choosing a timing randomly within an interval, at execution time. Existing industrial approaches use a new instruction `lwait (duration, delta)`, telling the execution engine to draw a value in the interval [`duration - delta, duration + delta`]. If the instruction appears within a loop, a new value is drawn for each execution of the instruction. However, this slows the simulations without guaranteeing that interesting cases are explored.

1.3   Contributions and Structure of the Paper

Ensuring *timing-independence* can also be done in a more systematic way, by generating exactly the set of timings that yield different behaviors of the SoC. In this paper, we generalize the approach of [1] in order to generate alternative schedulings and alternative timings for a given data input. The result is of the same kind: we obtain a complete but not always minimal set of alternative executions, for a given data input. The idea is that, if the software works well for all these alternative executions, it is more robust. This is our notion of scheduler and timing independence.

The paper is structured as follows: section 2 presents an overview of SystemC, and some examples for illustrating the influence of the scheduling and the presence of loose timings. Section 3 recalls the results of [1] and section 4 describes our new algorithm for models with loose timings. We present our implementation and its evaluation in section 5, related work in section 6, and we conclude with section 7.

2   SystemC, Scheduling Problems, and Loose Timings

A TLM model written in SystemC is based on an *architecture*, i.e. a set of parallel components and connections between them. Each component has typed connection *ports*, and its behavior is given by a set of communicating *processes* that can be programmed in full C++. For managing processes, SystemC provides a *scheduler*, and several synchronization mechanisms: the low-level *events*, the synchronous *signals* that trigger an event when their value changes, and higher level mechanisms. The static architecture is built by executing the so-called *elaboration phase* (ELAB), which creates components and connections. Then the scheduler starts running the processes of the components, according to the informal automaton of figure 1-(a). Simulations of a SystemC model look like sequences of *evaluation phases* (EV). Signals *update phase* (UP) and *time elapse* (TE) separate them (see figure 1-(b)).

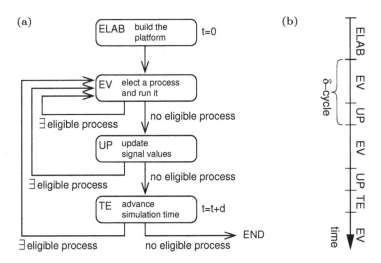

Fig. 1. (a) Automaton of the SystemC Scheduler; (b) Diagram of an execution

2.1   The SystemC Scheduler

The SystemC Language Reference Manual [6] describes the scheduler algorithm. At the end of the elaboration phase **ELAB**, some processes are *eligible*, some others are *waiting*. During the evaluation phase **EV**, eligible processes are run in an *unspecified order*, *non-preemptively*, and explicitly suspend themselves when reaching a *wait* instruction. A process may wait for some time to elapse, or for an event to occur. While running, it may access shared variables and signals, enable other processes by notifying events, or program delayed notifications. An eligible process cannot become "waiting" without being executed. When there is no more eligible process, signals values are updated (**UP**) and δ-delayed notifications are triggered, which can wake up processes. A δ-cycle is the duration between two update phases. Since there is no interaction between processes during the update phase, the order of the updates has no consequence. When there is still no eligible process at the end of an update phase, the scheduler lets time elapse (**TE**), and awakes the processes that have the earliest deadline. A notification of a SystemC event can be immediate, δ-delayed or time-delayed. Processes can thus be become eligible at any of the three steps EV, UP or TE. Besides events, processes can also communicate using shared variables, and higher level structures built with these two primitives.

2.2   Examples with Fixed Durations

To illustrate possible consequences of scheduling choices, let us introduce two small examples of SystemC programs. Figure 2 shows the example foo made of two processes P and Q. The example foo has three possible executions depending on the scheduling, leading to very different results. We describe them below, with the following notation: an execution is denoted by a sequence of process names (to show which process is elected) and strings of the form "$[t \xrightarrow{+d} D]$" that serve to show the **TE** phase of the scheduler; d represents the duration elapsed and D the new global date (these strings can be deduced from other information, but we include them for readability reasons). The three executions are:

- P;Q;P;$[t \xrightarrow{+20} 20]$;Q;P: this scheduling leads to the printing of "Ok".
- P;Q;P;$[t \xrightarrow{+20} 20]$;P;Q: the string "Ko" is printed. It is a typical case of *data-race*: x is tested before it has been set to 1.
- Q;P;$[t \xrightarrow{+20} 20]$;Q: the execution ends after three steps only. The "wait(e)" statement has been executed before any notification of event e. Since events are not persistent in SystemC, process P has not been woken up. It is a particular form of *deadlock*.

It is useful to test all executions of the foo example because they lead to different final states. But consider now the foobar example defined in figure 3. foobar has 30 possible executions, but only 3 different final states. 12 executions are equivalent to "R;P;Q;P;$[t \xrightarrow{+20} 20]$;R;Q;P", 12 to "R;P;Q;P;$[t \xrightarrow{+20} 20]$;R;P;Q" and 6 to "R;Q;P;$[t \xrightarrow{+20} 20]$;R;Q". Our method for scheduler-independence would generate only 3 executions, one for each final state (or equivalence class).

```
void top::P() {          void top::Q() {
wait(e);                 e.notify();
wait(20);                x = 0;
if (x) cout << "Ok\n";   wait(20);
else cout << "Ko\n";}    x = 1;}
```

Fig. 2. The foo example

```
void top::P()
   as in example foo       void top::R() {
void top::Q()                 wait(20);
   as in example foo       }
```

Fig. 3. The foobar example

```
void P() {                          void Q() {
  lwait(3,d1);   // t₁               lwait(6,d3);   // t₃
  wait(e);                           e.notify();
  lwait(40,d2);  // t₂               x = 0;
  if (x) cout << "Ok\n";             lwait(24,d4);  // t₄
  else cout << "Ko\n";}              x = 1;}
```

Fig. 4. The foochi example

2.3 Examples with Loose Durations

Figure 4 presents a new version foochi of the foo example, with loose durations. To execute this example, we must choose a value for t_1 between 3-d1 and 3+d1, a value for t_2 between 40-d2 and 40+d2, etc.

If d1 = d2 = d3 = d4 = 0, then all delays are fixed and there are only two valid and equivalent executions (the index on process names is used to identify the occurrence): $P_1; Q_1$ or $Q_1; P_1$ followed by $[t \xrightarrow{+3} 3]; P_2; [t \xrightarrow{+3} 6]; Q_2; P_3; [t \xrightarrow{+24} 30]; Q_3; [t \xrightarrow{+16} 46]; P_4$. P_1 and Q_1 occur at $T = 0ns$, P_2 at $T = 3ns$, Q_2 and P_3 at $T = 6ns$. Next Q_3 runs at $T = 24 + 6 = 30ns$. At last, the string "Ok" is displayed by P_4 at $T = 6 + 40 = 46ns$.

Giving non-null values to the di allows to test the robustness of the program. If we take d1 = d2 = d3 = d4 = 2, then it is possible to permute the wait and the notification of the SystemC event e: we choose $t_1 = 5ns$ and $t_3 = 4ns$. With theses values, it is still impossible to permute Q_3 and P_4. If we increase d2 (resp. d4) to 10 (resp. 6), then Q_3 and P_4 may occur at the same time $T = 6+30 = 36ns$ ($30 = 24 + 6 = 40 - 10$). Next, playing with the indeterminism of the scheduler allows to execute P_4 before Q_3. We have found the two errors of the foo example again. The algorithm we describe in this paper generates timings and schedulings automatically, in order to find the executions that lead to these errors.

3   Relationships for Partial Order Reduction Techniques

In the whole section, the SUT is a SystemC program. We suppose that we have an independent tool for generating test cases that only contain the data. We call SUTD the object made of the SUT plus one particular test data. We have to generate a relevant set of schedulings and timings for this data.

3.1 Representation of the SUTD

When data is fixed, a SUT execution is entirely defined by its scheduling and its concrete timing. A scheduling is entirely defined by an element of $\mathcal{P}^*$ where $\mathcal{P}$ is the set of process identifiers. Not all the elements of $\mathcal{P}^*$ represent possible schedulings of the SUTD (because of the synchronization and timing constraints between processes). With each lwait(D,d) instruction present in the source code, we associate an identifier $\omega \in \Omega$; we note $B(\omega)$ (B stands for "*Bounds*") the interval $[D-d, D+d]$ and $\#_u(\omega)$ the number of times an execution of ω occurs in a scheduling u. A timing T is a function from pairs $(\omega, n) \in \Omega \times [1..\#_u(\omega)]$ to durations d. $T(\omega, n) = d$ means that we wait for a duration d when we execute the instruction identified by ω for the n-th time. The timing T is valid if and only if $\forall (\omega, n) \in \Omega \times [1..\#_u(\omega)], T(\omega, n) \in B(\omega)$.

We call *transition* one execution of one process in a particular scheduling. Each transition of a scheduling is identified by its process identifier indexed by the occurrence number of this process identifier in the scheduling. For example, in the scheduling pqp there are 3 transitions: p_1, q_1 and p_2, in that order. For a particular execution with a specified timing, the *date* of a transition is the value of the variable t of the scheduler (figure 1-(a)) when the transition occurs.

We will use letters p, q, r to denote processes, $p_i, q_j, \ldots$ to denote transitions and $u, v, \ldots$ to denote sub-sequences of schedulings. Indexes will be omitted when obvious by context.

3.2   Relationships

We recall some standard notions from the literature on partial order reduction techniques, that we will use for both scheduling and timing generation.

Dependent and Equivalent Transitions. The theory of partial order reduction relies on the definition of *dependent* transitions [7]. Let u be a valid scheduling, two transitions p_i and q_j are independent if not any of them has been enabled by the other, and if permuting them gives a new valid scheduling which still leads to the same final state. In all other cases, we say that p_i and q_j are *dependent*. Note that it is correct because, in SystemC, an enabled process cannot be disabled without being executed. We note D the set of all pairs of dependent transitions.

Two schedulings u and v are *equivalent*, noted $u \equiv v$, if and only if we can transform one into the other by successive permutations of independent transitions. As a consequence of the definition of the dependency relationship D, two equivalent schedulings lead to the same final state. In our testing approach for SystemC, we include the output checker into the SUT, which means that the detection of an error corresponds to a particular final state. Hence generating one scheduling of each equivalence class allows to detect all errors.

Causally Ordered and Permutable Transitions. Consider a scheduling u: we note $p_i <_u q_j$ if the transition p_i (the i-th execution of process p) occurs before the transition q_j (the j-th execution of process q) in u. We note $p_i \prec_u q_j$ and say that p_i and q_j are *causally ordered*, if we have $p_i <_v q_j$ for any scheduling v equivalent to u. In other words, p_i and q_j are causally ordered if we cannot permute them without permuting dependent transitions. Unlike the causal relationship, the *permutability relationship* is not a partial order. Two transitions are permutable if they can be permuted without permuting **other** dependent transitions. We note P the set of permutable transitions. The transitions p_i and q_j are *permutable* in the valid scheduling $u = u_1 p_i u_2 q_j u_3$, noted $(p_i, q_j) \in P$, if and only if: $\exists v_1, v_2$ such that $u_1 v_1 p_i q_j v_2 \equiv u_1 p_i u_2 q_j u_3$ and $u_1 v_1 q_j$ is a valid scheduling.

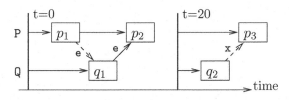

(a) `foo` with scheduling $p_1q_1p_2q_2p_3$

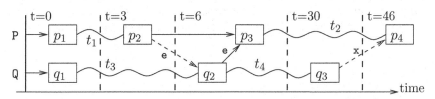

(b) `foochi` with scheduling $p_1q_1p_2q_2p_3q_3p_4$

and timing: $t_1 \mapsto 3, t_2 \mapsto 40, t_3 \mapsto 6, t_4 \mapsto 24$

Fig. 5. Dynamic Dependency Graphs

Dynamic Dependency Graph (DDG). The DDG represents the synchronizations of a particular scheduling. Fig. 5-(a) represents the scheduling P;Q;P;Q;P, denoted $p_1q_1p_2q_2p_3$, of the `foo` program of Fig. 2, and Fig. 5-(b) represents an execution of `foochi`. Each horizontal line is a process. Time elapses are represented by plain vertical lines if all delays are fixed, otherwise by dotted vertical lines. The curved lines represent loose durations. Each box is a process transition. Arrows between boxes indicate that the two transitions are causally ordered; we draw dashed arrows if the transitions are permutable, plain arrows otherwise. We may move some transitions on the horizontal axis, remaining among the *valid and equivalent schedulings*, provided we do not permute two boxes linked by an arrow, nor move a transition through a plain vertical line.

Computation of the Relationships. In practice, we can only compute an *approximation* of the dependency relationship: two independent transitions may be considered as dependent, but two dependent transitions are always considered as dependent. Consequently, the only risk is to generate useless schedulings.

We compute the dependency relationship for each new generated scheduling. Doing multiple dynamic computations is more precise than one static computation. For example, for a code like `Tab[h]=42` we know exactly which element of `Tab` is accessed, and whether the new value is different from the old one.

Two transitions are dependent if some reasons prevent their permutation, or else if they contain non-commutative actions on the same shared object (for example: `wait(e)` and `notify(e)`, or `x=0` and `x=x+1`). For the causal order and the relationship P, we have to compute a transitive closure. The principles of these algorithms are available in [5], or in [1] for SystemC-specific concerns. Here, we consider that D and P are computed without taking temporal constraints into account.

3.3   Generation of Schedulings

In this section, we rewrite the algorithm of [1] defined for the automatic generation of schedulings, in such a way that the generalization to timing generation becomes possible. The algorithm of [1] works on any SUTD with only fixed delays. First, we execute the SUTD with a random scheduling. Next, for each executed scheduling, we generate a new scheduling for each pair of dependent and permutable transitions. Figure 6 gives a definition of the main algorithm.

G_S(constraint set C):   *//initial call: $G_S(\emptyset)$*
    execute the SUTD according to C;
    $u=$ scheduling of the above execution;
    for all transitions p_i and q_j of u with $p_i <_u q_j$ such that:
        $(p_i, q_j) \in D \cap P$ and
        $date(p_i) = date(q_j)$ and   *//temporal constraints are treated here (*)*
        $\exists v, v \models C \wedge q_j <_v p_i$ do
        $G_S(C \cup$ "$q_j < p_i$");   *//constraint to be satisfied by new schedulings*
        $C = C \cup$ "$p_i < q_j$";   *//constraint satisfied by the current scheduling*

Fig. 6. Main algorithm for the generation of schedulings

We generate each scheduling in two steps. First, we build a set of *scheduling constraints* of the form "$p_i < q_j$". A constraint "$p_i < q_j$" is satisfied by a scheduling u if and only if the j-th occurrence of q does not occur before the i-th occurrence of p (formally: $q_j \in u \Rightarrow p_i \in u \wedge p_i <_u q_j$). The scheduling u satisfies a set of constraints C (noted $u \models C$) if and only if it satisfies all constraints of C. Next, we give this constraint set to a patched scheduler that elects processes according to the given constraints. Each new generated scheduling is more constrained than its father scheduling. Consequently, there are fewer and fewer new schedulings at each iteration. When the checker does not generate any new scheduling, we have a complete test suite. If we execute this algorithm until completion, we get at least one scheduling for each equivalence class.

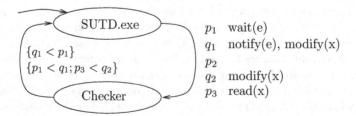

Fig. 7. First iteration of the analysis for the **foo** example

Figure 7 describes the first iteration of our tool on the `foo` example. The first execution activates processes p and q in the order $p_1 q_1 p_2 q_2 p_3$. The checker generates two new sets of constraints. One to permute p_1 and q_1 (unordered accesses to event e, first dashed arrow of figure 5-(a)) and the other to permute p_3 and q_2 (unordered accesses to shared variable x, second dashed arrow of figure 5-(a)). Following iterations do not generate other schedulings and we get at last 3 schedulings.

4   Conjoint Generation of Schedulings and Timings

4.1   The SystemC Models We Consider

First, we need to make the context of our work more precise. In this work, we restrict to SystemC programs whose executions have only one δ-cycle between two "time-elapse" phases. Indeed, the semantics of δ-cycle delays for abstract models with loose durations is unclear and such delays should not be used in timed TLM models. Moreover, for simplicity reasons, we do not consider delayed notifications. Finally, we consider that the global date (variable t of Figure 1-(a)) is private and cannot be accessed by processes. This means that the processes cannot use the timing annotations to perform functional effects. This is consistent with the context of several TLM models, where the timing annotations are added to a functional model, for performance evaluation only. We discuss this topic in the conclusion.

4.2   Main Ideas

With examples that use only fixed delays, two transitions cannot be permuted if they occur at different dates. This is no longer true for SUTDs with loose delays: an alternative concrete timing may allow or force the permutation of some transitions. Now, for all pairs of dependent transitions such that their permutation is not prevented by explicit synchronizations, we have to determine whether it exists a concrete timing which allows their permutation. If such timings exist, we have to choose one and to re-execute the SUTD with it. In the algorithm presented in section 3.3 above, it is the only point which has to be rewritten for the generation of timings; the rest is identical.

For an execution of the SUTD and a set of scheduling constraints, we compute the conjunction of all temporal constraints that must be satisfied. Fortunately, all temporal constraints give linear constraints whose variables are the $T(\omega, i)$ items. Consequently their conjunction gives a system of linear constraints S, which can be solved with linear programming techniques. If the system of constraints is built correctly, its solutions are valid timings which make the given set of scheduling constraints feasible. With the current semantics of the `lwait` instruction, S defines an octahedron [8] (all variable coefficients are in $\{-1, 0, 1\}$) but not an octagon [9] (a constraint may use more than two variables).

4.3   The Temporal Constraints

There are two sorts of temporal constraints. First, the solution must correspond to valid timings. So for all $(\omega, i) \in \Omega \times [1..\#(\omega)]$, we add the two constraints

$\inf(B(\omega)) < T(\omega, i)$ and $T(\omega, i) < \sup(B(\omega))$. Second, each scheduling constraint implies a temporal constraint.

In order to build temporal constraints implied by scheduling constraints, we need the following definition. With each transition p_i, we associate a *symbolic date* noted $sdate(p_i)$. A symbolic date is a sum of variables $T(\omega, i)$ and constants. We compute the symbolic date of a transition p_i as follows:

1. if p_i follows a `wait` with loose duration (p_{i-1} ended by a call to `lwait`), then: $sdate(p_i) = sdate(p_{i-1}) + T(\omega, n)$ where ω is the identifier of this `lwait` instruction and n its occurrence number.
2. if p_i follows a `wait` with fixed duration (p_{i-1} ended by a call to `wait(k)`), then: $sdate(p_i) = sdate(p_{i-1}) + k$;
3. if p_i as been enabled by an immediate notification from transition q_j, then: $sdate(p_i) = sdate(q_j)$;
4. if p is initially eligible, then $p_1 = 0$.

We illustrate these rules on the example `foochi` with $u = p_1 q_1 p_2 q_2 p_3 q_3 p_4$. Symbolic dates do not depend on the timing. We have $sdate(p_1) = sdate(q_1) = 0$ (rule 4); next $sdate(q_2) = t_3$ and $sdate(p_2) = t_1$ and $sdate(q_3) = t_3 + t_4$ (rule 1). According to rule 3 on immediate notifications, we have $sdate(p_3) = sdate(q_2) = t_3$ and so $sdate(p_4) = sdate(p_3) + t_2 = t_3 + t_2$ (rule 1).

Let "$p_i < q_j$" be a scheduling constraint, we build the associated temporal constraint as follows: we first evaluate $sdate(p_i)$ and $sdate(q_j)$, which yields two expressions e_1 and e_2; we then add to S the constraint "$e_1 \leq e_2$".

4.4   The Algorithm

Figure 8 presents the new algorithm. C is a set of scheduling constraints and u a scheduling. S is a linear program and the functions is_feasible and solution_of can be implemented with the simplex algorithm. On line (1), the timing T may be incomplete, i.e., the value for some `lwait` instructions may be unspecified. In this case, the simulation engine is free to choose any value in the given interval. Initially we call G_T with an empty set of scheduling constraints and an empty timing. Let T_u be the concrete timing of the current scheduling u. T_u is always a solution of the system of linear constraints S. In general, T_u is not a solution of the system built on line (2).

We describe the first call to G_T on the example `foochi` to illustrate this algorithm. If we ignore the temporal aspects, the analysis of $u = p_1 q_1 p_2 q_2 p_3 q_3 p_4$ generates two sets of constraints: $\{q_2 < p_2\}$ and $\{p_2 < q_2; p_4 < q_3\}$.

The first set of constraints $\{q_2 < p_2\}$ gives a linear system S' containing only the constraint $sdate(q_2) \leq sdate(p_2)$ which rewrites in $t_3 - t_1 \leq 0$. We must also respect bounds on variables: $t_1 \in [1, 5]$ and $t_3 \in [4, 8]$. We ask a solution to the linear programming library and get the solution $t_1 = t_3 = 4$. Finally, we call $G_T(\{q_2 < p_2\}, \{t_1 = 4, t_3 = 4\})$ (line (3) of the algorithm). These scheduling constraints and this timing lead to the first error of `foochi` cited at end of section 2.

The second set of constraints $\{p_2 < q_2; p_4 < q_3\}$ gives the two constraints $t_3 - t_1 \geq 0$ and $t_2 - t_4 \leq 0$. With the bounds $t_1 \in [1, 5]$, $t_2 \in [30, 50]$, $t_3 \in [4, 8]$

G_T(constraint set C, timing T):   //*initial call:* $G_T(\emptyset, \emptyset)$
    execute the SUTD according to C and T;   (1)
    $u=$ scheduling of the above execution;
    linear system $S = []$;
    for all $(\omega, i) \in \Omega \times [1..\#(\omega)]$ do
        $S = S \bullet (T(\omega, i) \in B(\omega))$;
    for all constraint "$p_i < q_j$" of C do
        $S = S \bullet (sdate(p_i) \leq sdate(q_j))$;
    for all transitions p_i and q_j of u with $p_i <_u q_j$ such that:
        $(p_i, q_j) \in D \cap P$ and
        $\exists v, v \models C \wedge q_j <_v p_i$ do
    if is_feasible($S \bullet (sdate(q_j) \leq sdate(p_i))$) then   (2)
        $T' =$ solution_of($S \bullet (sdate(q_j) \leq sdate(p_i))$);
        $G_T(C \cup "q_j < p_i", T')$;   (3)
        $C = C \cup "p_i < q_j"$;
        $S = S \bullet (sdate(p_i) \leq sdate(q_j))$;

Fig. 8. Main algorithm for the generation of timings

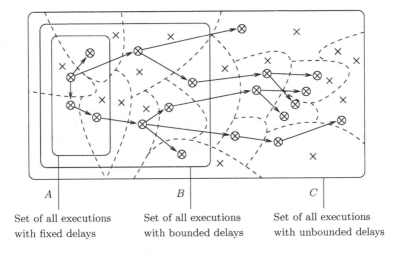

A	B	C
Set of all executions with fixed delays	Set of all executions with bounded delays	Set of all executions with unbounded delays

Fig. 9. Sets of all executions of the SUTD. The dashed lines delimit the equivalence classes. The surrounded crosses represent generated executions, with arrows from father to children. G_S returns the surrounded crosses of the set A, G_T those of B and G'_S those of C.

and $t_4 \in [18, 30]$, one solution is $t_1 = t_3 = 4$ and $t_2 = t_4 = 30$. Finally, we call G_T again with this set of constraints and this timing as arguments. This leads to the second error of `foochi`.

4.5   Elements for the Correctness of the Algorithm

In the general case, G_T generates **at least one** representant of each equivalence class, as G_S does. On this example, we have generated one element of each equivalence class. First, we have suppressed the condition *"the transitions p_i and q_j are not permutable if $date(p_i) \neq date(q_j)$"* (line (*) of Figure 6). We call G'_S the algorithm G_S in which this condition has been suppressed. Running G'_S on the SUTD generates a very large set E' of schedulings which are valid if all bounds of loose durations are extended to $[0, \infty[$. It is equivalent to removing all delays of the SUTD. E' contains at least one element of each equivalence class of this "untimed" version of the SUTD.

Second, we have encoded the temporal constraints into a linear system S. The only difference between G'_S and G_T is that G_T checks the feasibility of S. We know by construction that there exists an execution (u, T) which satisfies a set of scheduling constraints C if and only if the system S built from C is feasible. Hence G_T generates all elements of G'_S that satisfy the temporal constraints. Figure 9 represents the sets of executions generated by G_S, G'_S and G_T.

5   Case Study: The MPEG Decoder System

We have complemented our prototype for G_S with a prototype for G_T. Figure 10 gives an overview of this new prototype. We instrument the C++/SystemC source code with the SystemC front-end Pinapa [10] in order to detect the accesses to shared variables dynamically. We have chosen LP_SOLVE [11] to solve the linear systems.

We have evaluated the tool on a small industrial case-study. This system has 5 components: a master, a MPEG decoder, a display, a memory and a bus model. There are about 50 000 lines of code and only 4 processes. This is quite common in the more abstract models found in industry, because there is a lot of sequential code, and very few synchronizations. Complete models of SoCs are typically 3 to 6 times bigger than this MPEG decoder. The test is stopped after the third decoded image, which corresponds to 150 transitions. One simulation takes 0.39 s.

First, we run the G_S prototype on a timed version without loose delays. It generates **128 schedulings** in **1 mn 08 s**. No bug is found, which guarantees that this test-case will run correctly on any SystemC implementation. The total time spent splits into 50 s for running the SUTD 128 times and an overhead of 18 s for the additional computations. The experiments have been run on a Pentium 4 cadenced at 2.80 GHz.

The G_S prototype can be used on an untimed version too. This untimed version is obtained by replacing all timed instructions by their corresponding untimed instructions. But the prototype failed to run to completion because the scheduling space to explore is far too large. Indeed, removing time constraints allows a lot of new interleavings. For the untimed version, we estimate the number of relevant schedulings to about 2^{32}. It would take many years to execute them all. Most of this time would be spent exploring unrealistic interleavings.

The prototype of G_T allows to test bounded-delay versions which are intermediate between the fixed-delay version and the fully untimed version. We replace all instructions wait(d) by lwait(d,d*r). The number of valid interleavings

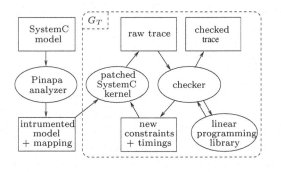

Fig. 10. The Prototype's Architecture

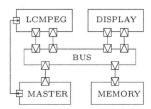

Fig. 11. Architecture of the MPEG decoder system

increases when the global variable r increases. The goal is to validate the SUTD with r as big as possible. We succeed in validating this MPEG decoder system with $r = 0.2$. The G_T prototype generates **3584 schedulings and timings** in **35 mn 11 s**. One must spend 23 mn 18 s to execute this system 3584 times. The overhead is about 11 mn 53 s. Our goal is to validate the system with $r = 0.5$ but the first attemps show that our prototype is not fast enough yet.

6   Related Work

The idea of interpreting timing annotations in a loose way is quite natural. It was already present in some modeling approaches based on fuzzy time (see, for instance, [12]). However, these approaches are often dedicated to the handling of imprecise functional information, while we focus on non-functional information.

The approach described in [13] has some similarities with ours. They run the formal verifier VINAS-P on a program with bounded delays to get test cases which exhibit "failures". Next, for each failure trace, they generate a system of linear constraints and solve it using an integer linear programming solver. Finally, they get new bounds for the delays specified in the program, which avoid failures. Static partial order reduction is used during the formal verification step. Like us, they found that the time spent to solve the generated linear programs is quite small compared with the total time spent. The technique used in our tool differs in two points: first we use *dynamic* POR, second the linear systems are used inside the POR algorithm and not afterwards.

As far as we know, there is no verification tool for SystemC programs with bounded delays yet. However, the tool LusSy [14] is able to translate automatically SystemC programs into synchronous automata for which numerous verification tools exist. Another approach would be to extend LusSy to translate SystemC programs into timed automata which can be verified with tools such as Kronos [15] or Uppaal [16] (this should be automatic; a *manual* translation of SystemC programs into some formal language is too much error prone). The approach described in this paper avoids the problem of relating a formal model with the source code; since it is developed for a testing framework, it scales better than verification techniques.

7   Conclusion and Further Work

In previous work, we presented a method to explore the set of valid schedulings of a SystemC program and a given data input. In this paper, we described a generalization to the exploration of valid timings. Exploring alternative timings may reveal more synchronization errors such as dead-locks or data-races, and violations of specified temporal constraints too. We work directly on the program so all errors found are true errors and not false warnings. The conjoint use of dynamic partial order reduction and linear programming allows to avoid redundant simulations of the system under test. As a result, we are now able to increase the test coverage of real size SoC models.

We have implemented this new algorithm. The current prototype is already efficient enough to cover exhaustively small timing variations (about 20%) of medium size SoC models, or parts of full big SoCs. We still have many possible improvements to study. First, using the pre-solve functionality of the LP_SOLVE library should reduce the overhead due to the computation of timings. Indeed, it seems we perform lots of redundant computations when solving the temporal constraints. Second, we still produce some redundant executions. The dynamic partial order reduction technique is not optimal; we can indeed get two schedulings which are equivalent according to the computed dependency relationship. In [5], P. Godefroid suggests the use of the sleep sets technique to eliminate some of them. In addition, computing a more precise dependency relationship will reduce the number of equivalence classes to cover. The dependency of two transitions depends mainly of the way they communicate. Up to now, we have only considered low level communication items (non-persistent events and shared variables). Higher level communication mechanisms (persistent events, for example) can be globally robust to the scheduler indeterminism although they perform dependent accesses locally. Taking them into account should reduce dramatically the total time spent. With these improvements, we hope to be able to cover wider timing variations, up to 40% or 50%.

Another further work concerns the restrictions imposed on the programs we validate. Currently, we forbid reading of the global date from the processes. For example, the following instruction is not allowed: if (date()<45) {A} else {B}, where date() returns the current global date. As a consequence of this restriction, the functional behavior of an execution depends only on its scheduling; the timing is only used to know whether the scheduling is valid, and to get an estimation of temporal performances of the final SoC. Instructions as above are not common in the models we have studied, however they might be more frequent or necessary in other domains; therefore extending our tool will be useful. Our idea is the following: first, we add to the scheduling representations virtual transitions of the form $\chi(t)$ meaning that the global date has just reached t. Next, we consider that a virtual transition $\chi(t)$ is: 1) dependent and permutable with all transitions which compare `date()` and t, and 2) causally ordered with the other virtual transitions. Thus it is possible to treat all expressions of the form `date()`$<k$ without modifying the main algorithm; it could be extended to multiple clocks with reset instructions but allowing all expressions using `date()` is a harder task.

References

1. Helmstetter, C., Maraninchi, F., Maillet-Contoz, L., Moy, M.: Automatic generation of schedulings for improving the test coverage of systems-on-a-chip. In: FMCAD, Springer (2006)
2. Ghenassia, F., ed.: Transaction-Level Modeling with SystemC. TLM Concepts and Applications for Embedded Systems. Springer (2005) ISBN 0-387-26232-6.
3. Rose, J., Swan, S.: SCV Randomization (2003)
   `www.testbuilder.net/reports/scv_randomization.pdf`.
4. Kuhn, T., Oppold, T., Winterholer, M., Rosenstiel, W., Edwards, M., Kashai, Y.: A framework for object oriented hardware specification, verification, and synthesis. In: DAC '01: Proceedings of the 38th conference on Design automation, New York, NY, USA, ACM Press (2001) 413–418
5. Flanagan, C., Godefroid, P.: Dynamic partial-order reduction for model checking software. In: Symposium on Principles of programming languages (POPL), New York, NY, USA, ACM Press (2005) 110–121
6. Open SystemC Initiative: SystemC v2.0.1 Language Reference Manual. (2003)
   `http://www.systemc.org/`.
7. Mazurkiewicz, A.: Trace theory. In: Advances in Petri nets 1986, part II on Petri nets: applications and relationships to other models of concurrency, New York, NY, USA, Springer-Verlag New York, Inc. (1987) 279–324
8. Clarisó, R., Cortadella, J.: The octahedron abstract domain. In Giacobazzi, R., ed.: Static Analysis, 11th International Symposium, SAS 2004, Verona, Italy, August 26-28, 2004, Proceedings. Volume 3148 of Lecture Notes in Computer Science., Springer (2004) 312–327
9. Miné, A.: The octagon abstract domain. In: WCRE. (2001) 310
10. Moy, M., Maraninchi, F., Maillet-Contoz, L.: Pinapa (2005)
    `http://greensocs.sourceforge.net/pinapa/`.
11. Berkelaar, M., et al.: Lp_solve (1996)
    `http://www.cs.sunysb.edu/~algorith/implement/lpsolve/implement.shtml`.
12. L. A. Kunzle, R. Valette, B.P.C.: Temporal reasoning in fuzzy time petri nets. Technical Report 98073, LAAS Toulouse (1998)
13. Yoneda, T., Kitai, T., Myers, C.J.: Automatic derivation of timing constraints by failure analysis. In: CAV '02: Proceedings of the 14th International Conference on Computer Aided Verification, London, UK, Springer-Verlag (2002) 195–208
14. Moy, M., Maraninchi, F., Maillet-Contoz, L.: LusSy: A toolbox for the analysis of systems-on-a-chip at the transactional level. In: International Conference on Application of Concurrency to System Design. (2005)
15. Bozga, M., Daws, C., Maler, O., Olivero, A., Tripakis, S., Yovine, S.: Kronos: A model-checking tool for real-time systems. In: Proc. 1998 Computer-Aided Verification, CAV'98. Volume 1427 of Lecture Notes in Computer Science., Vancouver, Canada, Springer-Verlag (1998)
16. Uppsala and Aalborg Universities: Uppaal (1994-2006)
    `http://www.uppaal.com/`.

Model-Based Testing of a WAP Gateway: An Industrial Case-Study

Anders Hessel and Paul Pettersson

Department of Information Technology, Uppsala University, P.O. Box 337,
SE-751 05 Uppsala, Sweden
{hessel,paupet}@it.uu.se

Abstract. We present experiences from a case study where a model-based approach to black-box testing is applied to verify that a Wireless Application Protocol (WAP) gateway conforms to its specification. The WAP gateway is developed by Ericsson and used in mobile telephone networks to connect mobile phones with the Internet. We focus on testing the software implementing the session (WSP) and transaction (WTP) layers of the WAP protocol. These layers, and their surrounding environment, are described as a network of timed automata. To model the many sequence numbers (from a large domain) used in the protocol, we introduce an abstraction technique. We believe the suggested abstraction technique will prove useful to model and analyse other similar protocols with sequence numbers, in particular in the context of model-based testing.

A complete test bed is presented, which includes generation and execution of test cases. It takes as input a model and a coverage criterion expressed as an observer, and returns a verdict for each test case. The test bed includes existing tools from Ericsson for test-case execution. To generate test suites, we use our own tool CO✓ER— a new test-case generation tool based on the real-time model-checker UPPAAL.

1 Introduction

Testing is the dominating technique used in industry to validate that developed software conforms to its specification. To improve the efficiency of testing, model-based testing has been suggested as an approach to automate the generation of the tests to be performed during testing. In model-based testing, a model is used to specify the desired behavior of the developed software, and the testing efforts aims at finding discrepancies between the behavior of an implementation and that specified by the model. This process can be automated by applying a test generation tool to produce the tests, and by automating the execution and validation of the tests using a test-execution tool.

Model-based test generation techniques have been studied thoroughly in the research community [Tre96, HLSU02, LMN05] and several applications to industrial systems have been reported, e.g., [BFG+00, LMNS05]. There is much less literature describing industrial applications of model-based testing techniques for real-time systems, i.e., systems that must react to stimuli and produce output in a timely fashion, i.e., real-time systems including, e.g., clients or servers using protocols with timing.

L. Brim et al. (Eds.): FMICS and PDMC 2006, LNCS 4346, pp. 116–131, 2007.

In this paper, we present experiences from applying a model-based approach to perform black-box conformance testing of a gateway developed by Ericsson. The gateway is used to connect mobile phone clients using the Wireless Application Protocol (WAP) with the Internet. We present how the specification of the transaction layer (WTP) and the session layer (WSP) have been described in the modeling language of timed automata [AD94]. The specific protocol used in the model is a connection oriented version, and the model includes scenarios where several transactions are associated with a session. In addition to the components constituting the WAP stack of the gateway, the model also contains automata modeling abstract behavior and assumptions imposed on the components in its environment, such as a web sever and terminals using the gateway.

A specific problem when modeling the WAP protocol is to model the sequence numbers, called Transaction Identifiers (TID), used in the exchanged packages, called Protocol Data Units (PDU). The protocol typically makes use of several TIDs with a domain of size 2^{15} using a sliding window of size 2^{14}. To make automatic analysis feasible, previous models of the protocol, used for model-checking the specification, have introduced a limit on the maximum allowed TID values, assuming that all behaviors of the protocol will be covered with a small maximum TID value [GB00]. We take a different approach and introduce an abstraction technique to handle TID values. It maintains the concrete TID values, so that they can be accessed in the abstract test-cases generated from the model.

To specify how thorough a test suite should test the WAP gateway, we select test cases following some particular coverage criterion, such as coverage of control states or edges in the model. As our model contains the environment of the system under test, a test-case generation tool can find out how the environment should behave to drive the system under test in a desired direction to fulfill a given coverage criterion. To formally specify coverage criteria, we apply results from our previous work [BHJP05], where we have proposed to use observer automaton with parameters as a formal specification language for coverage criteria. We show that the observer language is expressive enough to specify the coverage criteria used to test the WAP gateway.

To perform the actual testing, we have built a complete test bed that supports automated generation and execution of tests. It takes as input a network of timed automata and an observer automaton, and uses our tool UPPAAL CO√ER to generate an abstract test suite. UPPAAL CO√ER is a test generation tool based on the UPPAAL model checker [LPY97]. The test suite is compiled, by a tool named tr2mac [Vil05], into a script program that is executed by a test execution environment named TSC2, developed by Ericsson. TSC2 executes a script program by sending PDUs to the WAP gateway and observing the PDUs received in response. If unexpected packages or timing is observed the discrepancy is reported to a log file, and the testing proceeds with the next test case in the suite.

From testing the WAP gateway, we report the effect of executing test suites generated from extended versions of the edge, switch, and projection coverage criteria. In particular, we present two discrepancies between the model and the WAP gateway found during testing, and observe that both these problems were found in the rather small test suites satisfying the edge coverage criterion.

The rest of this paper is organized as follows: in the next section we give an informal description of the studied WAP gateway. In Section 3 we present the abstraction used to model sequence numbers in the model, presented in Section 4. In Section 5 we present the test generation and execution tools, and results from testing the gateway. We conclude the paper in Section 6, and then presents detailed models in an Appendix.

2 Wireless Application Protocol

The Wireless Application Protocol (WAP)[1] is a global and open standard that specifies an architecture for providing access to Internet services to mobile (hand-held) devices. It is typically used when a mobile phone is used to browse Web pages on the Internet, or when pictures or music are downloaded to a mobile phone. The WAP standard specifies both a protocol and a format, named Wireless Markup Language (WML) being the WAP analogy to HTML used by HTTP. The WML format also has a compressed binary encoding (WML/Binary) that is used during wireless communication to save bandwidth.

An overview of a WAP gateway architecture is shown in Figure 1. A WAP gateway converts between the WML content on the HTTP side, and WML/Binary on the mobile side. It also serves as a proxy for translating WAP requests to Internet protocols (e.g., HTTP). The WAP side of a gateway typically consists of the following protocol layers: Wireless Session Protocol (WSP), Wireless Transaction Protocol (WTP), Wireless Datagram Protocol (WDP), and a bearer layer such as e.g., GSM, CDMA, or UDP.

The internet side usually consists of the protocols Hypertext Transfer Protocol (HTTP), Transmission Control Protocol (TCP), and Internet Protocol (IP). The WDP layer and a bearer on the WAP side corresponds to the TCP/IP layers on the Internet side. The security layers Wireless Transport Layer Security (WTLS) on the WAP side and Secure Socket Layer (SSL) on the Internet side are optional and omitted in Figure 1.

WAP Terminal	WAP Gateway			Web Server
Application (WAE)	Proxy			WAP Application
Session (WSP)	WSP	HTTP		HTTP
Transaction (WTP)	WTP			
Transport (WDP)	WDP	TCP		TCP
Bearer (UDP)	UDP	IP		IP

Fig. 1. WAP Gateway Architecture

---

[1] The Wireless Application Protocol Architecture Specification is available at the web page `http://www.openmobilealliance.org/tech/affiliates/wap/wapindex.html`

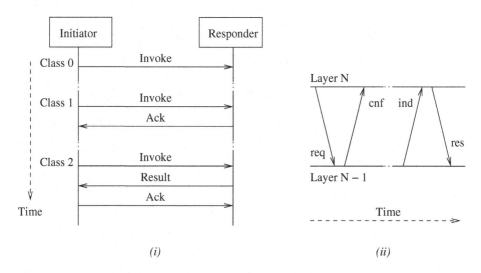

(i)   *(ii)*

Fig. 2. The three WTP transaction classes (*i*) and signaling terminology (*ii*)

The WAP specification defines two roles in the protocol. The part that starts a trans-action is called *initiator*, and the other part is called *responder*. For example, a mobile device is the initiator when it access data from the Internet, but it can also be the re-sponder if a (push) initiator sends out a message to the mobile device. Communication between initiator and responder is divided in three types of transaction *classes*, ranging from class 0 in which no acknowledgments are used, to class 2 that also send acknowl-edgments of results. The desired behavior the classes is shown in Figure 2(*i*).

In Figure 2(*ii*) the terminology for message signaling between layers in the WAP stack is illustrated. An upper layer requests (req) a service from the layer below, which then confirms (cnf) that the request has been handled. A message from a peer layer is indicated (ind) by the layer below and the upper layer response (res) to notify that the message is accepted. Some message types do not require response nor confirmation.

The data structures used to and from an upper layer in the WAP stack are called Service Data Units (SDUs). The WTP layer has its own peer messages, e.g. acknowl-edgment, and it conveys SDUs to and from its upper layers. The behavior of a WTP layer is specified in the WAP specification as a state machine. In practice, every new transaction is a new instance of the WTP state machine, and there can be many simul-taneous transactions.

The interfaces of a WAP stack layer are called Service Access Points (SAP). In this paper the Transport SAP (T-SAP), the Transaction SAP (TR-SAP), and the Session SAP (S-SAP) will be referenced.

Session Layer: The WSP layer is responsible for handling sessions in the WAP pro-tocol. A session is a collection of transactions from the same user that can be treated commonly. An example of a case when a session is convenient is when a user logs in to a Web server. When logged in, the session is used to authenticate subsequent requests.

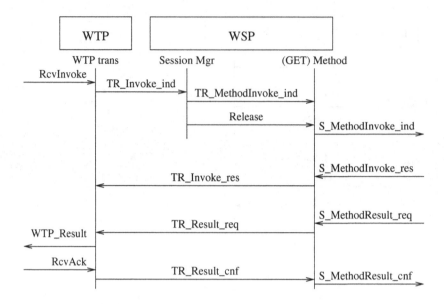

Fig. 3. Messages in the responder during a WSP GET request

If the session is disconnected (or aborted) all the transactions in the session will be aborted.

The session layer consists of two parts: a *Session Manager* that handles the connect and disconnect of a session, and a set of processes handling outstanding HTTP requests called *Methods*. For example, at a GET request a *GET-Method* process is spawned off to handle the request. A Method is associated with a WTP transaction and is terminated when the transaction terminates. In Figure 3, a sequence diagram shows WSP, and the underlying WTP layer, in a WAP responder stack during a successful GET request. Note how the Session Manager is only involved in the initialization of the WSP.

Transaction Layer: The WAP transaction layer handles the sending and re-sending of transactions. To separate transactions, each transaction is numbered with a unique sequence number, called *transaction identifier* (TID). New TIDs are created by the initiator by incrementing the last created TID value by one. The initiator can have several ongoing transactions with more than one responder, e.g., a server can push to several terminals. Therefore, a responder cannot be sure that each new transaction has a TID value incremented by exactly one.

The responder of a connection oriented session has a window of 2^{14} TIDs. The last TID value received from an initiator is saved in a variable named *lastTID*. The counter wraps around at $2^{15}-1$. When a new message arrives, it is directly accepted if the TID value is not increased more than 2^{14} times from *lastTID*. We will call such values *greater* than *lastTID*, and other values *less* than *lastTID*, except if the value is equal to *lastTID*.

If the bearer media reorders two messages so that the greater TID value arrives late, the later message is said to be an *out-of-order* message. When an out of order message arrives, the responder invokes a so-called *TID verification procedure* before it continues. The TID verification is performed by sending a special acknowledge message (with bit *TIDve* set). The initiator acknowledge (with bit *TIDok*) if it has an outstanding transaction with the same TID value.

If an initiator is out of synchronization with *lastTID* (e.g., after a reboot) it can avoid further TID verifications (using bit *TIDnew*). This forces a TID verification that will set *lastTID* to the TID of the *TIDnew* message. During TID verification no new transactions are started by the initiator, and the responder removes any old transactions.

3   Abstraction for Test Case Generation

As described, the TIDs of the messages play an important role in the WAP specification. An instance of the WAP protocol will typically make use of several TIDs from the domain 0 to $2^{15} - 1$, and a sliding window of size 2^{14}. Thus, the potential numbers of TID values will be infeasible for exhaustive model-based test-case generation — the generation algorithm will experience the so-called *state-space explosion problem* [Hol97]. To overcome this problem, previous applications of automatic verification techniques to the WAP protocol have limited the analysis to scenarios with only a single transaction [HJ04, GB00]. We will take a different approach and introduce an abstraction. It will allow us to deal with abstract TID values during the analysis of the model, while maintaining the concrete TID values so that concrete model traces can still be generated.

Concrete domain: We assume a set T of TID variables $t_0, \ldots, t_{N-1}$. To describe the semantics we use a *variable assignment* $v : T \rightarrow \{n \mid 0 \leq n \leq 2^{15}-1\} \cup \{\bot\}$, where $\bot$ represents the unassigned value. Initially all variables are unassigned. The variables can be compared with Boolean combinations of $t_i < t_j$ and $t_i \leq t_j$, and manipulated with the operations

$$
\begin{aligned}
t_i &= \textit{free} & v'(t_i) &= \bot \\
t_i &= t_j & v'(t_i) &= v(t_j) \\
t_i &= \textit{new}^+ & v'(t_i) &= \max(v) + 1 \\
t_i &= \textit{new}^- & v'(t_i) &= \min(v) - 1
\end{aligned}
$$

where v' is the resulting variable assignment, v the directly preceeding variable assignment, and $\max(v)$ and $\min(v)$ the maximum and minimum assigned integer values of all TIDs, respectively.

Abstract domain: We use a set A of abstract TID variables $a_0, \ldots, a_{N-1}$, and an abstract variable assignment $v_a : A \rightarrow \{n \mid 0 \leq n < N\} \cup \{\bot\}$. We assume that the set of abstract values is *tight* in the following sense: if $v_a(a_i) = k$ then there exists $v_a(a_j) = l$ for all $0 \leq l < k$.

Abstraction of Concrete TID values: We define the *abstraction function* $\alpha : T \rightarrow A$ to be the mapping, such that $\alpha(t_i) = 0$ if $\min(v) = v(t_i)$, $\alpha(t_i) < \alpha(t_j)$ if $v(t_i) < v(t_j)$, $\alpha(t_i) = \alpha(t_j)$ if $v(t_i) = v(t_j)$, $\alpha(t_i) = \bot$ if $v(t_i) = \bot$, and v_a is tight. A transition from the abstract state v_a to v'_a is possible if there exists a transition from v to v', $v_a = \alpha(v)$, and $v'_a = \alpha(v')$.

The proposed abstraction is sound in the sense that properties in the abstract state-space also hold in the concrete state-space. That is, if $v_a = \alpha(v)$, then the truth-value of $t_i < t_j$ or $t_i \leq t_j$ is the same for the corresponding abstract TIDs a_i and a_j. It can be shown that the abstract transition relation is *must* abstraction and thus under-approximates the concrete transition relation [LT88, BKY05].

Modeling and Analysis in UPPAAL: When modeling the WAP protocol, we shall use $t_i = new^+$, $t_i = t_j$, and $t_i = new^-$ to model assignment of new *correct* TID values, *existing* values, and values that are *out of order*, respectively. To implement the abstraction, we use UPPAAL's meta variables. Such variables are used to annotate models. They can be refered to in the model, but they are not considered when two states are compared during analysis. We declare the set of concrete TID variables T as a vector of meta variables, the set of abstract TID variables A as vector of ordinary integer variables, and apply the abstraction function to each state explored during state-space exploration[2]. In this way, the analysis will explore concrete states until the reachable abstract state-space is explored, while maintaining the concrete values to support generation of concrete test cases.

4   Testing Model

In this section, we describe our model of the WAP gateway. The model is emphasized on the software layers WTP and WSP. They have been modeled as detailed and close to the WAP specification as possible. Other parts of the gateway are modeled more abstractly, but without loss of externally observable behavior affecting the WTP and WSP layers. We have chosen to model the *connection oriented* version of the WAP protocol, where several outstanding transaction can be held together into a session. The model has been made with the intention to generate real system tests that can be executed over a physical connection. Obviously, the complexity of making this kind of system model and system test is much higher than to test each layer separately.

In Figure 4, an overview of the modeled automata and their conceptual connections is shown as a flow-graph. The nodes represent timed automata [AD94] and the edges synchronization channels or shared data, divided in two groups (with the small arrows indicating the direction of communication). The model is divided in two parts, the *gateway* model, and the *test environment* model. The test environment consists of the two automata Terminal and HTTP Sever. The gateway model is further divided in to a WTP part, a WSP part, and globally shared data and timers[3]. The WTP part consists of the service access point TSAP, two instances WTP0 and WTP1 of the WTP protocol, a WSP Session Manager, two instances Method 0 and Method 1 of the WSP methods, and a session service access point SSAP.

---

[2] We have implemented this in our UPPAAL CO√ER tool. The same affect can be achieved by annotating each edge in the model with a simple function, implementing the abstraction function.

[3] To improve the readability of Figure 4, we have omitted many edges to and from the automata Timer and Data Store.

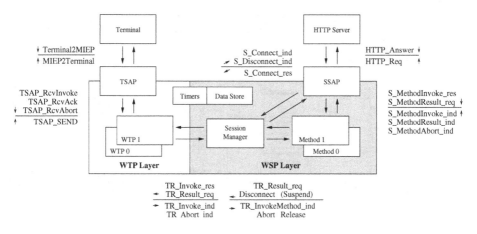

Fig. 4. Overview of the formal model

The idea of the model is to let the **Terminal** automaton model a mobile device that non-deterministically stimulates the gateway with input and receives its output. In a typical scenario, the Terminal requests a WML page from a web sever. The request goes through an instance of the WTP and WSP layers and further to a web sever. In case the page exists, it is sent back through the gateway, and is finally received in the Terminal. Such a scenario is depicted in Figure 3.

In the following, we briefly describe how the WAP gateway specification and the components in its environment have been modeled as a network of timed automata. Due to lack of space, several of the automata are not shown in detail in this paper, but can be found in [HP06].

4.1 Test Environment Model

The test environment consists of the two automata **Terminal** a **HTTP Server**. Messages from the terminal to the WAP gateway are modeled as the single synchronization **Terminal2MIEP**, and similar in the other direction (see Figure 4). When the synchronization occurs, a special set of global integer variables are assigned, which corresponds to the fields of the protocol headers, e.g., WTP Type, WTP Class, or WSP Connect. Our model is done so that any state preceding a **Terminal2MIEP** synchronization (similar in the other direction), contains all values of the variables that corresponds to fields of the modeled message. This is to facilitate the constructions of packets from model traces, which is needed in the later stage when traces are compiled in to concrete test cases.

As mentioned, another important design decision is to let the **Terminal** model initiate and control the whole interactions. A particular problem is to control the **HTTP server**. We have solved this by sending control messages encoded into the message content, from the terminal, all the way through the WAP gateway, to the **HTTP sever**. In this way, the **HTTP server** can be instructed to delay its response message, drop a message, or immediately return.

As the gateway model reacts to stimuli from **Terminal**, several instances of the WAP layers automata will become active simultaneously. We use a counter to keep track of

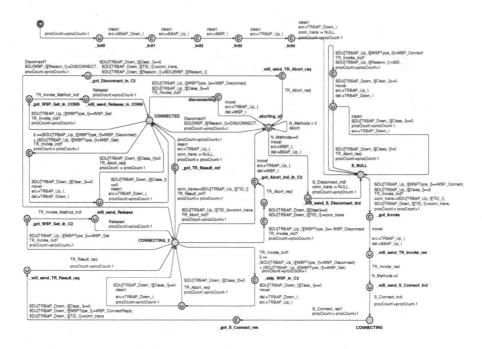

Fig. 5. The Session Manager automaton

the number of active automata in the gateway model that are not in a stable state, i.e., a state where it is idle and waiting for new input. The counter is used to restrict the Terminal from sending messages that will not be dealt with immediately. This scheme avoids unnecessary interleavings and reduces the state-space of the model.

How the TID Abstraction is modeled: In the Terminal automaton, TIDs are assigned when new PDUs are created, as described in Section 3. To use an existing TID value (i.e., to perform an assignment), or to free a TID variable (i.e., set it to $\perp$) is straightforward to model in UPPAAL. To model new^+ and new^-, we use two hidden variables MinTID and MaxTID that are initialized to $2^{14} - 1$ and 2^{14}, respectively. All TID variables t_i are initially $\perp$. The operation $t_i = new^+$ can now be modeled by assigning a variable ti the value of MaxTID followed by an incrementation of MaxTID, and dually for the operation $t_i = new^-$.

4.2 Gateway Model

The gateway model is a detailed timed automata description made with the intention to comply with the WAP specification as closely as possible. Communications between two layers are modeled as synchronization labels and an array of data representing the modeled fields values. All communications to or from WTP or WSP go via SAPs to mimic the real protocol.

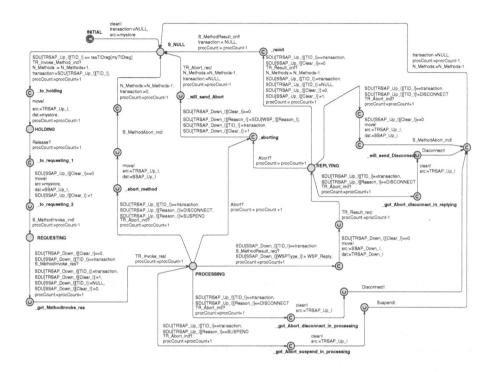

Fig. 6. The Method automaton

TSAP: As illustrated in Figure 4 the SAP below the WTP layer, called T-SAP, is modeled by automaton **TSAP** that converts the raw data fields sent over the Terminal2MIEP channel into signals that mimics a Transport SAP. In the upward direction, **TSAP** converts the WTP layer data into signals, e.g., RcvInvoke, RcvAck, and RcvAbort. In the downward direction **TSAP** merely copies the data to the environment (i.e., no headers to be added). The **TSAP** automaton also inspects the TID value and decides if the message should be delivered or dropped.

WTP layer: Two instances of the WTP layer are modeled, i.e., there can be two transactions active at the same time. An instance is activated when a message arrives with a TID that does not already exist in the layer. Successive messages with the same TID are directed to the activated instance. The WTP automata are named **WTP0** and **WTP1** and are instances of the same automaton template in UPPAAL. All messages from the WTP state machine of the WAP specification are modeled, including all types of aborts. The timers are also modeled, with the two intervals *acknowledge interval* A and *retry interval* R.

WSP layer: The WSP layer consists of two types of automata: session manager **Session Manager** shown in Figure 5, and two methods automata **Method0** and **Method1**, shown in Figure 6. The **Session Manager** is responsible for connections and disconnections of the session. It forwards incoming method invokes, e.g., when a WML page is requested. We model the GET method that, on the HTTP side, becomes a HTTP

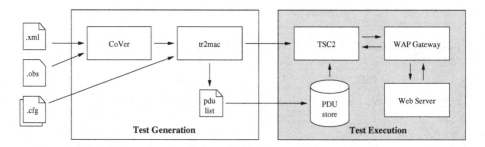

Fig. 7. Overview of the setup used for testing the WAP gateway

GET request. When a session is disconnected all methods are aborted. Each method has a corresponding outstanding transaction that it aborts. It is also possible to abort a individual method transaction without terminating the whole session.

SSAP: Above the WSP layer is the Session SAP. We model an automaton **SSAP** that mimics the gateway from the S-SAP to the communication with the HTTP server.

Timer: Timers are modeled by four instances of automaton **Timer**, two for each WTP layer automaton. A timer can be activated and deactivated by the WTP automaton. If a timer expires it sends a message to its WTP automaton.

Datastore: The automaton named **Datastore** manages data. Its memory is modeled as an array where the rows are "owned" by different automata. The columns represent fields in the PDUs. The **Datastore** automaton implements three convenient sub routines that can be used by the other automata in the gateway: **copy, clear,** and **move.** To not over-write data in an unintended way, the rows also include a **Clear** bit that is set when new data is allowed to be written.

5   Test Generation and Execution

The tool setup used for generating and executing tests at Ericsson is shown in Figure 7. The setup is divided in two parts, a test *generation* part for generating and transforming test cases into executable format, and a test *execution* part that executes the tests on the WAP gateway in a controlled computer network. In the following, we first describe the test criteria used as input to our test generation tool, then the test generation, and last how the tests were executed and some experiences.

5.1   Test Criteria

To specify how thorough a test suite should test a system, we select test cases following some given coverage criteria. Before presenting the criteria, we (informally) character-ize a stability property that will be used in all testing criteria. We say that the gateway model is in a *stable state* if all automata are in locations modeling idling states from which they need an (input) synchronization to proceed. In the system under test, this corresponds to a situation where the whole gateway is idle and waiting for some input from the environment, which implies that there are no transactions active in the gateway, and no other ongoing activity. We shall use a predicate named *stableState()* that is true only if the gateway model is in a stable state.

In Figure 8, the three coverage criteria used in this case study are formally specified as *observers with parameters* [BHJP05] [4].

Edge Coverage Observer: It is shown in Figure $8(i)$. Assume that P is a set of automata. The expression $edge(P)$ returns a value only if an automaton (in the set P) is active in a transition. The parameter E is then assigned to the edge of the active process in P. The observer then reaches state *gotEdge(E)*, where E is the assigned edge. The *gotEdge(E)* location has a true loop which allows it to stay in the location forever. When the *stableState()* macro becomes true, the observer reaches location *done(E)*, indicating that the edge E is covered.

Intuitively, the edge coverage observer specifies that a test suite should cover as many edges E of the automata in P as possible, given that after every E a state satisfying *stableState()* is reached. If the set P includes two or more automata from the same automaton template, we assume that $edge(P)$ is the same identifier for both automata if the same edge is traversed. That is, the edge is considered to be covered if it is traversed by any instance of the template.

Switch Coverage Observer: The observer in Figure $8(ii)$ is similar to the edge coverage observer, but it specifies that any two adjacent edges in the same automaton instance should be covered. In this case, it is crucial that the edges are from the same automaton. Therefore, we require that the automaton P that takes the first edge E, must also take the second edge $E2$.

Projection Coverage Observer: Figure $8(iii)$ shows an observer that specifies a projection criterion. It specifies that a pair of locations from the WTP layer, and the WSP layer should be covered. The macro *stackProj(WTP,WSP)* returns a pair of locations $(L, L1)$, where L is from a WTP automaton, and $L1$ is from a WSP automaton. It is further required that L and $L1$ are associated with the same transaction.

5.2 Test Generation

The problem of generating test cases is solved by the UPPAAL CO√ER tool, which extends the model-checking tool UPPAAL with capabilities for generating test suites [5]. It takes as input the timed automata model of the WAP gateway described in the previous section, and a coverage criterion specified as a parameterized observer (.xml and .obs in Figure 7, respectively). The output of UPPAAL CO√ER is a set of abstract test cases (or test specifications) represented as timed traces, i.e., alternating sequences of states, and delays or discrete transitions, in the output format of the UPPAAL tool.

---

[4] Due to lack of space, we refer the reader to [BHJP05] for a detailed description of the observer language.

[5] For more information about the UPPAAL CO√ER tool, see the web page http://user. it.uu.se/~hessel/CoVer/

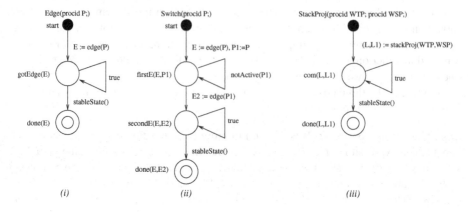

Fig. 8. The three observers used in the case study

Results: Table 1 shows the result of the test suite generation. Each row of the table gives the numbers for a given coverage criteria and the automata it covers (used as input). For example, WTP denotes **WTP0** and **WTP1** for which the tool has found 63 coverage items, i.e., edges in the WTP template. To cover the WTP edges a test suite of 16 test cases is produced. The number of transitions of the test suite is 1562. The test suite interacts with the system 92 times, i.e., 92 PDUs are communicated. We will discuss the rightmost column in the next subsection.

The table shows the result of the other test criteria as well. We note that, as expected, the switch coverage criterion requires many more test cases to be executed than edge coverage. We also note that it is more efficient to execute the test suites covering all templates at once, i.e., WTP, Session Manager, and Method, than to execute all the individual test suites. For example, the test suite with edge coverage in all templates sends 142 PDUs, whereas the sum of sent PDUs in the individual suites is 225. For switch coverage the numbers are 467 compared to 555 PDUs.

Table 1. Test generation and execution results

| Criteria | | Items | Test suite | | Test script | Failed tests |
Observer	Templates		cases	trans	PDUs	
Edge	WTP	63	16	1562	92	1
	Session Manager	46	12	1058	57	1
	Method	31	10	1497	76	0
	All	140	28	2548	142	2
Switch	WTP	109	44	5082	313	2
	Session Manager	76	28	3020	166	7
	Method	37	9	1495	76	0
	All	222	74	8129	467	10
StackProj	All	101	21	2129	114	0

5.3   Test Execution

The timed traces representing abstract test cases are converted to executable script programs by the tr2mac tool [Vil05], which also takes two configuration files as input (.cfg in Figure 7). In a trace, each action label and combination of variable values in the associated state, represents the parameters of a PDU to be sent or received, or a null operation (all internal actions are mapped to null operations). The files .cfg describe how to perform the translation for a given UPPAAL model, i.e., which labels to consider as external and where to put the state variable values in the PDUs. Each delay of a timed trace naturally represents a delay to be performed by the test program. The tr2mac program accumulates the delays between non-null operations and inserts the result in the script program.

The output of tr2mac is a script program that can be executed by the TSC2 test environment, and a list of partially instantiated PDUs that will be needed. The PDUs are fully instantiated at the time the script is executed in the test harness. The TID values and information about the specific test environment, e.g., the IP addresses, are filled in at execution time. In this way, many PDUs can be reused between different test cases (and the set of needed PDUs will eventually become stable).

When TSC2 executes a script, all listed PDUs must be available in the PDU store[6]. TSC2 will send PDUs to the WAP gateway and check that the expected response appear at the right time points. If this is not the case, TSC2 will report the discrepancy to a log file, and proceed with the next test script. During testing, TSC2 acts in place of the mobile device (i.e. the terminal). As described in the previous sections, the mobile device (and thus TSC2 when executing the generated test cases) thus controls the behavior of the surrounding computer network. The behavior of the web server is controlled by sending parameters in the PDUs that are interpreted as commands by a php script running on the web server.

Results: The test cases presented in the Table 1 have been executed on an in-house version of the WAP gateway at Ericsson. As shown in the rightmost column of Table 1 most of the test case went well. A few tests failed due to two discrepancies — one in the WTP automata and one in the Session Manager automaton.

The first discrepancy is in the WSP layer. The session manager is modeled to not accept any new *Connect* messages. Reading the WAP specification carefully, after finding this discrepancy, we conclude that it is allowed to accept new *Connect* messages and replace the current session if the layer above agrees. This problem in the model explains the discrepancy found with the test suite covering the edges of Session Manager, and the seven discrepancies found when executing the test suite with switch coverage in the Session Manager.

The second discrepancy is a behavior present in our model of the WTP layer but not in the tested WAP gateway. We found that no acknowledge is sent from the WTP state, RESULT_WAIT, when an (WTP) invoke is retransmitted and an acknowledgment has already been sent. The retransmission is required in the WTP specification [For01] but

---

[6] Currently, non-existing listed PDUs must be manually created. It is possible to automate also this step.

not performed by the implementation. This discrepancy was found both when running test suites covering the edge and switch criteria of the WTP template.

We also observe that the two discrepancies were both found when executing the edge covering test suites — one in the test suite for WTP, and the other in the test suite for Session Manager. The test suite with switch coverage finds the same discrepancies, but many times (as many as the erroneous edges appear in some switch). The suite with projection coverage did not find any discrepancies.

6 Conclusion

We have presented a complete test bed where test cases are automatically produced and executed, from a formal model and coverage criteria formally described as observers. The validity of the tests has been proven in a case study where test cases have been executed in a real test environment at Ericsson. The test generation techniques and the coverage criteria used have industrial strength as complete test suites have been generated for an industrial application, and discrepancies have been found between the model and the real system.

We have also presented an abstraction technique that can be used in models making use of sequence numbers with large domains. It preserves the relations needed when comparing sequence numbers in the WAP protocol, while the size of the analyzed state space is significantly reduced. We believe that the abstraction will be useful for specifying and analyzing models of other protocols.

Acknowledgment

We thank the other members of the ASTEC AuToWay project at Ericsson and Uppsala University: Tomas Aurell, Anders Axelssson, Johan Blom, Joel Dutt, Bengt Jonsson, Natalie Jost, John Orre, Payman Tavanaye Rashid, and Per Vilhelmsson.

References

[AD94]   R. Alur and D. L. Dill. A theory of timed automata. *Theoretical Computer Science*, 126(2):183–235, 1994.

[BFG+00]   Marius Bozga, Jean-Claude Fernandez, Lucian Ghirvu, Claude Jard, Thierry Jéron, Alain Kerbrat, Pierre Morel, and Laurent Mounier. Verification and test generation for the sscop protocol. *Science of Computer Programming*, 36(1):27–52, 2000.

[BHJP05]   J. Blom, A. Hessel, B. Jonsson, and P. Pettersson. Specifying and generating test cases using observer automata. In J. Gabowski and B. Nielsen, editors, *Proc. 4th International Workshop on Formal Approaches to Testing of Software 2004 (FATES'04)*, volume 3395 of *Lecture Notes in Computer Science*, pages 125–139. Springer–Verlag, 2005.

[BKY05]   Thomas Ball, Orna Kupferman, and Greta Yorsh. Abstraction for falsification. Technical Report MSR-TR-2005-50, Microsoft Research, June 2005.

[For01]   WAP Forum. Wireless transaction protocol, version 10-jul-2001. online, 2001. http://www.wapforum.org/.

[GB00]   S. Gordon and J. Billington. Analysing th wap class 2 wireless transaction protocol
            using colored petri nets. In M. Nielsen and D. Simpson, editors, *ICATPN 2000*, vol-
            ume 1825 of *Lecture Notes in Computer Science*, pages 207–226. Springer–Verlag,
            2000.

[HJ04]   Yu-Tong He and R. Janicki. Verification of the wap transaction layer. In *Software
            Engineering and Formal Methods*, pages 366–375, 2004.

[HLSU02]   H.S. Hong, I. Lee, O. Sokolsky, and H. Ural. A temporal logic based theory of test
            coverage. In J.-P. Katoen and P. Stevens, editors, *Tools and Algorithms for the Con-
            struction and Analysis of Systems : 8th International Conference, (TACAS'02)*, vol-
            ume 2280 of *Lecture Notes in Computer Science*, pages 327–341. Springer–Verlag,
            2002.

[Hol97]   G.J. Holzmann. The model checker SPIN. *IEEE Trans. on Software Engineering*,
            SE-23(5):279–295, May 1997.

[HP06]   Anders Hessel and Paul Pettersson. Model-based testing of a wap gateway: an in-
            dustrial case-study. Technical Report 2006-045, Department of Information Tech-
            nology, Uppsala University, 2006.

[LMN05]   K. G. Larsen, M. Mikucionis, and B. Nielsen. Online testing of real-time systems
            using uppaal. In J. Gabowski and B. Nielsen, editors, *Proc. 4th International Work-
            shop on Formal Approaches to Testing of Software 2004 (FATES'04)*, volume 3395
            of *Lecture Notes in Computer Science*, pages 79–94. Springer–Verlag, 2005.

[LMNS05]   Kim G. Larsen, Marius Mikucionis, Brian Nielsen, and Arne Skou. Testing real-
            time embedded software using uppaal-tron - an industrial case study. In *Proc. of the
            5th ACM International Conference on Embedded Software*, 2005.

[LPY97]   K. G. Larsen, P. Pettersson, and W. Yi. UPPAAL in a Nutshell. *Int. Journal on
            Software Tools for Technology Transfer*, 1(1–2):134–152, October 1997.

[LT88]   K.G. Larsen and G.B. Thomsen. A modal process logic. In *Proc. 3rd Int. Symp. on
            Logic in Computer Science*, 1988.

[Tre96]   J. Tretmans. Test generation with inputs, outputs, and quiescence. In T. Margaria
            and B. Steffen, editors, *Tools and Algorithms for the Construction and Analysis of
            Systems: 2nd Int. Workshop (TACAS'96)*, volume 1055 of *Lecture Notes in Com-
            puter Science*, pages 127–146. Springer–Verlag, 1996.

[Vil05]   Per Vilhelmsson. A test case translation tool - from abstract test sequences to con-
            crete test programs. Technical report, Department of Information Technology, Up-
            psala University, 2005.

Heuristics for ioco-Based Test-Based Modelling

(Extended Abstract)

Tim A.C. Willemse*

Institute for Computing and Information Sciences (ICIS)
Radboud University Nijmegen, The Netherlands
timw@cs.ru.nl

Abstract. Model-based conformance testing provides a mathematically sound technique to assess the quality of systems and check the correctness of a system with respect to a model. Most systems, however, are built or modified without documenting the (new) specifications, thereby limiting the use of model-based testing techniques. In this paper, we describe a method to obtain models automatically from an existing system, using model-based testing techniques relying on **ioco**-based testing. These models are useful for e.g. regression testing, or for the testing of different configurations of systems. We illustrate the effectiveness of our approach using a case-study in which we test mutants of the system against models that have been automatically extracted from the (correct) system.

1 Introduction

Much of today's systems engineering is predominantly evolutionary in nature. The bulk of the systems are modifications of existing systems. These modifications should in general lead to improvements of the quality of the system. An important tool in assuring that this is indeed the case is *regression testing*. Regression testing tests whether these modifications have no adverse effect on those parts of the systems that should not have been affected by the changes. Testing is mostly a manual and labour intensive process, often deprived of effective automation, leading to high costs and sometimes mediocre product quality. Current insights indicate that the testing effort typically consumes up to 50% of the total budget that is spent in developing a system, with regression testing consuming an almost disproportionately large amount [5,8] of the total budget.

Model-based testing is a mathematically sound analysis technique that is used to assess the level of quality of a system. The key idea is to use mathematical models of a system to automatically generate and execute tests. Proponents of the technique are quick to point out the benefits of this approach: the models are easier to understand and maintain, amenable to verification, and are less prone to complex changes, while the automation that can be achieved goes well beyond the mere automatic execution of manually crafted test cases.

While the technique has been shown to work well on real-life systems, it has its limitations. A major obstacle in applying the technique is rooted in the necessity to

---

* This work was carried out as part of the TANGRAM project under the responsibility of the Embedded Systems Institute. Tangram is partially supported by the Netherlands Ministry of Economic Affairs under grant TSIT2026.

L. Brim et al. (Eds.): FMICS and PDMC 2006, LNCS 4346, pp. 132–147, 2007.

have mathematical models of a system to start with. In practice these required models are often unavailable. Obtaining the models *a posteriori* from alternative sources, such as informal documentation and by conducting interviews, *etcetera*, is time consuming, or even impossible (e.g. for third-party systems or legacy systems). As a result, model-based testing is left without its engine.

The techniques we outline in this paper (collectively called test-based modelling techniques) are a step in the direction of applying model-based testing tools to many systems for which it is currently hard to obtain models. Our approach leans on the ideas from machine learning, such as initiated by Angluin [1]; it uses experiments to obtain *partial* models from running systems (i.e., actual implementations). While these models are useless for testing the same system again (when the learning is done properly, all tests should result in the verdict *pass*), they are valuable for other purposes, such as for regression testing or for testing different configurations of the same system.

The contributions of this paper are twofold: first, we provide an approximation-based basic algorithm, together with a set of heuristics, for constructing a model of a system based on counter-examples found by **ioco**-based model-based testing. This algorithm relies on a representation of the models using a subclass of suspension automata [11], called *valid* suspension automata. We show that in the **ioco**-setting, valid suspension automata have the exact same testing power as Labelled Transition Systems. Secondly, we have tested the hypothesis that a constructed model can effectively be used for regression testing and/or for testing of different configurations of the same system. This is demonstrated by running a prototype implementation of our algorithm on the *conference protocol*. The conference protocol is a well-known, mutant-based, benchmarking problem for testing (see e.g. [2]). The overall effectiveness of our approach is attested by the fact that 85% of all mutants of the correct system can be detected. Although the idea of using models, extracted from an implementation, for regression testing is not new (see e.g. [7]), to our knowledge, ours is the first study that actually quantifies the effectiveness of such an approach by means of mutant testing.

This paper is organised as follows. In Section 2, the testing theory **ioco** is outlined. In Section 3, we introduce our *test-based modelling* algorithm. Section 4 describes three heuristics to make the algorithm of Section 3 tractable in practice. Section 5 demonstrates the techniques using a case study. We conclude our contribution in Section 6.

Related Work. Berg *et al* [3] are among the few to have studied the effectiveness and applicability of Angluin's learning algorithm, and an optimisation thereof. The studied systems are generally small (up to 100 states). The authors conclude that the performance of Angluin's algorithm on prefix-closed automata comes close to its worst-case complexity, which they find disappointing, since reactive systems can usually be modelled using prefix-closed automata. Performance-wise, they remark that Angluin's algorithm has long execution times and a huge memory consumption. In [3], the information that is needed as input for Angluin's algorithm is extracted from formal models; this contrasts our experiments, which are conducted on real implementations from which we learn on-the-fly. Note that this also explains our long run-times when compared to [3].

Hungar *et al* [6,7] and also Margaria *et al* [9] build their work around Angluin's learning algorithm. Several domain-specific optimisations over this basic algorithm are discussed. The optimisations are fuelled by expert (human) knowledge. Such knowledge involves information concerning the symmetry of components and the independence of actions, and techniques to reduce the number of redundant membership queries that are generated by Angluin's algorithm. While these techniques are developed within the framework of testing of Finite-State Machines, most techniques described in these works seem complementary to the techniques we describe in this paper and it is very likely that these can be combined in some form.

Peled *et al* [10] advocate a different approach, combining model checking, testing and automata learning. Logical properties, given by domain experts, are checked against a model. Counter-examples are subsequently checked against the actual system and may lead to improvements of the model or to documented faults. FSM-based conformance testing is used when no counter-examples are found; the test outcome can again lead to a modified model. Related to this approach is the tool VeriSoft [4] by Godefroid, which can be used to verify *concurrent systems*. VeriSoft usually requires that all components of the concurrent system that is verified are deterministic. For the verification, it relies on model checking techniques, rather than testing techniques.

Most works are based on FSM-based testing, which usually relies on the assumption that the implementation behaves deterministically and/or has a finite number of states; our assumptions with respect to the system are more liberal, i.e. our technique can also deal with non-deterministic systems with infinite state spaces. Furthermore, our techniques do not require human intellect to drive the exploration technique, in contrast to the approaches using model checking techniques, which require interesting properties to be given by a human user.

2   Formal Testing Theory

The testing theory, used in this paper is based on *refusal testing* for Labelled Transition Systems. We briefly introduce the basic mathematical ingredients and the conformance relation **ioco** [11]. Most terminology is taken from [11].

Definition 1. *A labelled transition system (LTS) is a four-tuple* $\langle S, s_0, Act, \rightarrow \rangle$, *where S is a nonempty set of states, $s_0 \in S$ is the initial state, and, Act is a finite set of actions. The special action $\tau \notin Act$ denotes the* unobservable event; *we write Act_τ for $Act \cup \{\tau\}$. The relation $\rightarrow \subseteq S \times Act_\tau \times S$ is the transition relation; we write $s \xrightarrow{a} s'$ rather than $(s, a, s') \in \rightarrow$, and $\exists s' \in S. \ s \xrightarrow{a} s'$ is abbreviated to $s \xrightarrow{a}$. We use the name of the LTS and its initial state interchangeably.*

We restrict ourselves to LTSs that are *strongly converging*, i.e. have no infinite sequence of τ actions. The set of all LTSs over actions Act is henceforth denoted $\mathcal{L}(Act)$. We often distinguish between *input actions* Act_I and *output actions* Act_U, in which case we require $Act_I \cap Act_U = \emptyset$. We denote the set of all LTSs with inputs Act_I and outputs Act_U by $\mathcal{L}(Act_I, Act_U)$; we implicitly assume $Act = Act_I \cup Act_U$. For the remainder of this section, let $L = \langle S, s_0, Act, \rightarrow \rangle \in \mathcal{L}(Act_I, Act_U)$.

A set of actions $A \subseteq Act$ is a *refusal* of a state $s \in S$ when $\forall a \in A \cup \{\tau\}. \ s \xrightarrow{a} \not\rightarrow$, and we say that s *suspends on* A. For each state s of L that suspends on Act_U, we add a self-loop $s \xrightarrow{\delta} s$ to L; formally $\delta \notin \text{Act}$. We define Act_δ as $\text{Act} \cup \{\delta\}$. A state that suspends on Act_U is said to be *quiescent*.

Generalised transitions $\Longrightarrow \subseteq S \times \text{Act}_\delta^* \times S$ are given by the least set satisfying:

1. $s \xRightarrow{\epsilon} s$, with $s \in S$,
2. $s \xRightarrow{\sigma} s'$ if $s \xRightarrow{\sigma} s''$ and $s'' \xrightarrow{\tau} s'$, with $s, s', s'' \in S$ and $\sigma \in \text{Act}_\delta^*$,
3. $s \xRightarrow{\sigma a} s'$ if $s \xRightarrow{\sigma} s''$ and $s'' \xrightarrow{a} s'$, with $s, s', s'' \in S$, $\sigma \in \text{Act}_\delta^*$ and $a \in \text{Act}_\delta$.

We abbreviate $\exists s' \in S. \ s \xRightarrow{\sigma} s'$ with $s \xRightarrow{\sigma}$ and $s \not\xRightarrow{\sigma}$ abbreviates not $s \xRightarrow{\sigma}$. We define the following shorthands for all $n \in \mathbb{N}$, $s \in S$, $S' \subseteq S$ and $\sigma \in \text{Act}_\delta^*$:

1. $init(s) = \{a \in \text{Act}_\tau \mid s \xrightarrow{a} \}$,
2. $s\text{-}traces(s) = \{\sigma \in \text{Act}_\delta^* \mid s \xRightarrow{\sigma} \}$,
3. $s\text{-}traces_n(s) = \{ \sigma \in s\text{-}traces(s) \mid |\sigma| < n\}$,
4. $traces(s) = \text{Act}^* \cap s\text{-}traces(s)$,
5. $der(s) = \{s' \mid \exists \sigma \in \text{Act}^*. \ s \xRightarrow{\sigma} s'\}$,
6. $S' \ after \ \sigma = \{s' \mid \exists s \in S'. \ s \xRightarrow{\sigma} s'\}$. We write $s \ after \ \sigma$ rather than $\{s\} \ after \ \sigma$.

We say that the behaviour starting in a state s is *deterministic* if:

$$\forall \sigma \in traces(s). \ \forall t, t' \in s \ after \ \sigma. \ t = t' \tag{1}$$

We say that L is *input-enabled* when:

$$\forall s' \in der(s_0). \ \forall a \in \text{Act}_I. \ s' \xRightarrow{a} \tag{2}$$

$L \in \mathcal{L}(\text{Act}_I, \text{Act}_U)$ is called an *input/output transition system* (IOTS) when L is input-enabled. The set of all IOTSs over inputs Act_I and outputs Act_U is denoted $\mathcal{IO}(\text{Act}_I, \text{Act}_U)$.

Conformance Testing is the act of assessing whether an implementation of a system does what is prescribed by a specification of the system. We focus on a conformance relation for dynamic behaviours, called **ioco**. Let $S' \subseteq S$. We denote the set of outputs —including quiescence— that can be observed from states in S', by $out(S')$:

$$out(S') = \{x \in \text{Act}_U \mid \exists s \in S'. \ x \in init(s)\} \cup \{\delta \mid \exists s \in S'. \ s \xrightarrow{\delta} s\} \tag{3}$$

The conformance relation **ioco** is defined as follows:

Definition 2. *Let $L \in \mathcal{L}(\text{Act}_I, \text{Act}_U)$ be a specification, and $I \in \mathcal{IO}(\text{Act}_I, \text{Act}_U)$ an implementation. I is a **ioco**-correct implementation of L, denoted I **ioco** L, when:*

$$\forall \sigma \in s\text{-}traces(L). \ out(I \ after \ \sigma) \subseteq out(L \ after \ \sigma) \tag{4}$$

Example 1. As an example of the **ioco**-implementation relation, we consider the two input-output transition systems $L_1, L_2 \in \mathcal{IO}(\{m?\}, \{c!, t!\})$, depicted in Fig. 1. Both model a coffee-vending machine, where $m?$ represents the insertion of money, $c!$ represents coffee and $t!$ represents tea. We find that L_1 **ioco** L_2 (i.e. an implementation may be more selective in its output), but not L_2 **ioco** L_1 (i.e. an implementation may not produce unpredictable outputs). Note that by removing transition $t!$ from L_1, L_1 **ioco** L_2 no longer holds, because we then introduce a possibility to observe quiescence in L_1, which is not allowed by L_2.

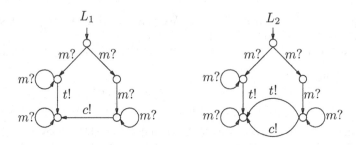

Fig. 1. Two input-output transitions systems

Since the model for the implementation I is not necessarily known, proving that I **ioco** L holds is usually not feasible, which is why *tests* are often derived from L that can be executed on the running implementation I to obtain confidence that I **ioco** L holds (or not). Tretmans [11] provides a detailed study of **ioco**, and also gives a sound and complete test case derivation algorithm for testing for **ioco** conformance. This algorithm underlies the tool TorX [2]. Note that the completeness result says that a test can be derived to detect any non-conformance, not that it *will* be detected.

Testing for **ioco**-correctness is in practice not exhaustive, since e.g. infinite behaviours of a system (if present) are never tested, due to the finite nature of the testing activity. We weaken general **ioco** to n-bounded **ioco** which makes the finiteness in depth explicit.

Definition 3. *Let $L \in \mathcal{L}(Act_I, Act_U)$ be a specification and let $I \in \mathcal{IO}(Act_I, Act_U)$ be an implementation. Let $n \in \mathbb{N}$ be an arbitrary natural number. We say that I is an n-bounded **ioco**-correct implementation, denoted I n-**ioco** L, when:*

$$\forall \sigma \in \text{s-traces}_n(L). \text{ out}(I \text{ after } \sigma) \subseteq \text{out}(L \text{ after } \sigma) \tag{5}$$

n-Bounded **ioco**-correctness guarantees that all behaviours of the implementation which are of length smaller than n are followed by an observation that is permitted by the specification. Behaviours of length n or larger are ignored.

3 Test-Based Modelling

In practice, most systems (e.g. legacy systems and third party components), do not come with an adequate (in)formal specification, which means that model-based testing techniques cannot be applied. Theoretically, this problem could be solved by employing *automata learning* techniques, such as Angluin's learning algorithm [1], to obtain these models. However, to be industrially applicable as a technique, a practical learning algorithm should be able to deal with systems that have very large state spaces, usually even infinite ones (which prohibits the use of most FSM-based techniques), Angluin's algorithm currently seems to be unfit for such systems [3].

Most research focuses on optimising Angluin's algorithm. We take a different approach, one that is orthogonal to the representation problem that is solved by Angluin's algorithm. In Section 3.3, we outline our test-based modelling algorithm, which can be used to obtain a *partial* model from a system. The algorithm relies on **ioco**-based test techniques. In Section 4, we discuss three heuristics that make the algorithm of Section 3.3 applicable for industrially sized systems.

3.1 Representing Models: Valid Suspension Automata

The non-deterministic behaviour of a system is a major source of complexity when learning its model by experimenting. A straightforward determinisation of the learnt model is in general impossible without compromising **ioco** conformance. We therefore recall the definition of *suspension automata* (SA) [11].

Suspension automata are deterministic LTSs with explicit inputs, outputs and a quiescence label δ, which is considered to be an output, and no τ-transitions. We denote the set of all SAs over inputs Act_I and outputs Act_U by $\mathcal{L}_\delta(\mathrm{Act}_I, \mathrm{Act}_U)$. We have $\mathcal{L}_\delta(\mathrm{Act}_I, \mathrm{Act}_U) \subseteq \mathcal{L}(\mathrm{Act}_I, \mathrm{Act}_U \cup \{\delta\})$. Tretmans [11] describes a transformation $\Delta{:}\mathcal{L}(\mathrm{Act}_I, \mathrm{Act}_U) \to \mathcal{L}_\delta(\mathrm{Act}_I, \mathrm{Act}_U)$ that satisfies the following property:

Theorem 1 (Tretmans [11]). *Let $L \in \mathcal{L}(\mathrm{Act}_I, \mathrm{Act}_U)$ be a specification, and let $\Delta(L)$ be its SA, with initial state s_δ. Then, for all implementations I:*

$$I \textbf{ ioco } L \text{ iff } \forall \sigma \in traces(s_\delta).\ out(I \text{ after } \sigma) \subseteq out(s_\delta \text{ after } \sigma) \tag{6}$$

The implications are that we can use the suspension automaton obtained from a specification when testing for **ioco**-conformance instead of the specification itself. We write I **ioco** M for a suspension automaton M when I is **ioco**-conform to a specification represented by M. There is, however, a large class of suspension automata that do not correspond to specifications given by LTSs, as illustrated below.

Example 2. Consider suspension automaton M_1 from Fig. 2. M_1 models an anomalous system: it produces an output *after* an observation of quiescence, and, it has a state in which the system is neither quiescent, nor does it produce output. Next, consider

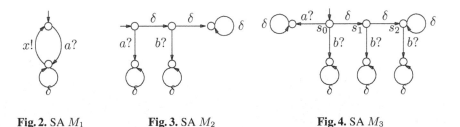

Fig. 2. SA M_1 **Fig. 3.** SA M_2 **Fig. 4.** SA M_3

suspension automaton M_2 (Fig. 3). The trace $\delta\ b?$ is a valid trace in M_2, the trace $b?$ is not. Hence, here the observation of quiescence *adds* new possibilities, which is impossible in SAs derived from LTSs. Further, M_2 is "instable" after the observation of quiescence: M_2 allows for a $b?$ after one observation of δ, but not after two observations of δ. M_3 on the other hand, does represent the behaviour of an SA that could have been the result from translating an LTS to an SA.   □

In view of the preceding example, we introduce the following terminology. Let $M = \langle S, s_\delta, \text{Act}_\delta, \rightarrow \rangle \in \mathcal{L}_\delta(\text{Act}_I, \text{Act}_U)$.

1. M is *non-blocking* when:
    $$\forall s \in der(s_\delta). \; \exists a \in \text{Act}_U \cup \{\delta\}. \; s \xrightarrow{a}$$
2. M is *quiescent reducible* when:
    $$\forall s \in der(s_\delta). \; \forall \sigma \in \text{Act}_\delta^*. \; \delta\sigma \in traces(s) \Rightarrow \sigma \in traces(s)$$
3. M is *anomaly-free* when:
    $$\forall s \in der(s_\delta). \; \forall a \in \text{Act}_U. \; \delta a \notin traces(s)$$
4. M is *stable* when:
    $$\forall s \in der(s_\delta). \; \exists \Sigma \subseteq \text{Act}_\delta^*. \; \forall \sigma \in \delta^+. \; \forall s' \in S. \; s \xRightarrow{\sigma} s' \Rightarrow traces(s') = \Sigma$$

Intuitively, M is stable whenever the behaviours *after* observing quiescence are not changed by new observations of quiescence: if $s \xrightarrow{\delta} s' \xrightarrow{\delta} s''$, then $traces(s') = traces(s'')$. When M is non-blocking, quiescent reducible, anomaly-free and stable, we say that M is *valid*, otherwise M is *not valid*. For LTSs and their suspension automata we have the following result:

Proposition 1. *Let L be an LTS. Then $\Delta(L)$ is valid.*

Proof. In order to show validity of $\Delta(L)$, we must show that $\Delta(L)$ is non-blocking, quiescent-reducible, anomaly-free and stable. Each property easily follows from the definition of the translation function Δ. ☐

This means that validity is a requirement that is respected by all suspension automata that can be derived by translating LTSs. The following theorem states that for each valid suspension automaton we can find at least one LTS, proving that for testing, valid SAs can be used rather than LTSs.

Theorem 2. *Let $M \in \mathcal{L}_\delta(\text{Act}_I, \text{Act}_U)$ be a valid SA. Then, there is an LTS $L \in \mathcal{L}(\text{Act}_I, \text{Act}_U)$, such that for all implementations I:*

$$I \text{ ioco } M \text{ iff } I \text{ ioco } L$$

Proof (Sketch). Let $M = \langle S, s_\delta, \text{Act}_\delta, \rightarrow \rangle$ be a valid SA. We define the relation $\sqsubseteq$ on states of an SA as $s \sqsubseteq t$ iff $traces(s) \subseteq traces(t)$, and we define the equivalence relation $\equiv$ on states as $s \equiv t$ iff $s \sqsubseteq t$ and $t \sqsubseteq s$. Let $L = \langle S_{/\equiv}, [s_\delta]_\equiv, \text{Act}, \rightarrow_L \rangle$ be an LTS with state-space $S_{/\equiv}$ consisting of $\equiv$-equivalence classes of S, initial state $[s_\delta]_\equiv$ the $\equiv$-equivalence class of s_δ and $\rightarrow_L$ defined as:

1. if $x \in \text{Act}$ and $s \xrightarrow{x} t$, then also $[s]_\equiv \xrightarrow{x}_L [t]_\equiv$,
2. if $s \xrightarrow{\delta} t$ and $s \not\equiv t$ then $[s]_\equiv \xrightarrow{\tau}_L [t]_\equiv$.

We refer to L as the *canonical specification*, induced by SA M. Then L satisfies the following three properties:

1. $traces(s_\delta) = s\text{-}traces([s_\delta]_\equiv)$,
2. for all $\sigma \in \text{Act}_\delta^*$, $out(s \text{ after } \sigma) = out([s]_\equiv \text{ after } \sigma)$,
3. for all $\sigma \in \text{Act}_\delta^*$, $\sigma \in traces(s)$ iff $out(s \text{ after } \sigma) \neq \emptyset$.

Combined, these properties lead to $I \text{ ioco } M$ iff $I \text{ ioco } L$ for all implementations I. ☐

3.2 Learning Hypothesis and Oracles

ioco-Based testing is rooted in several assumptions, collectively known as the *testing hypothesis*, the most important assumption being that implementations can be modelled using input/output transition systems [11]. These assumptions make testing practically applicable. We strengthen the testing hypothesis with the following assumption, leading to the *learning hypothesis*:

> all output actions that can follow an experiment (sequence of inputs and outputs) can, and will be observed by conducting the same experiment a finite (*a priori* known) number of times.

Note that the learning hypothesis quantifies the fairness of the resolution of a non-deterministic choice in a system, without attaching real values to this resolution. The learning hypothesis provides us with a powerful oracle: the system-under-test itself.

3.3 Algorithm

Let $I \in \mathcal{IO}(\text{Act}_I, \text{Act}_U)$ be an (unknown model of an) implementation of a system. The algorithm presented in Fig. 5 (hereafter referred to as the TBM-algorithm) automatically constructs a suspension automaton $\mathcal{H} \in \mathcal{L}_\delta(\text{Act}_I, \text{Act}_U)$, such that I **ioco** $\mathcal{H}$ holds on termination of the algorithm. First we define the following shorthands:

$$d\text{-}traces(s) = \{\sigma \in traces(s) \mid \forall s' \in s \text{ } after \text{ } \sigma. \forall a \in \text{Act}_U \cup \{\delta\}. \text{ } s' \not\xrightarrow{a}\}$$

$$\begin{cases} q\text{-}red(epsilon) = \epsilon \\ q\text{-}red(\delta \, \sigma) \quad = \sigma \\ q\text{-}red(a \, \sigma) \quad = a \, q\text{-}red(\sigma) \end{cases}$$

Theorem 3. *On termination of the TBM-algorithm, with inputs $N \in \mathbb{N}$ and $I \in \mathcal{IO}(\text{Act}_I, \text{Act}_U)$, a valid SA $\mathcal{H}$ has been constructed that satisfies I **ioco** $\mathcal{H}$.*

Proof (Sketch). Implementation I can be modelled as a valid SA (Proposition 1). For anomaly-freeness, stability and quiescent reducibility, we observe that the set of traces of $\mathcal{H}$ is, at all times, a subset of the suspension traces of I; since I is anomaly-free, also $\mathcal{H}$ is anomaly-free; since I is stable and since $\mathcal{H}$ adds δ-loops following an observation of δ (line 4), $\mathcal{H}$ is stable; since I is quiescent reducible and since all inputs are added in each (reachable) state of $\mathcal{H}$, also $\mathcal{H}$ is quiescent reducible. Non-blockingness of $\mathcal{H}$ of traces starting in state s_ϵ of length $n - 1$ or smaller is respected in the inner iteration (lines 3-8), and non-blockingness of all traces starting in a reachable node of $\mathcal{H}$ is ensured in lines 12-14. I **ioco** $\mathcal{H}$ holds as a result of the postcondition I N-**ioco** $\mathcal{H}$ of the outer iteration in lines 3-8 and the closure in lines 12-14. $\square$

The TBM-algorithm computes a tree-like hypothesis (with δ-loops) that is such that I is at least N-bounded **ioco** correct w.r.t. $\mathcal{H}$. The *learning phase* (lines 3–8) is the most crucial part of the algorithm. In this iteration, the hypothesis $\mathcal{H}$ is tested for $n+1$-bounded **ioco**-correctness, and, possibly modified to cope with counterexamples (lines 5-6). The *extension phase* (line 9), extends the $n+1$-bounded **ioco**-correct hypothesis

Input: implementation I with inputs Act_I and outputs Act_U, and an $N \in \mathbb{N}$.
Output: Suspension automaton $\mathcal{H} = \langle S, s_\epsilon, \text{Act}_\delta, T \rangle$, where:
-   $S = \{s_\sigma \mid \sigma \in \Sigma\}$, with $\Sigma = \text{Act}_\delta^* \setminus \text{Act}_\delta^* \, \delta\delta \, \text{Act}_\delta^*$
-   T is computed by the algorithm.

```
1.  n, T := 0, ∅;
2.  do n ≠ N →
3.      do ¬(I (n+1)-ioco s_ε) →
4.          choose σx from {σ'x' ∈ Σ | |σ'| = n ∧ x' ∈ out(I after σ') \ out(s_σ')};
5.          if x = δ → T := T ∪ {(s_σ, δ, s_σδ), (s_σδ, δ, s_σδ)};
6.          [] x ≠ δ → T := T ∪ {(s_σ, x, s_σx)};
7.          fi;
8.      od;
9.      T := T ∪ {(s_ρ, a, s_ρa) ∈ S × Act_I × S | |ρ| = n ∧ s_ρ ∈ der(s_ε)};
10.     n := n + 1;
11. od;
12. T := T ∪ {(s_ρ, x, s_ρ) ∈ S × Act_U × S | ρ ∈ d-traces(s_ε) ∧ q-red(ρ) = ρ}
13.         ∪{(s_ρ, δ, s_ρδ), (s_ρδ, δ, s_ρδ) ∈ S × {δ} × S | ρ ∈ d-traces(s_ε) ∧ q-red(ρ) = ρ}
14.         ∪{(s_ρ, x, s_q-red(ρ) x) ∈ S × Act \ Act_I × S | ρ ∈ d-traces(s_ε) ∧ ρ ≠ q-red(ρ)};
```

Fig. 5. Algorithm for learning the SUT

at each node at depth n with new input transitions. Robustness of the hypothesis is achieved in a third phase, viz. the *closure phase* (line 12–14). This phase is required to ensure that the constructed suspension automaton is non-blocking and ensures general **ioco**-conformance, rather than N-bounded **ioco**-correctness.

The size of the state-space of the hypothesis that is learnt by TBM-algorithm is bound from below by $|\text{Act}_\delta \setminus \text{Act}_U|^N$ and from above by $|\text{Act}_\delta|^N$. The number of experiments (tests) that are needed is also bound from below by $M \cdot |\text{Act}_\delta \setminus \text{Act}_U|^N$, where M is the maximal number of times an experiment must be repeated to observe all outputs that might follow; in practice, this number is rather optimistic, since the non-deterministic behaviour of the system may prevent an experiment from running to completion. Statistics may be used to find out the expected number of experiments, but we leave this as a topic for future research.

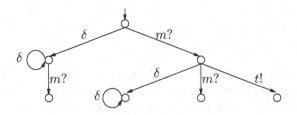

Fig. 6. Hypothesis for IOLTS L_2 when n is incremented to 2

Example 3. Applying the TBM-algorithm with $N \geq 2$ on IOTS L_2 of Fig. 1, we obtain the hypothesis of Fig. 6 after variable n of the algorithm has been incremented to 2 (line 10). The depicted hypothesis is constructed as follows: initially, the hypothesis consists of the state s_ϵ only, and the only experiment preventing I 1-**ioco** s_ϵ is an observation of quiescence; the hypothesis is extended with a δ-transition and a δ-loop. The transition $m?$ is subsequently added in line 9. In the next iteration, the two experiments violating I 2-**ioco** s_ϵ are $m?t!$ and $m?\delta$, so the hypothesis is extended accordingly, *etcetera.*

4   Heuristics

As a consequence of the large number of required experiments, the TBM-algorithm has little practical significance. Our hypothesis is that the extension phase of the TBM-algorithm is a root cause in the exponential blow-up of the state-space, since the number of different outputs that can follow an experiment is for most sensible systems severely limited. Reducing the number of newly introduced inputs therefore leads to a large reduction in the state-space that is built. Consequently, the number of experiments needed to build and validate the hypothesis is also reduced. Not all inputs can be removed without compromising the correctness of the TBM-algorithm, only some can. However, valid suspension automata always remain non-blocking and anomaly-free by removing input transitions.

Proposition 2. *Let* $M = \langle S, s, Act_\delta, \rightarrow \rangle \in \mathcal{L}_\delta(Act_I, Act_U)$ *be a valid suspension automaton. The SA* $M' = \langle S, s, Act_\delta, \mapsto \rangle \in \mathcal{L}_\delta(Act_I, Act_U)$, *where* $\mapsto = \rightarrow_I \cup ((S \times (Act_\delta \setminus Act_I) \times S) \cap \rightarrow)$, *in which* $\rightarrow_I \subseteq (S \times Act_I \times S) \cap \rightarrow$ *is an arbitrary relation, is non-blocking and anomaly-free.*

Proof. Follows from the fact that the transition relation $\mapsto$ still coincides with $\rightarrow$ on output transitions, and from the assumption that M is valid.   □

By removing input transitions ad random, a valid suspension automaton may become non-quiescent reducible or unstable:

Example 4. Let M_3 be given by the suspension automaton of Fig. 4 (page 137). Clearly, M_3 is a valid suspension automaton. Removing the transition $s_0 \xrightarrow{b?}$ will make M_3 non-quiescent reducible. Removing transition $s_2 \xrightarrow{b?}$ will make M_3 unstable.   □

In the next sections, we study three heuristics that allow us to safely prune the state-space of the hypothesis dynamically, i.e. the heuristics *preserve the validity of the computed suspension automaton.* This means that stability and quiescent reducibility are not affected by the heuristics. In the remainder of this section, we assume the heuristics are defined for the hypothesis $\mathcal{H}$, calculated by the TBM-algorithm.

4.1   Input Causality

The first heuristic that we study utilises the logs of the interactions of a system with its environment, which are often available for diagnostic purposes.

Definition 4. *A usage profile of I is a finite, non-empty set $U(I) \subseteq traces(I)$.*

Usage profiles are merely traces; their added value lies in the fact that they implicitly define causal relations between the possible stimuli.

Definition 5. *Let $I \in \mathcal{IO}(Act_I, Act_U)$ be an implementation, and let $U(I)$ be a usage profile. Input causality is defined as a relation $< \ \subseteq (Act_I \cup \{\perp\})^2$, where $\perp$ is a reserved constant, and:*

$$\begin{cases} \perp < b \text{ iff } \exists \sigma \in Act_U^*, \sigma' \in Act^*. \ \sigma b \sigma' \in U(I) \\ a < b \text{ iff } \exists \sigma, \sigma'' \in Act^*, \sigma' \in Act_U^*. \ \sigma a \sigma' b \sigma'' \in U(I) \\ \perp < \perp \text{ iff not } \exists \sigma, \sigma' \in Act^*, b \in Act_I. \ \sigma b \sigma' \in U(I) \end{cases} \tag{7}$$

Remark 1. Input causality does not require a usage profile *per se*: it can also be derived from available partial specifications or manually constructed via interviews. It involves high-level information, which often does not need deep knowledge about the system. Modifying the input causality relation by hand can be used to select and isolate behaviours that have to (should) be avoided in learning the system.

Note that it is possible to have inputs a that are never followed by another input, i.e. $\forall b \in Act_I. \ a \not< b$. We close the input causality relation as follows:

Definition 6. *Let $<$ be the input causality for a usage profile $U(I)$. Then the circular input causality $<_c$ is defined as:*

$$\forall a \in Act_I \cup \{\perp\}, b \in Act_I. \ a <_c b \text{ iff } (a < b \vee \perp < \perp) \vee (\forall c \in Act_I. \ a \not< c \wedge \perp < b)$$

We introduce the function $trailing(\sigma)$, with $\sigma \in Act_\delta^*$, defined inductively as

$$\begin{cases} trailing(\epsilon) = \perp \\ trailing(\sigma a) = a & \text{if } a \in Act_I \\ trailing(\sigma a) = trailing(\sigma) & \text{if } a \notin Act_I \end{cases}$$

Let $T_{cw} = \{(s_\sigma, a, s_{\sigma a}) \in S \times Act_I \times S \mid |\sigma| = n \wedge s_\sigma \in der(s_\epsilon) \wedge trailing(\sigma) <_c a \}$. Then heuristic 1 is obtained by replacing the assignment to T in line 7 in the TBM-algorithm with the following assignment: $T \ := \ T \cup T_{cw}$.

4.2 Penalty Functions

The selection of the right inputs can also be based on information derived from the hypothesis model itself. In particular, we aim at quantifying the amount of information a particular behaviour (i.e. a trace) adds to the hypothesis. We start with the basic observation that the length of the largest interval of inputs, after removing observations of quiescence, in a behaviour is a good indicator for the amount of its information. Let $\lambda : Act_\delta^* \to \mathbb{N}$ be the function that returns the length of the largest subsequence of input actions (not counting possible observations of quiescence) in a behaviour:

$$\lambda(\sigma) = \max\{n \mid \exists a_1, \dots, a_n \in Act_I. \ \exists \sigma', \sigma'' \in Act_\delta^*. \ \sigma = \sigma' a_1 \delta^* \dots a_n \delta^* \sigma''\} \tag{8}$$

When $\lambda(\sigma) > t$ for some threshold $t \in \mathbb{N}$, it is reasonable to consider the information in behaviour σ too low to invest in further investigating this behaviour. Let $T_{pf} = \{(s_\sigma, a, s_{\sigma a}) \in S \times Act_I \times S \mid |\sigma| = n \wedge s_\sigma \in der(s_\epsilon) \wedge \lambda(\sigma) \leq t\}$. Heuristic 2 is then obtained by replacing the assignment to T in line 7 in the TBM-algorithm with the following assignment: $T \ := \ T \cup T_{pf}$.

4.3 Non-repetitive Quiescence

Repetitive quiescence is a powerful tool in the test-based modelling as it enables one to find out which behaviours lead to outputs, which never do, and which lead to non-deterministic behaviour when both quiescence and actual outputs are valid observations. The observation of quiescence is also quite costly: in practice, it takes time to conclude that no output will come. Disabling the notion of repetitive quiescence turns the TBM-algorithm into an algorithm for test-based modelling with respect to a slightly weaker testing relation, known as **ioconf** [11]. Let $T_q = \{(s_\sigma, a, s_{\sigma a}) \in S \times \text{Act}_I \times S \mid |\sigma| = n \wedge s_\sigma \in der(s_\epsilon) \wedge (out(s_\sigma) = \{\delta\} \Rightarrow s_\sigma \overset{\delta}{\nrightarrow} s_\sigma)\}$. Heuristic 3 is obtained by replacing the assignment to T in line 7 with the following assignment: $\texttt{T} := \texttt{T} \cup \texttt{T}_q$.

4.4 Combining Heuristics

All of the heuristics proposed in the previous sections are complementary, which means that all heuristics can be combined. Let X be a non-empty subset of $\{cw, pf, q\}$. A combination of heuristics is achieved by replacing line 7 of the TBM-algorithm with the following assignment: $\texttt{T} := \texttt{T} \cup (\bigcap_{x \in X} \texttt{T}_x)$.

Proposition 3. *The TBM-algorithm in combination with any non-empty subset of heuristics 1,2 and 3, yields a valid suspension automaton.*

Proof (Sketch). Because of Proposition 2, only stability and quiescent reducibility must be shown for heuristics 1,2 and 3. For stability, we note that this is not affected by any of the heuristics, since for each reachable state s of $\mathcal{H}$, we have s *after* $\sigma = s$ *after* σ' for all $\sigma, \sigma' \in \delta^+$. For quiescent reducibility, we note that heuristic 3 (non-repetitive quiescence) by definition cannot conflict with quiescent reducibility. For heuristic 1 (input causality), we note that for a trace $\sigma\delta\sigma' \in traces(s_\epsilon)$, we find that $trailing(\sigma) = trailing(\sigma\delta)$, and, combined with the fact that implementation I is quiescent reducible, we find that also $\sigma\sigma' \in traces(s_\epsilon)$. For heuristic 2 (penalty functions), we observe that $\lambda(\sigma\delta^+\sigma') = \lambda(\sigma\sigma')$ for all $\sigma, \sigma' \in \text{Act}_\delta^*$, meaning that if $\sigma\delta^+a \in traces(s_\epsilon)$, for $a \in \text{Act}_I$, then also $\sigma a \in traces(s_\epsilon)$ (note that because $\mathcal{H}$ is anomaly-free, $a \notin \text{Act}_U$), and, because implementation I is also quiescent reducible, we find that also the hypothesis $\mathcal{H}$ is quiescent reducible. For the combination of heuristics, we observe that the intersection of the behaviours of two valid suspension automata that are derived from the same valid suspension automaton yields a valid suspension automaton. □

5 Experimental Data: The Conference Protocol

The conference protocol provides a rudimentary *chatbox service* to users participating in a conference. A conference is formed by a collection of users that can exchange messages with all conference partners in that conference. The unbounded number of messages that can be exchanged makes the system effectively infinite-state. The partners in a conference can change dynamically using *join* and *leave* primitives. Different conferences can exist at the same time, but a user can only participate in at most one conference at a time. The conference protocol relies on the service provided by UDP, i.e. data packets may get lost or duplicated or be delivered out of sequence but are never corrupted or misdelivered.

We have used our approach for learning and testing a running ANSI-C implementation of the *conference protocol*. This setup was previously used to benchmark testing theories [2] using *mutant testing*[1]. The mutants are ANSI-C implementations of the conference protocol that have been derived from the correct implementation by deliberately injecting a single error. These erroneous implementations are categorised in three different groups: *no outputs*, *no internal checks* and *no internal updates*. The first group contains implementations that sometimes fail to send output when they are required to do so. The second group contains implementations that do not correctly check whether they are allowed to participate in a conference, and the third group contains implementations that do not correctly administrate the set of conference partners. Given the large set of documented mutants, the conference protocol makes for an ideal setup for measuring the efficacy of the approach for regression testing and/or for the testing of different configurations.

5.1 Experiments

Setup. Table 1 lists the characteristics of the derived hypotheses. The hypotheses were derived from running the –what is believed to be– correct implementation of the conference protocol, connected to a prototype implementation of our TBM-algorithm. Two usage profiles were used in our experiments, and these were also used to determine the size of the input interface (the set Act_I) when the input causality was used. The first usage profile (I) has $|Act_I| = 19$ and is chiefly a run of the conference protocol in which all parties behave "optimally". The second usage profile (II) has $|Act_I| = 31$ and consists of three runs which combine aspects of "optimal" behaviour with "bad weather" behaviour. Each hypothesis represents the best hypothesis that can be guaranteed by experimenting with the implementation for 48 hours. For the operationalisation of quiescence we adopted the standard approach in testing by setting a time-out of 3 seconds on the observation of output (i.e. we observe quiescence when the system did not produce output for two seconds when asked for output). The learning hypothesis was operationalised by conducting each derivable experiment 15 times.

Figures 7 and 8 show the growth characteristics in terms of number of states for a given depth for each computed hypothesis. This is an important indicator as it can be used to estimate the overall run-time that is required to guarantee a certain depth-of-correctness. For instance, hypothesis I-6 is more likely to reach depth-of-correctness 15 than e.g. I-7. Additional learning time can therefore best be put into I-6.

Test Results. The computed hypotheses were subsequently used to test the 27 mutants of the system. For this, we used standard model-based testing techniques. We used a test suite consisting of tests that aimed at covering each output transition (including quiescence) of a used hypothesis. The test results are listed in Table 2. In some cases, it was not immediately clear whether the test-failure was due to an incorrect hypothesis

---

[1] The conference protocol implementation and its mutants, together with a more detailed description, are available via http://fmt.cs.utwente.nl/ConfCase/

Table 1. Characteristics of the computed hypotheses (I-1 through II-15). N indicates the N-bounded **ioco** correctness that could be achieved and S gives the number of states at depth $N + 1$ (note that these figures do not include states introduced by the closing phase). An 'x' for 'cw' and/or 'q' indicates that heuristic 1 and/or 3 was used. A figure for 'pf' indicates the threshold for heuristic 2. UP marks whether (the set of inputs of) usage profile I or II was used.

	I-1	I-2	I-6	I-7	I-8	I-14	I-15	II-1	II-2	II-6	II-7	II-8	II-14	II-15
N	2	6	10	7	12	7	8	2	5	6	6	11	5	6
S	8,488	826	1,326	1,819	1,295	1,264	1,795	28,123	1,521	829	3,363	1,626	1,045	1,746
cw		x	x	x	x	x	x		x	x	x	x	x	x
pf		1		1	2	2				1		1	2	2
q			x	x			x				x	x		x
UP	I	I	I	I	I	I	I	II	II	II	II	II	II	II

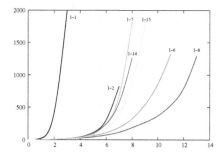

Fig. 7. Growth characteristics for the hypotheses with inputs determined by usage profile I

Fig. 8. Growth characteristics for the hypotheses with inputs determined by usage profile II

(recall that each experiment was conducted 15 times, which may have been too conservative for some experiments) or the mutant. These cases were resolved by hand using the informal documentation and a formalisation thereof.

5.2 Analysis and Discussion

The derived hypotheses are remarkably effective at singling out the mutants. The combined detection power of hypotheses I-8 and II-8 is 85% of all mutants.

Analysing the influence of depth-of-correctness on the defect detection capability, we find that usage profile I and usage profile II give slightly different results. For usage profile I, defect detection at a given depth-of-correctness is smaller than defect detection at the same depth for usage profile II. Since usage profile II includes "bad weather" behaviour, this may suggest that most robustness issues can be found at relatively small depths. This may be explained from the fact that programming for robustness is generally trickier than programming for nominal behaviour. Issues with nominal behaviour only show at greater depth. An explanation for this may be the increase in intrinsic complexity in nominal behaviours with depth.

Table 2. Test results obtained by testing mutants of the conference protocol against the derived hypotheses. An 'x' indicates that the mutant was discovered.

Mutant	I-1	I-2	I-6	I-7	I-8	I-14	I-15	II-1	II-2	II-6	II-7	II-8	II-14	II-15
100			x	x	x	x			x	x	x	x	x	x
111		x	x	x	x	x	x		x	x	x	x	x	x
384		x	x	x	x	x	x		x	x	x			x
548									x	x	x	x	x	x
674	x	x	x	x	x	x	x	x	x	x	x	x	x	x
687		x		x		x			x	x	x	x	x	x
293														
398											x			
444														
666														
214				x										
247		x	x	x	x	x	x		x	x	x	x	x	x
276		x	x	x	x	x	x		x	x	x	x	x	x
289											x			
294											x			
332											x			
345		x		x						x	x			
348		x		x		x					x			
358														
462									x	x	x	x	x	x
467		x	x	x	x	x	x			x	x	x	x	x
738									x	x	x	x	x	x
749		x	x	x	x	x	x		x	x	x	x	x	x
777				x										
836		x	x	x	x				x	x	x	x	x	x
856		x	x	x		x								
945											x			

It is also clear from the test results that there is no single combination of heuristics that should be used, although experience with other combinations of heuristics and different usage profiles (not reported here) shows that the usage profiles appear to be a minimum requirement; rather, the combination of several heuristics to compute different hypotheses appears to be more effective. The effect of the heuristics is clearly illustrated by the great difference in detection power of the computed models without heuristics (only I-1 and II-1), and with heuristics (all other hypotheses).

6   Conclusion

We have described a pragmatic approach to obtaining models of a system using black-box testing techniques, with the goal of using these models for regression testing. The approach is demonstrated using a well-known case study and the effectiveness is illustrated using mutant testing. The results of the case study, viz. the detection of 85% of all mutants illustrates that the approach is feasible, and, moreover, effective for regression-testing, or for the testing of different configurations.

Still, there is also some room for improvement, as approximately 15% of the mutants avoid detection. Concerning issues for future research, we feel that it is important to develop additional heuristics and use techniques from statistics, such that we can stretch the detection rate over 85% *within* a period of 48 hours. The issue of cleverer ways to represent a hypothesis becomes more important with the increase of the state-space. While our experiments show that for now, representation is not yet an issue, it will become problematic when experiments are run for weeks rather than days. At that point, representation techniques such as employed and developed by Angluin [1] become important. Reconciling Angluin's L* algorithm with **ioco**-based testing may, however, be quite tricky, if not impossible, as (1) all transformations have to respect the validity of suspension automata, and (2) the basic starting assumptions are different (e.g. **ioco**-based testing does not require the implementation to consist of a finite number of states).

Acknowledgement. Jan Tretmans is thanked for pointing out an error in an earlier version of this paper.

References

1. D. Angluin. Learning regular sets from queries and counterexamples. *Information and Computation*, 2(75):87–106, 1987.
2. A. Belinfante, J. Feenstra, R.G. de Vries, J. Tretmans, N. Goga, L. Feijs, S. Mauw, and L. Heerink. Formal test automation: A simple experiment. In G. Csopaki, S. Dibuz, and K. Tarnay, editors, *Testcom '99*, pages 179–196. Kluwer, 1999.
3. T. Berg, B. Jonsson, M. Leucker, and M. Saksena. Insights to angluin's learning. In S. Etalle, S. Mukhopadhyay, and A. Roychoudhury, editors, *Proceedings of SVV 2003*, volume 118 of *ENTCS*, pages 3–18. Elsevier, 2005.
4. P. Godefroid. Verisoft: A tool for the automatic analysis of concurrent reactive software. In *Proceedings of CAV'97*, volume 1254 of *LNCS*, pages 476–479. Springer-Verlag, 1997.
5. M.J. Harrold. Testing: A roadmap. In A. Finkelstein, editor, *ICSE - Future of SE Track*, pages 61–72. ACM, 2000.
6. H. Hungar, T. Margaria, and B. Steffen. Domain-specific optimization in automata learning. In W.A. Hunt Jr. and F. Somenzi, editors, *Proceedings of CAV'03*, volume 2725 of *LNCS*, pages 315–327. Springer-Verlag, 2003.
7. H. Hungar, T. Margaria, and B. Steffen. Test-based model generation for legacy systems. In *IEEE international test conference (ITC)*, pages 971–980, 2003.
8. H.K.N. Leung and L.J. White. Insights into regression testing. *Journal of Software Maintenance: Research and Practice*, 2:209–222, 1990.
9. T. Margaria, H. Raffelt, and B. Steffen. Knowledge-based relevance filtering for efficient system-level test-based model generation (to appear). *Innovations in Systems and Software Engineering*, 1(2):147–156, 2005.
10. D. Peled, M.Y. Vardi, and M. Yannakakis. Black box checking. In J. Wu, S.T. Chanson, and Q. Gao, editors, *Proceedings of FORTE/PSTV*, volume 156, pages 225–240. Kluwer, 1999.
11. J. Tretmans. Test generation with inputs, outputs and repetetive quiescence. *Software — Concepts and Tools*, 17(3):103–120, 1996.

Verifying VHDL Designs with Multiple Clocks in SMV[*]

A. Smrčka[1], V. Řehák[2], T. Vojnar[1], D. Šafránek[2], P. Matoušek[1], and Z. Řehák[2]

[1] FIT BUT, Brno, Czech Republic
{matousp,smrcka,vojnar}@fit.vutbr.cz
[2] FI MU, Brno, Czech Republic
{xsafran1,xrehak,xrehak5}@fi.muni.cz

Abstract. The paper considers the problem of model checking real-life VHDL-based hardware designs via their automated transformation to a model verifiable using the SMV model checker. In particular, model checking of asynchronous designs, i.e., designs driven by multiple clocks, is discussed. Two original approaches to compiling asynchronous VHDL designs to the SMV language such that errors possibly arising from the asynchronicity are preserved are proposed. The paper also presents results of experiments with using the proposed methods for verification of several real-life asynchronous components of an FPGA-based router being developed within the Liberouter project.

1 Introduction

The most recent verification technologies for design of hard-wired ASIC-based hardware or FPGA firmware offer highly developed industrial verification tools which give hardware designers a good support to minimise errors in the design of hardware synthesised from high-level descriptions usually written in languages like VHDL or Verilog. Such tools can be basically divided into two groups—simulation and testing, and formal verification tools. Tools of the first group are focused on simulation of gate-level signal behaviour and are commonly used, according to our experience, by hardware designers as a necessary support of hardware development. Tools of the second group augment the non-exhaustive simulation approach by model checking (formal assertion-based verification) of entire Register Transfer Level (RTL) hardware description [13,4], or checking of equivalence between an RTL description and the respective behavioural description [5,2]. However, because of limitations caused by the state explosion problem, these tools still lack the property of being usable by verification non-experts. In the case of, otherwise highly automated, model checking tools, the reason is that intricate abstraction methods are needed to fight the state explosion. Especially, such abstraction

---

[*] This research has been supported by the CESNET activity "Programmable hardware". Zdeněk Řehák has been partially supported by the Academy of Sciences of the Czech Republic grant No. 1ET408050503. Vojtěch Řehák has been partially supported by the research centre "Institute for Theoretical Computer Science (ITI)", project No. 1M0021620808. David Šafránek has been supported by the Grant Agency of Czech republic (GA CR) grant No. 201/06/1338, Aleš Smrčka and Tomáš Vojnar have been supported by the GA CR No. 102/04/0780, and Petr Matoušek by the grant GA CR No. 102/05/0723.

L. Brim et al. (Eds.): FMICS and PDMC 2006, LNCS 4346, pp. 148–164, 2007.

methods must be employed carefully to avoid any critical underapproximation potentially introduced in the model being verified.

The most fundamental abstraction used in verification of hardware is the abstraction of the physical latency of a signal value change, the so-called *zero-delay*. Our recent experience gained during verification of an FPGA-based design in the Liberouter project [10] shows that such abstraction cannot be used for verification of some typical parts of common FPGA hardware designs. More specifically, the zero-delay abstraction is inadequate for designs controlled by clocks of two or more mutually asynchronous clock domains. Especially, functional verification of clock domain crossing (CDC) signals behaviour requires a special care. At the same time, even though hardware designers typically use some standard constructions to deal with CDC, they may be omitted by mistake or a wrong mechanism wrt. the assumptions used in the rest of the design may be used, and so there is a real need to check for possible errors related to asynchronicity. Moreover, errors introduced due to an unexpected behaviour of CDC signals cannot be easily found by standard simulation and testing tools.

The Liberouter project is aimed at the development of a high-speed network monitoring and routing hardware [8,7] in the form of add-on cards for standard PCs. The design of these cards is based on FPGA technology. We have been employing various formal methods for verification of the design since the beginning of the project [12,9]. In this paper, we generalise our approach [6] of a direct temporal logic-based formal verification of VHDL hardware description using Cadence SMV [13] for the case of asynchronous hardware. Moreover, although we present our approach in a framework specific for our project, we believe that it offers a general idea of how verification of asynchronous hardware can be done even in different settings.

1.1 Related Work

There are simulation and testing approaches [1] which deal with transient behaviour of designs. However, all these methods are incomplete because of the non-exhaustive nature of design behaviour analysis.

The approach of [11] requires the design with CDC signals to be transformed into a design extended with additional combinational logic which models the potential misbehaviour of CDC signals. Assertion-based verification is then applied to the resulting design. The number of combinational logic elements added in this transformation increases exponentially with the number of asynchronous clocks, thus the state explosion of the resulting design complicates the verification. Moreover, there is no simplification in the sense of automated detection of those parts of the design for which the discussed transformation is necessary for a correct verification. Detection of CDC signals is realised at the verification phase itself, hence the state explosion cannot be overcome anyway in this method. Moreover, there are no arguments showing the generality of the approach. The approach is illustrated on a simple example only and no discussion of its efficiency is given.

Our approach offers a solution based on an extension of every critical gate to incorporate the delayed behaviour. Additionally, we also introduce an approximate solution which suffers much less from the state explosion. In contrast to the work mentioned in the previous paragraph, we focus on generality of our approach. Moreover, we also evaluate the efficiency of our approach on a real case study.

1.2 Our Contribution

In this paper, the problem of the above mentioned inadequacy of the zero-delay abstraction for multi-clock designs is carefully discussed and a general verification solution for dealing with such designs is established. The proposed solution comprises a detection of the relevant parts of the design for which the zero-delay abstraction cannot be employed and furthermore defines a way of how such design parts are transformed and verified using Cadence SMV. Besides the accurate solution, we also propose a solution based on a safe overapproximation of the reachable states. According to our practical experience, this solution is precise enough to handle various non-trivial real-life case studies while offering much better performance results. The proposed methods are demonstrated and compared on a real verification case study taken from the Liberouter project.

To the best of our knowledge, in the literature there is currently no general fully automated model checking solution for formal verification of designs controlled by asynchronous clocks. Moreover, our approach employs the Cadence SMV model checking tool which supports temporal logics (LTL, CTL). These logics are more expressive then traditional assertion languages used in many industrial verification tools.

The structure of the paper is the following. Section 2 brings a brief introduction to digital elements in digital hardware design, explains the case of situations when the synchronisation problem occurs, and presents a way of formalising elementary hardware entities in SMV. Section 3 describes precisely our methods how to find critical signal paths in the design and how to verify the system with respect to the considered properties. Section 4 illustrates our solution on a real example.

2 Formalising a Hardware Design

In this section, we shortly introduce elementary digital circuits and present our approach to their formalisation in SMV. We are mainly concerned about precise modelling which considers timing delays and unstable behaviour of the circuits. The issue is the most critical for design and verification of synchronous digital circuits. In order to prove that the design is correct using verification techniques, we have to (1) build a formal model of the circuit that reflects the examined properties including the timing behaviour, and (2) successfully verify the model using a model checker.

2.1 Preliminaries

In our work, we deal with logical circuits—discrete electronic circuits composed of basic entities like gates, flip-flops, and latches. A *gate* is a logical circuit with one or more inputs that produces an output based on the current input values. The most well-known are AND-, OR-, NOT-gates (or NAND-, NOR-gates) that are fundamental elements of every logical circuit. A gate is usually called a *combinational circuit*, or a combinational logic, as its output depends only on the current input combination [14].

Logical circuits that are able to store a value (they work like a register) are called *sequential logical circuits*. An output of a sequential circuit depends not only on its current inputs, but also on the past sequences of inputs. Formally, we can describe the behaviour of a sequential logical circuit using a finite-state machine.

We distinguish two basic kinds of sequential logical circuits—latches and flip-flops. A *latch* is a sequential circuit that continuously watches all of its inputs and changes its outputs at any time, independently of a clock signal. A *flip-flop* is a sequential circuit that normally samples its inputs and changes its outputs only at the instants determined by a clock tick. Common sequential circuits are D-latch, S-R latch, J-K flip-flop, etc.

2.2 Transient Behaviour

When dealing with the transient behaviour, we have to take into account what happens when the signal changes between two adjacent states, e.g., on a falling edge (the signal changes from a low level to a high level), or on a rising edge (from a high level to a low level). In real circuits, changes of a signal take a nonzero time. The amount of time that the output of a logical circuit requires to change its state is called the *transition time*.

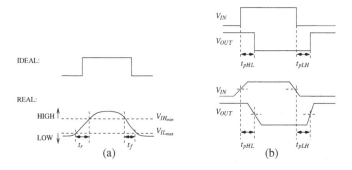

Fig. 1. (a) Transition times, (b) propagation delays

Fig. 1(a) shows the rise time t_r and the fall time t_f of a signal in a logical circuit. This time information indicates how long an output voltage takes to pass through the "undefined" region between the LOW and HIGH levels of signal.

The initial part of a transition before reaching the value $V_{IL_{max}}$, resp. $V_{IH_{min}}$, is not included in the rise- or fall-time value. Instead, it forms another parameter called a *propagation delay* t_p. The propagation delays t_{pHL} and t_{pLH} represent the amount of time that it takes for a change of the input signal to produce a change of the output signal, see Fig. 1(b). Finally, t_{pHL} is the time between an input change and the corresponding output change when the output is changing from HIGH to LOW, and t_{pLH} is the time between an input change and the output change when the output is changing from LOW to HIGH (cf. Fig. 1(a).

2.3 Synchronisation Between Two Clock Domains

The transient behaviour described above is usually not considered in an abstract model obtained when a hardware design specified by VHDL is transformed into an input language of a verification tool. We call this kind of abstraction the *zero delay abstraction*. In general, omitting the transient behaviour in the abstract model can lead to incorrect results. In this section, we explain the synchronisation problem that may cause the zero delay abstraction to produce incorrect results in cases of asynchronous designs. In the next section, we propose a precise way of modelling the transient behaviour.

If there is only one clock signal in the design, we do not need to care about propagation delays and transition times. In such a case, the transient behaviour of any circuit has no influence on the other parts of the design because every signal becomes stable after the same period, and we may assure the period to be long enough for the signals to stabilise—this issue is ensured by common hardware development tools. A *synchronisation problem* occurs if two or more communicating circuits are controlled by different clocks. Fig. 2 demonstrates the synchronisation problem between two directly connected gates X and Y. Gate X is controlled by clock C1, gate Y by C2, X has two output signals A and B, B is a negated version of A. When clock C2 is enabled at time t_{err}, both signals A and B are in the process of changing. At this moment, their state is undefined—both signals can be read out by gate Y either as 1 or 0 because their values are not stable yet. This is the critical moment for the circuit behaviour and its modelling.

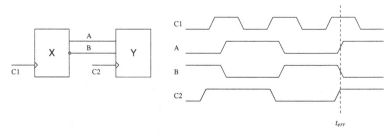

Fig. 2. The synchronisation problem between two clock domains

In our work, we propose a technique how to model this behaviour in order to verify properties on a real-world design. In the analysis, we use a notion of a *clock domain*. A clock domain is a part of the circuit. It is the maximal set of gates that are enabled by the same clock signal. From the point of view of synchronisation, *critical gates* are the gates on a signal path connecting different clock domains. A non-consistent behaviour can appear while reading data transferred from gate X in domain D_1 (enabled by signal C_1) at gate Y in domain D_2 (controlled by signal C_2), see Fig. 2.

To eliminate inconsistencies caused by the transient behaviour, designers typically use Gray code, mux-synchronised signals, handshake synchronizers, or asynchronous queues. Gray code is useful to guarantee a correct transfer of an integer variable whose next value differs only by one digit from the previous one. The method of multiplexer synchronised signals ensures that in one moment in time only one signal value may change. Handshake synchronizers, asynchronous queues, and other techniques not mentioned in this paper are more general. Here, our concern is how to properly model the transient behaviour in order to verify circuits where it appears.

2.4 Digital Circuits Design in VHDL and SMV

For the model checking approach, we need to specify the model formally as a finite state transition system where states represent the current signal values and transitions represent their discrete changes. For this purpose, we use the *Cadence SMV* language [13] which allows us to encode such a model. Moreover, using the SMV tool, we can prove the properties of the circuits that we are interested in. For specification of such properties, we use a temporal logic. In this section, we describe how this modelling is done. In particular, we demonstrate our technique of formalising a hardware design described by VHDL. However, the approach is not dependent on a certain language and can easily be adapted to other specification languages, e.g., VERILOG.

Each state of a transition system can be expressed as a vector of current values of signals at a particular discrete point of time. In the timing diagram depicted in Fig. 3, states are represented as columns of 0s and 1s denoting the LOW and the HIGH level of signals (HIGH corresponds to 1 and LOW to 0). For elementary circuits controlled by only one clock, we assume the *zero delay abstraction* to be used, which means abstracting from the transient behaviour. Each transition (verification step) models the *instantaneous change* of some signals with respect to their current values contained in the source state. The target state then contains the new values of the signals being changed.

A combinational logic is captured directly by the notion of states. Relations between signal values in a particular state specify a logical function of some combinational logic elements. As the transition time has no influence on the behaviour of a combinational logic, the zero delay abstraction fits here well. The modelling of sequential logic elements is more involved. In particular, a change of an output signal value in a sequential circuit is modelled by a transition between states.

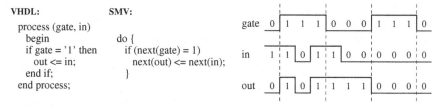

Fig. 3. Latch in Cadence SMV

In the case of a latch, any change of the out signal is guarded by a simple condition which requires the gate signal to have the HIGH level value. Encoding of a latch in SMV is showed in Fig. 3. An example of a trace of the respective transition system is depicted in the right-hand part of the figure. In every state in which gate is 1, the signal out has the same value as the signal in; otherwise, it keeps its previous value. Note that this behaviour is independent of any clock signal. Due to this asynchrony, the zero delay abstraction does not violate soundness of the model.

In contrary to the latch case, modelling of a flip-flop is more complicated. More specifically, in the case of a flip-flop circuit, whenever the current value of the clock signal is LOW and the next value is HIGH, the next value of the output signal is set to the current value of input. In Fig. 4 there is an SMV encoding of this behaviour and an example of its trace.

Above, we have shown how we encode elementary design entities in SMV. Below, we describe our general approach of modelling compositions of these elementary entities with correct treating of the transient behaviour whenever it cannot be abstracted.

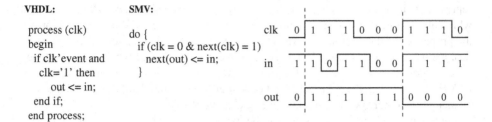

VHDL:

```
process (clk)
begin
  if clk'event and
     clk='1' then
     out <= in;
  end if;
end process;
```

SMV:

```
do {
  if (clk = 0 & next(clk) = 1)
     next(out) <= in;
}
```

Fig. 4. Flip-Flop in Cadence SMV

3 Modelling Asynchronous Behaviour

In this section, we propose two ways of modelling asynchronous VHDL designs in SMV which preserve errors possibly caused by the asynchronicity. In particular, we are interested in preserving *reachability of stable input and output values and state signals combinations* of the circuits. By *stable signal values*, we understand the values that are obtained after a circuit is given a sufficient time to stabilise, i.e., values that one can eventually observe when there is no change in clock signals. Moreover, the reasoning can be generalised to preservation of sequences of stable signal values allowing one to verify complex temporal properties.

An undesirable state can happen if a sequential gate reads an unstable signal value and then it changes to a stable value. As we have already indicated, common VHDL development tools (e.g., Leonardo [3]) check that signal paths within the same clock domain are not too long wrt. the used clock frequency, and thus that the signals are given sufficient time to stabilise. If the verified system has to be connected to systems such that some input/output signal goes from one clock domain to another domain, the entire combined system should be re-checked using the methods we propose here. Thus, *we ignore the possibility of obtaining unstable signal values within one clock domain.*

We further suppose that *the only asynchronicity in the circuits we consider is due to the clock signals.* This corresponds to the assumption that the set and reset signals which may also be used to control sequential circuits are all connected together (i.e., there is just one set and/or reset signal for the whole design).

Both of the approaches we propose are based on modifying the behaviour of the so-called *critical signal paths* between two clock domains. In the first approach, we modify every gate on a critical path to make its output undefined (arbitrarily zero or one) for a single verification step whenever a change occurs. In the second approach, we introduce a special component called a *destabilizer* at the end of every critical path. This component produces an undefined output for a number of verification steps corresponding to the accumulated delay of the critical path.

We argue that the first mentioned approach enables us to detect all the possible erroneous signal combinations as described above, and at the same time, no overapproximation is (in most usual practical cases) involved. However, there is a price to be payed for this due to an increased number of state variables contributing to the state explosion problem. On the other hand, the second approach is a safe overapproximation that may work in a number of practically interesting situations in a much faster way than the first approach, but it may sometimes raise false alarms. Note that we *suffice with focusing on only the critical paths* as we suppose the design to be already checked by the above mentioned common VHDL development tools which assure us that within a particular clock domain, all the signals always stabilise before they are sensed by sequential gates.

Below, we first formalise the notion of critical paths and then explain both of the approaches we propose in detail.

3.1 Critical Signal Paths and Critical Gates

In order to precisely define the notion of critical gates, we view a particular VHDL *hardware design* in an abstract way as a triple $H = (S, C, G)$ where:

- S is a finite set of *signals*.
- C is a finite set of *clock signals*, $C \cap S = \emptyset$. In order to obtain a more regular description, we introduce a special clock signal $\perp \notin C \cup S$ that we associate with combinational gates. We denote $C_{\perp} = C \cup \{\perp\}$.
- $G \subseteq C_{\perp} \times 2^S \times 2^S$ is a finite set of *gates* (combinational logic gates, flip-flops, latches). A gate is represented as a tuple consisting of its clock signal (which is $\perp$ for combinational gates), a set of input signals, and a set of output signals.

For a hardware design $H = (S, C, G)$, a *signal path* $\pi = \langle g_1 s_1 g_2 s_2 \ldots s_{n-1} g_n \rangle$ of length $n > 1$ is a connected sequence of gates and signals such that $\forall j \in \{1, \ldots, n-1\} : g_j = (c_j, I_j, O_j) \in G \wedge g_{j+1} = (c_{j+1}, I_{j+1}, O_{j+1}) \in G \wedge s_j \in O_j \cap I_{j+1}$. We denote $\Pi(H)$ the set of all signal paths of H, and for a signal path $\pi \in \Pi(H)$, we denote $\Gamma(\pi)$ the multiset of all the gates which appear in π and $\Sigma(\pi)$ the set of all signals in π. For a path $\pi = \langle g_1 s_1 g_2 s_2 \ldots s_{n-1} g_n \rangle$, we call $\gamma_i(\pi) = g_1$ the input gate, $\gamma_o(\pi) = g_n$ the output gate, $\sigma_i(\pi) = s_1$ the input signal, and $\sigma_o(\pi) = s_{n-1}$ the output signal.

We partition the set of gates G of a hardware design $H = (S, C, G)$ into subsets called *clock domains* that contain gates driven by the same clock signal. For $c \in C_{\perp}$, the clock domain is $D_c = G \cap (\{c\} \times 2^S \times 2^S)$.

The set R_c of *gates critical wrt. a domain* D_c, $c \in C$, is the set of gates which occur on signal paths leading to D_c and that are connected to the gates in D_c via combinational gates only. Equivalently, for a domain D_c, critical gates are all the gates on the signal paths that start by a sequential gate lying in a different clock domain (including this sequential gate) and lead via combinational gates to a sequential gate in D_c (excluding this terminal gate). Formally, $R_c = \{g_1 \in G \setminus D_c \mid \exists n > 1 \ \exists s_1, \ldots, s_{n-1} \in S \ \exists g_2, \ldots, g_{n-1} \in D_{\perp} \ \exists g_n \in D_c : \langle g_1 s_1 g_2 s_2 \ldots s_{n-1} g_n \rangle \in \Pi(H)\}$ for a hardware design $H = (S, C, G)$. The set $R(H)$ of *critical gates of* H is then simply the union of all the gates critical wrt. the particular domains of H, i.e., $R(H) = \bigcup_{c \in C} R_c$.

Finally, a *critical signal path* of length $n > 1$ in a hardware design $H = (S, C, G)$ is a signal path $\rho = \langle g_1 s_1 g_2 s_2 \ldots s_{n-1} g_n \rangle \in \Pi(H)$ that consists of critical gates, i.e., $\forall i \in \{1, \ldots, n-1\} : g_i \in R(H)$, and goes from one clock domain to another one, i.e., $g_1 \in D_{c_1}, g_2 \ldots g_{n-1} \in D_{\perp}, g_n \in D_{c_2}, c_1 \neq c_2, c_1 \neq \perp, c_2 \neq \perp$. We denote $\rho(H)$ the set of all critical signal paths in H.

3.2 Extending All Critical Gates

We now discuss in detail the approach when we extend the behaviour of every gate on a critical path to make its output random whenever there is a change of the stable value in its output. The fact that we make the output random stems from the reality where a signal does not sharply change from 0 to 1 (or vice versa) but goes through some rising (or falling) edge. When the signal is sensed by some sequential gate on such an edge, one cannot predict its value. Note that when there is no change in the output, no modification is necessary.

The basic principle of our transformation is the following. To model the impact of rising and falling edges in the output of critical gates, we replace every output of every critical gate by a new state signal—we call it a *delayed output*. The values of a delayed output are given by the states of the finite automaton in Fig. 5(a). The arcs represent the original (zero-delayed) output signal defined by a function $f(i_1,\ldots,i_n)$ where $i_1, \ldots, i_n$ are input signals of the gate. For example, when the delayed output is 0 and the original output changes to 1, the automaton goes to R, and the delayed output becomes R (i.e., "rising"). Only then, provided the original output does not change, it transfers to 1. Similarly, for a change of the original output from 1 to 0, the delayed output goes from 1 to F ("falling") and then changes to 0.

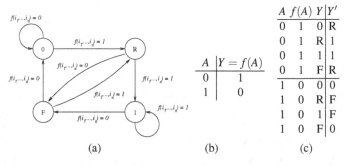

A	$Y = f(A)$
0	1
1	0

A	$f(A)$	Y	Y'
0	1	0	R
0	1	R	1
0	1	1	1
0	1	F	R
1	0	0	0
1	0	R	F
1	0	1	F
1	0	F	0

(a)   (b)   (c)

Fig. 5. (a) The finite automaton implementing a delayed output with the rising and falling edges of signals, (b) the transition table of the zero-delayed NOT-gate, (c) delayed extended NOT-gate

As an example, let us consider an inverter (a NOT-gate with the function $f(A) = \neg A$ where A is the only input signal) which is a critical gate. We extend this gate with the delayed output as shown in the table in Fig. 5(c). In the table, Y' is the future value of the delayed output. Note that a gate that was originally a combinational one becomes a gate with a state now.

Further, as digital gates are designed to handle only 0 and 1 values, we model the R and F values as a random choice between 0 and 1 in the final model (which we denote as the so-called x-value in the following).

To continue with our example, suppose that the input of the inverter (NOT-gate) is a signal controlled by a clock $C1$ and that both the input and the output are sensed by some sequential gate controlled by a clock $C2$. When the gates are modelled as zero-delayed, cf. Fig. 6(a), we will never see that the sequential gate can sense both the signals as equal (which we may suppose to cause real erroneous situations). This will become visible in our model as depicted in Fig. 6(b)—see x-values depicted as crosses in the figure.

A problem with the above extension of gates arises when there exist two paths linking some sequential gates via combinational gates only such that one of them stays within a

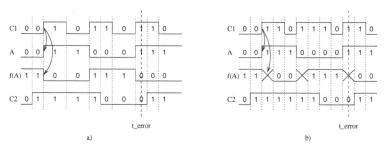

Fig. 6. The input and output of the NOT-gate sensed as (a) zero-delayed and (b) delayed

single clock domain, the other one goes from one domain to a different one, and the two paths intersect each other. More precisely, the problem arises when there exist signal paths $\pi_1 = \langle g_{1,1}s_{1,1} \ldots s_{1,n_1-1}g_{1,n_1} \rangle$, $\pi_2 = \langle g_{2,1}s_{2,1} \ldots s_{2,n_2-1}g_{2,n_2} \rangle \in \Pi(H)$ of a hardware design $H = (S, C, G)$ for $n_1, n_2 > 1$ and some domains $c_1, c_2, c_3 \in C$, $c_2 \neq c_3$ such that $g_{1,1}, g_{1,n_1} \in D_{c_1}$, $g_{2,1} \in D_{c_2}$, $g_{2,n_2} \in D_{c_3}$, $\forall i \in \{1,2\}$ $\forall j \in \{2,...,n_i - 1\} : g_{i,j} \in D_\perp$, and $\Gamma(\pi_1) \cap \Gamma(\pi_2) \neq \emptyset$. In such a situation, we need to extend the gates in $\Gamma(\pi_1) \cap \Gamma(\pi_2)$ for the path π_2, but to keep their original function within π_1. To achieve this, before the above described extension, we pre-process the circuit by replacing every gate $g_{2,i} = (\{\perp\}, I, O) \in \Gamma(\pi_1) \cap \Gamma(\pi_2)$ within the path π_2 by two gates $g'_{2,i} = (\{\perp\}, I, O \setminus \sigma(\pi_2))$ and $g''_{2,i} = (\{\perp\}, I, O \setminus \sigma(\pi_1))$ with the same behaviour. We call the new gate g'' a *duplicate*. For further analysis, let n_{dup} denote the number of new output signals produced by duplicates.

Extending Simple Combinational Logic Gates in SMV. So far, we have described the main principle of our technique of modelling asynchronous VHDL designs such that errors possibly arising due to the asynchronicity are preserved. We now have a look at how to apply this principle on transforming concrete gates from VHDL to SMV. We start with the simple case of combinational logic gates.

Recall the zero-delayed model of a given design described in Section 2.4. In such a model, circuits of combinational logic gates (NOT, AND, OR, NAND, NOR) are translated to SMV simply in the form of logic expressions. Now, we have to (1) define state-bearing *delaying modules* for every type of a critical combinational gate that appears in our design, (2) instantiate these modules (one instance for each particular critical combinational gate), and (3) change the interconnection of the original zero-delayed model such that the delayed outputs are used instead of the zero-delayed ones for every critical combinational gate.

A *state-bearing delaying module for a given combinational gate* has the same input and output signals as the original gate, but the output is computed according to the way described in the previous section. To implement the delaying functionality with the interleaved random signals corresponding to the automaton from Fig. 5(a), the module has an internal state variable in which we remember the output of the original gate computed according to its function (NOT, OR, ...) and we send it to the new output with a delay of one step (if there is no change in it). To detect the changes in signals, we may conveniently use the possibility of referring to the next values of signals offered by

SMV. To illustrate this construction on a concrete example, we give below a delaying module for a NAND gate (described in the SMV syntax).

```
module delayed_nand(out, in1, in2) {
    input in1 : boolean;
    input in2 : boolean;
    output out : boolean;
    orig_out : boolean;
    -- the original NAND function
    next(orig_out) := ~(next(in1) & next(in2));
    -- the delayed output
    if (orig_out = next(orig_out)) next(out) := orig_out;
    else next(out) := {0,1}; -- a random choice
}
```

Then, if there is used, e.g., an assignment z := w | ~(x & y); somewhere, we declare a new signal for the delayed output of the NAND over x and y, a new instance of the delayed NAND computing this delayed signal, and we use this signal instead of ~(x & y);. The construction is shown below with the delayed output of the NAND sent to a delayed OR module whose implementation is very similar to the delayed NAND and is not given here due to space limitations.

```
nand_output : boolean;
nand_module : delayed_nand(nand_output, x, y);
or_module : delayed_or(z, w, nand_output);
```

Extending More Complex Gates in SMV. More complex gates including flip-flops, latches, and complex combinational gates like multiplexers are modelled as separate SMV modules. We now have to create duplicates of such modules, extend them by new internal signals to hold the original output, and define the outputs of these new modules as delayed versions of the original outputs (interleaved with the random phases) much like in the above case of simple combinational gates. For instance, a delayed D flip-flop could then look as shown below.

```
module delayed_D(set, reset, in, clk, delayed_out) {
    input set : boolean; input reset : boolean;
    input in : boolean;  input clk : boolean;
    output delayed_out : boolean; -- the delayed output
    orig_out : boolean;           -- the original output
    do {                          -- an initialisation phase
        if (set) init(orig_out) := 1;
        else if (reset) init(orig_out) := 0;
        else if (clk) init(orig_out) := in;
        init(delayed_out) := init(orig_out);
    }
    do {                          -- computing the original output
        if (next(set)) next(orig_out) := 1;
        else if (next(reset)) next(orig_out) := 0;
        else if (~clk & next(clk)) next(orig_out) := in;
    }
    ------- the delay-based extension -- computing the delayed output -------
    if (orig_out = next(orig_out)) next(delayed_out) := orig_out;
    else next(delayed_out) := {0,1}; -- a random choice
}
```

A Justification of the Construction. The *extension of only the critical gates* is justified by our assumption that common VHDL development tools are used to check that in all single clock domains, all signals have always enough time to stabilise before being sensed by sequential gates. Moreover, we suppose that input and output signals of the entire checked design will be used within the same time domain as the gates which consume these signals.

As for the extension of critical gates, the modification makes their output *non-deterministic for a single verification step* if the changed input would lead to a change in the original output. If this change is permanent, the extension is clearly justified because when the signal is rising from 0 to 1 or falling from 1 to 0, it can be sensed in an unpredictable way by the adjacent logic. On the other hand, when there is no change in the output, no extension is needed. An interesting situation is when there is a change in the output, but a temporary one only (the so-called hazard)—i.e., there is a rising and immediately a falling edge (or vice versa). In such a case, our approach introduces two random phases, which is again justified for most common-life cases as it is difficult to guarantee that the generated peak or drop in the signal would never be sensed (in any case, a design that would depend on this, would not be very clean).

The above justification is, however, valid only from the point of view of monitoring a single signal. When we look at *reachable combinations of multiple signal values*, the length of the random phase (the phase with x-value(s)) is also important. We make it uniformly one verification step long which requires some further considerations. In fact, in general, such an approach can introduce an underapproximation or overapproximation though it does not happen in most practical situations (and it can be statically checked whether such a situation arises or not). In particular, such cases can arise *when the involved gates significantly differ in their delays*.

Let us first consider the case of *two critical paths with a different length* (a generalisation to more such paths is straightforward). Suppose we have two critical paths ρ_1, ρ_2 of lengths n_1, n_2 such that $n_1 < n_2$. If the accumulated delay of the gates in ρ_1 is smaller than in ρ_2, clearly the output of ρ_1 will stabilise before the output of ρ_2, which corresponds to our model. On the other hand, if the accumulated delay of the gates in ρ_1 is equal or greater than in ρ_2, we need to keep the random phase longer than one step per gate in ρ_1 in order to obtain the desirable combination of two x-values at the ends of both paths. A similar reasoning can then be employed in the case of *two equally long paths*. If the accumulated delay of one of the paths was longer than the other one, we would need to exclude the possibility of obtaining two undefined results. However, we suppose that such conditions do not arise (which is usually the case and which can be checked statically given the design and the descriptions of the used gates).

3.3   Extending Signal Paths

The previous section provides a method of modelling the progressive delay of a critical signal propagation (and of the associated random phases when its value is changing) via an extension of every critical gate. This method is rather precise but may cause a significant state-space explosion due to the number of the newly introduced state signals. Below, we try to avoid this explosion by introducing a less precise, approximate model that can, according to our experience, still be sufficient in many practical cases. In this approach, we do not extend every single critical gate, but instead, we put a special new gate called a *destabilizer* on every output of a critical signal path.

As a basis which we try to overapproximate in the new approach, let us summarise how the process of stabilisation of a signal $\sigma_o(\rho)$ in a critical signal path ρ looks like in the previous approach when we extend every critical gate by the delaying and randomising phase. In that case, a critical gate can be viewed as a generator of stable and unstable values. If more critical gates are sequentially connected (they all appear in the same critical signal path ρ), the unstable values are propagated through all critical gates on the path, and every gate delays its new output value. The new defined value of the signal $\sigma_i(\rho)$ influences the signal $\sigma_o(\rho)$ after the delay equal to the sum of delays of all gates on ρ without the last gate $\gamma_o(\rho)$. When $\sigma_i(\rho)$ changes its value, it can cause a temporary instability—the adjacent gates switch their output value through a rising or falling edge when the value of the signal is not unambiguously defined, and the undefined value is propagated to further gates. Due to modelling the delay of one gate as one step, it takes L steps to influence $\sigma_o(\rho)$ by $\sigma_i(\rho)$ where $L = |\Gamma(\rho)| - 1$, i.e., unstable values of the signal $\sigma_o(\rho)$ can occur in at most L steps.

The principle of the approximate approach we propose is to replace the progressive generation of unstable signals by having a single new gate called a *destabilizer* which will generate all possible combinations of x-values of a signal for a period of L steps. The destabilizer will be connected to the output signal of a critical signal path $(\sigma_o(\rho))$ where x-values can become visible. We create one destabilizer for every set of critical signal paths having the same output signal. The destabilizer starts to generate x-values if one of the input signals of these signal paths changes its value.

Formally, a *destabilizer over a critical path* ρ in a design $H = (S,C,G)$ is a gate $\delta_\rho = (\bot, \alpha(\rho) \cup \{\sigma_o(\rho)\}, \{\omega\})$ to be added into G where $\alpha(\rho) = \{\sigma_i(\rho') \mid \rho' \in \rho(H) \wedge \sigma_o(\rho') = \sigma_o(\rho) \wedge \gamma_o(\rho') = \gamma_o(\rho)\}$ is the set of input signals to be monitored (it is the set of input signals of all critical signal paths sharing the output with ρ) and $\omega \notin S \cup C \cup \{\bot\}$ is a new unique signal representing the output of δ_ρ. The original output signal $\sigma_o(\rho)$ of the given critical path ρ (and of the adjoining paths) becomes an input of δ_ρ and is sent to the output of δ_ρ after the phase of instability implemented by δ_ρ is over. Apart from introducing δ_ρ, we have to change the gate originally connected to ρ, i.e., $\gamma_o(\rho)$, such that it senses the output of δ_ρ. In particular, if $\gamma_o(\rho) = (c,I,O)$, we replace it by $\gamma_o'(\rho) = (c, (I \setminus \{\sigma_o(\rho)\}) \cup \{\omega\}, O)$.

The behaviour of a destabilizer δ_ρ is defined by the finite automaton shown in Fig. 7—for brevity, the automaton is described with one bounded counter whose possible values are not included directly in the state-transition control. Let $v(\alpha) \neq v'(\alpha)$ for a set of monitored signals α denote that some signal in α is changing its value (i.e., its current value differs from the value in the next step). If the destabilizer is in the D state—when it has a defined value (in particular, $\sigma_o(\rho)$) on its output—and one of the monitored signals changes its value, the destabilizer switches to the X state and produces on its output the x-value, i.e., randomly 0 or 1. The destabilizer will hold in the X state for a period of L verification steps where L is the number of critical gates in

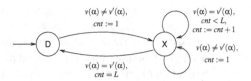

Fig. 7. The automaton describing the behaviour of a destabilizer

the longest critical signal path which the destabilizer is connected to, i.e., L is the maximum of $|\Gamma(\rho')| - 1$ for $\rho' \in \rho(H) : \sigma_o(\rho') = \sigma_o(\rho) \wedge \gamma_o(\rho') = \gamma_o(\rho)$.

Destabilizers in SMV. Let us consider a general destabilizer for n critical signal paths with L being the length of the longest of these paths. In SMV, we can implement the destabilizer as the following module with input signals in_1, ..., in_n to be connected to the monitored inputs of the covered critical paths, the input signal out (the original output to be delayed), and the new output signal omega.

```
module Destabilizer(in_1, ..., in_n, out, omega) {
    output omega : boolean;
    input out : boolean;
    input in_1 : boolean;
    ...
    input in_n : boolean;

    cnt : 0..L;          -- L is a constant value  L = |Γ(ρ)| - 1
    init(cnt) := 0;
    init(omega) := init(out);
    next(cnt) := case {
      -- one of the monitored signals is changing
        (in_1!=next(in_1)) |
        ...              |
        (in_n!=next(in_n))           : 1;       -- to state X
      -- the counter reaches the maximum and all monitored signals hold
        cnt=L & (in_1=next(in_1)) &
               ...                &
               (in_n=next(in_n))    : 0;        -- to state D (cnt=L-1)
      -- the counter is in (0;L) and all monitored signals hold
        cnt>0 & (in1=next(in_1)) &
               ...               &
               (in2=next(in_n))    : cnt+1; -- to state X
      -- all signals are stable
        1                          : 0;       -- to state D
    }
    next(omega) := case {
        next(cnt)=0 : next(out);   -- cnt==0: propagate a defined value
        next(cnt)>0 : {0,1};       -- cnt>0: output x-value
    }
}
```

To illustrate how a destabilizer is connected to the rest of a modelled design, let us consider a signal o whose stable value is computed as a function comb implemented by a combinational logic with inputs $\alpha = \{$ s_1, ..., s_n $\}$ and which is at the end of a critical path. Let Z be the output gate consuming o. Z is a sequential gate that is in a different clock domain than the gates from which the inputs s_1, ..., s_n are taken. In SMV, this would correspond to the code fragment below.

```
o := function_comb(s_1, ..., s_n);
Z_m : Z(..., o, ...);
```

To introduce a destabilizer, we define a new delayed output omega, instantiate a destabilizer with delayed_o as its output, connect the original output o as an input of the destabilizer, and replace the original output at the input of Z with omega.

```
o := function_comb(s_1, ..., s_n);
omega : boolean;
destabil_m : Destabilizer(s_1, ..., s_n, o, omega);
Z_m : Z(..., omega, ...);
```

A Justification of the Construction. We are interested in proving that no dangerous stable combination of signals is reachable even though there is a possibility that some undefined signal values on critical signal paths will be sensed and registered. Therefore a method which overapproximates the influence of working with undefined signal values on the reachable stable combinations of signals is a sound solution.

A destabilizer is connected to the output of several critical paths. In the previously described method based on extending all gates in critical signal paths, it takes at most $L = |\Gamma(\rho)| - 1$ steps to stabilise the output signal if the input signal of any critical path changes (provided ρ is the longest path). A destabilizer produces x-values for L steps if any of the input signals changes. Thus, the destabilizer method will generate all the combinations of signals to be sensed and become stable as in the method based on extending all gates in critical signal paths and may be even more. Therefore, it is a safe overapproximation of the extension of all gates in critical signal paths.

However, if a model checker returns a counterexample in a model using destabilizers, we cannot be sure if it reflects a possible behaviour of the real system. In such a case, we must use a more precise model based on the extension of all critical gates and perform the verification once again. One could also think of performing the check only on the given path and possibly using the extension of all critical gates only on this path. A proper investigation of such an approach is a part of our future work.

We said that destabilizers often save a number of state variables compared to the method of extending all critical gates. Let us examine when this approach is efficient wrt. the number of state variables. The method based on extending all gates in a critical signal path creates one new binary state variable per a critical gate (for a critical signal path $\rho \in \Pi(H)$, this means $|\Gamma(\rho)| - 1$ new variables) plus n_{dup} state variables for duplicated state signals—we mean the duplication due to the case where $\rho \in \rho(H), \pi \in \Pi(H), \pi \not\subseteq \rho(H), \Gamma(\rho) \cap \Gamma(\pi) \neq \emptyset$. One destabilizer can replace the extension of all critical gates that is needed in the first method on more than one critical signal paths. The number of gates in these critical paths is $\lambda = |G_d| - 1$ for $G_d = \bigcup_{i=1}^{n} \Gamma(\rho_i)$ where $\sigma_o(\rho_1) = \sigma_o(\rho_2) = \cdots = \sigma_o(\rho_n)$, $n \geq 1$. The method of signal path extension adds to the system three types of variables: (a) a binary variable of the new output—the ω signal, (b) a counter of unstable values of the range $[0; \lambda]$ (i.e., the size of the counter is $\lceil log(\lambda + 1) \rceil$), and (c) n_{div} duplicated state signals for the destabilizer due to the division of input gates (which may appear when combining the method of destabilizers with extending all critical gates as explained in the next paragraph). The method using destabilizers pays off if $\lambda + n_{dup} > \lceil log(\lambda + 1) \rceil + 1 + n_{div}$, hence in the case of $n_{dup} = n_{div} = 0$, we get $\lambda \geq 5$.

Combining Both Methods. To achieve a satisfying ratio between a model accuracy and its state space size, we are able to combine both proposed methods in one model. We are interested in behaviours when an unstable value is registered and propagated further to the design. Both methods are able to stabilise the signal with the same delay (the delay of L steps). Therefore, we can apply both methods on different critical signal paths. By selecting which of the methods should be used on a certain critical signal path, we can fine-tune the verification process by trading the accuracy of the result (due to the overapproximation by destabilizers) for the model complexity (the extension of all critical gates). Such a combination is safe if we avoid the specific case when both methods influence each other as discussed below.

Consider a circuit where two critical signal paths begin in the same gate and continue with a different signal, i.e., $\rho_1, \rho_2 \in \Pi(H)$, $\rho_1 \neq \rho_2$, $g = \gamma_i(\rho_1) = \gamma_i(\rho_2)$, and $\sigma_i(\rho_1) \neq \sigma_i(\rho_2)$. When we use the extension of all critical gates on the first signal path and the destabilizer on the second path, the first method extends the gate $g = \gamma_i(\rho_1)$ with a delayed output. However, we must also preserve its zero-delayed behaviour for the second method, and so the shared starting gate g must be *divided* into two separate gates g_1 and g_2 such that if $g = (c, I, O)$, then $g_1 = (c, I, O \setminus \{\sigma_i(\rho_2)\})$ and $g_2 = (c, I, O \setminus \{\sigma_i(\rho_1)\})$. Let n_{div} be the number of duplicated state signals caused by the division of all such gates in the model.

A similar problem appears if two critical paths with an application of both methods share some of the intermediate gates. For every pair of the critical signal paths $\rho_1, \rho_2 \in \Pi(H)$, $\rho_1 \neq \rho_2$, and all shared gates $\Gamma_{1,2} = (\Gamma(\rho_1) \setminus \{\gamma_i(\rho_1), \gamma_o(\rho_1)\}) \cap (\Gamma(\rho_2) \setminus \{\gamma_i(\rho_2), \gamma_o(\rho_2)\}) \neq \emptyset$, we have to *duplicate* every shared gate $\forall g \in \Gamma_{1,2}$ and every common signal $\forall s \in \Sigma(\rho_1) \cap \Sigma(\rho_2)$.

4   Experiments

We tested our approach on two asynchronous queues from the libraries of the Liberouter project—namely, `asfifo-bram` and `asfifo-dist`. Each of the components uses a different type of memory and has a slightly different control part. For `asfifo-bram`, we checked the property that the control part does not allow to rewrite unread data with new data. For `asfifo-dist`, we checked that the component correctly sets the so-called status data on its output which informs about the saturation of the queue.

Table 1 shows results of our experiments. Suffixes in the first column mean the following: (i) *no-check* is the case when no extension is performed, (ii) *all-gates* is the case when all critical gates are extended, (iii) *destabil* means that destabilizers are used instead of extending all the gates.

Table 1. Verification results

case	vars no.	time	mem
asfifo-bram-no-check	36	4.83 s	132607
asfifo-bram-all-gates	220	inf.	inf.
asfifo-bram-destabil	44	37.52 s	2446796
asfifo-dist-no-check	44	4550.07 s	9861121
asfifo-dist-all-gates	48	30556.7 s	25878822

Column *vars no.* gives the number of binary state variables, *time* is the verification time, and *mem* is the number of allocated BDD nodes.

There are eight critical signal paths in `asfifo-bram` and two critical paths in `asfifo-dist`. We can see from the number of state variables in `asfifo-bram` that there are many critical gates to extend when extending all critical gates (the number of state variables increases to 220) whereas the destabilizer-based approach found only two places for a destabilizer (which rapidly decreases the extensions needed). For `asfifo-dist`, we can see a big difference in time and the number of BDD nodes used for a slight difference in the number of state variables. Such a contrast is caused by the nondeterminism in the model—one random value $\{0,1\}$ divides the further state-space exploration into two directions (the first for value 0, the second for 1).

5 Conclusion

We have introduced two original approaches to modelling asynchronous hardware designs using the input language of the commonly employed Cadence SMV model checker. One of these approaches is quite precise, but may contribute to the state explosion problem in a significant way. The other approach can be much more efficient as it is based on an overapproximation of the reachable states. The approach is, however, still precise enough to allow one to prove interesting properties on various real-life hardware designs as we have illustrated by our experiments. Both of these methods may be modified to be used together with a different model checker than Cadence SMV and represent a contribution to the state-of-the-art in verifying hardware designs by allowing one to deal with asynchronous circuits.

References

1. P. Rashinka et al. *System-on-a-chip Verification*. Methodology & Techniques. Kluwer, 2001.
2. R.K. Brayton et al. VIS: A System for Verification and Synthesis. In *Proc. of CAV'96*, LNCS 1102, 1996. Springer.
3. Mentor Graphics. *Leonardo Synthesis*, 2005.
4. Mentor Graphics. *0-In Formal Verification Data Sheet*, 2006.
5. Mentor Graphics. *Formal Pro Data Sheet*, 2006.
6. J. Holeček, T. Kratochvíla, V. Řehák, D. Šafránek, and P. Simeček. Verification Process of Hardware Design in Liberouter Project. Technical Report 5/2004, CESNET, 2004.
7. J. Kořenek, T. Pečenka, and M. Žádník. NetFlow Probe Intended for High-Speed Networks. In *Proc. of FPL'05*. IEEE Computer Society, 2005.
8. J. Kořenek, P. Zemčík, and T. Martínek. FPGA-Based Platform for Network Applications. In *Proc. of DDECS'05*. University of West Hungary, 2005.
9. T. Kratochvíla, V. Řehák, and D. Šafránek. Formal Verification of a FIFO Component in Design of Network Monitoring Hardware. In *Proc. of CESNET 2006 Conference*, 2006.
10. Liberouter Project Homepage. http://www.liberouter.org.
11. T. Ly, N. Hand, and Ch. Ka kei Kwok. Formally Verifying Clock Domain Crossing Jitter Using Assertion-Based Verification. In *Proc of DVCon'04*, 2004.
12. P. Matoušek, A. Smrčka, and T. Vojnar. Modeling, Analysis, and Verification of SCAMPI2. Technical Report 8/2005, CESNET, 2005.
13. K.L. McMillan. *Cadence SMV Manual*, 2006.
14. J. F. Wakerly. *Digital Design: Principles and Practices*. Prentice-Hall, 3rd edition, 2001.

Verified Design of an Automated Parking Garage

Aad Mathijssen and A. Johannes Pretorius

Department of Mathematics and Computer Science
Technische Universiteit Eindhoven
P.O. Box 513, 5600 MB Eindhoven, The Netherlands
{a.h.j.mathijssen,a.j.pretorius}@tue.nl

Abstract. Parking garages that stow and retrieve cars automatically are becoming viable solutions for parking shortages. However, these are complex systems and a number of severe incidents involving such garages have been reported. Many of these are related to safety issues in software. We apply verification techniques to develop a software design for an automated parking garage. This design meets a number of safety requirements. We provide a software architecture that allows one to split implementation, safety and algorithmic aspects of the software. Consequently, we give a high-level description of the safety aspects and verify a number of safety requirements on this model. Also, we briefly discuss how this analysis is simplified by using a custom visualization tool.

1 Introduction

Many large cities cope with parking shortages. Traditionally, this has been dealt with by building parking garages below street level or by erecting multi-storey parking arcades. However, large parts of the floor area cannot be used for parking since driving lanes need to be provided. Automated parking garages do not require drivers to park their cars themselves. Instead, cars are placed into parking spaces fully automatically, using a combination of hardware and software. The area needed by such placement mechanisms is usually much less than that needed for driving lanes. This drastically increases parking capacity. Apart from being space efficient, automated parking garages often serve as status symbols for companies or city councils.

Automated parking garages are complex systems. This is reflected by their complex hardware. It is even more evident if one considers some of the incidents involving such systems [1]. These range from users obtaining the wrong car, or no car at all, to cars and equipment being reduced to rubble. The latter is a so-called *safety issue:* the system causes irrecoverable damage to cars or to itself.

In this article we treat safety aspects involved in the software design of a typical automated parking garage. By the time that we were consulted, the hardware design of the investigated system had been finalized. As a result, it is completely fixed and far from optimal regarding safety. This puts an extra burden on the software. Unfortunately, this seems to be a frequent mind-set when designing integrated systems: *"don't worry, we'll make it work with software"*.

L. Brim et al. (Eds.): FMICS and PDMC 2006, LNCS 4346, pp. 165–180, 2007.

The approach we take is to obtain a high-level behavioural description of the system. Safety requirements are verified on each state of this model. By identifying violations of the requirements, we are able to discover shortcomings and improve our specification to ensure safety. Process algebras are well suited for such verified design. We use the new mCRL2 language and toolset [2,3,4] to describe system behaviour and to verify requirements. mCRL2 succeeds and extends μCRL [5,6] with which a number of complex systems have been analysed [7,8,9].

In Sect. 2 we describe the automated parking garage in more detail. Based on this description, we define our goals in Sect. 3. In Sect. 4 we discuss how we conceptually divide the system software into three layers: a hardware abstraction layer, a safety layer and a logical layer. This allows us to concentrate on the safety layer, which we argue is essential for ensuring that the system is safe. In Sect. 5, we describe the design of the safety layer. We follow this with a discussion of implementation issues in Sect. 6. We also describe a simple visualization plug-in for the mCRL2 toolset and the insights we gained by using it. We conclude in Sect. 7.

2   Operational Description

The garage we consider was commissioned by property developers and its hardware designed by a company specialising in automated parking systems. It is due to be installed below street level in the basement of an existing building.

Access to the garage is provided by a vertical lift shaft with a door at street level. A single car can be driven into the lift through this door. When the driver and passengers have exited the car and the lift, the car is automatically lowered to an intermediate level, rotated 180° horizontally, lowered to the basement and stowed using a number of conveyor belts and shuttles. To retrieve a car, the same system of conveyor belts and shuttles is used to bring the car to the lift with which it is raised to street level. Since the car had been rotated before, it now faces the street.

The system provides a number of security and safety checks during check-in and check-out of a car. This includes reading a transponder card and checking a database of registered users before opening the lift door. As the car is driven into the lift, the driver is provided with cues to ensure a correct positioning. There is also a check to ensure that the handbrake is engaged. Before lowering the car to the basement, the lift is scanned to ensure that there are no living beings present.

In the remainder of this article, we consciously abstract from hardware details. We also restrict ourselves to the vertical lift and the basement level parking garage. We do not consider the mechanisms put in place for regulating traffic outside the lift, correctly positioning the car in the lift, or cues to enter and leave the lift. We do this to tightly draw the bounds of our scope. It also allows us to focus on the most important safety aspects of the system.

We assume the operation of the system is initiated every time a car is positioned appropriately in the lift at street level or when a request for retrieving a car is received. The lift can be in one of three vertical positions: street level, rotation level or basement level. At rotation level, the lift is able to rotate 180° horizontally, provided that there are no cars positioned immediately adjacent to the lift shaft (on either side) at basement level. The floor of the lift consists of a conveyor belt. When the lift is at the basement level this conveyor belt is able to move sideways (see the description below). The most complex and interesting part of the system is the basement level. Here the movement of cars is facilitated by a number of conveyor belts and shuttles. This is illustrated in the floor plan of the basement in Fig. 1.

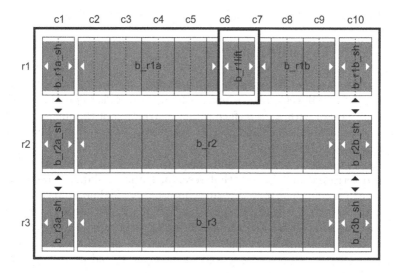

Fig. 1. Floor plan of the parking garage, basement level

As shown in Fig.1, the garage is divided into three rows (r1, r2 and r3) and ten columns (c1–c10). Conveyor belts are represented by grey rectangles with arrows on their ends and are identified by labels such as *b_r1a_sh*. The arrows indicate their direction of movement. Columns c1 and c10 contain three shuttles each. In each of these columns one shuttle may be tilted upwards on its long end facing the wall. This results in an open position to which adjacent lowered shuttles may be moved. A tilted shuttle may also move to a new row position behind lowered shuttles (this implies that it is possible for two shuttles to be in the same row and column position, provided that one is tilted and the other lowered). Black arrows indicate the directions in which shuttles can move. Similar to the lift, every shuttle contains a conveyor belt that can move sideways.

The lift shaft is in row r1. Notice that it is not placed over a full position, but intersects two columns (c6 and c7). This is due to the construction of the building in which the garage is to be installed (and beyond the control of the engineers who designed the parking installation). More importantly, this implies that it must be possible to move cars half-column distances in the first row. For this reason, every column in row r1 is also divided into an a (left) and b (right) part as indicated by the dashed lines in Fig. 1. We use this same convention in naming the conveyor belts. Hence, b_r1a_sh refers to the conveyor belt of the shuttle on the left-hand side of row r1, and so forth.

It is possible for adjacent conveyor belts to move simultaneously to function as a single larger conveyor belt. For instance, b_r3a_sh and b_r3 can be moved in unison. The system hardware can determine whether any (half-)position is free or occupied. For any column in r1, it is possible to determine the status of its a (left) and b (right) part. It is possible to determine whether there is a lowered, a tilted or no shuttle at all in any row of c1 and c10. Furthermore, the current height of the lift and its status (free or occupied) can be determined.

3   Problem Description

We have mentioned that hardware design is outside the scope of this article. It is also not our goal to develop algorithms. Instead, our aim is to provide specialists in algorithm design with an interface to an abstraction of the underlying hardware that guarantees the safe and correct operation of the system. This provides a clear separation of concerns.

Placement and retrieval algorithms need to ensure that cars are efficiently stowed and retrieved in a fashion that resembles a large sliding puzzle. Even if these algorithms contain errors, the safety interface should not allow the parking garage or the cars in it to get damaged. It needs to specify the necessary checks and restrictions that guarantee the execution of only safe or legal moves. For example, when an algorithm requests that a car be moved to a position that is already occupied by another car, the safety layer should not allow this. The safety interface must also be able to report on the success or failure of issued commands. Properly designed algorithms should be able to respond to such feedback in an appropriate fashion.

4   Conceptual System Design

We now provide a high-level software design for the automated parking garage.

4.1   Architecture

Our aim is to specify a safety interface that sits between placement and retrieval algorithms and the abstract hardware of the automated parking garage. This interface must allow only safe or legal instructions and report on their success or failure. To achieve this, we introduce a three-layered architecture consisting of a logical layer (LL), a safety layer (SL) and a hardware abstraction layer (HAL) (see Fig. 2). With this division into layers, the safety layer ensures the safe operation of the system independently of the particular algorithms that are implemented and without being concerned with hardware implementation issues.

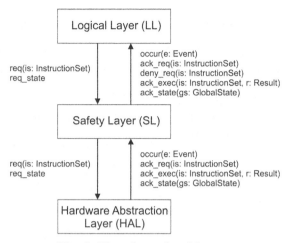

Fig. 2. Three-layered architecture

Data. The following data are communicated between the layers:

- *Event*: an event outside the scope of our design that has an impact on the system. We identify the following events:
  - *add_car*: a new car enters the lift.
  - *remove_car*: a car is removed from the lift.
- *InstructionSet*: a set of instructions to be executed concurrently by the HAL. It consists of a number of elements of type *Instruction*. The notion of a set of instructions allows for the execution of multiple instructions that apply to non-overlapping areas of the basement. For instance, with a single request it is possible to issue different instructions for moving conveyor belts as long as the belts in question do not overlap (see next section).
- *Instruction*: a single instruction that the hardware should execute. Instructions should be implemented by the HAL (see Sect. 4.2). There are 5 different instructions:
  - *move_belts(bs: BeltSet, d: Direction, ms: MoveSize)*: move the set of belts *bs* in direction *d* by a distance of size *ms* (half or full position).
  - *move_shuttles(shs: ShuttleSet, o: ShuttleOrientation, d: Direction)*: move the set of shuttles *shs* in orientation *o* (lowered or tilted upwards) in direction *d* by a distance of one row interval.
  - *tilt_shuttle(p: ShuttlePosition, o: ShuttleOrientation)*: lower or tilt the shuttle in positions *p* and orientation *o* to the orientation that is the opposite of *o*.
  - *move_lift(h: Height)*: move the lift to vertical position *h*.
  - *rotate_lift*: rotate the lift 180° horizontally.
- *Result*: indicates whether a set of instructions has been executed successfully (*ok*) or whether it has failed (*fail*).
- *GlobalState*: the current system state. That is, for every position whether it is free or occupied (*FloorState*), for every shuttle whether it is lowered or tilted upwards (*ShuttleState*), and for the lift its current vertical position and also whether it is free or occupied (*LiftState*).

Interactions. To facilitate communication between the different layers, we introduce the following interactions:

- *occur(e: Event)*: the occurrence of an event *e*. When the HAL detects *e*, the SL is informed by the action *occur(e)*. The SL informs the LL by issuing a similar *occur(e)* action. For the sake of design modularity, the LL is not directly informed by the HAL.
- *req(is: InstructionSet)*: request the execution of instructions *is*. A request from the LL to execute instructions is propagated to the HAL via the SL.
- *ack_req(is: InstructionSet)*: a signal from the SL that the instructions in *is* are safe.
- *deny_req(is: InstructionSet)*: a signal from the SL that the instructions in *is* are unsafe. The SL makes no subsequent requests to the HAL.
- *ack_exec(is: InstructionSet, r: Result)*: the instructions in *is* have been completed with result *r*. The HAL issues an *ack_exec(is, r)* action to the SL. Consequently, the SL issues this action to the LL.
- *req_state*: request the current global state of the system.
- *ack_state(gs: GlobalState)*: communicate the current global state from the HAL to higher layers. This is done in response to a *req_state* action.

4.2 Hardware Abstraction Layer (HAL)

We assume that the HAL serves as a coherent interface to all individual hardware components in the garage. The HAL receives requests for sets of instructions from the SL (action *req*). For each set of instructions the HAL attempts to execute the individual instructions and reports back on the result of the attempt (action *ack_exec*). For the specification of the SL to yield the intended results, instructions must be implemented correctly by the HAL. We assume that this is the case. Apart from executing instructions, the HAL also provides the SL with the current system state before and after issuing any instructions. Such a system state is constructed by the HAL using sensors that monitor the status of the conveyor belts, the shuttles and the lift.

4.3 Logical Layer (LL)

The LL allows for the development of algorithms by experts who can plug their specifications into the SL. These algorithms may contain errors that trigger the request of unsafe instructions. Due to the safety layer, such requests are harmless and will be blocked. More concretely, the LL utilises the SL by requesting that sets of instructions be executed. The SL reports back to the LL in the form of *ack_req*, *deny_req* and *ack_exec* actions. It also informs the LL of events that have occurred (a new car to stow or the removal of an existing car). The logical layer should respond to such feedback appropriately.

4.4 Safety Layer (SL)

The SL sits between the LL and the HAL. It receives requests (*req*) from the LL, which it acknowledges (*ack_req*) or denies (*deny_req*), based on whether the instruction is safe for the current state. After an acknowledgement is sent, the request is passed on to the HAL. In other cases the SL passes information between the HAL and the LL. We treat the SL in more detail in the next section.

5   Verified Design of the Safety Layer

In this section, we identify the safety requirements for the SL and we develop a specification in mCRL2, for which these should be satisfied. Consequently, we verify that this is indeed the case. A more detailed account of the analysis can be found in the corresponding technical report [10]. The full mCRL2 specification and verification code is also included in the report.

5.1   Informal Requirements

The SL should meet the following safety requirements:

1. Conveyor belts:
   (a) When a car is moved from one belt to another, both belts should move in the same direction.
   (b) Cars should never be moved into walls.
   (c) Cars should never be moved to a belt that is not available (when a shuttle is tilted, or when the lift belt is not at the basement level).
2. Shuttles:
   (a) Shuttles should never be moved into a wall.
   (b) When moving shuttles, no shuttles should be damaged.
   (c) When moving shuttles, cars should not be damaged.
   (d) When tilting a shuttle, no shuttles should be damaged.
   (e) When tilting a shuttle, cars should not be damaged.
3. Lift:
   (a) When moving the lift, cars should not be damaged.
   (b) When rotating the lift, cars should not be damaged.

5.2   Specification of Data Types

The data types described in Sect. 4.1 can be translated into mCRL2 in a relatively straightforward way:

```
sort
    Instruction      = struct move_belts(R1BeltSet, DirCol, MoveSize)
                       | move_belts(R2BeltSet, DirCol, MoveSize)
                       | move_belts(R3BeltSet, DirCol, MoveSize)
                       | move_shuttles(ShuttlePosSet, ShuttleOrientation, DirRow)
                       | tilt_shuttle(ShuttlePos, ShuttleOrientation)
                       | move_lift(LiftHeight)
                       | rotate_lift;
    InstructionSet = List(Instruction);% representing a set of instructions
    Event            = struct add_car | remove_car;
    Result           = struct ok | fail;
    GlobalState    = struct glob_state(fs : FloorState, shs : ShuttleState, ls : LiftState);
```

The ambiguity of the definition of *Instruction* is resolved by the fact that *R1BeltSet, R2BeltSet* and *R3BeltSet* are different types. These types are defined in fashion similar to the above definition. Note that the data language of mCRL2 is fully higher-order and we use this to implement some data types as functions. For instance, the datatype *FloorState* is defined as *FloorPos* → *OccState*. That is, a function from floor positions to occurrence states indicating whether a position is free or occupied.

Allowed Instruction Sets. The informal requirements introduced in Sect. 5.1 apply to the *InstructionSet* data type. In our specification of the SL we use an *allowed* function on sets of instructions to determine whether they are safe. A set of instructions *is* is allowed if:

1. *is* specifies at least one instruction.
2. The instructions in *is* do not *overlap*. That is, the positions on which the instructions operate are pairwise disjoint. Consequently, it is safe to execute the instructions in *is* simultaneously.
3. Each individual instruction in *is* is allowed.

Formulated in mCRL2:

```
map
   allowed : InstructionSet × GlobalState → Bool;
   % allowed(is, gs) indicates if instruction set is is allowed given global state gs
   allowed : Instruction × GlobalState → Bool;
   % allowed(i, gs) indicates if instruction i is allowed given global state gs
   overlap : Instruction × InstructionSet → Bool;
   % overlap(i, is) indicates if instruction i overlaps with any of the instructions in is
var
   gs : GlobalState;
   i, j : Instruction;
   is : InstructionSet;
eqn
   allowed([ ], gs)        = false;
   allowed(i ▷ [ ], gs)     = allowed(i, gs);
   allowed(i ▷ j ▷ is, gs) = allowed(i, gs) ∧ ¬overlap(i, j ▷ is) ∧ allowed(j ▷ is, gs);
```

Here × represents the Cartesian product and ▷ represents the list cons operation. We are now left with the task of defining the functions *overlap* and *allowed*. We elaborate on the latter, which is the least trivial.

Allowed Instructions. The core of the *allowed* function on instruction sets is an *allowed* function on individual instructions. We describe this function for every instruction.

move_belts(bs: BeltSet, d: Direction, ms: MoveSize) is allowed if:

1. *bs* contains at least one conveyor belt.
2. All conveyor belts in *bs* directly border each other (this also implies that they must be in the same row).
3. All conveyor belts in *bs* are available (this applies to belts on the lift and on shuttles).
4. At least one position of size *ms* (full or half) is free at the end of the set of belts specified. This free position is on the side indicated by *d*.
5. If the specified belts are in row r1, there is no car with one half on a belt in *bs* and the other half on a neighbouring belt not in *bs*.

move_shuttles(shs: ShuttleSet, o: ShuttleOrientation, d: Direction) is allowed if:

1. *shs* contains at least one shuttle.
2. All shuttles in *shs* border each other (this implies that they are all in column c1 or c10).
3. All specified shuttles are available in the orientation specified by *o* (lowered or tilted).
4. There is an open position at the end of *shs* in orientation *o* and direction *d*. This ensures that there is an open position for the shuttles to move to.
5. For every lowered r1 shuttle *s* in *shs*, there is no car with one half on *s* and the other half on a neighbouring belt.

tilt_shuttle(p: ShuttlePosition, o: ShuttleOrientation) is allowed if:

1. It is not the case that there is both a lowered and a tilted shuttle at the position specified by *p*.
2. If *o* is lowered, there is no car on the shuttle (fully or partially).

move_lift(h: Height) is allowed if:

1. *h* is not the current height.
2. If the current height is basement level, there are no cars with one half on the lift and the other half on a neighbouring belt.

rotate_lift is allowed if:

1. The lift is at rotation level.
2. Three half-positions on both sides of the lift are free. This prevents cars in these positions from being damaged by the rotation mechanism.

As an illustrative example of how the *allowed* function has been formally defined, we provide its definition for the *rotate_lift* instruction below. The complete formal specification of the *allowed* function can be found in [10].

```
var
    fs : FloorState;
    shs : ShuttleState;
    ls : ListState;
eqn
    allowed(rotate_lift, glob_state(fs, shs, ls)) =
        height(ls) ≈ rotate ∧
        free([pos_r1(c5, pa), pos_r1(c5, pb), pos_r1(c6, pa),
              pos_r1(c7, pb), pos_r1(c8, pa), pos_r1(c8, pb)], fs);
```

Here $\approx$ denotes the equality function on data types.

5.3   Specification of Behaviour

For the specification of the behaviour of the SL we note the following:

– At any point in time, the SL processes a single set of instructions. Multiple sets of instructions would complicate the system without having performance benefits (instead of buffering instruction sets in the LL, they would also have to be buffered in the SL).

- We do not take the message passing of the system state or external events into account, as this does not impact safety.

The interactions of Sect. 4.1 are specified by splitting them into *actions* representing the send and receive parts, as illustrated below. The *Layer* parameters indicate the sending and receiving layer of the action, respectively.

sort
    Layer = **struct** logical | safety | hardware;

act
    snd_req, rcv_req : Layer × Layer × InstructionSet;
    snd_ack_req, rcv_ack_req : Layer × Layer × InstructionSet;
    snd_deny_req, rcv_deny_req : Layer × Layer × InstructionSet;
    snd_ack_exec, rcv_ack_exec : Layer × Layer × InstructionSet × Result;
    snd_state, rcv_state : Layer × Layer × GlobalState;
    snd_event, rcv_event : Layer × Layer × Event;

Finally, using the actions defined above, the behaviour of the SL is specified as follows:

sort
    ProcState = **struct** ps_idle | ps_ack_deny | ps_req | ps_exec | ps_ack_exec;

proc
    SL(ps : ProcState, gs_sl : GlobalState, is : InstructionSet, r : Result) =
      (ps ≈ ps_idle) →
        ($\sum_{\text{isa:InstructionSet}}$ valid(isa) → rcv_req(logical, safety, isa) ·
        SL(ps_ack_deny, gs_sl, isa, r)
)
    +
      (ps ≈ ps_ack_deny) →
        (allowed(is, gs_sl) →
          (snd_ack_req(safety, logical, is) · SL(ps_req, gs_sl, is, r)) ⋄
          (snd_deny_req(safety, logical, is) · SL(ps_idle, gs_sl, is, r))
)
    +
      (ps ≈ ps_req) →
        snd_req(safety, hardware, is) · SL(ps_exec, gs_sl, is, r)
    +
      (ps ≈ ps_exec) →
        ($\sum_{\text{ra:Result}}$ rcv_ack_exec(safety, hardware, is, ra) ·
        SL(ps_ack_exec, nextstate(is, ra, gs_sl), is, ra)
)
    +
      (ps ≈ ps_ack_exec) →
        snd_ack_exec(safety, logical, is, r) · SL(ps_idle, gs_sl, is, r)
    +
      (ps ≈ ps_idle) →
        ($\sum_{\text{e:Event}}$ possible(e, gs_sl) → rcv_event(hardware, safety, e) ·
        SL(ps, nextstate(e, gs_sl), is, r)
)
    ;

init
    SL(ps_idle, init_gs, [ ], ok);

This specifies a process SL with 4 parameters, representing the current state of the process (ps) and the garage (gs_sl), and the instruction set (is) and execution result (r) that are to be processed. The behaviour is a collection of alternatives formed from condition-action-result sequences. A summation over a data type indicates a choice over all elements of that data type. Finally, we use three additional functions: *valid* ensures that the lists we use to model sets do not contain duplicates, *possible* indicates whether it is possible for an event to occur, and *nextstate* returns the new state of the system. We do not provide specifications of these functions here.

5.4   Reductions

Due to the enormous number of possible instruction sets that can be requested and executed, it is impossible to perform simulation, let alone verification, on the behavioural specification. This section describes a number of reductions we apply to enable verification. The corresponding specifications can be found in [10].

Reduction 1. Abstract from sets of instructions by focusing on single instructions only.

On the one hand this abstraction is dangerous, because sets of instructions are an essential part of the system. On the other hand, the core safety issue lies in the *allowed* function applied to single instructions. Furthermore, the number of possible system configurations remains the same, since the result of executing a set of instructions concurrently is the same as executing them sequentially. This implies that in the corresponding state space the number of states remains fixed, but the number of transitions is reduced substantially.

   Although the former reduction makes it possible to perform simulation, it is not very effective. The aim is to focus on logical mistakes and not hardware failures. For this reason, we also abstract from non-essential messages.

Reduction 2. Abstract from requests and acknowledgements. It is assumed that instructions are executed successfully by the HAL.

The state space corresponding to the specification after applying the above reductions is still prohibitively large. It consists of a calculated total of 6.4×10^{11} (640 billion) states, and a multiple of this in transitions. Hence, we apply one last abstraction.

Reduction 3. The number of positions of the belts is reduced to the minimum that retains the behavioural characteristics of the original configuration. This entails the following. The positions on the conveyor belts b_r2 and b_r3 are reduced to two positions each (see Fig. 3). Also, belts b_r1a and b_r1b are reduced to $1\frac{1}{2}$ full positions (or 3 half positions) each.

The resulting state space has 3.3×10^6 (3.3 million) states and 9.8×10^7 (98 million) transitions, which existing verification tools can manage. Although strictly speaking we are not concerned with proving deadlock-free behaviour, we note that this state space contains no deadlock.

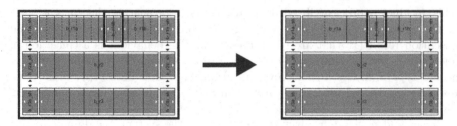

Fig. 3. Reduction of the floor plan

5.5   Formal Requirements and Verification

We verify our safety requirements by extending the specification with *error* actions that are only executed when a requirement is violated. Hence, the requirements are fulfilled when the state space does not contain any error actions. To do this, we translate the high-level requirements from Sect. 5.1 to a lower level of detail. For example, requirement 3(a) is translated to the following.

For all heights h the instruction *move_lift(h)* should not be allowed if both:

1. The lift is at the basement level.
2. The lift contains a car placed halfway on the lift.

This is translated to mCRL2 as the condition-action-result sequence shown below, and is appended to the original specification.

$$\sum_{i:\text{Instruction},lh:\text{LiftHeight}}(i \approx \text{move\_lift}(lh) \land \text{valid}(i) \land \text{allowed}(i, gs\_sl) \land$$
$$\text{ls}(gs\_sl) \approx \text{ls\_basement} \land$$
$$\neg\text{free}(\text{positions}(b\_r1lift), \text{fs}(gs\_sl)) \land$$
$$\neg(\text{even\_occ}(\text{positions\_b\_r1}([b\_r1a\_sh, b\_r1a]), \text{fs}(gs\_sl)) \land$$
$$\quad \text{even\_occ}(\text{positions\_b\_r1}([b\_r1b, b\_r1b\_sh]), \text{fs}(gs\_sl)))$$
$$) \rightarrow \text{error}(\text{req3a}, 1) \cdot \delta$$

Extra care is taken to specify the enabling conditions of the error actions: the use of elements of the definition of the *allowed* function are avoided as much as possible, since mistakes in the original specification could carry over to the verification. When we extend the original specification in this fashion, it does not contain any errors. This means that all the requirements are fulfilled.

We conclude this section with some figures. The complete specification contains 991 lines of mCRL2 code, whereas the verification code contains 217 lines of mCRL2, amounting to a total of 1208 lines. Verification took 35 hours and 16 minutes on a single PC (3 GHz CPU, 4 GB RAM), and 5 hours and 38 minutes on a cluster of 34 CPUs (3 GHz CPU, 2 GB RAM). The specification and analysis of the safety layer required approximately 480 man hours to complete.

6   Discussion

Before we draw conclusions, we elaborate on two issues. We discuss how visualization helped us during the analysis. Also, we mention some issues regarding the implementation of software based on our specification.

6.1 Visualization

During specification we often resorted to simulating the behaviour of the system using the mCRL2 toolset. The simulator tool allows us to quickly and incrementally check whether our specification results in the behaviour we had anticipated. This is opposed to generating and examining an entire state space which is quite a time consuming undertaking. However, we soon realised that interpreting the text-based output of the simulator is arduous, not entirely intuitive, and prone to human error.

To address these problems and inspired by other visualization initiatives for systems analysis [11,12], we implemented a very simple visualization tool as a plug-in to the simulator. This tool receives the current system state from the simulator and maps it onto a simple 2D floor plan of the parking garage (see Fig. 4). The visualization uses visual cues to indicate the vertical lift position and whether a specific position is *occupied* (red or dark grey), *free* (green or medium gray) or *unavailable* (light gray). Tilted shuttles are also shown. After selecting a new transition, the visualization is updated and the user is able to analyse the system using this representation. The plug-in is distributed with the mCRL2 toolset [4].

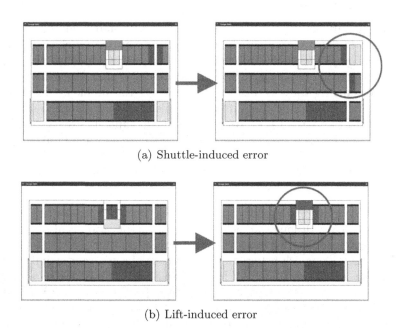

(a) Shuttle-induced error

(b) Lift-induced error

Fig. 4. Mistakes identified with the visualization plug-in

Using our visualization tool we discovered a number of problems related to the fact that cars may be moved by half positions in row r1. For instance, we moved a car toward the side of the garage and positioned it with one half on a conveyor belt and one half on a shuttle. To our surprise, it was possible to subsequently move the shuttle, literally tearing the car in half (see Fig. 4(a))! This first bug was relatively easy to fix. A similar problem occurred when two cars were positioned side-by-side on the lift, each with one half on a neighbouring conveyor belt. In this case, despite our best efforts to explicitly check for such a situation, it was possible to move the lift upward, tearing two cars in half (see Fig. 4(b)). This turned out to be a harder problem to solve and involved keeping track of the number of half-positions occupied in row r1 (see Sect. 5.5).

We found the representation of our visualization tool to be intuitively clear and easy to understand. We also believe that this mode of analysis saved a great amount of time. Since we could follow cars as they were transported down the lift and moved to new positions using the conveyor belts and shuttles, we were able to construct potentially dangerous scenarios, such as those discussed above relatively easily. This allowed us to identify and correct a number of problems early on. These included mistakes on our part as well as unknown complexities about the system setup. Although all requirements should also be checked during formal verification, we emphasise that this rests on the assumption that *all relevant questions have been identified and formalised*. By visualizing the current state it is possible to identify issues that may not have been noted otherwise.

6.2   Implementation

As far as software development is concerned, the next step would be to use the specification of data types and behaviour discussed in this article as a starting point for an implementation. Moreover, we believe that reuse of the *allowed* function is of crucial importance. Should software be designed and implemented without considering this, we believe that some of the problems we identified and addressed could easily creep into the implementation despite considerable precaution on the part of the programmers. Unfortunately, we know of cases where such an approach was not taken and where both cars and vital equipment were damaged [1].

Before starting to implement the safety layer, the following aspects require further investigation:

– We have only formally verified the specification for *individual* instructions (see Sect. 5.5). Although we believe that the specification is also correct for sets of instructions, this cannot be guaranteed.
– We do not distinguish between the occurrence of a *recoverable* and an *unrecoverable* hardware failure. All failures are assumed to be recoverable. Furthermore, execution of a set of instructions only gives one result which holds for all instructions. For more detailed error handling, the execution of individual instructions should also return results. That is, after the execution of a set of instructions, some elements may return *ok* while others may return *fail*.
– In practice, the events *add_car* and *remove_car* are not atomic. They need to be split up into a *begin* and *end* part. This results in additional safety requirements. For example, it should be impossible to execute a *move_lift* instruction between the *begin* and *end* part of an event.

Although we have not investigated the *efficiency* of the automated parking garage we foresee a performance challenge in terms of the timely stowing and recovery of cars in practice.

7 Conclusion

We have described the verified design of an automated parking garage. We proposed a system design consisting of three layers: a logical layer, a safety layer and a hardware abstraction layer. We have discussed the verified design of the safety layer. Verification guarantees that in every valid configuration of the system, no damage can occur due to the execution of unsafe instructions. We argue that our work comprises the essence of the system design regarding safety. We recommend that a future implementation should closely follow this design.

With regard to the analysis process, although formal verification is necessary to ensure that requirements are never violated, we want to stress that simulation should not be underestimated. All defects in the specification were found using simulation. Also, simulation allowed us to identify and address interesting behavioural characteristics that would probably not have been included in the requirements otherwise. In particular, we found visually supported simulation to be extremely effective. In this way we were able to gain insight into the system in a way that goes further than simply listing and verifying requirements.

Finally, in this case study software development only started after the hardware design was finished. We argue that both hardware and software experts should be involved in the entire design process to ensure that an optimal solution is found. For this reason, we argue that the current combination of hardware and software is far from optimal.

Acknowledgements

We thank Bas Ploeger and Muck van Weerdenburg for their input and suggestions. Hannes Pretorius is supported by the Netherlands Foundation for Scientific Research (NWO) under grant 612.065.410.

References

1. Verdult, E.: In de prak geparkeerd. De Ingenieur **7** (2005) 32–35
2. Groote, J.F., Mathijssen, A., Van Weerdenburg, M., Usenko, Y.S.: From μCRL to mCRL2: motivation and outline. In: Proc. Workshop on Algebraic Process Calculi: The First Twenty Five Years and Beyond. BRICS NS-05-3 (2005) 126–131
3. Groote, J.F., Mathijssen, A., Ploeger, B., Reniers, M., Van Weerdenburg, M., Van der Wulp, J.: Process algebra and mCRL2, IPA basic course on formal methods 2006. www.mcrl2.org (2006)
4. mCRL2: mCRL2 homepage (2006) www.mcrl2.org.
5. Groote, J.F., Ponse, A.: The syntax and semantics of μCRL. In: Algebra of Communicating Processes, Workshops in Computing. (1994) 26–62
6. Groote, J.F., Reniers, M.: Algebraic process verification. In: Handbook of Process Algebra. Elsevier (2001) 1151–1208

7. Fokkink, W., Groote, J.F., Pang, J., Badban, B., Van de Pol, J.: Verifying a sliding window protocol in μCRL. In: Proc. 10th Int'l Conf. Algebraic Methodology and Software Technology. Number 3116 in LNCS, Springer (2004) 148–163
8. Groote, J.F., Pang, J., Wouters, A.G.: Analysis of a distributed system for lifting trucks. J. Logic and Algebraic Programming **55**(1–2) (2003) 21–56
9. Pang, J., Fokkink, W., Hofman, R., Veldema, R.: Model checking a cache coherence protocol for a Java DSM implementation. In: Proc. International Parallel and Distributed Processing Symposium (IPDPS'03), IEEE CS Press (2003)
10. Mathijssen, A., Pretorius, A.J.: Specification, analysis, and verification of an automated parking garage. Technical Report 05-25, Technische Universiteit Eindhoven (2005)
11. Pretorius, A.J., Van Wijk, J.J.: Multidimensional visualization of transition systems. In: Proc. 9th Int'l Conf. Information Visualization (IV05), IEEE CS Press (2005) 323–328
12. Van Ham, F., Van de Wetering, H., Van Wijk, J.J.: Interactive visualization of state transition systems. IEEE Transactions on Visualization and Computer Graphics **8**(4) (2002) 319–329

Evaluating Quality of Service for Service Level Agreements

Allan Clark and Stephen Gilmore

Laboratory for Foundations of Computer Science, The University of Edinburgh,
Edinburgh, Scotland

Abstract. Quantitative analysis of quality-of-service metrics is an important tool in early evaluation of service provision. This analysis depends on being able to estimate the average duration of critical activities used by the service but at the earliest stages of service planning it may be impossible to obtain accurate estimates of the expected duration of these activities. We analyse the time-dependent behaviour of an automotive rescue service in the context of uncertainty about durations. We deploy a distributed computing platform to allow the efficient derivation of quantitative analysis results across the range of possible values for assignments of durations to the symbolic rates of our high-level formal model of the service expressed in a stochastic process algebra.

1 Introduction

Service-oriented computing is an important focus area for industrial computer systems, highlighting the crucial interplay between service provider and service consumer. Service-level agreements (SLAs) and service policies are key issues in this domain. An SLA typically incorporates a time bound and a probability bound on a particular path through the system. It will make clear the metric against which the service is being judged, how the service provision will be measured, and the penalty to be exacted if the service is not delivered with the agreed level of quality of service (QoS). We are concerned here with the quantitative core of an SLA and wish to answer formally questions of the form "Will at least 90% of all requests receive a response within 3 seconds?" which has as a probability bound "at least 90%", as a time bound "within 3 seconds", and as the path through the system "from request to response".

An SLA needs to be established in the early specification phase for a commissioned service, and the service provider needs to ensure not later than that point in time that the SLA is credible. High-level formal modelling is helpful here because it allows us to pose precise questions about a formal model of the service to be provided and to answer them using efficient, proven analysis tools [1]. The difficulty at the early specification phase is to know whether we can match the quantitative constraints of customers' requests against the efficiency or performance of the implementation of our service. In the early specification phase in model-driven software development we have no measurement data which we can use to parameterise our high-level quantitative model (since the implementation

L. Brim et al. (Eds.): FMICS and PDMC 2006, LNCS 4346, pp. 181–194, 2007.

has not yet been built), leading to uncertainty about the values of the rate constants to be used in the computation of the passage-time quantiles needed to answer the questions about satisfaction of QoS constraints.

This uncertainty is manageable in practice because although we may not know precisely the value of the rate constants to be used in the model we may know a range of values within which they will lie. The problem then is simply to evaluate our model against our SLA measure a (possibly large) number of times. This can be done by performing a parameter sweep across the range of possible values for the rates. If each of these computations leads to the conclusion that the SLA can be met, then we can accept it even in the presence of uncertainty about the rate values. However, if any of the computations leads to the conclusion that the SLA cannot be met, then we must revise the SLA to loosen the time or probability bounds which it mandates and see if this weaker SLA is still acceptable to the service consumer. An alternative would be to try to improve some of the rates at which key activities are performed, in order to fulfil the stricter SLA and avoid the need to weaken the time or probability bounds. To help with identifying the key rates in the model we need to investigate the sensitivity of the model to changes in individual rates. To do this we evaluate our chosen measure for each rate repeatedly while varying the rate throughout its range of allowable values. This will allow us to identify those rates which have a major impact on performance if varied and those rates which impact on performance little.

Specifically, we are addressing in the present paper analysis methods and tools for the efficient computation of cumulative distribution functions (CDFs) which decide whether an SLA will be met. Set against this means of evaluating SLAs by parameter sweep is the cost of the many numerical computations needed to calculate the many CDFs required. The approach which we follow here is to evaluate simultaneously many runs of the Markov chain analyser used. Parameter sweep is an approach which falls into the class of problems commonly known as "embarrassingly parallelizable". That is, there are many independent copies of the code being run in isolation with none of the complexities of management of synchronisation points which are usually associated with parallel codes. In this setting a simple approach based on a network of workstations architecture will be effective in delivering the computational effort needed.

We used the Condor [2] high-throughput computing platform to distribute the necessary SLA computation across many hosts. Condor is a widely-used long-standing workload management system. A recent paper presenting the key ideas is [3].

We model our service in the PEPA process algebra [4]. Our models are compiled into stochastic Petri nets by the Imperial PEPA Compiler, ipc, and these are analysed by the Hydra release of the DNAmaca Markov chain analyser [5], a state-of-the-art stochastic Petri net tool which computes the passage-time quantiles needed in the computation of a CDF used in the evaluation of an SLA.

PEPA models submitted to ipc must be Cyclic PEPA [6], formed by the composition of co-operating sequential components. Each of the sequential components at the leaves of the process tree is viewed as a finite state automaton with timed Markovian transitions and converted into a Petri net state machine. ipc then recurses back up the process tree composing these nets until it has produced a single net representing the complete PEPA model.

2   Related Work

Our use of Hydra on a distributed workload management system such as Condor is different in nature from previous work on using Hydra on distributed-memory parallel machines (examples include [7]) and distributed compute clusters (examples include [8]). One difference is that we initiate our Hydra execution from a PEPA model, via ipc, and are therefore using Markovian modelling exclusively ([8] addresses semi-Markov models). In work such as [7], [8] and [9] the emphasis is on *grande* modelling, where detailed models of systems are evaluated in the setting of many component replications. Due to the multitude of possible interleavings of the local states of each of these subcomponents it is not uncommon for such grande modelling to give rise to statespaces of order 10^6 [8], 10^7 [7], 10^8 [9], or 10^9 [10]. Although such sizes might seem modest if compared to the sizes of models analysed by *non-quantitative* procedures these dimensions place these analysis problems on the edge of tractability for Markovian analysis.

In contrast to the above, the style of modelling which we are using here is diminutive. Most nodes in our Condor cluster are typical desktop Pentium 4 PCs, with 1 CPU and with 1Gb of RAM. Each of these must be able to solve our modelling problem independently. The difference is that the prior work cited above is solving very large models a relatively small number of times whereas we are solving relatively small models a very large number of times.

An alternative method of answering the same question about SLAs would be first to encode the statement of the QoS measure as a formula in Continuous Stochastic Logic (CSL) [11] and then to model-check the formula against the PEPA model using the PRISM probabilistic symbolic model checker [12]. Computationally, this solution procedure would be very similar to the method which we employ, using uniformisation [13,14] to compute the transient analysis result needed from the continuous-time Markov chain representation underlying the PEPA model.

While this approach would have been successful for solving one run of the numerical computing procedure required we believe that we would have found difficulty in hosting multiple runs of PRISM on the Condor platform. As a batch processing system Condor has a notion of execution context called a *universe*. The ipc and Hydra modelling tools which we used run as native executables in Condor's vanilla universe. Java applications run on Condor's java universe (developed in [15]). However, PRISM combines both Java code and native C code in its use of the CUDD binary decision diagram library [16] via the Java Native Interface. The general approach to running Java code with JNI calls under Condor would be to execute the JVM under the vanilla universe because the java universe cannot guarantee to provide necessary libraries for the native code part of PRISM. However, this would in general require first copying the JVM binary onto the remote machine before execution of PRISM could begin. This would impose a heavy penalty on run-time which would offset significantly the advantages to be gained from Condor-based distribution.

3   Markovian Process Algebras

Markovian process algebras such as PEPA extend classical process algebras by associating an exponentially-distributed random variable with each activity representing the average rate at which this activity can be performed. The random variable X is said to have an exponential distribution with parameter λ ($\lambda > 0$) if it has the distribution function

$$F(x) = \begin{cases} 1 - e^{-\lambda x} & \text{for } x > 0 \\ 0 & \text{for } x \leq 0 \end{cases}$$

The mean, or expected value, of this exponential distribution is

$$\mu = E[X] = \int_{-\infty}^{\infty} x\lambda e^{-\lambda x} dx = \frac{1}{\lambda}$$

An activity in a PEPA model takes the form $(\alpha, \lambda).P$ ("perform activity α at exponentially-distributed rate λ and behave as process P"). The high-level expression of the model includes a symbolic rate variable λ. The model is evaluated against a valuation which assigns numerical values to all of the symbolic rates of the model.

All activities in a PEPA model are timed, and via the structured operational semantics of the language, PEPA models give rise to continuous-time, finite-state stochastic processes called Continuous-Time Markov Chains (CTMCs).

The relationship between the process algebra model and the CTMC representation is the following. The process terms (P_i) reachable from the initial state of the PEPA model by applying the operational semantics of the language form the states of the CTMC (X_i). For every set of labelled transitions between states P_i and P_j of the model $\{(\alpha_1, r_1), \ldots, (\alpha_n, r_n)\}$ add a transition with rate r between X_i and X_j where r is the sum of $r_1, \ldots, r_n$. The activity labels (α_i) are necessary at the process algebra level in order to enforce synchronisation points, but are no longer needed at the Markov chain level.

A CTMC can be represented by a set of states X and a transition rate matrix R. The matrix entry in position r_{ij} is λ if it is possible for the CTMC to transition from state i to state j at rate λ. An infinitesimal generator matrix Q is formed from the transition rate matrix by normalising the diagonal elements to ensure that each row sums to zero. The generator matrix is usually sparse.

3.1   Transient Analysis and Uniformisation

Investigation of SLAs requires the transient analysis of a CTMC. That is, we are concerned with finding the transient state probability row vector $\pi(t) = [\pi_0(t), \ldots, \pi_{n-1}(t)]$ where $\pi_i(t)$ denotes the probability that the CTMC is in state i at time t. Transient and passage-time analysis of CTMCs proceeds by uniformisation [13,14]. The generator matrix, Q, is "uniformized" with:

$$P = Q/q + I$$

where $q > \max_i |Q_{ii}|$. This process transforms a CTMC into one in which all states have the same mean holding time $1/q$.

Passage-time computation is concerned with knowing the probability of reaching a designated target state from a designated source state. It rests on two key sub-computations. First, the time to complete n hops ($n = 1, 2, 3, \ldots$), which is an Erlang distribution with parameters n and q. Second, the probability that the transition between source and target states occurs in exactly n hops.

3.2   Model Checking

A widely-used logic for model checking properties against continuous-time Markov chains is Continuous Stochastic Logic (CSL) [11]. The well-formed formulae of CSL are made up of *state formulae* ϕ and *path formulae* ψ. The syntax of CSL is below.

$$\phi ::= true \mid false \mid a \mid \phi \wedge \phi \mid \phi \vee \phi \mid \neg \phi \mid \mathcal{P}_{\bowtie p}[\psi] \mid \mathcal{S}_{\bowtie p}[\phi]$$
$$\psi ::= X\,\phi \mid \phi\,U^I\,\phi \mid \phi\,U\,\phi$$

where a is an atomic proposition, $\bowtie \in \{<, \leq, >, \geq\}$ is a relational parameter, $p \in [0, 1]$ is a probability, and I is an interval of $\mathbb{R}$. Derived logical operators such as implication ($\Rightarrow$) can be encoded in the usual way.

Paths of interest through the states of the model are characterised by the *path formulae* specified by $\mathcal{P}$. Path formulae either refer to the next state (using the X operator), or record that one proposition is always satisfied until another is achieved (the until-formulae use the U-operator).

Performance information is encoded into the CSL formulae via the time-bounded until operator (U^I) and the steady-state operator, $\mathcal{S}$. The evaluation of time-bounded until formulae against a CTMC in a CSL-based model checker such as PRISM [12] or MRMC [17] proceeds by transient analysis using uniformisation and a numerical procedure such as the Fox-Glynn algorithm [18].

3.3   Sensitivity Analysis

Due to the roles which activities play in creating the dynamics of our stochastic process algebra model it may be that increasing the rate of one activity increases the score obtained by the model on our chosen performance measure of interest. Conversely, increasing the rate of another activity may decrease the score which we get. Changing one rate a little may vary the score a lot. Changing another rate a lot might only vary the score a little. The study of how changes in performance depend on changes in parameter values in this way is known as *sensitivity analysis*.

Our main aim here is to determine that our SLA is met across all of the possible combinations of average values of rates across all their allowable ranges.

However, by collecting the results where one rate is varied we can examine the sensitivity of our measure with respect to that rate, at no added computational cost.

The practical relevance of sensitivity analysis is that we may find that the model is relatively insensitive to changes in one of the rates. In this case we need not spend as much effort in trying to determine precisely the exact average value of this rate. This effort would be better directed to determining the values of rates for which the model has been shown to be sensitive. Further, sensitivity analysis will identify the most critical areas to improve if failing to meet an SLA.

4   Case Study: Automotive Crash Scenario

Our case study concerns the assessment of an SLA offered by an automotive collision support service. The scenario with which these systems are concerned is road traffic accidents and dispatch of medical assistance to crash victims. Drivers wishing to use the service must have in-car GPS location tracking devices with communication capabilities and have pre-registered their mobile phone information with the service.

The scenario under study considers the following sequence of events.

– A road traffic accident occurs. The car airbag deploys.
– Deployment of the air bag causes the on-board safety system to report the car's current location (obtained by GPS) to a pre-established accident report endpoint.
– The service at the reporting endpoint attempts to call the registered driver's mobile phone.
– If there is no answer to the call then medical assistance is dispatched to the reported location of the car (presuming that the driver has been incapacitated by injuries sustained in the accident).

There may be many possible reasons why the driver does not answer the phone. The phone may be turned off; its battery may be flat; the phone may be out of network range; the driver may have switched to a new telephone provider, and not informed the collision support service; the phone may not be in the car; it may have been smashed on impact; or many other possibilities.

The accident reporting service cannot know the exact reason why the driver does not answer the phone. They only know that an accident has happened which was serious enough to cause the airbag to be deployed, and that the driver has not confirmed that they do not need medical assistance. In this setting they will dispatch medical help (even if sometimes this will mean that help is sent when it is not absolutely necessary).

The SLA related to this scenario concerns the response time of the passage from the deployment of the airbag to the dispatch of medical assistance. The parameters of our modelling study are:

– the rate at which information on the location of the car—and any other pertinent information such as speed on impact, engine status, and other

diagnostic information obtained from the on-board diagnostic systems and controllers—can be reported to the accident reporting service;
- the time taken to confirm that the driver is not answering their mobile telephone; and
- the time taken to contact the emergency services to dispatch medical assistance.

None of these parameters are known exactly, but their average values are known to lie within a range of acceptable operation. We are, of course, interested in worst case bounds on passage-time quantiles and also in best case analysis but also in the variety of possible responses in between.

4.1 PEPA Model

In this section we consider the sequence of events which begins with the deployment of the airbag after the crash and finishes with the dispatch of the medical response team. The first phase of the sequence is concerned with relaying the information to the remote service, reporting the accident. When the diagnostic report from the car is received the service processes the report and matches it to the driver information stored on their database.

$$Car_1 \stackrel{def}{=} (airbag, r_1).Car_2$$
$$Car_2 \stackrel{def}{=} (reportToService, r_2).Car_3$$
$$Car_3 \stackrel{def}{=} (processReport, r_3).Car_4$$

The second phase of this passage through the system focuses on the attempted dialogue between the service and the registered driver of the car. We consider the case where the driver does not answer the incoming call because this is the case which leads to the medical response team being sent.

$$Car_4 \stackrel{def}{=} (callDriversPhone, r_4).Car_5$$
$$Car_5 \stackrel{def}{=} (timeoutDriversPhone, r_5).Car_6$$

The service makes a final check on the execution of the procedure before the decision is taken to send medical help. At this stage the driver is awaiting rescue.

$$Car_6 \stackrel{def}{=} (rescue, r_6).Car_7$$
$$Car_7 \stackrel{def}{=} (awaitRescue, r_7).Car_1$$

This takes us to the end of the passage of interest through the system behaviour.

4.2 Rates Constants and Ranges

All timings are expressed in minutes, because that is an appropriate granularity for the events which are being modelled. Thus a rate of 1.0 means that something happens once a minute (on average). A rate of 6.0 means that the associated activity happens six times a minute on average, or that its mean or expected duration is ten seconds, which is an equivalent statement. A table of the ranges of average rate values used appears in Table 1.

4.3   Sensitivity Analysis for the Automotive Crash Scenario

We consider how the cumulative distribution function for the passage from airbag deployment to dispatch of medical assistance is affected as the values of the rates r_2 to r_6 are varied as specified in Table 1. The results are presented in Figure 1.

Table 1. Minimum and maximum values of the rates from the model

Rate	Value min	max	Meaning
r_1	600.0	600.0	an airbag deploys in 1/10 of a second
r_2	2.0	10.0	the car can transmit location data in 6 to 30 seconds
r_3	0.5	1.5	it takes about one minute to register the incoming data
r_4	1.5	2.5	it takes about thirty seconds to call the driver's phone
r_5	1.0	60.0	give the driver from a second to one minute to answer
r_6	0.25	3.0	vary about one minute to decide to dispatch medical help
r_7	1.0	1.0	arbitrary value — the driver is now awaiting rescue

What we see from these results is that variations in upstream rates (near the start of the passage of interest) such as r_2, r_3 and r_4 have less impact overall than variations in downstream rates (near the end of the passage of interest) such as r_5 and r_6. This is true even when the scale over which the upstream rates are varied is much more than the scale over which the downstream rates are varied (for example, contrast variation in r_2 against variation in r_6).

The conclusion to be drawn from such an observation is that, if failing to meet a desired QoS specified in an SLA then it is better to expend effort in making a faster decision to dispatch medical help (governed by rate r_6) than to expend effort in trying to transmit location data faster (governed by rate r_2), over the range of variability in the rates considered in the present study.

Another use of this sensitivity data would be to find an optimum time to hold while waiting for the driver to answer the phone. The optimisation problem to be solved here is to decide how long to wait before terminating the call in case of non-answer. If the service providers wait too long then they risk failing to meet their SLA. If they wait too little then they risk dispatching medical assistance when it is not actually necessary. In this case the sensitivity graph of rate r_5 shows a portion where changes in rate value have little impact and so targeting the lowest rate here gives the driver more time to answer the phone.

A further kind of graph which can be drawn is depicted in Figure 2. To produce this graph we have held constant the time and varied two of the rates involved, r_5 and r_6. From this kind of graph one can analyse how the probability of completion by a chosen time bound can depend on the relationship between two of the rates. In this graph we can see that when the rate r_5 is low, as in the front line of the graph, then varying the rate r_6 has little effect. However the back line of the graph shows that when rate r_5 is high, varying rate r_6 has a greater effect.

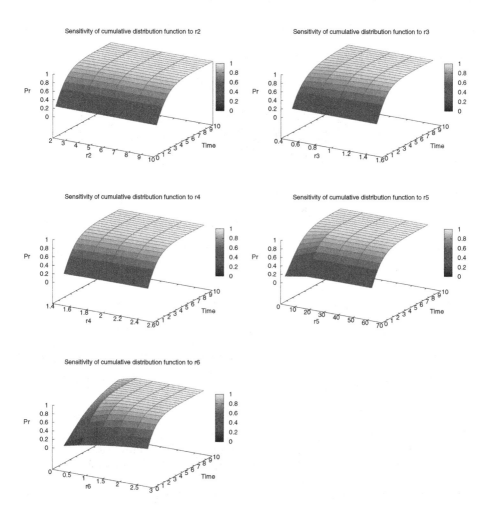

Fig. 1. Graphs of cumulative distribution function sensitivity to changes in rates for the passage from airbag deployment to dispatch of medical assistance

The reverse relationship between rates r_5 and r_6 is also true. The model we used was a linear model, which means that there were few paths through the model. In particular the action *rescue* governed by the rate r_6 cannot be performed until the action *timeoutDriversPhone*, regulated by rate r_5, has occurred. Also once the *timeoutDriversPhone* action has occurred there is nowhere for the model to go but to a *rescue* action. This means that if either of the two rates associated with these two actions is very low, then that action will be the bottleneck for that part of the model. Varying the other rate will have less effect.

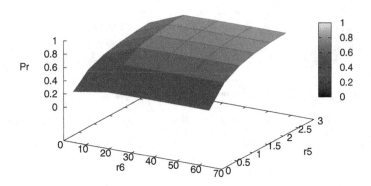

Fig. 2. Graph of probability of completion against variation in the rates r_5 and r_6, for a fixed time value

5   Relation to Model Checking

In this section we consider how the results expressed above relate to model checking a CSL formula against our model of the system. Expressed as a CSL formula an example of the kind of question which we are asking is the following.

$$airbag \Rightarrow \mathcal{P}_{>0.9}[true\ U^{[0,10]}\ rescue]$$

In words, this says "If the airbag in the car deploys, is it true with probability at least 0.9 that the rescue service will be sent within 10 minutes?"

We consider a more general form of the question which is the following

$$airbag \Rightarrow \mathcal{P}_{\bowtie p}[true\ U^{[0,10]}\ rescue]$$

We consider this for all relations $\bowtie\ \in\ \{<,\leq,>,\geq\}$ and for all values of the probability bound $0 \leq p \leq 1$. Further, we answer these general formulae not for only a single assignment of values to symbolic rate variables (as would be the case for conventional model checking) but across the range of assignments presented in Figure 1.

In order to determine upper and lower bounds on the probability with which the rescue service is dispatched within 10 minutes we can simply plot the probability computed via transient analysis against experiment number. Each mapping of rate values onto symbolic rate names is an experiment.

The graph of computed probability against experiment number for the first fifty experiments is shown in Figure 3. Experiments are grouped whereby a group contains about five evaluations of the CDF corresponding to the SLA for five assignments of concrete rate values to one of the symbolic rates r_2 to r_6. This shows slightly more than the first eight groups of experiments.

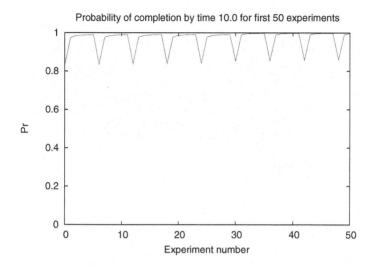

Fig. 3. Graph of probability of completing the passage from airbag deployment to medical assistance dispatch within ten minutes plotted against experiment number over the first fifty experiments

The graph of computed probability against experiment number for all the 3750 experiments is shown in Figure 4. At this level of granularity it is not easy to pick out groups of runs but one can see that all experiments achieve at least a minimum QoS that at least 83% of calls to the service will lead to medical assistance being dispatched within 10 minutes.

One use of these graphs is to identify all of the combinations of average rate values which allow the service to satisfy an SLA which requires their quality of service to be above a specific threshold. For example, say that the service providers wish to, or need to, meet the SLA that the rescue service is dispatched within 10 minutes in 92% of cases of airbag deployment. The graph in Figure 4 identifies all of the combinations of parameter values which achieve this bound, or do better. Some of these might be much easier to realise than others so the service could meet its QoS requirement by striving for those combinations of average rates for individual actions of the system such as taking the decision to dispatch medical help (at rate r_6).

6   Further Work

Our future programme of work on using ipc and Hydra on the Condor distributed computing platform is directed towards making better use of the support which Condor provides for distributed computing. This will include the use of the **standard** universe which will allow checkpointing within a run, and allow a long-running Hydra computation to be migrated in-run from a machine claimed by a user onto a presently-idle machine.

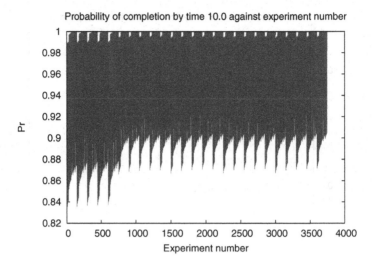

Fig. 4. Graph of probability of completing the passage from airbag deployment to medical assistance dispatch within ten minutes plotted against experiment number over all 3750 experiments

In this work we have made the conceptually convenient simplification of thinking of Hydra as a single, indivisible application which accepts a stochastic Petri net as input and returns as its output a CDF showing passage-time quantiles. While this is an accurate conceptual description Hydra is in fact structured as a collection of independent components (a parser, a state-space generator, a functional analyser, a solver and a uniformiser). The application which we think of as Hydra is a high-level driver executing these components in the order described above.

The opportunity which this gives us for the future is to structure Hydra as a directed acyclic graph (DAG) of component tasks. To run Hydra on Condor in this way we would specify the inputs and outputs from each sub-component (state-space generator, functional analyser and others) and connect these together replacing Hydra's top-level driver with the appropriate use of Condor's DAG manager (DAGman). This would offer a greater range of possibilities for component deployment on our Condor pool.

7   Conclusions

The automotive rescue case study used in this paper gives rise to a relatively small continuous-time Markov chain, the unit solution cost of which is not excessive. However, when repeatedly re-running this solution procedure for different parameter values these small costs quickly start to add up. The Condor distributed computing system allowed us to execute these many copies of the job simultaneously.

The parallel structure of the joint computation was very simple; running a sequential application multiple times. No dynamic process creation was required within an individual run, and no inter-process communication was needed. A full-blown parallel computing infrastructure such as PVM or MPI would have been excessive but Condor suited our problem very well.

The style of analysis which we pursue here is embarrassingly parallelizable, meaning that the throughput of jobs increases linearly with the number of machines available. This means that if given access to a larger Condor pool, or the ability to connect Condor pools together, then the rate at which jobs can be processed continues to grow and is not capped by an inherent bound on problem scalability. Thus the combination of ipc, Hydra and Condor as a modelling and experimentation framework provides a strong platform on which to conduct larger and more complex experiments.

Acknowledgements

The authors are supported by the SENSORIA project (EU FET-IST Global Computing 2 project 016004). We are grateful to Angelika Zobel and Nora Koch of F.A.S.T. München for the specification of the automotive case study. We modified the open-source software tool ipc developed and made freely available by Jeremy Bradley. We ran our models on the Condor cluster provided in the School of Informatics at Edinburgh and benefited from advice from Chris Cooke on using this effectively.

References

1. William J Knottenbelt. Generalised Markovian analysis of timed transition systems. MSc thesis, University of Cape Town, South Africa, July 1996.
2. Condor project homepage. Website with documentation and software, University of Wisconsin-Madison, April 2006. http://www.cs.wisc.edu/condor/.
3. Douglas Thain, Todd Tannenbaum, and Miron Livny. Distributed computing in practice: the Condor experience. *Concurrency - Practice and Experience*, 17(2-4):323–356, 2005.
4. J. Hillston. *A Compositional Approach to Performance Modelling*. Cambridge University Press, 1996.
5. J.T. Bradley and W.J. Knottenbelt. The ipc/HYDRA tool chain for the analysis of PEPA models. In *Proc. 1st International Conference on the Quantitative Evaluation of Systems (QEST 2004)*, pages 334–335, Enschede, Netherlands, September 2004.
6. J. Hillston and M. Ribaudo. Stochastic process algebras: a new approach to performance modeling. In K. Bagchi and G. Zobrist, editors, *Modeling and Simulation of Advanced Computer Systems*. Gordon Breach, 1998.
7. Nicholas J Dingle, Peter G Harrison, and William J Knottenbelt. Uniformization and hypergraph partitioning for the distributed computation of response time densities in very large Markov models. *Journal of Parallel and Distributed Computing*, 64:908–920, 2004.

8. Jeremy T Bradley, Nicholas J Dingle, Peter G Harrison, and William J Knottenbelt. Distributed computation of passage time quantiles and transient state distributions in large semi-Markov models. In *Performance Modelling, Evaluation and Optimization of Parallel and Distributed Systems*, Nice, April 2003. IEEE Computer Society Press.

9. W J Knottenbelt, P G Harrison, M S Mestern, and P S Kritzinger. A probabilistic dynamic technique for the distributed generation of very large state spaces. *Performance Evaluation*, 39(1–4):127–148, February 2000.

10. R. Mehmood and Jon Crowcroft. Parallel iterative solution method for large sparse linear equation systems. Technical Report UCAM-CL-TR-650, Computer Laboratory, University of Cambridge, UK, October 2005.

11. A. Aziz, K. Sanwal, V. Singhal, and R. Brayton. Verifying continuous time Markov chains. In *Computer-Aided Verification*, volume 1102 of *LNCS*, pages 169–276. Springer-Verlag, 1996.

12. M. Kwiatkowska, G. Norman, and D. Parker. PRISM: Probabilistic symbolic model checker. In A.J. Field and P.G. Harrison, editors, *Proceedings of the 12th International Conference on Modelling Tools and Techniques for Computer and Communication System Performance Evaluation*, number 2324 in Lecture Notes in Computer Science, pages 200–204, London, UK, April 2002. Springer-Verlag.

13. W. Grassmann. Transient solutions in Markovian queueing systems. *Computers and Operations Research*, 4:47–53, 1977.

14. D. Gross and D.R. Miller. The randomization technique as a modelling tool and solution procedure for transient Markov processes. *Operations Research*, 32:343–361, 1984.

15. Al Globus, Eric Langhirt, Miron Livny, Ravishankar Ramamurthy, Marvin Solomon, and Steve Traugott. JavaGenes and Condor: Cycle-scavenging genetic algorithms. In *Proceedings of the ACM Conference on Java Grande*, pages 134–139, San Francisco, CA, 2000.

16. F. Somenzi. *CUDD: CU Decision Diagram Package*. Department of Electrical and Computer Engineering, University of Colorado at Boulder, February 2001.

17. J.-P. Katoen, M. Khattri, and I. S. Zapreev. A Markov reward model checker. In *Proceedings of the Second International conference Quantitative Evaluation of Systems (QEST)*, pages 243–244. IEEE CS Press, 2005.

18. Bennett L. Fox and Peter W. Glynn. Computing Poisson probabilities. *Communications of the ACM*, 31:440–445, 1988.

Simulation-Based Performance Analysis of a Medical Image-Processing Architecture

P.J.L. Cuijpers[1] and A.V. Fyukov[2]

[1] Technische Universiteit Eindhoven
Den Dolech 2, 5600 MB Eindhoven, The Netherlands
[2] Philips Research
Prof. Holstlaan 4, 5656 AA Eindhoven, The Netherlands

Abstract. In this paper, we show a simulation method for performance prediction of medical image processing chains, based on the real-time calculus of [9]. In particular, we focus on estimating the latency and throughput of a given image processing chain and its distribution over hardware resources. The architectural level of abstraction of the real-time calculus approach makes our method flexible, so that different design decisions can be studied using similar models. The choice for simulation rather than the usual algebraic analysis of real-time calculus equations, gives us the possibility to include a number of performance relevant implementation details in our models for which analytical estimates are not available.

1 Introduction

In the field of medical imaging systems, a great variety of consumers exist, leading to a great variety of requirements, features, and budget. As a consequence, architects of medical image processing systems have to make the tradeoff between general purpose hardware, in order to gain flexibility in cost and functionality, and dedicated hardware, in order to gain high performance in terms of throughput and latency. Furthermore, although the physics behind the imaging is different for each product, the image processing is often similar. This means that the aforementioned tradeoff has to be made over and over again, for products that have a comparable software architecture.

In this paper, we model a core part of the architecture of image processing systems, the image transfer engine. This engine is designed to handle the passing of image data between both general purpose and dedicated hardware resources. It takes a so-called image processing graph (see Figure 1 in section 2) as input. This graph depicts the order in which an image is processed by several algorithms and depicts which algorithms run on which processing units. The engine then distributes the execution of image processing algorithms according to this graph.

The goal of our case study, is to develop a method for predicting the throughput and latency of a given image processing graph when implemented using the image processing engine. Previously, we developed an (unpublished) analytic formula, based on the work of [7], giving a quick, but rough, best-case analysis of latency

L. Brim et al. (Eds.): FMICS and PDMC 2006, LNCS 4346, pp. 195–210, 2007.

and throughput. This formula was used to eliminate infeasible image processing graphs in an early design phase. The simulation method presented in this paper serves as a follow-up analysis, and gives a more accurate estimate by taking a number of performance relevant implementation details of the engine into account. Whenever possible, we keep an architectural level of abstraction in our models and, as a result, performance estimates for large image processing graphs (for example 10 algorithms over 16 resources) can be made with a relatively low effort. Even when the modeling is done by hand, performance estimates can be made in a couple of hours, provided the right measurements are already available.

As a mathematical formalism underlying our simulations, we choose the real-time calculus of [9]. This formalism is based on the network calculus of [3]. To the best of our knowledge, simulation of real-time calculus formulas has not been used in industrial case studies before. We are aware of a number of studies in which performance bounds were estimated algebraically using real-time calculus (see for example [8,10]), but this analysis is not possible on our models due to a number of implementation details in the engine. For example, the engine splits images into image parts, and processes those image parts as separate entities (see section 2). In real-time calculus, it is difficult to perform an algebraic analysis on the processing of separate entities, since this requires quantization of data streams, for which no theory is available yet. In comparison, the analytic estimates of [7,2] were abandoned because they are not suited to analyze the way in which our engine handles the creation of overlap between image parts. This creation of overlap is necessary for some image processing algorithms, and turns out to be expensive in terms of latency when applied at the wrong point in the image processing graph.

Compared to more established formalisms like timed/colored petri-nets [4] and queuing theory [5], that are also fit for simulation, real-time calculus has the advantage that it allows an easy description of the preemptive scheduling of resources. This is relevant, since the engine allows multiple algorithms running on the same resource in a preemptive way. Another advantage of the real-time calculus approach, is that it supports the architectural level of abstraction that we are aiming for. An alternative candidate in this respect, would be to use a language like VHDL, as in [6].

The remainder of this paper is structured as follows. In section 2, we describe the generic image processing features of the image transfer engine, and give the real-time calculus equations that characterize each feature. In section 3, we discuss the measurements that we used to validate our models and to characterize the individual image processing algorithms. Furthermore, we discuss the results of some of our simulations. In section 4, we discuss our conclusions regarding the applicability of real-time calculus for performance analysis of real-time image processing graphs through simulation.

2   Modeling the Image Transfer Engine

In this section, we discuss the workings of the image transfer engine, and our real-time calculus model of it. The first subsection gives an overview of the engine,

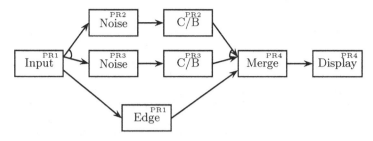

Fig. 1. An image processing graph with hardware mapping

the ensuing subsections each discuss one particular factor that plays a role in determining the throughput and latency of an image processing chain.

2.1   Image Processing Graphs

High throughput in image processing can be achieved by *pipelining*, i.e. by splitting the image processing into several consecutive steps that are executed by different resources, or by *scattering*, i.e. by cutting the image into parts which are processed separately on different resources. A third option is *parallel processing*, which means that the image processing is split into several synchronous steps that are later combined to form the final image. The difference between scattering and parallel processing, is that with scattering the image is divided into parts that are all processed in the same way, while with parallel processing the image is processed as a whole by different algorithms. Often scattering requires some redundancy in the computations and data transfer, because the separate image parts need to overlap, while parallel processing is in turn harder to implement, and very much depends on the kind of processing that is desired. Incidentally, the *creation of overlap* gives rise to additional latency, as we will see further on in this section. The various ways of image processing lead to the intuitive notion of viewing an image processing chain as a graph in which:

- Nodes represent basic image processing algorithms, and are labeled with the resource on which the algorithm runs;
- Edges represent communication lines in a pipeline. Depending on the nodes they connect, different kinds of communication (shared memory, LAN, etc.) may be implied;
- Multiple edges model parallel processing of an image by different subgraphs;
- A fan of edges (decorated by an arc) models a scattering of image parts over a number of (identical) subgraphs.

Figure 2 shows a (simplified) BNF-definition of our image processing graphs, as it is used by the image processing engine.

An example of an image processing graph is depicted in Figure 1. This graph shows how resource PR1 takes an image stream from the network (Input) and performs a (2-)scattered execution of a noise-reduction algorithm (Noise) and a contrast/brightness algorithm (C/B), running on resources PR2 and PR3. In

```
<Graph> ::= {<Node>}              ; A graph is a collection of nodes
 <Node> ::= Node Begin
            Label     <String> ; Name of the node
            Resource  <String> ; Name of the targeted resource
            Algorithm <String> ; Name of the algorithm
            Overlap   <Int>    ; Necessary amount of overlap
            Input     {<Port>} ; Sync. input from 0 or more ports
            Output    {<Port>} ; Sync. output to 0 or more ports
            End Node
 <Port> ::= {<String>}             ; Each port scatters or gathers 0 or
                                   ; more nodes, represented by their labels
```

Fig. 2. BNF definition of an image processing graph

parallel, there is an edge-detection algorithm (Edge), running on resource PR1. The result is synchronized using a merge algorithm (Merge) and displayed on a screen (Display), using resource PR4.

What is missing in the image processing graphs, is how the distribution of a resource over multiple algorithms is scheduled. For example, one might want to give the input node of the graph higher priority than all other nodes to prevent the loss of images, while all other nodes have equal priority with respect to each other. Whether this is a good choice is still a subject of debate, and the decisions made in our image processing engine are temporary in that respect. Therefore, we allow different kinds of scheduling in our model.

Summarizing, we recognize the following factors to influence the performance of an image processing graph.

- Basic image processing algorithms
- Pipelining
- Parallel processing and synchronization
- Scattering and gathering
- Overlap creation
- Connections between resources
- Resource scheduling

In the remainder of this section, we will treat each of these factors separately. We give constitutive equations for each of the factors, and combine these equations into a model for the image processing graph as a whole.

2.2   Basic Image Processing Algorithms

The starting point of real-time calculus, is to consider cumulative request streams $R(t)$ [pixel] and cumulative resource streams $C(t)$ [operations] in a system. In our case study, the request stream models the total number of image parts that has passed through a certain part of the graph at a certain time, while the resource stream models the total amount of processing power that has been offered by the individual resources. An image processing algorithm is represented by an

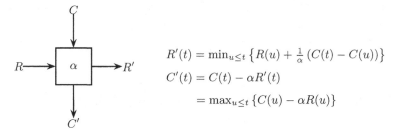

$$R'(t) = \min_{u \leq t} \left\{ R(u) + \tfrac{1}{\alpha} \left(C(t) - C(u) \right) \right\}$$

$$C'(t) = C(t) - \alpha R'(t)$$

$$= \max_{u \leq t} \left\{ C(u) - \alpha R(u) \right\}$$

Fig. 3. Basic processing in Real-time Calculus

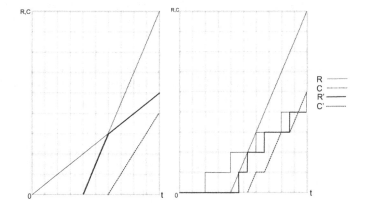

Fig. 4. Example of a data flow (left) and a quantized data flow (right)

abstract processing unit that describes how a cumulative input stream $R(t)$ and a cumulative resource stream $C(t)$ are transformed into a cumulative output stream $R'(t)$ and cumulative stream $C'(t)$ of unused resources. In our model, this transformation is based on the (constant) weight α $[\frac{\text{operations}}{\text{pixel}}]$ of the algorithm, representing the amount of resources that is needed to process one image pixel. For each algorithm, we then find the constitutive equations given in figure 3. These equations are adapted from [9].

The equations express that, in an interval $[u, t]$, the number of processed requests is limited by the amount of resources $C(t) - C(u)$ that arrives in this interval. Furthermore, by taking $u = t$, we see that this number can never exceed the total number of requests $R(t)$ at time t. Conversely, the number of unused resources can be found by subtracting what is used, $\alpha R'(t)$, from what is delivered, $C(t)$. Note, that these equations are only valid if we assume that requests are buffered and that processing power is the dominating resource. Furthermore, the factor α suggests that the resource usage is independent of the content of the data and linear in its size. This assumption, however, is only essential for the analytic treatment of the equations. In our simulations, α does not have to be constant. A movie with changing image content may for example be reflected by a change in α over time.

An example of a data flow that results from the real-time calculus equations, has been depicted in the left graph of Figure 4. We have taken a steady stream of requests $R(t) = t$ and a delayed stream of resources $C(t) = \max(3t - 6, 0)$ for this example.

The smallest data unit that occurs in our image transfer engine is known as an *image part*. Image parts still contain many pixels, and the size S [pixel] of an image is always a multiple of the size s [pixel] of an image part. Usually, whenever an image part is completely processed by an image processing algorithm, the engine will transfer that part to the next algorithm. In our model, this requires quantizing of the data. Both the input image stream and the output image stream of an algorithm should be quantized to fit the packet-size at the input and output. In order to be generic, we use s_i [pixel] for the packet-size at the input and s_o [pixel] for the packet-size at the output. Usually, we will have $s_i = s_o = s$, but when an algorithm reads or writes for example a complete image at a time, these values may change. For the quantized model of an algorithm we find the following equations. Note, that by writing down these equations, we leave the domain for which analytic results are available.

$$R'(t) = s_o \left\lfloor \min_{u \leq t} \left\{ \frac{s_i}{s_o} \left\lfloor \frac{R(u)}{s_i} \right\rfloor + \frac{1}{\alpha s_o} \left(C(t) - C(u) \right) \right\} \right\rfloor$$
$$C'(t) = \max_{u \leq t} \left\{ C(u) - \alpha s_i \left\lfloor \frac{R(u)}{s_i} \right\rfloor \right\}$$

In the right graph of Figure 4 we have shown graphically how the quantization affects the data flow. As input we have taken $R(t) = \lfloor t \rfloor$ and $C(t) = \max(3t-6, 0)$.

Some image processing algorithms allow for a division of an image into parts only if the parts have sufficient overlap. The overlap is discarded by the algorithm after processing, which complicates the equations further, because the amount of pixels that leave the algorithm is smaller than the amount of pixels that enter it. Furthermore, overlap may be cumulative, which means that if two algorithms are processing images after each other, the first algorithm will have to process the overlap for the second algorithm as if it was a real part of the image. Consequently, the influence of the overlap needed for an algorithm can be accounted for in the value of α, while the cumulative overlap cannot. In our equations we take o_i to be the overlap at the input and $o_o \leq o_i$ to be the overlap at the output of an algorithm. The difference $o_o - o_i$ then gives us the overlap that is discarded by the algorithm after processing. Note, that the package size increases with the added overlap, and that the overlap is 0 whenever the package size is that of an image rather than that of an image part. The basic model of an image processing algorithm as we'll use it in the remainder of this paper, is then given by the following equations.

$$R'(t) = (s_o + o_o) \left\lfloor \min_{u \le t} \left\{ \frac{s_i + o_o}{s_o + o_o} \left\lfloor \frac{R(u)}{s_i + o_i} \right\rfloor + \frac{1}{\alpha(s_o + o_o)} (C(t) - C(u)) \right\} \right\rfloor$$

$$C'(t) = \max_{u \le t} \left\{ C(u) - \alpha(s_i + o_o) \left\lfloor \frac{R(u)}{s_i + o_i} \right\rfloor \right\}$$

2.3   Pipelining, Parallel Processing and Synchronization

Suppose we have two image processing algorithms, 0 and 1. For each of the algorithms we have the equations that were developed in the previous paragraph. On top of that, the algorithms may be combined in one or more ways, depending on the way in which they interact. The easiest interaction is when the output of process 0 serves as input for process 1 (or vice versa). Algebraically, this gives us the additional equation:

$$R_1(t) = R'_0(t).$$

When two algorithms are executed in parallel, their inputs are equal.

$$R(t) = R_0(t) = R_1(t).$$

Furthermore, their outputs need to be synchronized in some way. Abstracting from the precise way in which this is done, we may assume that the synchronization depends on data from both algorithm 0 and algorithm 1. So, only image parts that have been processed by both can be processed by the synchronization. Hence, synchronization can be modeled using a minimum operation. The output $R'(t)$ of the synchronized algorithms becomes:

$$R'(t) = \min \left\{ R'_0(t), R'_1(t) \right\}$$

Note, that for these equations to hold, we need to assume that algorithms process their data in the order in which they receive it.

2.4   Scattering and Gathering

As we discussed before, it is possible to distribute the processing of an image over multiple processors by splitting the image into parts. Our engine uses round-robin scheduling for this. In terms of real-time calculus, distribution leads to a division on the input signal. Furthermore, round-robin distribution leads to a bias on the signal, depending on the input rank. Assuming that the incoming image stream $R(t)$ is quantized into parts of size s with overlap o, a scattering to n processes $R_i(t)$, with $0 \le i < n$, we obtain the following family of equations:

$$R_i(t) = (s + o) \left\lfloor \frac{R(t) + (n - i)(s + o)}{n(s + o)} \right\rfloor$$

On the outgoing streams, addition can be used to model the gathering of image parts. Round-robin gathering assures that image parts exit the system in the same order as in which they arrived. Round-robin gathering can be modeled using an addition in which each outgoing stream synchronizes with the previous one, while the first outgoing stream synchronizes with a biased version of the last one.

$$R'(t) = \min \{R_0(t), R_{n-1}(t) + s + o\} + \sum_{1 \leq i < n} \min \{R_i(t), R_{i-1}(t)\}$$

As with parallel processing, this still assumes that the individual algorithms process the requests in the order in which they arrive.

2.5   Overlap Creation

In subsection 2.2 we saw that the basic algorithms can only decrease the amount of overlap on an image part. When, at some point in the image processing graph, the amount of overlap needs to increase, the image transfer engine makes use of so-called temporal overlap. In other words, the processing of a part is delayed until a second part arrives, from which the desired overlap may be constructed. In practice, outer parts of an image have only half the overlap compared to the other parts. This fact is ignored in our modeling of basic image processing algorithms, because there it only has a small effect on the total computation times. However, in the case of temporal overlap, the difference between inner and outer parts is relevant because the last part of an image does not need to be delayed. Given an input stream $R(t)$, an image size S, an image part size s, input overlap o_i and output overlap $o_o \geq o_i$, we obtain the following formula for the output stream $R'(t)$.

$$R'(t) = (s + o_o) \max \left\{ \left\lfloor \frac{R(t)}{(s + o_i)} - 1 \right\rfloor, \frac{S}{s} \left\lfloor \frac{sR(t)}{S(s + o_i)} \right\rfloor \right\}$$

The effect of this formula is depicted graphically in Figure 5. As one can see in this figure, the arriving image parts are delayed except for the last image part, and the total output is greater than the input due to the creation of redundant data.

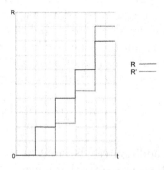

Fig. 5. Example of temporal overlap creation (4 image parts per image)

Fig. 6. A subgraph modeling a connection between resources

2.6   Connections Between Resources

If two algorithms run on the same resource they can communicate, for example, through shared memory. This takes a negligible amount of time compared to the actual image processing, so that the models for pipelining, parallel processing and scattering presented earlier are valid. When communication takes place over, for example, a network connection, we need to model the bandwidth and latency characteristics of this communication medium. Furthermore, the communication may even put an additional load on the sending and receiving resources as well.

To take the influence of connections between resources into account, we simply add the subgraph depicted in Figure 6 at every place in the graph where a connection is necessary according to hardware mapping. Figure 6 depicts the way in which a connection can be treated as a series of three algorithms. The first and the last algorithm model the added resource load due to the connection, the second algorithm, which has its own private resource, models the bandwidth and latency of the connection itself. Note, that we assume here that the same connection is never used twice. If that happens, this can of course be modeled by sharing the relevant resources.

2.7   Resource Scheduling

In this subsection, we focus on the scheduling of resources. Whenever there are multiple algorithms running on the same resource, the basic models of these algorithms need to be connected. Suppose that algorithm 0 and algorithm 1 run on the same resource. Then, we can schedule them by either giving one priority over the other, or by giving them equal priority.

Scheduling, in our system, is always preemptive. This means that resources that are left unused by one algorithm can always be used by another algorithm that runs on the same resource. In the case that algorithm 0 has priority over algorithm 1, this leads to the following equation.

$$C_1(t) = C_0'(t).$$

And symmetrically for the case where 1 obtains priority over 0.

When algorithm 0 and 1 have equal priority, we need a more elaborate scheduling method. The equations need to split a continuous resource stream, so we cannot use the round-robin method that we applied when scattering images. Furthermore, the equations need to take into account which of the algorithms need resources at all. If, for example, algorithm 0 does not need any resources, then algorithm 1 should be provided with the full amount. Whether an algorithm needs resources is easy to see by subtracting the output from the input. This difference gives us the amount of buffering in the process. Of course, one needs to take differences due to overlap into account in this comparison, so an algorithm needs resources (has a non-empty buffer) whenever $\frac{R(t)}{s+o_i} > \frac{R'(t)}{s+o_o}$. The scheduling of a resource C over n algorithms C_i, with $0 \le i < n$ is then described using the following equations, in which $C(t)$ is assumed to be (piece-wise) differentiable.

$$\frac{\partial}{\partial t}C_i(t) = \begin{cases} 0 & ; \frac{R_i(t)}{s+o_{i,i}} = \frac{R'_i(t)}{s+o_{o,i}} \\ X(t) & ; \frac{R_i(t)}{s+o_{i,i}} > \frac{R'_i(t)}{s+o_{o,i}} \end{cases}$$

$$X(t) = \frac{1}{\sum_{0 \le j < n} \begin{cases} 0 & ; \frac{R_j(t)}{s+o_{i,i}} = \frac{R'_j(t)}{s+o_{o,i}} \\ 1 & ; \frac{R_j(t)}{s+o_{i,i}} > \frac{R'_j(t)}{s+o_{o,i}} \end{cases}} \frac{\partial}{\partial t}C(t)$$

Note that the assumption that $C(t)$ is piece-wise differentiable is fair. We usually use a ramp-function ($C(t) = C \cdot t$) to model a processing resource, and the processing algorithms turn a piece-wise differentiable function $C(t)$ into a piece-wise differentiable function $C'(t)$, as long as the request stream $R(t)$ is piece-wise continuous.

3   Results

In this section, we discuss the measurements that were carried out on an actual implementation of the image processing engine to validate our model, and to establish the parameters necessary for simulation. Furthermore, we show the outcome of a simulation of the example graph of Figure 1, and discuss the insights we obtained about the engine through our simulations.

3.1   Measurements

Measurements on an actual implementation of the image processing engine were needed for two reasons. Firstly, to obtain parameters for the individual algorithms to use in the simulations described in the next subsection, and secondly, to validate the assumptions that were made while modeling the system. For those measurements, the setup depicted in figure 7 was used. The Source and Sink algorithm were equipped with a time-stamping mechanism to be able to measure latency and throughput with an accuracy in the order of milliseconds.

Note, that the parameter α, the processing per pixel of an algorithm, cannot be measured directly. It can be derived from measuring the maximum throughput achieved by an algorithm, using the following relation:

$$\alpha = \frac{C}{S \cdot T},$$

where α $[\frac{\text{operations}}{\text{pixel}}]$ is the weight of the algorithm, C $[\frac{\text{operations}}{\text{sec}}]$ is the processor speed, S $[\frac{\text{pixel}}{\text{image}}]$ is the image size and T $[\frac{\text{images}}{\text{sec}}]$ is the measured maximum throughput of the algorithm. Note, that this formula assumes a 100% utilization,

Fig. 7. Measurement setup

which was obtained by running the algorithms in isolation. Any deviations due to interference with the Source and Sink that were running on a second processor turned out to be negligible.

To summarize, we made the following assumptions during our modeling:

- *Resource usage depends linearly on the size of the image.*
  By changing the size of the images, the image parts and the overlap, we confirmed that the relation between data size and resource usages is linear with 10% accuracy. Note, however, that our graphs consisted mainly of filtering algorithms. Algorithms for image compression, for example, may not fit this assumption. In that case, the modeling of α needs to be extended.
- *Resource usage is independent of the image content.*
  Unfortunately, we have not been able to verify the content independence using measurements. At the time of our research, no Source capable of producing different images was available. Independency of the filtering algorithms was concluded from the way they are implemented. Still, if content dependent algorithms are introduced, a time-dependent α could be used to reflect the changing of content.
- *Processing power is the dominant resource.*
  When there are no feedback loops, the assumption that processing power is the dominant resource coincides with the statement that the latency of an algorithm equals the reciprocal of the throughput. Note, that to validate this, we can correct for the processing time of Sink and Source using measurements on a void algorithm. For the majority of the algorithms, the difference between the latency measurements and the predictions based on throughput was within 10%. Two algorithms deviated more severely. One of those is a very fast algorithm, for which the throughput measurements were probably inaccurate. The other is suspected of having an internal feedback loop, but more elaborate measurements or investigations into the code are needed to verify this.
- *Image parts do not overtake each other during processing in a node.*
  This was one of the functional requirements of the image transfer engine.

3.2 Simulations

The models we have discussed form a mixed set of max-plus and differential equations. For the simulation of such a mixed system, Matlab/Simulink offers only one possible simulation method: fixed step Euler integration. This method is very stable, but slow when high accuracy is needed. For our purposes it sufficed,

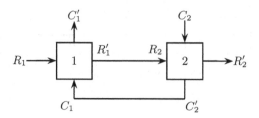

Fig. 8. Algebraic Loop

since the accuracy of the measurements on which we based our parameters was a more limiting factor than simulation accuracy.

The most important problem with our simulations, was the possibility of algebraic loops. When, for example, the first process (1) in a pipeline has low priority, and second process (2) has high priority on the same processor, we get the situation as in figure 8. The value of R_2 depends on the value of R_1', which in turn depends on the value of C_1, which depends on the value of C_2', which depends on the value of R_2. Such a recursive situation cannot be simulated in Matlab/Simulink without introducing a small delay between C_2' and C_1, which causes additional inaccuracies and in general may lead to wrong solutions. We have not found a convincing solution for this problem yet. One alternative could be to solve the equations numerically using, for example, Mathematica. But when trying this we encountered the problem that the numerical methods available to us gave wrong estimates of the minima, unless they were fed with suitable initial points to start their search. Since the Matlab/Simulink approach gave satisfactory solutions for our models, we decided to stick to that approach.

As an example of our simulations, we will discuss the outcome of a simulation of the example graph in Figure 1. The simulations have been carried out using Matlab/Simulink [1], a well-known simulation tool for engineering purposes. Each of the equations of section 2 has been modeled as a signal-processing block in Simulink, and those blocks have been tied together according to the image processing graph. The building of the Simulink model from an image processing graph was not done automatically. However, it was built by following the procedure by which the engine implements the image processing graph. Therefore, we expect that it can be automated in the future if the need arises. To give the reader an impression of the resulting Simulink model, we have depicted it in figure 9. The greyed boxes coincide with the elements that also occur in the original image processing graph, the white boxes were added to model communication connections, overlap creation, scattering, gathering etc.

In the left part of Figure 10, we have depicted the image streams as they were measured at several places in our model. Each image is split into ten parts, which results in an image stream consisting of ten 'steps'. From left to right, we first see the slightly delayed arrival of parts over the input network. Second, we see the image stream as it is read by the Input algorithm. Third, we see the image stream as it has passed from PR1 to PR2. Fourth, we see the image stream after overlap has been created. This stream, which contains bigger parts than the others, was scaled down to make it easier to see the effect of overlap creation. For example, one should observe that overlap creation introduces latency in the header-part, but not in the footer-part of an image. Fifth, we show the image stream after the Noise and C/B algorithms were applied. Sixth we show the image stream after the passage from PR2 to PR3 is made, and seventh, we show how the separate parts are processed for displaying. The maximum horizontal distance between the incoming image stream and the displayed image stream is the latency of the total image processing. This gives us one of the two performance parameters that we are interested in.

The other performance parameter of interest, throughput, can be found by adapting the framerate and studying both the image stream and the resource usage. In the right part of Figure 10, we have depicted the resource usage or, rather, the left-overs of all resources present in the model. Whenever one of these lines is horizontal, the resource is in use, when the line is rising, there is an abundance of that particular resource. Resource PR1 can be recognized because it is the first one to have a horizontal line. That is the resource where the image processing begins. The two graphics cards of PR2 are loaded in a similar way, be it with a one-image-part phase difference, and therefore have similar characteristics in the Figure. PR3 is the last to process an image, and therefore the last to start rising again.

The resource with the least waste, forms the bottleneck of the system. In our case, this is PR1. By increasing the framerate, we increase the resource usage. In the left of Figure 11 we show the image processing at the maximal framerate. Note, that the tenth image part is finished only after a new image has entered the pipeline. The middle of Figure 11 shows the resource usage at that framerate, and shows that the usage of PR1 is at its maximum (viz. a horizontal line).

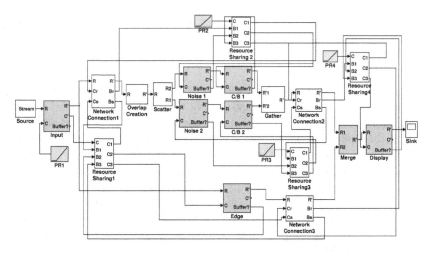

Fig. 9. Simulink model of the example image processing graph

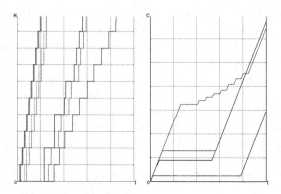

Fig. 10. Simulation of an image stream (left) and resource stream (right), with 10 parts per image

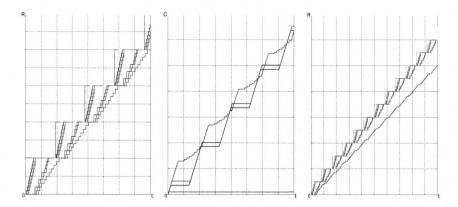

Fig. 11. Simulation of an image stream (left) and resource stream (middle), at full load, and an image stream (right), when overloaded

The right of Figure 11 illustrates how the image processing streams become divergent if the framerate is increased above the maximum load of the system. The divergence occurs at the end of the image processing stream, where the fast results of the upper stream (Noise and C/B) are combined with the results of the overloaded lower stream (Edge).

Although the image processing graph of figure 1 is only a simple example, we have made simulations of image processing graphs of much greater complexity with relative ease. Regrettably, we cannot show the results of these due to industrial confidentiality, but the graphs are similar in character. Furthermore, comparison with actual implementations of the graphs showed an accuracy of our predictions of 10-20%.

4   Conclusions

In this paper, we have shown a simulation method for performance prediction of medical image processing chains. Using the real-time calculus modeling paradigm, we found max-plus and differential equations that describe the dynamic behavior of image processing. Using Matlab/Simulink we found numerical solutions of those equations. We chose real-time calculus as a paradigm because it allows easy modeling of preemptive scheduling techniques, and chose simulation because the standard algebraic analysis of real-time calculus did not fit the intricacies of our image transfer engine. To calibrate our models, we characterized each of the image processing algorithms by a single value, obtained through throughput measurements on the algorithms in isolation.

As a first conclusion, we find the presented simulation method to be suitable for performance predictions of medical image processing chains, especially when implementation details need to be included in the model. Simulation seems to be most suitable in the later stages of the design phase, when modeling is used to optimize the image processing graphs and scheduling strategies. In an early design phase, it is hard to determine how much detail is needed to make accurate predictions. Admittedly, we were lucky to find that the image processing algorithms in our case studies were all content independent and linear in their resource use. This might be a consequence of the type of medical imaging on which we were working and is, of course, not true for general image processing. Compression algorithms, and some de-noising algorithms, are infamous for their content dependence, for example. Still, we are convinced that it is possible to account for non-linearities and dependencies, by making the factor α dependent on time and image size. As a matter of future research, we are planning to use a similar simulation approach for the modeling of a more complex architecture, in which image processing is only a part of the desired functionality. There, content independence must certainly be abandoned.

A second conclusion, is that a simulation model gives new insights in the workings of a system. It allows estimates of values that are hard to measure in practice. In section 3, we have seen estimates of resource consumption and of latencies half way down the image processing graph. Using these estimates we found that the performance decreases due to a low bandwidth or high processing time is amplified by the creation of overlap. Based on this insight, a change in the engine was proposed so that overlap creation can be more flexibly positioned. This change is expected to result in a latency decrease of a few milliseconds. Additionally, the estimates gave insight in resource load balancing, on which alternative image processing graphs were based. If these insights had to be obtained from measurements, instrumentation of the code would have been necessary, which influences the systems performance. Simulation models give insight in the behavior of a system without making such changes.

Acknowledgments. We would like to thank Henk Obbink and Jan Friso Groote for their feedback, and Stichting Toegepaste Wetenschappen (Grant EWI.4877) for funding this project.

References

1. Matlab/Simulink. http://www.mathworks.com.
2. D.T. Altilar and Y. Paker. Optimal scheduling algorithm for parallel video processing. In *The 1998 International Conference on Multimedia Computing and Systems*, pages 245–248, Austin, Texas, USA, June 1998.
3. J-Y. Le Boudec and P. Thiran. *Network Calculus: A Theory of Deterministic Queuing Systems for the Internet*, volume 2050 of *Lecture Notes in Computer Science*. Springer, Berlin, 2001.
4. K. Jensen. *Coloured Petri nets: basic concepts, analysis methods and practical use*. Springer, Berlin, 1992-1997.
5. L. Kleinrock. *Queuing systems, Volume 1: theory*. John Wiley, New York, 1975.
6. P. Schwarz and U. Donath. Simulation-based performance analysis of distributed systems. In *International Workshop Parallel and Distributed Real-Time Systems*, pages 244–249, Geneva, Switzerland, 1997.
7. J. Subhlok and G. Vondran. Optimal latency-throughput tradeoffs for data parallel pipelines. In *Eighth Annual ACM Symposium on Parallel Algorithms and Architectures*, pages 62–71, Padua, Italy, June 1996.
8. L. Thiele, S. Chakraborty, M. Gries, and S. Künzli. A framework for evaluating design tradeoffs in packet processing architectures. In *DAC '02: Proceedings of the 39th conference on Design automation*, pages 880–885, New York, NY, USA, 2002. ACM Press.
9. L. Thiele, S. Chakraborty, and M. Naedele. Real-time calculus for scheduling hard real-time systems. In *Proc. IEEE International Symposium on Circuits and Systems (ISCAS)*, volume 4, pages 101–104, 2000.
10. E. Wandeler, L. Thiele, M. Verhoef, and P. Lieverse. System architecture evaluation using modular performance analysis - a case study. In *1st International Symposium on Leveraging Applications of Formal Methods (ISoLA)*, 2004.

BLASTing Linux Code*

Jan Tobias Mühlberg and Gerald Lüttgen

Department of Computer Science, University of York, York YO10 5DD, U.K.
{muehlber,luettgen}@cs.york.ac.uk

Abstract. Computer programs can only run reliably if the underlying operating system is free of errors. In this paper we evaluate, from a practitioner's point of view, the utility of the popular software model checker BLAST for revealing errors in Linux kernel code. The emphasis is on important errors related to memory safety in and locking behaviour of device drivers. Our conducted case studies show that, while BLAST's abstraction and refinement techniques are efficient and powerful, the tool has deficiencies regarding usability and support for analysing pointers, which are likely to prevent kernel developers from using it.

1 Introduction

Today's application software critically depends on the reliability, safety and security of the underlying operating system (OS). However, due to their complicated task of managing a system's physical resources, OSs are difficult to develop and even more difficult to debug. Quite frequently major errors stay undiscovered until they are exploited in security attacks or are found "by accident".

In recent years, automatic approaches to discover OS bugs via runtime checks or source code analysis have been explored. Despite the fact that many of these approaches do not focus on an exhaustive analysis, they still helped developers to detect hundreds of safety problems in the Linux and BSD OS kernels. Most of the programming errors found were either related to *memory safety* or incorrect *locking behaviour* [6]. Here, "memory safety" typically is interpreted as the property that an OS component never de-references an invalid pointer, since this would cause the program to end up in an undefined state. "Correct locking behaviour" means that functions that ensure mutual exclusion on the physical resources of a system are called in a way that is free of deadlocks and starvation. Both classes of problems are traceable by checking whether an OS component complies with basic usage rules of the program interface provided by the kernel.

Software model checking. By having the potential of being exhaustive and fully automatic, *model checking*, in combination with *abstraction* and *refinement*, is a successful technique used in software verification [7]. Intensive research in this area has resulted in software model checkers like Bandera [9] for Java programs or SLAM/SDV [1], MAGIC [5] and BLAST [16] (*Berkeley Lazy Abstraction Software verification Tool*) for analysing C source code. The major advantage

---

* Research funding was provided by the EPSRC under grant GR/S86211/01.

of these tools over model-based model checkers such as Spin [17] is their ability to automatically abstract a model from the source code of a given program. User interaction should then only be necessary in order to provide the model checker with a specification, against which the program can be checked. Since complete formal specifications are not available for most programs, verification will usually be relative to a partial specification that covers the usage rules of the *Application Program Interface* (API) used by the program. However, up to now all releases of SLAM are restricted to verifying properties for Microsoft Windows device drivers and do not cover memory safety problems [19], while BLAST and MAGIC are able to verify a program against a user defined temporal safety specification and thus allows checking of arbitrary C source code.

The BLAST Toolkit . This popular toolkit implements an advanced abstraction algorithm, called "lazy abstraction" [15], for building a model of some C source code, and model-checking algorithm for checking whether some specified label placed in the source code is reachable. This label can either be automatically introduced by instrumenting the source with an explicit temporal safety specification, be added via `assert()` statements, or be manually introduced into the source. In any case, the input source file needs to be preprocessed using a standard C preprocessor like `gcc`. In this step, all header and source files included by the input file under consideration are merged into one file. It is this preprocessed source code that is passed to BLAST to construct and verify a model using *predicate abstraction*.

This Paper. In this paper we investigate to which extent software model checking as implemented in BLAST can aid a practitioner during OS software development. To do so, we analyse whether BLAST is able to detect errors that have been reported for recent releases of the Linux kernel. We consider programming errors related to *memory safety* (cf. Sec. 3) and *locking behaviour* (cf. Sec. 4). The code examples utilised in this paper are taken from releases 2.6.13 and 2.6.14 of the Linux kernel. They have been carefully chosen by searching the kernel's change log for fixed memory problems and fixed deadlock conditions, in a way that the underlying problems are representative for memory safety and locking behaviour as well as easily explainable without referring to long source code listings.[1] Our studies use version 2.0 of BLAST, which was released in October 2005.

The focus of our work is on showing at what scale a give problem statement and a program's source code need to be adapted in order to detect an error. We discuss how much work is required to find a certain usage rule violation in a given snippet of a Linux driver, and how difficult this work is to perform in BLAST. Due to space constraints, we cannot present all of our case studies in full here; however, all files necessary to reproduce our results can be downloaded from `www.cs.york.ac.uk/~muehlber/blast/`.

Related Studies with BLAST. BLAST has been applied for the verification of memory safety as well as locking properties before [3,13,16,14]. In [3], the use

---

[1] All source code used is either included or referenced by a *commit key* as provided by the source code management system *git* which is used in the Linux kernel community; see `www.kernel.org` for further information on *git* and Linux.

of CCURED [21] in combination with BLAST for verifying memory safety of C source code is explained. This is done by inserting additional runtime checks at all places in the code where pointers are de-referenced. BLAST is then employed to check whether the introduced code is reachable or can be removed again. The approach focuses on ensuring that only valid pointers are de-referenced along the execution of a program, which is taken to mean that pointers must not equal NULL at any point at which they are de-referenced. However, invalid pointers in C do not necessarily equal NULL in practise. In contrast to [3], we will interpret pointer invalidity in a more general way and conduct our studies on real-world examples rather than constructed examples.

A methodology for verifying and certifying systems code on a simple locking problem is explained in [16], which deals with the spinlock interface provided by the Linux kernel. *Spinlocks* ensure that a kernel process can spin on a CPU without being preempted by another process. The framework studied in [16] is used to prove that calls of spin_lock() and spin_unlock() in Linux device drivers always alternate. In contrast to this work, our case studies will be more detailed and thereby will be providing further insights into the usability of BLAST.

2   Programming Errors in OS Code

There is quite a long list of commonly found OS errors. While most of them mainly affect a system's safety, others have a security-related background. An insightful study of OS errors has been published in [6]; see Table 1 for a summary of its results. The study shows that the majority of programming errors in OS code can be found in device drivers. Its authors highlight that most errors are related to problems causing either deadlock conditions or driving the system into undefined states by de-referencing invalid pointers.

Although memory safety problems have a direct impact on an OS's reliability, API rules for OS kernels are usually described in an informal way. For example, in the Linux device driver handbook [8, p. 61] it is stated that one "should never pass anything to *kfree* that was not obtained from *kmalloc*" since, otherwise, the system may behave in an undefined way. The functions kmalloc() and kfree() are kernel-space functions which are used to dynamically allocate and de-allocate memory, respectively. Another common example are buffer overrun errors, where data is written beyond the size of an allocated area of memory, thus overwriting unrelated data.

Correct locking of resources is another major issue causing problems in OS code. As shown in [6], deficiencies resulting in deadlocks in the Linux and BSD kernels make up a large amount of the overall number of errors found. In the documentation explaining the API of the Linux kernel, quite strict rules about the proper use of functions to lock various resources are stated. For example, in [8, p. 121], one of the most basic rules is given as follows: "Neither semaphores nor spinlocks allow a lock holder to acquire the lock a second time; should you attempt to do so, things simply hang." The rational for this lies in the functionality provided by spinlocks: a kernel thread holding a lock is spinning on

Table 1. Results of an empirical study of OS errors [6]

% of Bugs	Rule checked
63.1%	**Bugs related to memory safety**
38.1%	Check potentially NULL pointers returned from routines.
9.9%	Do not allocate large stack variables (> 1K) on the fixed-size kernel stack.
6.7%	Do not make inconsistent assumptions about whether a pointer is NULL.
5.3%	Always check bounds of array indices and loop bounds derived from user data.
1.7%	Do not use freed memory.
1.1%	Do not leak memory by updating pointers with potentially NULL realloc return values.
0.3%	Allocate enough memory to hold the type for which you are allocating.
33.7%	**Bugs related to locking behaviour**
28.6%	To avoid deadlock, do not call blocking functions with interrupts disabled or a spinlock held.
2.6%	Restore disabled interrupts.
2.5%	Release acquired locks; do not double-acquire locks.
3.1%	**Miscellaneous bugs**
2.4%	Do not use floating point in the kernel.
0.7%	Do not de-reference user pointers.

one CPU and cannot be preempted until the lock is released. Another important rule is that any code holding a spinlock cannot relinquish the processor for anything except for serving interrupts; especially, the thread must never sleep because the lock might never be released in this case [8, p. 118].

3   Checking Memory Safety

This section focuses on using BLAST for checking usage rules related to memory safety, for which we have analysed several errors in different device drivers. The examples studied by us include use-after-free errors in the kernel's SCSI[2] and InfiniBand[3] subsystems. The former is the *small computer system interface* standard for attaching peripheral devices to computers, while the latter is an industry standard designed to connect processor nodes and I/O nodes to form a system area network. In each of these examples, an invalid pointer that is not NULL is de-referenced, which causes the system to behave in an undefined way. This type of bug is not covered by the work on memory safety of Beyer et al. in [3] and cannot easily be detected by runtime checks.

The example we will study here in detail is a use-after-free error spotted by the Coverity source code analyser (www.coverity.com) in the I2O subsystem

---

[2] Commit 2d6eac6c4fdaa69656d66c80754d267be233cc3f.
[3] Commit d0743a5b7b837334cb414b773529d51de3de0471.

of the Linux kernel (cf. Sec. 3.1). To check for this bug in BLAST we first specify a temporal safety specification in the BLAST specification language. Taking this specification, BLAST is supposed to automatically generate an instrumented version of the C source code for analysis (cf. Sec. 3.2). However, due to an apparent bug in BLAST, this step fails for our example, and we are therefore forced to manually instrument our code by inserting ERROR labels at appropriate positions (cf. Sec. 3.3). However, it will turn out that BLAST does not track important operations on pointers, which is not mentioned in BLAST's user manual and without which our example cannot be checked (cf. Sec. 3.4).

3.1   The I2O Use-After-Free Error

The I2O subsystem bug of interest to us resided in lines 423–425 of the source code file drivers/message/i2o/pci.c. The listing in Fig. 1 is an abbreviated version of the file pci.c before the bug was fixed. One can see that function i2o_iop_alloc() is called at line 330 of the code extract. This function is defined in drivers/message/i2o/iop.c and basically allocates memory for an i2o_controller structure using kmalloc(). At the end of the listing, this memory is freed by i2o_iop_free(c). The bug in this piece of code arises from the call of put_device() in line 425, since its parameter c->device.parent causes an already freed pointer to be de-referenced. The bug has been fixed in commit d2b0e84d195a341c1cc5b45ec2098ee23bc1fe9d, by simply swapping lines 424 and 425 in the source file.

```
drivers/message/i2o/pci.c:            330   c = i2o_iop_alloc();
  300   static int __devinit
        i2o_pci_probe(                 423   free_controller:
        struct pci_dev *pdev,          424   i2o_iop_free(c);
  301   const struct pci_device_id     425   put_device(
        *id)                                   c->device.parent);
  302   {
  303   struct i2o_controller *c;      432   }
```

Fig. 1. Extract of drivers/message/i2o/pci.c

This bug offers various different ways to utilise BLAST. A generic temporal safety property for identifying bugs like this would state that *any pointer that has been an argument to kfree() is never used again* unless it has been reallocated. A probably easier way would be to check whether *the pointer c in i2o_pci_probe() is never used again after i2o_iop_free() has been called* with c as its argument. Checking the first, more generic property would require us to put function definitions from other source files into pci.c, since BLAST considers only functions that are available in its input file. Therefore, we focus on verifying the latter property.

Checking for violations even of the latter, more restricted property will lead to a serious problem. A close look at the struct `i2o_controller` and its initialisation in the function `i2o_iop_alloc()` reveals that `i2o_controller` contains a function pointer which can be used as a "destructor". As is explained in BLAST's user manual, the "current release does not support function pointers"; they are ignored completely. Further, the manual states that "correctness of the analysis is then modulo the assumption that function pointer calls are irrelevant to the property being checked." This assumption is however not always satisfied in practise, as we will see later in our example.

3.2   Verification with a Temporal Safety Specification

Ignoring the function pointer limitation, we developed the temporal safety specification presented in Fig. 2. The specification language used by BLAST is easy to understand and allows the assignment of status variables and events. In our specification we use a global status variable `allocstatus_c` to cover the possible states of the struct c of our example, which can be set to 0 meaning "not allocated" and 1 meaning "allocated". Furthermore, we define three events, one for each of the functions `i2o_iop_alloc()`, `i2o_iop_free()` and `put_device()`. All functions have special preconditions and calling them may modify the status of c. The special token $? matches anything. Intuitively, the specification given in Fig. 2 states that `i2o_iop_alloc()` and `i2o_iop_free()` must be called alternately, and `put_device()` must only be called when c has not yet been freed. Note that this temporal safety specification does not cover the usage rule for `i2o_iop_free()` and `put_device()` in general. We are using one status variable to guard calls of `i2o_iop_free()` and `put_device()` regardless of its arguments. Hence, the specification will work only as long as there is only one pointer to an `i2o_controller` structure involved.

Using the specification of Fig. 2, BLAST should instrument a given C input file by adding a global status variable and error labels for all violations of the

```
global int allocstatus_c = 0;          event
                                        {
event                                     pattern { i2o_iop_free($?); }
{                                         guard   { allocstatus_c == 1 }
  pattern { $? = i2o_iop_alloc(); }       action  { allocstatus_c = 0; }
  guard   { allocstatus_c == 0 }        }
  action  { allocstatus_c = 1; }
}                                       event
                                        {
                                          pattern { put_device($?); }
                                          guard   { allocstatus_c == 1 }
                                        }
```

Fig. 2. A temporal safety specification for `pci.c`

preconditions. The instrumentation is done by the program `spec.opt` which is part of the BLAST distribution. For our example taken from the Linux kernel, we first obtained the command used by the kernel's build system to compile `pci.c` with `gcc`. We appended the option `-E` to force the compilation to stop after preprocessing, resulting in a C source file containing all required parts of the kernel headers. This step is necessary since BLAST cannot know of all the additional definitions and include paths used to compile the file. Unfortunately, it expands `pci.c` from 484 lines of code to approximately 16k lines, making it difficult to find syntactical problems which BLAST cannot deal with. Despite spending a lot of effort in trying to use `spec.opt`, we never managed to get this work. The program mostly failed with unspecific errors such as **Fatal error: exception Failure("Function declaration not found")**. Finding such an error in a huge source without having a line number or other hint is almost impossible, especially since `gcc` compiles the file without any warning. We constructed several simplifications of the preprocessed file in order to trace the limitations of `spec.opt`, but did not get a clear indication of what the source is. We suspect it might be a problem with parsing complex data structures and inline assembly imported from the Linux headers.

Given the bug in BLAST and in order to demonstrate that our specification indeed covers the programming error in `pci.c`, we developed a rather abstract version of `pci.c` which is shown in Fig. 3. Using this version and the specification of Fig. 2, we were able to obtain an instrumented version of our source code without encountering the bug in `spec.opt`. Running BLAST on the instrumented version then produced the following output:

```
$ spec.opt test2.spc test2.c
[...]
$ pblast.opt instrumented.c
[...]
Error found! The system is unsafe :-(
```

In summary, the example studied here shows that the specification used in this section is sufficient to find the bug. However, the approach required by BLAST has several disadvantages. Firstly, it is not automatic at all. Although we ended up with only a few lines of code, it took quite a lot of time to produce this code by hand and to figure out what parts of the original `pci.c` are accepted by BLAST. Secondly, the methodology only works if the bug is known beforehand, hence we did not learn anything new about unwanted behaviour of this driver's code. We needed to simplify the code to an extent where the relation to the original source code may be considered as questionable. The third problem lies in the specification used. Since it treats the allocation and de-allocation as something similar to a locking problem, we would not be able to use it in a piece of code that refers to more than one dynamically allocated object. A more generic specification must be able to deal with multiple pointers. According to [2], such a generic specification should be possible to write by applying a few minor modifications such as defining a "shadow" control state and replacing $?

```
test2.h:                              test2.c:
#include <stdio.h>                     #include "test2.h"
#include <stdlib.h>
                                       i2o_controller *i2o_iop_alloc
typedef struct device                    (void)
{                                      { i2o_controller *c;
 int parent;                             c = malloc(
} device;                                  sizeof(struct i2o_controller));
                                         return (c); }
typedef struct i2o_controller
{                                      void i2o_iop_free
 struct device device;                   (i2o_controller *c)
} i2o_controller;                      { free (c); }

i2o_controller *i2o_iop_alloc          void put_device (int i) { }
 (void);
void i2o_iop_free                      int main (void)
 (i2o_controller *c);                  { i2o_controller *c;
void put_device (int i);                 c = i2o_iop_alloc ();
                                         i2o_iop_free (c);
                                         put_device (c->device.parent);
                                         return (0); }
```

Fig. 3. Manual simplification of `pci.c`

with $1. However, in practise the program generating the instrumented C source file failed with obscure error messages.

3.3 Verification Without a Temporal Safety Specification

Since BLAST could not deal with verifying the original pci.c using an explicit specification of the use-after-free property, we will now try and manually instrument the source file so that our bug can be detected whenever an ERROR label is reachable.

When conducting our instrumentation, the following modifications were applied by hand to pci.c and related files:

1. A variable unsigned int alloc_status was added to the definition of struct i2o_controller in include/linux/i2o.h.
2. The prototypes of i2o_iop_alloc() and i2o_iop_free() were removed from drivers/message/i2o/core.h.
3. The prototype of put_device() was deleted from include/linux/device.h.
4. C source code for the functions put_device(), i2o_iop_free(), i2o_iop_release() and i2o_iop_alloc() was copied from iop.c and drivers/base /core.c into pci.c. The functions were modified such that the new field alloc_status of a freshly allocated struct i2o_controller is set to 1 by

i2o_iop_alloc(). i2o_iop_free() no longer de-allocates the structure but checks whether alloc_status equals 1 and sets it to 0; otherwise, it jumps to the ERROR label. put_device() was modified to operate on the whole struct i2o_controller and jumps to ERROR if alloc_status equals 0.

By feeding these changes into the model checker it is possible to detect duplicate calls of i2o_iop_free() on a pointer to a struct i2o_controller, as well as calls of put_device() on a pointer that has already been freed. Even calls of i2o_iop_free() and put_device() on a pointer that has not been allocated with i2o_iop_alloc(), should result in an error report since nothing can be said about the status of alloc_status in such a case.

After preprocessing the modified source files and running BLAST, we get the output "Error found! The system is unsafe :-(". Even after we reduced the content of i2o_pci_probe() to something quite similar to the main() function shown in Fig. 3 and after putting the erroneous calls of put_device() and i2o_iop_free() in the right order, the system was still unsafe from BLAST's point of view. It took us some time to figure out that BLAST does not appear to consider the content of pointers at all.

3.4   The Problem with BLAST and Pointers

We demonstrate this apparent shortcoming of BLAST regarding handling pointers by means of another simple example, for which BLAST fails in tracing values behind pointers over function calls.

```
test5.c:                                17
   1  #include <stdlib.h>               18  int main (void)
   2                                     19  {
   3  typedef struct example_struct      20     example_struct p1;
   4  {                                  21
   5     void    *data;                  22     init (&p1);
   6     size_t size;                    23     if (p1.data != NULL ||
   7  } example_struct;                           p1.size != 0)
   8                                     24     { goto ERROR; }
   9                                     25     else
  10  void init (example_struct *p)      26     { goto END; };
  11  {                                  27
  12    p->data = NULL;                  28  ERROR:
  13    p->size = 0;                     29     return (1);
  14                                     30
  15    return;                          31  END:
  16  }                                  32     return (0);
                                         33  }
```

Fig. 4. An example for pointer passing

As can be seen in the code listing of Fig 4, label ERROR can never be reached in this program since the values of the components of our struct are explicitly set by function init(). However, BLAST produces the following output:

```
$ gcc -E -o test5.i test5.c
$ pblast.opt test5.i
[...]
Error found! The system is unsafe :-(
Error trace:
23 :: 23: Pred((p1@main).data!=0) :: 29
-1 :: -1: Skip :: 23
10 :: 10: Block(Return(0);) :: -1
12 :: 12: Block(* (p@init ).data = 0;* (p@init ).size = 0;) :: 10
22 :: 22: FunctionCall(init(&(p1@main))) :: -1
-1 :: -1: Skip :: 22
 0 ::  0: Block(Return(0);) :: -1
 0 ::  0: FunctionCall (__BLAST_initialize_test5.i()) :: -1
```

This counterexample shows that BLAST does not correlate the pointer p used in init() and the struct p1 used in main(), and assumes that the if statement in line 23 evaluates to true. After adding a line "p1.data = NULL; p1.size = 0;" before the call of init(), BLAST claims the system to be safe, even if we modify init() to reset the values so that they differ from NULL (and 0).

We were able to reproduce this behaviour in similar examples with pointers to integer values and arrays. Switching on the BDD-based alias analysis implemented in BLAST also did not solve the problem. The example shows that BLAST does not only ignore function pointer calls as stated in its user manual, but appears to assume that all pointer operations have no effect. This limitation is not documented in the BLAST manual and renders BLAST almost unusable for the verification of properties related to our understanding of memory safety.

3.5   Results

Our experiments on memory safety show that BLAST is able to find the programming error discovered by the Coverity checker. Out of eight examples, we were able to detect two problems after minor modifications to the source code, and three after applying manual abstraction. Three further programming errors could not be traced by using BLAST. Indeed, BLAST has some major restrictions. The main problem is that BLAST ignores variables addressed by a pointer. As stated in its user manual, BLAST assumes that only variables of the same type are aliased. Since this is the case in our examples, we initially assumed that our examples could be verified with BLAST, which is not the case. Moreover, we encountered bugs and deficiencies in spec.opt which forced us to apply substantial and time consuming modifications to source code. Most of these modifications and simplifications would require a developer to know about the error in advance. Thus, from a practitioner's point of view, BLAST is not of much help in finding unknown errors related to memory safety. However, it needs to be mentioned that BLAST was designed for verifying API usage rules of a different type than those required for memory safety. More precisely, BLAST is intended for proving the adherence of pre- and post-conditions denoted by integer values and for ensuring API usage rules concerning the order in which certain functions are called, regardless of pointer arguments, return values and the effects of aliasing.

4   Checking Locking Properties

Verifying correct locking behaviour is something used in almost all examples provided by the developers of BLAST [2,16]. In [16], the authors checked parts of the Linux kernel for correct locking behaviour while using the *spinlock* API and stated that BLAST showed a decent level of performance during these tests. Spinlocks provide a very simple but quite efficient locking mechanism to ensure, e.g., that a kernel thread may not be preempted while serving interrupts. The kernel thread acquires a certain lock by calling `spin_lock(l)`, where `l` is a previously initialised pointer to a struct `spinlock_t` identifying the lock. A lock is released by calling `spin_unlock()` with the same parameter. The kernel provides a few additional functions that control the interrupt behaviour while the lock is held. By their nature, spinlocks are intended for use on multiprocessor systems where each resource may be associated with a special spinlock, and where several kernel threads need to operate independently on these resources. However, as far as concurrency is concerned, uniprocessor systems running a preemptive kernel behave like multiprocessor systems.

```
global int lockstatus = 2;

event
{
  pattern { spin_lock_init($?); }
  guard    { lockstatus == 2 }
  action   { lockstatus = 0; }
}

event
{
  pattern { spin_lock($?); }
  guard    { lockstatus == 0 }
  action   { lockstatus = 1; }
}

event
{
  pattern { spin_unlock($?); }
  guard    { lockstatus == 1 }
  action   { lockstatus = 0; }
}

event
{
  pattern { $? = sleep($?); }
  guard    { lockstatus == 0 }
}
```

Fig. 5. A temporal safety specification for spinlocks

Finding examples for the use of spinlocks is not difficult since they are widely deployed. While experimenting with BLAST and the spinlock functions on several small components of the Linux kernel we experienced that it performs well with functions using only one lock. We focused on functions taken from the USB subsystem in *drivers/usb/core*. Due to further unspecific parse errors with the program `spec.opt` we could not use a temporal safety specification directly on the kernel source. However, in this case we were able to generate the instrumented source file and to verify properties by separating the functions under consideration from the remaining driver source and by providing simplified header files.

In Fig. 5 we provide our basic temporal safety specification for verifying locking behaviour. Variable `lockstatus` encodes the possible states of a spinlock; the initial value 2 represents the state in which the lock has not been initialised, while 1 and 0 denote that the lock is held or has been released, respectively. The pattern within the specification varies for the different spinlock functions used within the driver source under consideration, and the specification can easily be extended to cover forbidden functions that may sleep. An example for a function `sleep()` is provided in the specification of Fig. 5.

Difficulties arise with functions that acquire more than one lock. Since all spinlock functions use a pointer to a struct `spinlock_t` in order to identify a certain lock, and since the values behind pointers are not sufficiently tracked in BLAST, we were forced to rewrite parts of the driver's source and the kernel's spinlock interface. Instead of the pointers to `spinlock_t` structs we utilise global integer variables representing the state of a certain lock. We have used this methodology to verify an example of a recently fixed deadlock[4] in the Linux kernel's SCSI subsystem. In Fig. 6 we provide an extract of one of the functions modified in the fix. We see that the spinlocks in this example are integrated in more complex data structures referenced via pointers. Even worse, this function calls a function pointer passed in the argument `done` in line 1581, which was the source of the deadlock before the bug was fixed. To verify this special case, removing the function pointer and providing a dummy function `done()` with a precondition assuring that the lock on `shost->host_lock` is not held is needed. However, we were able to verify both the deadlock condition before the fix had been applied, as well as deadlock freedom for the fixed version of the source.

During our experiments we analysed several other examples of deadlock conditions. The more interesting examples are the spinlock problem explained above,

```
1564 int ata_scsi_queuecmd(struct        1571 ap = (struct ata_port *)
       scsi_cmnd *cmd, void                      &shost->hostdata[0];
       (*done)(struct scsi_cmnd *))    1573 spin_unlock(shost->host_lock);
1565 {                                   1574 spin_lock(&ap->host_set->lock);
1566 struct ata_port *ap;
1567 struct ata_device *dev;            1581 done(cmd);
1568 struct scsi_device
       *scsidev = cmd->device;         1597 spin_unlock(&ap->host_set->lock);
1569 struct Scsi_Host                   1598 spin_lock(shost->host_lock);
       *shost = scsidev->host;          1600 }
```

Fig. 6. Extract of `drivers/scsi/libata-scsi.c`

---

[4] Commit d7283d61302798c0c57118e53d7732bec94f8d42.

and another one in the SCSI subsystem,[5] as well as a bug in a IEEE1394 driver[6]. We were able to detect the locking problems in all of these examples and proved the fixed source files to be free of these bugs.

Results. Out of eight examples for locking problems we were able to detect only five. However, when comparing our results with the conclusions of the previous section, BLAST worked much better for the locking properties because it required fewer modifications to the source code. From a practitioner's point of view, BLAST performed acceptable as long as only one lock was involved. After considerable efforts in simplifying the spinlock API — mainly removing the use of pointers and manually adding error labels to the spinlock functions — we also managed to deal with multiple locks. However, we consider it as fairly difficult to preserve the behaviour of functions that may sleep and therefore must not be called under a spinlock. Even for large portions of source code, BLAST returned its results within a few seconds or minutes, on a PC equipped with an AMD Athlon 64 processor running at 2200 MHz and 1 GB of RAM. Hence, BLAST's internal slicing and abstraction techniques work very well.

We have to point out that the code listing in Fig. 6 represents one of the easily understandable programming errors. Many problems in kernel source code are more subtle. For example, calling functions that may sleep is something that needs to be avoided. However, if a driver calls a function not available in source code in the same file as the driver under consideration, BLAST will only be able to detect the problem if there is an event explicitly defined for this function.

5   Issues with BLAST

This section highlights various shortcomings of the BLAST toolkit which we experienced during our studies. We also present ideas on how BLAST could be improved in order to be more useful for OS software verification.

Lack of Documentation. Many problems while experimenting with BLAST were caused by the lack of consistent documentation. For example, a significant amount of time could have been saved in our experiments with memory safety, if the BLAST manual would state that almost all pointer operations are ignored. An in-depth discussion of the features and limitations of the alias analysis implemented in BLAST would also be very helpful to have.

Non-support of Pointers. The fact that BLAST does not properly support the use of pointers, in the sense of Sec. 3.4, must be considered as a major restriction, and made our experiments with the spinlock API rather difficult. The restriction forces one to carry out substantial and time consuming modifications to source code. Furthermore, it raises the question whether all important predicates of a given program can be preserved in a manual step of simplification. In some of our experiments we simply replaced the pointers used by the spinlock functions

---

[5] Commit `fe2e17a405a58ec8a7138fee4ebe101858b636e0`.

[6] Commit `910573c7c4aced8fd5f45c334cc67862e3424d92`.

with integers representing the state of the lock. This is obviously a pragmatic approach which does not reflect all possible behaviour of pointer programs. However, it turned out that it is expressive enough to cover the usage rules of the spinlock API. As such modifications could be introduced into the source code automatically, we consider them as an interesting extension for BLAST.

The missing support of function pointers has already been mentioned in Sec. 3. It is true that function pointers are often used in both application space and OS development. In most cases their effect on the program execution can only be determined at run-time, not statically at compile-time. Therefore, we assume that simply skipping all calls of function pointers is acceptable for now.

Usability. There are several issues regarding BLAST's usability which are probably easy to fix, but right now they complicate the work with this tool. Basically, if a piece of C source is accepted by an ANSI C compiler, it should be accepted by BLAST rather than raising uninformative error messages.

A nice improvement would be to provide wrapper scripts that automate preprocessing and verification in a way that BLAST can be used with the same arguments as the compiler. It could be even more useful if functions that are of interest but from other parts of a given source tree, would be copied in automatically. Since we obviously do not want to analyse the whole kernel source in a single file, this should be integrated into BLAST's abstraction/model checking/refinement loop.

6   Related Work

Much work on techniques and tools for automatically finding bugs in software systems has been published in recent years.

Runtime Analysis. A popular runtime analysis tool which targets memory safety problems is Purify (`www-306.ibm.com/software/awdtools/purify/`). It mainly focuses on detecting and preventing memory corruption and memory leakage. However, Purify and other such tools, including Electric Fence (`perens.com/FreeSoftware/ElectricFence/`) and Valgrind (`valgrind.org`), are meant for testing purposes and thereby only cover the set of program runs specified by the underlying test cases. An exhaustive search of a programs state space, as is done in model checking, is out of the scope of these tools.

Static Analysis and Abstract Interpretation. Static analysis is another powerful technique for inspecting source code for bugs. Indeed, most of the memory safety problems within the examples of this paper had been detected earlier via an approach based on system-specific compiler extensions, known as *meta-level compilation* [11]. This approach is implemented in the tool Coverity (`www.coverity.com`) and was used in [6]. A further recent attempt to find bugs in OS code is based on abstract interpretation [10] and presented in [4]. The authors checked about 700k lines of code taken from recent versions of the Linux kernel for correct locking behaviour. The paper focuses on the kernel's spinlock interface and problems related to sleep under a spinlock. Several new bugs in the Linux kernel were found during the experiments. However, the authors suggest that their approach could be improved by adopting model checking techniques. An overview of the advantages and disadvantages of static analysis versus model checking can be found in [12].

Case Studies with BLAST. We have already referred to some such case studies in the introduction. Two project reports of graduate students give further details on BLAST's practical use. In [20], Mong applies BLAST to a doubly linked list implementation with dynamic allocation of its elements and verifies correct allocation and de-allocation. The paper explains that BLAST was not powerful enough to keep track of the state of the list, i.e., the number of its elements. Jie and Shivkumar report in [18] on their experience in applying BLAST to a user level implementation of a virtual file system. They focus on verifying correct locking behaviour for data structures of the implementation and were able to successfully verify several test cases and to find one new error. However, in the majority of test cases BLAST failed due to documented limitations, e.g., by not being able to deal with function pointers, or terminated with obscure error messages. Both studies were conducted in 2004 and thus based on version 1.0 of BLAST. As shown in this paper, BLAST's current version has similar limitations.

7   Conclusions and Future Work

We exposed BLAST to analysing 16 different OS code examples of programming errors related to memory safety and locking behaviour. Details of the examples which we could not show here due to a lack of space, can be found at `www.cs.york.ac.uk/~muehlber/blast/`. In our experience, BLAST is rather difficult to apply by a practitioner during OS software development. This is because of (i) its limitations with respect to reasoning about pointers, (ii) several issues regarding usability, including bugs in `spec.opt`, and (iii) a lack of consistent documentation. Especially in the case of memory safety properties, massive changes to the source code were necessary which essentially requires one to know about a bug beforehand. However, it must be mentioned that BLAST was not designed as a memory debugger. Indeed, BLAST performed considerably better during our tests with locking properties; however, modifications on the source code were still necessary in most cases.

BLAST performed nicely on the modified source code in our examples for locking properties. Even large portions of C code — up to 10k lines with several locks, status variables and a relatively complex program structure — were parsed and model checked within a few minutes on a modern PC. Hence, the techniques for abstraction and refinement as implemented in BLAST are quite able to deal with most of the problems analysed in this paper. If its limitations are ironed out, BLAST is likely to become a very usable and popular tool with OS software developers in the future.

Regarding future work we propose that our case study is repeated once the most problematic errors and restrictions in BLAST are fixed. An analysis allowing one to draw *quantitative* conclusions concerning BLAST's ability of finding certain programming problems could then give results that are more interesting to kernel developers. To this end, metrics for the evaluation of BLAST are required, as is a more precise classification of the chosen examples.

Acknowledgements. We thank Radu Siminiceanu for his constructive comments and suggestions on a draft of this paper.

References

1. Ball, T. and Rajamani, S. K. Automatically validating temporal safety properties of interfaces. In *SPIN 2001*, vol. 2057 of *LNCS*, pp. 103–122.
2. Beyer, D., Chlipala, A. J., Henzinger, T. A., Jhala, R., and Majumdar, R. The BLAST query language for software verification. In *PEPM 2004*, pp. 201–202. ACM Press.
3. Beyer, D., Henzinger, T. A., Jhala, R., and Majumdar, R. Checking memory safety with BLAST. In *FASE 2005*, vol. 3442 of *LNCS*, pp. 2–18.
4. Breuer, P. T. and Pickin, S. Abstract interpretation meets model checking near the 10^6 LOC mark. In *AVIS 2006*. To appear in ENTCS.
5. Chaki, S., Clarke, E., Groce, A., Ouaknine, J., Strichman, O., and Yorav, K. Efficient verification of sequential and concurrent C programs. *FMSD*, 25(2–3):129–166, 2004.
6. Chou, A., Yang, J., Chelf, B., Hallem, S., and Engler, D. R. An empirical study of operating system errors. In *SOSP 2001*, pp. 73–88. ACM Press.
7. Clarke, E. M., Grumberg, O., and Peled, D. A. *Model checking.* MIT Press, 2000.
8. Corbet, J., Rubini, A., and Kroah-Hartmann, G. *Linux Device Drivers.* O'Reilly, 3rd edition, 2005.
9. Corbett et al, J. C. Bandera: Extracting finite-state models from Java source code. In *ICST 2000*, pp. 439–448. SQS Publishing.
10. Cousot, P. and Cousot, R. On abstraction in software verification. In *CAV 2002*, vol. 2404 of *LNCS*, pp. 37–56.
11. Engler, D. R., Chelf, B., Chou, A., and Hallem, S. Checking system rules using system-specific, programmer-written compiler extensions. In *OSDI 2000*. USENIX.
12. Engler, D. R. and Musuvathi, M. Static analysis versus software model checking for bug finding. In *VMCAI 2004*, vol. 2937 of *LNCS*, pp. 191–210.
13. Henzinger, T. A., Jhala, R., and Majumdar, R. Race checking by context inference. In *PLDI 2004*, pp. 1–13. ACM Press.
14. Henzinger, T. A., Jhala, R., Majumdar, R., and Sanvido, M. A. A. Extreme model cecking. In *Verification: Theory & practice*, vol. 2772 of *LNCS*, pp. 232–358, 2003.
15. Henzinger, T. A., Jhala, R., Majumdar, R., and Sutre, G. Lazy abstraction. In *POPL 2002*, pp. 58–70. ACM Press.
16. Henzinger et al, T. A. Temporal-safety proofs for systems code. In *CAV 2002*, vol. 2404 of *LNCS*, pp. 526–538.
17. Holzmann, G. J. *The SPIN model checker.* Addison-Wesley, 2003.
18. Jie, H. and Shivaji, S. Temporal safety verification of AVFS using BLAST. Project report, Univ. California at Santa Cruz, 2004.
19. Microsoft Corporation. Static driver verifier: Finding bugs in device drivers at compile-time. www.microsoft.com/whdc/devtools/tools/SDV.mspx.
20. Mong, W. S. Lazy abstraction on software model checking. Project report, Toronto Univ., Canada., 2004.
21. Necula, G. C., McPeaki, S., and Weimer, W. CCured: Type-safe retrofitting of legacy code. In *POPL 2002*, pp. 128–139. ACM Press.

A Finite State Modeling of AFDX Frame Management Using Spin

Indranil Saha and Suman Roy

Honeywell Technology Solutions Lab Pvt. Ltd.
151/1, Doraisanipalya, Bannerghatta Road,
Bangalore 560 076, India
{indranil.saha, suman.roy}@honeywell.com

Abstract. Data exchange with strong data transmission time guarantees is necessary in the internal communication of an aircraft. The Avionics Full Duplex Switched Ethernet (AFDX) has been developed for this purpose. Its design is based on the principle of a switched network with physically redundant links to support availability. It should also be tolerant to transmission and link failures in the network. Recent research on an industrial case study by Anand et. al. reveals that AFDX frame management design is vulnerable to faults such as network errors, network babbling etc. Their proposed modifications, though are able to solve these problems, degrades the performance of network in terms of delay at receiving end and delay before the receiving end-system gets reset. They also do not present any performance analysis. We propose new solutions to alleviate these problems in AFDX frame management design, formally model it in Spin incorporating our proposed solution, thus also showing a finite state modeling of the above is possible. We also verify some of its relevant properties and carry out a performance analysis of the same.

Keywords: Industrial case study, ARINC, AFDX frame management design, finite state modeling, verification, LTL, fault tolerance, Spin model checker.

1 Introduction

As the complexity of avionics systems has grown for both flight-critical items and passenger entertainment, so has the need for increased bandwidth of on-board data buses. The desire for rapid deployment with minimal development and implementation costs, such as wiring, has driven the industry to explore existing off-the-shelf technologies. Both Boeing and Airbus have explored commercial Ethernet technology to build a next-generation avionics data bus. This research has resulted in the development of Avionics Full-Duplex Switched Ethernet (AFDX) [4], based upon IEEE 803.2 Ethernet technology [13], but adding specific functionality to provide a deterministic network with guaranteed service. The Avionics Full Duplex Switched Ethernet (AFDX) is a special application of a network compliant with ARINC 664. Although 802.3 Ethernet offers high speed and low cost due to widespread commercial usage, it does not offer the robustness required for an avionics system. The primary drawback of IEEE 802.3 is the lack of guaranteed bandwidth and Quality of Service (QoS). The AFDX attempts to solve these issues with key enhancements to provide deterministic timing and reliable

L. Brim et al. (Eds.): FMICS and PDMC 2006, LNCS 4346, pp. 227–243, 2007.

delivery of messages. Deterministic timing is achieved through communication over virtual links (VL) that have a bounded bandwidth and frame delivery interval. Communication over redundant channels is used to achieve reliable delivery of the messages. A frame management mechanism is responsible for checking integrity of message frames and managing the redundancy before delivering the messages to the application. Therefore, the frame management forms an important component of the AFDX design and has to be guaranteed against design flaws: this highlights its importance as an industrial case study.

Recently Anand et.al. [1] have developed a formal model of the AFDX frame management to ascertain the reliability properties of the design. To capture the temporal semantics, they have modeled the system as a network of timed automata [2] and use UPPAAL [7] to model-check for the desired properties expressed in CTL. Their analysis detects that the design of the AFDX frame management is vulnerable to faults such as network errors, network babbling etc which led to unwarranted resets and dropped frames if they arrived out-of-order. To fully utilize the redundancy in messages and use this redundancy to detect faults, they propose including a priority queue at the receiving end which helps detect network babble on a channel, and deliver frames in sequence to the application even if they arrive out-of-order. To reduce the probability of erroneous resets, they suggest communicating redundant copies of the reset message. But their solution suffer from two major limitations: it increases delay at the receiving end-system to deliver frames to the upper level of protocol stack, and it also increases delay before the receiving end system reset.

We address these issues, and provide new solutions to alleviate these problems. We propose two modifications towards that by providing a signature for each data frame and a variable to keep track of the sequence number of the last frame delivered to the upper level of the protocol stack. The receiver can authenticate each message it receives by using its signature which provides a protection against the network babble. The Redundancy Checking is efficiently performed using the variable "psn" and a queue which holds the frames coming to the receiver out of order. Incorporating these modifications we model AFDX frame management design in PROMELA language. We specify the desired properties in LTL, and model-check those properties by using Spin model checker [12]. We also present a performance analysis of our model which was not present in an earlier work [1].

The remainder of this paper is organized as follows: In Section 2, we briefly describe AFDX frame management design, describe the modifications proposed by Anand et. al. [1], and the drawback of their proposed modification. In this section, we also introduce our modification over original AFDX design, and explains how these modifications help to alleviate the drawbacks that arise in [1]. We briefly discuss on discrete time extension of Spin in Section 3. In Section 4 we describe our model, and in Section 5 we present the verification results, and analyze them. Section 6 finally concludes the paper.

2   AFDX Frame Management

AFDX network consists of a number of End-Systems, the function of which is to provide services, which guarantee a secure and reliable data exchange to the partition soft-

ware. The heart of an AFDX network is the virtual link (VL). Each VL builds a unidi-
rectional logic path from one source ES to one or more destination ESes. Each VL is
allocated dedicated bandwidth, the amount being defined by the system integrator. The
total bandwidth of all created VLs cannot exceed the maximum available bandwidth of
the network, and the bandwidth allocated to a given VL is reserved to that link. Fundamental to an AFDX network is guaranteed service: both the bandwidth and maximum
end-to-end latency of the link are guaranteed. However, there is no guarantee of packet
delivery. Transmission acknowledgements and retransmission requests must be handled
at the application level.

Reliable frame delivery in the AFDX design is ensured by utilizing redundant links.
This basic idea of network redundancy is shown in Figure 1. End-systems communicate
over multiple communication channels with the effect that communication is protected
against loss of one complete network. The redundancy scheme operates on a per link
basis in the following manner: A transmitting end-system prepares some data and passes
it to the communication protocol stack. Here, a sequence number is added to each frame
to enable the receive function to reconstruct a single ordered stream of frames without
duplication before delivery to the receiving partition. The sequence numbers are one
octet long with a range from 0 to 255 and are incremented on each successive frame.
After 255, the sequence number is wrapped around to 1. The sequence number 0 is
reserved for communicating reset. In the default mode, each frame is sent across both
of the channels and the redundancy is taken care at the receiving end-system.

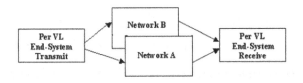

Fig. 1. Network Redundancy Concept

Upon reception, an algorithm in the communications stack (below IP layer) uses a
"First Valid Wins" policy. This means that the first frame to be received from either network channel with the next valid sequence number is accepted and passed up the stack
to the receiving partition. When the second frame is received with this sequence number, it is simply discarded. Figure 2 shows the redundancy management at the receiving
end-system. Redundancy Manager (RM) is placed after the Integrity Checker (IC). Under fault-free network operation, the IC simply passes the frames that it has received
on to the RM, independently for each network. If there are faults (based on sequence
number), the IC has the task to eliminate invalid frames. For each network the IC tests
each frame for a sequence number in the interval: $[PSN \oplus 1, PSN \oplus 2]$ where Previous Sequence Number (PSN) is the sequence number of the previous frame received
(but not necessarily forwarded) on this VL. The operator $\oplus$ takes the wrap-around of
sequence numbers into account. For example, if PSN = 254, then $PSN \oplus 1 = 255$ and
$PSN \oplus 2 = 1$.

The network channel is responsible for deliveringr frames from the transmitting end-
system to the receiving end-system. Different kinds of network faults may arise with

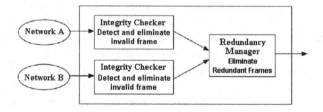

Fig. 2. Redundancy Management at the Receiving End-System

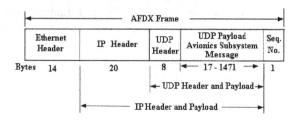

Fig. 3. AFDX Frame Format

their detrimental impact on the frame management. We consider two kinds of network faults here:

1. *Arbitrary drop of frame due to channel error:* Due to some error in the channel a frame may be arbitrarily dropped from the channel, which does not reach the receiver.
2. *Network Babble:* Arbitrary frame can be generated in the channel and delivered to the receiver.

In practice, however, it is commonly assumed that the probability of error in consecutive frames is close to zero. Also, when a babbled frame is generated in the channel, the probability that the next frame which reach the receiver is also a babbled frame is insignificant. To model AFDX protocol, we have taken these assumptions into consideration, as was done in the modeling of AFDX protocol by Anand et. al. [1].

The AFDX frame format is shown in Figure 3. The destination and source addresses are contained in the Ethernet Header. The actual IP address information is contained in the IP Structure block. The UDP structure identifies the appropriate application port. The AFDX payload ranges from 17 to 1471 bytes. Payload sizes less than 17 bytes must be padded to maintain a minimum length of 17 bytes. The one-byte sequence number is used to maintain ordinal integrity within a given VL. The maximum frame size is set for each VL and is represented by the parameter L_{MAX}. The range of this parameter is between 60 and 1514 bytes.

There are some temporal aspects of AFDX frame management system mentioned below:

BAG. The data flow on the links is controlled by the transmitting end-systems according to the Bandwidth Allocation Gap (BAG). The BAG values are the time slices allocated for an end-system to transmit data on a VL. This time is defined in milliseconds and is typically some exponent of two.

Jitter. The ES may introduce jitter when transmitting frames for a given VL. This jitter is defined as the interval beginning from the start of the BAG to the occurrence of the first bit of the frame transmitted through the VL.

TDRF. Time Delay for Redundant Frame is defined as the maximum time difference between the sending of the redundant copies of a frame on the two channels.

Resetdelay. This is the time that an endsystem spends as it is reset, and come to the normal operational mode.

Latency. Latency is defined as the time for a frame that it spends in the channel. Maximum and minimum values of latency are denoted by Maximum Channel Latency (L_{max}) and Minimum Channel Latency (L_{min}).

Skewmax. It is the maximum time difference between the reception of two redundant frames by the receiver.

2.1   Modeling of AFDX Design in UPPAAL

In [1], Anand et. al. developed a formal model of the AFDX frame management to ascertain the reliability properties of the design. They modeled the system as a network of timed automata and used UPPAAL to model-check the desired properties expressed in CTL. In their work, they haven't considered the *jitter* time. Their analysis revealed that the AFDX frame management is vulnerable to faults such as arbitrary dropping of frames and network babble. They considered the following three reliability properties:

– A babbling frame is never accepted by the receiver.
– A receiving end-system reset implies a transmitting end-system reset.
– If a valid and non-redundant frame is delivered, then it is not discarded.

They considers two conditions under which they verifies the above three properties:

(a) $Skewmax < (BAG - L_{max} + L_{min})$:
Under this condition, the frames arrive in order, i.e., a redundant frame on the second channel arrives the receiver before the successive frame on the first channel. When model-checked by UPPAAL, the first two properties had been proved to be non-valid, while the third one was valid.

(b) $Skewmax > (BAG - L_{max} + L_{min})$:
The frames arrive out of order to the receiver, i.e., in this case it is possible that the redundant frame on the second channel arrives the receiver after the successive frame arrives on the first channel. When model-checked by UPPAAL, all the three properties had been proved to be non-valid.

The counterexample that was generated for the first property is that if one of the network babbles such that the babbling frame number is either $PSN \oplus 1$ or $PSN \oplus 2$, then this is accepted and in this process, the legitimate frame from the other network gets rejected even though it is delivered successfully. The counterexample for the second property is that if a network babbles a reset frame (frame with sequence number 0), then that results in the receiving end-system getting erroneously reset. For the third property, counterexample shows that when the faster of the two networks delivers successive invalid and valid frames before the slower network can deliver the first one, the receiving end-system accepts the second frame from the faster network and considers the first frame (which is valid) on the slower network as invalid and discards it.

2.2   Modifications of AFDX Design Suggested

As a remedy of the above problems, the authors proposed two modifications in the original AFDX protocol. The first modification is the introduction of an integrity check with queuing module instead of the distinct IC and RM modules in the original design. Under this modification, the first property and the third property becomes valid, offering better data integrity and QoS. But the drawback of the modification is that it introduces an additional delay of as high as $(L_{max} + BAG - L_{min})$, over the latency *Skewmax* of the original AFDX design. The second modification has two aspects. It deals with the second property which is not valid in case of original AFDX design due to network babble. To achieve tolerance to one channel babble, one extra network channel can be introduced, which adds a significant overhead. Otherwise instead of sending one frame 0 through one channel, two reset messages are sent on both the channels. The disadvantage here is that it increases the delay before the receiver gets reset.

2.3   Further Improvement of the Frame Management Design

To improve the AFDX frame management design, we propose two modifications on the original AFDX design. The first two properties of AFDX deals with network babble. By checking only the sequence number, it is not possible for the Integrity Checker to decide whether a frame is legitimate frame or babbled frame. To provide the IC the way to detect a babbled frame we propose to introduce a new field in the original AFDX frame. This field is like a signature [15] of the frame sequence number. To generate the signature, any hash function [15] can be used. At the receiving end, the receiver can now perform a message authentication [14] like operation to verify whether the frame is legitimate. This replaces the IC part of original AFDX design. Note that the signature does not add much overhead to the message sent from the transmitting end as it only increases the length of the AFDX frame by 1 byte.

The second modification is on Redundancy Manager. It maintains a variable *psn* which denotes the sequence number of the last frame it has delivered to the upper level of the protocol stack. Also it maintains a queue to store the frames which reach the RM out of order. When the RM gets a legitimate frame from the IC of either channel, it checks whether a frame with the same sequence number is already in the queue. If that is the case, then the frame is delivered to the upper level of the protocol stack. If the frame is not present in the queue, then it checks whether the sequence number of the incoming frame is $(psn \oplus 1)$. If it is so, then the RM accepts the frame and sends it immediately to the upper level of the protocol stack. If the sequence number of the frame is less than $(psn \oplus 1)$, then the RM simply discards the frame, as the frame with the same sequence number has been already accepted. If the sequence number of the incoming frame is greater than $(psn \oplus 1)$, the frame is enqueued. Whenever a frame is delivered to the upper level of the protocol stack, the *psn* value is changed to the sequence number of that frame. Then the queue is examined to check whether it contains a frame with sequence number $(psn \oplus 1)$. If it is so, then the frame is delivered, and again the same process is repeated.

In our design, as a signature is sent with every transmitted frame, a babbled frame can not affect the performance of the network, whatever the sequence number of the babbled frame may be. The IC never passes a babbled frame to the RM. As a result, a babbled frame with sequence number 0 can not reset the receiver. So the first two properties of AFDX design should be satisfied. Let us explain the case of the third property by an example. We consider the *Skewmax* parameter to be arbitrarily large. Suppose, in the first channel, Frame 1 (frame with sequence number 1) has been accepted by the IC, and the RM delivers the frame to the upper level of the protocol stack. Frame 1 is also received by the IC of channel 2 and discarded by the RM. Now frame 2 is dropped on Channel 1. There may be two cases. Frame 2 may be dropped in the second channel also. If that is the case, then Frame 3 on any channel, which comes first to the RM is enqueued. Whenever Frame 3 Comes through the other channel, the frame is dequeued and passed to the upper level of the protocol stack. If Frame 2 is not dropped on the second channel, then whenever RM gets it, it delivers Frame 2 to the upper level and also, it dequeues the successive frames from the queue, and delivers them. Note that the number of the elements present in the queue depends on the parameter *Skewmax*. In both the cases, delivery of a frame is not delayed more than *Skewmax* time unit, so the frame delivery delay of the original AFDX protocol is maintained in our design. The problem of erroneous reset of receiver is also removed without any overhead in terms of number of channels and delay before the receiver resets.

3   Discrete Time in Promela and Spin

Spin is a tool for automatically model checking distributed systems [12]. Spin checks properties of communication protocols, modeled in the Promela language, by exploring their state space. Promela is a non-deterministic guarded-command language for modeling systems of concurrent processes that can interact via shared variables and message channels. Interaction via message channels can be either synchronous or asynchronous with arbitrary buffer capacities, and arbitrary number of message parameters. Given a concurrent system modeled by a Promela program, Spin can check for deadlock, dead code, violations of user specified assertions, and temporal properties expressed by LTL formulas. When a violation of a property is detected, Spin reports a scenario, i.e., a sequence of transitions, violating this property.

The time ordering of actions in a Promela program is implicit and depends on the (fixed) sequential composition of statements within each one of the component processes, as well as on the (unspecified) interleaving of statements from different processes. This time relation is only *qualitative*, meaning that we do not know the exact time interval that will elapse between two events. This can be a hindrance when systems are to be verified whose correct functioning depends on timing parameters. One faces the same problem while trying to model AFDX in Promela, it requires the provision of explicitly expressing time in Spin. There are few literatures on time extensions of

Spin [5,6,17]. We shall be considering the work of [5,6] as it will be sufficient for our purpose. This extension allows one to quantify (discrete) time elapse between events, by specifying the time slice in which they occur. This extension is fully compatible with the partial order reduction algorithm. Although the real-time extension of Spin [17] is more general that it can model Timed Automata with real-valued clocks, it is not compatible with the partial order reduction algorithm.

In the discrete time model, time is divided into slices of equal length indexed by natural numbers. The actions are then framed into those slices, obtaining in that way a measure for the elapsed time between events belonging to different slices. Within a slice however, we only know the relative ordering between events, as in the time free case. The elapsed time between events is measured in ticks of a global digital clock that is increased by one with every such tick.

The basic idea behind simulation is to execute the system time slice by time slice. Recalling that the execution of statements in Spin is asynchronous and interleaved, the basic problem is how to avoid interleaving of actions belonging to different time slices. The authors implement this synchronization scheme by extending Promela with a new variable type `timer` corresponding to discrete time countdown timers, three new statements `set`, `expire` and `tick` that operate on the new type, and a special timing process `Timers` which is the demon process that uses `ticks` to decrease the timer values. *The implementation can be done entirely on user level, without any additional changes in the Spin source code*, for example, with the following Promela macro definitions and timer process.

```
#define timer byte
#define set(tmr,val) (tmr=val)
#define expire(tmr) (tmr==0) /*timeout*/
#define tick(tmr) if :: tmr>0 -> tmr=tmr-1 :: else fi

proctype Timers()
do :: timeout -> atomic{ tick(tmr1); tick(tmr2) } od
```

`Timers` consists of an endless do iteration that realizes the passage of time. It runs concurrently with the other processes of the system. The key idea of the concept is the usage of `timeout` - a predefined Promela statement that becomes true when no other statement within the system is executable. By guarding ticks with timeout, we ensure that no process will proceed with an action from the next time slice until the other processes have executed all actions from the current time slice.

Within a process, statements are divided into time slices by putting `set` and `expire` at the beginning and end, respectively, of each time slice. For instance, assuming that we have declared timer `tmr`, and that A, B and C are nonblocking Promela statements, the sequence,

```
set(tmr,1); A; B; expire(tmr); C
```

means that A and B will be executed in same time slice, while C belongs to the next time slice. The `expire` statement is a synchronization point where the process waits for tmr to become zero. This can be done only by `Timers`, i.e., only when all active timers are decreased. Thus, it is guaranteed that C will be executed in the next time slice. In fact, `set` is only a labeling of the time slice (some sort of reading of the global digital clock is assumed in this time model) and it can be permuted with the statements from the time slice that it labels (in our case A and B).

It is often convenient to use derived macros for modeling various delays. For instance, one tick delay and unbounded nondeterministic delay are implemented, by the following macros

```
#define delay(tmr,x) set(tmr,x); expire(tmr)
#define udelay(tmr) do ::delay(tmr,1) ::break od
```

In the unbounded nondeterministic delay, at each iteration a nondeterministic choice is made whether the loop will be broken and the process will proceed with the execution of a new statement, or the decision will be delayed for the next time slice. In a similar way a nondeterministic bounded delay up to a certain number of ticks, or a nondeterministic delay within lower and upper bounds can be modeled.

It is noteworthy that, because of the independence of the timing implementation from the other parts of Spin's source code, the expressivity of the timing framework is in fact augmented with the introduction of new features on Spin, we shall address it as DT-Spin.

4   Modeling Modified AFDX Frame Management Design in Promela

We model the AFDX frame management system in Promela. This model captures the temporal aspects of the frame management such as BAG, transmission delay of redundant frame, transmitter jitter, transmitter reset delay and channel latency. In our model, there are four components: the transmitting end system, two channels, and the receiving end system. These four components are modeled as four active processes.

4.1   Transmitting End-System

The Bandwidth Allocation Gap (BAG) of the transmitter is modeled by a timer *bag*. Once it expires, a new BAG starts immediately. At the beginning of a new BAG, the *bag* timer is set to the BAG value 16, and a boolean variable *rchk* which denotes transmitter reset is set to 0. Transmitter *jitter* is randomly set to any value between 1 to 3 time units. The Transmitter has to wait for that much time to transmit the first of the two redundant frames. It is randomly decided by the *randomreset* function whether the Transmitter will be reset or it will continue sending frames, a boolean variable *reset* is used for this purpose. If it is 0, then the Transmitter generates the hashed value messagedigest through the Channel 1, the current transmitted frame being represented by the variable *tfr*. A timer *tdrf* is set to the value TDRF which represents the maximum delay of the Transmitter to send the redundant frame through Channel 2. The same frame with the same *messagedigest* is sent through Channel 2 before the timer *tdrf* expires. When the timer *tdrf* expires, *tfr* is updated to the sequence number of the next frame to be transmitted. If the current transmitted frame is less than 255, then the *tfr* is updated to $tfr + 1$, if the current transmitted frame is 255, then it is made 1. If the *reset* variable is 1, the transmitter will be reset, the boolean variable *rchk* is set to 1. A frame with sequence number 0 along with its corresponding *messagedigest* is sent in the same way as any other frame described through Channel 1 and 2. There is delay of HRD time units corresponding to the hardware reset at the Transmitter, which is modeled by the timer *resetdelay*. Then the *tfr* is set to 1 to model the fact that after reset the Transmitter again starts sending frames beginning with sequence number 1. At this point Transmitter resets some flag variables, they will be discussed while describing the models of the channels and Receiver processes. The Promela code of the Transmitter process is described in the following Listing 1.

4.2 Network Channel

In our model, there are two processes Channel1 and Channel2 corresponding to the two channels in the system. The design of these two channels are identical. We represent the model of Channel 1 in Listing 2. Following [1] we consider two types of errors in Channel 1.

1. Arbitrary drop of frame due to channel error: Due to some error in the channel a frame may be arbitrarily dropped from the channel, and it does not reach the receiver. To generate this error, we use an inline function randomerrorinchannel1. The boolean variable *error1* denotes the presence of error in Channel 1. If *error1* is 0, then the frame obtained from the transmitter is delivered successfully to the receiver. An array of boolean variable *ec1flag[255]* is used to keep track of which frames are in error during the transmission. The latency of the Channel 1 has been modeled by using inline function *randomlatencyinchannel1*. This function randomly sets the latency for a frame to be transmitted to an arbitrary value between MINLATENCY and MAXLATENCY, which are two system parameters. The variable *latency1* represents the latency of a frame in Channel 1.

2. Network Babble: Due to network babble arbitrary frame can be generated in the channel and can be delivered to the receiver. The function *randombabbleinchannel1* randomly decides if a babbled frame has been generated in Channel 1. The variables *babble1* denotes the generation of a babbled frame in Channel 1. If *babble1* is 1 then the babbled frame is generated randomly with a sequence number between 0 to 255. Also, the hashed value *messagedigest* for the babbled frame is generated randomly which also takes value between 0 to 255.

4.3 Receiving End-System

When the Receiver gets a frame from Channel 1 or Channel 2, it first verifies the frame to check whether it is babbled or not. This is performed by the *verify* function. By this function the receiver, knowing the hash function, generates the signature for the incoming frame, and checks if it matches with the messagedigest field of the incoming frame. If they do not match then the receiver decides the received frame to be babbled,

Listing 1. Model of the Transmitting End-System

```
proctype Transmitter() {
    byte j;
    do
    :: expire(bag) ->
        set(bag, BAG);
        rchk = 0;
        randomjitter();
        delay(transmitterjitter, jitter);
        randomreset();
        if
        :: reset == 0 ->
            generatemessagedigest(tfr);
            channelt1 ! tfr, messagedigest;
            set(tdrf, TDRF);
            channelt2 ! tfr, messagedigest;
            do
            :: expire(tdrf) ->
                if
                :: tfr < 255 -> tfr = tfr + 1;
                :: else -> tfr =1;
                fi;
                break;
            od;
        :: reset == 1 ->
            rchk =1;
            tfr = 0;
            generatemessagedigest(tfr);
            channelt1 ! tfr, messagedigest;
            set(tdrf, TDRF);
            channelt2 ! tfr, messagedigest;
            do
            :: expire(tdrf) ->
                delay(resetdelay, HRD);
                tfr = 1; j = 0;
                do
                :: j < 256 ->
                    ec1flag[j] = 0;
                    ec2flag[j] = 0;
                    rfflag[j] = 0;
                    j++;
                :: j == 256 -> break;
                od;
                break;
            od;
        fi;
    od
}
```

Listing 2. Model of Channel 1

```
proctype Channel1() {
    byte j;
    byte cfr1, cmd1;
    randombabbleinchannel1();
    do
    :: babble1 == 1 ->
        generatebabbleframeforchannel1();
        channelr1! babblefrm1,
        randommsgedigest1;
        babble1 = 0;
    :: channelt1 ? cfr1, cmd1 ->
        randomerrorinchannel1();
        if
        :: error1 == 0 ->
            ec1flag[cfr1] = 1;
            randomlatencyinchannel1();
            delay(channeldelay1, latency1);
            channelr1 ! cfr1, cmd1;
        :: error1 == 1 ->
            delay(channeldelay1, MAXLATENCY);
            ec1flag[cfr1] = 0;
        fi;
        randombabbleinchannel1();
    od;
}
```

and sets the value of a boolean variable *babblechk* to 1, otherwise *babblecheck* is set to 0. If *babblechk* is 1, it is simply made 0. If *babblechk* is 0, *i.e.*, when the received frame is not a babbled one, the Receiver checks if the received frame number is 0. In that case, a boolean variable *resetflag* is set to 1 which represents the fact that the Receiver is reset. A variable *psnr*, which denotes the currently received frame is set to 0. A list is maintained with the Receiver to hold the frames which arrives at the receiving end out of order. If the Received frame is not 0, then it is checked if a frame with the same number is already in the list. If that is the case then the frame is delivered to the upper level of the protocol stack. This is done by the *deliverframe* function (Listing 3). In this function, after delivering the first frame it is checked whether the other frames in the list are in order. Then all those frames are delivered to the upper level of the protocol stack.

The frames which are delivered are modeled by an array *rfflag[256]*. If a frame is successfully delivered then the corresponding array element is made 1. If the received frame is not present in the list, then it checks if it is the next expected frame ($rfr == psnr + 1$). If it is so, then the frame and the other enlisted frames those are in order are delivered by the *deliverframe* function. If the received frame number is more than the expected frame number ($rfr > psnr + 1$) then the frame is inserted into the list by *insertframeinlist* function. If the received frame number is less than the expected

Listing 3. Inline Function to Deliver Frames to the Upper Level of the Protocol Stack

```
inline deliverframe(element) {
    byte j, k;
    rfflag[element] = 1;
    psnr = element;
    j =0;
    do
    :: psnr < 255 ->
        if
        :: listelement[j] == psnr +1 ->
            rfflag[listelement[j]] = 1;
            psnr = listelement[j];
            j++;
        :: listelement[j] != psnr + 1 ->
            break;
        fi;
    :: psnr == 255 ->
        if
        :: listelement[j] == 1 ->
            rfflag[listelement[j]] = 1;
            psnr = listelement[j];
            j++;
        :: listelement[j] != 1 ->
            break;
        fi;
    od;
    k = j;
    do
    :: k < numoflistelements ->
        listelement[k] = listelement[k-j];
        k++;
    :: k >= numoflistelements ->
        break;
    od;
    numoflistelements = numoflistelements - j;
}
```

frame number ($rfr < psnr + 1$), the frame is simply discarded. The part in which the Receiver process receives a frame from Channel 1 is shown in Listing 4.

5   Verification Results and Analysis

In the model of AFDX frame management design we check our specification against the following properties. Integer time verification (digitization) techniques suffice if the problem of whether all real numbered behaviors of a system satisfy a property can be reduced to the question of whether the integral observations satisfy a (possibly modified) property [11]. This reduction is possible for qualitative properties for timed transitions

Listing 4. Part of the Model of the Receiving End-System

```
atomic {
    verify(rfr1, rmd1);
    if
    :: babblechk == 0 ->
        if
        :: rfr1 != 0 ->
            ispresentinlist(rfr1);
            if
            :: ispresentflag == 0 ->
                if
                :: rfr1 = psnr + 1 ->
                    deliverframetoendsystem(rfr1);
                :: rfr1 > psnr + 1->
                    insertframeinlist(rfr1);
                :: rfr1 < psnr + 1 ->
                fi;
            :: ispresentflag == 1 ->
                deliverframetoendsystem(rfr1);
            :: else ->
            fi;
        :: rfr1 ==0 ->
            resetflag = 1;
        psnr = 0;
        fi;
    :: babblechk == 1->
        babblechk = 0;
    fi;
}
\vspace{-2mm}
```

systems. Since we will be considering only qualitative properties (no explicit statement of time is involved in the properties) we can use discretized models.

Progression of Time (POT). Naturally we would like to avoid situations when the passage of time is blocked (referred to as *zero cycle* in [6]). We do this by checking the system against the property $\Box\Diamond$ timeout.

Rejection of Babbling Frame (RBF). A babbling frame is never accepted by the receiver. We model this as: a babbling channel on either channel is rejected by the receiver.

$$\Box((p \lor q) \to \Diamond r),$$

where $p \stackrel{\text{def}}{=} babble1 == 1, q \stackrel{\text{def}}{=} babble2 == 1, r \stackrel{\text{def}}{=} babblechk == 1.$

Reset at both ends (RST). A receiving end-system reset implies a transmitting end-system reset.

$$\Box(s \rightarrow t),$$

where $s \stackrel{\text{def}}{=} resetflag == 1, t \stackrel{\text{def}}{=} rchk == 1.$

Data Consistency (DC). If a valid and non-redundant frame is delivered then it is not discarded. We model this as: if both the redundant copies of a frame are not in error, then eventually that frame will be received by the receiver.

$$\Box((p_1 \wedge q_1) \rightarrow \Diamond r_1),$$

where $p_1 \stackrel{\text{def}}{=} ec1flag[1] == 1, q_1 \stackrel{\text{def}}{=} ec2flag[1] == 1, r_1 \stackrel{\text{def}}{=} rfflag[1] == 1.$

Table 1. Computational resources required for the basic model

Properties	States stored	States matched	Transitions usage (visited + matched)	Time (in min.)
POT	2.65978e+06	8.20632e+06	1.35252e+07	21
RBF	2.65039e+06	7.69169e+06	1.1812e+07	19
RST	2.53634e+06	3.08398e+06	5.62032e+06	6
DC	272152	271036	814228	< 1

We use xspin on an Intel (R) P4 machine with speed 2.60 GHz and RAM 256 MB on a platform of Windows 2000. Table 1 illustrates the computational resources required for state space generation for the properties verified. (with the partial order reduction option kept on). All the properties are proved to be valid as expected for our modified model. RBF is valid as the receiving end is able to authenticate the message it receives. Since any babbled reset frame is not accepted RST is also valid. The validity of DC follows from the fact that any frame that comes out of order is inserted into the queue and later on delivered to upper level of the protocol stack at an appropriate time.

6 Conclusion

The ARINC-664 [3] is a commercial standard for the avionics communication architecture. The AFDX [4] is a vendor specific implementation of this standard. It is based on the 802.3 standard Ethernet with enhancements to ensure determinism and reliability. An overview of a switched Ethernet avionics network along with testing challenges are identified in [16]. Their work mainly concentrates on hardware testing of various modules through simulation. The first verification effort on AFDX is reported in [1]. The authors formally model and analyze the design of the AFDX frame management under different faults. Their model was developed using UPPAAL, a freely available tool [7] that allows modeling with a flavor of timed automata, called the Timed Safety

Automata [8]. The model-checker in UPPAAL allows specifying queries using a simplified version of CTL.

We model AFDX frame management design in Promela language and specify the properties in LTL and model check those properties in Spin [12]. A finite state analysis of the design has produced very encouraging results though we have used a model of discrete time. We do also stress that discrete-time models are sufficient for a large class of practical applications [11]. In [1] no performance analysis of the modeling and verification experiment has been provided. That is why we could not compare the UPPAAL model and our Spin model in terms of memory and time requirement to verify the desired properties, though it might be a useful work. In future we are planing to model our modified AFDX protocol in UPPAAL, and compare its performance with that of the model written in Spin. Also, we plan to design the frame management in a modeling framework based on event calenders [9] that would enable us to capture a dense time semantics.

In [10], Gong *et. al.* have studied authentication in the Byzantine agreement in tolerating hybrid and link faults by adding a signature field to the message. In fault-tolerant systems based on state machine approach, replicated processors are required to agree on a single-source data (such as sensor samples). This is called the Byzantine Agreement. There are some protocols which achieve Byzantine Agreement. By adding authentication to variants of Oral Messages protocol the authors have able to show the increase in the number faults tolerated by the protocols in presence of the authentication mechanism, The protocols do not also compromise their innate fault tolerance if those assumptions were violated. Further, assuming authentication they also show that one of these protocols can tolerate as many hybrid faults as the classical Signed Messages protocol. Using their framework it could be interesting to study whether our AFDX frame management scheme would meet Byzantine Agreement.

Acknowledgement. The authors would like to thank Darren Cofer and Madhukar Anand for helpful suggestions about the problem.

References

1. Anand, M., Vestal, S., Dajani-Brown, S., Lee, I:. Formal Modeling and Analysis of the AFDX Frame Management Design. Proceedings of 9th IEEE International Symposium on Object and component-oriented Real-time distributed Computing (2006).
2. Alur R., Dill, D. L.: A Theory of Timed Automata. Theoretical Computer Science, Vol. 126 (2) (1994) 183–235.
3. ARINC. Specification 664: Aircraft Data Network, Part 7 - Deterministic Networks. (Draft 2) (Oct 10, 2003).
4. ARINC. Arinc Project Paper 664: Aircraft Data Network, Part 7 - Avionics Full Duplex Switched Ethernet (afdx) Network (2005).
5. Bošanački, D., Dams, D.: Integrating Real Time into Spin: A Prototype Implementation. Proceedings of the FORTE/PSTV XVIII conference. Kluwer (1998) 423-439.
6. Bošanački, D., Dams, D.: Discrete-Time Promela and Spin. Proceedings of Formal Techniques in Real-Time and Fault-Tolerant Systems FTRFT. LNCS, Vol. 1486. Springer-Verlag, (1998) 307-310.

7. Behrmann, G., David, A., Larsen, K.G.: A Tutorial on UPPAAL. In 4th International School on Formal Methods for the Design of Computer, Communication, and Software Systems, SFM-RT 2004. LNCS, Vol. 3185. Springer-Verlag, (2004) 200–236.

8. Bengtsson, J., Yi, W.,: Timed automata: Semantics, algorithms and tools. Lecture Notes on Concurrency and Petri Nets, W. Reisig and G. Rozenberg (eds.). LNCS, Vol. 3098. Springer-Verlag (2004).

9. Dutertre, B., Sorea, M.: Modeling and Verification of a Fault-Tolerant Real-Time Startup Protocol using Calendar Automata. Proceedings of FORMATS/FTRTFT'04 (2004).

10. Gong, L, Lincoln, P., Rushby, J.: Byzantine Agreement with Authentication: Observations and Applications in Tolerating Hybrid and Link Faults. Presented at Dependable Computing for Critical Applications–5, Champaign, IL. IEEE Computer Society Press (19995) 139-157.

11. Henzinger, T., Manna, Z., Pnueli, A., What good are digital clocks? Proceedings of the ICALP'92. LNCS, Vol. 623. Springer-Verlag (1992) 545–558.

12. Holtzman, G. J.: The SPIN Model Checker, Primer and Reference Manual. Addison-Wesley (2003).

13. IEEE. Std.802.3:Information Technology. (1998).

14. Menezes, A. J., van Oorschot, P. C., Vanstone, S. A.: Handbook of Applied Cryptography. CRC Press, Fifth reprint (2001).

15. Stinson, D. G.: Cryptography: Theory and Practice. 2nd Edition, Chapman & Hall/CRC (2002).

16. Bisson K., Troshynski, T.: Switched Ethernet Testing for Avionics Applications. Proceedings of IEEE Systems Readiness Technology Conference (2003) 546–550.

17. Tripakis, S., Courcoubetis, C.: Extending Promela and Spin for Real Time. Proceedings of TACAS'96. LNCS, Vol. 1055. Springer-Verlag (1996).

UML 2.0 State Machines:
Complete Formal Semantics Via Core State Machines*

Harald Fecher and Jens Schönborn

Christian-Albrechts-University at Kiel, Germany
hf@informatik.uni-kiel.de, jes@informatik.uni-kiel.de

Abstract. UML has become the standard modeling language for object-oriented systems. The informal description of UML and its continuous extension cause many ambiguities. Therefore, a formal semantics for UML is necessary, especially for formal reasoning and tool development. We present a formal semantics of UML 2.0 state machines, which are used for modeling the reactive behavior of objects, by (i) deriving core state machines with fewer design features and a precise syntax, (ii) developing a formal semantics for core state machines, and (iii) presenting a complete transformation from UML 2.0 state machines to core state machines. Such a transformational approach provides the opportunity of easy adaption to future changes of the semantics of UML state machines.

1 Introduction

UML [8] has become the standard modeling language for object-oriented systems. It constitutes the de-facto-standard for industrial applications in many areas - especially in the object-oriented domain, but it also gains in importance for modeling embedded real-time systems. Its advantages are given by a great variety of intuitive and mostly well-known notations for different kinds of information to be specified: requirements, static structure, interactive and dynamic behavior, as well as physical implementation structures. However, it suffers from an insufficiently precise definition. This and the continuous extension of UML cause many ambiguities and inconsistencies, see, e.g., [9, 3, 10]. Therefore, a formal semantics for UML is necessary, especially for formal reasoning and tool development.

A standard technique to handle such high complexities is to derive a sublanguage, sometimes called core language, for which a precise syntax and a formal semantics are defined. Then the semantics of the original language is given via transformation into the core language. Having such a transformational approach for UML state machines semantics provides, e.g., the opportunity of easy adaption to future changes and independent examination and tool development can be build on the core languages.

In this paper we focus on defining a complete formal semantics of single UML 2.0 state machines, which are one of the most important constituents of UML, since they are widely used for modeling the reactive behavior of objects. UML state machines have evolved from Harel's statecharts [6] and their object-oriented version [5]. In particular, our contributions are:

---

* Part of this work is financially supported by DFG project Refism (FE 942/1-1).

L. Brim et al. (Eds.): FMICS and PDMC 2006, LNCS 4346, pp. 244–260, 2007.

- In Section 3, we present core state machines consisting of composite and final states, regions, choice and entry/exit pseudostates, internal/external transitions, do actions, and event deferral.
- In Section 4, we present a formal semantics of core state machines in terms of transition systems, which are chosen as semantical model in order to enhance readability. A translation of our semantics to abstract state machines [4], which are more suitable for verification, can be straightforwardly defined.
- In Section 5, we give a transformation from UML 2.0 state machines into core state machines such that a precise semantics coincident with the UML standard is obtained. In particular, all aspects of single UML 2.0 state machines, i.e., join, fork, junction, choice, entry, exit, history, initial pseudostates, do, entry, exit actions, event deferral, completion, local, internal, external, conflicting transitions, and priority relations between transitions are handled. Parameters on events, which are omitted for readability, can straightforwardly be added. By this transformation, we rule out the ambiguities and inconsistencies of UML 2.0 state machines observed earlier by us in [3], where possible solutions are illustrated.
- Especially, we handle the following non-trivial aspects that are in our opinion not adequately handled in the literature: choice pseudostates (including the decision which state is left at which point in time); the order of execution of actions of compound transitions (including entry/exit pseudostates); transitions pointing to a history pseudostate from inside its containing region; the effect that event deferral can have priority over transition firing.

Note that core state machines can also be reused as semantical basis for other variations of statecharts.

Related work. For an overview of existing formal semantics of UML state machines see [1], where 26 different approaches to the semantics are well compared. We only discuss the most relevant works in detail. All of the cited papers there, except of [11] and a technical report of us [2] consider previous versions of UML state machines, i.e., they do not deal with UML 2.0 state machines. This is significant, since there have been major changes and additions in the syntax and semantics, i.e., entry/exit pseudostates are allowed at any composite state, the concept of local transitions has been added, and event deferral can have priority over transition firing. None of these challenging aspects are considered in [11], where only a small subset of UML 2.0 state machines is considered. In contrast to our technical report [2], we now handle entry/exit pseudostates at any composite state and the fact that event deferral can have priority over transition firing, as well as choice pseudostates and completion transitions. It is not obvious how the existing semantics can be extended to handle exit/entry pseudostates at any composite state, i.e., how to define a formalization for the order of execution of the actions of compound transitions.

The paper that handles most state machines aspects is [7]. Besides the new aspects of UML 2.0 state machines, the authors do not address in detail the order of execution of actions (which already occurs in earlier UML versions by, e.g., the usage of join/fork pseudostates). All other works mentioned in [1] handle fewer aspects than [7].

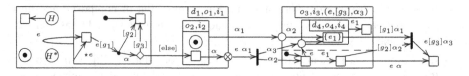

Fig. 1. A UML 2.0 state machine. Here we depict states as rectangular, final states as circles surrounding a solid filled smaller circle, shallow (deep) history pseudostates as circles containing 'H' (resp. 'H*'), initial/junction pseudostates as solid filled circles, join/fork as fat lines, choice pseudostates as diamond-shaped symbols, and entry (exit) pseudostates as small circles (resp., as small circles with a cross) on the border of the state. Regions are separated by dashed lines. The set of events deferred at a state is written inside the state. Transition labels divide or are written closely to the transition, where guard true and action skip are omitted. Events are written as e, guards as g, and transition actions as α, possibly attached with indices. One of the transitions outgoing a choice or a junction pseudostate may be labeled with guard [else]. Transitions with an additional label $\star$ have type local. Do, exit, entry actions and internal transitions are written, if present, in a small box in the upper right corner of the corresponding state via d, o, i, $(e[g]\alpha)$, respectively.

2   Informal Description of UML 2.0 State Machines

Before we give the informal description, we refer to Figure 1, where a state machine is illustrated. Note that this picture is mainly used to illustrate our transformation in Section 5 and therefore is not always meaningful, e.g., the final states are meaningless, since no transitions pointing to them.

The basic concepts of UML 2.0 state machines are states and transitions between states. A state may contain regions (called direct subregions of that state) and a region must contain states (called direct substates of that region) such that this hierarchy yields a tree structure. A configuration describes the currently active states, where exactly one direct substate of an active region must be active and all regions of an active state must be active. Entering a state (via firing a transition) corresponds to its activation whereas exiting a state corresponds to its deactivation. A state may have *entry* actions (executed when the state is entered), *exit* actions (executed when the state is left), and *do* actions ((partly) executed as long as the state is active). In the following, executing do actions means (partial) execution of such actions. The environment may send events to the state machine. These are collected in the event pool of the state machine. A state machine may either execute do actions of active states or may dispatch a single event from its event pool to trigger transitions. UML state machines follow the *run-to-completion* assumption, i.e., "an event occurrence can only be taken from the pool and dispatched if the processing of the previous current occurrence is fully completed" [8, p. 546]. Furthermore, a dispatched event that does not trigger transitions is either discarded or deferred, if there is an active state that is specified to defer the corresponding event. When a state completes its do actions and only final states (that are special states without outgoing transitions) are active in its subregions, then a completion transition[1] of

---

[1] Encoded via compound transitions having no event.

that state, selected depending on the guard, becomes enabled. The completion transition has to be fired before another event can be dispatched.

Besides its source and target, a transition consists of an event (optional), a guard (a boolean expression), and actions. Join and fork pseudostates, which may also be source and target of transitions, are used to collect different transitions into a compound transition having a set of sources and a set of targets. Note that further pseudostates, which will be discussed later, are used to obtain more complex compound transitions. A compound transition is enabled if its source state is currently active, its event is dispatched from the event pool, and its guard evaluates to true. Among the enabled transitions a maximal set of pairwise conflict-free elements is fired. Two compound transitions are in conflict if the intersection of the sets of states that will be left by firing these transitions is non empty. An active state s will be exited by firing transition t if, roughly speaking, the target of t is not a substate of s. A non-active state s will be entered by firing transition t if, roughly speaking, (i) s is the target of t, (ii) the target of t is a substate of s or (iii) s is an element of a recursively defined chain of substates (by using initial pseudostates) from the target of t. Furthermore, a priority relation determining which one of conflicting and enabled compound transitions will fire exists. But this relation does not resolve nondeterminism completely. Roughly speaking compound transitions having deeper nested source states have priority. The firing of a compound transition t leads, in this order, to (i) exiting the corresponding states together with the execution of their exit actions, (ii) the execution of the actions of t, and (iii) entering the corresponding states together with the execution of their entry actions. The order of the action execution can be changed (to a certain degree) by using exit and entry pseudostates: the actions of the states and transitions that are above the exit (below the entry) pseudostates are executed after the actions of the states and transitions that are below the exit (resp., above the entry) pseudostates w.r.t. state hierarchy.

Further pseudostates are junction pseudostates, that are a shorthand notation for the set of transitions obtained by combining any incoming with any outgoing transition; choice pseudostates lead to a new decision, where the effects of the previously executed transitions are taken into account when determining the outgoing transition to be fired; history pseudostates activate those substates of the region, to which the history pseudostate belongs, that were active when the region was the last time active. The shallow-history pseudostates consider only the direct substates of a region r, whereas deep history pseudostates consider also deeper nested substates. In case r was not active before or the last active direct substate of r is a final state, the history default transition, that is the (unique) transition leaving the history pseudostate, is fired instead. Furthermore, a transition can be external, local, or internal. An internal transition does not exit any state and a local compound transition does not exit its source state, but its substates.

3   Syntax of Core State Machines

Core state machines, derived from UML 2.0 state machines, use only composite and final states, regions, do actions, event deferral, and choice, entry, exit pseudostates. No interlevel transitions, i.e., transitions crossing a state border, are allowed, instead additional exit, entry pseudostates are used. Default exit and entry must be explicitly modeled. Exit and entry pseudostates are used as junction as well as join (resp., fork) pseudostates in some sense and have, therefore, a slightly augmented meaning as in UML 2.0. We use three different kinds of exit pseudostates: a normal one, a priority relevant one, and a completion relevant one, which is only 'enabled' if the do actions of the corresponding state have terminated (but not necessarily its corresponding regions). States are only allowed as sources and targets of internal transitions. Two additional predicates, occurring in guards of transitions, are used for the modeling of history entry. This construct classification is summarized below.

core constructs		derived constructs
unmodified	modified	
composite and final states, regions, do actions, event deferral, choice, external/local transitions, completion	exit (pr, npr, cp) and entry pseudostates	interlevel transitions, join/fork, junction, history, exit and entry pseudostates, internal transitions, initial pseudostates

Definition 1 (States & regions). S denotes a set of states, partitioned into composite, final, exit, entry, and choice states, denoted by S_{com}, S_{fin}, S_{exit}, S_{entry}, and S_{choice}, respectively. Furthermore, S_{exit} is partitioned into priority, non-priority, and completion (relevant) exit states, denoted by S_{exit}^{pr}, S_{exit}^{npr}, and S_{exit}^{cp}, respectively. Set S is consistent with a set of regions R and parent function parent if the outermost region, denoted by ϵ, is contained in R, parent maps composite, final, and choice states to regions, maps regions (different from ϵ) and entry states to composite states, and maps exit states to composite or final states such that the derived containing relation $\succ$ defined as the transitive closure of $\{(z, \mathsf{parent}(z)) \mid z \in S \cup R \setminus \{\epsilon\}\}$ is irreflexive.

Note that for technical reasons we also allow that exit states belong to final states and not only to composite states. In the following, we assume fixed S, R, and parent such that S is consistent w.r.t. R and parent. Furthermore, $\succ$ denotes the derived containing relation from parent and $\succeq$ denotes the reflexive closure of $\succ$. Moreover, functions $\mathsf{stateOf} : S \to (S_{com} \cup S_{fin} \cup S_{choice})$ and $\mathsf{regOf} : S \to R$ yield the deepest composite, final, or choice state (resp. region) that contains the argument. Formally:

$$\mathsf{stateOf}(s) = \begin{cases} s & \text{if } s \in S_{com} \cup S_{fin} \cup S_{choice} \\ \mathsf{parent}(s) & \text{otherwise} \end{cases}$$

$$\mathsf{regOf}(s) = \mathsf{parent}(\mathsf{stateOf}(s))$$

In the following definition, we introduce the sets of actions, events, and guards, whose elements are, e.g., used as transition labels.

Definition 2 (Actions). An action is a sequence of atomic actions (like changing value of attributes, sending signals, and creating new objects). In the following, we will use symbol Actions to denote the set of all actions. Let skip $\in$ Actions denote the termination of the sequence execution. Furthermore, let $(\mathcal{B}, \mathsf{Actions}, \leadsto, \sqrt{})$ be a labeled transition system having a labeled termination predicate, i.e., $\mathcal{B}$ is the set of transition *system states,* $\rightsquigarrow \subseteq \mathcal{B} \times$ Actions $\times \mathcal{B}$, *and* $\sqrt{} \subseteq \mathcal{B} \times$ Actions, *where* $(B, \alpha) \in \sqrt{}$ *indicates that an execution of* α *which leads to termination is possible. To simplify definitions, we assume* skip $\in \mathcal{B}$ *with* (skip, skip) $\in \sqrt{}$ *and* $\forall (B, \alpha, B') \in \rightsquigarrow : B \neq$ skip.

Note that $\mathcal{B}$ is later used to model interleaving points. More precisely, $B \in \mathcal{B}$ encodes, roughly speaking, a set of sequences of actions; between every action of such a sequence ϑ an interleaving point exists, i.e., another action (of a transition firing in parallel) can be executed before ϑ is continued. Note that do actions can interleave at any point, not necessarily at the modeled interleaving points. In particular, transitions of the state machines will be labeled with elements of $\mathcal{B}$ instead of Actions, compare with Section 5.

Definition 3 (Events/guards). *Set* $\mathcal{E}$ *denotes the set of all* events *and set* $\mathcal{G}$ *denotes a set of boolean expressions, which depend on global information such as the attribute values of the objects. Furthermore, the atomic predicates* wla *and* nab *are contained in* $\mathcal{G}$, *where* wla *indicates that the target state of the transition having* wla *as guard was last active and* nab *indicates that the region of the target state of the transition having* nab *as guard was not active before. These two atomic predicates are later used to model UML 2.0 history pseudostates.*

Next we define what are allowed transitions between states:

Definition 4 (Transitions). *A transition* t *w.r.t. a set of states* $\mathcal{S}$ *is a tuple* (s_1, e, g, B, s_2) *such that:*

- $s_1 \in \mathcal{S} \setminus \mathcal{S}_{\text{fin}}$ *(i.e.,* $s_1 \in \mathcal{S}_{\text{exit}} \cup \mathcal{S}_{\text{entry}} \cup \mathcal{S}_{\text{choice}} \cup \mathcal{S}_{\text{com}}$*) is called its* source state,
- $s_2 \in \mathcal{S}$ *its* target state *where*
  - *exactly the internal transitions have composite states as sources or as target, in which case the source and target must also be equal, i.e.,*
    $(s_1 \in \mathcal{S}_{\text{com}} \vee s_2 \in \mathcal{S}_{\text{com}}) \Rightarrow s_1 = s_2$
  - *transitions targeting exit pseudostates have exit pseudostates as source, i.e.,*
    $s_2 \in \mathcal{S}_{\text{exit}} \Rightarrow s_1 \in \mathcal{S}_{\text{exit}}$,
  - *exit pseudostates may only be the source of transitions targeting exit pseudostates at exactly one level higher in the state hierarchy or targeting non-exit pseudostate states at the same level of hierarchy, i.e.,*
    $(s_1 \in \mathcal{S}_{\text{exit}} \wedge s_2 \in \mathcal{S}_{\text{exit}}) \Rightarrow$ stateOf(stateOf(s_1)) $=$ stateOf(s_2) *and*
    $(s_1 \in \mathcal{S}_{\text{exit}} \wedge s_2 \notin \mathcal{S}_{\text{exit}}) \Rightarrow$ regOf(s_2) $=$ regOf(s_1),
  - *transitions outgoing from exit pseudostates of final states may only target exit pseudostates, i.e.,* stateOf(s_1) $\in \mathcal{S}_{\text{fin}} \Rightarrow s_2 \in \mathcal{S}_{\text{exit}}$,
  - *transitions outgoing from entry pseudostates may only have targets at one level of hierarchy downwards, i.e.,*
    $s_1 \in \mathcal{S}_{\text{entry}} \Rightarrow$ stateOf(stateOf(s_2)) $=$ stateOf(s_1), *and*
  - *choice pseudostates must have targets at the same level of hierarchy, i.e.,*
    $s_1 \in \mathcal{S}_{\text{choice}} \Rightarrow$ regOf(s_1) $=$ regOf(s_2).
- $e \in \mathcal{E} \cup \{\emptyset\}$ *is called its* necessary event *(which has to be provided to enable the transition), where events may not occur at transitions leaving entry or choice pseudostates, i.e.,* $e \neq \emptyset \Rightarrow s_1 \in \mathcal{S}_{\text{exit}} \cup \mathcal{S}_{\text{int}}$,

- $g \in \mathcal{G}$ is called its guard, *constraining the necessary condition for the enabling of the transition, and*
- $B \in \mathcal{B}$ is called its action encoding.

The projections of transitions to the corresponding components are denoted by π_{sor}, π_{ev}, π_{gua}, π_{act}, and π_{tar}, respectively. Furthermore, the direct subregions of a composite state $s \in \mathcal{S}_{\text{com}}$ are given by

$$\text{dsr}(s) = \{r \in \mathcal{R} \mid \text{parent}(r) = s\}$$

Now we are ready to present the syntax of core state machines, where $\mathbb{P}(U)$ denotes the power set of set U:

Definition 5 (Core state machines). *A core state machine M is a tuple*

$$((\mathcal{S}, \mathcal{R}, \text{parent}), \text{doAct}, \text{defer}, \mathbb{T}, s_{\text{start}}, \text{Var}, \sigma_{\text{init}}) \ , \ \textit{where}$$

- $\mathcal{S}$ *is a set of states that is consistent w.r.t. the set of regions $\mathcal{R}$ and with function parent,*
- $\text{doAct} : \mathcal{S}_{\text{com}} \rightarrow \text{Act}$ *assigns to each state the do action that can be executed when the state is active,*
- $\text{defer} : \mathcal{E} \rightarrow \mathbb{P}(\mathcal{S}_{\text{com}})$ *assigns to each event those states in which it will be deferred,*
- $\mathbb{T}$ *is a set of transitions w.r.t. $\mathcal{S}$, where $\mathbb{T}_{\text{int}}$ denotes the set of the singleton sets of internal transitions, i.e., $\mathbb{T}_{\text{int}} = \{\{t\} \mid t \in \mathbb{T} \wedge \pi_{\text{sor}}(t) \in \mathcal{S}_{\text{com}}\}$,*
- $s_{\text{start}} \in \mathcal{S}_{\text{com}}$ *its initial state belonging to the uppermost region and having no subregions, i.e., $\text{regOf}(s_{\text{start}}) = \epsilon \wedge \text{dsr}(s) = \emptyset$,*
- Var *a set of variables ranging over some fixed domain, and*
- $\sigma_{\text{init}} \in \text{VarAss}$ *its initial variable assignment, where VarAss denotes the set of all possible variable assignments over Var.*

Note that if an entry pseudostate s is 'active' and there is a direct subregion 'of' s for which no enabled transition outgoing s points to (which is, in particular, the case if the state contains a region that does not contain a state), a deadlock occurs (this situation corresponds to the absence of initial pseudostates in UML state machines). A similar case arises if there is no enabled transition leaving an 'active' choice pseudostate. Note that this situation is ill-formed in UML 2.0 [8, p. 523].

In the following, $((\mathcal{S}, \mathcal{R}, \text{parent}), \text{doAct}, \text{defer}, \mathbb{T}, s_{\text{start}}, \text{Var}, \sigma_{\text{init}})$ denotes a fixed core state machine M. Next we define the compound transitions CoTr of a core state machine. A compound transition is either a set consisting of one internal transition ($\in \mathbb{T}_{\text{int}}$) or a collection of (non-internal) transitions such that a single outermost state is exited. Note that here, contrary to UML state machines, only transitions outgoing exit pseudostates are collected in a compound transition. This is formalized by using function $\Upsilon : \mathcal{S}_{\text{exit}} \rightarrow \mathbb{P}(\mathbb{P}(\mathbb{T}))$, where $\Upsilon(s)$ collects all sets of transitions 'below' s that can belong to a compound transition that 'includes' s. Formally:

$$\Upsilon(s) = \{ \textstyle\bigcup_{r \in \text{dsr}(s)} (\{f(r)\} \cup F(r)) \mid f : \text{dsr}(s) \rightarrow \mathbb{T} \wedge F : \text{dsr}(s) \rightarrow \mathbb{P}(\mathbb{T}) \wedge$$
$$\forall r \in \text{dsr}(s) : \pi_{\text{tar}}(f(r)) = s \wedge \text{regOf}(\pi_{\text{sor}}(f(r))) = r \wedge F(r) \in \Upsilon(\pi_{\text{sor}}(f(r)))\}$$

$$\text{CoTr} = \{\{t\} \cup T \mid t \in \mathbb{T} \wedge \pi_{\text{sor}}(t) \in \mathcal{S}_{\text{exit}} \wedge \pi_{\text{tar}}(t) \notin \mathcal{S}_{\text{exit}} \wedge T \in \Upsilon(\pi_{\text{sor}}(t))\} \cup \mathbb{T}_{\text{int}}$$

Note that exit states not targeted by transitions from all direct subregions may not occur in a compound transition. In order to simplify definitions, we also allow that different events may occur in a compound transition. This is not problematic, since compound transitions where more than one event occurs cannot be enabled.

4 Formal Semantics of Core State Machines

A history maps a region r to its direct substate that was active the last time the region was left. If the region was not active before (or a final state was last active), r is mapped to the default value $\perp$.[2] Therefore, the set of histories is

$$\mathcal{H} = \{H : \mathcal{R} \to \mathcal{S}_{\text{com}} \cup \mathcal{S}_{\text{fin}} \cup \{\perp\} \mid \forall r \in \mathcal{R} : H(r) \neq \perp \Rightarrow r = \mathsf{regOf}(H(r))\},$$

Configurations describe a snapshot of a state machine execution. They are introduced below, where we, in order to simplify the definition, allow configurations that cannot occur during execution.

Definition 6. *A csm-configuration C w.r.t. M is a tuple $(\sigma, \mathcal{A}, \text{do}, H, \alpha, \ddot{s}, \beta, T, \ddot{T})$ where*

- *$\sigma \in \mathsf{VarAss}$, denoting the current variable assignment,*
- *$\mathcal{A} \subseteq \mathcal{S}_{\text{com}} \cup \mathcal{S}_{\text{fin}}$, denoting which states are currently active,*
- *$\text{do} : \mathcal{S}_{\text{com}} \to \mathsf{Act}$ denoting the corresponding do actions which remain to be executed,*
- *$H \in \mathcal{H}$, denoting its current history information,*
- *$\alpha \in \mathsf{Actions}$, denoting the action that has to be executed next w.r.t. transition execution,*
- *$\ddot{s} \in \{\emptyset\} \cup \mathcal{S}_{\text{fin}} \cup \mathcal{S}_{\text{exit}} \cup \mathcal{S}_{\text{entry}} \cup \mathcal{S}_{\text{choice}}$, denoting the (pseudo)state that has to be activated after α is completed,*
- *$\beta \subseteq \mathcal{B} \times (\{\emptyset\} \cup \mathcal{S}_{\text{fin}} \cup \mathcal{S}_{\text{exit}} \cup \mathcal{S}_{\text{entry}} \cup \mathcal{S}_{\text{choice}})$, denoting the currently executing transitions (i.e., remaining actions and target states),*
- *$T \in \mathsf{CoTr} \cup \{\emptyset\}$, denoting the currently executing compound transition, and*
- *$\ddot{T} \subseteq \mathsf{CoTr}$, denoting the compound transitions that are left to be executed in order to complete the run-to-completion step.*

The initial csm-configuration is

$$(\sigma_{\text{init}}, \{s_{\text{start}}\}, \mathsf{doAct}, \{(\epsilon, s_{\text{start}})\} \cup \{(r, \perp) \mid r \in \mathcal{R} \setminus \{\epsilon\}\}, \mathsf{skip}, \emptyset, \emptyset, \emptyset, \emptyset).$$

In the following we give some preliminaries for the definition of the relation between csm-configurations.

We assume that a function eval : $(\mathsf{VarAss} \times \mathcal{H} \times \mathcal{S}) \to \mathbb{P}(\mathcal{G})$, that evaluates the guards, is given such that wla holds in $\mathsf{eval}(\sigma, H, s)$ if 's' was the last active state of the corresponding region, i.e., $\text{wla} \in \mathsf{eval}(\sigma, H, s) \Leftrightarrow H(\mathsf{regOf}(s)) = \mathsf{stateOf}(s)$, and nab holds in $\mathsf{eval}(\sigma, H, s)$ if the region of 's' was not visited before or a final state was

---

[2] Note that the history information is ambiguous in UML 2.0 [8], e.g., it is not clear if the last active subconfiguration instead of the subconfiguration generated by the corresponding last active states is chosen, see [3] for more detail.

last active there, i.e., nab $\in$ eval(σ, H, s) $\Leftrightarrow$ $H(\text{regOf}(s)) \in \{\bot\} \cup \mathcal{S}_{\text{fin}}$. A compound transition is enabled for trigger $e \in \mathcal{E} \cup \{\emptyset\}$, variable assignment σ, active states $\mathcal{A}$, history H, and current do actions of the active states: if the sources of its transitions are active, if the triggers of all of its transitions are in e, if the guards of its transitions evaluate to true, and if the do actions are terminated for its transitions having elements from $\mathcal{S}_{\text{exit}}^{\text{cp}}$ as its sources. Formally:

$$\text{Enable}_{e,\sigma,\mathcal{A},H,\text{do}} = \Big\{ T \in \text{CoTr} \mid \forall t \in T : \text{stateOf}(\pi_{\text{sor}}(t)) \in \mathcal{A} \wedge \pi_{\text{ev}}(t) \subseteq \{e\} \wedge$$
$$\pi_{\text{gua}}(t) \in \text{eval}(\sigma, H, \pi_{\text{tar}}(t)) \wedge (\pi_{\text{sor}}(t) \in \mathcal{S}_{\text{exit}}^{\text{cp}} \Rightarrow \text{do}(\text{stateOf}(\pi_{\text{sor}}(t))) = \text{skip}) \Big\}$$

Two compound transitions are in conflict if their states that have to be left (for an internal transition: the set consisting of its source state) are not disjoint. Formally:

$$\text{Conflict} = \{(T_1, T_2) \in \text{CoTr} \times \text{CoTr} \mid \text{stateOf}(\pi_{\text{sor}}(T_1)) \cap \text{stateOf}(\pi_{\text{sor}}(T_2)) \neq \emptyset\}$$

Note that two internal transition of the same state are in conflict with each other. Note that in UML no two internal transitions of the same state can be enabled at the same time [8, p. 539]. A compound transition T_1 has priority over another one T_2 if every priority relevant source state of T_1 is a substate of a priority relevant source state of T_2, i.e., $\text{PrBelow}(T_1, T_2) \Longleftrightarrow \forall t_1 \in T_1 : \pi_{\text{sor}}(t_1) \in \mathcal{S}_{\text{exit}}^{\text{pr}} \cup \mathcal{S}_{\text{com}} \Rightarrow \exists t_2 \in T_2 : \pi_{\text{sor}}(t_2) \in \mathcal{S}_{\text{exit}}^{\text{pr}} \cup \mathcal{S}_{\text{com}} \wedge \text{stateOf}(\pi_{\text{sor}}(t_2)) \succeq \text{stateOf}(\pi_{\text{sor}}(t_1))$, and one of the highest priority relevant source states of T_1 is a proper substate. The later fact is here equivalent to the existence of a priority relevant source state of T_2, for which no upper or at the same level priority relevant source state of T_1 exists, i.e., $\text{PrStrBelow}(T_1, T_2) \Longleftrightarrow \exists t_2 \in T_2 : \pi_{\text{sor}}(t_2) \in \mathcal{S}_{\text{exit}}^{\text{pr}} \cup \mathcal{S}_{\text{com}} \wedge \forall t_1 \in T_1 : \pi_{\text{sor}}(t_1) \in \mathcal{S}_{\text{exit}}^{\text{pr}} \cup \mathcal{S}_{\text{com}} \Rightarrow \neg(\text{stateOf}(\pi_{\text{sor}}(t_1)) \succeq \text{stateOf}(\pi_{\text{sor}}(t_2)))$:

$$\text{Priority} = \{(T_1, T_2) \in \text{CoTr} \times \text{CoTr} \mid \text{PrBelow}(T_1, T_2) \wedge \text{PrStrBelow}(T_1, T_2)\}$$

Note that the outermost prioritized exit pseudostates decide about priority. A set of compound transitions is fire-able if it is a non-empty maximal set of enabled and conflict-free compound transitions such that no enabled compound transition with higher priority exists. The non-emptiness is used to model deferral of an event, which is only possible if no corresponding fire-able compound transition exists. Formally:

$$\text{Fireable}_{e,\sigma,\mathcal{A},H,\text{do}} = \{ \ddot{T} \subseteq \text{Enable}_{e,\sigma,\mathcal{A},H,\text{do}} \mid \ddot{T} \neq \emptyset \wedge \forall T' \in \text{Enable}_{e,\sigma,\mathcal{A},H,\text{do}} \setminus \ddot{T} :$$
$$(\forall T \in \ddot{T} : (T', T) \notin \text{Priority}) \wedge (\exists T \in \ddot{T} : (T, T') \in \text{Conflict}) \wedge$$
$$\forall T_1, T_2 \in \ddot{T} : (T_1, T_2) \in \text{Conflict} \Rightarrow T_1 = T_2 \}$$

In the following, we assume that a function calc : $(\text{Actions} \times \text{VarAss}) \to (\mathcal{L} \times \text{Actions} \times \text{VarAss})$, calculating the effect of action execution (observable communication [encoded via elements of a given set $\mathcal{L}$], remaining actions, and obtained variable assignment), is given. Furthermore, $f[x \mapsto v]$, that is straightforwardly extended to sequences $(x_i \mapsto v_i)^{i \in I}$, denotes the function that is everywhere equal to f except on x (if it is in its range) where it is equal to v.

The rules defining the relation between csm-configurations is given in Table 1, where a transition step without a label corresponds to an internal step. The rules are explained

Table 1. Configuration steps

$$\text{do-act} \quad \frac{\begin{array}{c} s \in \mathcal{A} \cap \mathcal{S}_{\mathrm{com}} \quad \mathrm{do}(s) \neq \mathsf{skip} \\ \mathrm{calc}(\mathrm{do}(s), \sigma) = (\ell, \alpha', \sigma') \quad \alpha = \mathsf{skip} \Rightarrow \ddot{s} = \emptyset \end{array}}{(\sigma, \mathcal{A}, \mathrm{do}, H, \alpha, \ddot{s}, \beta, T, \ddot{T}) \xrightarrow{\ell} (\sigma', \mathcal{A}, \mathrm{do}[s \mapsto \alpha'], H, \alpha, \ddot{s}, \beta, T, \ddot{T})}$$

$$\text{cur-act} \quad \frac{\alpha \neq \mathsf{skip} \quad \mathrm{calc}(\alpha, \sigma) = (\ell, \alpha', \sigma')}{(\sigma, \mathcal{A}, \mathrm{do}, H, \alpha, \ddot{s}, \beta, T, \ddot{T}) \xrightarrow{\ell} (\sigma', \mathcal{A}, \mathrm{do}, H, \alpha', \ddot{s}, \beta, T, \ddot{T})}$$

$$\text{next-tr-1} \quad \frac{(B, \ddot{s}) \in \beta \quad B \overset{\alpha}{\leadsto} B' \quad \beta' = \{(B', \ddot{s})\} \cup \beta \setminus \{(B, \ddot{s})\}}{(\sigma, \mathcal{A}, \mathrm{do}, H, \mathsf{skip}, \emptyset, \beta, T, \ddot{T}) \rightarrowtail (\sigma, \mathcal{A}, \mathrm{do}, H, \alpha, \emptyset, \beta', T, \ddot{T})}$$

$$\text{next-tr-2} \quad \frac{(B, \ddot{s}) \in \beta \quad (B, \alpha) \in \sqrt{} \quad \beta' = \beta \setminus \{(B, \ddot{s})\}}{(\sigma, \mathcal{A}, \mathrm{do}, H, \mathsf{skip}, \emptyset, \beta, T, \ddot{T}) \rightarrowtail (\sigma, \mathcal{A}, \mathrm{do}, H, \alpha, \ddot{s}, \beta', T, \ddot{T})}$$

$$\text{next-com} \quad \frac{\begin{array}{c} T' \in \ddot{T} \setminus \mathbb{T}_{\mathrm{int}} \quad \beta = \{(\mathsf{skip}, \pi_{\mathrm{sor}}(t)) \mid t \in T' \wedge \forall t' \in T' : \\ \neg(\mathrm{stateOf}(\pi_{\mathrm{sor}}(t)) \succ \mathrm{stateOf}(\pi_{\mathrm{sor}}(t'))) \} \end{array}}{(\sigma, \mathcal{A}, \mathrm{do}, H, \mathsf{skip}, \emptyset, \emptyset, T, \ddot{T}) \rightarrowtail (\sigma, \mathcal{A}, \mathrm{do}, H, \mathsf{skip}, \emptyset, \beta, T', \ddot{T} \setminus \{T'\})}$$

$$\text{next-int} \quad \frac{\{t\} \in \ddot{T} \cap \mathbb{T}_{\mathrm{int}} \quad \beta = \{(\pi_{\mathrm{act}}(t), \emptyset)\}}{(\sigma, \mathcal{A}, \mathrm{do}, H, \mathsf{skip}, \emptyset, \emptyset, T, \ddot{T}) \rightarrowtail (\sigma, \mathcal{A}, \mathrm{do}, H, \mathsf{skip}, \emptyset, \beta, \{t\}, \ddot{T} \setminus \{\{t\}\})}$$

$$\text{next-completion} \quad \frac{\ddot{T} \in \mathrm{Fireable}_{\emptyset, \sigma, \mathcal{A}, H, \mathrm{do}} \quad T' \in \ddot{T}}{(\sigma, \mathcal{A}, \mathrm{do}, H, \mathsf{skip}, \emptyset, \emptyset, T, \emptyset) \rightarrowtail (\sigma, \mathcal{A}, \mathrm{do}, H, \mathsf{skip}, \emptyset, \emptyset, T, \{T'\})}$$

$$\text{next-trigger} \quad \frac{e \in \mathcal{E} \quad \mathrm{Fireable}_{\emptyset, \sigma, \mathcal{A}, H, \mathrm{do}} = \emptyset \quad \ddot{T} \in \mathrm{Fireable}_{e, \sigma, \mathcal{A}, H, \mathrm{do}}}{(\sigma, \mathcal{A}, \mathrm{do}, H, \mathsf{skip}, \emptyset, \emptyset, T, \emptyset) \xrightarrow{e} (\sigma, \mathcal{A}, \mathrm{do}, H, \mathsf{skip}, \emptyset, \emptyset, T, \ddot{T})}$$

$$\text{defer} \quad \frac{\mathrm{defer}(e) \cap \mathcal{A} \neq \emptyset \quad \mathrm{Fireable}_{e, \sigma, \mathcal{A}, H, \mathrm{do}} = \emptyset}{(\sigma, \mathcal{A}, \mathrm{do}, H, \mathsf{skip}, \emptyset, \emptyset, T, \emptyset) \xrightarrow{\mathrm{defer}(e)} (\sigma, \mathcal{A}, \mathrm{do}, H, \mathsf{skip}, \emptyset, \emptyset, T, \emptyset)}$$

$$\text{a-fin} \quad \frac{\ddot{s} \in \mathcal{S}_{\mathrm{fin}} \quad H' = (H[(r \mapsto \bot)^{r \in \mathcal{R} \cap \uparrow \{\mathrm{regOf}(\ddot{s})\}}])}{(\sigma, \mathcal{A}, \mathrm{do}, H, \mathsf{skip}, \ddot{s}, \beta, T, \ddot{T}) \rightarrowtail (\sigma, \mathcal{A} \cup \{\ddot{s}\}, \mathrm{do}, H', \mathsf{skip}, \emptyset, \beta, T, \ddot{T})}$$

$$\text{a-ch} \quad \frac{\ddot{s} \in \mathcal{S}_{\mathrm{choice}} \quad t \in \mathbb{T} \quad \pi_{\mathrm{sor}}(t) = \ddot{s} \quad \pi_{\mathrm{gua}}(t) \in \mathrm{eval}(\sigma, H, \pi_{\mathrm{tar}}(t))}{(\sigma, \mathcal{A}, \mathrm{do}, H, \mathsf{skip}, \ddot{s}, \beta, T, \ddot{T}) \rightarrowtail (\sigma, \mathcal{A}, \mathrm{do}, H, \mathsf{skip}, \emptyset, \beta \cup \{(\pi_{\mathrm{act}}(t), \pi_{\mathrm{tar}}(t))\}, T, \ddot{T})}$$

$$\text{a-en} \quad \frac{\begin{array}{c} \ddot{s} \in \mathcal{S}_{\mathrm{entry}} \quad \mathrm{do}' = \mathrm{do}[\mathrm{stateOf}(\ddot{s}) \mapsto \mathrm{doAct}(\mathrm{stateOf}(\ddot{s}))] \\ f : \mathrm{dsr}(\mathrm{stateOf}(\ddot{s})) \to \mathbb{T} \quad \beta' = \beta \cup \bigcup_{r \in \mathrm{dsr}(\mathrm{stateOf}(\ddot{s}))} \{(\pi_{\mathrm{act}}(f(r)), \pi_{\mathrm{tar}}(f(r)))\} \\ \forall r \in \mathrm{dsr}(\mathrm{stateOf}(\ddot{s})) : \pi_{\mathrm{sor}}(f(r)) = \ddot{s} \wedge \pi_{\mathrm{gua}}(f(r)) \in \mathrm{eval}(\sigma, H, \pi_{\mathrm{tar}}(t)) \end{array}}{(\sigma, \mathcal{A}, \mathrm{do}, H, \mathsf{skip}, \ddot{s}, \beta, T, \ddot{T}) \rightarrowtail (\sigma, \mathcal{A} \cup \{\mathrm{stateOf}(\ddot{s})\}, \mathrm{do}', H, \mathsf{skip}, \emptyset, \beta', T, \ddot{T})}$$

$$\text{a-ex-1} \quad \frac{\begin{array}{c} \ddot{s} \in \mathcal{S}_{\mathrm{exit}} \quad \forall (B, \ddot{s}') \in \beta : \ddot{s}' \neq \ddot{s} \quad \forall s \in \mathcal{A} : \neg(\mathrm{stateOf}(\ddot{s}) \succ s) \quad t \in T \\ \pi_{\mathrm{sor}}(t) = \ddot{s} \quad \beta' = \beta \cup \{(\pi_{\mathrm{act}}(t), \pi_{\mathrm{tar}}(t))\} \quad H' = H[\mathrm{regOf}(\ddot{s}) \mapsto \mathrm{stateOf}(\ddot{s})] \end{array}}{(\sigma, \mathcal{A}, \mathrm{do}, H, \mathsf{skip}, \ddot{s}, \beta, T, \ddot{T}) \rightarrowtail (\sigma, \mathcal{A} \setminus \{\mathrm{stateOf}(\ddot{s})\}, \mathrm{do}, H', \mathsf{skip}, \emptyset, \beta', T, \ddot{T})}$$

$$\text{a-ex-2} \quad \frac{\ddot{s} \in \mathcal{S}_{\mathrm{exit}} \quad \exists B : (B, \ddot{s}) \in \beta \vee \exists s \in \mathcal{A} : \mathrm{stateOf}(\ddot{s}) \succ s}{(\sigma, \mathcal{A}, \mathrm{do}, H, \mathsf{skip}, \ddot{s}, \beta, T, \ddot{T}) \rightarrowtail (\sigma, \mathcal{A}, \mathrm{do}, H, \mathsf{skip}, \emptyset, \beta, T, \ddot{T})}$$

below: RULE do-act describes an atomic action execution of a do action of an active composite state, where condition $\alpha = \text{skip} \Rightarrow \ddot{s} = \emptyset$ ensures that the entry of a state finishing the execution of a corresponding transition cannot be interleaved by a do action. Note that a do action can also execute at any point during the execution of actions of transitions. RULE cur-act describes the next atomic action execution of the atomic action sequence currently being executed. RULES next-tr-1 and next-tr-2 select from the transitions currently being fired ($(B, \ddot{s}) \in \beta$) a new atomic action sequence α (determined from $B \overset{\alpha}{\leadsto} B'$, resp. $(B, \alpha) \in \sqrt{}$) that will be executed next. This is only possible if no action has to be executed and no pseudostate has to be activated ($\ddot{s} = \emptyset$). In next-tr-2 , contrary to next-tr-1 , the target of the transition has to be activated after the execution of α, since this completes the firing of the transition.

RULE next-com determines the next non-internal compound transition T' from $\ddot{T}$ which will be fired, that is only possible if the previous fired compound transition is completed: no state has to be activated, no action and no transition remain to be executed. Furthermore, the deepest source exit pseudostates of T' are remembered to be activated. This is done by using special transitions formed by deepest source exit pseudostates of T' as targets and skip as actions. These transitions determine β. RULE next-int determines the next internal transition $\{t\}$ of $\ddot{T}$ which will be fired, that is only possible if the previously fired compound transition is finished. RULE next-completion determines the next trigger-free compound transition (which corresponds in UML to transitions triggered by completion) that will be fired. This is only possible if the previous set of compound transitions is completely executed (which corresponds in UML to the termination of the previous run to completion step). RULE next-trigger is similar to Rule next-completion except that transitions triggered by an event are considered. Note that completion transitions have priority over triggered transitions, which is ensured by $\text{Fireable}_{\emptyset,\sigma,\mathcal{A},H,\text{do}} = \emptyset$ stating that no completion transition is enabled. RULE defer describes the deferral of events, which is possible if a state that defers the event is active and no completion transition and no compound transition having this trigger is enabled.

RULE a-fin activates a final state $\ddot{s}$ directly contained in region $\ddot{r} = \text{regOf}(\ddot{s})$ and resets the history information of all subregions of $\ddot{r}$ to $\perp$, since they are now considered as not visited before [3]. RULE a-ch activates a choice pseudostate, where it is immediately determined which of its currently enabled outgoing transitions is fired. RULE a-en activates an entry pseudostate s, thereby the composite state s' to which s belongs becomes active and the current do action of s' is reset to the do action specified in the state machine, i.e., it starts from the beginning also in the case of history entry. Furthermore, as for choice pseudostates, it is immediately determined for every direct subregion which one of the currently enabled outgoing transitions of state s is fired. RULES acti-ex-1 and acti-ex-2 deal with the activation of exit pseudostates, that will not happen if there is a transition with a source below the exit pseudostate, w.r.t. state hierarchy, which has not yet been completely executed (Rule acti-ex-2). In the case of activation (Rule acti-ex-1) the unique transition from T having the exit pseudostate as source is added to β. Furthermore, the state to which the exit pseudostate belongs is deactivated and the history information of the exited region is adapted.

5   Embedding of UML 2.0 State Machines

Many ambiguities in UML 2.0 state machines are resolved here along our suggestions given in [3]. Another ambiguity, which is not mentioned in [3] concerns the influence of event deferral on enabling transitions: "The conflict resolution [between deferring or consuming] follows the triggering priorities, where nested states override enclosing states. In case of a conflict between states in different orthogonal regions, a consumer state overrides a deferring state."[8, p. 536]. Consider, e.g., the two transition having event e_1 in Figure 1. Will the above transition fire, since the enabling the lower transition avoids the deferral of the event? We decide that a compound transition with trigger e is disabled if it has a source state that has a deeper state which defers e. Thus in our example the upper transition will not fire in contrast to the other one.

The transformation of UML 2.0 state machines is divided into 5 succeeding steps. In the following, prototype transitions are transitions with no event, with guard true, and with action skip, except that the label is explicitly specified differently. Furthermore, the transition system encoding the transitions' actions in core state machines is built upon a simple process algebra consisting of actions, sequential composition, and parallel composition without synchronization mechanism. Weak-compound transitions combine transitions connected via join, fork, and junction pseudostates. Note that we decide to use a not optimal transformation w.r.t. space, in order to increase understandability. In order to increase comprehension, the UML 2.0 state machine of Figure 1 is transformed along the different steps. Besides the resolving of junction pseudostates, the complexity of the transformation is in $\mathcal{O}(n \cdot t)$, where n is the number of states and t the number of transitions.

Step 1: Here some simplifications are made: Replace every guard 'else (resp., otherwise)' at a transition t, by the negation of the disjunction of the guards of the other transitions outgoing from the source of t. Replace a transition with a set of events as trigger by copies of the transition, one for each event in the set, which yields the event label of that copy. Resolve junction pseudostates, by introducing for every pair of incoming and outgoing transitions a new transition labeled with the union of the events (must be empty or singleton), with the conjunction of the guards, and the actions combined via the sequential composition of the process algebra. Next, we ensure that no choice, entry, exit pseudostate can occur in two different compound transitions: Copy choice, entry, exit pseudostates, and adapt (including copying) the transitions such that every choice and entry pseudostate has exactly one incoming transition, every exit pseudostate has exactly one outgoing transition, and every direct subregion of the state corresponding to an exit (entry) pseudostate has at most one transition pointing to (resp., leaving) this exit (resp., entry) pseudostate. After applying Step 1 to the UML 2.0 state machine from Figure 1 we obtain:

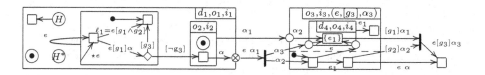

Step 2: In this step sources and targets become exit, resp., entry pseudostates and further modifications making clear which states are left, resp., entered are made: For every local transition t having its target below its source s add a new entry pseudostate at s, which becomes the new target of t (note that t remains local), and add a prototype transition from the new entry pseudostate to the original target of t. Every weak-compound transition of the current state machine is labeled by its event, by the conjunction of its transitions' guards, and by a process algebra term encoding its transitions' actions. Every exit pseudostate that does not have an incoming transition becomes a priority relevant exit pseudostate, the other exit pseudostates become non-priority relevant exit pseudostates. To every composite state add a so called default entry pseudostate. For every transition t outgoing a composite state s, add a new completion (priority) exit pseudostate to s if t belongs to a completion (resp., if t belongs to a non-completion) compound transition and this exit pseudostate becomes the new source state of the transition. Every transition targeting a composite state is redirected such that its target becomes the composite state's default entry pseudostate. Next, we make explicit which states of a compound transition are left (resp., entered): Divide by a new choice pseudostate every weak-compound transition whose sources are different from choice pseudostates and whose sources and targets are in two orthogonal regions (i.e., none contains the other). This new choice pseudostate belongs to the deepest region that contains all sources (and join pseudostates). The label of the old weak-compound transition is written at the weak-compound transition pointing to the new choice pseudostate, whereas the weak-compound transition leaving the new choice pseudostate with no event, with guard true, and with action skip as label. Thereafter, relocate every choice pseudostate to the outermost region that can be reached via a chain of transitions starting from the choice pseudostate, where transitions crossing regions reach also the lowest region containing both those regions.[3] After applying Step 2 on our running example we obtain, where circled p (n, c) indicates priority (resp., non-priority, completion) exit pseudostates:

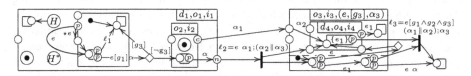

Step 3: Intuitively, in this step a transition is divided by an exit (resp., entry) pseudostate, where it crosses the border of a state. In order to handle also join and fork pseudostates the transformation is precisely given: For every weak-compound transition T having interlevel transitions, add a non-priority exit pseudostate at every composite state that will be left by T and that strictly contains a source of T, and add an entry pseudostate at every composite state that will be entered by T and that strictly contains a target of T. Then connect those new pseudostates for T as well as the sources and

---

[3] In our interpretation, transitions between orthogonal regions lead to leaving (and entry) the lowest containing composite state. Note that the other interpretation that only the regions of the lowest containing composite state and not the state itself are left and entered can also be handled via transformation to core state machines.

targets of T with non-interlevel prototype transitions along the transition path of T. The event, guard, and action of T are written (temporarily till the end of Step 5) at T's target if it is an exit pseudostate[4], at T's source if it is an entry pseudostate, and at the outermost transition added for T otherwise. Different transitions labels at an exit (resp., entry) pseudostate, which all correspond to a single compound transition (ensured by Step 1), are transformed into a single label, by taking the union of the events (must be empty or singleton), the conjunction of the guards, and the actions combined via the parallel composition of the process algebra. Remove all interlevel transitions and all join/fork pseudostates. Finally, internal transitions are replaced via transitions having the corresponding label and having the corresponding state as source and target. After applying Step 3 on our running example we obtain:

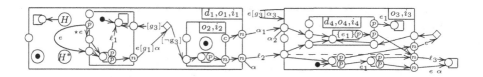

Step 4: Default exit and entry are obtained as follows: To every composite or final state add a non-priority exit pseudostate, called its default exit pseudostate. To every composite state add for every event e a non-priority exit pseudostate, called its default exit pseudostate w.r.t. e. Note that default exit pseudostates w.r.t. events are used for modeling the fact that deferral of events can disable transitions. Furthermore, every priority exit pseudostate s is considered as an exit pseudostate w.r.t. event e if s belongs to a compound transition that has trigger e. For every exit pseudostate s that is different from a completion exit pseudostate and from an exit pseudostate w.r.t. an event and for every direct subregion r of stateOf(s) such that no transition pointing to s exists in r, add prototype transitions from the default exit pseudostate of every composite/final state of r to s. For completion exit pseudostates add transitions in the same way except that only the default exit pseudostates of final states are used as sources. For an exit pseudostate w.r.t. e add transitions in the same way except that default exit pseudostates w.r.t. e are used at composite states (final states use their default exit pseudostate) and only composite states that do not defer event e are allowed.[5] For every entry pseudostate s and direct subregion r of stateOf(s) such that no transition outgoing s exists in r, add a default transition from s to the initial pseudostate of r (if present).[6] History entry

---

[4] Note that if a compound transition T has an exit (entry) pseudostate as target (resp., source) then T has exactly one target (resp., source).

[5] The transformation follows our decision that a transition t_1 has priority over t_2 when every source of t_1 is below or equal a source of t_2 and (one is strictly below or there is a subregion for which t_2 has a source but not t_1).

[6] Note that UML 2.0 provides a variation point for default entry if no initial pseudostate exists [8, p. 532]. The first alternative is an ill-defined behavior, as we interpret it. The second one is not to activate any state of such regions (using partial configurations). The second interpretation can be handled by transformation as follows: an initial pseudostate pointing to a new state having no entry, exit, do actions, and no regions, is added to every region that has no initial pseudostate.

is obtained as follows: The guards of transitions leaving history pseudostates are conjunctively extended by predicate nab. Add an entry pseudostate to every composite state for which an upper region has a deep history pseudostate. These newly introduced entry pseudostates are called the deeper-history entry pseudostates of the corresponding states. Add non-interlevel prototype transitions having guard wla (i) from shallow history pseudostates to default entry pseudostates, (ii) from deep history pseudostates to deeper-history entry pseudostate, and (iii) from deeper-history entry pseudostates to deeper-history entry pseudostates or final states. Finally, transform history and initial pseudostates into choice pseudostates, except of the initial pseudostate belonging to the outermost region which becomes an exit pseudostate of the initial state s_{start}, which also is added. After applying Step 4 on our running example, we obtain the following structure: Here, only the relevant exit pseudostates are depicted (e.g., the default exit points on the outermost states and those pointing to them are omitted) and the default entry pseudostates on states not containing regions are used there for the deeper-history entry pseudostates.

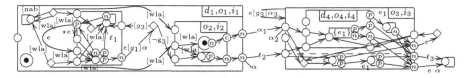

Step 5: In the final step exit and entry actions are transformed: For every composite state s (different from s_{start}), we introduce a new composite state $\tilde{s}$ that (i) belongs to the region to which s belonged, (ii) contains exactly one region that exactly contains s, (iii) has the do actions of s (the do action of s becomes skip), (iv) has a non-priority exit pseudostate for every priority or non-priority exit pseudostate of s, and (v) has a completion exit pseudostate for every completion exit pseudostate of s. Transitions between the exit (entry) pseudostates of s and their corresponding exit (resp., entry) pseudostates of $\tilde{s}$ are added. These transitions are labeled with the labels of the corresponding exit (entry) pseudostates of s, if present, and with no event, with guard true, and with action skip, otherwise. The exit (resp., entry) actions of s are sequentially attached after (resp., before) the action of every outgoing (resp., incoming) transition of exit (resp., entry) pseudostates of s, which corresponds to the new introduced transitions. This sequentially attaching is done via the sequential process algebra operator. External transitions targeting entry (outgoing from exit) pseudostates of s are redirected such that they are targeting (resp., outgoing from) the corresponding entry (resp., exit) pseudostates of $\tilde{s}$. Finally, all entry/exit actions at a state and all labels written at entry (exit) pseudostates are removed. After applying Step 5 on our running example we obtain the following structure: Here, only the relevant composite states are copied and the non relevant entry points are removed.

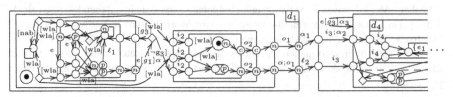

6   Conclusion

To structure the cumbersome process of resolving the ambiguities and removing the inconsistencies in the semantics of UML state machines (as published by the OMG) we propose a new strategy: Introduce core state machines with their precise semantics. These core state machine contain all essential features of UML state machines in a compact way. Then transform UML state machines to these core state machine. Thereby we have presented a complete, formal semantics of single UML 2.0 state machines.

Because of the low space complexity of the transformation, core state machines yield an appropriate basis model for verification of UML 2.0 state machines and probably also for other statecharts variations: tools can be based on core state machines and, e.g., UML 2.0 state machines are handled via transformation. Thus more independent tool support can be developed. In our opinion, core state machines are optimal in the sense that the syntax of core state machines cannot be further reduced by maintaining the hierarchical structure and by maintaining the expressive power of UML 2.0 state machines. Furthermore, core state machines have even more expressive power than UML state machines, e.g., a more specific history entry can be defined.

Note that do actions can (partly) be executed at any point in time provided that the corresponding state is active. This big amount of interleaving points leads to a large state explosion. Here, the core state machines' explicitly modeled action-interleaving points (modeled by encoding actions via a state of a labeled transition systems) are also appropriate for handling the interleaving with the do actions: Modify the semantics such that do actions may only execute at the interleaving points of the transitions. Furthermore, action-interleaving can also be used to model more atomic executions inside do actions by slightly modifying the syntax and semantics. Another possible variation in the semantics of core state machines is to allow in case of history entry that do actions continue their execution at those positions when the corresponding state was exited. Note that the behavior of UML 2.0 state machines is not totally clear in this situation.

Future work will be the modeling of communication between state machines, the development of formal semantics taking further UML diagrams into account, as well as the development of tool support for core state machines.

References

[1] M. L. Crane and J. Dingel. On the semantics of uml state machines: Categorization and comparison. Technical Report 501, Queen's University, 2005.

[2] H. Fecher, M. Kyas, and J. Schönborn. Semantic issues in UML 2.0 state machines. Technical Report 0507, Christian-Albrechts-Universität zu Kiel, 2005.

[3] H. Fecher, J. Schönborn, M. Kyas, and W. P. de Roever. 29 new unclarities in the semantics of uml 2.0 state machines. In *ICFEM*, volume 3785 of *LNCS*, pages 52–65. Springer, 2005.

[4] Y. Gurevich. Evolving algebras 1993: Lipari guide. In *Specification and Validation Methods*, pages 9–36. Oxford University Press, 1995.

[5] D. Harel and A. Naamad. The STATEMATE Semantics of Statecharts. *ACM Transactions on Software Engineering and Methodology*, 5(4):293–333, 1996.

[6] D. Harel, A. Pnueli, J. P. Schmidt, and R. Sherman. On the formal semantics of statecharts (extended abstract). In *LICS*, pages 54–64. IEEE Computer Society Press, 1987.

[7] Y. Jin, R. Esser, and J. W. Janneck. A method for describing the syntax and semantics of uml statecharts. *Software and System Modeling*, 3(2):150–163, 2004.

[8] Object Management Group. *UML Superstructure Specification, v2.0 formal/05-07-04*, 2005.

[9] G. Reggio and R. Wieringa. Thirty one problems in the semantics of uml 1.3 dynamics. In *OOPSLA'99 workshop, Rigorous Modelling and Analysis of the UML: Challenges and Limitations*, 1999.

[10] A. J. H. Simons and I. Graham. 30 things that go wrong in object modelling with uml 1.3. In *Behavioral Specifications of Businesses and Systems*, pages 237–257. Kluwer Academic, 1999.

[11] X. Zhan and H. Miao. An approach to formalizing the semantics of uml statecharts. In *ER*, volume 3288 of *LNCS*, pages 753–765. Springer, 2004.

Automated Incremental Synthesis of Timed Automata*

Borzoo Bonakdarpour and Sandeep S. Kulkarni

Department of Computer Science and Engineering,
Michigan State University,
East Lansing, MI 48824, USA
{borzoo, sandeep}@cse.msu.edu
http://www.cse.msu.edu/~{borzoo,sandeep}

Abstract. In this paper, we concentrate on incremental synthesis of timed automata for automatic addition of different types of bounded response properties. Bounded response – that *something good* will happen soon, in a certain amount of time – captures a wide range of requirements for specifying real-time and embedded systems. We show that the problem of automatic addition of a bounded response property to a given timed automaton while maintaining maximal non-determinism is NP-hard in the size of locations of the input automaton. Furthermore, we show that by relaxing the maximality requirement, we can devise a sound and complete algorithm that adds a bounded response property to a given timed automaton, while preserving its existing universally quantified properties (e.g., MTL). This synthesis method is useful in adding properties that are later discovered as a crucial part of a system. Moreover, we show that addition of interval-bounded response, where the good thing should not happen sooner than a certain amount of time, is also NP-hard in the size of locations even without maximal nondeterminism. Finally, we show that the problems of adding bounded and unbounded response properties are both PSPACE-complete in the size of the input timed automaton.

Keywords: Timed automata, Transformation, Synthesis, Real-time, Bounded liveness, Bounded response, Formal methods.

1 Introduction

As the traditional approaches to software development turn out to be inefficient in many cases (e.g., due to maintenance, resolving bugs, etc.), *correct-by-construction* approaches to treat software development as a true form of engineering gains more attention. *Automated program synthesis* is the problem of designing an algorithmic method to find a program that satisfies a mathematical model (i.e., a required set of properties) that is correct-by-construction. The synthesis problem has mainly been studied in two contexts: synthesizing programs from specification, where the entire specification is given, and synthesizing programs from existing programs along with a fully or partially available new specification. In approaches where the entire specification must be

---

* This work was partially sponsored by NSF CAREER CCR-0092724, DARPA Grant OSURS01-C-1901, ONR Grant N00014-01-1-0744, NSF grant EIA-0130724, and a grant from Michigan State University.

available, changes in specification, e.g., addition of a new property, requires us to begin from scratch. By contrast, in the latter approach, it is possible to *reuse* an existing program and, hence, the previous efforts made for synthesizing it. Since it may not be possible to anticipate all the necessary required properties at design time, this approach is especially useful in program maintenance, where the program needs to be modified so that it satisfies a new property of interest.

In order to *add* a new property to a program there are two ways: (1) *comprehensive redesign*, where the designer introduces new behaviors (e.g., by introducing new variables, or adding new computation paths), or (2) *local redesign*, where the designer removes behaviors that violate the property of interest, but does not add any new behaviors. While the former requires the designer to verify all other properties of the new program, the latter ensures that certain existing universally quantified properties (e.g., LTL and MTL) are preserved.

Depending upon the choice of formulation of the problem and expressiveness of specifications and programs, the class of complexity of synthesis methods varies from polynomial time to undecidability. In this paper, we focus on incremental synthesis methods that add properties typically used for specifying timing constraints. This approach is opposite to those synthesize arbitrary specifications and, hence, belong to high classes of complexity. More specifically, we study the problem of incremental addition of different types of *bounded response* properties – that something good will happen soon, in a certain amount of time – to Alur and Dill's timed automata [1], while preserving existing Metric Temporal Logic (MTL) specification [2]. A more practical application of the results presented in this paper is in aspect-oriented programming. Indeed, our synthesis methods is close in spirit to automated *weaving* of real-time aspects.

1.1 Related Work

In the context of untimed systems, in the pioneering work [3, 4], the authors propose methods for synthesizing the synchronization skeleton of programs from their temporal logic specification. More recently, in [5, 6, 7], the authors investigate algorithmic methods to locally redesign fault-tolerant programs using their existing fault-intolerant version and a partially available safety specification. In [8], the authors introduce a synthesis algorithm that adds UNITY properties [9] such as leads-to (which is an unbounded response property) to untimed programs.

Controller synthesis is the problem of finding an automaton (called *controller*) such that its parallel composition with a given automaton (called *plant*) satisfies a set of properties [10]. Synthesis of real-time systems has mostly been formulated in the context of timed controller synthesis. In the early work [11, 12, 13], the authors investigate the problem, where the given program is a *deterministic* timed automaton and the specification is modeled as a deterministic *internal* winning condition on the state space of the plant. The authors also assume that the controller can use *unlimited* resources (i.e., the number of new clocks and guards that compare the clocks to constants). Similarly, in [14], the authors solve the reachability problem in timed games. Deciding the existence of a winning condition with the formulation presented in [11, 12, 13, 14] is shown to be EXPTIME-complete in [15].

In [16, 17], the authors address the problem of synthesizing timed controllers with limited resources. Similar to the aforementioned work, the plant is modeled by a deterministic timed automaton, but the specification is given by an *external* nondeterministic timed automaton that describes *undesired* behavior of the plant. With this formulation, the synthesis problem is 2EXPTIME-complete. However, if the given specification remains nondeterministic, but describes *desired* behavior of the plant the problem turns out to be undecidable.

In [18], the authors propose a synthesis method for timed games, where the game is modelled as a timed automaton, the winning condition is described by TCTL-formulae, and unlimited resources are available. In [19], the authors consider concurrent two-person games given by a timed automaton played in real-time and provide symbolic algorithms for solving them with respect to all ω-regular winning conditions. In both approaches, deciding the existence of a winning strategy is EXPTIME-complete.

1.2 Contributions

In our work, we consider (i) the case where the entire specification of the program is not given to the synthesis algorithm; and (ii) *nondeterministic* timed automata. In fact, we study how the *level of nondeterminism* affects the complexity of synthesis methods. The main results in this paper are as follows:

- We show that adding a bounded response property while maintaining maximal nondeterminism is NP-hard in the size of the locations of the given timed automaton.
- Based on the above result and the NP-hardness of adding two bounded response properties without maximal nondeterminism [1], we focus on addition of a single bounded response property to a time automaton without maximal nondeterminism. In fact, we present a surprising result that by dropping the maximality requirement we can devise a simple *sound* and *complete* transformation algorithm that adds a bounded response property to a timed automaton while existing MTL properties. Note that since our algorithm is complete, if it fails to synthesize a solution then it informs the designer that a more comprehensive (and expensive) approach *must* be used. Moreover, since the complexity of our algorithm is comparable with that of model checking, the algorithm has the potential to provide timely insight to the designer about how the given program needs to be modified to meet the required bounded response property. Thus, in this paper, we extend the results presented in [8] to the context of timed automata.
- We show that adding *interval-bounded response*, where the good thing should not happen sooner than a certain amount of time, is also NP-hard in the size locations of the given timed automaton even without maximal nondeterminism.
- We show that the problems of adding bounded and *unbounded response* (also called *leads-to*) properties are both PSPACE-complete in the size of the input timed automaton.

---

[1] In [8], it is shown that adding two unbounded response properties to an untimed program is NP-hard. The same proof can be easily extended to the problem of adding two bounded response properties to a timed automaton.

Table 1 compares the complexity of our approach and other synthesis methods in the literature. A natural question is "since direct synthesis of limited MTL to bounded response properties is PSPACE-complete, what is the advantage of our method over direct synthesis?". There are two advantages:

- Since we incrementally add properties to a given timed automaton while preserving its existing MTL specification, we do not need to have this specification at hand. This is particularly useful when the existing specification includes properties whose automated synthesis is undecidable (e.g., $\Diamond_{=\delta}q$) or lies in classes of complexity higher than PSPACE.
- The second advantage of our approach is in cases where the given timed automaton is designed manually for ensuring that it is efficient. Since in our approach, existing computations are preserved it has the potential to preserve the efficiency of the given timed automaton.

Table 1. Complexity of different synthesis approaches

Adding Bounded Response (This paper)	Direct Synthesis from MTL [20]	Timed Control Synthesis [16, 17]	Timed Games [18, 13, 14, 11, 19]
PSPACE-*complete*	EXPSPACE-*complete*	2EXPTIME-*complete*	EXPTIME-*complete*

Organization of the paper. In Section 2, we present the preliminary concepts. In Section 3, we formally state the problem of addition of an MTL property to an existing timed automaton. We describe the NP-hardness result for adding bounded response with maximal nondeterminism in Section 4. Then, in Section 5, we present a sound and complete algorithm for adding bounded response to timed automata without maximal nondeterminism. In Section 6, we present the complexity of addition of interval-bounded response and unbounded response properties. Finally, we make the concluding remarks and discuss future work in Section 7.

2 Preliminaries

Let AP be a set of *atomic propositions*. A state is a subset of AP. A *timed state sequence* is an infinite sequence of pairs $(\sigma, \tau) = (\sigma_0, \tau_0), (\sigma_1, \tau_1)...$, where σ_i ($i \in \mathbb{N}$) is a state and $\tau_i \in \mathbb{R}_{\geq 0}$, and satisfies the following constraints:

1. *Initialization*: $\tau_0 = 0$.
2. *Monotonicity*: $\tau_i \leq \tau_{i+1}$ for all $i \in \mathbb{N}$.
3. *Progress*: For all $t \in \mathbb{R}_{\geq 0}$, there exists j such that $\tau_j \geq t$.

2.1 Metric Temporal Logic

We briefly recap the syntax and semantics of *point-based* MTL. Linear Temporal Logic (LTL) specifies the *qualitative part* of a program. MTL introduces real time by constraining temporal operators, so that one can specify the *quantitative part* as well. For instance, the constrained eventually operator $\Diamond_{[1,3]}$ is interpreted as "eventually within 1 to 3 time units both inclusive".

Syntax. Formulae of MTL are inductively defined by the grammar: $\phi ::= p \mid \neg\phi \mid \phi_1 \wedge \phi_2 \mid \phi_1 \mathcal{U}_I \phi_2$, where $p \in AP$ and $I \subseteq \mathbb{R}_{\geq 0}$ is an open, closed, half-open, bounded, or unbounded interval with endpoints in $\mathbb{Z}_{\geq 0}$. For simplicity, we use $\Diamond_I \phi$ and $\Box_I \phi$ instead of $true\,\mathcal{U}_I \phi$ and $\neg \Diamond_I \neg \phi$. We also use pseudo-arithmetic expressions to denote intervals. For instance, "≤ 4" means $[0, 4]$.

Semantics. For an MTL formula ϕ and a timed state sequence $(\sigma, \tau) = (\sigma_0, \tau_0), (\sigma_1, \tau_1)...$, the satisfaction relation $(\sigma_i, \tau_i) \models \phi$ is defined inductively as follows:

$(\sigma_i, \tau_i) \models p$ iff $\sigma_i \models p$ ($\sigma_i \models p$ iff $p \in \sigma_i$ and we say σ_i is a p-state);

$(\sigma_i, \tau_i) \models \neg\phi$ iff $(\sigma_i, \tau_i) \not\models \phi$;

$(\sigma_i, \tau_i) \models \phi_1 \wedge \phi_2$ iff $(\sigma_i, \tau_i) \models \phi_1 \wedge (\sigma_i, \tau_i) \models \phi_2$;

$(\sigma_i, \tau_i) \models \phi_1 \mathcal{U}_I \phi_2$ iff there exists $j > i$ such that $\tau_j - \tau_i \in I$ and $(\sigma_{i'}, \tau_{i'}) \models \phi_1$ for all i', where $i \leq i' < j$, and $(\sigma_j, \tau_j) \models \phi_2$.

A timed state sequence (σ, τ) satisfies the formula ϕ if $(\sigma_0, \tau_0) \models \phi$.

The formula ϕ defines a set $\mathcal{L}$ of timed state sequences that satisfy ϕ. We call this set a *property*. A *specification* Σ is the conjunction of a set of properties. In this paper, we focus on a standard class of real-time properties defined as follows. An *interval-bounded response* property is of the form $\mathcal{L}_I \equiv \Box(p \rightarrow \Diamond_{[\delta_1, \delta_2]} q)$, where $p, q \in AP$ and $\delta_1, \delta_2 \in \mathbb{Z}_{\geq 0}$, i.e., it is always the case that a p-state is followed by a q-state within δ_2, but not sooner than δ_1 time units. A special case of $\mathcal{L}_I$ is in which $\delta_1 = 0$ known as *bounded response* property and is of the form $\mathcal{L}_B \equiv \Box(p \rightarrow \Diamond_{\leq \delta} q)$, i.e., it is always the case that a p-state is followed by a q-state within δ time units. An *unbounded response* (or *leads-to*) property is defined as $\mathcal{L}_\infty \equiv \Box(p \rightarrow \Diamond_{[0,\infty)} q)$, i.e, it is always the case that a p-state is eventually followed by a q-state.

2.2 Timed Automata

A *clock constraint* over the set X of clock variables is a Boolean combination of formulas of the form $x \preceq c$ or $x - y \preceq c$, where $x, y \in X$, $c \in \mathbb{Z}_{\geq 0}$, and $\preceq$ is either $<$ or $\leq$. We denote the set of all clock constraints over X by $\Phi(X)$. A *clock valuation* is a function $\nu : X \rightarrow \mathbb{R}_{\geq 0}$ that assigns a real value to each clock variable. Furthermore, for $\tau \in \mathbb{R}_{\geq 0}$, $\nu + \tau = \nu(x) + \tau$ for every clock x. Also, for $Y \subseteq X$, $\nu[Y := 0]$ denotes the clock valuation for X which assigns 0 to each $x \in Y$ and agrees with ν over the rest of the clock variables in X.

Definition 2.1. A *timed automaton* $\mathcal{A}$ is a tuple $\langle L, L^0, \psi, X, E \rangle$, where

- L is a finite set of *locations*,
- $L^0 \subseteq L$ is a set of *initial locations*,
- $\psi : L \rightarrow 2^{AP}$ is a labeling function assigning to each location the set of atomic propositions true in that location,

- X is a finite set of clocks, and
- $E \subseteq (L \times 2^X \times \Phi(X) \times L)$ is a set of *switches*. A switch $\langle s_0, \lambda, \varphi, s_1 \rangle$ represents a transition from location s_0 to location s_1 under clock constraint φ over X, such that it specifies when the switch is enabled. The set $\lambda \subseteq X$ gives the clocks to be reset with this switch.   □

The semantics of a timed automaton is as follows. A *state* of a timed automaton is a pair (s, ν), such that s is a location and ν is a clock valuation for X at location s. The labeling function for states is defined by $\psi'((s, \nu)) = \psi(s)$. Thus, if $p \in \psi(s)$, s is a p-location (i.e., $s \models p$) and (s, ν) is a p-state for all ν. An initial state of $\mathcal{A}$ is (s_{init}, ν_{init}) where $s_{init} \in L^0$ and ν_{init} maps the value of all clocks in X to 0. *Transitions* of $\mathcal{A}$ are of the form $(s_0, \nu_0) \rightarrow (s_1, \nu_1)$. They are classified into two types:

- **Delay:** for a state (s, ν) and a time increment $\tau \in \mathbb{R}_{\geq 0}$, $(s, \nu) \xrightarrow{\tau} (s, \nu + \tau)$.
- **Location switch:** for a state (s_0, ν) and a switch $(s_0, \lambda, \varphi, s_1)$ such that ν satisfies the clock constraint φ, $(s_0, \nu) \rightarrow (s_1, \nu[\lambda := 0])$.

We use the well-known *railroad crossing problem* [21] as a running demonstration throughout the paper. The original problem comprises of three timed automata, but we only consider the TRAIN automaton (cf. Figure 1-a). The TRAIN automaton models the behavior of a train approaching a railroad crossing. Initially, the train is far from the gateway of the crossing. It announces approaching the gateway by resetting the clock variable x. The train is required to start crossing the gateway after at least 2 minutes. It passes the gateway at least 3 minutes after approaching the gateway. Finally, there is no constraint on reaching the initial location.

We now define what it means for a timed automaton $\mathcal{A}$ to satisfy an MTL specification Σ. An infinite sequence $(s_0, \nu_0, \tau_0), (s_1, \nu_1, \tau_1)...$, where $\tau_i \in \mathbb{R}_{\geq 0}$, is a *computation* of $\mathcal{A}$ iff for all $j > 0$ (1) $(s_{j-1}, \nu_{j-1}) \rightarrow (s_j, \nu_j)$ is a transition of $\mathcal{A}$, (2) the sequence $\tau_0 \tau_1 ...$ satisfies initialization, monotonicity, and progress, and (3) $\tau_j - \tau_{j-1}$ is consistent with $\nu_j - \nu_{j-1}$. We write $\mathcal{A} \models \Sigma$ and say that timed automaton $\mathcal{A}$ *satisfies* specification Σ iff every computation of $\mathcal{A}$ that starts from an initial state is in Σ. Thus, $\mathcal{A} \models (\square(p \rightarrow \Diamond_{\leq \delta} q))$ iff any computation of $\mathcal{A}$ that reaches a p-state, reaches a q-state within δ time units. If $\mathcal{A} \not\models \Sigma$, we say $\mathcal{A}$ *violates* Σ.

2.3   Region Automata

Timed automata can be analyzed with the help of an equivalence relation of finite index on the set of states [1]. Given a timed automaton $\mathcal{A}$, for each clock $x \in X$, let c_x be the largest constant in the guards of switches of $\mathcal{A}$ that involve x, where $c_x = 0$ if x does not occur in any guard. Two clock valuations ν, μ are *clock equivalent* if (1) for all $x \in X$, either $\lfloor \nu(x) \rfloor = \lfloor \mu(x) \rfloor$ or both $\nu(x), \mu(x) > c_x$, (2) the ordering of the fractional parts of the clock variables in the set $\{x \in X \mid \nu(x) < c_x\}$ is the same in μ, and (3) for all $x \in \{y \in X \mid \nu(y) < c_y\}$, the clock value $\nu(x)$ is an integer if and only if $\mu(x)$ is an integer. A *clock region* ρ is a clock equivalence class. Two states (s_0, ν_0) and (s_1, ν_1) are *region equivalent*, written $(s_0, \nu_0) \equiv (s_1, \nu_1)$, if (1) $s_0 = s_1$ and (2) ν_0 and ν_1 are clock equivalent. A *region* is an equivalence class with respect to $\equiv$. Also, region equivalence is a *time-abstract bisimulation* [1].

Using the region equivalence relation, we construct the *region automaton* of $\mathcal{A}$ (denoted $R(\mathcal{A})$) as follows. Vertices of $R(\mathcal{A})$ are regions. Edges of $R(\mathcal{A})$ are of the form $(s_0, \rho_0) \rightarrow (s_1, \rho_1)$ iff for some clock valuations $\nu_0 \in \rho_0$ and $\nu_1 \in \rho_1$, $(s_0, \nu_0) \rightarrow (s_1, \nu_1)$ is a transitions of $\mathcal{A}$. Figure 1-b shows the region automaton of the TRAIN automaton.

We say a region (s_0, ρ_0) of region automaton $R(\mathcal{A})$ is a *deadlock region* iff for all regions (s_1, ρ_1), there does not exist an edge of the form $(s_0, \rho_0) \rightarrow (s_1, \rho_1)$. The definition of a *deadlock state* is analogous. A clock region β is a *time-successor* of a clock region α iff for each $\nu \in \alpha$, there exists $\tau \in \mathbb{R}_{>0}$, such that $\nu + \tau \in \beta$, and $\nu + \tau' \in \alpha \cup \beta$ for all $\tau' < \tau$. We call a region (s, ρ) a *boundary region*, if for each $\nu \in \rho$ and for any $\tau \in \mathbb{R}_{>0}$, ν and $\nu + \tau$ are not equivalent. A region is *open*, if it is not a boundary region. A region (s, ρ) is called *end region*, if $\nu(x) > c_x$ for all clocks x.

3   Problem Statement

Given are a timed automaton $\mathcal{A}\langle L, L^0, \psi, X, E\rangle$ and an MTL property $\mathcal{L}$ (either $\mathcal{L}_I, \mathcal{L}_B$, or $\mathcal{L}_\infty$). Our goal is to find a timed automaton $\mathcal{A}'\langle L', L'^0, \psi', X', E'\rangle$, such that $\mathcal{A}' \models \mathcal{L}$ and for any MTL specification Σ, if $\mathcal{A} \models \Sigma$ then $\mathcal{A}' \models \Sigma$.

Since we require that $\mathcal{A}' \models \Sigma$, if L' contains locations that are not in L, then $\mathcal{A}'$ includes computations that are not in Σ and as a result, $\mathcal{A}'$ may violate Σ. Hence, we require that $L' \subseteq L$ and $L'^0 \subseteq L^0$. Moreover, if E' contains switches that are present in E, but are guarded by weaker timing constraints, or E' contains switches that are not present in E at all then $\mathcal{A}'$ includes computations that are not in Σ. Hence, we require that E' contains a switch $\langle s_0, \lambda, \varphi', s_1\rangle$, only if there exists $\langle s_0, \lambda, \varphi, s_1\rangle$ in E, such that φ' is stronger than φ. Furthermore, extending the state space of $\mathcal{A}$ by introducing new clock variables under the above circumstances is legitimate. Finally, we require ψ' to be equivalent to ψ. Thus, the synthesis problem is as follows:

Problem Statement 3.1.   Given $\mathcal{A}\langle L, L^0, \psi, X, E\rangle$ and an MTL property $\mathcal{L}$, identify $\mathcal{A}'\langle L', L'^0, \psi', X', E'\rangle$ such that

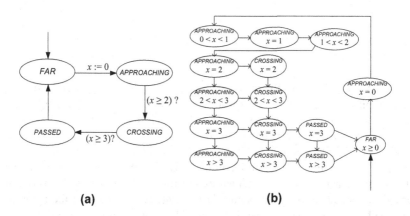

(a)   **(b)**

Fig. 1. (a) TRAIN automaton. (b) Region automaton of TRAIN automaton.

(C1) $L' \subseteq L, L'^0 \subseteq L^0$
(C2) $\psi' = \psi$
(C3) $X \subseteq X'$
(C4) $\forall \langle s_0, \lambda, \varphi', s_1 \rangle \in E' : (\exists \langle s_0, \lambda, \varphi, s_1 \rangle \in E : (\varphi' \Rightarrow \varphi))$
(C5) $\mathcal{A}' \models \mathcal{L}$
(C6)   For any MTL specification Σ: $((\mathcal{A} \models \Sigma) \Rightarrow (\mathcal{A}' \models \Sigma))$ $\square$

Notice that constraint $(C6)$ implicitly implies that the synthesized program is not allowed to have deadlock states. This constraint is known as the *non-blocking condition* in the literature of controller synthesis. Furthermore, constraint $(C6)$ is similar to *language inclusion condition* in controller synthesis where the set of uncontrollable transitions is empty. Note that, based on Problem Statement 3.1, since we allow synthesis methods to remove states and transitions of a timed automaton, such methods are appropriate to preserve universally quantified properties only. In fact, constraints of Problem Statement 3.1 do not suffice to preserve existential properties of a program (e.g., TCTL).

Soundness and completeness.   We say that an algorithm for the synthesis problem is *sound* iff its output meets the constraints of the Problem Statement 3.1. We say that an algorithm for the synthesis problem is *complete* iff it finds a solution to the Problem Statement 3.1 iff there exists one.

4   Adding Bounded Response Properties with Maximal Nondeterminism

In this section, we show that the synthesis problem in Problem Statement 3.1 for adding a bounded response property while maintaining maximal nondeterminism is NP-hard in the size of locations of the input timed automaton. We show this result by a reduction from the Vertex Splitting Problem [22] in directed acyclic graphs (DAG).

Given a timed automaton $\mathcal{A}$ and property $\mathcal{L}_B \equiv \Box(p \rightarrow \Diamond_{\leq \delta} q)$, we say that the synthesized timed automaton $\mathcal{A}'$ is *maximally nondeterministic* iff $\mathcal{A}'$ meets all the constraints of Problem Statement 3.1 and its set of transitions is maximal. Maintaining maximal nondeterminism is desirable in the sense that it increases the potential for future successful incremental synthesis. Indeed, in our framework, maximal nondeterminism is similar to the concept of *weakest controller* in the literature of controller synthesis.

The DAG Vertex Splitting Problem (DVSP).   Let $G\langle V, A \rangle$ be a weighted DAG and v_s, v_t be arbitrary source and target vertices in G. Let G/Y denote the DAG when each vertex $v \in Y$ is split into vertices v^{in} and v^{out} such that all arcs $(v, u) \in A$, where $u \in V$, are replaced by arcs of the form (v^{out}, u) and all arcs $(w, v) \in A$, where $w \in V$, are replaced by arcs of the form (w, v^{in}). In other words, the outgoing arcs of v now leave vertex v^{out} while the incoming arcs of v now enter v^{in}, and there is no arc between v^{in} and v^{out}. The DAG vertex splitting problem is to find a vertex set Y, where $Y \subseteq V$ and $|Y| \leq i$ (for some positive integer i), such that the length of the longest path of G/Y from v_s to v_t is bounded by a prespecified value d. In [22], the authors show that DVSP is NP-hard.

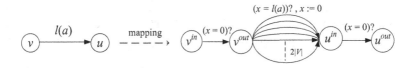

Fig. 2. Mapping DVSP to MNBRAP

We now show that the problem of adding a bounded response property while maintaining maximal nondeterminism is NP-hard.

Instance. A timed automaton $\mathcal{A}\langle L, L^0, \psi, X, E\rangle$, a bounded response property $\mathcal{L}_B \equiv \square(p \to \lozenge_{\leq\delta}q)$, and a positive integer k, where $|E| \geq k$.

Maximally Nondeterministic Bounded Response Addition Problem (MNBRAP). Does there exist a timed automaton $\mathcal{A}'\langle L', L'^0, \psi', X', E'\rangle$, such that $|E'| \geq k$ and $\mathcal{A}'$ meets the constraints of the Problem Statement 3.1?

Theorem 4.1. MNBRAP is NP-hard in the size of locations of the input timed automaton.

Proof. We reduce DVSP to MNBRAP. The reduction maps a weighted DAG $G\langle V, A\rangle$ and integers d and i to a timed automaton $\mathcal{A}$ and integers δ and k, respectively.

Mapping. Let $G\langle V, A\rangle$ be any instance of DVSP whose longest path is to be bounded by d. Let $l(a)$ be the length of an arc $a \in A$. We construct a timed automaton $\mathcal{A}$ as follows (cf. Figure 2). Each vertex $v \in V$ is mapped to a pair of locations v^{in} and v^{out} in $\mathcal{A}$. The set of initial locations of $\mathcal{A}$ is the singleton $L^0 = \{v_s^{in}\}$, where v_s is the source vertex in G. Switches of $\mathcal{A}$ consist of two types of switches as follows:

- We include switches of the form $v^{in} \xrightarrow{(x=0)?} v^{out}$ for all v in V. The clock constraint $(x = 0)$ is used to force computations of $\mathcal{A}$ not to wait at location v^{in}.
- We add $2|V|$ number of parallel switches of the form $v^{out} \xrightarrow{(x=l(a))?,\ x:=0} u^{in}$, for all arcs $a = (v, u) \in A$ of length $l(a)$.

Let the set of clock variables of $\mathcal{A}$ be the singleton $X = \{x\}$. Finally, let $v_s^{in} \models p$, $v_t^{out} \models q$, $k = |E| - i$, and $\delta = d$. Other locations may satisfy arbitrary atomic propositions except p and q.

Reduction. We need to show that vertex $v \in Y$ in G must be split if and only if the switch $v^{in} \xrightarrow{(x=0)?} v^{out}$ must be removed from $\mathcal{A}$. We distinguish two cases:

- *DVSP $\longrightarrow$ MNBRAP:* Suppose the answer to DVSP is the set Y, where $|Y| \leq i$. Hence, after splitting all $v \in Y$ the length of the longest path of G is at most d. Now, we show that we can synthesize a timed automaton $\mathcal{A}'$ from the mapped timed automaton $\mathcal{A}\langle L, \{v_s^{in}\}, \psi, \{x\}, E\rangle$ as an answer to MNBRAP. It is easy to see that if we remove switches of the form $v^{in} \xrightarrow{(x=0)?} v^{out}$ (for all $v \in Y$)

from E to obtain E', the maximum delay between locations v_s^{in} and v_t^{out} in $\mathcal{A}'$ becomes at most δ. Recall that, $\delta = d$ and $k = |E| - i$. Therefore, $\mathcal{A}' \models \mathcal{L}_B$ and $|E'| \geq |E| - i = k$. Other constraints of the Problem Statement 3.1 are immediately met by construction of $\mathcal{A}'$.

- *MNBRAP* $\longrightarrow$ *DVSP*: Suppose the answer to MNBRAP is $\mathcal{A}'\langle L', L'^0, \psi', \{x\}, E'\rangle$, where $|E'| \geq k$ and the maximum delay to reach v_t^{out} from v_s^{in} is at most δ. Note that, $L'^0 = \{v_s^{in}\}$. Since the number of switches removed from E is at most $|E| - k$, $k = |E| - i$, and $i \leq |V|$, we could not have removed switches of the form $v^{out} \xrightarrow{(x=l(a))?,\ x:=0} u^{in}$. This is because there are $2|V|$ of such switches and, hence, their removal would not change the maximum delay. Thus, we should have removed switches of the form $v^{in} \xrightarrow{(x=0)?} v^{out}$ from E to bound the maximum delay. Indeed, these switches identify the set Y of vertices that should be split in G, i.e, $Y = \{v \mid (v \in V) \wedge ((v^{in}, v^{out}) \in (E - E'))\}$. It is easy to see that by removing the set Y from V the length of the longest path of G becomes at most d. $\qquad \square$

5   Adding Bounded Response Properties Without Maximal Nondeterminism

In this section, we show that by relaxing the maximality constraint, we can solve the Problem Statement 3.1 in polynomial time in the size of locations of the input timed automaton. A possible approach to add a bounded response property to a timed automaton is as follows. First, we construct an auxiliary timed automaton $\mathcal{A}_2$ accepting all behaviors of the given bounded response property. Then, we construct the product of $\mathcal{A}_2$ and the given timed automaton $\mathcal{A}_1$ (denoted $\mathcal{A}_1 \otimes \mathcal{A}_2$). Although this approach is semantically correct, it does not meet the constrains of the Problem Statement 3.1. In particular, construction of the product alone may introduce deadlock states to $\mathcal{A}_1 \otimes \mathcal{A}_2$. As a result, some of the infinite computations of $\mathcal{A}_1$ become finite in $\mathcal{A}_1 \otimes \mathcal{A}_2$ and, hence, existing MTL properties are not preserved, which in turn violates the constraint ($C6$) of the problem statement. Thus, we need a more "behavior-aware" approach.

Since our synthesis algorithm constructs and manipulates a specific weighted directed graph introduced by Courcoubetis and Yannakakis as a solution to the maximum delay problem in timed automata [23], we review this problem in Subsection 5.1. In Subsection 5.2, we describe our synthesis algorithm.

5.1   The Maximum Delay Problem in Timed Automata

The maximum delay problem is as follows. Given a timed automaton $\mathcal{A}$, a source location and clock valuation, what is the latest time that a target location can appear along a computation of $\mathcal{A}$? We first construct the region automaton $R(\mathcal{A})\langle S, T\rangle$, where S is the set of regions and T is the set of edges. Then, we transform the region automaton to an ordinary weighted directed graph (called MaxDelay digraph). Let the subroutine ConstructMaxDelayGraph do this transformation as follows. It takes a region automaton $R(\mathcal{A})\langle S, T\rangle$, a set X of source regions, and a set Y of target regions, where $X, Y \subseteq S$, as input, and constructs a MaxDelay digraph $G\langle V, A\rangle$. Vertices of G consist of the regions in $R(\mathcal{A})$ with the addition of a source vertex v_s and a target vertex v_t.

Notation: We denote the weight of an arc (v_0, v_1) by $Weight(v_0, v_1)$. Let f denote a function that maps each region in $R(\mathcal{A})$ to its corresponding vertex in G, i.e., $f(r)$ is a vertex that represents region r in G. Also, let f^{-1} denote the inverse of f, i.e., $f^{-1}(v)$ is the region of $R(\mathcal{A})$ that corresponds to vertex v in G. Likewise, let F be a function that maps a set of regions in $R(\mathcal{A})$ to the corresponding set of vertices in G and F^{-1} be its inverse. Finally, for a boundary region r with respect to clock variable x, we denote the value of x by $r.x$ (equal to some constant in $\mathbb{Z}_{\geq 0}$).

Arcs of G consist of the following:

- Arcs of weight 0 from v_s to all vertices in $F(X)$, and from all vertices in $F(Y)$ to v_t.
- Arcs of weight 0 from v_0 to v_1, if $f^{-1}(v_0) \rightarrow f^{-1}(v_1)$ is a location switch in $R(\mathcal{A})$.
- Arcs of weight $c' - c$, where $c, c' \in \mathbb{Z}_{\geq 0}$ and $c' > c$, from v_0 to v_1, if $f^{-1}(v_0)$ and $f^{-1}(v_1)$ are both boundary regions with respect to clock variable x_i, such that $f^{-1}(v_0).x_i = c$, $f^{-1}(v_1).x_i = c'$, and there exists a path in $R(\mathcal{A})$ from $f^{-1}(v_0)$ to $f^{-1}(v_1)$, which does not reset x_i.
- Arcs of weight $c' - c - \epsilon$, where $c, c' \in \mathbb{Z}_{\geq 0}$, $c' > c$, and $0 < \epsilon \ll 1$, from v_0 to v_1, if (1) $f^{-1}(v_0)$ is a boundary region with respect to clock variable x_i, (2) $f^{-1}(v_1)$ is an open region whose time-successor $f^{-1}(v_2)$ is a boundary region with respect to clock variable x_i, (3) $f^{-1}(v_0) \rightarrow f^{-1}(v_1)$ represents a delay transition in $R(\mathcal{A})$, and (4) $f^{-1}(v_0).x_i = c$ and $f^{-1}(v_2).x_i = c'$.
- Self-loop arcs of weight ∞ at vertex v, if $f^{-1}(v)$ is an end region.

In order to compute the maximum delay between X and Y, it suffices to find the longest distance between v_s and v_t in G.

5.2   The Synthesis Algorithm

In this subsection, we present a sound and complete algorithm, Add_BoundedResponse (cf. Figure 3), for solving the Problem Statement 3.1 with respect to $\mathcal{L}_B \equiv \Box(p \rightarrow \Diamond_{\leq \delta} q)$. The core of the algorithm is straightforward. It begins with an empty digraph and builds up a subgraph of the MaxDelay digraph by adding paths of length at most δ that start from the set of vertices that represents p-regions in G to the set of vertices that represents q-regions. Then, it adds the rest of vertices and arcs while ensuring that no new paths from p-regions to q-regions are introduced. In order to ensure completeness, the algorithm preserves p-regions.

We now describe the algorithm in detail. First, in order to keep track of time elapsed since p have become true, we add an extra clock variable t to $\mathcal{A}$ as a timer. Moreover, the maximum value that t would be compared with is δ (lines 1-2). Next, we construct the region automaton $R(\mathcal{A})\langle S, T\rangle$, where S is the set of regions and T is the set of edges (Line 3). Let the function $g : AP \rightarrow 2^S$ calculate the set of regions with respect to an arbitrary atomic proposition ap as follows:

$$g(ap) = \{(s_1, \rho_1) \mid (s_1 \models ap) \land$$
$$(\exists (s_0, \rho_0) \mid (((s_0, \rho_0), (s_1, \rho_1)) \in T) : (s_0 \not\models ap))\}$$

```
Add_BoundedResponse(𝒜⟨L, L⁰, ψ, X, E⟩ : timed automata, ℒ_B ≡ □(p → ◇_{≤δ}q))
{
        X := X ∪ {t}; c_t := δ;                                                                    (1)
        ∀⟨s₀, λ, φ, s₁⟩ | (⟨s₀, λ, φ, s₁⟩ ∈ E ∧ (s₀ ⊭ p ∧ s₁ ⊨ p)) : λ := λ ∪ {t};                  (2)
        R(𝒜)⟨S, T⟩ := ConstructRegionAutomaton(𝒜);                                                 (3)
        Repeat
                IsQRemoved := false;                                                                (4)
                G⟨V, A⟩ := ConstructMaxDelayGraph(R(𝒜), g(p), g(q));   \\ Defined in Subsection 5.1  (5)
                G'⟨V', A'⟩ := ConstructSubgraph(G, δ);                                               (6)

                R(𝒜')⟨S', T'⟩ := {};                                                                (7)
                S' := F⁻¹(V');                                                                      (8)
                T' := {(r₀, r₁) | (r₀, r₁) ∈ T ∧ (f(r₀), f(r₁)) ∈ A'} ∪
                        {(r₁, r₂) | (r₁, r₂) ∈ T ∧ (f(r₁), f(r₂)) ∉ A' ∧
                        ∃r₀ : Weight(f(r₀), f(r₁)) = 1 − ε};                                         (9)
                while (∃r₀ | r₀ ∈ S' : (∀r₁ | r₁ ∈ S' : (r₀, r₁) ∉ T'))                              (10)
                        S' := S' − {r₀}; T' := T' − {(r, r₀), (r₀, r) | r ∈ S'};                     (11)
                        if r₀ ∈ g(q) then                                                           (12)
                                IsQRemoved := true;                                                 (13)
                                S := S − {r₀}; T := T − {(r, r₀), (r₀, r) | r ∈ S}; break;           (14)
                until (IsQRemoved = false);
                if {(s, ρ) | (s, ρ) ∈ S' ∧ s ∈ L⁰ ∧ (∀x, ν | (ν ∈ ρ ∧ x ∈ X) : ν(x) = 0)} = {} then
                        declare failure; exit;                                                      (15)
                𝒜' := ConstructTimedAutomata(R(𝒜'));                                               (16)
                return 𝒜';                                                                          (17)
}
ConstructSubgraph(G⟨V, A⟩ : MaxDelay digraph, δ : integer)
{
        G'⟨V', A'⟩ = {};                                                                            (18)
        for all vertices v such that (v_s, v) ∈ A                                                   (19)
                if the length the shortest path 𝒫 from v to v_t is at most δ then                   (20)
                        V' := V' ∪ {u | u is on 𝒫};                                                 (21)
                        A' := A' ∪ {a | a is on 𝒫};                                                 (22)
        A' := A' ∪ {(u, v) | (u, v) ∈ A ∧ (u ∉ V' ∨ (u, v_t) ∈ A')};                                (23)
        V' := (V' ∪ {u | (∃v : (u, v) ∈ A' ∨ (v, u) ∈ A')}) − {v_s, v_t};                           (24)
        return G'⟨V', A'⟩;                                                                          (25)
}
```

Fig. 3. The synthesis algorithm for adding bounded response

We now reduce our problem to the problem of bounding the length of longest path in ordinary weighted digraphs. Towards this end, we first generate the MaxDelay digraph $G\langle V, A\rangle$ (Line 5), as described in Subsection 5.1. Then, we invoke (Line 6) the subroutine ConstructSubgraph (lines 18-25) which takes a MaxDelay digraph G and an integer δ as input. It generates a subgraph G' whose longest path from v_s to v_t is bounded by δ. Recall that v_s and v_t are additional source and target vertices connected to $F(g(p))$ and $F(g(q))$, respectively. We now begin with an empty digraph and add a certain number of paths in polynomial order of $|S|$. To this end, first, we include the shortest path from each vertex in $F(g(p))$ to v_t, provided its length is at most δ (lines 19-22). Then, we add the rest of the vertices and arcs to G' (lines 23-24) while ensuring that no new paths are added from v_s to v_t.

After invoking ConstructSubgraph, we transform G' back to a region automaton $R(\mathcal{A}')$ (lines 7-9). Next, due to pruning some vertices and arcs in ConstructSubgraph, we remove deadlock regions from $R(\mathcal{A}')$ (lines 10-11). However, in order to ensure that this removal does not break the completeness of our algorithm, we should consider the case where a q-region becomes a deadlock region (lines 12-14). In case the removal of deadlock regions leaves no initial regions, the algorithm declares failure and terminates (Lines 15). Otherwise, it constructs the timed automaton $\mathcal{A}'$ out of $R(\mathcal{A}')$ and terminates successfully (lines 16-17).

Let us now consider the TRAIN automaton presented in Section 2 (cf. Figure 1-a). Our goal is to bound the delay of revisiting the initial location within at most 4 minutes. To this end, we add the property $\mathcal{L}_B \equiv \Box(APPROACHING \rightarrow \Diamond_{\leq 4} FAR)$ to the TRAIN automaton. Since $\delta = 4$, we have $c_x = 4$ when generating the region automaton. Next, we construct the MaxDelay digraph. It is easy to observe by adding 12 shortest paths, we includes all computations that satisfy $\mathcal{L}_B$. Figure 4-a shows the synthesized region automaton and Figure 4-b shows the the final timed automaton.

Theorem 5.1. The algorithm Add_BoundedResponse is sound and complete. □

Theorem 5.2. The problem of adding a bounded response property to a timed automaton is in PSPACE. □

6 Adding Interval-Bounded and Unbounded Response Properties

We first consider automatic addition of an interval-bounded response property $\mathcal{L}_I \equiv \Box(p \rightarrow \Diamond_{[\delta_1, \delta_2]} q)$ to a timed automaton, where $\delta_1 > 0$. As an intuition, let us use the algorithm Add_BoundedResponse to add $\mathcal{L}_I$. Since the required response time has a lower bound, the subroutine ConstructSubgraph has to enumerate and ignore all the paths whose lengths are less than δ_1. Obviously, this enumeration cannot be done in polynomial time in the size of region automata.

Theorem 6.1. The problem of adding an interval-bounded response property to a timed automaton is NP-hard in the size of the locations of the input timed automaton.

Proof. The proof is a simple reduction from the *longest path problem* to an instance of the problem, where $\mathcal{L}_I \equiv \Box(p \rightarrow \Diamond_{[\delta_1, \infty)} q)$. Figure 5 illustrates the mapping of a digraph G to a timed automaton $\mathcal{A}$. It is easy to see that if G has a path of length at least

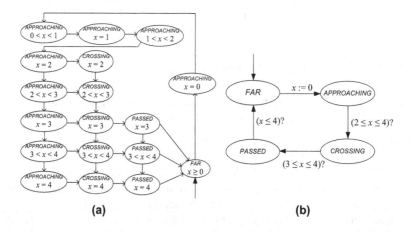

Fig. 4. (a) Synthesized region automaton (b) Synthesized TRAIN automaton

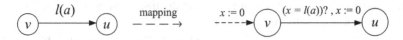

Fig. 5. Mapping the longest path problem to addition of interval-bounded response

δ_1 from a source vertex v_s to a target vertex v_t then $\mathcal{A}$ can be transformed to a timed automaton $\mathcal{A}'$ whose delay from v_s to v_t is at least δ_1 time units and vice versa.   □

Next, we discuss the problem of addition of unbounded response (also called leads-to) properties.

Theorem 6.2. The problem of addition of an unbounded response property to a timed automaton is PSPACE-complete in the size of the input timed automaton.

Proof. Since this problem is an instance of adding bounded response, membership to PSPACE follows from Theorem 5.2 immediately. We now show that the problem is PSPACE-hard. To this end, we reduce the *reachability problem* in timed automata [23] (whether a location s_1 is reachable from another location s_0) to an instance of our problem.

Mapping. Let the timed automaton $\mathcal{A}$ be any instance of the reachability problem. We map $\mathcal{A}$ to an instance of our problem as follows. Let $\mathcal{A}^*$ be an automaton identical to $\mathcal{A}$ with the following modifications. Let $s_0 \models p$ and $s_1 \models q$. Other locations of $\mathcal{A}^*$ may satisfy arbitrary atomic propositions except p and q. Let s_0 be the only initial location of $\mathcal{A}^*$. We also add a self-loop at s_1.

Reduction. If s_1 is reachable from s_0 in $\mathcal{A}$ then there exists a computation in $\mathcal{A}^*$ that starts from s_0 and ends at s_1. A timed automaton $\mathcal{A}'$ constructed from this computation plus the self-loop at s_1 satisfies $\mathcal{L}_\infty$ and meets the constraints of Problem Statements 3.1. Now, we show the other direction. Let us assume that the answer to the decision problem is affirmative and we can synthesize a timed automaton $\mathcal{A}'$ from $\mathcal{A}^*$ such that $\mathcal{A}' \models \mathcal{L}_\infty$. Then $\mathcal{A}'$ should contain both s_0 and s_1. This means that s_1 is reachable from s_0. Otherwise, $\mathcal{A}'$ would not satisfy $\mathcal{L}_\infty$.   □

Since an unbounded response property is an instance of bounded and interval-bounded response properties, problems of adding those properties are also PSPACE-hard.

Corollary 6.3. The problem of adding a bounded response property to a timed automaton is PSPACE-complete in the size of the input timed automaton.   □

Remark 6.4. The time complexity of adding an unbounded response property to a timed automaton with maximal nondeterminism in terms of transitions remains open in this paper. However, we refer the reader to [8], where the authors introduce a synthesis algorithm for adding leads-to properties to an untimed program, while maintaining maximal nondeterminism in terms of reachable states of the given program.

We summarize the complexity of problems of addition of different types of response properties in Table 2.

Table 2. Complexity of adding response properties in the size of the locations

Bounded Response		Unbounded Response		Interval-Bounded Response
Maximal (Sec. 4)	NonMaximal (Sec. 5)	Maximal (Sec. 6)	NonMaximal (Sec. 6)	(Sec. 6)
NP-hard	*P*	see Rem. 6.4	*P*	*NP-hard*

7   Conclusion and Future Work

In this paper, we focused on automated incremental synthesis of timed automata by adding various types of bounded response properties, while preserving its existing Metric Temporal Logic (MTL) specification. Unlike specification-based methods, in our approach, we start with an existing program rather than specification and, hence, the previous efforts made for synthesizing the input program are reused.

First, we showed the problem of addition of a bounded response property to a timed automaton while maintaining maximal nondeterminism is NP-hard in the size of locations of the input automaton. Then, we presented a simple sound and complete transformation algorithm that adds a bounded response property to a timed automaton (without maximal nondeterminism), such that the automaton continues to satisfy its existing MTL specification. The complexity of the algorithm is polynomial in the size of region automata. Furthermore, we showed that the problem of addition of interval-bounded response properties is also NP-hard. Moreover, we showed that adding bounded and unbounded response properties are PSPACE-complete in the size of the input timed automaton.

Detailed region automata are not an efficient finite representation of timed automata in terms of space complexity. On other hand, zone automata [24] are more efficient finite representation of timed automata used in model checking techniques. Since our goal was to evaluate complexity classes for adding bounded response, we focused on region automata. However, an interesting improvement step is modifying Add_BoundedResponse, so that it manipulates a zone automaton rather than a detailed region automaton.

In many hard real-time systems (e.g., mission-critical systems) meeting deadlines in the presence of faults is a necessity. As future work, we plan to study the problem of automatic addition of fault-tolerance to existing fault-intolerant real-time systems. More specifically, we plan to extend the theory of automated addition of fault-tolerance to untimed programs [5,6,7] to the context of real-time programs. In particular, we plan to study how time-bounded recovery can be achieved in the presence of faults using the results presented in this paper.

References

1. R. Alur and D. Dill. A theory of timed automata. *Theoretical Computer Science*, 126(2): 183–235, 1994.
2. R. Alur and T.A. Henzinger. Real-Time Logics: Complexity and Expressiveness. *Information and Computation*, 10(1):35–77, May 1993.

3. E.A. Emerson and E.M. Clarke. Using branching time temporal logic to synthesize synchronization skeletons. *Science of Computer Programming*, 2(3):241–266, 1982.
4. Z. Manna and P. Wolper. Synthesis of communicating processes from temporal logic specifications. *ACM Transactions on Programming Languages and Systems*, 6(1):68–93, 1984.
5. S. S. Kulkarni and A. Arora. Automating the addition of fault-tolerance. In *Formal Techniques in Real-Time and Fault-Tolerant Systems (FTRTFT)*, pages 82–93, 2000.
6. S. S. Kulkarni, A. Arora, and A. Chippada. Polynomial time synthesis of Byzantine agreement. In *20th Symposium on Reliable Distributed Systems (SRDS)*, pages 130–140, 2001.
7. S. S. Kulkarni and A. Ebnenasir. Automated synthesis of multitolerance. In *International Conference on Dependable Systems and Networks (DSN)*, pages 209–219, 2004.
8. A. Ebnenasir, S. S. Kulkarni, and B. Bonakdarpour. Revising UNITY programs: Possibilities and limitations. In *9th International Conference on Principles of Distributed Systems (OPODIS)*, 2005.
9. K. M. Chandy and J. Misra. *Parallel Program Design: A Foundation*. Addison-Wesley, 1988.
10. W. M. Wonham P. J. G. Ramadge. The control of discrete event systems. *Proceedings of the IEEE*, 77(1):81–98, January 1989.
11. H. Wong-Toi and G. Hoffmann. The control of dense real-time discrete event systems. In *30th International Conference on Decision and Control*, pages 1527–1528, 1991.
12. O. Maler, A. Pnueli, and J. Sifakis. On the synthesis of discrete controllers for timed systems. In *12th Annual Symposium on Theoretical Aspects of Computer Science (STACS)*, pages 229–242, 1995.
13. E. Asarin, O. Maler, A. Pnueli, and J. Sifakis. Controller synthesis for timed automata. In *IFAC Symposium on System Structure and Control*, pages 469–474, 1998.
14. E. Asarin and O. Maler. As soon as possible: Time optimal control for timed automata. In *Hybrid Systems: Computation and Control (HSCC)*, pages 19–30, 1999.
15. T. A. Henzinger and P. W. Kopke. Discrete-time control for rectangular hybrid automata. *Theoretical Computer Science*, 221(1-2):369–392, 1999.
16. D. D'Souza and P. Madhusudan. Timed control synthesis for external specifications. In *19th Annual Symposium on Theoretical Aspects of Computer Science (STACS)*, pages 571–582, 2002.
17. P. Bouyer, D. D'Souza, P. Madhusudan, and A. Petit. Timed control with partial observability. In *Computer Aided Verification (CAV)*, pages 180–192, 2003.
18. M. Faella, S. LaTorre, and A. Murano. Dense real-time games. In *Logic in Computer Science (LICS)*, pages 167–176, 2002.
19. L. de Alfaro, M. Faella, T. A. Henzinger, R. Majumdar, and M. Stoelinga. The element of surprise in timed games. In *International Conference on Concurrency Theory (CONCUR)*, 2003.
20. R. Alur, T. Feder, and T.A. Henzinger. The benefits of relaxing punctuality. *Journal of the ACM*, 43(1):116–146, 1996.
21. N. G. Leveson and J. L. Stolzy. Analyzing safety and fault tolerance using time petri nets. In *International Joint Conference on Theory and Practice of Software Development (TAPSOFT) on Formal Methods and Software*, pages 339–355, 1985.
22. D. Paik, S.M. Reddy, and S. Sahni. Deleting vertices to bound path length. *IEEE Transation on Computers*, 43(9):1091–1096, 1994.
23. C. Courcoubetis and M. Yannakakis. Minimum and maximum delay problems in real-time systems. In *Computer-Aided Verificaion (CAV)*, pages 399–409, 1991.
24. R. Alur, C. Courcoubetis, N. Halbwachs, D. L. Dill, and H. Wong-Toi. Minimization of timed transition systems. In *International Conference on Concurrency Theory (CONCUR)*, pages 340–354, 1992.

SAT-Based Verification of LTL Formulas

Wenhui Zhang*

Laboratory of Computer Science
Institute of Software, Chinese Academy of Sciences, Beijing, China
zwh@ios.ac.cn

Abstract. Bounded model checking (BMC) based on satisfiability testing (SAT) has been introduced as a complementary technique to BDD-based symbolic model checking of LTL properties in recent years and a lot of successful work has been done with this approach. The basic idea is to search for a counter example of a particular length and to generate a propositional formula that is satisfied iff such a counter example exists. An over approximation of the length that need to be checked in order to certify that the system is error free is usually too big, such that it is not practical to use this approach for checking systems that are error free with respect to given properties. Even if we know the exact threshold, for a reasonably large system, this threshold would possibly also be large enough to make the verification become intractable due to the complexity of solving the corresponding SAT instance. This study is on a different direction and the aim of this study is verification of valid properties. We propose an approach to (partly) avoid the use of the completeness threshold as the verification criteria when checking systems that are error free with respect to LTL properties. The benefit of the use of this approach may be very large compared to the use of the completeness threshold. Though, Prasad, Biere and Gupta pointed out in a survey paper [19] that, currently, the strength of SAT-based verification techniques lies primarily in falsification, this study explores the strength of SAT-based techniques for verification and the case study shows that this is a promising approach.

1   Introduction

Model checking has been successfully used in the last decade for the formal verification of finite state systems. It is considered as one of the most practical applications of theoretical computer science in the verification of concurrent systems. However the practical applicability of model checking is limited by the state explosion problem which could be caused by for instance, the representation of currency of operations by their interleaving. Therefore much effort has been put into the research aiming at minimizing models. The methods include application of cone of influence reduction [1], semantic minimization [20], state

---

* Supported by the National Natural Science Foundation of China under Grant No. 60373050, 60421001 and 60573012, and the National Grand Fundamental Research 973 Program of China under Grant No. 2002cb312200.

L. Brim et al. (Eds.): FMICS and PDMC 2006, LNCS 4346, pp. 277–292, 2007.

information compression [11], abstraction techniques [6,14], partial order reductions [22,23], symmetry reductions [10], compositional techniques for splitting verification tasks [8,1], case-based partition techniques [15,24], and BDD based symbolic techniques for compactly representing transition relations and system states [5,4].

Bounded model checking (BMC) based on satisfiability testing (SAT) has been introduced as a complementary technique to BDD-based symbolic model checking of LTL properties [3]. A lot of successful work has been done with this approach [2,19]. The basic idea is to search for a counter example of a particular length and to generate a propositional formula that is satisfied iff such a counter example exists. The efficiency of this method is based on the observation that if a system is faulty then only a fragment of its state space is sufficient for finding an error. Given a finite transition system M, an LTL formula φ and a natural number k, a BMC procedure decides whether there exists a computation in M of length k or less that violates φ. SAT based BMC is performed by generating a propositional formula which is satisfiable if and only if such a path exists. BMC is conducted in an iterative process where k is incremented until either (i) an error is found, (ii) the problem becomes intractable due to the complexity of solving the corresponding SAT instance, or (iii) k reaches some pre-computed completeness threshold which indicates that M satisfies φ. If we have given M and φ such that M satisfies φ, then the practical value of this approach depends on the existence of a relatively small value of the completeness threshold. Computing an exact value of the completeness threshold for a given model and formula is difficult. A general over approximation of the completeness threshold is $|M| \cdot 2^{|\varphi|}$ where $|M|$ is the size of the model and $|\varphi|$ is the size of the formula. This approximation is obviously impractical for checking systems that are error free with respect to given properties. For reducing this approximation, completeness threshold has been studied for several types of LTL formulas [13,7].

As stated in [13], knowing the completeness threshold is essential for making BMC complete. Without it, there is no way of knowing whether the property holds or rather the bound is not sufficiently high. Even if we know the completeness threshold, for a reasonably large system, this threshold would possibly be large enough to make the verification become intractable due to the complexity of solving the corresponding SAT instance. This study is on a different direction that proposes an approach that (partly) avoids this problem and may prove whether the property holds without knowing a completeness threshold. This kind of research has also been considered in [2] for simple liveness properties of the form Fp. There is also a lot of work on proving safety properties based on SAT, the related works are for instance, proving safety properties by using induction [21,16], conservative abstraction with counter example guided refinement [9], and interpolation based transition relation approximation for generating facts relevant with respect to given properties [12]. In this work, we study LTL properties in general.

2   Propositional Linear Temporal Logic

Propositional linear temporal logic (LTL) is a logic introduced by Pnueli as a specification language for concurrent programs [18]. Let AP be a set of proposition symbols. The set of LTL formulas is defined as follows:

- Every member of AP is an LTL formula.
- Logical connectives of LTL include: $\neg$, $\wedge$, $\vee$, and $\rightarrow$.
  If φ and ψ are LTL formulas, then so are $\neg\varphi$, $\varphi \wedge \psi$, $\varphi \vee \psi$, and $\varphi \rightarrow \psi$.
- Temporal operators include: X, F, G, U, and R.
  If φ and ψ are LTL formulas, then so are: $X\varphi$, $F\varphi$, $G\varphi$, $\varphi U \psi$, and $\varphi R \psi$.

2.1   Semantics of LTL

The formal semantics of LTL is defined with respect to paths of a Kripke structure. Let $M = \langle S, T, I, L \rangle$ be a Kripke structure where S is a set of states, $T \subseteq S \times S$ is a transition relation which is total, $I \subseteq S$ is a set of initial states and $L : S \rightarrow 2^{AP}$ is a labeling function. Let φ be a temporal formula. Let $\pi = \pi_0 \pi_1 \cdots$ be a path of M and π^i be the subpath of π starting at π_i. We define the relation φ holds on π, denoted $\pi \models \varphi$, as follows.

$$
\begin{aligned}
\pi &\models p && \text{iff } p \in L(\pi_0) \\
\pi &\models \neg\varphi && \text{iff } \pi \not\models \varphi \\
\pi &\models \varphi \wedge \psi && \text{iff } \pi \models \varphi \text{ and } \pi \models \psi \\
\pi &\models \varphi \vee \psi && \text{iff } \pi \models \varphi \text{ or } \pi \models \psi \\
\pi &\models \varphi \rightarrow \psi && \text{iff } \pi \models \varphi \text{ implies } \pi \models \psi \\
\pi &\models X\varphi && \text{iff } \pi^1 \models \varphi \\
\pi &\models F\varphi && \text{iff } \exists k \geq 0. \pi^k \models \varphi \\
\pi &\models G\varphi && \text{iff } \forall k \geq 0. \pi^k \models \varphi \\
\pi &\models \varphi U \psi && \text{iff } \exists k \geq 0. \forall j < k. (\pi^k \models \psi \wedge \pi^j \models \varphi) \\
\pi &\models \varphi R \psi && \text{iff } \forall j \geq 0. (\pi^j \models \psi) \vee \exists k \geq 0. ((\pi^k \models \varphi) \wedge (\forall j \leq k. (\pi^j \models \psi)))
\end{aligned}
$$

For simplicity, we call a Kripke structure a model. An LTL formula φ is *true* in the model M, denoted $M \models \varphi$, iff φ is *true* on all paths starting from an arbitrary initial state of M.

2.2   Bounded Semantics of LTL Formulas in NNF

An LTL formula is in negation normal form (NNF), if the symbol $\rightarrow$ does not appear in the formula and $\neg$ is applied only to proposition symbols. Every formula can be transformed into a formula in NNF by using the following rules:

$$
\begin{aligned}
\varphi \rightarrow \psi &= \neg\varphi \vee \psi & \neg(\varphi \wedge \psi) &= (\neg\varphi \vee \neg\psi) \\
\neg(\varphi \vee \psi) &= (\neg\varphi \wedge \neg\psi) & \neg X\varphi &= X\neg\varphi \\
\neg F\varphi &= G\neg\varphi & \neg G\varphi &= F\neg\varphi \\
\neg(\varphi U \psi) &= \neg\varphi R \neg\psi & \neg(\varphi R \psi) &= \neg\varphi U \neg\psi
\end{aligned}
$$

In the following, we only consider LTL formulas in NNF. Let $M = \langle S, T, I, L \rangle$ be a model and $k \in \mathbf{N}$. Let $\pi = \pi_0 \pi_1 \cdots$ be an infinite path of M. If $u = \pi_0 \cdots \pi_k$

and $v = \pi_l \cdots \pi_k$ for some $0 \leq l \leq k$, we call $\pi = u \cdot v^\omega$ a (k,l)-loop. If π is a (k,l)-loop for some $0 \leq l \leq k$, we call π a k-loop.

Definition 1 (Bounded Semantics for a Loop). *Let $k \geq 0$ and π be a k-loop. Then an LTL formula φ is valid on π with bound k, written $\pi \models_k \varphi$, iff $\pi \models \varphi$.*

Definition 2 (Bounded Semantics without a Loop). *Let $k \geq 0$ and π be a path which is not a k-loop. Then an LTL formula φ is valid on π with bound k, written $\pi \models_k \varphi$, iff $\pi \models_k^0 \varphi$ where:*

$$\pi \models_k^i p \quad \textit{iff } p \in L(\pi_i)$$
$$\pi \models_k^i \neg p \quad \textit{iff } \pi \not\models_k^i p$$
$$\pi \models_k^i \varphi \wedge \psi \quad \textit{iff } \pi \models_k^i \varphi \textit{ and } \pi \models_k^i \psi$$
$$\pi \models_k^i \varphi \vee \psi \quad \textit{iff } \pi \models_k^i \varphi \textit{ or } \pi \models_k^i \psi$$
$$\pi \models_k^i X\varphi \quad \textit{iff } i < k \textit{ and } \pi \models_k^{i+1} \varphi$$
$$\pi \models_k^i F\varphi \quad \textit{iff } \exists j \in \{i, ..., k\}.\pi \models_k^j \varphi$$
$$\pi \models_k^i G\varphi \quad \textit{iff false}.$$
$$\pi \models_k^i \varphi U\psi \quad \textit{iff } \exists j \in \{i, ..., k\}.\forall n \in \{i, ..., j-1\}.(\pi \models_k^j \psi \wedge \pi \models_k^n \varphi)$$
$$\pi \models_k^i \varphi R\psi \quad \textit{iff } \exists j \in \{i, ..., k\}.((\pi \models_k^j \varphi) \wedge \forall n \in \{i, ..., j\}.(\pi \models_k^n \psi))$$

Note that $\pi \models_k^i G\varphi$ is *false* by definition. This is explained by that a global property can only be witnessed by an infinite path (or a path with a loop).

Theorem 1. *Let M be a model, φ an LTL formula. Then $M \not\models \varphi$ iff there is a path π and a $k \geq 0$ such that $\pi \models_k \neg\varphi$.*

3   Encoding the Model in SAT-Formulas

Since we have $F\varphi = true\, U\varphi$ and $\varphi R\psi = (\psi U(\varphi \wedge \psi)) \vee G\psi$, we only consider formulas of the form $\varphi \vee \psi, \varphi \wedge \psi, X\varphi, G\varphi, \varphi U\psi$ constructed from propositions and the negation of propositions.

Given a model M, an LTL formula φ and a bound k, we will construct encodings for the pair (M, φ). Let $u_0, ..., u_k$ be a finite sequence of states on a path π. We first define $[[M]]_k$ to be a formula representing that $u_0 \cdots u_k$ is a finite prefix of a valid path of M.

Definition 3 (Transition Relation). *Let $M = \langle S, T, I, L \rangle$ be a model and $k \geq 0$.*

$$[[M]]_k := I(u_0) \wedge \bigwedge_{i=0}^{k-1} T(u_i, u_{i+1})$$

This translation of transition relation corresponds to that in [3]. Let $M = \langle S, T, I, L \rangle$ be a model. Let u, w (possibly with subscripts) represent individual states. Let $p \in AP$ be a proposition symbol and $p(u)$ represent the propositional formula representing the states in which p is *true* according to L. For a state and a formula, we first present the encoding for (formula,state) pair as done in [3] (however with a slightly different version). Then we propose an encoding for (formula,state) pair for the purpose of verification.

3.1 Encoding of LTL Formulas

Let min() be the minimum operation and $s(i, k, l)$ denote

$$\text{if } (k = i) \text{ then } l \text{ else } i + 1.$$

Definition 4 (Translation of LTL formulas). *Given a state $u \in \{u_0, ..., u_k\}$ and a formula φ, the encoding is denoted by $[[\varphi, u]]_{k,l}$.*

$$
\begin{aligned}
[[p, u]]_{k,l} &= p(u) \\
[[\neg p, u]]_{k,l} &= \neg p(u) \\
[[\varphi \vee \psi, u]]_{k,l} &= [[\varphi, u]]_{k,l} \vee [[\psi, u]]_{k,l} \\
[[\varphi \wedge \psi, u]]_{k,l} &= [[\varphi, u]]_{k,l} \wedge [[\psi, u]]_{k,l} \\
[[X\varphi, u_i]]_{k,l} &= [[\varphi, u_{s(i,k,l)}]]_{k,l} \\
[[G\varphi, u_i]]_{k,l} &= \bigwedge_{j=\min(i,l)}^{k} [[\varphi, u_j]]_{k,l} \\
[[\varphi U\psi, u_i]]_{k,l} &= \bigvee_{j=i}^{k}([[\psi, u_j]]_{k,l} \wedge \bigwedge_{t=i}^{j-1}[[\varphi, u_t]]_{k,l}) \vee \\
&\quad \bigwedge_{t=i}^{k}[[\varphi, u_t]]_{k,l} \wedge \bigvee_{j=l}^{i-1}([[\psi, u_j]]_{k,l} \wedge \bigwedge_{t=l}^{j-1}[[\varphi, u_t]]_{k,l})
\end{aligned}
$$

where $[[\varphi, u_{-1}]]_{k,l} = false$.

In the above definition, u_{-1} is a special symbol used only for the purpose of uniform formula representation (avoiding specification of different cases explicitly). In the real transformation, formulas containing this symbol are to be replaced by *true* or *false* according to their meaning, for instance, $[[p \vee q, u_{-1}]]_{k,l}$ must be replaced by *false* and not by $[[p, u_{-1}]]_{k,l} \vee [[q, u_{-1}]]_{k,l}$. In addition, we define $T(u_k, u_{-1}) = true$. The subscript (k, l) in the definition indicates that the path is a (k, l)-loop for $l \geq 0$, otherwise the path is considered loop free.

Definition 5. $[[M, \varphi]]_k := [[M]]_k \wedge \bigvee_{l=-1}^{k}(T(u_k, u_l) \wedge [[\varphi, u_0]]_{k,l})$.

The encoding of $[[M, \varphi]]_k$ corresponds to that in [3] with some modification, i.e. a condition $\bigwedge_{l=0}^{k} \neg T(u_k, u_l)$ representing loop-free-ness is removed (or more precisely, replaced by *true*)[1]. This change does not affect the satisfiability of the formula. This fact is to be established and presented as Theorem 2.

Lemma 1. $[[\varphi, u_0]]_{k,-1} \rightarrow [[\varphi, u_0]]_{k,l}$ for $l \in \{0, ..., k\}$.

---

[1] This is not only a matter of representational simplicity. With this clause in the formulation, we would not be able to prove Lemma 3 and then the proof of Theorem 5 would be different and more complicated.

Proof: We prove a more general property

$$[[\varphi, u_i]]_{k,-1} \rightarrow [[\varphi, u_i]]_{k,l} \text{ for } i \in \{0, ..., k\} \text{ and } l \in \{0, ..., k\}$$

by structural induction. The case is trivial for φ being a proposition or negation of a proposition. Assume the induction hypothesis.

- The case is trivial for φ being a conjunctive or disjunctive formula.
- If $\varphi = X\varphi_0$, then
  $[[\varphi, u_i]]_{k,-1}$ is either *false* ($i = k$) or the same as $[[\varphi_0, u_{i+1}]]_{k,-1}$ ($i < k$).
  In the latter case, $[[\varphi, u_i]]_{k,l} = [[\varphi_0, u_{i+1}]]_{k,l}$.
  Therefore, according to the induction hypothesis, $[[\varphi, u_i]]_{k,-1} \rightarrow [[\varphi, u_i]]_{k,l}$.
- If $\varphi = G\varphi_0$, then $[[\varphi, u_i]]_{k,-1}$ is *false*. Therefore $[[\varphi, u_i]]_{k,-1} \rightarrow [[\varphi, u_i]]_{k,l}$.
- If $\varphi = \varphi_0 U \varphi_1$, then $\bigvee_{j=-1}^{i-1}([[\varphi_1, u_j]]_{k,-1} \wedge \bigwedge_{t=-1}^{j-1}[[\varphi_0, u_t]]_{k,-1}) = false$.
  Therefore $[[\varphi, u_i]]_{k,-1} = \bigvee_{j=i}^{k}([[\varphi_1, u_j]]_{k,-1} \wedge \bigwedge_{t=i}^{j-1}[[\varphi_0, u_t]]_{k,-1})$.
  Then, according to the induction hypothesis,
  $[[\varphi, u_i]]_{k,-1} \rightarrow \bigvee_{j=i}^{k}([[\varphi_1, u_j]]_{k,l} \wedge \bigwedge_{t=i}^{j-1}[[\varphi_0, u_t]]_{k,l})$.
  Since the right side of the implication is a disjunctive part of $[[\varphi, u_i]]_{k,l}$, we
  obtain $[[\varphi, u_i]]_{k,-1} \rightarrow [[\varphi, u_i]]_{k,l}$.   □

Theorem 2. *Let M be a model, φ be an LTL formula. Let $k \geq 0$. There is a path π of M such that $\pi \models_k \varphi$ iff $[[M, \varphi]]_k$ is satisfiable.*

Theorem 2 corresponds to the normal soundness theorem of bounded LTL model checking [3]. As explained, the only different in the encoding $[[M, \varphi]]_k$ and that in [3] is that a condition representing loop-free-ness is removed. The fact that this change does not affect the satisfiability of the formula can be proved easily based on Lemma 1.

3.2   Encoding of LTL Formulas for Verification

Definition 6 (Translation of LTL formulas for Verification). *Given a state $u \in \{u_0, ..., u_k\}$ and a formula φ, the encoding is denoted by $[[\varphi, u]]_k^v$.*

$[[p, u]]_k^v$	$= p(u)$
$[[\neg p, u]]_k^v$	$= \neg p(u)$
$[[\varphi \vee \psi, u]]_k^v$	$= [[\varphi, u]]_k^v \vee [[\psi, u]]_k^v$
$[[\varphi \wedge \psi, u]]_k^v$	$= [[\varphi, u]]_k^v \wedge [[\psi, u]]_k^v$
$[[X\varphi, u_i]]_k^v$	$= [[\varphi, u_{i+1}]]_k^v$
$[[G\varphi, u_i]]_k^v$	$= \bigwedge_{j=i}^{k}[[\varphi, u_j]]_k^v$
$[[\varphi U \psi, u_i]]_k^v$	$= \bigvee_{j=i}^{k}([[\psi, u_j]]_k^v \wedge \bigwedge_{t=i}^{j-1}[[\varphi, u_t]]_k^v) \vee \bigwedge_{t=i}^{k}[[\varphi, u_t]]_k^v$

where $[[\varphi, u_{k+1}]]_k^v = true$.

Definition 7. $[[M, \varphi]]_k^v := [[M]]_k \wedge [[\varphi, u_0]]_k^v$.

In the following, we shall establish that there is no path π and $k \geq 0$ such that $\pi \models_k \varphi$ if there is some i such that $[[M, \varphi]]_i^v$ is unsatisfiable.

Definition 8. $[[M, \varphi, u_i]]_k^v := [[M]]_k \wedge [[\varphi, u_i]]_k^v$.

Proposition 1. *For all $i \in \{0, ..., k\}$, the following equivalences holds:*

(1) $[[M, \varphi_0 \vee \varphi_1, u_i]]_k^v = [[M, \varphi_0, u_i]]_k^v \vee [[M, \varphi_1, u_i]]_k^v$

(2) $[[M, \varphi_0 \wedge \varphi_1, u_i]]_k^v = [[M, \varphi_0, u_i]]_k^v \wedge [[M, \varphi_1, u_i]]_k^v$

(3) $[[M, X\varphi, u_i]]_k^v = [[M, \varphi, u_{i+1}]]_k^v$

(4) $[[M, G\varphi, u_i]]_k^v = \bigwedge_{j=i}^{k} [[M, \varphi, u_j]]_k^v$

(5) $[[M, \varphi U\psi, u_i]]_k^v = \bigvee_{j=i}^{k}([[M, \psi, u_j]]_k^v \wedge \bigwedge_{t=i}^{j-1}[[M, \varphi, u_t]]_k^v) \vee \bigwedge_{t=i}^{k}[[M, \varphi, u_t]]_k^v$

Proof: We only prove the first equivalence. The others are similar. We have

$$[[M, \varphi_0 \vee \varphi_1, u_i]]_k^v$$
$$= [[M]]_k \wedge [[\varphi_0 \vee \varphi_1, u_i]]_k^v$$
$$= [[M]]_k \wedge ([[\varphi_0, u_i]]_k^v \vee [[\varphi_1, u_i]]_k^v)$$
$$= [[M, \varphi_0, u_i]]_k^v \vee [[M, \varphi_1, u_i]]_k^v$$

This was what needed to be proved.

Lemma 2. $[[M, \varphi, u_i]]_{k+1}^v \rightarrow [[M, \varphi, u_i]]_k^v$ *for $i \in \{0, ..., k\}$.*

Proof: This can be proved based on structural induction on φ. The proof is straightforward and is omitted.

Theorem 3. $[[M, \varphi]]_{k+1}^v \rightarrow [[M, \varphi]]_k^v$.

Proof: This follows directly from Lemma 2.

Theorem 4. $[[M, \varphi]]_k \rightarrow [[M, \varphi]]_k^v$.

Proof: Since $[[M, \varphi]]_k = [[M]]_k \wedge \bigvee_{l=-1}^{k}(T(u_k, u_l) \wedge [[\varphi, u_0]]_{k,l})$ and $[[M, \varphi]]_k^v = [[M]]_k \wedge [[\varphi, u_0]]_k^v$, it is sufficient to prove that $[[\varphi, u_0]]_{k,l} \rightarrow [[\varphi, u_0]]_k^v$. We prove

$$[[\varphi, u_i]]_{k,l} \rightarrow [[\varphi, u_i]]_k^v \text{ for } i \in \{0, ..., k\} \text{ and } l \in \{0, ..., k\}$$

by structural induction. The case is trivial for φ being a proposition or negation of a proposition. Assume the induction hypothesis.

- The case is trivial for φ being a conjunctive or disjunctive formula.
- If $\varphi = X\varphi_0$, we have two cases.
  For $i = k$, we have $[[\varphi, u_i]]_k^v = true$. Therefore $[[\varphi, u_i]]_{k,l} \rightarrow [[\varphi, u_i]]_k^v$.
  For $i < k$, we have $[[\varphi, u_i]]_{k,l} = [[\varphi_0, u_{i+1}]]_{k,l}$ and $[[\varphi, u_i]]_k^v = [[\varphi_0, u_{i+1}]]_k^v$.
  Therefore, according to the induction hypothesis, $[[\varphi, u_i]]_{k,l} \rightarrow [[\varphi, u_i]]_k^v$.
- If $\varphi = G\varphi_0$, then
  $[[\varphi, u_i]]_{k,l} = \bigwedge_{j=i}^{k}[[\varphi_0, u_j]]_{k,l} \wedge \bigwedge_{j=\min(i,l)}^{i-1}[[\varphi_0, u_j]]_{k,l}$
  $[[\varphi, u_i]]_k^v = \bigwedge_{j=i}^{k}[[\varphi_0, u_j]]_k^v$.
  Therefore, according to the induction hypothesis, $[[\varphi, u_i]]_{k,l} \rightarrow [[\varphi, u_i]]_k^v$.

- If $\varphi = \varphi_0 U \varphi_1$, then

$[[\varphi_0 U \varphi_1, u_i]]_{k,l}$

$= \bigvee_{j=i}^{k}([[\varphi_1, u_j]]_{k,l} \wedge \bigwedge_{t=i}^{j-1}[[\varphi_0, u_t]]_{k,l}) \vee$

$\bigwedge_{t=i}^{k}[[\varphi_0, u_t]]_{k,l} \wedge \bigvee_{j=l}^{i-1}([[\varphi_1, u_j]]_{k,l}^m \wedge \bigwedge_{t=l}^{j-1}[[\varphi_0, u_t]]_{k,l})$

$[[\varphi_0 U \varphi_1, u_i]]_k^v = \bigvee_{j=i}^{k}([[\varphi_1, u_j]]_k^v \wedge \bigwedge_{t=i}^{j-1}[[\varphi_0, u_t]]_k^v) \vee \bigwedge_{t=i}^{k}[[\varphi_0, u_t]]_k^v.$

Therefore, according to the induction hypothesis, $[[\varphi, u_i]]_{k,l} \rightarrow [[\varphi, u_i]]_k^v$.

Lemma 3. *If* $[[M]]_k \wedge [[\varphi, u_0]]_{k,-1}$ *is satisfiable, then* $[[M]]_{k+1} \wedge [[\varphi, u_0]]_{k+1,-1}$ *is satisfiable.*

Proof: Let $u_0, ..., u_k$ be a set of states (each represented by a set of literals) that satisfy $[[M]]_k \wedge [[\varphi, u_0]]_{k,-1}$. Since the transition relation in M is total, there is a state u_{k+1} such that $T(u_k, u_{k+1})$. We prove that $u_0, ..., u_k, u_{k+1}$ is a set of states that satisfies $[[M]]_{k+1} \wedge [[\varphi, u_0]]_{k+1,-1}$. Since $[[M]]_k \wedge [[\varphi, u_0]]_{k,-1}$ and $T(u_k, u_{k+1})$, then $[[M]]_{k+1} = [[M]]_k \wedge T(u_k, u_{k+1})$ is *true*. Then it is sufficient to prove that

$$[[\varphi, u_i]]_{k,-1} \rightarrow [[\varphi, u_i]]_{k+1,-1} \text{ for all } i \in \{0, ..., k\}.$$

This can then be proved based on structural induction. The proof is omitted.

Lemma 4. *Let* l *be non-negative. If* $[[M]]_k \wedge T(u_k, u_l) \wedge [[\varphi, u_0]]_{k,l}$ *is satisfiable, then* $[[M]]_{k+1} \wedge T(u_{k+1}, u_{l+1}) \wedge [[\varphi, u_0]]_{k+1,l+1}$ *is satisfiable.*

Proof: Let $u_0, ..., u_k$ be a set of states that satisfy $[[M]]_k \wedge T(u_k, u_l) \wedge [[\varphi, u_0]]_{k,l}$. Let $u_{k+1} = u_l$. We prove that $u_0, ..., u_k, u_{k+1}$ is a set of states that satisfies $[[M]]_{k+1} \wedge T(u_{k+1}, u_{l+1}) \wedge [[\varphi, u_0]]_{k+1,l+1}$. We have

$$[[M]]_{k+1} \wedge T(u_{k+1}, u_{l+1})$$
$$= [[M]]_k \wedge T(u_k, u_{k+1}) \wedge T(u_{k+1}, u_{l+1})$$
$$= [[M]]_k \wedge T(u_k, u_l) \wedge T(u_l, u_{l+1})$$
$$= [[M]]_k \wedge T(u_k, u_l)$$

Since $[[M]]_k \wedge T(u_k, u_l) \wedge [[\varphi, u_0]]_{k,l}$, then $[[M]]_{k+1} \wedge T(u_{k+1}, u_{l+1})$ is *true*. Then it is sufficient to prove that

$$[[\varphi, u_i]]_{k,l} \rightarrow [[\varphi, u_i]]_{k+1,l+1} \text{ for all } i \in \{0, ..., k\}.$$

This can then be proved based on structural induction. The proof is omitted.

Theorem 5. *If* $[[M, \varphi]]_k$ *is satisfiable, then* $[[M, \varphi]]_{k+1}$ *is satisfiable.*

Proof: Suppose that $[[M, \varphi]]_k = [[M]]_k \wedge \bigvee_{l=-1}^{k}(T(u_k, u_l) \wedge [[\varphi, u_0]]_{k,l})$ is *true*. Then $[[M]]_k \wedge (T(u_k, u_l) \wedge [[\varphi, u_0]]_{k,l})$ is *true* for some $l \in \{-1, 0, ..., k\}$. There are two cases $l = -1$ and $l \in \{0, ..., k\}$. In the former case, Lemma 3 implies that $[[M]]_{k+1} \wedge (T(u_{k+1}, u_{-1}) \wedge [[\varphi, u_0]]_{k+1,-1})$ is satisfiable. Therefore $[[M, \varphi]]_{k+1}$ is satisfiable. In the latter case, Lemma 4 implies that $[[M]]_{k+1} \wedge (T(u_{k+1}, u_{l+1}) \wedge [[\varphi, u_0]]_{k+1,l+1})$ is satisfiable. Therefore $[[M, \varphi]]_{k+1}$ is satisfiable also in this case.

Theorem 6. *If* $[[M, \varphi]]_k^v$ *is unsatisfiable for some* k, *then* $M \models \neg\varphi$.

Proof: Suppose that $M \models \neg\varphi$ does not hold. Then there is a path π of M and a $k' \geq 0$ such that $\pi \models_{k'} \varphi$ according to Theorem 1. Then $[[M, \varphi]]_{k'}$ is satisfiable according to Theorem 2. Then $[[M, \varphi]]_n$ is satisfiable for $n \geq k'$ according to Theorem 5. Then $[[M, \varphi]]_n^v$ is satisfiable for $n \geq k'$ according to Theorem 4. Choose n' such that $n' \geq k$ and $n' \geq k'$. Then $[[M, \varphi]]_{n'}^v$ is satisfiable. Then $[[M, \varphi]]_{k''}^v$ is satisfiable for all $n' \geq k''$ according to Theorem 3. This contradicts with that $[[M, \varphi]]_k^v$ is unsatisfiable, since $n' \geq k$. This proves the theorem.

4   SAT-Based Verification

Theorem 6 provides a theoretical basis for verification and Theorem 2 provides a theoretical basis for error detection. The theorems suggest the following combination of verification and error detection approach. Let M be a model and φ be a temporal formula to be verified.

- Start with $k = 0$;
- If $[[M, \neg\varphi]]_k^v$ is unsatisfiable, report that $M \models \varphi$ is valid;
- If $[[M, \neg\varphi]]_k$ is satisfiable, report that $M \models \varphi$ does not hold;
- If a completeness threshold is reached, report that $M \models \varphi$ is valid;
- Increase k and repeat the process.

Note that $\neg\varphi$ represents the formula in NNF corresponding to $\neg\varphi$. In many cases, as will be demonstrated in the case study, the procedure may terminate before reaching a completeness threshold. However, in the general case, it may be necessary to repeat the process until a completeness threshold is reached. For instance, if we have the trivial property $\varphi = G\,true$, which is $true$ for all systems, then we have $[[M, \neg\varphi]]_k = false$ and $[[M, \neg\varphi]]_k^v = I(u_0) \wedge \bigwedge_{i=0}^{k-1} T(u_i, u_{i+1})$. Then the first one is unsatisfiable and the second is always satisfiable. The above approach can only terminate when a completeness threshold is reached.

This is a theoretical formulation. In practice, for a reasonably large system, the threshold would possibly be large enough to make the verification become intractable due to the complexity of solving the corresponding SAT instance, and the process will be interrupted by time or memory constraints.

In the rest of this section, we discuss some types of simple properties which can then be a background for the case-study of the use of this approach for verification in the next section.

A Safety Property: A simple safety property is of the forms pRq where p and q are propositions. For verifying this property, we need to calculate $[[M, \neg pU\neg q]]_k^v$. This formula expands to

$$I(u_0) \wedge \bigwedge_{i=0}^{k-1} T(u_i, u_{i+1}) \wedge (\bigvee_{j=0}^{k}(\neg q(u_j) \wedge \bigwedge_{t=0}^{j-1} \neg p(u_t)) \vee \bigwedge_{t=0}^{k} \neg p(u_t))$$

Therefore $M \models pRq$ if there is a k such that

$$I(u_0) \wedge \bigwedge_{i=0}^{k-1} T(u_i, u_{i+1}) \wedge (\bigvee_{j=0}^{k}(\neg q(u_j) \wedge \bigwedge_{t=0}^{j-1} \neg p(u_t)) \vee \bigwedge_{t=0}^{k} \neg p(u_t))$$

is unsatisfiable.

A Co-Safety Property: A simple co-safety property is of the form pUq where p and q are propositions. For verifying this property, we need to calculate $[[M, \neg pR\neg q]]_k^v$. This formula is equivalent to $[[M, (\neg qU(\neg q \wedge \neg p)) \vee G\neg q]]_k^v$ which expands to

$$I(u_0) \wedge \bigwedge_{i=0}^{k-1} T(u_i, u_{i+1}) \wedge \bigvee_{j=0}^k (\neg q(u_j) \wedge \neg p(u_j) \wedge \bigwedge_{t=0}^{j-1} \neg q(u_t)) \vee \bigwedge_{t=0}^k \neg q(u_t))$$

Therefore $M \models pUq$ if there is a k such that

$$I(u_0) \wedge \bigwedge_{i=0}^{k-1} T(u_i, u_{i+1}) \wedge (\bigvee_{j=0}^k (\neg p(u_j) \wedge \bigwedge_{t=0}^j \neg q(u_t)) \vee \bigwedge_{t=0}^k \neg q(u_t))$$

is unsatisfiable. Furthermore, we have the following lemma.

Lemma 5. *if $M \models pUq$, then there is a k such that*

$$I(u_0) \wedge \bigwedge_{i=0}^{k-1} T(u_i, u_{i+1}) \wedge (\bigvee_{j=0}^k (\neg p(u_j) \wedge \bigwedge_{t=0}^j \neg q(u_t)) \vee \bigwedge_{t=0}^k \neg q(u_t))$$

is unsatisfiable.

Proof: We prove that if

$$I(u_0) \wedge \bigwedge_{i=0}^{k-1} T(u_i, u_{i+1}) \wedge (\bigvee_{j=0}^k (\neg p(u_j) \wedge \bigwedge_{t=0}^j \neg q(u_t)) \vee \bigwedge_{t=0}^k \neg q(u_t))$$

is satisfiable for all k, then $M \not\models pUq$, i.e. $[[M, \neg pR\neg q]]_{k'}$ is satisfiable for some k'. We have

$$
\begin{aligned}
&[[M, \neg pR\neg q]]_k \\
=\ &[[M, (\neg qU(\neg q \wedge \neg p)) \vee G\neg q]]_k \\
=\ &I(u_0) \wedge \bigwedge_{i=0}^{k-1} T(u_i, u_{i+1}) \wedge \\
&\bigvee_{l=-1}^k (T(u_k, u_l) \wedge [[(\neg qU(\neg q \wedge \neg p) \vee G\neg q), u_0]]_{k,l}) \\
=\ &I(u_0) \wedge \bigwedge_{i=0}^{k-1} T(u_i, u_{i+1}) \wedge \\
&([[[(\neg qU(\neg q \wedge \neg p) \vee G\neg q), u_0]]_{k,-1} \vee \\
&\bigvee_{l=0}^k (T(u_k, u_l) \wedge [[(\neg qU(\neg q \wedge \neg p) \vee G\neg q), u_0]]_{k,l})) \\
=\ &I(u_0) \wedge \bigwedge_{i=0}^{k-1} T(u_i, u_{i+1}) \wedge \\
&(\bigvee_{j=0}^k (\neg q(u_j) \wedge \neg p(u_j) \wedge \bigwedge_{t=0}^{j-1} \neg q(u_t)) \vee \\
&\bigvee_{l=0}^k (T(u_k, u_l) \wedge (\bigvee_{j=0}^k (\neg q(u_j) \wedge \neg p(u_j) \wedge \bigwedge_{t=0}^{j-1} \neg q(u_t)) \vee \bigwedge_{j=0}^k \neg q(u_j)))) \\
=\ &I(u_0) \wedge \bigwedge_{i=0}^{k-1} T(u_i, u_{i+1}) \wedge \\
&(\bigvee_{j=0}^k (\neg p(u_j) \wedge \bigwedge_{t=0}^j \neg q(u_t)) \vee \bigvee_{l=0}^k (T(u_k, u_l) \wedge \bigwedge_{j=0}^k \neg q(u_j))))
\end{aligned}
$$

The difference between $[[M, \neg pR\neg q]]_k^v$ and $[[M, \neg pR\neg q]]_k$ is $T(u_k, u_l)$ for some $k \geq l \geq 0$. Since the transition relation is total, there is some k and l such that $T(u_k, u_l)$ is *true*. This proves the lemma. $\square$

Corollary 1. $M \models pUq$ *iff there is a k such that*

$$I(u_0) \wedge \bigwedge_{i=0}^{k-1} T(u_i, u_{i+1}) \wedge (\bigvee_{j=0}^{k} (\neg p(u_j) \wedge \bigwedge_{t=0}^{j} \neg q(u_t)) \vee \bigwedge_{t=0}^{k} \neg q(u_t))$$

is unsatisfiable.

Proof: This follows from the Lemma 5 and Theorem 5.

A Liveness Property: Naturally, Fp is a special case of qUp. By simplifying the previously obtained equation, we have

$$[[M, G\neg p]]_k^v = I(u_0) \wedge \bigwedge_{i=0}^{k-1} T(u_i, u_{i+1}) \wedge \bigwedge_{i=0}^{k} \neg p(u_i)$$

Then according to Corollary 1, $M \models Fp$ iff there is a k such that

$$I(u_0) \wedge \bigwedge_{i=0}^{k-1} T(u_i, u_{i+1}) \wedge \bigwedge_{i=0}^{k} \neg p(u_i)$$

is unsatisfiable. Note that this is consistent with the liveness property of the form Fp considered in [2] where the translation of $M \models Fp$ is as follows:

$$[[M, Fp]]_k = I(u_0) \wedge \bigwedge_{i=0}^{k-1} T(u_i, u_{i+1}) \rightarrow \bigvee_{i=0}^{k} p(u_i)$$

Then $M \models Fp$ iff there is a k such that $[[M, Fp]]_k$ is valid.

5   A Case Study

We consider verification of properties of the form pUq and pRq of a mutual exclusion algorithm. We first present our tool for verification, and then the experimental results.

5.1   Verification Tool: VERBS

We have developed a tool called VERBS (VERification Based on Sat) based on our satisfiability checking tool BOSCH (BOolean Satisfiability CHecker)[2]. The input to the tool is as follows:

- a file containing the specification of state variables;
- a file containing the specification of initial states in CNF format;
- a file containing the specification of the transition relation in CNF format;
- a file containing the specification of the property;
- a number k representing the length of transition ($k = 0, 1, 2, ...$).

Currently the subset of LTL formulas handled by the tool is of the forms $\varphi U \psi$ and $\varphi R \psi$, where φ, ψ are propositional formulas in DNF format. The tool first converts all these information to a CNF formula and then calls BOSCH for satisfiability checking.

---

[2] A tool based on DPLL and similar principles as the tool for parallel execution of stochastic search procedures on reduced SAT instances [25].

5.2   Presentation of the Case

Let a, b be variables of enumeration type which have respectively the domain $\{s_0, ..., s_3\}$ and $\{t_0, ..., t_3\}$. Let x, y, t be variables of boolean type. Let the system consist of two processes: A and B with the following specification in a first order transition system [17]:

Process A:

$$
\begin{aligned}
a = s_0 &\longrightarrow (y, t, a) := (1, 1, s_1) \\
a = s_1 \wedge (x = 0 \vee t = 0) &\longrightarrow (a) := (s_2) \\
a = s_2 &\longrightarrow (y, a) := (0, s_3) \\
a = s_3 &\longrightarrow (y, t, a) := (1, 1, s_1)
\end{aligned}
$$

Process B:

$$
\begin{aligned}
b = t_0 &\longrightarrow (x, t, b) := (1, 0, t_1) \\
b = t_1 \wedge (y = 0 \vee t = 1) &\longrightarrow (b) := (t_2) \\
b = t_2 &\longrightarrow (x, b) := (0, t_3) \\
b = t_3 &\longrightarrow (x, t, b) := (1, 0, t_1)
\end{aligned}
$$

Let the initial state be $a = s_0 \wedge b = t_0 \wedge x = y = t = 0$. We consider two properties:

1. One of the processes reached the critical region ($a = s_2 \vee b = t_2$) releases the property that the system is either at the initial state ($a = s_0 \wedge b = t_0$) or some is waiting to enter the critical region ($x = 1 \vee y = 1$);
2. The value of y and t is consistent ($y = t$) unless both processes have tried to get into the critical region ($a \geq s_1 \wedge b \geq t_1$) and this continues until some process exited the critical region ($a = s_3 \vee b = t_3$).

Let boolean variables a_0 and a_1 represent the variable a such that $a_0 = i \wedge a_1 = j$ meaning $a = s_{2i+j}$, and b_0 and b_1 represent b such that $b_0 = i \wedge b_1 = j$ meaning $b = t_{2i+j}$. Then each state is represented by a tuple $(a_0, a_1, b_0, b_1, x, y, t)$. Let $V = \{a_0, a_1, b_0, b_1, p, q, r\}$. The system can be represented by boolean formulas as follows:

$$
\begin{aligned}
&I(a_0, a_1, b_0, b_1, x, y, t) \equiv \\
&\quad x = 0 \wedge y = 0 \wedge t = 0 \wedge a_0 = 0 \wedge a_1 = 0 \wedge b_0 = 0 \wedge b_1 = 0
\end{aligned}
$$

$$
\begin{aligned}
&T(a_0, a_1, b_0, b_1, x, y, t, a'_0, a'_1, b'_0, b'_1, x', y', t') \equiv \\
&\quad a_0 = 0 \wedge a_1 = 0 \wedge y' = 1 \wedge t' = 1 \wedge a'_1 = 1 \wedge same(V \setminus \{y, t, a_1\}) \vee \\
&\quad a_0 = 0 \wedge a_1 = 1 \wedge (x = 0 \vee t = 0) \wedge a'_0 = 1 \wedge a'_1 = 0 \wedge same(V \setminus \{a_0, a_1\}) \vee \\
&\quad a_0 = 1 \wedge a_1 = 0 \wedge y' = 0 \wedge a'_1 = 1 \wedge same(V \setminus \{y, a_1\}) \vee \\
&\quad a_0 = 1 \wedge a_1 = 1 \wedge y' = 1 \wedge t' = 1 \wedge a'_0 = 0 \wedge same(V \setminus \{y, t, a_0\}) \\
&\quad b_0 = 0 \wedge b_1 = 0 \wedge x' = 1 \wedge t' = 0 \wedge b'_1 = 1 \wedge same(V \setminus \{x, t, b_1\}) \vee \\
&\quad b_0 = 0 \wedge b_1 = 1 \wedge (y = 0 \vee t = 1) \wedge b'_0 = 1 \wedge b'_1 = 0 \wedge same(V \setminus \{b_0, b_1\}) \vee \\
&\quad b_0 = 1 \wedge b_1 = 0 \wedge x' = 0 \wedge b'_1 = 1 \wedge same(V \setminus \{x, b_1\}) \vee \\
&\quad b_0 = 1 \wedge b_1 = 1 \wedge x' = 1 \wedge t' = 0 \wedge b'_0 = 0 \wedge same(V \setminus \{x, t, b_0\})
\end{aligned}
$$

where $same(S)$ represents $v'_1 = v_1 \wedge \cdots \wedge v'_n = v_n$ for the set of propositions $S = \{v_1, ..., v_n\}$. Let

$$p_1 \equiv (a_0 = 1 \wedge a_1 = 0 \vee b_0 = 1 \wedge b_1 = 0)$$
$$q_1 \equiv (a_0 = 0 \wedge a_1 = 0 \wedge b_0 = 0 \wedge b_1 = 0) \vee (x = 1 \vee y = 1)$$
$$p_2 \equiv (a_1 = 1 \vee a_0 = 1) \wedge (b_1 = 1 \vee b_0 = 1) \vee (y = 0 \wedge t = 0 \vee y = 1 \wedge t = 1)$$
$$q_2 \equiv (a_0 = 1 \wedge a_1 = 1 \vee b_0 = 1 \wedge b_1 = 1)$$

We check the two properties: $M \models p_1 R q_1$ and $M \models p_2 U q_2$.

Property 1: For $M \models p_1 R q_1$, we check the satisfiability of $[[M, \neg(p_1 R q_1)]]_k$ and $[[M, \neg(p_1 R q_1)]]_k^v$ for $k = 0, 1, 2, ...$, until the first formula is satisfiable, the second formulas is unsatisfiable, or the completeness threshold is reached. Here, we only consider the use of $[[M, \neg(p_1 R q_1)]]_k^v$ to the verification of the property (since verification is the main concern of this paper). Let $V_i = \{u_{i,0}, ..., u_{i,6}\}$ and $same(S)$ represent $u_{i+1,j} = u_{i,j}$ for each $u_{i,j} \in S$. We have

$$[[M, \neg(p_1 R q_1)]]_k^v = I(u_0) \wedge \bigwedge_{i=0}^{k-1} T(u_i, u_{i+1}) \wedge [[\neg(p_1 R q_1), u_0]]_k^v$$

where

$$I(u_0) \equiv \neg u_{04} \wedge \neg u_{05} \wedge \neg u_{06} \wedge \neg u_{00} \wedge \neg u_{01} \wedge \neg u_{02} \wedge \neg u_{03}$$

$$\begin{aligned}
T(u_i, u_{i+1}) \equiv \\
&\neg u_{i,0} \wedge \neg u_{i,1} \wedge u_{i+1,5} \wedge u_{i+1,6} \wedge u_{i+1,1} \wedge same(V_i \setminus \{u_{i,5}, u_{i,6}, u_{i,1}\}) \vee \\
&\neg u_{i,0} \wedge u_{i,1} \wedge (\neg u_{i,4} \vee \neg u_{i,6}) \wedge u_{i+1,0} \wedge \neg u_{i+1,1} \wedge same(V_i \setminus \{u_{i,0}, u_{i,1}\}) \vee \\
&u_{i,0} \wedge \neg u_{i,1} \wedge \neg u_{i+1,5} \wedge u_{i+1,1} \wedge same(V_i \setminus \{u_{i,5}, u_{i,1}\}) \vee \\
&u_{i,0} \wedge u_{i,1} \wedge u_{i+1,5} \wedge u_{i+1,6} \wedge \neg u_{i+1,0} \wedge same(V_i \setminus \{u_{i,5}, u_{i,6}, u_{i,0}\}) \vee \\
&\neg u_{i,2} \wedge \neg u_{i,3} \wedge u_{i+1,4} \wedge \neg u_{i+1,6} \wedge u_{i+1,3} \wedge same(V_i \setminus \{u_{i,4}, u_{i,6}, u_{i,3}\}) \vee \\
&\neg u_{i,2} \wedge u_{i,3} \wedge (\neg u_{i,5} \vee u_{i,6}) \wedge u_{i+1,2} \wedge \neg u_{i+1,3} \wedge same(V_i \setminus \{u_{i,2}, u_{i,3}\}) \vee \\
&u_{i,2} \wedge \neg u_{i,3} \wedge \neg u_{i+1,4} \wedge u_{i+1,3} \wedge same(V_i \setminus \{u_{i,4}, u_{i,3}\}) \vee \\
&u_{i,2} \wedge u_{i,3} \wedge u_{i+1,4} \wedge \neg u_{i+1,6} \wedge \neg u_{i+1,2} \wedge same(V_i \setminus \{u_{i,4}, u_{i,6}, u_{i,2}\})
\end{aligned}$$

$$\begin{aligned}
[[\neg(p_1 R q_1), u_0]]_k^v \equiv \\
&\bigvee_{j=0}^{k}((u_{j,0} \vee u_{j,1} \vee u_{j,2} \vee u_{j,3}) \wedge \neg u_{j,4} \wedge \neg u_{j,5} \wedge \\
&\bigwedge_{t=0}^{j-1}((\neg u_{t,0} \vee u_{t,1}) \wedge (\neg u_{t,2} \vee u_{t,3}))) \vee \bigwedge_{t=0}^{k}((\neg u_{t,0} \vee u_{t,1}) \wedge (\neg u_{t,2} \vee u_{t,3}))
\end{aligned}$$

Let us use $\varphi(k)$ to denote the conjunction of the above formulas. By feeding files with formulas representing the initial states, the transition relation and the property in required format into VERBS, we obtain that $\varphi(0)$, $\varphi(1)$ and $\varphi(2)$ are satisfiable, while $\varphi(3)$ is unsatisfiable and this proves $M \models p_1 R q_1$.

The result of running VERBS provides information to be interpreted as a path, if the result is satisfiable. For instance, for $k = 2$ and $\varphi(2)$ satisfiable, we can extract the following path from the information:

$$a_0 = 0, a_1 = 0, b_0 = 0, b_1 = 0, x = 0, y = 0, t = 0$$
$$a_0 = 0, a_1 = 1, b_0 = 0, b_1 = 0, x = 0, y = 1, t = 1$$
$$a_0 = 0, a_1 = 1, b_0 = 0, b_1 = 1, x = 1, y = 1, t = 0$$

This path information could sometimes be useful for error location, if the property is not valid. For instance, if we check $M \models Gp_2$ with $k = 4$, we obtain a path with a loop as follows.

$$a_0 = 0, a_1 = 0, b_0 = 0, b_1 = 0, x = 0, y = 0, t = 0$$
$$a_0 = 0, a_1 = 1, b_0 = 0, b_1 = 0, x = 0, y = 1, t = 1$$
$$a_0 = 1, a_1 = 0, b_0 = 0, b_1 = 0, x = 0, y = 1, t = 1$$
$$a_0 = 1, a_1 = 1, b_0 = 0, b_1 = 0, x = 0, y = 0, t = 1$$
$$a_0 = 0, a_1 = 1, b_0 = 0, b_1 = 0, x = 0, y = 1, t = 1$$

This is a path with a loop that starts from the second state and has length 3. With this path information, we know that the 4-th state of this path violates p_2. Therefore Gp_2 does not hold in M. Then we may conclude that either Gp_2 is not a necessary requirement of such a model or the model should be modified in order to avoid such a path.

Property 2: For $M \models p_2 U q_2$, we check the satisfiability of $[[M, \neg(p_2 U q_2)]]_k$ and $[[M, \neg(p_2 U q_2)]]_k^v$ for $k = 0, 1, 2, ...$, until the first formula is satisfiable, the second formulas is unsatisfiable, or the completeness threshold is reached. We have

$$[[M, \neg(p_2 U q_2)]]_k^v = I(u_0) \wedge \bigwedge_{i=0}^{k-1} T(u_i, u_{i+1}) \wedge [[\neg(p_2 U q_2), u_0]]_k^v$$

where $I(u_0)$ and $T(u_i, u_{i+1})$ are the same as that already specified previously, and $[[\neg(p_2 U q_2), u_0]]_k^v$ is as follows:

$$\bigvee_{j=0}^{k}((\neg u_{j,0} \wedge \neg u_{j,1} \vee \neg u_{j,2} \wedge \neg u_{j,3}) \wedge (\neg u_{j,5} \wedge \neg u_{j,6}) \wedge (u_{j,5} \wedge u_{j,6}) \wedge$$
$$\bigwedge_{t=0}^{j}((\neg u_{t,0} \vee \neg u_{t,1}) \wedge (\neg u_{t,2} \vee \neg u_{t,3}))) \vee \bigwedge_{t=0}^{k}((\neg u_{t,0} \vee \neg u_{t,1}) \wedge (\neg u_{t,2} \vee \neg u_{t,3}))$$

Let $\psi(k)$ denote the conjunction of this formula and $I(u_0) \wedge \bigwedge_{i=0}^{k-1} T(u_i, u_{i+1})$. We obtain that $\psi(0), \psi(1), \psi(2), \psi(3)$ are satisfiable, while $\psi(4)$ is unsatisfiable and this proves $M \models p_2 U q_2$.

Table 1. Experimental Data

Property	k	Variables	Clauses	SAT	Property	k	Variables	Clauses	SAT
$\varphi(k)$	0	7+2	13	yes	$\psi(k)$	0	7+2	18	yes
	1	14+11	127	yes		1	14+11	137	yes
	2	21+20	243	yes		2	21+20	258	yes
	3	28+29	361	no		3	28+29	381	yes
						4	35+38	506	no

Summary: Table 1 is a summary of the experimental data on a Sun Blade 1000 with 750 MHz and 512 MB. The number of variables is divided into two parts: the number of variables representing the states and that of auxiliary variables used in the transformation of the formula into CNF. The time used by BOSCH for satisfiability checking is negligible.

6   Concluding Remarks

We have presented encodings of pairs of model and formula in SAT for the purpose of both verification of valid properties and error detection, in which the encoding with the emphasis on error detection is basically the same as that in [3], and proposed an approach to verify $M \models \varphi$ in the following way.

- Start with $k = 0$;
- If $[[M, \neg\varphi]]_k^v$ is unsatisfiable, report that $M \models \varphi$ is valid;
- If $[[M, \neg\varphi]]_k$ is satisfiable, report that $M \models \varphi$ does not hold;
- If a completeness threshold is reached, report that $M \models \varphi$ is valid;
- Increase k and repeat the process.

The case-study presented in the previous section shows that this approach is useful for checking formulas that are valid in a model (though, there are also weaknesses of the approach, cf. the discussion in Section 4), in the sense that the iteration stopped before a completeness threshold is reached. Although the system presented is simple with the completeness threshold bounded by a relatively small number, it is easy to construct systems by extending the model, such that the completeness threshold is larger than any given number, while the verification can still stop when k reaches respectively 3 and 4 for the given properties. Therefore the benefit of the use of this approach could be arbitrary large compared to the use of the completeness threshold, and this extends the practical capability of SAT based model checking to the verification of valid properties.

In a survey paper [19], Prasad, Biere and Gupta pointed out that, currently, the strength of SAT-based verification techniques lies primarily in falsification. This is a remark on verification related to general temporal properties. For simple properties, there has been a lot of work and report of success, for instance, for proving simple safety and liveness properties [21,16,12,2]. This study explores the strength of SAT-based techniques for verification of general LTL properties and the case study shows that this is a promising approach for certain types of applications as demonstrated in the case study.

Acknowledgments. The author thanks anonymous referees for their constructive critics and comments that helped improving this paper.

References

1. S. Berezin and S. Campos and E. M. Clarke. Compositional Reasoning in Model Checking. Proceedings of COMPOS'97. Lecture Notes in Computer Science 1536: 81-102. 1998.
2. A. Biere, A. Cimmatti, E. Clarke, O. Strichman, and Y. Zhu. Bounded Model Checking. Advances in Computers 58, Academic Press, 2003.
3. A. Biere, A. Cimmatti, E. Clarke, and Y. Zhu. Symbolic Model Checking without BDDs. LNCS 1579:193-207. TACAS 99.

4. J. R. Burch, E. M. Clarke, K. L. McMillan, D. L. Dill, and J. Hwang. Symbolic model checking: 10^{20} states and beyond. IEEE Symposium on Logic in Computer Science 5: 428-439, 1990.
5. R. Bryant. Graph based algorithms for boolean function manipulation. IEEE Transaction on Computers 35(8):677-691. 1986.
6. E. M. Clarke, O. Grumberg and D. E. Long. Model Checking and Abstraction. ACM Transactions on Programming Languages and Systems 16(5): 1512-1542, 1994.
7. E. M. Clarke, D. Kroening, J. Ouaknine, and O. Strichman. Completeness and Complexity of Bounded Model Checking. VMCAI 2004: 85-96.
8. E. M. Clarke, D. E. Long and K. L. McMillan. Compositional Model Checking. IEEE Symposium on Logic in Computer Science 4: 353-362, 1989.
9. Satyaki Das and David L. Dill. Successive Approximation of Abstract Transition Relations. LICS 2001: 51-60.
10. E. Allen Emerson and A. P. Sistla. Symmetry and model checking. Formal Methods in System Design 9:105-131. 1995.
11. J. Gregoire. Verification Model Reduction through Abstraction. Formal Design Techniques VII, 280-282, 1995.
12. Ranjit Jhala and Kenneth L. McMillan. Interpolation and SAT-based Model Checking. CAV 2003: 1-13.
13. D. Kroening, O. Strichman. Efficient Computation of Recurrence Diameters. VM-CAI 2003: 298-309.
14. C. Loiseaux, S. Graf, J. Sifakis, A. Bouajjani and S. Bensalem. Property preserving abstractions for the verification of concurrent systems. Journal of Formal methods in System Design 6:1-35. 1995.
15. K. L. McMillan. Verification of Infinite State Systems by Compositional Model Checking. Lecture Notes in Computer Science 1703:219-234. CHARME 1999.
16. Leonardo de Moura, Harald Ruess, Maria Sorea. Bounded Model Checking and Induction: From Refutation to Verification. CAV 2003: 14-26.
17. Doron A. Peled. Software Reliability Methods. Springer-Verlag. 2001.
18. A. Pnueli. A temporal logic of concurrent programs. Theoretical Computer Science 13:45-60. 1981.
19. Mukul R. Prasad, Armin Biere, Aarti Gupta. A survey of recent advances in SAT-based formal verification. STTT 7(2): 156-173 (2005).
20. V. Roy and R. de Simone. Auto/Autograph. In Computer Aided Verification. DIMACS series in Discrete Mathematics and Theoretical Computer Science 3: 235-250, June 1990.
21. Mary Sheeran, Satnam Singh and Gunnar Stålmarck. Checking Safety Properties Using Induction and a SAT-Solver. FMCAD 2000: 108-125.
22. A. Valmaru. Stubborn sets for reduced state space generation. LNCS 483(ICATPN'89):491-515. 1989.
23. P. Wolper and P. Godefroid. Partial-order methods for temporal verification. LNCS 715(CONCUR'93):233-246. 1993.
24. W. Zhang. Combining Static Analysis and Case-based Search Space Partitioning for Reducing Peak Memory in Model Checking. Journal of Computer Science and Technology 18(6):762-770, 2003.
25. W. Zhang, Z. Huang, and J. Zhang. Parallel Execution of Stochastic Search Procedures on Reduced SAT Instances. Lecture Notes in Computer Science 2417:108-117. Springer-Verlag. 2002.

jmle: A Tool for Executing JML Specifications Via Constraint Programming

Ben Krause and Tim Wahls

Department of Mathematics and Computer Science
Dickinson College
P.O. Box 1773
Carlisle, PA 17013, USA
{krauseb, wahlst}@dickinson.edu

Abstract. Formal specifications are more useful and easier to develop if they are executable. In this work, we describe a system for executing specifications written in the Java Modeling Language (JML) by translating them to constraint programs, which are then executed via the Java Constraint Kit (JCK). Our system can execute specifications written at a high level of abstraction, and the generated constraint programs are Java implementations of the translated specifications. Hence, they can be called directly from ordinary Java code.

1 Introduction

The ability to execute a formal specification while it is being developed greatly eases the development process. Running a specification allows the developer to validate that the meaning of the specification is what was intended, providing strong intuition that the specification is correct and complete. As formal specifications are intrinsically abstract, this ability to get "hands on" experience with a specification makes developing and understanding the specification much easier. Additionally, executable formal specifications can serve as prototypes of the final implementation, and test oracles for back-to-back testing of that implementation. These benefits are accessible to nontechnical users, as they do not require reading mathematical notation, understanding proofs of system properties, and so on. Given these benefits, it is not surprising that a large number of techniques for implementing specifications have been developed [1,2,3,4,5].

In this work, we describe the jmle tool, which is used to execute specifications written in the Java Modeling Language (JML) [6]. JML is a behavioral interface specification language for Java - class definitions and method prototypes are written using Java syntax, and a JML class specification can only be correctly implemented by a Java class definition. JML is also a model-based specification language - the language provides a rich set of mathematical types (sets, sequences, bags, functions, relations, ...), which are implemented as Java classes. Each method is specified with first order pre- and postconditions written over these types, as well as the built-in types of Java. An example of a JML specification is presented in Section 3.

L. Brim et al. (Eds.): FMICS and PDMC 2006, LNCS 4346, pp. 293–296, 2007.

jmle executes JML specifications by translating them to constraint programs. It is important that executability does not compromise the abstraction and freedom from implementation bias that makes JML specifications useful, and using constraint programming techniques allows specifications written at a relatively high level of abstraction to be executed. The resulting constraint programs are executed using the Java Constraint Kit (JCK) [7], a system for creating Java implementations of constraint solvers. All parts of our system are implemented in Java, so users do not need to install any additional programming environments, and our system is completely compatible with existing tools for JML (as described in [6]). The programs that we generate are Java implementations of the corresponding specifications, and so can be called directly from Java code.

2   Implementation of jmle

We have adapted jmlc (the JML tool that generates runtime assertion checking code) [8] to automatically compile JML specifications to JCK programs as follows:

- a JML class specification is compiled to a Java class
- the model (specification only) fields become actual fields of this class
- each JML method specification is compiled to a method implementation.

The body of each translated method creates goal constraints corresponding to the original JML specification. When the method is called, these constraints become the initial constraint store, which is then simplified using special-purpose JCK solvers. The solvers can execute a large subset of JML, including \old expressions (which allow pre-state values to be used in postconditions), universally and existentially quantified assertions where the domain of the quantified variable can be determined and is finite, and nondeterministic specifications (which are executed via backtracking). The system will report an error at compile time for specifications that use features outside of this subset. Additionally, jmle will fail to execute specifications that use only these features if they do not provide sufficient information to allow the system to construct post-state values, or to simplify all of the constraints in the store. In these situations, jmle will throw an exception to indicate that it could not execute the specification.

We considered each of the Java primitive types and the JML classes implementing the JMLCollection interface (that is, the classes representing mathematical sets, sequences, bags, functions and relations) as constraint domains, and defined constraints corresponding to each operation on each of these types. We then implemented solvers for each of these domains using JCK rewriting rules. Targeting our solvers specifically for Java and JML types allowed us to compensate somewhat for the performance disadvantages of a Java implementation (as compared to the solvers found in full constraint programming languages).

3   Example

The following JML specification of class `IntList` demonstrates the kind of implicit and abstract specifications that jmle can execute. Instances of class `IntList` contain a list of integers, modeled as a `JMLObjectSequence` holding `java.lang.Integer` objects. `JMLObjectSequence` is a `JMLCollection` class that implements sequences in which elements are compared using `==` (rather than the `equals` method). The constructor and other natural methods of the class have been omitted in the interest of space.

```
//@ model import org.jmlspecs.models.JMLObjectSequence;

public class IntList {
  //@ public model JMLObjectSequence theList;

  /*@ assignable theList;
      ensures theList.int_size() == \old(theList.int_size()) &&
       (\forall Integer i; \old(theList.has(i));
         theList.count(i) == \old(theList.count(i))) &&
       (\forall int j; 0 <= j && j < \old(theList.int_size()) - 1;
         ((Integer) theList.itemAt(j)).intValue() <=
             ((Integer) theList.itemAt(j + 1)).intValue()); */
  public void sort();
}
```

The postcondition for the `sort` method asserts that the pre- and post-state values of the model field `theList` are of the same size, and then uses a universal quantifier to state that the post-state value of `theList` contains the same number of occurrences of each element as occurs in the pre-state value. Together, these assertions ensure that the post-state value is a permutation of the pre-state value. The final universally quantified assertion forces the post-state value to be sorted. When this specification is executed, the `count` constraints on the post-state value are used to search partial permutations of the pre-state value (backtracking as soon as an unsorted prefix is discovered) until a sorted permutation is found. As the running time is exponential in the length of the sequence, only small inputs (up to about 5 elements) can be used for validating this specification.

jmle first compiles this specification to a JCK program, and then to ordinary Java bytecode that uses JCK library code. Hence, the compiled specification appears to client code exactly as any Java implementation of the JML specification would (except that it is much larger and slower than a hand-coded implementation). The specification can then be executed using ordinary Java "driver" code that creates an instance of the class and calls its methods, by writing JUnit tests for the class specification, or in any other manner that a hand-coded implementation could be used. This client code can then be re-used without modification when testing other implementations of the specification.

4   Conclusion

jmle is related to several other systems that translate specifications to constraint programs (such as [1,5]), and particularly the jml-tt tool [3], which animates JML specifications. One practical difference is that these other systems do not translate specifications to implementations that can be called directly from client code. Rather, specifications are animated using an external interface. Additionally, jml-tt does not provide constraint support for executing specifications that use the JMLCollection classes.

Although jmle can execute a large subset of JML, much remains to be done. Java and JML constructs that are currently not supported include exceptional behavior specifications, signals clauses, history constraints, inheritance of specifications from interfaces, and the features added in Java 1.5. Perhaps the most critical area for future work is using jmle to execute specifications that are being developed in industrial applications, in order to investigate the usefulness of the system in practice. As such, we encourage anyone who is interested in obtaining and evaluating jmle to contact the second author via email.

References

1. Grieskamp, W.: A computation model for Z based on concurrent constraint resolution. In Bowen, J.P., Dunne, S., Galloway, A., King, S., eds.: ZB 2000: Formal Specification and Development in Z and B, First International Conference of Z and B Users. Volume 1878 of Lecture Notes in Computer Science., York, UK, Springer-Verlag (2000) 414 – 432
2. Wahls, T., Leavens, G.T., Baker, A.L.: Executing formal specifications with concurrent constraint programming. Automated Software Engineering **7**(4) (2000) 315 – 343
3. Bouquet, F., Dadeau, F., Legeard, B., Utting, M.: Symbolic animation of JML specifications. In: Proceedings of the International Conference on Formal Methods 2005 (FM'05). Volume 3582 of Lecture Notes in Computer Science., Springer-Verlag (2005) 75 – 90
4. Wahls, T.: Compiling formal specifications to Oz programs. In van Roy, P., ed.: MOZ 2004, The Second International Mozart/Oz Conference. Volume 3389 of Lecture Notes in Computer Science., Springer-Verlag (2005) 66 – 77
5. Leuschel, M., Butler, M.: ProB: A model checker for B. In Araki, K., Gnesi, S., Mandrioli, D., eds.: FME 2003: Formal Methods. LNCS 2805, Springer-Verlag (2003) 855–874
6. Burdy, L., Cheon, Y., Cok, D., Ernst, M., Kiniry, J., Leavens, G.T., Leino, K.R.M., Poll, E.: An overview of JML tools and applications. International Journal on Software Tools for Technology Transfer (STTT) **7**(3) (2005) 212–232
7. Abdennadher, S., Krämer, E., Saft, M., Schmauss, M.: JACK: A Java constraint kit. In Hanus, M., ed.: Electronic Notes in Theoretical Computer Science. Volume 64., Elsevier (2002)
8. Cheon, Y., Leavens, G.T.: A runtime assertion checker for the Java Modeling Language (JML). In Arabnia, H.R., Mun, Y., eds.: Proceedings of the International Conference on Software Engineering Research and Practice (SERP '02), Las Vegas, Nevada, USA, June 24-27, 2002, CSREA Press (2002) 322–328

Goanna—A Static Model Checker

Ansgar Fehnker[1], Ralf Huuck[1], Patrick Jayet[2,*], Michel Lussenburg[2,*], and Felix Rauch[1]

[1] National ICT Australia Ltd. (NICTA)[**] and University of New South Wales, Locked Bag 6016, NSW 1466, Australia
[2] Department of Computer Science, Swiss Federal Institute of Technology (ETH), CH-8092 Zurich, Switzerland

Abstract. In this work we present Goanna, the first tool that uses an off-the-shelf model checker for the static analysis of C/C++ source code. We outline its architecture and show how syntactic properties can be expressed in CTL. Once the properties have been defined the tool analyses source code automatically and efficiently. We demonstrate its applicability by presenting experimental results on analysing OpenSSL and the GNU coreutils.

1 Introduction

Formal design and analysis techniques are successfully applied to hardware. In fact, model checking parts of the chip design is common practice. However, the application of verification technology to existing and complex software has been much less successful.

The reasons are manifold: Full formal verification as done by interactive theorem proving is expensive. It requires a lot of time and expertise, making it often impractical for software that has a short life cycle, is not highly safety-critical, or suffers from a high pressure to market. Algorithmic verification techniques have to deal with software's infinite state space, requiring abstraction techniques to make properties of interest decidable. Suitable abstractions are typically hard to compute and the overall interaction required by the user in order to apply them to real-life software are often considerable.

One area that has been successful is static analysis [1,2]. Approaches such as abstract interpretation, data flow analysis and other static checking techniques have made it into several industrial strength tools.

In this work we present Goanna [3], a static analysis tool for C/C++ source code based on model checking. It uses the NuSMV [4] model checker as the underlying verification engine, allows the specification of user defined properties

---

[*] This work was carried out while visiting NICTA.

[**] National ICT Australia is funded by the Australian Governments Department of Communications, Information Technology and the Arts and the Australian Research Council through Backing Australias Ability and the ICT Research Centre of Excellence programs.

L. Brim et al. (Eds.): FMICS and PDMC 2006, LNCS 4346, pp. 297–300, 2007.

and scales well to commercial size software. Since Goanna does not require any user interaction it makes it particularly suited to be integrated into the software development process. Moreover, it is the first step of bringing static analysis and software model checking closer together by providing one uniform framework.

2   Technology

The basic ideas of solving static analysis problems by model checking have been first developed by Steffen and Schmidt [5]. While their main focus has been on developing a safe approximation of the program's behaviour to check for safety properties, we abandon in some cases the soundness of the analysis for effectiveness. This means we can check for full CTL including (syntactic) liveness properties.

The CTL model checking problem is encoded in two steps and we illustrate this by a simple example. First we define the atomic propositions of interest we like to reason about, e.g., whether a variable is declared, used, or assigned a value. For a variable named x we write $decl_x$, $used_x$ and $assigned_x$ for the respective propositions. We use a pattern matching approach to relate certain patterns on a program's abstract syntax tree (AST) with propositions of interest. In a second step we automatically extract the control flow graph (CFG) of a program and label it with the previously determined propositions.

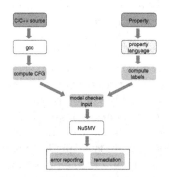

Fig. 1. Goanna architecture

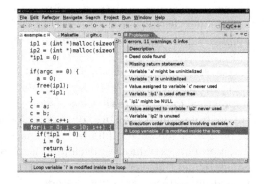

Fig. 2. Goanna results in Eclipse

The translation of an annotated CFG into a NuSMV model is rather straight-forward and the encoding can be done in an efficient way resulting in a small state space. Properties of interest can then be expressed as CTL formulae over this model. E.g., checking for uninitialised variables can be expressed as follows:

$$AG\ decl_x \Rightarrow (A\ \neg used_x\ W\ assigned_x)$$

This means we require that on all program paths if a variable is declared it must not be used until it has a value assigned or it will not be used at all. We use the weak until operator W here to include the second possibility. The latter can also point to unused variables, which is checked separately.

Our tool chain is depicted in Figure 1. We use gcc as a front end, as one of its features allows us to easily output the AST of C/C++ programs in an intermediate language. We parse the AST and on the one hand generate the CFG from it and on the other hand match patterns on the AST, which constitute the atomic propositions of a CTL formula expressing the desired property. We label the CFG with atomic propositions where their respective patterns were matched. Once the patterns and the CTL formula have been specified, the translation of the C/C++ source code into a suitable NuSMV model and its checking is fully automatic.

The current implementation is developed in OCaml. Goanna is easily integrated in Makefiles and, thus, is automatically supported by development environments such as Eclipse. A screen shot of Goanna running in combination with Eclipse can be found in Figure 2. As a result we obtain a seamless integration into the overall software development process.

3   Application

To evaluate the applicability of our tool, we examine two real-world open-source software packages: The GNU coreutils[1], which provide basic file, shell and text manipulation utilities (59 kLoC[2]), and the *OpenSSL*[3] toolkit implementing the Secure Sockets Layer (SSL) and Transport Layer Security (TLS) protocols (260 kLoC). We analyse the source code of these two packages on a recent 3.4 GHz Xeon-processor-based server.

Analysing the whole source with our current Goanna tool (which has not yet been optimised) takes slightly less than 2 minutes for the coreutils and slightly less than 29 minutes for OpenSSL. The latter is somewhat distorted by a single pathological file that takes almost 12 minutes to analyse. In practice, analysis times are typically much shorter, because the analysis can be done incrementally on the set of recently changed files only and a more in-depth study of Goanna's analysis times shows that a large majority of source files is analysed quite quickly. In fact, 72% of all source files in the coreutils are analysed in less than 1 second and 95% under 5 seconds. Similarly, for OpenSSL 83% of all files are analysed in under 1 second and again 95% under 5 seconds.

Note that the current prototype has not yet been optimised regarding execution time. Hence, there is still a lot of room for performance improvements, for example by optimising the search in the AST for patterns of interest (which currently contains redundant searches for different properties), the OCaml library we use to conduct the search on the AST (which is convenient to use but not efficient), or by changing the way in which we use NuSMV (which is

---

[1] http://www.gnu.org/software/coreutils/
[2] LoC = Lines of Code, kLoC = 1000 Lines of Codes
[3] http://www.openssl.org/

currently invoked with rather large chunks of source code at the time that could be reduced to smaller pieces).

Looking at the memory requirements of our tool we find that the maximum memory consumption of the analysis is about 65 MiB to analyse the coreutils and about 113 MiB for OpenSSL respectively. This is in both cases much below the limit set by todays PCs used by developers.

The above numbers show that the tool is already quite usable in practice. A full evaluation of course requires also an analysis of the precision of the tool, with looking at the number of real bugs found and the number of false positives reported. Such a study is very time consuming and we are still in the process of qualitatively evaluating Goanna regarding its precision. Preliminary results indicate that the precision of our approach is comparable to standard static analysis.

4   Conclusion

In this work we presented Goanna, the first static analyser purely based on an off-the-shelf model checker. We demonstrated that the approach scales well to real-life software, making it suitable for the integration into the overall software development process.

While Goanna is fast, it is not yet more precise than traditional static analysis. However, we anticipate to improve on this by incorporating more semantic-based software model checking techniques such as predicate abstraction [6]. The foundation of this integration has been laid by having a uniform framework for static analysis as well as traditional model checking.

References

1. Engler, D.R., Musuvathi, M.: Static analysis versus software model checking for bug finding. In: "VMCAI '04: 5th Intl. Conference Verification, Model Checking and Abstract Interpretation". (2004) 191–210
2. Blanchet, B., Cousot, P., Cousot, R., Feret, J., Mauborgne, L., Miné;, A., Monniaux, D., Rival, X.: Design and implementation of a special-purpose static program analyzer for safety-critical real-time embedded software. (2002) 85–108
3. NICTA: The Goanna Project. (http://ertos.nicta.com.au/research/goanna/)
4. Cimatti, A., Clarke, E., Giunchiglia, E., Giunchiglia, F., Pistore, M., Roveri, M., Sebastiani, R., Tacchella, A.: NuSMV Version 2: An OpenSource Tool for Symbolic Model Checking. In: Proc. International Conference on Computer-Aided Verification (CAV 2002). Volume 2404 of LNCS., Springer (2002)
5. Schmidt, D.A., Steffen, B.: Program analysis as model checking of abstract interpretations. In: SAS '98: Proceedings of the 5th International Symposium on Static Analysis, London, UK, Springer-Verlag (1998) 351–380
6. Ball, T., Cook, B., Levin, V., Rajamani, S.K.: SLAM and Static Driver Verifier: Technology transfer of formal methods inside Microsoft. In: IFM 2004: 4th International Conference on Integrated Formal Methods. Volume 2999 of LNCS., Springer-Verlag (2004) 1–20

Parallel SAT Solving in Bounded Model Checking*

Erika Ábrahám[1,3], Tobias Schubert[1], Bernd Becker[1],
Martin Fränzle[2], and Christian Herde[2]

[1] Albert-Ludwigs-Universität Freiburg, Germany
[2] Carl von Ossietzky Universität Oldenburg, Germany
[3] RWTH Aachen, Germany

Abstract. Bounded Model Checking (BMC) is an incremental refutation technique to search for counterexamples of increasing length. The existence of a counterexample of a fixed length is expressed by a first-order logic formula that is checked for satisfiability using a suitable solver.

We apply communicating parallel solvers to check satisfiability of the BMC formulae. In contrast to other parallel solving techniques, our method does not parallelize the satisfiability check of a single formula, but the parallel solvers work on formulae for different counterexample lengths. We adapt the method of constraint sharing and replication of Shtrichman, originally developed for sequential BMC, to the parallel setting. Since the learning mechanism is now parallelized, it is not obvious whether there is a benefit from the concepts of Shtrichman in the parallel setting. We demonstrate on a number of benchmarks that adequate communication between the parallel solvers yields the desired results.

1 Introduction

The term *Bounded Model Checking* [16,8] refers to symbolic analysis techniques checking finite unravelings of transition systems for satisfaction of a formal specification. While originally being confined to a refutation technique based on an incremental search for counterexamples of increasing length, there are now several extensions to recognize fixed points and allow system verification (see e.g. [12]). Basically, given a system together with a specification, the existence of counterexamples of increasing length $k = 0, 1, \ldots$ is expressed by first-order formulae φ_k that are checked for satisfiability by a solver suitable for the underlying logic. For discrete systems a SAT solver is used, while the analysis of linear hybrid automata, for example, requires the application of a combined SAT-LP solver. Some popular solvers are, e.g., zChaff [24], BerkMin [15], MiniSAT [13], HySat [14], MathSAT [5], CVC Lite [6], and ICS [10].

Given the high computational cost of checking large BMC instances and driven by the advent of affordable multiprocessor machines, research recently focusses on the development of *parallel* BMC techniques, too. The main line of research applies parallel solvers to the *same* BMC instance, that means, the solvers work on the satisfiability

---

* This work was partly supported by the German Research Council (DFG) as part of the Transregional Collaborative Research Center "Automatic Verification and Analysis of Complex Systems" (SFB/TR 14 AVACS).

L. Brim et al. (Eds.): FMICS and PDMC 2006, LNCS 4346, pp. 301–315, 2007.

check of the same formula φ_k. Thereby, the overall search space is divided into disjoint parts which are then treated by the involved processes.

Parallel SAT algorithms can be traced back to at least 1994, where Böhm and Speckenmeyer presented an approach for a transputer system with up to 256 processors [9]. In subsequent years, a number of more advanced implementations have been developed. Two of the most powerful distributed SAT solvers nowadays are PaSAT [27] and PaMira [25]. Both tools use many of the latest improvements in sequential SAT solving, e.g., conflict-driven learning combined with non-chronological backtracking, various efficient decision heuristics, and zChaff's concept of watched literals. Additionally, PaMira employs *Early Conflict Detection BCP* and *Implication Queue Sorting* [20]. Both features together result in a significantly reduced number of clauses the BCP stage has to deal with, and by this substantially increase the overall performance.

PaSAT and PaMira also support the exchange of information about the problem instance under consideration, usually encoded as *conflict clauses*. In traditional parallel SAT solvers the processes independently generate conflict clauses for their own usage (in [27] also referred to as lemmas). Every conflict clause, generated by a conflicting assignment of the variables, is a piece of information that the corresponding process has learnt about the problem and that might be helpful to cut off parts of the search space. If the solvers share their knowledge, consisting of their conflict clauses, then this information enables them to avoid descending into parts of the search tree that have already been proven to be unsatisfiable by other solvers. If a solver, receiving a conflict clause, is currently analyzing such an unsatisfiable sub-tree then it can immediately stop its analysis of the current part of search tree. Thus exchanging conflict clauses is helpful in increasing the performance of the overall system.

In this work we introduce a different kind of parallelization of BMC: instead of applying a distributed SAT solver to a single BMC instance, we do concurrently address the satisfiability check for *different* counterexample lengths through parallel solvers.

In a naive setting, without relating the SAT-checks of different BMC instances, such a parallelization would immediately provide ideal, *linear* speedup. Solvers optimized towards BMC do, however, exploit constraints of earlier SAT-checks to aggressively prune the search space of the subsequent ones (see e.g. [26,14,2]). These pruning techniques are developed for sequential execution. Our primary goal is to preserve linear speedup even when parallelizing such optimized BMC engines.

The BMC formulae φ_k for different ks describe similar problems, i.e., the formulae have some common sub-formulae. We make use of this fact and let the parallel solvers exchange information in the form of conflict clauses. However, knowledge sharing is not as simple as before: In parallel SAT solvers like PaSAT or PaMira, as described above, the solvers communicate conflict clauses in order to help each other with information which part of the state space does not need to be searched through. Without modification, this method does not work in our case when the different solvers have to solve different problems: a conflict clause, generated by some solver, may result from clauses that some of the other solvers do not have in the clause set they have to satisfy and thus those other solvers must not make use of that conflict clause.

In [14,2] we dealt with *constraint sharing and replication (CSR)* in the style of Shtrichman [26]. Recall, that sequential BMC defines a sequence of SAT problems

$\varphi_0, \varphi_1, \ldots$, which are checked sequentially one after the other. CSR can be seen as a method of communicating at the interface between the different BMC SAT problems: the conflict clauses after the SAT check of one problem are analyzed and used to prune the check of the following BMC problems when possible. Constraint sharing re-uses those conflict clauses whose generation involved only clauses that are part of the next SAT problem, too. Constraint replication shifts conflict clauses in time: if all clauses involved in the generation of a conflict clause are present in the next SAT check with the same variables but at different computation depth, i.e., with different indices, then we can insert that conflict clause after renaming the variables accordingly. Constraint replication can also be applied on-the-fly. In that case, shifted copies of new conflict clauses are added immediately after conflict resolution, when possible.

In the context of the AVACS project [1] we are interested in the analysis of linear hybrid automata. Linear hybrid automata are transition systems with mixed discrete-continuous behavior. Additionally to the discrete part, time passes while control stays in the locations, and the values of the real-valued variables evolve continuously according to some linear flows.[1] Consequently, the BMC formulae for linear hybrid automata are not only Boolean combinations of Boolean variables, but additionally of some linear constraints over the real-valued variables.

In [14,2] we showed that CSR speeds up the satisfiability checks remarkably not only for discrete systems (e.g. circuits) but also for linear hybrid automata. Our experience shows that in the mixed discrete-continuous case the search in the real domain, involving some LP solving techniques, is very time-consuming. Thus, for the hybrid case CSR is especially important to make use of the conflicts found in the real domain.

Now, if we start several SAT solvers running in parallel and solving BMC problems for different counterexample lengths *independently using CSR*, the expected speedup of CSR plus the linear speedup due to parallelization will not be reached. The reason is the following: In sequential BMC with CSR, each BMC instance is solved completely before the next check starts. As CSR re-uses the conflict clauses, the forthcoming check will not run into the same conflicts again. However, in the parallel case, if the different solvers do not communicate, they may find the same conflict independently, thus wasting time.

Even if the solvers communicate, yielding constraint sharing, we need to apply constraint replication to the communicated clauses immediately after communication, in order to get the same speedup as in the sequential case for each of the solvers. Without immediate constraint replication, the different solvers often find the same problem at different time instances. This entails on the one hand unnecessarily finding the same conflict twice, and on the other hand increased constraint propagation time: constraint replication at the beginning of the SAT checks may produce lots of subsumed clauses.

In this paper we integrate the standard parallel SAT-solving paradigm and CSR in the context of BMC. We parallelize the learning algorithm using communicating SAT solvers such that we can keep the speedup of the sequential case for each of the parallel solvers and at the same time, due to parallelization, the experiments show an additional linear speedup.

---

[1] The linearity of the flows allows us to express the BMC formulae in a decidable logic for which efficient solvers are available.

The rest of the paper is structured as follows: Section 2 deals with BMC and SAT solving, and Section 3 describes our parallelization technique. In Section 4 we present the experimental results, and finally we draw conclusions in Section 5.

2   Bounded Model Checking

We first give a short review of bounded model checking [16,8] and briefly describe how state-of-the-art SAT solvers check satisfiability of propositional formulae. In this paper we restrict ourselves to safety properties; for lifeness properties see e.g. [8].

2.1   Encoding Finite Transition Systems

Given a finite transition system, its initial condition and transition relation can be described by propositional formulae $Init(s)$ and $Trans_t(s, s')$ for all $t \in T$ with T the set of transitions, where s and s' explicitly denote the free variables occurring in the given formulae: $s = (v_0, \ldots, v_m)$ contains all variables and $s' = (v'_0, \ldots, v'_m)$ copies of them in order to describe the target valuation after a transition.

Let $Safe(s)$ be a propositional formula describing a safety property of the system. Counterexamples of a fixed length k, i.e., runs of length k violating the property $Safe$ in their final state, can be described by the following formula:

$$\varphi_k(s_0, \ldots, s_k) = Init(s_0) \wedge \left(\bigwedge_{i=0,\ldots,k-1} \bigvee_{t \in T} Trans_t(s_i, s_{i+1}) \right) \wedge \neg Safe(s_k) .$$

Starting with $k = 0$ and iteratively increasing $k \in \mathbb{N}$, BMC checks whether the BMC instances $\varphi_0, \varphi_1, \varphi_2, \ldots$ are satisfiable. The algorithm terminates at depth k if φ_k is satisfiable, i.e., an unsafe state is reachable from an initial state in k steps.

2.2   Satisfiability Checking

The formulae φ_k describing counterexamples of length k are checked for satisfiability by a traditional SAT solver.

First, the Boolean formula is transformed into a *conjunctive normal form* (CNF). In order to keep the formula as small as possible, auxiliary Boolean variables are used to build the CNF [30]. A formula in CNF-form is a conjunction of *clauses*, while each clause is the disjunction of *literals*. We distinguish between positive literals being Boolean variables, and negative literals being negated ones.

In order to satisfy the formula, each of the clauses must be satisfied, i.e., at least one literal in each clause must be true. The SAT solver *assigns values* to the variables in an iterative manner. After each *decision*, i.e., free choice of an assignment, the solver *propagates* the assignment by searching for *unit-clauses*, i.e., clauses in that all literals but one are already false; the remaining literal is implied to be true, since otherwise the clause would not be satisfied.

If two unit-clauses imply different values for the same variable, a *conflict* occurs. In this case a conflict analysis can take place which results in *nonchronological back-tracking* and *conflict learning* [22,33]. Intuitively, the solver applies resolution to some unit-clauses, using the implication tree, and inserts a new *conflict clause* thereby strengthening the problem constraints and restricting the state space for further search.

For performing the experiments of Section 4, we developed our own SAT solver, which – from a top level point of view – works quite similarly to zChaff [24] and Berk-Min [15]. While not being as optimized as other state-of-the-art solvers, it incorporates most of the algorithms employed by modern SAT engines to accelerate the search process, like conflict-driven learning, non-chronological backtracking, and watched literals. The development of our own solver was necessary for our experiments, since there is no parallel solver available which supports constraints over the reals, as necessary for checking hybrid automata.

Our tool exploits the concept of lazy theorem proving [7] to provide a decision procedure for LinSAT formulae, i.e. CNFs where the atoms can be both propositional variables and linear inequations over the reals. It tightly integrates a Davis-Putnam style SAT solver with a linear programming (LP) routine, combining the virtues of both methods: LP adds the capability of solving large conjunctive systems of linear inequalities over the reals, whereas the SAT solver accounts for fast Boolean search and efficient handling of disjunctions (see e.g. [32,5,7,11]). The basic idea of the integration is to build a Boolean abstraction of the hybrid problem by replacing each non-propositional constraint occuring in the input formula by a fresh auxiliary Boolean variable. The SAT solver checks the satisfiability of a Boolean abstraction, while the LP solver checks the consistency of the assignments in the real domain.

2.3 Symmetries of BMC Problems

The formulae of BMC problems have a special structure: they describe computations, starting from an initial state, executing k transition steps, and leading to a state violating the specification. Accordingly, the set of clauses generated by the SAT solver can be grouped into clauses describing (1) the initial condition (*I-clauses*), (2) one of the transitions (*T-clauses*), and (3) the violation of the specification (*S-clauses*). Furthermore, the T-clauses can be grouped into k groups describing the k computation steps. Those k T-clause groups describe the same transition relation, but at different time points. That means, they are actually the same up to variable renaming. For example, some BMC problem for counterexample length $k = 3$ could be represented by a clause set like this:[2]

I-clauses	*T-clauses*	*S-clauses*
$(x_0 \vee y_0), \dots$	$(x_0 \vee y_1 \vee \overline{z}_0), \dots, (x_1 \vee \overline{y}_1 \vee z_0)$	$(y_3 \vee z_3), \dots$
	$(x_1 \vee y_2 \vee \overline{z}_1), \dots, (x_2 \vee \overline{y}_2 \vee z_1)$	
	$(x_2 \vee y_3 \vee \overline{z}_2), \dots, (x_3 \vee \overline{y}_3 \vee z_2)$	

We say that a T-clause describing the ith transition step is a $T_{[i-1,i]}$-clause, since it involves state-vector components with indices $i-1$ to i; we call $i-1$ the *lower boundary* and i the *upper boundary* of the clause. Similarly, I-clauses are also called $I_{[0,0]}$-clauses

---

[2] The value of a Boolean variable v in the ith state of the computation is denoted by v_i, the value of its negation by $\overline{v}_i$.

and S-clauses in iteration k also $S_{[k,k]}$-clauses. We also write $T_{[i,\leq j]}$ when being unspecific about the upper boundary $i \leq j' \leq j$; we use similar notation for I- and S-clauses and lower boundaries. Furthermore we say that we *shift* a clause by d meaning that we replace each variable index i by $i + d$.

2.4 Constraint Sharing and Replication

Usually, the conflict clauses learned during the SAT check of a BMC instance φ_k get removed before the satisfiability check of the next BMC instance φ_{k+1}. However, they can also be partially re-used in the style of Shtrichman [26], thereby excluding search paths from the SAT search already before the search starts: If a conflict clause is the result of a resolution applied to clauses that are present also in the next BMC iteration, then the same resolution could be applied in the new setting, too, and thus we can keep those conflict clauses. Furthermore, if all clauses used for resolution to generate a conflict clause are present with a shifted instance, then the same resolution could be made using the shifted instances. Accordingly, we distinguish between the following conflict clause types:

- $I_{[0,j]}$-*conflict-clauses* are the result of resolution applied to $I_{[0,\leq j]}$- and possibly $T_{[\geq 0,\leq j]}$-(conflict-)clauses. They can be re-used without any modification in all iterations $k' \geq j$.
- $S_{[i,k]}$-*conflict-clauses* are the result of resolution applied to $S_{[\geq i,k]}$- and possibly $T_{[\geq i,\leq k]}$-(conflict-)clauses. They can be re-used in all iterations $k' \geq k - i$ when shifted by $k' - k$.
- $T_{[i,j]}$-*conflict-clauses* are the result of resolution applied to (conflict) clauses of type $T_{[\geq i,\leq j]}$. They can be inserted in iteration $k' \geq j - i$ in all instances shifted by $-i, \ldots, k' - j$.
- *IS-conflict-clauses* are the result of resolution applied to (conflict) clauses of both types I and S. They cannot be re-used in other iterations.

In a sequential setting, a single solver is used to check all the BMC formulae for incremental counterexample lengths. Thereby, the conflict clauses can be re-used in the above manner: before each iteration k, the conflict clauses generated in the iterations less than k are analyzed and adapted to the depth k. Alternatively, T-conflict-clauses can also be replicated on-the-fly directly after their generation, within the width of the current BMC instance.

2.5 Extension to Linear Hybrid Automata

The previously presented approach can be naturally extended to BMC of linear hybrid automata. *Hybrid automata* [3,18] are a formal model to describe systems with combined discrete and continuous behavior. We consider the class of *linear hybrid automata*, whose behavior can be described by Boolean combinations of linear (in)equations over real-valued variables.

Applying BMC, counterexamples of a linear hybrid automaton can be encoded similarly to that of a finite transition system. In the hybrid case the underlying logic is the existential fragment of the first-order logic over $(\mathbb{R}, +, <, 0, 1)$, i.e., formulae are the

Boolean combinations of (in)equations over linear terms using real-valued variables. The satisfiability check of those formulae is done by a combined SAT-LP solver. For a detailed description of the encodings, the satisfiability checks, and for optimizations see [2].

3   Parallel BMC

We are going to transfer the BMC technique into a parallel setting. Assume n solvers running in parallel, where each solver checks a different BMC instance of the same system for satisfiability. An additional master process makes the book-keeping of the BMC problems already checked and assigns the unresolved instances to the distributed solvers. When becoming idle due to completion of its previous instance, each solver asks the master process which counterexample length to check next. Starting at 0, the master distributes the problem instances in the order of increasing unraveling depth.

After receiving the first BMC instance to check, each solver generates the corresponding clause set and starts the satisfiability check.

If one of the solver runs into a conflict, it generates a conflict clause, which is then sent to the master process. In addition to the literals constituting the clause, the solver sends the conflict's type and boundaries. For example, the sequence of literals of a $T_{[i,j]}$-conflict-clause is augmented with the information that it is a T-clause with boundaries i to j. IS-conflict-clauses are not sent, since they cannot be re-used in other iterations. After sending, the solver replicates the conflict clause, if possible, and the SAT algorithm continues. During replication, we remember which clause is the highest instance of the conflict, i.e., the one shifted by the highest value. To avoid multiple copies, only the highest instance will be shifted in future.

In order to benefit from conflict clauses generated by other solvers, each solver frequently fetches from the master new conflict clauses sent by the other solvers. Note that solvers receiving some clauses do actually process a BMC instance of another length than the sending solver does. Therefore, a solver checking iteration k may receive a $T_{[i,j]}$-conflict-clause with $j - i > k$. In this case, the solver must not yet make use of the clause, but may of course memorize it for later use when it attacks a larger BMC instance.

Thus each receiving solver checks whether it can currently make use of the received conflict clause. If so, the clause and possible replications get inserted into the solver's clause set. S-clauses get shifted into the right position before insertion. Again, when replicating T-clauses, the highest instance is marked. It is important that received conflict clauses are replicated on-the-fly directly after their reception, and not later before the next satisfiability check: If different shifted instances of the same conflict are found or received, the solver would replicate all of them before the next check, resulting in multiple copies of the same clauses. That would increase propagation time.[3] Replicating on-the-fly alleviates this problem, since all processes insert all possible shifted instances within a small time frame, such that the probability that two solvers find the same conflict in the same or in a different instance is significantly reduced (see Section 4 for some experimental results).

---

[3] One could also employ subsumption checks to avoid this effect.

Otherwise, if the width of the conflict is too large for the current iteration of the receiver, the clause is inserted as a *silent* clause: though it is syntactically stored, it will not influence the current SAT check.

Before a solver starts a new iteration, it adds possible new replications of the already active T-conflict-clauses, adapts the S-conflict-clauses, and deletes all IS-conflict-clauses. Note that, in order to reduce subsumption, only the highest instances get shifted with all possible positive values, and the new highest instances get marked. Besides that, the solver checks which silent clauses may be activated and eventually replicated. In the above example, the solver may make use of the previously silent $T_{[i,j]}$-conflict-clause when the new iteration k' that the solver is going to check is at least $j - i$. In this case the conflict clause shifted by $-i, \ldots, k' - j$ can be added to the clause set.

The above mechanisms aim at preserving linear speedup from parallelization even if constraint sharing is used, a mechanism that suits the sequential world better. Communication between the solvers has the role of knowledge transfer, such that none of the solvers has disadvantages from the fact that it does not compute each BMC instance incrementally, but skips over some that get computed by the others. In the next section we show by means of benchmarks that without exchanging conflict clauses, the effect of constraint sharing and replication in the parallel case does not yield the same speedup as in the sequential setting.

4   Experimental Results

We implemented a prototype SAT solver which works mainly as described in Section 2.2. For communication we use MPICH2 [17], an implementation of the Massage Passing Interface (MPI) standard. It is worth to mention that our approach works well only if communication is *very fast*. To satisfy this requirement, we designed the communication as simple as possible. It is very important that a process does not loose time by checking incoming messages if no message is there, or that it does not have to wait long when sending. Direct synchronous communication between the solvers seems to be disadvantageous, since the processes have to wait for each other. MPICH supports buffered, i.e., asynchronous communication, only in a restricted manner: there is a fast algorithm to check whether there have arrived some messages along some channels, but it can happen that a process must wait when sending if the buffer is full. For that reason, we introduce an additional master process acting as a communication hub and providing sufficient buffer capacity (see also [19,23] for such master-solutions). The master receives messages from the solvers, buffers copies for all other solvers, and forwards them when the solvers are ready to receive. This way communication can proceed without long waiting times. Thus we have one more process, but the solvers themselves need negligible time for communication (for experimental results see Figure 3).

For our experiments we used a network of 4 computers each having two AMD Opteron(tm) 250/252 processors with 2400-2600 MHz, 1024 kB L2 cache, and between 4 and 16 GB of main memory. We measured the relative performance of 1, 2, and 5 parallel solvers supported by a master process. We performed experiments with communicating solvers using constraint sharing and replication. To test the effectiveness of these algorithmic enhancements, we also measured the running times when the solvers do not use constraint sharing and replication or when no communication takes place.

The running times (except in Figure 3) are given as the CPU times per processor for each BMC iteration. For each iteration, the CPU time per processor is computed as the runtime of that instance divided by the number of parallel solvers. Thus the depicted values correspond to the system time: the sum of the values for the iterations 0 to k is approximately the system time up to iteration k.

The running times contain the CPU times for the SAT checks including the communication times as well as the times needed for the generation of the BMC problems for the different counterexample lengths. We have run each experiment 4 times and show the average results below.

To give an example of a discrete benchmark, we applied BMC to check invariants of UsbPhy (Universal Serial Bus), taken from the VIS benchmark suite [28,31]. As for hybrid automata, we applied BMC to Fischer's mutual exclusion protocol [21] for 2, 3, and for 4 processes. The specification states the mutual exclusion property, i.e., that at each time point there is at most one process in its critical section. The Railroad Crossing [18] is a further hybrid benchmark. It consists of 3 parallel automata modeling a train, a railroad crossing gate, and a controller. The specification requires that the gate is always fully closed when the train is close to the railroad crossing. Further hybrid benchmarks are a model of an elastic approach to train distance control and a model of a Renault Clio 1.9 DTI RXE, equipped with a simple cruise controller as reported in [29].[4] To test the behavior also for deep counterexample search, we have chosen invariant safety properties, i.e., there exists no counterexample for the systems used, but for the elastic train train control at depth 22.

Figure 1 shows results for different settings for Fischer's protocol for 4 processes. Figure 1 a) motivates CSR by comparing the running times for a single solver with and without CSR. For all the benchmarks applied, CSR leads to substantially shorter running times.

Figure 1 b) shows what happens when parallelizing the solver with applying CSR but without communicating information between the solvers. I.e., CSR is only applied locally on a per-solver basis. The speedup due to parallelization is very small; the running times are sometimes even longer for the parallelized version than for the sequential setting. The reason is illustrated in Figure 1 c) by listing the number of conflicts in each iteration. Without communication, the number of conflicts may increase when employing more solvers. When a solver has computed a problem instance k and starts to compute a new instance $k' > k$, then during the computation of the new instance k' it will find conflicts that already occurred in other solvers computing instances between k and k'. However, since the solver computing k' is not informed about those conflicts, it may run into the same conflicts again.

To complete the picture, Figure 1 d) compares the running times when using CSR with and without communication between the solvers. Figure 1 e) shows the

---

[4] These two hybrid benchmarks are very complex in the real domain, i.e., the satisfiability check of their BMC instances requires a massive usage of the LP-solver. This yields, at least for deep BMC instances, long running times even for only a few conflicts.

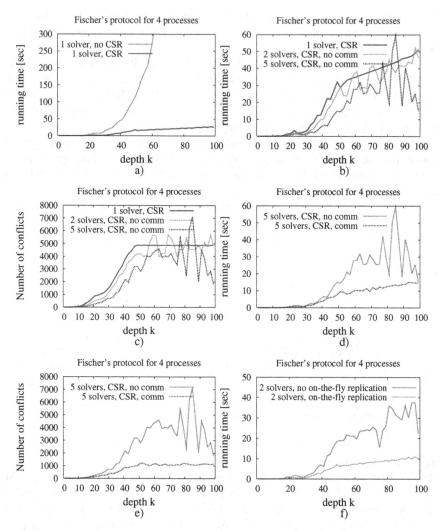

Fig. 1. CPU times per processor and iteration in different settings for Fischer's protocol for 4 processes

corresponding number of conflicts for each iteration. Communication between the solvers massively reduces the increment of the conflicts with a growing number of solvers. We observe that communication becomes more and more important when increasing the number of solvers, since the number of iterations that are skipped over by a solver after finishing instance k and before starting a new instance k' increases, and so the number of conflict clauses the solver did not get informed about. The last diagram f) of Figure 1 shows for two communicating solver using CSR the effect when not applying on-the-fly constraint replication, but replicating only at the beginning of a new SAT check.

Figure 2 shows the running times for the different benchmarks, when applying parallelized CSR and communication. We obtain, that the running times of the sequential

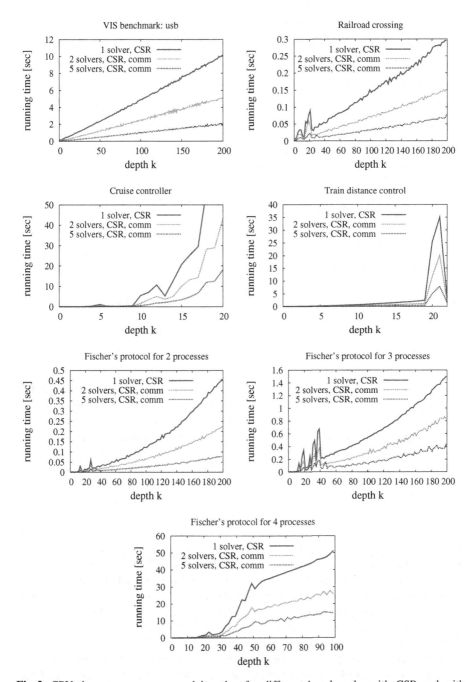

Fig. 2. CPU times per processor and iteration for different benchmarks with CSR and with communication

Bench-mark	depth k	M	1 solver		2 solvers		5 solvers		10 solvers	
			Time	C	Time	C	Time	C	Time	C
usb	200	1	973 (0)	13	487 (0)	13	201 (0)	13	99 (0)	13
		2	990 (0)	1	491 (0)	1	197 (0)	1	100 (0)	1
		3	– (–)	–	504 (< 1)	1	201 (< 1)	1	103 (< 1)	1
Railroad crossing	200	1	798 (0)	72	399 (0)	72	165 (0)	72	81 (0)	72
		2	14 (0)	3	8 (0)	5	7 (0)	10	10 (0)	17
		3	– (–)	–	7 (< 1)	3	3 (< 1)	4	1 (< 1)	6
Cruise controller	20	1	2254(0)	798	1129(0)	798	454 (0)	798	225 (0)	798
		2	317 (0)	262	278 (0)	275	183 (0)	387	148 (0)	582
		3	– (–)	–	158 (< 1)	240	67 (< 1)	235	37 (< 1)	240
Train distance control	22	1	120 (0)	9	62 (0)	9	27 (0)	9	13 (0)	9
		2	85 (0)	8	50 (0)	8	22 (0)	9	10 (0)	10
		3	– (–)	–	49 (< 1)	7	20 (< 1)	8	10 (< 1)	9
Fischer 2	200	1	242 (0)	258	121 (0)	258	47 (0)	258	23 (0)	258
		2	16 (0)	6	9 (0)	10	5 (0)	24	3 (0)	46
		3	– (–)	–	8 (< 1)	6	3 (< 1)	5	1 (< 1)	6
Fischer 3	200	1	5688(0)	10830	2815(0)	10830	1093(0)	10830	552 (0)	10830
		2	63 (0)	265	39 (0)	517	27 (0)	1222	24 (0)	2323
		3	– (–)	–	35 (1)	330	17 (2)	360	8 (3)	297
Fischer 4	100	1	nn (nn)	nn	nn (nn)	nn	3945(0)	43514	1971(0)	43514
		2	1186(0)	3268	1054(0)	6086	787 (0)	11944	820 (0)	23045
		3	– (–)	–	637 (11)	3289	341 (15)	3658	277 (9)	4259

Fig. 3. Total running times. Notations: Time=total SAT check time for all iterations up to depth k (average communication time per solver in brackets) in seconds, C=average number of conflicts per iteration, M=method. We distinguish the methods (1) without CSR and without communication, (2) with CSR but without communication, and (3) with CSR and with communication.

solver using CSR, which is already substantially shorter than without CSR, can be further improved by a linear factor when using our parallel approach with communication.

Finally, Figure 3 shows for each benchmark the total running times, i.e., the sum of the running times for all instances, up to the shown depth. We distinguish the methods (1) without CSR, (2) with CSR but without communication, and (3) with CSR and with communication. Besides the running times, the average total communication time per solver is given in brackets. Note, that the communication is very fast; for most benchmarks it amounts to less than 1 second. Additionally, the average number of conflicts per iteration is listed. Again, the results are presented for 1, 2, and for 5 solvers. To give an impression of the behavior for more massive parallelism, we also list the results for 10 parallel solvers. However, since we had only 8 CPUs but 11 processes (10 solvers and a master), the listed running times, i.e., the average CPU times per solver, do not correspond to the real system times observed, but state an estimated running time for 11 processors calculated based on measurements stemming from a time-sharing execution.

Since one single solver cannot communicate, the corresponding fields are not filled. By nn we denote that the computation was timed out because the total running time reached the timeout threshold of 10000 seconds.

To conclude the results, the experiments show that communication between parallel solvers using CSR yields an additional linear speedup to the improvement of CSR. Without communication, the effect of CSR gets worse with an increasing number of solvers.

5 Conclusions

In this paper we introduced a parallel SAT solving technique for bounded model checking. The parallelization is different from existing approaches: instead of solving a single problem instance using parallel solvers, we let different solvers solve different BMC instances. In order to speed up the search, we apply constraint sharing and replication and let the solvers communicate the conflict clauses found during their SAT checks. The experiments performed show that the positive effect of constraint sharing and replication can only be preserved under parallelization if the solvers communicate the conflict clauses among themselves. With communication, the full advantage of sequential CSR can be maintained in the concurrent setting, yielding linear speedup from parallelization.

The efficiency of other parallelization techniques strongly depends on how the state space gets split. The experiments show that our parallelization technique is stable: Each BMC instance is solved by a single solver, and thus we do not have to split the state space. With parallelized CSR we obtain a remarkable and consistent speedup for all benchmarks used. As for future work, we will compare our results with the application of other parallel SAT-solvers.

Furthermore, motivated by the positive findings obtained using our approach, we will combine both kinds of parallelization: on the one hand, instead of having a single solver checking each BMC instance, we will use a group of solvers for this purpose that work in parallel on the same problem by sharing the search space, similarly to PaSAT and PaMira. On the other hand, we will parallelize those solver groups as described in this paper to check for existence of counterexamples of different lengths. This combined approach we will build on the HySAT solver [14] which is more efficient than the prototype solver employed for these experiments.

Acknowledgements. We thank Marc Herbstritt for supplying us with benchmarks. We thank Henrik Bohnenkamp, Peter Schneider-Kamp, and Ivan Zapreev for their valueable comments on the paper.

References

1. AVACS: Automatic Verification and Analysis of Complex Systems.
   http://www.avacs.org.
2. E. Ábrahám, B. Becker, F. Klaedke, and M. Steffen. Optimizing bounded model checking for linear hybrid systems. In R. Cousot, editor, *Proc. of VMCAI'05*, volume 3385 of *LNCS*, pages 396–412. Springer-Verlag, 2005.
3. R. Alur, C. Courcoubetis, T. Henzinger, P. Ho, X. Nicollin, A. Olivero, J. Sifakis, and S. Yovine. The algorithmic analysis of hybrid systems. *Theoretical Computer Science*, 138:3–34, 1995.
4. R. Alur and D. A. Peled, editors. *Procceedings of the 16th International Conference on Computer Aided Verification, CAV'04, Boston, MA, USA, July 13-17, 2004*, volume 3114 of *LNCS*. Springer-Verlag, 2004.
5. G. Audemard, P. Bertoli, A. Cimatti, A. Kornilowicz, and R. Sebastiani. A SAT based approach for solving formulas over boolean and linear mathematical propositions. In A. Voronkov, editor, *Proc. of CADE'02*, volume 2392 of *LNAI*. Springer-Verlag, 2002.

6. C. Barrett and S. Berezin. CVC Lite: A new implementation of the cooperating validity checker. In Alur and Peled [4], pages 515–518.

7. C. Barrett, D. Dill, and A. Stump. Checking satisfiability of first-order formulas by incremental translation to SAT. In *Proc. of CAV'02*, 2002.

8. A. Biere, A. Cimatti, E. Clarke, and Y. Zhu. Symbolic model checking without BDDs. In W. R. Cleaveland, editor, *Proc. of TACAS'99*, volume 1579 of *LNCS*, pages 193–207. Springer-Verlag, 1999.

9. M. Böhm and E. Speckenmeyer. A Fast Parallel SAT-Solver – Efficient Workload Balancing. *Annals of Mathematics and Artificial Intelligence*, 17(3–4):381–400, 1996.

10. L. de Moura and H. Rueß. An experimental evaluation of ground decision procedures. In Alur and Peled [4], pages 162–174.

11. L. de Moura, H. Rueß, J. Rushby, and N. Shankar. Embedded deduction with ICS. In B. Martin, editor, *Proc. of HCSS'03*, 2003.

12. L. de Moura, H. Rueß, and M. Sorea. Bounded model checking and induction: From refutation to verification. In W. J. Hunt and F. Somenzi, editors, *Proc. of CAV'03*, number 2725 in LNCS, pages 14–26. Springer-Verlag, 2003.

13. N. Eén and N. Sörensson. An extensible SAT-solver. In E. Giunchiglia and A. Tacchella, editors, *Proc. of SAT'03*, volume 2919 of *LNCS*, pages 502–518. Springer-Verlag, 2003.

14. M. Fränzle and C. Herde. Efficient proof engines for bounded model checking of hybrid systems. *ENTCS*, 133:119–137, 2005.

15. E. Goldberg and Y. Novikov. BerkMin: A Fast and Robust SAT-Solver. In *Proc. of DATE'02*, pages 142–149, 2002.

16. J. F. Groote, J. W. C. Koorn, and S. F. M. van Vlijmen. The safety guaranteeing system at station Hoorn-Kersenboogerd. In *Proc. of Compass'95*, pages 57–68. National Institute of Standards and Technology, 1995.

17. W. Gropp, E. Lusk, N. Doss, and A. Skjellum. A high-performance, portable implementation of the MPI message passing interface standard. *Parallel Computing*, 22(6):789–828, 1996.

18. T. Henzinger. The theory of hybrid automata. In *Proc. of LICS'96*, pages 278–292. IEEE, Computer Society Press, 1996.

19. F. Holmén, M. Leucker, and M. Lindström. UppDMC – a distributed model checker for fragments of the μ-calculus. In L. Brim and M. Leucker, editors, *Proc. of PDMC'04*, volume 128/3 of *Electronic Notes in Computer Science*. Elsevier Science Publishers, 2004.

20. M. Lewis, T. Schubert, and B. Becker. Speedup Techniques Utilized in Modern SAT Solvers – An Analysis in the MIRA Environment. In *8th International Conference on Theory and Applications of Satisfiability Testing*, 2005.

21. N. Lynch. *Distributed Algorithms*. Kaufmann Publishers, 1996.

22. J. Marques-Silva and K. Sakallah. GRASP: A Search Algorithm for Propositional Satisfiability. *IEEE Transactions on Computers*, 48(5):506–521, 1999.

23. I. Melatti, R. Palmer, G. Sawaya, Y. Yang, R. M. Kirby, and G. Gopalakrishnan. Parallel and distributed model checking in Eddy. In *Proc. of SPIN'06*, pages 108–125, 2006.

24. M. W. Moskewicz, C. F. Madigan, Y. Zhao, L. Yang, and S. Malik. Chaff: Engineering an efficient SAT solver. In *Proc. of DAC'01*, pages 530–535, 2001.

25. T. Schubert, M. Lewis, and B. Becker. PaMira – a Parallel SAT Solver with Knowledge Sharing. In *6th International Workshop on Microprocessor Test and Verification*, 2005.

26. O. Shtrichman. Accelerating bounded model checking of safety formulas. *Formal Methods in System Design*, 24(1):5–24, 2004.

27. C. Sinz, W. Blochinger, and W. Küchlin. PaSAT – Parallel SAT-Checking with Lemma Exchange: Implementation and Applications. In *Proc. of LICS'01*, 2001.

28. The VIS Group. VIS: A system for verification and synthesis. In *Proc. of CAV'96*, volume 1102 of *LNCS*, pages 428–432. Springer-Verlag, 1996.

29. F. D. Torrisi. *Modeling and Reach-Set Computation for Analysis and Optimal Control of Discrete Hybrid Automata.* Doctoral dissertation, ETH Zürich, 2003.
30. G. Tseitin. On the complexity of derivations in propositional calculus. In *Studies in Constructive Mathematics and Mathematical Logics.* 1968.
31. VIS Benchmark Suite. http://vlsi.colorado.edu/~vis.
32. S. A. Wolfman and D. S. Weld. The LPSAT engine & its application to resource planning. In T. Dean, editor, *Proc. of 16th International Joint Conference on Artificial Intelligence*, pages 310–315, 1999.
33. L. Zhang, C. Madigan, M. Moskewicz, and S. Malik. Efficient Conflict Driven Learning in a Boolean Satisfiability Solver. In *IEEE/ACM International Conference on Computer-Aided Design*, 2001.

Parallel Algorithms for Finding SCCs in Implicitly Given Graphs*

Jiří Barnat and Pavel Moravec

Department of Computer Science, Faculty of Informatics
Masaryk University Brno, Czech Republic

Abstract. We examine existing parallel algorithms for detection of strongly connected components and discuss their applicability to the case when the graph to be decomposed is given implicitly. In particular, we list individual techniques that parallel algorithms for SCC detection are assembled from and show how to assemble a new more efficient algorithm for solving the problem. In the paper we also report on a preliminary experimental study we did to evaluate the new algorithm.

1 Introduction

The problem of finding strongly connected components (SCCs), known also as SCC decomposition, is one of the basic graph problems that finds its applications in many research fields even beyond the scope of computer science. An efficient algorithmic solution to this problem is due to Tarjan [20] who showed that given a graph with n vertices and m edges, it is possible to identify and list all strongly connected components of the graph in $O(n + m)$ time and $O(n)$ space. Besides Tarjan's serial algorithm, several parallel algorithms have been designed to solve the problem. Tarjan's algorithm (and its variants) strongly rely on the depth-first search post-ordering of vertices whose computation is known to be *P*-complete [19], and thus, difficult to be parallelized. Therefore, parallel algorithms avoid the depth-first search of the graph and build on different approaches.

A parallel algorithm relying on matrix multiplication was described in [14] and further improved in [10,1]. The algorithm works in $O(log^2 n)$ time in the worst case, however, to achieve the complexity it requires $O(n^{2.376})$ parallel processors. As graphs that we are typically dealing with in practice contain millions of vertices the algorithm is practically unusable and is only interesting from the theoretical point of view. Another parallel algorithm for finding SCCs was given in [12]. Its general idea is to repeatedly pick a vertex of the graph and identify the component the vertex belongs to using two parallel reachability procedures. The algorithm proved to be efficient enough in practice, which resulted in several theoretical improvements of it [17,15]. The worst time complexity of the algorithm is $O(n \cdot (n + m))$, nevertheless, the algorithm exhibits $O(m \cdot log n)$ expected time [12].

---

* This work has been partially supported by the Grant Agency of Czech Republic grant No. 201/06/1338.

L. Brim et al. (Eds.): FMICS and PDMC 2006, LNCS 4346, pp. 316–330, 2007.

In this paper, we discuss known as well as suggest new techniques used for parallel SCC decomposition, and we explore their restrictions if they are applied to implicitly given graphs. Efficient parallel algorithms for SCC decomposition will find their application in distributed formal verification tools such as DiVinE [2], CADP [13], DUPPAAL [4], LiQuor [8], etc. Namely, they will allow the tools to verify stochastic systems, compute τ-confluence, or verify systems with fairness constraints or properties given by other than Büchi automata.

The rest of the paper is organized as follows. We recapitulate basic terms and definitions in Section 2, describe known and new techniques used in parallel algorithms for solving the problem in Section 3, and list known parallel algorithms along with their pseudo-codes in Section 4. In Section 5 we report on an experimental study we performed, and in Section 6 we conclude the paper with several remarks and plans for future work.

2   Preliminaries

We start by brief summary of basic terms and definitions. Let V be a set of vertices, $E \subseteq V \times V$ a set of directed edges, and $v_0 \in V$ a vertex. We denote by $G = (V, E, v_0)$ a directed graph with initial vertex v_0.

Let $G = (V, E, v_0)$ be a directed graph. A sequence of edges $(u_0, u_1), (u_1, u_2)$, $\ldots, (u_{n-1}, u_n)$ is called a *path* from vertex u_0 to vertex u_n. We say that vertex v *is reachable* from vertex u if there is a path from u to v or $u = v$. A *strongly connected component* (SCC) is a subset $C \subseteq V$ such that for any vertices $u, v \in C$ u is reachable from v. A strongly connected component C is *maximal* if there is no strongly connected component C' such that $C \subsetneq C'$. A maximal strongly connected component C is *trivial* if C is made of a single vertex c and $(c, c) \notin E$. Henceforward, we speak of maximal strongly connected components as of strongly connected components.

Let W_G be the set of all strongly connected components of graph $G = (V, E, v_0)$. A directed graph of strongly connected components of graph G is defined as $SCC(G) = (W_G, H_G, w_0)$, where w_0 is the component that contains the initial vertex v_0, and $H_G \subseteq W_G \times W_G$ is the set of edges between members of W_G. $(w_1, w_2) \in H_G$ if there are vertices $u_1 \in w_1$ and $u_2 \in w_2$ such that $(u_1, u_2) \in E$. Note that the graph of strongly connected components of any directed graph is acyclic.

A graph could be given in many ways. For purpose of this paper (and according to our needs) we consider graphs that are given implicitly. A graph is given implicitly if it is defined by its initial vertex and a function returning immediate successors of arbitrary vertex. Within the context of implicitly given graphs there are some restrictions the algorithms have to follow. If an algorithm requires any piece of information that cannot be concluded from the implicit definition of the graph, the algorithms have to compute the information first. For example, there is no way to directly identify immediate predecessors of a given vertex from the implicit definition of the graph. If the algorithm needs to enumerate immediate predecessors, then all the predecessors must be computed and stored first.

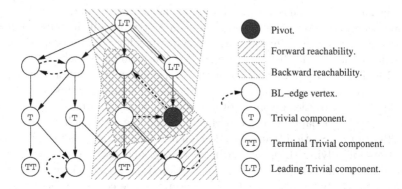

Fig. 1. Component detection, identified subgraphs, and trivial components

Similarly, to number vertices of an implicitly given graph means to enumerate all its vertices first. For numbering vertices of implicitly given graphs a parallel procedure was introduced in [13]. Note that vertices of an implicitly given graph are trivially reachable from the initial vertex.

The reason for dealing with implicitly given graphs comes from practice. In many cases, the description of rules according to which the graph could be generated is more space efficient than the enumeration of all vertices and edges. The difference might be quite significant. For example, in the context of model checking [9], the implicit definition of the graph is up to exponentially more succinct compared to the explicit one. This is commonly referred to as the state explosion problem [9].

3   List of Techniques

Before describing individual parallel algorithms we give the basic principles and list common techniques that all later given algorithms use. We hope this allow us to describe the algorithms and analyze their behavior in more compact and clear way.

Basic Principle

All parallel algorithms we present in Section 4 build on the same technique that was originally presented in [12]. The graph to be decomposed is split into two parts. The *decomposed* part of the graph consisting of already identified components, and the *not-yet-decomposed* part of the graph consisting of vertices that have not been classified into strongly connected components yet. The basic step of each algorithm consists of picking a vertex from the *not-yet-decomposed* part of the graph, the so called *pivot*, and identifying the component the selected vertex belongs to. Having a pivot, the strongly connected component the pivot belongs to is determined as the intersection of sets of all predecessors and successors of the given pivot [12]. The structure of all algorithms is then a simple loop in which the basic step is repeated until the *not-yet-decomposed* part becomes empty. The basic step is illustrated on the example graph depicted in Figure 1. Note that the *not-yet-decomposed* part of the graph is further structured as explained below.

Reachability Relation

Computation of the reachability relation is the core procedure used in all the algorithms. The task of the procedure is to identify all vertices that are reachable from a given vertex. The standard breadth-first or depth-first traversals of the graph can be employed to do so using $O(n)$ space and $O(n + m)$ time.

The reachability procedures are the first place where parallelism appears in the algorithms. The parallelization of a reachability procedure became the standard technique [6,7,21,16]. The so called *partition function* is used to assign every vertex of the graph to a single processor that is responsible for exploration of the vertex. Every processor participating the parallel computation maintains its own set of already explored vertices and its own list of vertices to be explored. If a vertex has been explored previously (it is in the set of explored vertices), then its re-exploration is omitted, otherwise, its immediate successors are generated and distributed into lists of vertices to be explored according to the partition function.

The algorithms we describe in the next section use, in addition to the notion of *forward reachability*, the notion of *backward reachability*. The task of a backward reachability procedure is to identify all vertices that a given vertex can be reached from. The procedure for backward reachability mimics the behavior of the procedure for the forward reachability except it uses immediate predecessors instead of immediate successors during graph traversal. While forward reachability can be performed using only the implicit definition of the graph, the backward reachability, as explained above, requires a list of immediate predecessors to be computed and stored for every vertex first.

Trivial Strongly Connected Components

Considering the basic algorithmic approach to SCC decomposition, the detection of trivial components is quite inefficient. If the pivot itself is a trivial component, both forward and backward reachability procedures perform useless work. There is rather small improvement in omitting the backward reachability procedure in the case the forward procedure did not hit the pivot, however, the forward procedure still performs $O(n + m)$ work. Therefore, any technique that prevents trivial components from becoming pivots has significant impact on practical performance of the algorithm.

A possible approach for doing so builds on the elimination of leading and terminal trivial components from the *not-yet-decomposed* part of the graph. In particular, every vertex that has zero predecessors must be a trivial component and as such it can be immediately removed (along with all incident edges) from the *not-yet-decomposed* part of the graph. Removing such a vertex may, however, produce new vertices without predecessors that can be removed in the same way. We refer to this recursive elimination technique as to the *One-Way-Catch-Them-Young* elimination (OWCTY) [11]. The technique can be applied in the analogue way also to vertices without successors (Reversed OWCTY). The improved version of the basic parallel algorithm that perform OWCTY elimination procedures before selection of the pivot was described in [15]. We stress that only leading and terminal trivial components may be identified in this way. Trivial components that are neither leading nor terminal may still be chosen as pivots. The graph depicted in Figure 1 contains all three types of trivial components: leading trivial components (LT), terminal trivial components (TT), and trivial components that are neither leading nor terminal (T).

Regarding implicitly given graphs the OWCTY elimination techniques suffer from the difficulty of identifying vertices with zero predecessors or zero successors. Basically, a complete reachability of the *not-yet-decomposed* part of the graph has to be performed to list those vertices. This reachability does not increase the theoretical complexity, however, it may play significant role in the practical performance of the algorithm.

Finally, let us mention that in many cases trivial components of the graph are of a little interest. Therefore, it make sense to save running time by avoiding their explicit enumeration that can be done using a single additional reachability procedure.

Pivot Selection

Pivot selection plays a significant role in the complexity of the algorithm. Imagine we always pick a pivot belonging to a component that has no descendant components in the component graph of the *not-yet-decomposed* part. Due to the acyclicity of the component graph such a component always exists. Having such a pivot all vertices belonging to the corresponding component can be identified using only a single forward reachability initiated at the pivot and restricted to the *not-yet-decomposed* part of the graph. Decomposing the graph to SCCs in this manner results in a linear time procedure. Unfortunately, to pick pivots so that the condition above is satisfied means to pick pivots in the depth-first search post-ordering, which is, as stated in the introduction, difficult to be done in parallel. Since the optimal pivot selection is difficult, pivots are typically selected randomly. A random pivot selection leads to $O(m \cdot \log n)$ expected time as claimed in [12].

In the explicit case, we can presuppose that vertices are numbered. Therefore, picking a random pivot corresponds to the generation of a random number. However, the problem occurs if a pivot has to be selected among vertices of the *not-yet-decomposed* part of the graph. As we are not aware of any $O(1)$ time and $O(1)$ space technique for a single pivot selection, we suggest a technique whose complexity is $O(n)$ space and $O(n)$ time if time and space complexity are summed for all pivot selection procedures called within a single run of the algorithm. The technique is applicable to implicitly given graphs as well. First, each participating processor enqueues newly discovered vertices in a local queue when doing the very first forward reachability of the graph. Then, a new pivot

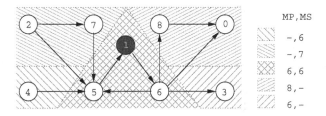

Fig. 2. Subgraphs identified with maximal predecessors (MP) and maximal successors (MS) if the propagations of MPs and MSs are initiated at pivot vertex

can be selected among the heads of the local queues. However, if the vertex on the head of a local queue belongs to the *decomposed* part of the graph, it is dequeued and the next head is considered to be a candidate for pivot selection. Moreover, in the case of implicitly given graphs, the procedure organizing vertices into local queues can be combined with the procedure computing the immediate predecessors of vertices producing thus no overhead at all.

As we are typically not interested in trivial components, we suggest a completely new improvement in pivot selection. The idea is to prevent some trivial strongly connected components from being selected as pivots. We achieve this with the definition of the so called *candidate set*, i.e. the set of vertices among which pivots are chosen. Our intention is to terminate the algorithm once all candidate pivots have been selected and the corresponding components identified. If the candidate set contains initially at least one vertex for every non-trivial component of the graph, it must be the case that after the algorithm terminates the remaining *not-yet-decomposed* part of the graph is made of trivial components only. Generally, the smaller the candidate set is, the fewer trivial components are chosen as pivots. What we use for computing the candidate set is the concept of the so called *back-level edge* [3]. It is known that every cycle, and thus every non-trivial strongly connected component, contains at least one back-level edge, which is an edge that leads from a vertex with some distance from the initial vertex of the graph to a vertex with equal or smaller distance from the initial vertex of the graph. Let us call the destination vertex of a back-level edge a *BL-edge* vertex. We suggest the candidate set to be the set of *BL-edge* vertices. Note that *BL-edge* vertices can be computed during the initial reachability procedure using the level-synchronized breadth-first search of the graph [3]. As depicted in the graph in Figure 1, some trivial components can never become pivots considering *BL-edge* vertices as pivot candidates.

Independent Subgraphs

In every iteration of the outermost loop of the basic algorithm the *not-yet-decomposed* part of the graph is split into several disjoint subgraphs. Let alone the identified component, these are the subgraph induced by vertices out of the component but explored during the forward reachability, subgraph induced by vertices out of the component but explored during the backward reachability,

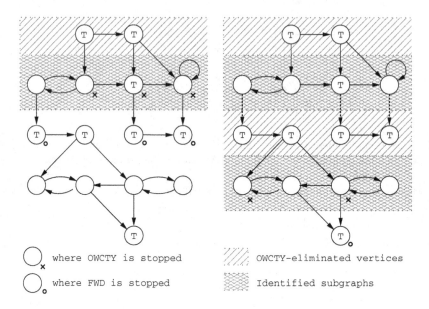

Fig. 3. Two steps of OWCTY-BWD-FWD independent subgraph identification

and subgraph induced by vertices that were not explored in that iteration at all. See example in Figure 1. An important observation [12] is that decomposing one of these subgraphs into strongly connected components is completely independent of the decomposition of other subgraphs. Therefore, the subgraphs may be viewed as if they were three independent graphs for the next step of the algorithm, which introduces two major improvements. First, three independent decomposition procedures may be performed in parallel increasing thus the amount of parallelism, second, every independent procedure may be restricted to explore vertices within the subgraph avoiding thus useless exploration of vertices out of the subgraph. Let us call the number of independent subgraphs produced in every iteration of the outermost loop (excluding the identified component) the *degree of parallelism* of the algorithm. Note that the number of the independent subgraphs grows exponentially with the number of iterations. Thus, if p is the number of available processors and d is the degree of parallelism, then after $log_d(p)$ iterations the number of independent subgraphs may exceed the number of available processors.

In the case of implicitly given graphs, vertices of a given subgraph are partitioned among processors according to the partition function. Therefore, all the single decomposition procedures share all processors participating the computation. Unfortunately, this requires to perform as many independent distributed termination detection procedures as there are single decomposition procedures running in parallel, which is quite technically involved and may actually be a reason for preventing individual decomposition procedures from being executed concurrently in practice. Also note that considering independent subgraphs, efficient pivot selection becomes complicated. In particular, we are not aware of any technique that could be used for selection of a random pivot from a subgraph without actually performing the whole subgraph exploration first. Also identifying leading and terminal trivial components in a subgraph results in a reachability procedure performed on the subgraph before the subgraph is decomposed. That is why we did not considered the leading and terminal trivial components elimination in all of the algorithms.

There is a technique that allows to identify more than three subgraphs in a single iteration [17]. Suppose the vertices of the graph are arbitrarily linearly ordered. Then, the maximal preceding vertex and maximal succeeding vertex can be computed for any vertex of the graph using an $O(n \cdot m)$ procedure [5]. If the forward and backward reachability procedures are extended to propagate maximal preceding and succeeding vertices, respectively, new subgraphs can be identified according to the maximal predecessors and successors associated to vertices in the subgraph. All vertices of the strongly connected component that the selected pivot belongs to, must have the same maximal predecessor and successor. Due to the pivot selection the maximal predecessors are computed only in the subgraph induced by vertices reachable from the pivot (forward reachability) while the maximal successors are computed for vertices that can reach the pivot (backward reachability). A possible result after a single iteration on a subgraph is depicted in Figure 2. In the original approach described in [17], the maximal predecessors and successors were computed over the complete graph. Regarding the number of identified components none of the approaches is better.

In the following we suggest a completely new technique to identify independent subgraphs in $O(n + m)$ time. The technique employs OWCTY elimination technique succeeded with backward and forward reachability procedures. A graph and two steps of the new technique performed on the graph are depicted in Figure 3. The OWCTY elimination procedure, if initiated from the vertex with zero predecessors, eliminates all leading trivial components and visits some vertices of all components immediately reachable from the eliminated trivial ones. Visited but not eliminated vertices are shown as vertices with a little cross. A backward reachability performed from vertices with the little cross identifies one independent subgraph. Note that this subgraph contains exactly all strongly connected components immediately reachable from the eliminated trivial components. Having the subgraph a forward reachability procedure restricted to the subgraph is performed from the vertices with little cross. This procedure stops on vertices outside the subgraph but immediately reachable from the subgraph (vertices with the little circle). Among these vertices there might be some that have predecessors only in the previously identified subgraph. These vertices must be trivial components, and therefore, they can be used as vertices to start the next OWCTY elimination procedure from. Figure 3 shows two successive steps of the subgraph identifying procedure OWCTY-BWD-FWD. We stress that the procedure may detect many independent subgraphs while performing only $O(n + m)$ work.

4   Algorithms

Having described all the techniques, we can now present individual algorithms. All pseudo-codes listed below describe the core parts of the algorithms. We neither list the initial reachability procedure that must be performed in order to compute the predecessor function in the implicit case, nor we list many technical details related to implementation, parallelization, distribution, etc.

F-B

The F-B algorithm [12] is the basic algorithm that all other presented algorithms build on. In the following pseudo-code, we describe a single procedure that is initially called for the complete set of vertices of the graph to be decomposed and then called recursively for identified independent subgraphs. A pivot is selected using procedure PIVOT and the set of vertices reachable in forward and backward manner are computed using parallel reachability procedures FWD and BWD. Both reachability procedures have two parameters. Besides the vertex or vertices to start from, each reachability procedure is also given a set of vertices that its exploration is limited to. This ensures that given a subgraph, the procedure will explore only immediate successors or predecessor of vertices within the subgraph. The sets of vertices as computed by forward and backward reachability procedures are referred to as F and B, respectively. Having computed both sets F and B, a new component is identified as the intersection of F and B, and recursive calls for three new subgraphs are made. Note that if it is necessary, the procedure is able to select pivots among given set of candidates.

```
 1  proc F-B(V, candidates)
 2     if (V ≠ ∅)
 3        then p := PIVOT(V ∩ candidates)
 4             F := FWD(p, V)
 5             B := BWD(p, V)
 6             SCCs := SCCs ∪ {F ∩ B}
 7             in parallel do
 8                F-B(F ∖ B, candidates)
 9                F-B(B ∖ F, candidates)
10                F-B(V ∖ (F ∪ B), candidates)
11             od
12     fi
13  end
```

In our experimental study we also considered a slightly modified version of the basic algorithm. In particular, we implemented a version in which the backward reachability procedure was restricted to the vertices discovered by the preceding forward reachability procedure, i.e. line 5 in the pseudo-code is changed to

$$B := BWD(p, F).$$

This modification decrease the degree of parallelism, but produce a procedure where exploration of some vertices is omitted compared to the original algorithm. One could tend to see this technique as an improvement, however, our experiments proved that neither of the versions was significantly better then the other. Our explanation for the lack of improvement in some cases is that the subgraphs identified as $(V \smallsetminus (F \cup B))$ become actually larger causing thus more work to be done in subsequent recursive calls to the procedure.

MP-MS

Algorithm MP-MS [17] extends the previous algorithm with the maximal predecessors and maximal successors concept. Compared to algorithm F-B, the improvement is in the subgraph detection, see Section 3. In order to compute the maximal predecessors and successors, parallel procedures FWD and BWD have to be replaced with new parallel procedures FWD-MAXPRED and BWD-MAXSUCC, respectively. Besides computing the same reachability relation as procedures FWD and BWD, the new procedures also identify subgraphs according to the maximality of predecessors or successor and return lists of those vertices whose order is used to refer to a subgraph. These $SuccList$ and $PredList$ are then used to perform parallel recursive calls on identified subgraphs. See the pseudo-code below. Recall that the time complexity of both new procedures is $O(n \cdot m)$, which is worse than if simple reachability procedures are used. However, the bad complexity is paid off with the degree of parallelism being much higher compared to the degree of parallelism of algorithm F-B. Finally, let us mention that also algorithm MP-MS is capable of selecting pivots among given set of candidates.

```
1  proc MP-MS(V, candidates)
2    if (V ≠ ∅)
3      then p := PIVOT(V ∩ candidates)
4           F, PredList := FWD-MAXPRED(p, V)
5           B, SuccList := BWD-MAXSUCC(p, V)
6           SCCs := SCCs ∪ {F ∩ B}
7           in parallel do
8               MP-MS(V ∖ (F ∪ B), candidates)
9               MP-MS(F[k, −], candidates) foreach k ∈ PredList
10              MP-MS(B[−, k], candidates) foreach k ∈ SuccList
11          od
12   fi
13 end
```

O-B-F

Algorithm O-B-F is completely a new algorithm we suggest in this paper. The core idea of the algorithm is to partition the component graph to the so called O-B-F levels and then call any algorithm (F-B in our case) to decompose individual levels of the component graph into strongly connected components. Recall that the component graph can be partitioned to those levels in linear time using the new technique described in Section 3.

The procedure O-B-F performs the detection of levels in the level by level manner. It is started with the complete set of vertices as the graph to be decomposed, and with the initial vertex as the vertex to start the exploration from. In every single call of the procedure one O-B-F level is detected. The set of remaining vertices, denoted with V, is appropriately shrunk, candidates for initial vertices of V (the so called *Seeds*) are computed, and two procedures are initiated in parallel. First, a procedure to decompose the subgraph identified with the O-B-F level, second, procedure O-B-F to identify other levels in the remaining set V. Recursive calls to procedure O-B-F terminates when all the levels are recognized and the set of remaining vertices is empty.

Every single O-B-F level is detected using standard procedures. First of all, leading trivial components of the remaining graph are eliminated using procedure OWCTY. The procedure computes the set of leading trivial components (*Eliminated*) and the set of vertices on which the elimination process stopped (*Reached*). Eliminated vertices are removed from set V of remaining vertices and the standard backward reachability procedure is performed from vertices in *Reached* and restricted to vertices in V. As the backward procedure is restricted to V, it computes exactly vertices belonging to the top most level in the component graph of V. These vertices (denoted with B) are removed from set V of remaining vertices and the decomposition of the level is initiated as an independent parallel procedure. Note that the set of potential pivots can be restricted to vertices in *Reached* because every strongly connected component belonging to the level must contain at least one vertex from *Reached*. A forward reachability (FWD-SEEDS) is also performed on vertices in B in order to identify vertices immediately below the current level, which are exactly vertices that become *Seeds* for the next call to procedure OWCTY in the next recursive call of the procedure O-B-F. Note that vertices in *Seeds* that belong to non-trivial strongly connected components are moved directly to set *Reached* within procedure OWCTY.

```
1  proc O-B-F(V, Seeds)
2    if (V ≠ ∅)
3      then Eliminated, Reached = OWCTY(Seeds, V)
4           V := V ∖ Eliminated
5           B := BWD(Reached, V)
6           V := V ∖ {B}
7           F, Seeds := FWD-SEEDS(Reached, B)
8           in parallel do
9              F-B(B, B)
10             O-B-F(V, Seeds)
11          od
12   fi
13 end
```

5   Experimental Evaluation

We have implemented and experimentally evaluated quite a few algorithms described in this paper. The algorithms were implemented using the DiVinE Library [2] as the library providing support for parallel and distributed generation of implicitly given graphs. The common library used gives approximately the same level of enhancement of all implementations, thus, the experimental comparison is quite fair. All experiments were conducted on a network of ten Intel Pentium 4 2.6 GHz workstations each having 1 GB of RAM and 100Mbps switched Ethernet connection.

The graphs we use to evaluate our implementations come from DiVinE Library distribution. They are listed in Table 1 along with their important characteristics, namely, the number of vertices (**Vertices**), number of edges (**Edges**), numbers of trivial and non-trivial strongly connected components (**T. SCCs**, **N. SCCs**), and the time needed for sequential decomposition into strongly connected components using Tarjan's algorithm (**Tarjan**). Value $n.a.$ means that the sequential decomposition algorithm exceeded available amount of RAM. For the purpose of the distributed experiments, all the graphs were distributed using the default hash-based partition function implemented in DiVinE Library.

We implemented and experimentally evaluated six different algorithms. Algorithms **F-B**, **MP-MS**, and **O-B-F** directly correspond to algorithms presented in Section 4. Algorithm **F-RB** is the modified version of algorithm **F-B**, i.e. the version where the backward reachability procedure is restricted to vertices explored during the preceding forward reachability procedure. If the name of the algorithm is extended with suffix (**B**), then the algorithm was initiated considering *BL-edge* vertices as pivot candidates. We have not implemented the modification of algorithms **F-B** and **MP-MS** that includes elimination of leading and terminating trivial components on the given subgraph before the subgraph is decomposed [15,18]. The reason is that we are not aware of any technique that would identify vertices with zero predecessors or zero successors in the given subgraph without actually exploring the subgraph first, which makes the approach inefficient in the case of implicitly given graphs.

All our implementations explicitly avoid concurrent performance of the decomposition procedures on independent subgraphs. In particular, if an independent decomposition procedure is about to be initiated, its assignment is stored and its initiation postponed. There are several reasons for this. First, the number of processors we have at our hand is very limited. Therefore, parallel procedures would very soon produce a non-trivial overhead caused by switching the context of CPUs depreciating thus the measured values. Second, as already mentioned in Section 3, appropriate termination detection becomes technically involved if independent parallel procedures share CPUs. Moreover, pivot selection within the given subgraph would generally introduce additional reachability procedure performed on every discovered independent subgraph if the subgraphs should be decomposed in parallel. And third, as the algorithms perform parallel reachability procedures most of the time, we have not observed idling of individual workstations. Therefore, we believe that the parallelism of the decomposition

Table 1. Summary of graphs

Name	Vertices	Edges	T. SCCs	N. SCCs	Tarjan
DrivingPhilsK3	6307240	12950475	16	1	4:51
DrivingPhilsK3_4	10301529	24055321	3170354	2680	10:27
Elevator12_2	8591334	89419176	2004966	2	13:21
Lifts6	16364845	50088312	7231789	8052	n.a.
LookUpProc10_3	16562363	33464135	1603283	2	n.a.
MutBak4	9384762	31630895	1881088	15	30:07
MutMcs4	1241948	4456310	9718	39	33
Phils14_1	9565935	124357142	531442	28	n.a.
Pet6err	1060048	6656522	208436	25075	4:29
Rether9_2	7663993	9624242	81831	5	16:38
Train8_2	11740214	37389502	5273750	50858	3:10:44

Table 2. Runtimes (hours:minutes:seconds)

Graph	F-B	F-B (B)	F-RB (B)	MP-MS	MP-MS (B)	O-B-F
DrivingPhilsK3	2:13	1:58	2:08	17:20	22:43	1:57
DrivingPhilsK3_4	n.a.	3:41:37	n.a.	n.a.	n.a.	4:30:36
Elevator12_2	n.a.	n.a.	n.a.	n.a.	n.a.	9:06
Lifts6	n.a.	5:15:46	n.a.	n.a.	n.a.	5:47:44
LookUpProc10_3	n.a.	n.a.	n.a.	n.a.	n.a.	16:36
MutBak4	n.a.	2:31:31	1:42:31	n.a.	n.a.	1:29:09
MutMcs4	7:32	37	23	26:21	34:32	23
Phils14_1	2:42:03	18:36	18:30	n.a.	n.a.	21:31
Pet6err	n.a.	n.a.	n.a.	n.a.	n.a.	4:53:47
Rether9_2	1:13:01	27:57	8:23	4:13:29	2:14:05	17:11
Train8_2	n.a.	2:09:54	1:52:21	n.a.	n.a.	n.a.

procedures would bring nothing but increased complexity of the implementations. Actual runtimes needed by all the algorithms to decompose the graphs are reported in Table 2. Value *n.a.* denotes now that the runtime of the algorithm exceeded 10 hours time limit.

We find the experimental results very interesting. First, we were slightly surprised with the practical inefficiency of the algorithm based on maximal predecessors and maximal successors. Its performance is far beyond performance of other algorithms proving that the decomposition into many subgraphs is not worth unless it is done in $O(n + m)$ time. Second, quite interesting result is that the restriction of the set of vertices that can be selected for pivots play significant role in practice. Note that in the case of algorithm **F-B**, the *BL-edge* vertices yielded roughly speed up of to ten. In the case of algorithm **MP-MS** they did not generally help at all, for which we blame the procedures with $O(n \cdot m)$ time complexity whose bad performance cut off any improvements made in pivot selection. Third, algorithm **O-B-F** proved to have big potential as it was the fastest algorithm in many cases, and sometimes even the only algorithm that was able to perform the decomposition within the given time limit. Finally, let us mention that according to our preliminary experiments, there were cases where the parallel algorithms if executed on ten workstations, outperformed even the optimal Tarjan's algorithm.

6 Conclusion and Future Work

In this paper we tried to list and evaluate all known techniques used in parallel algorithms for decomposition of implicitly given graphs into strongly connected components, and compare the parallel algorithms that exploit them. We also introduced two completely new techniques that the parallel algorithms can employ. In particular, we suggested how *BL-edge* vertices can be profited from if they are used as pivot candidates, and how the graph can be decomposed into subgraphs preserving SCCs using linear time and parallel technique OWCTY-BWD-FWD. Both newly suggested techniques have shown their superior strength in our experimental study.

We would especially like to emphasize that the newly suggested procedure shows not only practical usefulness, but also a theoretically interesting behavior. In particular, it may be proved that graphs whose components exhibit a chain-like structure, can be decomposed in parallel in the optimal linear time. Generally, using the technique we are able to give a parallel algorithm for solving the SCC decomposition problem working in $O(h \cdot (n + m))$ time, where h is the maximal number of strongly connected components on an acyclic path in a single *O-B-F* level.

Although, the preliminary results are encouraging, we are well aware of the immaturity of our experimental evaluation. We intend to perform thorough experimental study on larger set of inputs including algorithms with elimination of leading and terminal trivial components in the future. We also intend to improve implementations of the algorithms, in particularly, we would like to come up with a reasonable pivot selection procedure that would allow us to implement and experimentally evaluate virtually concurrent decomposition of the independent subgraphs. Finally, we intend to incorporate the best algorithms in the distributed verification environment DiVinE, so that the tool is capable of distributed and parallel verification of stochastic systems as well as verification of properties given by other than Büchi automata.

Let us also mention that we have tried to come up with some algorithms that avoid backward reachability procedure being thus perfectly suitable for the decomposition of implicitly given graphs. However, all our attempts resulted in algorithms whose practical performance was quite poor and discouraging.

References

1. Nancy Amato. Improved processor bounds for parallel algorithms for weighted directed graphs. *Inf. Process. Lett.*, 45(3):147–152, 1993.
2. J. Barnat, L. Brim, I. Černá, P. Moravec, P. Ročkai, and P. Šimeček. Divine – a tool for distributed verification. To appear in proceedings of CAV 2006.

3. J. Barnat, L. Brim, and J. Chaloupka. Parallel Breadth-First Search LTL Model-Checking. In *18th IEEE International Conference on Automated Software Engineering (ASE'03)*, pages 106–115. IEEE Computer Society, Oct. 2003.

4. G. Behrmann. A performance study of distributed timed automata reachability analysis. In *Proc. Workshop on Parallel and Distributed Model Checking*, volume 68 of *Electronic Notes in Theoretical Computer Science*. Elsevier Science Publishers, 2002.

5. L. Brim, I. Černá, P. Moravec, and J. Šimša. Accepting Predecessors are Better than Back Edges in Distributed LTL Model-Checking. In *5th International Conference on Formal Methods in Computer-Aided Design (FMCAD'04)*, volume 3312 of *LNCS*, pages 352–366. Springer-Verlag, 2004.

6. S. Caselli, G. Conte, and P. Marenzoni. Parallel state space exploration for GSPN models. In G. De Michelis and M. Diaz, editors, *Applications and Theory of Petri Nets 1995*, volume 935 of *LNCS*, pages 181–200. Springer-Verlag, 1995.

7. G. Ciardo, J. Gluckman, and D.M. Nicol. Distributed State Space Generation of Discrete-State Stochastic Models. *INFORMS Journal of Computing*, 1997.

8. Frank Ciesinski and Christel Baier. LiQuor: A tool for Qualitative and Quantitative Linear Time analysis of Reactive Systems, 2006.

9. E. M. Clarke, O. Grumberg, and D. A. Peled. *Model Checking*. The MIT Press, Cambridge, Massachusetts, 1999.

10. Richard Cole and Uzi Vishkin. Faster optimal parallel prefix sums and list ranking. *Inf. Comput.*, 81(3):334–352, 1989.

11. K. Fisler, R. Fraer, G. Kamhi, M. Y. Vardi, and Z. Yang. Is there a best symbolic cycle-detection algorithm? In *Proc. Tools and Algorithms for Construction and Analysis of Systems*, volume 2031 of *LNCS*, pages 420–434. Springer, 2001.

12. Lisa K. Fleischer, Bruce Hendrickson, and Ali Pinar. On identifying strongly connected components in parallel. *Lecture Notes in Computer Science*, 1800:505–511, 2000.

13. H. Garavel, R. Mateescu, and I.M Smarandache. Parallel State Space Construction for Model-Checking. In *Proceedings of the 8th International SPIN Workshop on Model Checking of Software (SPIN'01)*, volume 2057 of *LNCS*, pages 200–216. Springer-Verlag, 2001.

14. Hillel Gazit and Gary L. Miller. An improved parallel algorithm that computes the bfs numbering of a directed graph. *Inf. Process. Lett.*, 28(2):61–65, 1988.

15. William McLendon III, Bruce Hendrickson, Steven J. Plimpton, and Lawrence Rauchwerger. Finding strongly connected components in distributed graphs. *J. Parallel Distrib. Comput.*, 65(8):901–910, 2005.

16. F. Lerda and R. Sisto. Distributed-memory model checking with SPIN. In *Proceedings of the 6th International SPIN Workshop on Model Checking of Software (SPIN'99)*, volume 1680 of *LNCS*. Springer-Verlag, 1999.

17. S. Orzan. *On Distributed Verification and Verified Distribution*. PhD thesis, Free University of Amsterdam, 2004.

18. S.M. Orzan and J.C. van de Pol. Detecting strongly connected components in large distributed state spaces. Technical Report SEN-E0501, CWI, 2005.

19. John H. Reif. Depth-first search is inherently sequential. *Information Processing Letters*, 20(5):229–234, June 1985.

20. R. Tarjan. Depth first search and linear graph algorithms. *SIAM Journal on computing*, pages 146–160, 1972.

21. U.Stern and D. L. Dill. Parallelizing the murφ verifier. In O. Grumberg, editor, *Proceedings of Computer Aided Verification (CAV '97)*, volume 1254 of *LNCS*, pages 256–267. Springer-Verlag, 1997.

Can Saturation Be Parallelised?[*]
On the Parallelisation of a Symbolic State-Space Generator

Jonathan Ezekiel[1], Gerald Lüttgen[1], and Radu Siminiceanu[2]

[1] University of York, York, YO10 5DD, UK
{jezekiel,luettgen}@cs.york.ac.uk
[2] National Institute of Aerospace, Hampton VA 23666, USA
radu@nianet.org

Abstract. Symbolic state-space generators are notoriously hard to parallelise. However, the Saturation algorithm implemented in the SMART verification tool differs from other sequential symbolic state-space generators in that it exploits the locality of firing events in asynchronous system models.

This paper explores whether event locality can be utilised to efficiently parallelise Saturation on shared-memory architectures. Conceptually, we propose to parallelise the firing of events within a decision diagram node, which is technically realised via a thread pool. We discuss the challenges involved in our parallel design and conduct experimental studies on its prototypical implementation. On a dual-processor dual-core PC, our studies show speed-ups for several example models, e.g., of up to 50% for a Kanban model, when compared to running our algorithm only on a single core.

1 Introduction

Automated verification, such as temporal-logic model checking [6], relies on efficient algorithms for computing state spaces of complex system models. To avoid the well-known state-space explosion problem, symbolic algorithms working on *decision diagrams*, usually BDDs, have proved successful in practice [5, 14]. Several efforts have been made to implement these algorithms on parallel computer platforms, most notably on networks of workstations and on PC clusters [8, 9, 10, 15, 16]. The efforts range from simple approaches that essentially implement BDDs as two-tiered hash tables [15, 16] to sophisticated approaches relying on *slicing* BDDs [9], and techniques for *workstealing* [8]. However, the resulting implementations show only very limited speed-ups, which is not surprising given that state-space generation is essentially an irregular task.

Saturation [4], as implemented in the verification tool SMART [3], is a symbolic state-space generation algorithm with unique features (cf. Sec. 2). It is intended for asynchronous system models that are based on an interleaving semantics, and exploits the local effect of firing events on state vectors by locally

---

[*] Research funding was provided by the EPSRC under grant GR/S86211/01.

L. Brim et al. (Eds.): FMICS and PDMC 2006, LNCS 4346, pp. 331–346, 2007.
© Springer-Verlag Berlin Heidelberg 2007

manipulating MDDs [12], which are a generalised version of BDDs. Saturation has proved orders of magnitude more time- and memory-efficient than other symbolic algorithms [4], including the one implemented in the popular NuSMV model checker [5]. Hence, the question arises whether the locality of events can also be utilised for parallelising Saturation in order to achieve further speedups. Previous approaches to parallelising Saturation have focused on data parallelism [2, 1], but not on parallelising the algorithm itself.

This paper investigates the parallelisability of the Saturation algorithm for shared-memory architectures, such as multi-processor, multi-core PCs. At first sight, this is a challenging endeavor since Saturation relies on relatively lightweight operations for processing or "saturating" MDD nodes. Indeed, the algorithm's key operation is firing a single event from a given MDD node. However, this operation is not an entity that can easily be parallelised, since newly generated nodes are saturated themselves before the saturation of the node under consideration continues. In this sense, Saturation is a greedy algorithm.

Almost two years of studies have given us a detailed understanding of what is needed to efficiently parallelise the firing of events within Saturation (cf. Sec. 3). Key to the algorithm is how to manage the dependency of tasks without forcing computation threads to frequently idle. To this end, we propose a task queue for storing tasks that need to be processed, from which available compute nodes can pick jobs. However, letting the operating system manage tasks is very costly, due to the overheads involved when creating threads. Consequently, we implement our own thread pool that minimises these overheads. Another challenge is how to group firings of events such that our tasks, while still being lightweight, become sizable. Our solution here is to consider firing several events for a given node within the same task.

We have implemented our algorithm on a PC with two dual core Intel processors. Our experimental studies (cf. Sec. 4) show speed-ups of up to 50% when running the parallel algorithm on four processors instead of one, for large systems with densely connected MDD nodes, such as a Kanban model. Indeed, the algorithm's efficiency depends on the studied models, and improvements over the optimised sequential version of Saturation have proved to be hard to achieve. We carefully justify our results with the help of *Intel Threading Tools* [www.intel.com/software/products/threading/], which provides valuable insights into the locking behavior and processor idle times of our algorithm. The analysis also shows that our parallelisation is quite efficient in terms of utilising computation resources. The answer to the question posed in this paper's title is "yes", however speed-ups over the sequential algorithm are model dependent.

2   Saturation

The introduction of *Binary Decision Diagrams* (BDDs) [6] has revolutionised the field of model checking. BDDs offer a compact encoding for large sets of states when performing the next-state computation in a single, symbolic operation. However, despite the clear advantage over explicit exploration algorithms, the traditional monolithic BDD approach has been inherently a breadth-first search (BFS) strategy, or a variant of it [14]. For complex systems, however, the symbolic BFS algorithm usually suffers from an excessive peak memory consumption, thus failing to build the entire state space even when the final BDD is much smaller than the intermediate peak.

The Saturation algorithm [4] is radically different from its symbolic predecessors. It consists of a series of small, nested fixed point operations that are guided by the current shape of the decision diagram, with the goal of systematically *saturating* decision diagram nodes in a bottom-up fashion. The building block of this strategy is the firing of an individual event in an individual node, which encodes a subset of states, in contrast to computing the entire next-state function on the entire current set of states. This finer-grain decomposition of symbolic operations is more flexible, by allowing more efficient firing orders, while exploiting the *event locality* property, which is inherently present in concurrent, asynchronous systems. In our setting, the system is *structured* if it consists of a collection of subsystems, such that the global system state can be written as a vector of *local* states and the effect of an event on the system state can be expressed as the composition of the local effects of the event on each subsystem. For structured systems, an encoding of sets of states with Multi-way Decision Diagrams (MDDs) is more natural, for several reasons. Firstly, the one-to-one correspondence between a state variable and the level in the MDD is always apparent. Secondly, MDD nodes allow one to exploit the key operation of *in-place updates* [4] which accelerates the exploration.

A decision diagram node is said to be *saturated* if it encodes a local fixed point with respect to the subset of events that affect its level and the levels below. The global fixed point strategy is therefore *chaotic*, which can be shown to be correct as long as the firing order of events is *fair*, i.e., each event is considered often enough. To allow chaotic exploration, the system's model requires a disjunctively partitioned transition relation and must obey the interleaving semantics when firing events.

In contrast to traditional, BFS-oriented approaches, Saturation is extremely efficient. It performs lightweight decision diagram manipulations in contrast to the heavyweight, monolithic image computation of its symbolic counterparts. The greedy strategy of saturating every node immediately upon its creation, by pre-empting the undergoing event firing operation, results in a series of recursive, preemptive firings, which leads to a reduction of the peak MDD size. The intuition behind this is that *only* saturated nodes can be part of the final state-space representation. Also, once a node is saturated, it does not need to be considered for further exploration. The bottom-up order of saturating nodes ensures that all descendants are already saturated when a node is considered for saturation. Since the complexity of symbolic algorithms is closely related to the number of nodes in the decision diagram as opposed to the number of encoded states, Saturation is significantly more efficient than BFS. It is up to several orders of magnitude faster and memory efficient on classic asynchronous systems [4].

Paradoxically, the properties of Saturation make its efficient parallelisation extremely difficult. Given the doubly-recursive dependencies of the saturation and event firing routines, the algorithm is sequential by nature and heavily optimised, leaving little room for further improvements.

3   Parallel Saturation

State-space generation algorithms are difficult to parallelise due to the characteristics of the process. Tasks such as applying the next state function are irregularly sized, are dependent upon each other and have to synchronise frequently. These characteristics can introduce high parallel overheads. Irregular tasks cause load-imbalance, and dependencies between tasks compound the problem. While there are a number of techniques to load-balance irregular tasks, frequent synchronisation can only be avoided by making tasks as large and independent as possible. We exploit event locality to achieve this. Creating parallel tasks from event firings allows parts of the MDD to be constructed independently since subsequent event firings are local to the resultant sub-MDD.

While we can exploit event locality to create independent tasks, local events often cannot be parallelised due to their efficiency. On the shared memory architectures we investigated, the cost of creating a parallel event to perform an in-place-update outweighs the cost of performing it. On a SPARC Solaris shared memory machine we approximated the cost of an in-place update as 1200ns, compared to 90000ns for creating a thread and 8000ns for allocating a task to an existing thread. An in-place update can also occur when an event firing fully utilises previous work that has been cached. The cost of retrieving information from a cache is only 900ns. We therefore group event firings together and only consider those events that do not result in in-place updates for parallel tasks.

To address irregularity we introduce a task queue to which parallel tasks can be added, and to load-balance the tasks we utilise a thread pool where a thread is mapped 1-to-1 to a processor core. An available thread picks a task from the queue and performs the work associated with it. However, fitting the Saturation algorithm into this load-balancing structure is difficult due to its mutually recursive nature. In particular, in order to prevent threads from suspending we have to eliminate sequential waits on the result of a parallel event firing. We achieve this by introducing upward arcs into the MDD structure, which directly replace recursive function calls waiting for work to complete. Instead, the function calls continue when parallel work is pending leaving the upward arcs to represent future updates on a node. Upward arcs allow a task that was created by firing an event on a node to continue the work on the node when it completes. Each node must keep track of the number of tasks operating on it in order to determine when it is saturated. We also allow work requests to be cached before they have been carried out in order to avoid duplicate work in parallel.

The result of mapping our ideas into code is shown in Fig. 1, with supporting functions described in Fig. 2. The code extends the one from the sequential version of Saturation [4], parallel code is highlighted in Fig. 1, dark-shaded code

---

Saturate(in k:lvl, p:idx)

> Update $\langle k.p \rangle$, not in $UT[k]$, in–place, to encode $\mathcal{N}^*_{\leq k}(\mathcal{B}(\langle k.p \rangle))$.

declare ops:$bool$; i:lcl;

1. $\langle k.p \rangle.saturating \Leftarrow true$;
2. $AddOp(k, p)$;
3. foreach $i \in \mathcal{S}^k$ do
4.   if $\langle k.p \rangle[i] \neq 0$ then $FireEvents(k, p, i)$;
5. $RemoveOp(k, p, ops)$;
6. if $!ops$ then $NodeSaturated(k, p)$;

FireEvents(in k:lvl, p:idx ,i:lcl)

> Fire e on $\langle k.p \rangle[i]$ when $\mathcal{N}^k_e(i) \neq 0$

declare e:evt; j:lcl; f,u:idx; $lock$:$bool$;

1. foreach $e \in \mathcal{E}^k$ do
2.   if $\mathcal{N}^k_e(i) \neq 0$
3. $f \Leftarrow RecFire(e, k-1, \langle k.p \rangle[i])$;
4. $lock \Leftarrow true$; if $f \neq 0$ then
5.   if $lock$ then
6. $Lock(\langle k.p \rangle.dw)$; $lock \Leftarrow false$;
7.   foreach $j \in \mathcal{N}^k_e(i)$ do
8. $u \Leftarrow Union(k-1, f, \langle k.p \rangle[j])$;
9.   if $u \neq \langle k.p \rangle[j]$ then
10. $\langle k.p \rangle[j] \Leftarrow u$; $lock \Leftarrow true$;
11. $Unlock(\langle k.p \rangle.dw)$;
12. $FireEvents(k, p, j)$;

NodeSaturated(in k:lvl, p:idx)

> Add $\langle k.p \rangle$ to $UT[k]$. Remove uparcs from $\langle k.p \rangle$.

declare $ops,lock$:$bool$; q:idx; i:lcl; l:lvl;

1. $q \Leftarrow p$; $Check(k, p)$;
2. if $k = K$ then $Terminate()$; return;
3. $l \Leftarrow k + 1$; $Lock(FC[k])$;
4. $Insert(FC[k], FCkey(k, q), p, true)$;
5. $Unlock(FC[k])$; $lock \Leftarrow true$;
6. while $GetUpArc(k, p, r, i)$ do
7.   if $lock$ then
8. $Lock(\langle l.r \rangle.dw)$; $lock \Leftarrow false$;
9. $u \Leftarrow Union(k, p, \langle l.r \rangle[i])$;
10.   if $u \neq \langle l.r \rangle[i]$ then
11. $\langle l.r \rangle[i] \Leftarrow u$;
12.   if $\langle l.r \rangle.saturating$ then
13. $Unlock(\langle l.r \rangle.dw)$; $lock \Leftarrow true$;
14. $FireEvents(l, r, i)$;
15. $RemoveOp(l, r, ops)$;
16.   if $!ops$ then
17.   if $\langle l.r \rangle.saturating$ then
18. $NodeSaturated(l, r)$;
19.   else
20. $QSaturate(l, r)$;
21. if $q \neq p$; then delete $\langle k.q \rangle$;

RecFire(in e:evt,l:lvl,q:idx,p:idx,i:lcl):idx

> Build an MDD rooted at $\langle l.s \rangle$, in $UT[l]$, encoding $\mathcal{N}^*_{\leq l}(\mathcal{N}_e(\mathcal{B}(\langle l.q \rangle)))$.

declare $\mathcal{L}$:set of lcl;
declare g,h,j:lcl;
declare f,u,s:idx;
declare sat,ops:$bool$;

1. if $l < Last(e)$ then return q;
2. $Lock(FC[l])$;
3. if $Find(FC[l], \{q, e\}, s, sat)$ then
4.   if $!sat$ then foreach $j \in \mathcal{N}^l_e(i)$ do
5. $SetUpArc(l, s, p, j)$;
6. $s \Leftarrow 0$;
7. $Unlock(FC[l])$; return s;
8. $s \Leftarrow NewNode(l, e, q)$;
9. foreach $j \in \mathcal{N}^l_e(i)$ do
10. $SetUpArc(l, s, p, j)$;
11. $AddOp(l, s)$;
12. $Insert(FC[l], \{q, e\}, s, false)$;
13. $Unlock(FC[l])$;
14. $\mathcal{L} \Leftarrow Locals(e, l, q)$;
15. while $\mathcal{L} \neq \emptyset$ do
16. $g \Leftarrow Pick(\mathcal{L})$;
17. $f \Leftarrow RecFire(e, l-1, \langle l.q \rangle[g])$;
18.   if $f \neq 0$ then
19. $Lock(\langle l.s \rangle.dw)$;
20.   foreach $h \in \mathcal{N}^l_e(g)$ do
21. $u \Leftarrow Union(l-1, f, \langle l.s \rangle[h])$;
22.   if $u \neq \langle l.s \rangle[h]$ then $\langle l.s \rangle[h] \Leftarrow u$;
23. $Unlock(\langle l.s \rangle.dw)$;
24. $RemoveOp(l, s, ops)$; if $!ops$ then
25.   if $DWarcs(l, s)$ then
26. $QSaturate(l, s)$;
27.   else $Remove(l, s)$; $s \Leftarrow 0$;
28. $s \Leftarrow 0$; return s;

Remove(in k:lvl, p:idx)

> Remove $\langle k.p \rangle$ and its uparcs.

declare ops:$bool$;l:lvl;
declare i:lcl;q:idx;

1. $Lock(FC[k])$;
2. $Insert(FC[k], FCkey(k, p), 0, true)$;
3. $Unlock(FC[k])$;
4. $l \Leftarrow k + 1$;
5. while $GetUpArc(k, p, q, i)$ do
6. $RemoveOp(l, q, ops)$;
7.   if $!ops$ then
8.   if $\langle l.q \rangle.saturating$ then
9. $NodeSaturated(l, q)$;
10.   else if $DWarcs(l, q)$ then
11. $QSaturate(l, q)$;
12.   else $Remove(l, q)$;
13. delete $\langle k.p \rangle$;

Fig. 1. Pseudo–code for the parallel node–saturation algorithm

facilitates tasks and removes mutual recursion, while light-shaded code shows locks ensuring correct synchronisation. An MDD node is written as $\langle k.p \rangle$, where k is the MDD level of the node and p is its unique index. The notation $\langle k.p \rangle[i]$ represents a downward arc from local state i. Information and locks on the node are denoted by $\langle k.p \rangle.information/lock$. The MDD nodes are stored in k hash tables, one per level, also called *unique tables* $UT[k]$, $1 < k \leq K$ where K is the

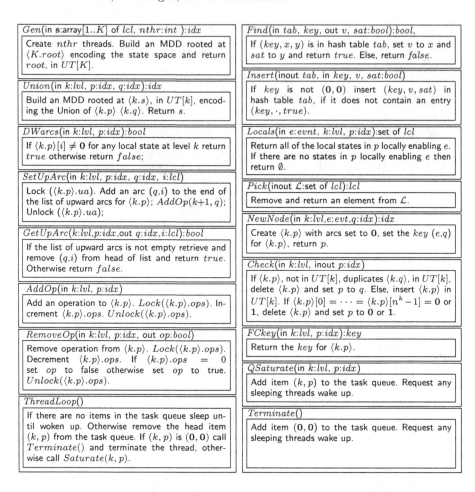

Fig. 2. Supporting function descriptions

height of the MDD. Work resulting from event firings is stored on a per level basis in a cache, the *firing cache* (*FC*), i.e., $FC[k]$, $1 < k \leq K$. The notation $\mathcal{S}^k$ refers to the local state space at level k, $\mathcal{E}^k$ indicates events where the highest level affected by the event is equal to k, and $\mathcal{N}$ refers to the next state function where $\mathcal{N}^k_e$ is the next state function with respect to the event e at level k.

Node Information: Each MDD node keeps track of the number of tasks that are currently working on it or that will perform work on it in the future (via upward arcs). The functions *AddOp* and *RemoveOp* allow current/pending task operations to be added and removed from a node respectively. The saturation status of the node is indicated by $\langle k.p \rangle.saturating$ and determines if a node with no remaining tasks is *saturated* from firing all events, or a newly created node waiting to be saturated. Nodes created from event firings store a *key* to add to the firing cache.

Initialisation: Function *Gen* creates an initial MDD representing the initial state set of the underlying system model and the threads in the thread pool. Each thread calls *ThreadLoop* to synchronise on the task queue. Tasks are added to the queue for the bottom nodes of the initial MDD.

Saturate: This function first indicates that the node has begun saturating by setting *saturating* to true. Since the saturation task is being performed by a thread, it registers the thread on the node via *AddOp*. It begins the process of exhaustively firing events on the node by calling *FireEvents* for each non zero state. Once it has fired the events the task is complete, and it calls *RemoveOp*. The *Saturate* function allows the thread to check the status of the node to see whether it is saturated. It can continue work on any nodes dependent upon the node reaching a fixpoint.

FireEvents: This function checks whether an event is enabled in the state being fired upon and calls *RecFire* to fire an enabled event. Successful firings result in the node being updated with the work carried out by the firing. Any updated nodes invoke a recursive call to *FireEvents* on the updated state.

RecFire: Uncompleted nodes discovered in the cache have upward arcs set from them to the calling node via *SetUpArc*. For new work, a node is created setting the *FC key* in the process. The thread registers with the new node and adds it to the *FC* as a work request. Upward arcs are set to the calling node. *RecFire* is recursively called to continue event firing then the thread de-registers from the node. Nodes at the bottom of the MDD generated by the event firing are either added to the task queue or removed if the event is disabled.

NodeSaturated: This function is called when a node is saturated. The node is checked into the unique table. *NodeSaturated* updates nodes dependent upon the saturated node via upward arcs, and allows the thread to continue working on them. The termination condition occurs when this function is called for the top level node.

We illustrate the parallel algorithm in Figs. 3 and 4 with an example for a thread pool of two threads. The disjunctively partitioned transition relation, for four events, is represented as an *event matrix* displayed in Fig. 3.*a*.

a) *Gen* generates the initial MDD. All nodes are marked as *not saturating*. None of the nodes have an FC key (*fc*) since the nodes are not created from a *RecFire* operation. Operations (*op*) is incremented for each upward arc set on a node. *Saturate* tasks are added to the task queue for the bottom nodes of the MDD, i.e., nodes $\langle 1.1 \rangle$ and $\langle 1.2 \rangle$. The sleeping threads are about to be woken by the new tasks.

b) The threads have woken and removed the tasks from the queue. They both call *Saturate* which marks each target node as *saturating* and increments *op* to indicate they are currently being operated upon by the *Saturate* task.

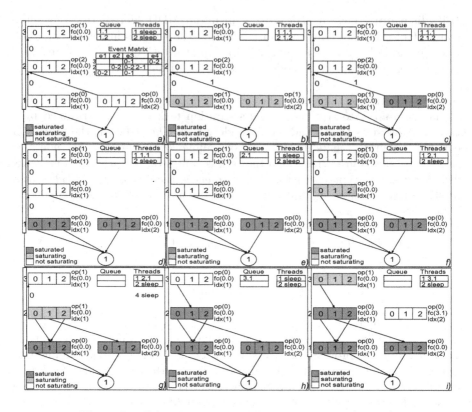

Fig. 3. Parallel node-saturation algorithm example (Part 1)

c) *Saturate(1,1)* makes a local update on ⟨1.1⟩ by firing event *e1*. *Saturate(1,2)* has completed since no events are enabled on ⟨1.2⟩ and has decremented *op* to zero. Since *op* is zero, *NodeSaturated* is called which marks the node as *saturated* and checks it into the *unique table*.

d) *Saturate(1,1)* has completed firing events and decremented *op* to zero, marking the node as *saturated*. *NodeSaturated(1,2)* removes the upward arc to ⟨2.1⟩ and replaces it with a downward arc, decrementing *op* for ⟨2.1⟩ in the process. Since *op* is nonzero, *NodeSaturated* terminates leaving Thread 2 to sleep.

e) *NodeSaturated(1,1)* removes the upward arc to ⟨2.1⟩ and replaces it with a downward arc and decrements the *op* for ⟨2.1⟩. Since *op* is now zero and the node is not *saturating*, a new *Saturate* task is added to the task queue for ⟨2.1⟩. *NodeSaturated* completes thus allowing the thread to return to sleep.

f) Thread 1 is woken up by the new task and removes it from the queue. It calls *Saturate(2,1)* which increments *op* and marks ⟨2.1⟩ as *saturating*.

g) Saturate(2,1) makes an in-place update on ⟨2.1⟩ by firing *e2* to set local state 2 to point to node ⟨1.1⟩.

h) Saturate(2,1) completes firing, decrements *op* and calls *NodeSaturated* which replaces the upwards arc to ⟨3.1⟩ with a downward arc and decrements *op*. Since

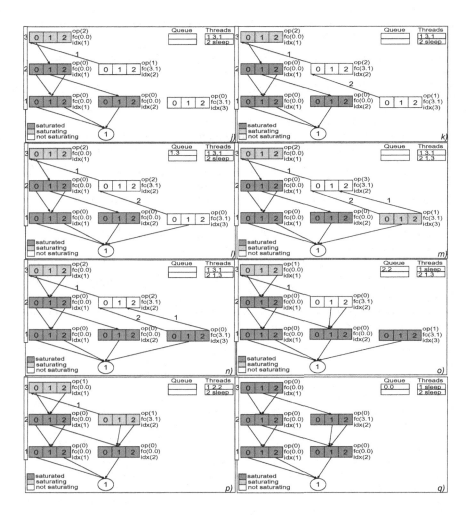

Fig. 4. Parallel node-saturation algorithm example (Part 2)

⟨3.1⟩ is not *saturating* and has no *op*, a task to *Saturate* ⟨3.1⟩ is added to the queue. *NodeSaturated* terminates allowing Thread 1 to return to sleep.

i) Thread 1 is woken by the addition of the task to the queue. It calls *Saturate(3,1)* which marks the node as *saturating* and increments *op*. *RecFire* is called for event *e3* which creates node ⟨2.2⟩ that contains an FC key *fc(3.1)*.

j) *RecFire* increments *op* on ⟨2.2⟩ and sets an upward arc to ⟨3.1⟩ incrementing *op* in the process. It recursively calls *RecFire* which creates node ⟨1.1⟩

k) *RecFire* increments *op* on ⟨1.3⟩ and sets an upward arc to ⟨2.2⟩ incrementing *op* in the process.

l) *RecFire* sets a downward arc from ⟨1.3⟩ to terminal node **1** and terminates decrementing *op* in the process. On termination, since *op* is zero and the node is *not saturating* a task to *Saturate* ⟨1.3⟩ is added to the task queue.

m) Thread 2 picks up the new task and calls *Saturate(1,3)* which marks the node as *saturating* and increments *op*. Meanwhile, Thread 1 has continued with *RecFire* and has discovered ⟨1.3⟩ as an *unsaturated* node in the firing cache, while firing *e3*, which sets an upward arc to ⟨2.2⟩ and increments *op*.

n) Node ⟨1.3⟩ has completed saturating and decrements *op* to 0 and marks the node as *Saturated*. Meanwhile, *RecFire* has completed on ⟨2.2⟩, decrementing *op*, and *Saturate* continues on ⟨3.1⟩ by firing *e4* to make a local update.

o) *Saturate* has completed on ⟨3.1⟩, decrementing *op* and returning Thread 1 to sleep. Since *op* is greater than 0, the node is not yet saturated. *NodeSaturated* has been called on ⟨1.3⟩ which has discovered the node is the same as node ⟨1.2⟩ while checking it into the *unique table*, and has removed the upward arcs, setting the downward arcs to this node. Since *op* is 0, a *Saturate* task is added to the queue for ⟨2.2⟩ and the thread goes to sleep.

p) Thread 1 takes the *Saturate* task for ⟨2.2⟩, setting the thread to *saturating* and incrementing *op*.

q) *Saturate* completes on ⟨2.2⟩, decrementing *op* to zero and calling *NodeSaturate* which replaces the upward arc to ⟨3.1⟩ with a downward arc and decrements *op*. Since *op* is 0 and the node is *saturating*, node ⟨3.1⟩ is now *Saturated*. Since this is the root node, *Terminate* is called which instructs the task queue to terminate the threads. The final MDD representing the state space is shown.

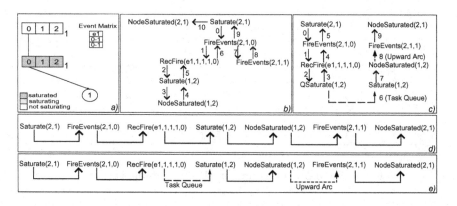

Fig. 5. The calling order of functions for the sequential and parallel algorithms

Correctness of the Algorithm

The algorithm in Fig. 1 can be expressed in terms of its sequential counterpart. Removing the highlighted parallel code gives us the sequential algorithm which is known to be correct [4]. Thus correctness of the parallel algorithm can be shown by demonstrating that the parallel code allows our algorithm to arrive at the same result and that locks prevent any data races. We can illustrate the calling structure of both sequential and parallel saturation using the example in Fig. 5a. The call graphs in Figs. 5b and 5c are the calling order of functions for the sequential and parallel code, respectively, where Fig. 5d and Fig. 5e further simplify the order. Function calls in the sequential version are directly replaced by the task queue and upward arcs in the parallel version. Since locks ensure that updating the node is atomic, firing events exhaustively will result in the same MDD shape for the saturated node as in the sequential version.

4   Experimental Results

We built a prototypical parallel algorithm using C and the POSIX `Pthreads` library [13]. To evaluate the algorithm we measured several aspects of the algorithms performance when utilising between one and four cores on a shared-memory machine. For comparison we also measured the performance of a C version of the sequential algorithm [4] on the same machine. The machine used for evaluation is a dual-processor, dual-core machine with 2GB of memory and Intel Xeon(TM) CPU 3.06GHz processors with 512kb cache sizes running Red-hat Linux AS 4, Redhat kernel 2.6.9-22.ELsmp with glibc 2.3.4-2.13. We applied the algorithm to Slotted Ring, Round Robin, Kanban, and a number of *randomly generated* models. The state space sizes varied between approximately $1.69x10^{10}$ and $4.53x10^{158}$ states. The traditional models have been used previously to evaluate the sequential algorithm [4]. In our results we have classified the event matrices by average *density*, i.e., the number of state updates within an event relative to the width of a node, and by the average number of *events per level*. Based on these properties we generated random models with a varying number of randomly generated events with similar matrix characteristics to the traditional models. Run times and relative memory against the sequential version are shown in Table 1, where N is either the number of nodes in a Slotted Ring network, the number of processes for the Round Robin protocol or the tokens in the Kanban system, and where # is a number identifying a random model.

Traditional Models: All of the results show speed-ups when running our parallel algorithm on four cores instead of one. The best parallelism is for a Kanban model with an approximate 50% speed-up. Despite this, however, the algorithm is still slower than the sequential version. It is most comparable to the sequential version for the Round Robin model with only a slight decrease in run-time for the highest value of N. The memory consumption of the parallel algorithm is greater for all models, varying between up to 28 times for the Slotted Ring model to less than 3 times for the Round Robin model.

Random Models: The results vary between speed-ups and slow-downs. The majority of the models show speed-ups when running the parallel algorithm on 4 cores instead of 1 core, but remain slower than the sequential version. Model 9 shows a slow-down of approximately 30% when running on 4 cores instead

Table 1. Experimental Results

	Sequential		1 Core		2 Cores		3 Cores		4 Cores	
	time	mem(b)	time	rmem	time	rmem	time	rmem	time	rmem
Slotted Ring (*Avg. Density* 0.40 *Avg. Events Per Level* 3.00)										
N	time	mem(b)	time	rmem	time	rmem	time	rmem	time	rmem
60	2.36	2002880	7.01	15.22	7.72	23.67	7.08	23.67	6.27	22.02
90	7.56	6109680	23.11	16.12	26.40	25.85	24.59	25.68	20.76	22.61
120	17.56	13726480	55.16	16.61	64.48	26.86	60.43	26.86	50.71	24.17
150	34.28	25933280	110.23	16.93	128.71	27.50	121.09	27.42	99.94	24.47
Random A (*Avg. Density* 0.40 *Avg. Events Per Level* 2.8)										
#	time	mem(b)	time	rmem	time	rmem	time	rmem	time	rmem
1	1.58	3665040	2.43	7.71	1.81	7.89	1.58	7.91	1.49	7.96
2	4.90	4603360	31.24	20.53	20.95	20.91	18.61	21.26	17.41	21.39
3	12.09	8927840	76.60	20.39	51.22	21.29	49.20	22.97	46.81	23.38
4	7.70	7813120	16.52	12.69	11.03	12.95	9.70	13.25	8.75	13.25
Round Robin (*Avg. Density* 0.19 *Avg. Events Per Level* 4.96-4.98)										
N	time	mem(b)	time	rmem	time	rmem	time	rmem	time	rmem
150	6.03	86462784	10.98	2.26	7.64	2.26	7.71	2.26	7.75	2.26
180	12.26	147830244	21.44	2.27	14.39	2.27	14.59	2.26	14.69	2.26
210	23.51	232961304	38.89	2.27	25.21	2.27	25.65	2.27	25.74	2.27
240	41.73	345743964	65.89	2.27	41.88	2.27	42.32	2.27	42.55	2.27
Random B (*Avg Density* 0.20 *Avg. Events Per Level* 4.41-4.54)										
#	time	mem(b)	time	rmem	time	rmem	time	rmem	time	rmem
5	6.99	44951280	12.40	3.38	9.25	3.42	8.27	3.39	8.27	8.07
6	15.20	73501020	26.81	3.43	18.66	3.46	16.76	3.44	16.00	3.45
7	16.90	55277700	30.53	4.67	21.53	4.70	19.62	4.68	18.76	4.67
8	1.62	17186280	3.15	3.34	2.51	3.35	2.35	3.33	2.28	3.32
Kanban (*Avg Density* 1.67-1.82 *Avg. Events Per Level* 1.50)										
N	time	mem(b)	time	rmem	time	rmem	time	rmem	time	rmem
15	0.64	1008188	1.15	2.74	0.71	3.02	0.70	3.56	0.70	4.70
20	2.85	3601728	5.98	2.77	3.52	3.05	3.34	4.19	3.32	5.32
25	10.08	9934868	22.91	2.80	12.79	3.22	12.31	4.77	12.27	6.65
30	29.73	23089108	73.24	2.83	39.96	3.36	37.32	5.33	36.65	6.74
Random C (*Avg Density* 1.74 *Avg. Events Per Level* 1.50)										
#	time	mem(b)	time	rmem	time	rmem	time	rmem	time	rmem
9	5.93	1378080	33.90	10.6	30.47	10.8	51.25	11.91	41.72	11.29
10	4.20	503440	5.33	7.65	3.11	7.76	2.50	7.90	2.32	8.00
11	7.02	874640	20.93	15.96	10.02	16.58	8.36	18.86	7.51	19.37
12	5.39	642640	10.43	10.54	6.03	10.92	4.78	10.65	4.17	10.60

of 1. Model 10 shows the best parallelism with a speed-up over 40%. Memory consumption increases for the parallel algorithm on all models and varies between approximately 5 and 25 times that of the sequential version.

Much of the extant research examines run-time, memory consumption and direct measurements on the state space for evaluating parallel algorithms. Our approach to evaluation is more thorough. We used several tools to evaluate the performance of our algorithm. We carefully selected our architecture in order to allow Intel Threading Tools, that only support Intel chips, to be used on the algorithm. Using the Thread Checker we verified that the locks were set correctly to avoid data races and would not interfere with the results. Using the Thread Profiler we obtained measurements of the parallel overheads, and how well the cores were utilised by the algorithm. To investigate the parallel effect on the construction of the state space we built a tool to visualise the MDD construction. To evaluate any code overheads we used the GNU Profiler [7]. Combining these tools with our results and direct measurements provided us with a great deal of insight into the performance of our algorithm.

Overheads: The run-time results and memory are affected by the overheads incurred by the parallel algorithm. High overheads prevent the parallel algorithm from competing with the sequential version. We saw two types of overhead, the parallel overhead incurred by the introduction of locks and threads, and the code overhead incurred by removing mutual recursion from the algorithm. The highest memory and run-time overhead comes from the use of upward arcs. Locks on the data structure accounted for less than 10% of the overhead on all models.

Extra Work: The order in which events are fired affects the amount of work the algorithm has to perform. Due to the dependencies between events, parallel events are often fired on smaller state sets than the sequential version. This creates more work and larger intermediate MDDs. The extra work can outweigh the benefits of parallelism. It also introduces higher overheads.

Parallelism: The number of parallel events and how well this causes the work to branch in parallel during construction affects the level of parallelism of the algorithm. The lower the parallelism, the lower the number of parallel tasks to perform. Low parallelism means cores are undersubscribed during construction.

We examined the event matrices as to whether overheads, extra work and parallelism could be determined by their properties. We chose to classify our models by properties that could influence parallelism. Our evaluation showed that the factors which affect whether the algorithm showed speed-ups are more complicated than the properties we chose. In order to determine how well a model can be parallelised we also need to look at how event orderings influence parallelism. Orderings can introduce spikes in performance between processors, which has been seen before in explicit parallel model checking [11]. This effect is greater in our algorithm since individual event firings produce larger state sets.

Our results are encouraging for models that have low overheads, are unaffected by extra work and show good parallelism. The overheads incurred by parallelism are too great, however, in order to show speed-ups over the sequential version. Given that Saturation is orders of magnitude more time- and memory-efficient than other symbolic algorithms [4], it would be difficult for our parallel algorithm to further improve over the sequential version. When we incur several penalties from parallelisation such as extra work, code to remove mutual recursion and parallel overheads, parallelism is likely to hinder rather than enhance the state-space construction process.

5   Related Work

For explicit state space generators, the algorithm is normally the key consideration for parallelisation [11]. For symbolic state-space generators, however, the complex data structure for storing states often needs to be investigated [2, 8, 9, 10, 15, 16]. The extant research on symbolic model checking has focused primarily on networks of workstations (NOW). We can classify the symbolic parallelisation approaches into a number of categories, and show that the one into which our work fits is unique from the previous work in this area.

Data Parallelisation (Memory): Most of the work on parallel symbolic state-space generation considers only how to parallelise the data structure. These approaches target the increased memory available on NOW by slicing the data structure and distributing it across processors of the NOW. The structure of decision diagrams has previously been sliced horizontally [2] and vertically [10, 15, 16]. Horizontal slicing scales well but prevents the state-space generation task from being speeded up, since each slice has to complete its work before the next slice begins its work. Finding a good vertical slicing is a non-trivial issue often leading to poor scalability. In order to facilitate scalability, load-balancing techniques need to be employed. The most advanced work in this area uses work-stealing techniques to distribute work dynamically [9].

Data and Algorithm Parallelisation (Memory/Time): Researchers have parallelised symbolic state-space generation algorithms in order to gain speed-ups from developing vertical slices on different processors of a NOW [8]. If the algorithm developing the slices has to frequently synchronise on the application of the imaging function, each round of computation is only as fast as the slowest time it takes for a slice to develop on a processor. In order to achieve speed-ups the research tackles the difficult task of removing the synchronous nature of the algorithm. The parallel algorithm allows slices to develop asynchronously while the imaging function is applied to create more work. The work is load-balanced using the workstealing techniques developed in [9]. For very large circuits this technique has proved to lead to a very efficient parallelisation showing up to an order of magnitude improvement in time efficiency.

Utilising Idle Processors (Memory/Time): Recent work has also considered ways to utilise idle processors during state-space construction [1]. The idle processors are used to perform and cache work that may be performed in future, while a main processor develops the state space. If work that the main processor requires has already been performed by another processor, the main processor retrieves it from the cache. This reduces the peak size of the data structure during state-space construction and improves time efficiency if the amount of utilised work performed by the idle processors is sufficient to overcome the overhead of allocating work to the processors and synchronising on the cache.

Algorithm Parallelisation(Time): Our approach is unique in that we consider how to parallelise only the algorithm itself. The primary goal is in improving time efficiency by utilising the extra processing power. Parallel overheads are addressed while leaving the data structure whole during state-space construction. A shared memory architecture is targeted in order to reduce the costs of synchronisation. In contrast to most other work, with the exception of [11], we have evaluated the performance characteristics of our parallel algorithm very carefully by combining several evaluation tools and techniques.

In [11] a shared memory architecture is used to parallelise an explicit state-space generation algorithm. The approach employs worksteating techniques in order to load-balance. Many of the parallelisation overheads are addressed by tailoring the parallelisation specifically to the selected architecture. The high optimisation of the algorithm for the architecture allows the parallel algorithm to overcome parallel overheads, showing good linear speed-ups for several models.

6   Conclusions and Future Work

We investigated whether the MDD-based Saturation algorithm for computing reachable state spaces of asynchronous system models can be parallelised on shared-memory architectures, such as multi-processor multi-core PCs. This is a challenging question since symbolic state-space generation is an irregular task.

The idea for parallelising Saturation was to consider the firing of events on a node as a task. Because Saturation is a mutual recursive algorithm, many relatively lightweight tasks are created which cannot be managed efficiently by the operating system. Instead, we implemented a task queue, which stores tasks awaiting processing, ourselves. Available threads running on dedicated processors then collect work from this queue, thereby minimising processor idle time. Our conceptual ideas and implementation strategy for the thread pool are not specific to Saturation and reusable for implementations of other parallel algorithms. We showed speed-ups for traditional models utilising four computing cores over a single core of up to 50%. However, speed-ups over the original sequential version of Saturation depend very much on the specific model studied.

Future work shall proceed along three orthogonal directions. Firstly, we wish to optimise our current implementation and explore heuristics for the order in which tasks are taken out of the thread pool. This order does not affect the correctness of our parallel algorithm but significantly its efficiency. Secondly, it should be investigated whether our ideas can be combined with those of [2] for efficiently parallelising Saturation for distributed-memory architectures, such as PC clusters. Thirdly, other approaches to further exploiting modern parallel computer architectures shall be explored, including the predictive firing of events suggested in [1].

References

[1] Chung, M.-Y. and Ciardo, G. A dynamic firing speculation to speedup distributed symbolic state-space generation. In *IPDPS*. IEEE, 2006.

[2] Chung, M.-Y. and Ciardo, G. Saturation NOW. *QEST*, pp. 272–281, IEEE, 2004.

[3] Ciardo, G., Jones, R., Miner, A., and Siminiceanu, R. SMART: Stochastic model analyzer for reliability and timing. *Tools of Measurement, Modelling and Evaluation of Computer-Communication Systems*, pp. 29–34, 2001.

[4] Ciardo, G., Lüttgen, G., and Siminiceanu, R. Saturation: An efficient iteration strategy for symbolic state-space generation. In *TACAS*, vol. 2031 of *LNCS*, pp. 328–342, 2001.

[5] Cimatti, A., Clarke, E. M., Giunchiglia, F., and Roveri, M. NUSMV: A new symbolic model checker. *STTT*, 2(4):410–425, 2000.

[6] Clarke, E. M., Grumberg, O., and Peled, D. A. *Model Checking*. MIT, 1999.

[7] Graham, S. L., Kessler, P. B., and McKusick, M. K. gprof: A call graph execution profiler (with retrospective). In *Best of PLDI*, pp. 49–57. ACM, 1982.

[8] Grumberg, O., Heyman, T., Ifergan, N., and Schuster, A. Achieving speedups in distributed symbolic reachability analysis through asynchronous computation. In *CHARME*, vol. 3725 of *LNCS*, pp. 129–145, 2005.

[9] Grumberg, O., Heyman, T., and Schuster, A. A work-efficient distributed algorithm for reachability analysis. In *CAV*, vol. 2725 of *LNCS*, pp. 54–66, 2003.

[10] Heyman, T., Geist, D., Grumberg, O., and Schuster, A. Achieving scalability in parallel reachability analysis of very large circuits. In *CAV*, vol. 1855 of *LNCS*, pp. 20–35, 2000.

[11] Inggs, C. P. *Parallel Model Checking On Shared Memory Architectures*. PhD thesis, University of Manchester, UK, 2004.

[12] Kam, T., Villa, T., Brayton, R., and S.-Vincentelli, A. L. Multi-valued decision diagrams: Theory and applications. *Multiple-Valued Logic*, 4(1-2):9–62, 1998.

[13] Lewis, B. and Berg, D. J. *Multithreaded programming with Pthreads*. Prentice-Hall, 1998.

[14] McMillan, K. L. *Symbolic Model Checking*. Kluwer, 1993.

[15] Milvang-Jensen, K. and Hu, A. J. BDDNOW: A parallel BDD package. In *FMCAD*, vol. 1522 of *LNCS*, pp. 501–507, 1998.

[16] Stornetta, T. and Brewer, F. Implementation of an efficient parallel BDD package. In *DAC*, pp. 641–644. ACM, 1996.

Distributed Colored Petri Net Model-Checking with CYCLADES

Christophe Pajault and Jean-François Pradat-Peyre

CEDRIC - CNAM Paris
292, rue St Martin, 75003 Paris
{christophe.pajault,peyre}@cnam.fr

Abstract. The major bottleneck of explicit model-checking tools is the limited amount of available memory. Distributed model-checking is an approach to tackle the combinatorial explosion problem. It consists in taking advantage of the aggregate of memory provided by a network of workstations to increase the amount of memory available for model-checking.

HELENA is the model-checker of the QUASAR tool suite for concurrent software verification. It is a high-level colored Petri net explicit sequential model-checker that implements several state-space reduction and efficient state representation mechanisms. HELENA is currently able to verify safety properties. In this paper we present CYCLADES, a distributed version of HELENA, that remains compatible with these reduction techniques. Several distribution mechanisms and some preliminary results are also provided.

1 Introduction

Concurrency introduces at the same time design facilities and reliability problems. Indeed, the interleaving of tasks execution leads to a high degree of concurrency and may be the source of subtle mistakes that are difficult to detect by simple simulations or human reasoning. Classically encountered problems are deadlock, starvation or more generally race conditions on shared resources.

Software model checking is a very efficient technique to track these problems since it can be fully automated and works directly at the program level. The main difficulty is to combat the combinatorial explosion problem induced by the interleaving between threads or processes. Four categories of techniques can be used to efficiently tackle this phenomenon:

- program/model reductions: some parts of the program can be useless w.r.t. the analyzed property; they can safety suppressed using a *slicing* approach [Wei84]. Some abstractions can be made on the model[CGL92] or some sequential actions of the program or of the corresponding model (when an equivalent model is built from the program for its analysis) may be merged into an atomic one whose effect is the composition of the effects of these statements. This transformation was initiated by Lipton [Lip75] with the notion

L. Brim et al. (Eds.): FMICS and PDMC 2006, LNCS 4346, pp. 347–361, 2007.

of *left* and *right movers*, developed by several authors [CL98, FQ03b, FQ03a] and explored in Petri nets formalisms in [Ber83], [PPP00] and in [HPP06].

- state graph reductions: when building the state graph, some techniques can be applied on-the-fly in order to reduce the number of states that have to be explored:
  - some enabled actions may be forgotten since they lead to an already visited state [GW93],
  - some enabled actions may be safely delayed [Val93],
  - some enabled actions may be executed simultaneously [VM97].
- states representation reduction: several techniques have been proposed to store and represent the state space efficiently. Bit state hashing [Hol87] does not store any state explicitly but maintains a vector of bits. This approach is a probabilistic verification technique like the hash-compact method [WL93] as it is does not consider the possible collision of state keys. The state collapse method [Hol97] is an efficient state compression used to reduce the amount of memory used per state. Another approach presented in [CKM01] propose to define a measure of progress (when it is possible) to enable the deletion of some useless states. BDD representations [McM93] can also be used but these techniques seems not useful when dealing with software models.
- state space distribution: this technique consists in distributing the state space among a cluster of workstations. The state space is thus divided in partitions. Each partition is owned by a single node. Every time a node n explores a new state s, it determines whether it is the owner of s or not. In the case when s is the owner of s, the algorithm works like the sequential algorithm. In the case when n is not the owner, it sends s to its owner and the works like s was a fully expanded state. Such a depth first search algorithm is presented in figure. 2.1.

Inside our software verification tool suite named Quasar [EKPPR03, EKP+05], the model-checker HELENA implements the first three techniques presented above: program slicing [Rou06] and static model reduction [EHPP04], on-the-fly graph reductions [EP06], state representation reduction [EPP05]. To make a step beyond, we decided to implement the fourth strategy: the state graph distribution. One of the difficulties is to keep the benefit of others used techniques, in particular, the one used for minimizing the state graph representation: the Δ marking method.

The paper is structured as follows. CYCLADES is presented in section 2. The adaptation of the Δ-marking method to a distributed environment is discussed in section 3. Section 4 briefly presents some work done in the scope of distributed model-checking while section 5 reports some experiments.

2   CYCLADES: A Distributed Version of Helena

HELENA [Eva05] is a high-level colored Petri net model-checker. It performs:

- static reduction of the net model: *Pre* and *Post-agglomerations* [PPP00] [HPP06] that statically reduce the colored Petri net before model-checking.

- partial-order reduction with stubborn sets computation [Val93]
- efficient storage and state representation with bit state hashing, hash-compact and state collapse methods. HELENA also proposes a new efficient storage mechanism called Δ-marking[EPP05] which consists in storing a large set of states in a non explicit way by storing only references to others states.

HELENA is the model-checker of QUASAR [1] [EKPPR03] which is a tool suite for the analysis of concurrent programs. QUASAR follows a four step process:

1. slicing: our slicer YASNOST [Rou06] removes parts of the source code which are not related to the investigated property
2. modeling: translation of the sliced code into a high-level Petri net
3. model-checking: analysis of the model with HELENA
4. error-reporting: when the targeted property is not verified, the faulty sequence of actions is displayed.

We present here CYCLADES, a distributed version of HELENA and some preliminary results. When parallelizing HELENA , one of our objective was to keep the three kinds of reductions available in a distributed environment.

Distribution of model-checking has no impact on static reductions as they are computed before the model-checking process. Stubborn sets computation, on the contrary, have to be modified as it uses the search stack which, in distributed model-checking, is no longer globally maintained. We will not discuss distributed partial-order computation in this paper as it is not yet implemented.

Then, distributed model-checking is not dependent on the internal state representation and storage in almost all the cases. But, as Δ-marking represents a state with a reference to one of its predecessors, problems could arise in distributed environment when the predecessor is not stored on the same node as the given state. We will present some modifications of the Δ-marking for a distributed environment in section 3.

2.1   Basic Algorithm

The basic algorithm of CYCLADES is presented in figure 2.1. The distributed exploration is started by calling the *START* procedure on each node. Each node gets its rank number with the *GET_RANK* call. The node with rank equal to *manager* works as the master node. This master node calls the *MANAGER* function that computes the initial state and sends it to its owner. Then it waits for incoming messages until termination is detected. The other nodes call the *WORKER* function. This function consists in waiting for incoming messages. When a state is received, a new depth-first search procedure is started, then statistics used for termination detection are sent to the master node.

The *DFS* procedure works as follows: when a node n explores a new state s', the partition is calculated with the *PARTITION* function. If s' does not belong to n, it is sent to its owner and considered as visited by n.

---

[1] http://quasar.cnam.fr/

START ()
1    $Q \leftarrow \emptyset$
2    $V \leftarrow \emptyset$
3    $termination \leftarrow false$
4    $rank \leftarrow$ GET_RANK()
5   if $rank = manager$ then
6   MANAGER()
7   else
8   WORKER()
9   end if

WORKER ()
1   while not $termination$ do
2        $Q \leftarrow Q \cup$ RECEIVE()
3   if RECEIVE_TERMINATION() then
4            $termination \leftarrow true$
5   else
6   while $Q \neq \emptyset$ do
7                $s \leftarrow$ POP(Q)
8   DFS(s)
9   end while
10   if $no\ incoming\ message$ then
11   SEND($statistics, manager$)
12   end if
13   end if
14   end while

MANAGER ()
1    $s_0 \leftarrow$ INITIAL()
2    $owner \leftarrow$ PARTITION(s_0)
3   SEND($s_0, owner$)
4   while not $termination$ do
5   //$Statistics\ sent\ by\ workers$
6        $Q \leftarrow Q \cup$ RECEIVE()
7        $termination \leftarrow$ IS_TERMINATED(Q)
8   end while
9   BROADCAST_TERMINATION()

DFS (s)
1   if $s \notin V$ then
2        $V \leftarrow V \cup \{s\}$
3        $A \leftarrow$ ENABLE(s)
4   for $a \in A$ do
5            $s' \leftarrow$ NEXT(s, a)
6            $owner \leftarrow$ PARTITION(s')
7   if $owner = rank$ then
8   DFS(s')
9   else
10   SEND($s', owner$)
11   end if
12   end for
13   end if

Fig. 1. Distributed DFS search algorithm

2.2   Partition Function

The partition function has a key role in distributed model-checking as it is the function that creates the state space partitions.

A first possible solution for the partition function is to use a simple hashing function (for example, the internal hashing function) that is applied when a state is stored in the state space. This solution, presented in [SD97] has been implemented in CYCLADES. Results presented in section 5 are really convincing and show that the state space is divided evenly among the workstations even for large models. However, this approach does not limit the number of generated communications.

The number of communications is the direct result of the partition function. Thus a good partition function is a function that limits the number of *cross-transitions*, i.e. an action of the model that generates an arc in the state space that links two states belonging to different partitions. Such an arc generates a communication when it is explored.

A solution to limit the number of cross-transitions has been presented in [LS99]. This solution is based on the observation that a global state of a system S can be seen as a vector of local states of the p processes of S. Thus, instead of applying the partition function to the entire vector, a solution could be to limit the partition function to a subset of the vector.

Let us consider the case when the chosen subset is reduced to a single process, the cross transitions are just the actions that modify the state of the designated process. Thus such a partition function results in a reduction of cross-transitions and then communications.

A similar approach based on [KP04] has been implemented in CYCLADES. A global state of a Petri net is a set of markings corresponding to the markings of each place of the net. To ensure a better locality and then reduce the number of communications, the partition function does not depend on the whole set of markings but on a subset of the places markings.

A good place subset for the partition function can be a subset describing a process. Contrary to Promela specifications, it is hard to identify process in a Petri nets. Thus we add the possibility for the user to specify the type of place for each place of the net. It is then possible to statically determine the different processes of the model. It is also possible in HELENA to specify explicitly a subset of places. However note that, even if it can be used independently, CYCLADES is the model-checker of the QUASAR tool suite and then is executed on Petri nets generated from a concurrent program. It is then easy, during modeling of the Petri net to specify the process places.

Results present in section 5 show that this approach results in a visible reduction of communications. However choosing a good partition is not easy and can, sometimes, result in a high load imbalance.

2.3 Reducing Communications

We present here two mechanisms used in CYCLADES to reduce the number of communications.

Message Buffering. The message buffering consists in sending several messages in a single communication. Considering k states that have to be sent to a node n, instead of sending k messages, a single message containing the k states can be sent to n. This solution efficiently reduces the number of communications. Results presented in the section 5 show that this approach is particularly efficient and reduces the verification time. However care must be taken with large buffer sizes to avoid inactivity as message buffering delays the message sending. Two approach have been implemented in the distributed version of HELENA. A simple timeout mechanism could achieve this goal: each sending buffer is coupled with a timeout. When the timeout expires, the buffer is sent even if it has not reached the maximal size.

A second less aggressive solution avoids the use of timeout. It consists in sending a request when a node is idle. To avoid a broadcast of the request that would generate a high number of communications and would lead to a network overload, when a node n_i is idle it sends a request to its neighbor n_{i+1}. If n_{i+1} maintains a non-empty buffer for n, it sends the buffer otherwise it propagates the request to its neighbor n_{i+2}. In the case when the request is propagated along the network back to n_i, n_i withdraw the request. This approach can lead to a better message buffering as an incomplete buffer will not be sent until a sending request is received.

We decided to use this last solution by default as it is the one that allows a better message buffering, especially in the case of a good partitioning of the state space.

State Caching. State caching is a technique to avoid the sending of redundant messages. Considering a node n that sends a state s, n stores s in a local cache. Thus, if s is explored again by n, it will not be sent again as it is in the cache. Experiments made in section 5 show that state-caching results in a visible diminution of messages and thus in a reduction of the execution time.

2.4   Construction of the Error Report

If an error is found during the state space exploration, HELENA must produce a trace of the sequence that leads to this error. In the sequential version, the trace is simply built by traversing the search stack.

In the distributed version, the stack is no longer maintained as each node only maintains a local search stack.

A first solution to this problem presented in [LS99] was implemented in CY-CLADES. It consists in sending the path p leading to s with the sent state s. Then when a node detects an error it is able to rebuild the sequence of actions that violates the property.

Another solution has been implemented in CYCLADES. The idea is to reduce the amount of memory used to store paths. For each state we store additional information that will help rebuilding the sequence of actions. This additional information is simply the address of the predecessor, the partition number of the predecessor and the id of the transition that generates the state. Note that this additional information has a fixed size.

Once an invalid state is explored, the node starts building the report by traversing the local search stack. When the bottom of the stack is reached, if the last state has a predecessor, a request is sent to the owner of this predecessor together with the current report. When receiving such a request, a node starts by getting the state stored at the given address then recalculates the enabling set of the state for the given transition id. The transition color and the state can then be added to the report. Then, if this state has a predecessor, the same process is executed until the initial state is reached.

As a state can have more than one predecessor, it would be possible to have more than one reference to a predecessor for each state. This solution would lead to an excessive memory overhead. Another possible solution would be to update the reference of the predecessor each time a predecessor with a smaller depth is explored which would result in a minimal error report. However this solution supposes that the depth of the predecessor should be stored and as maximal search depth cannot be statically known, the amount of memory used to store the depth could not be fixed. That is the reason why we decided not to update the predecessor of an already stored state.

The advantage of this approach is that the amount of memory used is reduced although the time used to build the report is increased but still negligible compared to the exploration.

2.5 Detection of Termination

The detection of termination is computed by the master node. Each time a worker node becomes idle, it sends a message to the manager with both its number of received and sent messages. When the manager detects that the global number of sent messages is equal to the number of received messages, termination is detected and a termination message is broadcasted.

A node is said to be idle when it has no more states in its state queue and no incoming message. These conditions are checked at line 6 and 10 of the *WORKER* procedure of figure 2.1.

Compared to the solution presented in [LS99], we avoid the sending of *busy* and *idle* messages used to notify the state of each node to the manager. It is not necessary for the manager to know exactly which nodes are busy and idle, it just has to know if at least one node is still working or will work. This is done by checking the number of overall sent and received states. The key of our algorithm is that a message is considered as received by a node when it has been completely treated. Thus, when a node sends its number of sent and received messages it is implicit that it is idle until it may receive a message. This solution leads to a reduction of communications to detect termination.

3 Dealing with Δ-Markings

In colored Petri nets, as in many other formalisms, the transition relation is a deterministic mechanism: the firing of a transition instance at a marking leads to a single marking. On the basis of this determinism, we proposed to store some markings of the reachability set in a non explicit way: instead of storing the actual value of a marking m, we only store a reference to one of its predecessors m' and a transition instance (t, c_t) whose execution leads from m' to m. Because of the determinism of the transition relation, this representation of m' is unambiguous although it is not canonical since a marking may have several predecessors. Markings stored in this manner are called Δ-markings and are said to be stored symbolically while markings stored in the usual way are said to be stored explicitly.

Storing a reference to a marking and a transition instance leads to better state representations, especially when the modeled system exhibits large state vectors. However, this representation presents a drawback: the test for checking whether or not a marking m is new or not can be significantly slowed down. This test usually entails comparing m to some marking(s) m' stored in the state space. The comparison can then be efficiently implemented by a bit vectors comparison. When the reachability set contains Δ-markings, the operation is more complicated. Let us assume that we have a sequence of markings $m_1, m_2, \ldots, m_n = m'$ such that m_1 is stored explicitly and each $m_i \neq m_1$ is stored as a Δ-marking which points to m_{i-1} with the binding (t_{i-1}, c_{i-1}) such that $m_{i-1}[(t_{i-1}, c_{i-1})\rangle m_i$. The idea is then to backtrack to m_1, and to apply to it the firing of bindings sequence $(t_1, c_1).(t_2, c_2) \ldots (t_{n-1}, c_{n-1})$ to have an "explicit view" of m'. Once this operation realized, the comparison of m and m' becomes straightforward.

We will call a *reconstitution* the operation which consists in finding the actual value from a Δ encoding, and the sequence of transition bindings which enables to reconstitute a marking will be called a *reconstituting sequence*. The principle of the reconstitution mechanism can be illustrated with the help of Figure 2. Let us suppose, for instance, that we have to reconstitute marking m. To do so, we will first have to backtrack to m'. Since it is not stored explicitly, we will then have to backtrack to m_0 and finally apply to it the reconstituting sequence $(t', c').(t, c)$. This operation allows us to retrieve the actual value of marking m.

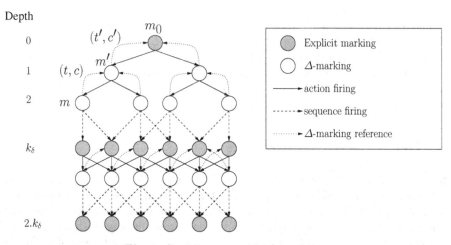

Fig. 2. A state-space with Δ-marking

The distributed environment implies some modifications of the Δ-marking as it represents a given state s' with reference to one of its predecessor s. A problem arises when s and s' belong to different partitions.

A first solution is to modify the representation of the non-explicit marking. The reference to the predecessor must take into account the localization (i.e. the partition) of the state. Thus, s' is represented by the transition color, the reference to its predecessor s and the partition number owning s. When s' has to be reconstructed a request is sent to the owner of s which reconstructs s and sends it back to the owner of s' for the construction of s'. It is obvious that such a solution would generate a lot of communications to reconstruct the Δ-markings.

Another approach is to modify the algorithm such that each sent state s is stored explicitly. Results presented in section 5 show that this solution does not generate extra communications. However, the efficiency of the method decreases as the number of nodes involved in the verification process increases (especially in the case of a uniform partitioning). That is because the probability that a state will be stored as a Δ-marking depends on the probability that a state belongs to the partition of its predecessor. The efficiency of distributed Δ-marking depends on the efficiency of the state space partition.

To increase the efficiency of distributed Δ−marking, let us consider the example presented in figure 3: s_j is a successor of s_i and s_k is a successor of s_j. Consider now a node n_I owner of the partition I and n_{II} owner of the partition II. In the basic case, both s_i, s_j and s_k will be stored explicitly. Inspired from the children look-ahead mechanism, it could be interesting to store s_j on n_{II} in order to store s_k as a Δ-marking.

Children look-ahead was presented in [LV01]. The aim is to reduce the number of messages. Look-ahead works as follow: when a state s_i is explored by a node n_1 and has to be sent to a node n_2, n_1 explores all the successors s_j of s_i. Each state s_j belonging to the partition of n_1 is store on n_1 and will not be sent back by n_2 when exploring s_i. This approach results in some cases in a significant reduction of communications but can sometimes lead to a runtime increase because states may be explored several times.

However we reduced this runtime overhead in the case of a state space partitioning based on the net structure as we can identify *cross-transitions*. Then only *cross-transitions* are relevant for the look-ahead computation as they are the only ones that can lead to a state belonging to a different partition. Thus, in the case of a structural partition, only *cross-transitions* are considered when computing children look-ahead.

When combining distributed Δ-marking with children look-ahead, we consider three cases:

1. considering s_j stored on n_{II}, s_k has to be stored as an explicit marking,
2. s_j is stored explicitly on n_{II} and then s_k can be stored as a Δ-marking,
3. s_j and s_k are both stored as Δ-markings on n_{II}

It is clear that the first case will never result in a more efficient storage because storing s_j on n_{II} will not result in Δ representation of s_k.

Consider now the second case, when s_j is stored explicitly on n_{II}. A better storage is obtained only when the storing s_j explicitly and s_k as a Δ-marking will consume less memory than storing s_k explicitly. In practice, we decided to store s_j on n_{II} when at least two successors of s_j belong to the partition II.

At least, it is obvious that in the last case, storing s_j and s_k on n_{II} leads to a more efficient storage than the basic mode. In that case, s_j is stored on n_{II} as a Δ-marking and on n_I as an explicit marking. Compared to the basic mode, instead of 3 explicit markings, this solution leads to 2 explicit markings and 2 Δ-markings and then to a reduction of the amount of memory needed for storage.

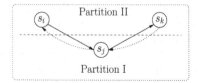

Fig. 3. A state-space with Δ-marking

This optimization yields good results especially with a partition function based on the net structure as it is possible to identify the cross-transitions. Thus only such transitions are used for the calculation of children look-ahead.

Moreover it is interesting to notice that the representation of a Δ-marking is very similar to the solution used for error report when storing reference on a predecessor. To build the error report no additional information is needed for Δ-markings as their representation already have a reference to a predecessor and the required informations. Thus, when using Δ-marking, only explicitly stored states need additional information to build the error report.

4   Related Works

Several works on distributed and parallel model-checking have been proposed.

A distributed version of the Murφ Verifier was presented in [SD97]. Based on this work, a first distributed version of the SPIN model-checker, reduced to the verification of safety properties, was proposed in [LS99]. The major innovation was the way to partition the state space. Authors exploit the structure of the state representation in SPIN to ensure a better degree of locality, i.e. a reduction of communications. A new version, allowing the verification of LTL properties was presented in [JBS01].

A very efficient model-checker for Petri net specification was presented in [BH02]. However the approach presented computes backward firing which, in our models is not always possible as it can lead to an infinity of markings.

In [GMS01], authors propose some algorithms for parallel state space construction for labeled transition systems(LTS) obtain from languages such as LOTOS.

All these approaches address exact and exhaustive verification issues. Another work, based on a probabilistic verification was presented in [KMHK98]. This approach performs a state enumeration with a low probability that some states can be omitted. At last, distributed symbolic model-checking was presented in [HGGS00].

5   Experiments

Evaluations were made on a cluster of computers with 512Mb of memory and 2.6Ghz processor and 100Mb/s network. Cyclades uses Open MPI for communications. All communications are buffered and asynchronous. CYCLADES generates code written in C.

Table 1 presents the evaluation of the state space partition on the sieve of Eratosthene example. The sieve of Eratosthene is used to find all primes inferior to a number k. The column N represents the number of nodes used for model-checking Min represents the minimal number of states stored on a node and Max, the maximum of states stored on a node. $Discrepancy$ presents the average difference of stored states on each node compared to the ideal load balance, ie. when each node stores an equal number of states. Then the $Communications$ column presents the total number of sent states during model-checking.

Table 1. State space partition - Sieve of Eratosthene (657 388 states/3 003 225 arcs)

N	Min	Max	Discrepancy	Communications
Partition based on the internal hashing function				
5	164 321	164 356	15	2 875 027
10	72 673	73 269	240	3 003 226
Partition based on Petri net structure				
5	110 378	218 487	38 696	593 707
10	49 534	89 558	29 060	2 389 351

We can see that the partition function based on the internal hashing function results in an efficient load balancing, ie. the discrepancy is low, but generates a high number of communications. This is because the probability that a successor of a state s belongs to the partition of s tends to be $1/N$. This probability is increased when using a partition function based on the net structure but this can lead to a high load imbalance.

As communications are very expensive compared to time spent for exploration, we decided to use partition based on the Petri net structure for the next experiments.

Table 2 presents some experiments made on three Petri net models. The first column represents the number of node used for model-checking. The next column reports the number of sent states and the execution time. Same evaluations with the state caching method are reported in the third column. The average hit rate in the state cache is also reported. All experiments were made with a partition function based on the net structure. The message buffer size was set to 1000 bytes. The size of the state cache was set to 1Mb. For each model, the number of states, arcs and the memory used to store the whole state space with the sequential algorithm are also reported.

The first model is the Sieve of Erathostene used to calculate prime numbers inferior to a number k. The next model is the database manager model which represents a system with a set of k database managers which communicates to maintain a consistent replica of a database. Then, the last model is a simple load balancer model with C clients an S servers. All these models are available in the HELENA distribution.

Table 2. Time and communications evaluations on some Petri net models

N	Basic algorithm		Basic algorithm + State Caching		
	Comm.	Time	Comm.	Time	Hits
Database manager			$(k = 13 - 6\ 908\ 734$ states $- 55\ 269\ 890$ arcs)		
				Memory used: 270.33 Mb.	
1	0	317s		–	
3	29 760 709	530s	6 902 180	296s	76%
5	42 515 299	344s	19 247 071	212s	54%
7	46 766 829	228s	28 256 056	163s	39%
Sieve of Eratosthene			$(k = 43 - 3\ 957\ 786$ states $- 20\ 039\ 199$ arcs)		
				Memory used: 226.85 Mb.	
1	0	170s		–	
3	2 519 061	174s	1 952 760	128s	23%
5	2 519 061	119s	2 106 749	102s	15%
7	3 128 650	93s	3 032 356	88s	10%
Load balancer			$(C = 6, S = 5 - 11\ 682\ 018$ states $- 59\ 980\ 779$ arcs)		
				Memory used: 367.77 Mb.	
1	0	396s		–	
3	18 022 501	419s	8 352 421	355s	53%
5	27 033 751	309s	17 981 575	267s	32%
7	27 033 751	190s	21 049 147	168s	21%

A first conclusion concerns the cost of communications. As we can see, for each model, using 3 nodes for verification (i.e. 2 working nodes and 1 manager) does not lead to a speedup. However, using 2 or 4 more working nodes always results in a reduction of the verification time except for the database manager model with 4 working nodes. That is because the number of arcs is very high compared to the number of nodes. As communications result from arcs, the database model generates a lot of communications which slow down the exploration time.

We also notice that state caching always reduce the number of communications with a direct impact on the execution time. Especially in the case when state are often revisited as in the database manager model.

Table 3 presents the experiments of CYCLADES with the Δ-marking storage method enable. Experiments for the basic distributed Δ-marking algorithm and for the algorithm with children look-ahead are presented. For each model, the time execution and the total number of both explicit and Δ marking are reported. The depth parameter of the Δ-marking algorithm was set to 10.

The optimization of the distributed Δ-marking algorithm performs a high rate of Δ-markings (and so an efficient memory saving). Furthermore, the time is reduced compared to the sequential algorithm. This is because the cost of communications is compensated by the time needed for state reconstruction.

This optimization finally leads to a very efficient memory usage in a distributed environment. Note that the locality degree of the partition function has a direct impact on the efficiency of the distributed Δ-marking algorithm.

Table 3. Evaluations of the Δ-marking in a distributed environment

N	Basic Algorithm			Algorithm + Look-ahead		
	explicit	Δ	time	explicit	Δ	time
Load balancer				(1 232 262 states – 5 897 781 arcs)		
1	123 207	1 109 055	73s	–	–	–
5	223 548	1 008 714	41s	112 319	1 119 943	48s
7	227 643	1 004 619	24s	173 473	1 058 789	29s
Database manager				(2 125 765 states – 15 588 960 arcs)		
1	241 561	1 884 204	269s	–	–	–
5	1 629 029	496 736	137s	1 046 920	1 078 845	159s
7	1 837 253	288 512	82s	1 379 173	746 592	93s
Eratosthene				(3 957 786 states – 20 039 199 arcs)		
1	395 781	3 562 005	610s	–	–	–
5	383 242	3 574 544	280s	356 562	3 601 224	291s
7	340 824	3 568 528	211s	333 669	3 624 117	225s

6   Conclusion and Future Works

In this paper we have presented a preliminary version of CYCLADES, a distributed high-level colored Petri net model-checker based on HELENA . Experiments show that we obtain a good memory repartition per node combined with a execution speedup as soon as the number of node is sufficient.

Moreover we have shown that some sophisticated state representation techniques, such as Δ-marking, can be efficiently distributed without fundamental modification of the sequential algorithm.

Experiments show that the execution time can be reduced when using efficient model-checking methods, such as Δ-marking, that increase the calculation time. Thus the communication time tends to be less important than the calculation time.

One of our future works is planned toward the computation of distributed partial-order reductions as it is one of the most efficient reduction technique. Moreover, as calculating the stubborn sets is time expensive, we can hope that distributed model-checking will result in good speedups, especially when combining stubborn sets computation with Δ-marking.

As Petri nets places invariants give informations about the behavior of the system, we think that it will help selecting good place subsets for a more efficient structural partitioning. Part of our future works will thus investigate this possibility.

References

[Ber83]   G. Berthelot. *Transformation et analyse de réseaux de Petri, applications aux protocoles.* Thèse d'état, Université Pierre et Marie Curie, Paris, 1983.

[BH02]   Alexander Bell and Boudewijn R. Haverkort. Sequential and distributed model checking of petri net specifications. *Electr. Notes Theor. Comput. Sci.*, 68(4), 2002.

[CGL92]   E. M. Clarke, O. Grumberg, and D. E. Long. Model checking and abstraction. In *POPL '92: Proceedings of the 19th ACM SIGPLAN-SIGACT symposium on Principles of programming languages*, pages 343–354, 1992.

[CKM01]   S. Christensen, L.M. Kristensen, and T. Mailund. A Sweep-Line Method for State Space Exploration. In *Proc. of TACAS'01*, volume 2031 of *LNCS*, pages 450–464. Springer-Verlag, 2001.

[CL98]   Ernie Cohen and Leslie Lamport. Reduction in TLA. In *International Conference on Concurrency Theory*, pages 317–331, 1998.

[EHPP04]   S. Evangelista, S. Haddad, and J.F. Pradat-Peyre. New coloured reductions for software validation. In *Work. on Discrete Event Systems*, 2004.

[EKP+05]   S. Evangelista, C. Kaiser, C. Pajault, J. F. Pradat-Peyre, and P. Rousseau. Dynamic tasks verification with QUASAR. In *Reliable Software Technologies - Ada-Europe 2005*, volume 3555 of *LNCS*. Springer-Verlag, 2005.

[EKPPR03]   S. Evangelista, C. Kaiser, J. F. Pradat-Peyre, and P. Rousseau. Quasar: a new tool for analysing concurrent programs. In *Reliable Software Technologies - Ada-Europe 2003*, volume 2655 of *LNCS*. Springer-Verlag, 2003.

[EP06]   Sami Evangelista and Jean-Franois Peyre. On the computation of stubborn sets of colored petri nets. In *Proc. 27th Intl. Conf. on the Application and Theory of Petri Nets and Other Models of Concurrency*, 2006.

[EPP05]   Sami Evangelista and Jean-François Pradat-Peyre. Memory efficient state space storage in explicit software model checking. In *Model Checking Software: 12th International SPIN Workshop*, volume 3639, page 43, 2005.

[Eva05]   Sami Evangelista. High level petri nets analysis with helena. In *ICATPN*, pages 455–464, 2005.

[FQ03a]   Cormac Flanagan and Shaz Qadeer. Transactions for software model checking. In Byron Cook, Scott Stoller, and Willem Visser, editors, *Electronic Notes in Theoretical Computer Science*, volume 89. Elsevier, 2003.

[FQ03b]   Stephen N. Freund and Shaz Qadeer. Checking concise specifications for multithreaded software. In *FTfJP 03: Formal Techniques for Java-like Programs*, 2003.

[GMS01]   Hubert Garavel, Radu Mateescu, and Irina Smarandache. Parallel state space construction for model-checking. In *SPIN '01: Proceedings of the 8th international SPIN workshop on Model checking of software*, pages 217–234. Springer-Verlag New York, Inc., 2001.

[GW93]   Patrice Godefroid and Pierre Wolper. Using partial orders for the efficient verification of deadlock freedom and safety properties. *Form. Methods Syst. Des.*, 2(2):149–164, 1993.

[HGGS00]   Tamir Heyman, Daniel Geist, Orna Grumberg, and Assaf Schuster. Achieving scalability in parallel reachability analysis of very large circuits. In *CAV*, pages 20–35, 2000.

[Hol87]   Gerard J. Holzmann. On limits and possibilities of automated protocol analysis. In *Proceedings of the IFIP WG6.1 Seventh International Conference on Protocol Specification, Testing and Verification VII*, pages 339–344. North-Holland, 1987.

[Hol97]   Gerard J. Holzmann. State compression in SPIN: Recursive indexing and compression training runs. In *Proc. of the 3th International SPIN Workshop*, 1997.

[HPP06]   S. Haddad and J.-F. Pradat-Peyre. New efficient petri nets reductions for parallel programs verification. *Parallel Processing Letters*, 16(1), 2006. to appear.

[JBS01]   L. Brim J. Barnat and J. Stríbrná. Distributed LTL model-checking in SPIN. In *Proceedings of the 8th international SPIN workshop on Model checking of software*, pages 200–216. Springer-Verlag New York, Inc., 2001.

[KMHK98]   William J. Knottenbelt, Mark Mestern, Peter G. Harrison, and Pieter S. Kritzinger. Probability, parallelism and the state space exploration problem. In *Computer Performance Evaluation (Tools)*, pages 165–179, 1998.

[KP04]   L. M. Kristensen and L. Petrucci. An approach to distributed state space exploration for coloured petri nets. In *Proc. 25th Int. Conf. Application and Theory of Petri Nets (ICATPN'2004)*, volume 3099, pages 474–483. Springer-Verlag, 2004.

[Lip75]   Richard J. Lipton. Reduction: a method of proving properties of parallel programs. *Commun. ACM*, 18(12):717–721, 1975.

[LS99]   Flavio Lerda and Riccardo Sisto. Distributed-memory model checking with SPIN. In *Proceedings of the 5th and 6th International SPIN Workshops on Theoretical and Practical Aspects of SPIN Model Checking*, pages 22–39. Springer-Verlag, 1999.

[LV01]   Flavio Lerda and Willem Visser. Addressing dynamic issues of program model checking. In *SPIN '01: Proceedings of the 8th international SPIN workshop on Model checking of software*, pages 80–102. Springer-Verlag New York, Inc., 2001.

[McM93]   Kenneth L. McMillan. *Symbolic Model Checking*. Kluwer Academic Publishers, Norwell, MA, USA, 1993.

[PPP00]   D. Poitrenaud and J.F. Pradat-Peyre. Pre and post-agglomerations for *LTL* model checking. In M. Nielsen and D Simpson, editors, *High-level Petri Nets, Theory and Application*, number 1825 in LNCS, pages 387–408. Springer-Verlag, 2000.

[Rou06]   Pierre Rousseau. A new approach for concurrent program slicing. In *26th International Conference on Formal Techniques for Networked and Distributed Systems, FORTE'06*, Lecture Notes in Computer Science, 2006. to appear.

[SD97]   Ulrich Stern and David L. Dill. Parallelizing the murphi verifier. In *CAV '97: Proceedings of the 9th International Conference on Computer Aided Verification*, pages 256–278, London, UK, 1997. Springer-Verlag.

[Val93]   Antti Valmari. On-the-fly verification with stubborn sets. In *Proceedings of the 5th International Conference on Computer Aided Verification*, pages 397–408. Springer-Verlag, 1993.

[VM97]   François Vernadat and François Michel. Covering step graph preserving failure semantics. In *Proceedings of the 18th International Conference on Application and Theory of Petri Nets*, pages 253–270. Springer-Verlag, 1997.

[Wei84]   M. Weiser. Program slicing. *IEEE Transactions on Software Engineering*, 10(4):352–357, 1984.

[WL93]   Pierre Wolper and Denis Leroy. Reliable hashing without collision detection. In *CAV*, pages 59–70, 1993.

Author Index

Ábrahám, Erika   301

Barnat, Jiří   316
Becker, Bernd   301
Bonakdarpour, Borzoo   261
Brim, Luboš   23, 84

Černá, Ivana   84
Clark, Allan   181
Cuijpers, P.J.L.   195

Ezekiel, Jonathan   331

Fecher, Harald   244
Fehnker, Ansgar   297
Fränzle, Martin   301
Fyukov, A.V.   195

Gilmore, Stephen   181

Hammer, Moritz   51
Helmstetter, C.   100
Herde, Christian   301
Hessel, Anders   116
Huuck, Ralf   297

Jayet, Patrick   297

Krause, Ben   293
Kulkarni, Sandeep S.   261

Lampka, Kai   35
Lussenburg, Michel   297
Lüttgen, Gerald   211, 331

Maillet-Contoz, L.   100
Maraninchi, F.   100

Mathijssen, Aad   165
Matoušek, P.   148
Moravec, Pavel   84, 316
Mühlberg, Jan Tobias   211

Pajault, Christophe   347
Pettersson, Paul   116
Pradat-Peyre, Jean-François   347
Pretorius, A. Johannes   165

Rauch, Felix   297
Řehák, V.   148
Řehák, Z.   148
Roy, Suman   227

Šafránek, D.   148
Saha, Indranil   227
Saïdi, Hassen   67
Schönborn, Jens   244
Schubert, Tobias   301
Siegle, Markus   35
Siminiceanu, Radu   331
Šimša, Jiří   84
Slobodová, Anna   1
Smrčka, A.   148

Vojnar, T.   148

Wahls, Tim   293
Walter, Max   35
Weber, Michael   51
Willemse, Tim A.C.   132

Zhang, Wenhui   277

Lecture Notes in Computer Science

For information about Vols. 1–4300

please contact your bookseller or Springer

Vol. 4429: C. Ullrich, J.H. Siekmann, R. Lu (Eds.), Cognitive Systems. X, 162 pages. 2007. (Sublibrary LNAI).

Vol. 4405: L. Padgham, F. Zambonelli (Eds.), Agent-Oriented Software Engineering VII. XII, 225 pages. 2007.

Vol. 4403: S. Obayashi, K. Deb, C. Poloni, T. Hiroyasu, T. Murata (Eds.), Evolutionary Multi-Criterion Optimization. XIX, 954 pages. 2007.

Vol. 4397: C. Stephanidis, M. Pieper (Eds.), Universal Access in Ambient Intelligence Environments. XV, 467 pages. 2007.

Vol. 4396: J. García-Vidal, L. Cerdà-Alabern (Eds.), Wireless Systems and Mobility in Next Generation Internet. IX, 271 pages. 2007.

Vol. 4394: A. Gelbukh (Ed.), Computational Linguistics and Intelligent Text Processing. XVI, 648 pages. 2007.

Vol. 4393: W. Thomas, P. Weil (Eds.), STACS 2007. XVIII, 708 pages. 2007.

Vol. 4392: S.P. Vadhan (Ed.), Theory of Cryptography. XI, 595 pages. 2007.

Vol. 4390: S.O. Kuznetsov, S. Schmidt (Eds.), Formal Concept Analysis. X, 329 pages. 2007. (Sublibrary LNAI).

Vol. 4385: K. Coninx, K. Luyten, K.A. Schneider (Eds.), Task Models and Diagrams for Users Interface Design. XI, 355 pages. 2007.

Vol. 4384: T. Washio, K. Satoh, H. Takeda, A. Inokuchi (Eds.), New Frontiers in Artificial Intelligence. IX, 401 pages. 2007. (Sublibrary LNAI).

Vol. 4383: E. Bin, A. Ziv, S. Ur (Eds.), Hardware and Software, Verification and Testing. XII, 235 pages. 2007.

Vol. 4381: J. Akiyama, W.Y.C. Chen, M. Kano, X. Li, Q. Yu (Eds.), Discrete Geometry, Combinatorics and Graph Theory. XI, 289 pages. 2007.

Vol. 4380: S. Spaccapietra, P. Atzeni, F. Fages, M.-S. Hacid, M. Kifer, J. Mylopoulos, B. Pernici, P. Shvaiko, J. Trujillo, I. Zaihrayeu (Eds.), Journal on Data Semantics VIII. XV, 219 pages. 2007.

Vol. 4378: I. Virbitskaite, A. Voronkov (Eds.), Perspectives of Systems Informatics. XIV, 496 pages. 2007.

Vol. 4377: M. Abe (Ed.), Topics in Cryptology – CT-RSA 2007. XI, 403 pages. 2006.

Vol. 4376: E. Frachtenberg, U. Schwiegelshohn (Eds.), Job Scheduling Strategies for Parallel Processing. VII, 257 pages. 2007.

Vol. 4373: K. Langendoen, T. Voigt (Eds.), Wireless Sensor Networks. XIII, 358 pages. 2007.

Vol. 4372: M. Kaufmann, D. Wagner (Eds.), Graph Drawing. XIV, 454 pages. 2007.

Vol. 4371: K. Inoue, K. Satoh, F. Toni (Eds.), Computational Logic in Multi-Agent Systems. X, 315 pages. 2007. (Sublibrary LNAI).

Vol. 4370: P.P Lévy, B. Le Grand, F. Poulet, M. Soto, L. Darago, L. Toubiana, J.-F. Vibert (Eds.), Pixelization Paradigm. XV, 279 pages. 2007.

Vol. 4369: M. Umeda, A. Wolf, O. Bartenstein, U. Geske, D. Seipel, O. Takata (Eds.), Declarative Programming for Knowledge Management. X, 229 pages. 2006. (Sublibrary LNAI).

Vol. 4368: T. Erlebach, C. Kaklamanis (Eds.), Approximation and Online Algorithms. X, 345 pages. 2007.

Vol. 4367: K. De Bosschere, D. Kaeli, P. Stenström, D. Whalley, T. Ungerer (Eds.), High Performance Embedded Architectures and Compilers. XI, 307 pages. 2007.

Vol. 4366: K. Tuyls, R. Westra, Y. Saeys, A. Nowé (Eds.), Knowledge Discovery and Emergent Complexity in Bioinformatics. IX, 183 pages. 2007. (Sublibrary LNBI).

Vol. 4364: T. Kühne (Ed.), Models in Software Engineering. XI, 332 pages. 2007.

Vol. 4362: J. van Leeuwen, G.F. Italiano, W. van der Hoek, C. Meinel, H. Sack, F. Plášil (Eds.), SOFSEM 2007: Theory and Practice of Computer Science. XXI, 937 pages. 2007.

Vol. 4361: H.J. Hoogeboom, G. Păun, G. Rozenberg, A. Salomaa (Eds.), Membrane Computing. IX, 555 pages. 2006.

Vol. 4360: W. Dubitzky, A. Schuster, P.M.A. Sloot, M. Schroeder, M. Romberg (Eds.), Distributed, High-Performance and Grid Computing in Computational Biology. X, 192 pages. 2007. (Sublibrary LNBI).

Vol. 4358: R. Vidal, A. Heyden, Y. Ma (Eds.), Dynamical Vision. IX, 329 pages. 2007.

Vol. 4357: L. Buttyán, V. Gligor, D. Westhoff (Eds.), Security and Privacy in Ad-Hoc and Sensor Networks. X, 193 pages. 2006.

Vol. 4355: J. Julliand, O. Kouchnarenko (Eds.), B 2007: Formal Specification and Development in B. XIII, 293 pages. 2006.

Vol. 4354: M. Hanus (Ed.), Practical Aspects of Declarative Languages. X, 335 pages. 2006.

Vol. 4353: T. Schwentick, D. Suciu (Eds.), Database Theory – ICDT 2007. XI, 419 pages. 2006.

Vol. 4352: T.-J. Cham, J. Cai, C. Dorai, D. Rajan, T.-S. Chua, L.-T. Chia (Eds.), Advances in Multimedia Modeling, Part II. XVIII, 743 pages. 2006.

Vol. 4351: T.-J. Cham, J. Cai, C. Dorai, D. Rajan, T.-S. Chua, L.-T. Chia (Eds.), Advances in Multimedia Modeling, Part I. XIX, 797 pages. 2006.

Vol. 4349: B. Cook, A. Podelski (Eds.), Verification, Model Checking, and Abstract Interpretation. XI, 395 pages. 2007.

Vol. 4348: S.T. Taft, R.A. Duff, R.L. Brukardt, E. Ploedereder, P. Leroy (Eds.), Ada 2005 Reference Manual. XXII, 765 pages. 2006.

Vol. 4347: J. Lopez (Ed.), Critical Information Infrastructures Security. X, 286 pages. 2006.

Vol. 4346: L. Brim, B. Haverkort, M. Leucker, J. van de Pol (Eds.), Formal Methods: Applications and Technology. X, 363 pages. 2007.

Vol. 4345: N. Maglaveras, I. Chouvarda, V. Koutkias, R. Brause (Eds.), Biological and Medical Data Analysis. XIII, 496 pages. 2006. (Sublibrary LNBI).

Vol. 4344: V. Gruhn, F. Oquendo (Eds.), Software Architecture. X, 245 pages. 2006.

Vol. 4342: H. de Swart, E. Orłowska, G. Schmidt, M. Roubens (Eds.), Theory and Applications of Relational Structures as Knowledge Instruments II. X, 373 pages. 2006. (Sublibrary LNAI).

Vol. 4341: P.Q. Nguyen (Ed.), Progress in Cryptology - VIETCRYPT 2006. XI, 385 pages. 2006.

Vol. 4340: R. Prodan, T. Fahringer, Grid Computing. XXIII, 317 pages. 2007.

Vol. 4339: E. Ayguadé, G. Baumgartner, J. Ramanujam, P. Sadayappan (Eds.), Languages and Compilers for Parallel Computing. XI, 476 pages. 2006.

Vol. 4338: P. Kalra, S. Peleg (Eds.), Computer Vision, Graphics and Image Processing. XV, 965 pages. 2006.

Vol. 4337: S. Arun-Kumar, N. Garg (Eds.), FSTTCS 2006: Foundations of Software Technology and Theoretical Computer Science. XIII, 430 pages. 2006.

Vol. 4335: S.A. Brueckner, S. Hassas, M. Jelasity, D. Yamins (Eds.), Engineering Self-Organising Systems. XII, 212 pages. 2007. (Sublibrary LNAI).

Vol. 4334: B. Beckert, R. Hähnle, P.H. Schmitt (Eds.), Verification of Object-Oriented Software. XXIX, 658 pages. 2007. (Sublibrary LNAI).

Vol. 4333: U. Reimer, D. Karagiannis (Eds.), Practical Aspects of Knowledge Management. XII, 338 pages. 2006. (Sublibrary LNAI).

Vol. 4332: A. Bagchi, V. Atluri (Eds.), Information Systems Security. XV, 382 pages. 2006.

Vol. 4331: G. Min, B. Di Martino, L.T. Yang, M. Guo, G. Ruenger (Eds.), Frontiers of High Performance Computing and Networking – ISPA 2006 Workshops. XXXVII, 1141 pages. 2006.

Vol. 4330: M. Guo, L.T. Yang, B. Di Martino, H.P. Zima, J. Dongarra, F. Tang (Eds.), Parallel and Distributed Processing and Applications. XVIII, 953 pages. 2006.

Vol. 4329: R. Barua, T. Lange (Eds.), Progress in Cryptology - INDOCRYPT 2006. X, 454 pages. 2006.

Vol. 4328: D. Penkler, M. Reitenspiess, F. Tam (Eds.), Service Availability. X, 289 pages. 2006.

Vol. 4327: M. Baldoni, U. Endriss (Eds.), Declarative Agent Languages and Technologies IV. VIII, 257 pages. 2006. (Sublibrary LNAI).

Vol. 4326: S. Göbel, R. Malkewitz, I. Iurgel (Eds.), Technologies for Interactive Digital Storytelling and Entertainment. X, 384 pages. 2006.

Vol. 4325: J. Cao, I. Stojmenovic, X. Jia, S.K. Das (Eds.), Mobile Ad-hoc and Sensor Networks. XIX, 887 pages. 2006.

Vol. 4323: G. Doherty, A. Blandford (Eds.), Interactive Systems. XI, 269 pages. 2007.

Vol. 4320: R. Gotzhein, R. Reed (Eds.), System Analysis and Modeling: Language Profiles. X, 229 pages. 2006.

Vol. 4319: L.-W. Chang, W.-N. Lie (Eds.), Advances in Image and Video Technology. XXVI, 1347 pages. 2006.

Vol. 4318: H. Lipmaa, M. Yung, D. Lin (Eds.), Information Security and Cryptology. XI, 305 pages. 2006.

Vol. 4317: S.K. Madria, K.T. Claypool, R. Kannan, P. Uppuluri, M.M. Gore (Eds.), Distributed Computing and Internet Technology. XIX, 466 pages. 2006.

Vol. 4316: M.M. Dalkilic, S. Kim, J. Yang (Eds.), Data Mining and Bioinformatics. VIII, 197 pages. 2006. (Sublibrary LNBI).

Vol. 4314: C. Freksa, M. Kohlhase, K. Schill (Eds.), KI 2006: Advances in Artificial Intelligence. XII, 458 pages. 2007. (Sublibrary LNAI).

Vol. 4313: T. Margaria, B. Steffen (Eds.), Leveraging Applications of Formal Methods. IX, 197 pages. 2006.

Vol. 4312: S. Sugimoto, J. Hunter, A. Rauber, A. Morishima (Eds.), Digital Libraries: Achievements, Challenges and Opportunities. XVIII, 571 pages. 2006.

Vol. 4311: K. Cho, P. Jacquet (Eds.), Technologies for Advanced Heterogeneous Networks II. XI, 253 pages. 2006.

Vol. 4310: T. Boyanov, S. Dimova, K. Georgiev, G. Nikolov (Eds.), Numerical Methods and Applications. XIII, 715 pages. 2007.

Vol. 4309: P. Inverardi, M. Jazayeri (Eds.), Software Engineering Education in the Modern Age. VIII, 207 pages. 2006.

Vol. 4308: S. Chaudhuri, S.R. Das, H.S. Paul, S. Tirthapura (Eds.), Distributed Computing and Networking. XIX, 608 pages. 2006.

Vol. 4307: P. Ning, S. Qing, N. Li (Eds.), Information and Communications Security. XIV, 558 pages. 2006.

Vol. 4306: Y. Avrithis, Y. Kompatsiaris, S. Staab, N.E. O'Connor (Eds.), Semantic Multimedia. XII, 241 pages. 2006.

Vol. 4305: A.A. Shvartsman (Ed.), Principles of Distributed Systems. XIII, 441 pages. 2006.

Vol. 4304: A. Sattar, B.-H. Kang (Eds.), AI 2006: Advances in Artificial Intelligence. XXVII, 1303 pages. 2006. (Sublibrary LNAI).

Vol. 4303: A. Hoffmann, B.-H. Kang, D. Richards, S. Tsumoto (Eds.), Advances in Knowledge Acquisition and Management. XI, 259 pages. 2006. (Sublibrary LNAI).

Vol. 4302: J. Domingo-Ferrer, L. Franconi (Eds.), Privacy in Statistical Databases. XI, 383 pages. 2006.

Vol. 4301: D. Pointcheval, Y. Mu, K. Chen (Eds.), Cryptology and Network Security. XIII, 381 pages. 2006.